The Battle Abbey Roll, With Some Account of the Norman Lineages

D1738369

THE
BATTLE ABBEY ROLL.

WITH SOME

ACCOUNT OF THE NORMAN LINEAGES.

BY THE

DUCHESS OF CLEVELAND.

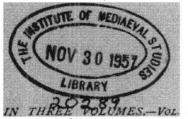

IN THREE VOLUMES.—VOL. II.

LONDON:
JOHN MURRAY, ALBEMARLE STREET.
1889.

LONDON :
PRINTED BY WILLIAM CLOWES AND SONS, LIMITED,
STAMFORD STREET AND CHARING CROSS.

THE BATTLE ABBEY ROLL.

Estrange: This name has always been stigmatized as an interpolation, on the ground of the generally accepted account of its origin, which—endorsed both by Glover and Dugdale—assigns to it a later date. "The Fitz Warine Chronicle tells us that William Peverel advertised through many lands a Tournament to be held at his Castle in the Peak, whereat he who acquitted himself best should have to wife Melette, Peverel's youngest niece, and with her the Lordship of Whittington in Shropshire:—that to this Tournament came Guarine de Metz of Lorrain (eventually the victor), also Owen Prince of Wales, and ten sons of John Duke of Brittany, and some others whose existence seems more or less fabulous. After the Tournament, says the same authority, Guy, the youngest of the ten brothers of Brittany, remained in England, and conquered with the sword many fair lands, and he was called Guy le Estrange, and from him came all the great Lords of England who have the surname of Estrange."—*Eyton's Salop.* The story rests solely upon tradition, and in some of its details is demonstrably false. If the tournament ever took place at all, it must have been between 1137, when Owen Gwynned succeeded to the sceptre of North Wales, and 1147, when the last Peverel, who was Lord of Whittington died. "The advent of Guy le Strange, as yet unmarried, at such a period, is irreconcilable with the fact that the three brothers, whom this narrative would make his sons, were all enfeoffed by Henry II. at a time when, according to the same narrative, the eldest of them could not have been of age."—*Ibid.* John Duke of Brittany is "unknown to any other record:" William Peverel's coheirs were not his nieces, but his sisters, and "neither of them was at any time wife of Guarin de Metz. "The sons of the latter are moreover found attesting deeds at a time when, according to this narrative, their father was yet unmarried, for it expressly says that he "had neither wife nor child."—*Ibid.* I think the authenticity of the legend may fairly be considered as disposed of.

But Eyton, after "a long search made in reference to this question," has provided a substitute for the imaginary Duke John of Brittany. He has discovered the true ancestor of the Le Stranges in Rodland or Ruald Extraneus, who witnesses two grants to the Norfolk Priory of Castle Acre, one by Roger Fitz-Wimer, Seneschal to the second William de Warrenne, Earl of Surrey (1089–1135) : and the other by Alan Fitz Flaald and Adeline his wife, the known ancestors of Fitz Alan, early in the reign of Henry I. Another deed, recently brought to light in the Castle-Acre chartulary, proves him to have been the father of John Le Strange, who in 1165 held a knight's fee in the Norfolk barony of these same Fitz Alans, and was the elder of the four brothers of which, at the accession of Henry II., the family was composed. Most probably they were of Breton lineage.

"But the tenure of a single Norfolk fee by Roland Le Strange was insignificant, and it is not for any paternal ancestry of the Stranges that we must look, if we wish to account for their great ascendency. As a race they were distinguished for their abilities in field and in council. They were distinguished yet more for the most steadfast loyalty. The feoffments of Henry Fitz Empress and William Fitz Alan I. were tributes to men of ascertained ability. For three long-lived and successive generations, the heads of this House were indefinitely trusted by contemporary Kings. For the same period no Le Strange ever betrayed such trust, or was suspected of betraying it."—*Ibid.*

The wife of Roland Extraneus, who was the daughter of Ralph Fitz Herlewin, or de Hunstanton, by Helewise de Plaiz, had two brothers who neither of them left issue ; and thus Hunstanton and their other Norfolk manors (five knight's fees in all) devolved on her eldest son John. She had three other sons, Hamon, Guy, and Ralph, who were all—as well as John—enfeoffed in Shropshire by Henry II. during the first years of his reign. Guy received Alveley ; Hamon, Cheswardine ; John, Ness (now Great Ness) ; and Ralph, Little Ercall. But John's was the only line that outlasted the century. Guy, Sheriff of Shropshire for fifteen years under Henry II., left one son who died in the prime of life in 1195 ; Hamo had died s. p. in 1160, and been succeeded by John as tenant in chief at Cheswardine ; and Ralph survived his only son Ronald, and died in 1194.

John, the common ancestor of the two great baronial families that bore the name, was the first of seven John Le Stranges, who followed each other in lineal succession as chiefs of a house "remarkable for longevity, activity, and loyal steadfastness." They had a castle and park at Cheswardine ; but the head of their Honour was the frontier fortress of Knockyn, traditionally said to have been founded by Guy the Viscount. Round this, their principal stronghold, " the Stranges gradually amassed an extent of territory which made them formidable even to their own suzerains the Fitz Alans, and constituted the Chatelleny or Fee of Knockyn." They were enterprising and energetic Barons Marcher. John II., who died in 1237, an old man of more than eighty, had spent fully fifty years of his life in the active discharge of the duties of his station. King John greatly favoured and trusted him, and he never swerved from his loyalty, but proved himself a faithful liegeman to the very end. In 1226, Henry III. acknowledged his "great services, large outlay, and losses," by the remission of some arrears due to the Crown. John III. was invested with even wider authority. In 1232 he was Constable of the three castles of Shrewsbury, Montgomery, and Bridgenorth, with "the greater trust or custody of the counties of Salop and Stafford:" and in 1240 had the further charge of the castle and county of Chester conferred upon him by a patent, "equivalent," says Eyton, "to appointing him to the high office of Justiciar of Chester." He was in arms against the Welsh even in advanced old age, summoned to parliament as a baron in 1260, and stood fast to the Crown throughout the brunt of the Barons' War. His younger son Hamo was equally and zealously loyal; but he had the mortification of seeing the elder, John IV., break away from the honoured traditions of his house, and join Simon de Montfort. During the brief supremacy of the barons, this younger John held his father's office of Constable of Montgomery, but "had small joy of his possession. In a midnight march through Kari, he was attacked by the Welsh, and two hundred of his men slain." He was not, with the other insurgent barons, compelled to compound for his estate after the battle of Evesham, being "probably shielded from punishment by the name he bore," but peaceably succeeded his father as second Lord Strange of Knockyn in 1269. He added materially to his influence and possessions by his marriage with Joan de Somery, daughter of Roger, Baron of Somery, and Nichola, sister and coheir of Hugh de Albini, the last Earl of Arundel of his line; and John V., following his father's example, again espoused an heiress, Maud, the only child of Roger D'Eivill of Walton D'Eivill in Warwickshire. Yet none of his successors ever attained the position in the county that had been held by the first Lord Strange. They were not slack of service in the field; nor backward in doing their duty there: and one, at least, of them made another great alliance. This was John VIII., nephew and heir of John VII., with whom the direct line of descent closed in 1323; and his wife was one of the coheirs of the last Lord Mohun of Dunster, and sister of Philippa Duchess of York, to whose share of the lands the Le Stranges in process of time succeeded. Their grandson, who died in 1461, was the last Lord Strange of Knockyn. He had been selected by Edward IV.'s up-start Queen as an eligible husband for one of her many portionless sisters, and married Jaquetta Widville, by whom he left an only child, Joan, the wife of George, son and heir-apparent of Thomas Stanley, the first Earl of Derby of that name. The Stanleys thus became representatives of the elder line of Le Strange, and held the barony till it lapsed into abeyance on the death of the fifth Earl.

The first Lord Strange of Knockyn left, besides his heir and successor, John IV., three younger sons, Hamo, Roger, and Robert. Hamo (already mentioned) was the loyal Sheriff of Shropshire who stood fast for the King when his elder brother joined Simon de Montfort, and was rewarded by splendid grants, comprising Stretton and the fortalice and hundred of Ellesmere. He went with Robert to the Crusade of 1270, in the train of Prince Edward, and died in Palestine. "The elder brother," says Eyton, " perished in the expedition ; the younger barely survived it." Hamo left no children, and Ellesmere passed, by Royal grant, to the next brother, Sir Roger, summoned to parliament as *Dominus de Ellesmere* in 1294; but he, too, was without an heir, and it reverted to the Crown on his death in 1311.

Robert, the last born of the family, had then been dead more than thirty-five years, Before their departure for the East, Hamo had enfeoffed him of Wrockwardine ; and his wife was the heiress of Whitchurch, Alianor de Blancminster (i.e. White Church). John, the eldest of their two sons, commonly known as Lord of Whitchurch, died s. p. when he was only twenty-three ; and Fulk, the second, succeeded in 1289 to "a very considerable inheritance. Thus, and by formal writ of Parliamentary summons, did Fulk Le Strange become first Baron of Blackmere ; the originator of that noble succession which, after twice merging in lines greater than itself, is now no longer represented by a Talbot or a Howard, but is in abeyance between the heirs general of these illustrious races."—*Ibid.* The name of Blackmere was adopted from the sombre lake adjoining the manor house of Whitchurch. The manor was held by the service of doing duty as Huntsman to Earl Warren, at the will and at the charges of the said Earl.

Fulk, "distinguished by various public offices and honours," and a baron by writ in 1308, was zealously engaged in all Edward I.'s wars, and became Lord of Corfham in right of his wife Eleanor Giffard, one of the daughters and coheirs of the great Clifford heiress by the second husband who had so cruelly wronged her. Their son John, the next Lord, was one of the soldier-peers of Edward III., whose armour was seldom doffed till it was laid aside in their coffins. Yet he did not fall in battle, but after a life spent amid the din of conflict and turmoil of arms, died peaceably in 1349. He had two sons ; Fulk, who never lived to be of age ; and John, who married Lady Mary Fitz Alan, and was the father of the last heir-male, John, fifth Lord Strange of Blackmere, and of a daughter named Ankaret. According to Dugdale, the son again died a minor in 1375 ; but he left a widow (Isabel de Beauchamp) and a child to inherit his barony. This child, Elizabeth Le Strange, can scarcely have been nine years old when she followed him to the grave in 1383 ; yet she was already the wife of Thomas de Moubray, Earl of Nottingham ; and Eyton even seems to imply that she left descendants ! On her death the succession reverted to her aunt Ankaret, then married to Sir Richard Talbot, who had summons to parliament in 1386 as *Richardo Talbot de Blakemere Ch'v'r;* and succeeded his father as Lord Talbot a few years afterwards.

Two other cadets of this great house remain to be noticed, Eubolo and Hamon, both sons of John V., the third Baron of Knockyn, by Maud D'Eivill, Lady of Walton. Eubolo—a knight banneret who had seen much service in the

Scottish wars—was the lover of the frail heiress, Alice de Lacy, Countess of Lincoln, who is said to have been repudiated by her first husband, the Earl of Lancaster, on his account, and promptly married him when she became a widow, He assumed in her right the title of Earl of Lincoln, but was summoned to parliament in 1326 only as *Euboloni le Estrange.* Edward II. had, as Eyton informs us, received several castles and manors from the Countess Alice "while she was single" (though, as she married at nine years old, this fact requires elucidation) : and Edward III., partly on that account, and partly because Eubolo was "a valued servant," bestowed upon them a munificent series of grants in 1330. These included the castle and hundred of Ellesmere, which, when Eubolo died s. p. five years afterwards, went to the head of the family, his nephew Roger, fifth Lord Strange of Knockyn.

Hamo, the youngest son, was enfeoffed in 1311 by his elder brother of Hunstanton in Norfolk, one of the original manors held by his ancestors, which, having been the cradle of his race, was the home of his descendants for the next four hundred and fifty years. "It is," says Camden, "the place where King Edmund resided nearly a whole year, endeavouring to get by heart David's Psalms in the Saxon language. But neither is it to be omitted on this account, that it has been the seat of the famous family of L'Estrange, knights, ever since the time of Ed. II." During this long period, there is little to record of their history. They several times appear on the roll of Sheriffs, and married the heiresses of Vernon, Hastings, and Coke of Norfolk—the latter being a granddaughter of Chief Justice Coke. Sir Nicholas Le Strange received a baronetcy from Charles I. : and it was with the fifth baronet, Sir Henry, that this illustrious name finally expired in 1760. Armine, his elder sister and coheir, was the wife of Nicholas Styleman of Snettisham in Norfolk, one of whose descendants, in 1839, adopted the name of Le Strange.

It is retained by Betton-Strange, and Ness-Strange, two of their former manors in Shropshire.

Estuteuille : This name, which is included in Wace's account of the Conqueror's companions, appears a second time on the Roll as Front-de-Bœuf. "The Sire d'Estoteville of the Roman de Rou was in all probability Robert, surnamed Frontdebœuf, Grantebœf, or, according to the French antiquaries, Grand-bois; but whether he was of Estouteville-sur-Cailly or Estouteville-sur-Mer may be an open question. There was a knightly family deriving its name from the former, one of whom, Nicholas, great-great-grandson of Robert, married Gunnor de Gant, the daughter of Hugh IV. de Gournay, in the twelfth century, and received with her in dower the manors of Beddingfield and Kimberley in Norfolk, which remained for many generations in the family. This Estouteville was formerly a *mouvance* or dependency on the fief of La Ferté-en-Brai, of which the Gournays were the lords, and it is therefore likely that Robert d'Estouteville followed Hugh II. de Gournay to England in the invading army.

" Some ten or eleven years previous to the Conquest, he was governor of the Castle of Ambrières, and stoutly defended it against Geoffrey Martel until relieved by the approach of Duke William. He could therefore not have been very young even at that time—say between twenty and thirty—and in 1066 he would have been between thirty and forty. Of his exploits at Senlac we hear nothing, and his name does not appear in Domesday, so we are ignorant of the reward, if any, which he received for his services. The latest mention of him is by Orderic, who records him as a witness to a confirmation charter of the Dean of Evreux to the Abbey of Ouche before the year 1089."—*J. R. Planché.*

Dugdale asserts that he was taken prisoner at the battle of Tinchebrai in 1106, when he would have been nearly eighty years of age ; but evidently confuses him with his son of the same name. Of this second Robert, Orderic speaks " as a brave and powerful baron, who was a strong partizan of the Duke " (Robert Court-heuse); " and superintended his troops and fortresses in the Pays de Caux." He also says (817) that d'Estouteville was slain fighting against Henry I. at Tinchebrai, and not, as other authorities aver, sent over to England to suffer the doom of life-long captivity. In either case, the whole of his possessions—which apparently included Roger de Moubray's former barony—were forfeited, and granted to the King's favourite, Nigel de Albini. His wife Erneburga, a Yorkshire heiress, whose father, Hugh, the son of Baldric, had been a great Saxon thane, brought him three sons ; Robert III. ; Osmund, who died at Joppa in Palestine ; and Patrick (omitted by Dugdale), to whom he gave the lordship of Skipwith in the East Riding.

Robert III. had been taken prisoner some little time before his father at the storming of Dives ; but, unlike him, was set at liberty, and returned home to enjoy at least some portion of his mother's inheritance, for in 1169, when Henry II. appointed him Sheriff of Yorkshire, he held between seven and eight knight's fees. He had fought valiantly at the great Northern victory, famous as the *Bellum Standardi,* and in 1173 was with Ranulph de Glanville and Bernard Baliol at the battle before Alnwick, where the King of Scots was taken prisoner. Some three years afterwards, feeling that his past services and actual position warranted him in making the attempt, he claimed from Nigel de Albini's son, Roger de Mowbray, the barony that had belonged to the first Roger de Mowbray, and of which Henry I. had deprived his father. It is said that the country generally favoured his claim ; and after a protracted suit, it was compromised by Mowbray's surrendering to him the Lordship of Kirkby Moorside, held by the service of nine knight's fees.

Robert de Stuteville—the name had been thus abbreviated by English habit of speech—was a considerable benefactor to the Church, for he founded two monasteries in Yorkshire, one at Rossedale and the other at Keldholme, and bestowed lands on two more. He was twice married ; first to Helewise . . . , who was the mother of William, his heir, and of two daughters ; and secondly to Sybil, the heiress of Philip de Valoines, who brought him Thorpenhow in Cumberland, and had one son named Eustace.

His successor, William, was a man of great power and account in the reign of Coeur de Lion, actively employed in all its troubles and dissensions; and having always taken part with Prince John in his various contests with the Regent Longchamp, was munificently rewarded on his accession to the throne. Not only was "the whole rule of the counties of Northumberland, Cumberland, and Westmorland, with all the castles therein, committed to his trust," but he likewise received a grant of the Honours of Knaresborough and Boroughbridge, with license to hold a fair and build a castle at each of his manors of Cottingham and Buttercramb in Yorkshire. Yet he was very far from being content. Seeing that he stood so high in the King's favour, he seized this propitious moment for reviving the ancient claim to Nigel de Albini's barony, that had been set to rest in his father's time; and after "great disputes," compelled Mowbray to buy him off at the price of nine more knight's fees, and a life rent of £12 a year. Then the two litigants were finally "made friends;" and shook hands before the King in the Bishop of Lincoln's house at Louth. Stuteville died in 1203, leaving two sons; of whom Robert, the elder, only survived him two years, and was a minor at the time of his death. Nicholas,* the second, who succeeded, was "one of the seven great Northern barons that wrested Magna Charta from King John," and were, as a necessary consequence, excommunicated by the Pope. He was again on the baronial side at the battle of Lincoln, where he was taken prisoner by the famous William Mareschal, Earl of Pembroke, and had to pay 1000 marks for his ransom, besides forfeiting both Knaresborough and Boroughbridge to the King, which were granted to the Justiciary Hubert de Burgh. His wife Gunnor, the widow of Robert de Gant, had given him only two daughters, of whom Margaret, the youngest, who was the wife of William Mastoc, died three years after him, leaving no children; and the whole splendid inheritance passed undivided to her sister Joan. Joan married Hugh de Wake; but "in regard she was so great an Inheritrix" called herself *Johanna de Stutevile* in her widowhood, instead of bearing her husband's name. She it was (and not, as usually avouched, Anne of Bohemia) who first rode on a side saddle in England; for the seal on her grant of Hessel to the Canons of Wharton, bears the impression "of a Woman riding sideway (as now is usual) holding the Bridle in her right Hand, and an Escoucheon with the Arms of Stutevile thereon, in her left Hand."

Eustace, the second son of Robert III., was, as I have said, through his

---

* Dugdale, in his pedigree, interpolates a second Nicholas, son of the first, thus crowding two generations into a space of twenty-seven years. Nicholas I. must have been very young in 1205, when he succeeded his elder brother, who did not live to be of age; yet Nicholas II. died in 1232, the father of two married daughters. It is obvious they were one and the same person.

mother the heir of Philip de Valoines; and held some property in Cumberland. I think that Dugdale, in the account he gives of him, must have skipped a generation: for it is clearly impossible that a man whose father was dead before 1172 should be "within age and under tuition" in 1205. It was probably a second Eustace who, the year after Nicholas de Stutevile's death, gave the King £1000 to have Cottingham and its appurtenances, but only succeeded in obtaining possession of it for fourteen weeks. He died in 1242; and his son Robert, though "born and bred up beyond Sea," was yet, by the King's favour, permitted to inherit, but appears to have had no descendants.

Two younger sons of Robert II. remain to be accounted for. Osmund, who died on pilgrimage in the Holy Land, married Isabel, daughter and heir of William Fitz Roger of Gressing Hall, and had two sons: 1. Robert, seated at Burton Agnes in Yorkshire, whose three daughters were his co-heirs: 2. William, who became the third husband of the great heiress, Margery de Say, and by "courtesy of England" held her two baronies of Burford and Richard's Castle till his death in 1259. She herself had died long before, leaving him two sons, the youngest of which, Robert, succeeded to Gressing Hall, and married Joan Talbot, a Lincolnshire heiress. Their son John, who was in arms against Henry III., was the father of Robert de Stutevile, whose wife, Eleanor de Genevere or de Genoure, was the widow of Alexander Baliol, and received from Queen Eleanor (the mother of Edward I.) a grant of " Mitford Castle and divers lands in Northumberland." He died in 1305, and the line ended with his son John in 1332. So, at least, says Dugdale; but Thoroton, in his *History of Notts*, derives these three last Stutevilles from a different ancestor, Henry de Stuteville —probably another son of Osmund's—who, "about 33 Henry II., gave account of £15 of the Fee of Kirkby, which was parted between him and Hubert Fitz Ralph." His son Robert married Leonia de Rennes, who brought him Diham, &c., in Nottinghamshire, and was the great-grandfather of the other Robert, already mentioned as the husband of Eleanor Baliol. It seems that John de Stutevile, who fought at Evesham, held one moiety of Hubert Fitz Ralph's barony, which goes far to prove this descent; but the pedigree is perplexed and perplexing, and evidently incomplete.

On the other hand, the numerous progeny of Patrick, Lord of Skipwith, has been minutely traced down to the present time. They took the name of their manor, but migrated from Yorkshire in the time of Henry III., when Sir William de Skipwith married Alice Thorpe, who brought him a great estate in Lincolnshire. They then settled in the latter county, and were subdivided into various branches, for I find mention of the Skipwiths of Utterby, the Skipwiths of Heburgh, the Skipwiths of Calthorpe, and the Skipwiths of Grantham and of Metheringham (who received a baronetcy that expired in 1756), besides the Skipwiths of Snore in Norfolk, &c. The parent stock from whence they sprung continued for many generations at Ormesby, and thence removed to Newbold

Hall. They gave several sheriffs to Lincolnshire, and two judges—father and son—to the King's Bench; one under Edward III., the other under his successor. "The collar of Esses," says an old writer, speaking of the latter, "now worn by judges, first introduced from the initial letters of *Sanctus Simon Simplicius*, an uncorrupted justicier in the primitive times, well suited this Sir William Skipwith, who died full of honour." In 1670 Fulwar Skipwith of Newbold Hall was created a baronet by Charles II., and the direct line ended with Sir Thomas in 1790. But a representative remains, descended from the youngest son of Sir William, Sheriff of the county of 18 Henry VIII., whose grandson Henry was seated at Prestwould Hall in Leicestershire, and received a baronetcy in 1622. Sir Guy, the third baronet, emigrated to America during Cromwell's usurpation; and the family remained for five generations in Virginia, where the grandfather of the present Sir Peyton was born.

The house of Estouteville was one of the greatest in Normandy, and flourished in the Pays de Caux up to the end of the last century. "Le Sieur Louis d'Estouteville" was the captain of the one hundred and nineteen gallant gentlemen that defended Mont St. Michel against the English in 1423.

Engaine: from Engen or Ingen, near Boulogne: a baronial name, that has travelled down to our own times under an English disguise as Ingham. "There are many places in England," says Morant, "named Gaynes, Engaines, D'Engains: one, for instance, near St. Neots in Huntingdonshire: another at Taversham in Cambridgeshire:" two, I may add, in Essex, Colne-Engaine and Gaines, held by Sir John Engaine in 1271 by the service of keeping the King's greyhounds; and one in Herefordshire, Aston Engen, now Aston Ingham. The original seat of the family was, however, at Senelai (Shenley) in Buckinghamshire, held *in capite* by Richard de Engen or Ingaine in 1086, with Redinges in Hunts. (Domesday). Another Richard, his descendant, Baron of Blatherwick in Northamptonshire, is entered in the *Liber Niger* as the tenant of Paganus de Dudley in Bucks, and held Pytchley by the sergeantry of destroying all "wolves, foxes, martrons and other vermin, in the counties of Northampton, Rutland, Oxford, Buckingham, Essex, and Huntingdon."* He was the founder of Finshed Priory, and married a daughter of the Earl of Oxford, Sara de Vere, by whom he left at his death, in 1208, two sons, both of which were engaged with the insurgent barons. Richard, the eldest, who died single in 1215, had thus forfeited his barony; but Vitalis, the other brother, received back his inheritance at the accession of Henry III. and obtained a rich wife, Rose, one of the three co-heiresses that divided the great Welsh Honour of Montgomery. He was the father of Vitalis, Henry, William, and John. Vitalis died young; Henry, who

* This tenure is entered in Domesday, when one William was lord of the manor; his predecessor in the time of the Confessor had been Alwyne "the Hunter:" and the celebrated Pytchley hounds of our own day hunt the same country, which can thus show a "sporting antiquity" of eight hundred years.

succeeded him in 1244, and fought on the barons' side at Evesham, was never married; William had no children; and thus the whole inheritance devolved on John. John's successor and namesake was summoned to Parliament from 1299 to 1321, but again had no heir, and was followed in 1322 by his brother Nicholas, who died two months after him, leaving two sons. The elder, according to the strange fatality that persistently attended the first-born of this house, again was without posterity. The second, another John, seated at Dyllington in Huntingdonshire, was a baron by writ in 1342, and the father of the two last male heirs that bore the name, John and Thomas. Both died s. p., John in his life-time, and Thomas, second Lord Engaine, in 1367. His great estates, lying in the counties of Huntingdon, Northants, Buckingham, Rutland, Oxon, Leicester, and Bedford, fell to their three sisters, Joyce de Goldington, Elizabeth de Pabenham, and Mary Bernak.

In addition to this baronial house, there were other families of the name. Ansfrid de Cormeilles, who held Aston in Herefordshire in 1086, was succeeded there by the Engaines, or Inghams, who continued in possession till the latter years of the fourteenth century. William de Inghayn presented to the rectory in 1306; and his son Simon, who adopted the name of his manor, was the father of Thomas, High Sheriff of the county in 1351. With Thomas's son Roger the line was brought to a close.—*Duncomb's Herefordshire.* In Cumberland Ralph de Engayne obtained the manor of Isal from Alan, the son of Earl Waltheoff, and married a great heiress, Ibria de Estrivers (see *Travers*), who brought him the barony of Burgh-upon-Sands, and the hereditary Forestership of Cumberland. Both passed to his only child Ada, who had two husbands, Sir Simon de Morville, and Lord Vaux of Gillesland. Sir Simon, we are told, was well stricken in years when he married her; and Ada's wanton fancy strayed to one of his squires, a comely Saxon youth, named Lyulph. But Lyulph, like another Joseph, was a loyal servant, deaf to the blandishments of his amorous mistress; and Ada, infuriated at finding herself scorned and rejected, played the part of Potiphar's wife, and charged him with attempting the very crime she had vainly solicited him to commit. Her husband, as credulous as Potiphar, implicitly believed her story; but here the analogy ends, for the Christian knight proved far crueller than his heathen prototype had been. Not content with a mere sentence of imprisonment, he ordered the unhappy squire to be thrown into a "leadful of scalding water," and actually boiled alive. Hutchinson, who retails this shocking story, bids us, however, remember, in justice to Ada de Engayne and her old husband, that it is borrowed from a monkish chronicler, who would assuredly endeavour to blacken their characters, for no better reason than that they were the parents of Sir Hugh de Morville, abominated by the Church for the murder of Thomas à Beckett (see *Morville*).

The name of Engayne had not died out with Ada's father; for his grandson Sir Hugh granted to Gilbert de Engayne—evidently a kinsman—the manor of

Clifton in Westmorland, where his posterity continued till the reign of Edward III. The daughter of the last male heir, another Gilbert, married William de Wybergh.

Though the Engaines became Inghams in Herefordshire, they had no connection with the Norfolk family of that name, which also attained baronial rank. Their arms were entirely different. The Engaines bore *Gules* a fesse indented between seven cross-crosslets, four in chief and three in base *Or.*

Chalmers, in his *Caledonia*, states that "Berengarius de. Engain, a noble Anglo-Norman, was one of the followers of Earl David, to whom he gave lands in Scotland after his accession to the throne." Berengarius was a benefactor of Jedburgh Abbey.

Estriels: mis-spelt; it should be, as it is in Duchesne's copy, Escriols, or Criol—a name that appears again on the Roll in its Anglicized form of Kiriell. "It derived from Robert, Count of Eu, whose younger son Robert obtained from him Criol, or Crieul, near Eu. He had been previously in possession of Criol, as appears by one of his charters to the Abbey of Tréport (Gall. Christ. xi. col. 13, Instr.)"—*The Norman People.* In Domesday it is written Cruel. "Robertus Cruel" held Esseborne (Ashburnham) in Sussex of his kinsman the Earl of Eu, who then governed the Rape of Hastings, and I think there can be no reasonable doubt that he was the progenitor of the Ashburnhams. But they themselves claim a remoter ancestry. "My poor and plaine Pen," writes Fuller, with genuine enthusiasm, "is willing, though unable, to add any lustre to this Family of stupendous Antiquitie. The chiefe of this name was Highe Sheriff of Sussex and Surrey, anno 1066, when William Duke of Normandy invaded England, to whom King Harold wrote to assemble the *posse Comitatum* to make effectual resistance against that Foreigner. The Original hereof, an honorable Heireloome (worth as much as the Owners thereof would value it at), was lately in the possession of this Familie; a Familie wherein the Eminency hath equalled the Antiquity thereof, having been Barons of England in the Reign of King Henry the Third." There is certainly no record of any such barony, and I fear King Harold's writ is not forthcoming either. In point of fact, this Saxon descent rests on the sole authority of Francis Thynne, one of the inventive heralds of the time of Queen Elizabeth, who tells us that "Bertram Ashburnham, a Baron of Kent, was Constable of Dover Castle in 1066; which Bertram was beheaded by William the Conqueror, because he did so valiantly defend the same against the Duke of Normandy." There are, however, various difficulties to be met in this pedigree, in addition to the historical fact that Dover Castle, though styled "the lock and key of the whole kingdom," surrendered to the Conqueror without striking a blow. Bertram's two sons, Philip and Michael, are said to have been also executed; but his grandson Reginald reappears in possession of the estate, as one of the benefactors of Battle Abbey. Now the name of the Saxon owner of Ashburnham, as given in Domesday, was Sewardus, and not Bertram,* and there is no evidence to show that the posterity of Robert de Cruel were ever dispossessed. According to the common practice of those days, they styled themselves De Ashburnham, bearing their paternal name conjointly during five or six generations. Thus it seems evident that Reginald de Ashburnham, who bestowed some lands and two salt-works on the monks of La Bataille, and his son Stephen, who confirmed the gift, and sold lands, as "Steven de Cuell" to Robertsbridge Abbey (Mon. i. 916), were in reality of the Norman race that received Ashburnham at the Conquest. Their beautiful domain has been transmitted by direct male descent to the present Earls of Ashburnham, who are probably—though far from admitting the fact themselves —the last remaining representatives of this great baronial house.

Its chief seat was in Kent, where, as Leland tells us, " Creal was a Man of very faire Land, ontylle it felle to be devydid.

"Sum say Folchestone Parke was his, and then it cam to the Clintons. Costinghaungre was Creal's Lordship, of sum now corruptely caullid Westenhanger. . .

" Certen of the Crealles were honorably biried at S. Radegund.

" Creaulles were greate Benefactors to Houses of Religion in Est Kent, as appereth by their Armes in many Glase-Windois.

" The name of Finiox thus cam ynto Kent about King Edwarde II. Dayes. One Creaulle was a Prisoner in Bologne in Fraunce, and much desiring to be at Liberte made his Keper to be his Frend, promysing hym Landes in Kent if he wold help to deliver him. Whereapon they both toke secrete Passage and cam to Kent, and Creal performed his Promise : so that after his Keper or Porter apon the cause was namid Finiox."

This is one of the families belonging to East Kent of which Mr. Planché remarks that we hear much, and know but little, "although their ancient coats are still to be seen quartered in so many atchievements, and studding the roof of Canterbury Cathedral." The first mentioned is John de Criol, who in 1194 gave the church of Sarres in Thanet to Ledes Priory, and was the father of four sons, Bertram, Simon, William, and Nicholas. Of the three younger we know no more than that Nicholas married a Clifford, and left three co-heiresses ; but Bertram, the heir, was a man of note and importance, styled, from his large possessions in the county, the Great Lord of Kent. " Some misdemeanour (it seems) this Bertram had committed, for which in 15 Hen. III. he was commanded to quit the Countrey ; nevertheless, by the mediation of friends, he got leave to stay, upon condition he should not come to Court ; and the next year' following he obtain'd so much credit with the King, that he was then constituted Sheriff of Kent, in which trust he continued until the end of the first half of

* By a strange irony of fate, Francis Thynne selected for his Saxon hero the very un-Saxon name of Bertram, which happened to be an hereditary one in the house of Criol.

23 Hen. III."—*Dugdale.* He was also Sheriff of Essex and Herts, with the custody of two royal castles, Dover and Rochester, and left three sons, John, Simon, and Nicholas (of whom presently). John, whose wife brought him the manor of Estwell, had a writ of military summons to oppose the Welsh under Llewellyn in 1256, and died in 1262. He, again, had four sons. The eldest, a second Bertram, was splendidly matched with Alianor, one of the four co-heiresses of Hamo de Crevecoeur and Maud d'Avranches, the great heiress of Folkestone, who was dowered with half the hundred of Folkestone and half the manor of Hythe. He forfeited his lands by joining Simon de Montfort, but " made his composition " on the accession of Edward I. He died in 1308, leaving two sons, John and Bertram,* who successively died s. p., and a daughter Joan, married to Sir Richard de Rokesley, whose children eventually divided this great inheritance. One married Sir William Baude, the other Walter de Patteshull and Thomas de Poynings, but had a son only by her second husband.

Nicholas, the youngest son of the Great Lord of Kent (according to Planché, for Dugdale names him before his brother), received, like him, a summons to serve against the Welsh in 1256, and six years later was appointed Sheriff of Kent, and Warden of the Cinque Ports, at that time charged with the whole maritime defence of the realm. He was likewise Constable of Rochester. He married the widow of Sir Henry de Sandwich, Joan, sole daughter and heir of William de Auberville, in whose right she was Lady of Westenhanger; and their son Nicholas, having attended Edward I. in his foreign wars, was summoned to Parliament in 1296. But this summons was never repeated to his descendants, though they continued for five more generations. The next heir, Nicholas III., was Admiral of the Fleet in 1324, from the Thames mouth southwards, and "imploy'd by the King to prevent the landing of Queen Isabel and her son Prince Edward, and to infest the French Merchants upon the Western Coasts." The last was Sir Thomas Kiriell (for so the name had now become written), whose fortunes were wrecked with the House of Lancaster. " He was made a Knight of the Garter by Henry VI., but was never installed, and was beheaded in 1461 by order of Edward IV., having been taken prisoner in the fatal battle of St. Albans."—*Planché.* His only child, Alice, married Sir John Fogg of Repton.

Croxton-Cryol, or Keryel, which had been granted to the first Bertram de Criol by Henry III. in 1242, preserves their name in Leicestershire, though now best known as the property of the Duke of Rutland, and the scene of an annual race-meeting. Several junior branches survived the extinction of the main line, and amongst them was probably the Herefordshire family which gave birth to

---

* Bertram held two of his manors by a singular tenure : " to provide one man called a *Vautrer*, to lead three greyhounds, when the King should go into Gascoign, as long as a pair of Shoes of Fourpence price would last."—*Dugdale.*

the "Man of Ross." Their descent is traced from their first settlement in the county in 1295; and the name, then spelt Crull, or Cryll, gradually merged into Kyrle. They bore one of the chevrons of the Criols (though in a changed tincture, and with the addition of three fleurs-de-lis), and were seated at Walford Court, from whence Robert Kyrle, "a stony-hearted rebel," who was a captain of Cromwell's troopers, is said to have bombarded Goodrich Castle during the Civil War. Pope's hero, John Kyrle, was the nephew of this Robert's father, James, High Sheriff of Herefordshire (married to a niece of John Hampden's), and himself the son of a younger brother, who left him only a narrow income :

> "Of debts and taxes, wife and children clear,
> This man possest—500 pounds a year."

Yet, by thrift and self-denial, he found means to be munificent in good works, and to accomplish, in his 87 years of life—for " he had his hour measured him by a large glass "—all that needed to be done in his native place. How much this was—how far beyond what seemed possible even to his " boundless charity " is a never-ending marvel, and brings home to us all a lesson we should do well to learn.*

> "Who hung with woods yon mountain's sultry brow?
> From the dry rock who bade the waters flow?
> Not to the skies in useless columns tost,
> Or in proud falls magnificently lost,
> But clear and artless, pouring through the plain,
> Health to the sick, and solace to the swain.
> Whose causeway parts the vale with shady rows?
> Whose seats the weary traveller repose?
> Who taught that heaven-directed spire to rise?
> 'The Man of Ross,' each lisping babe replies.
> Behold the market-place with poor o'erspread !
> The Man of Ross divides the weekly bread :
> He feeds yon almshouse, neat, but void of state,
> Where Age and Want sit smiling at the gate ;
> Him portion'd maids, apprentic'd orphans blest,
> The young who labour, and the old who rest.
> Is any sick ? the Man of Ross relieves,
> Prescribes, attends, the medicine makes and gives.

---

* Since writing the above, I have met with the following passage in one of Dr. Johnson's letters : " Wonders are willingly told and willingly heard. The truth is, that Kirle was a man of known integrity and active benevolence, by whose solicitations the wealthy were persuaded to pay contributions to his charitable schemes; this influence he obtained by an example of liberality, exerted to the utmost extent of his power, and was thus enabled to give more than he had. This account Mr. Victor received from the minister of the parish, and I have preserved it that the praise of a good man, being made more credible, may be more solid."

Is there a variance? Enter but his door,
Balk'd are the courts, and contest is no more.
Despairing quacks with curses fled the place,
And vile attorneys, now a useless race."

This noble-hearted man died in 1724.

Walford Court, the family seat, had passed away to the Gwyllyms through a daughter of the rebel captain's in the previous century. A younger brother, of Much Marcle in the same county, was created a baronet by Charles I., but the line expired with his grandson in 1679.

Esturny; for L'Estourmi, the true version of the name, as given on the Dives Roll; without any doubt a *sobriquet*, and, I am bound to add, to me, at least, incomprehensible. In England the first letter was often dropped, and it became Sturmy, Sturmid (as in Domesday), Stormey, Sturmer, Sturmyn, &c., while in Normandy it has survived to the present day as Etourmy. Jean L'Estourmi, a younger brother of the two companions-in-arms of the Conqueror, had remained at home; and became the ancestor of "a family that from the most remote antiquity held a high rank among the nobles of the province." —*Nobiliaire de Normandie.* In the seventeenth century they were Seigneurs de St. Privat; and in 1721 of Joinville. They bear *D'azur à une fontaine d'argent, surmontée d'un renard couché de même.* Nothing can well be more unlike the coat of the English house: *Argent*, three demi-lions rampant *Gules.*

The two brothers who came over at the Conquest, Richard and Ralph, were both land-owners in 1086; Richard, as the elder, held of the King, and Ralph as a mesne-lord under him in Hants, Wilts, and Surrey. Cowsfield-Esturmy in Wiltshire, and Lysse-Sturmy, in Hampshire, were two of his manors. His descendants continued, for a long succession of generations, Foresters in fee of Savernake. "The Esturmies," says Camden, "from the time of King Henrie the Second were by right of inheritance the Bailiffes and Guardians of the Forest of Savernac lying hard by, which is of great name for plentie of good game, and for a kinde of Ferne there, that yeeldeth a most pleasing savour. In remembrance thereof, their Hunter's horn of a mighty bignesse and tipt with silver, the Earle of Hertford keepeth unto this day, as a monument of his progenitors.* They founded the Hospital of the Holy Trinity at Easton, near Marlborough, where a Master (appointed at their presentation to the Bishop), was bound to have his "continual residence, to keep hospitality, and to find five priests to say daily masses for the founder's souls." Besides this "great inheritance" in Wiltshire, they possessed in Hampshire "large holdings at Odiham, Dogmersfield, Winchfield, and Elvetham. In 1206 Henry Esturmy paid at Porchester sixty out of one hundred capons promised in consideration of leave to break up land at Culefield; and in 1280 another Henry was summoned to show warrant for his taking the assize of bread and beer at Elvetham, and pleaded that his ancestors had enjoyed the privilege since the time of King Richard I."—*Woodward's*

Hampshire. A third Henry, who was Sheriff of Wilts in 1362, and married Margaret, daughter and co-heir of Sir John de L'Ortie of Axford, was the father of the last of the line, Sir William Esturmy of Chedham and Wolf's Hall, living temp. Richard II. His only daughter Maud married Roger Seymour, ancestor of the Dukes of Somerset, to whom the great domain of the Esturmies thus accrued. His descendants, transplanted into Wiltshire from their distant home on the Welsh border, held it close upon three hundred years. At length, on the death of William, third Duke of Somerset, who died unmarried in 1671 at the early age of twenty, it passed to his only surviving sister, Lady Elizabeth. She became the wife of Thomas Bruce, second Earl of Aylesbury and third Earl of Elgin, and died in childbed in 1696, leaving a son and a daughter. The son left no heir-male, and at his death in 1747 the estates devolved on the youngest son of his sister, Elizabeth, Countess of Cardigan, who was created Earl of Ailesbury. When the second Earl received a Marquessate in 1821, he took the title of Viscount Savernake, from the magnificent forest over which the Esturmies had so long held sway.

The family was represented in many other parts of England—in the Eastern Counties, in Worcestershire, Shropshire, and Yorkshire. In Shropshire, "the first of this race," says Eyton, "that occurs to my notice is Hugh Esturmi, amerced five marks in 1176 for trespass in the Forests of Worcestershire." This Hugh Esturmi came from Sussex, where his father exchanged some land near Chichester with the Earl of Arundel; and Hugh himself received from the same Earl—William de Albini, the first of the name—a grant of half a knight's fee in Offham.—v. *Dallaway's Sussex.* There is no further mention of the family in Sussex, and their connection with Shropshire had ceased in the first part of the fourteenth century. Stanford-Sturmy and Sutton-Sturmy bear their name in Worcestershire. "We find in the old White Book of the Bishopric, *Willielmus Esturmy tenet Rushoke de dono domini Regis.* They continued in possession in the reign of Ed. I., when Geoffrey Sturmy held it of the barony of William de Beauchamp, and it belonged to many lords of that name. Laurence Sturmy is reported in the Exchequer to have had it 28 Ed. I.; it then descended to Harry Sturmy, and 20 Ed. III. to Henry Sturmy his heir. Sutton-Sturmy was in early ages the habitation of that Sturmy who distinguished himself by his zeal for the recovery of the Holy Land, and is buried in Tenbury church. This memorable name of Sturmy ended in Rushoke 7 Hen. VI., and the lands were dispersed among the general heirs of Henry Sturmy."—*Nash's Worcestershire.* Robert Sturmy was knight of the shire in 1309 and 1315; and summoned for service against the Scots in 1322.

The Yorkshire Esturmies (there, again, abbreviated to Sturmy) were Lords of Dromonby, in Cleveland, for four generations; their heiress married a younger son of Sir Robert Constable of Flamborough.—*Grave's Cleveland.* William Sturmy, in 1316, was joint Lord of Worsall, Faceby, and Skutterskelfe in Yorkshire.—*Palgrave's Parliamentary Writs.* At the same date, and in the same record, we find John Sturmy, joint Lord of Stratton and Thorp, Fritton, Skelton, and Hardwick; and Walter Sturmy, joint Lord of Surlingham, Rockwell, and Brandon; both in Norfolk. John was Admiral of the Fleet in 1325. Robert le Sturmy had received Stratton by grant from the Malherbes; "and gave his name to Sturmyn's or Sturmer's Manor, of which his son was Lord in 1262. The heiress of this family, Anne Sturmer, married Ralph Drury in the time of Edward IV."—*Blomfield's Norfolk.* Another contemporary family was seated at Buxhall in Suffolk: of whom Sir William Esturmy was High Sheriff of Norfolk and Suffolk from 1210 to 1214. "In 1254 his grandson held the manor of Buxhall. About 1367 the last Sir William Esturmy died, leaving one daughter Rhosia, married to William Clement of Stow."—*Hollingworth's History of Stowmarket.*

The name is found in Somersetshire in 1669; and certainly existed for 100 years after that; for it is inscribed on a pyramid of variegated marble in Cheltenham Church, which bears the three demi-lions that appertained to it, and commemorates Henry Sturmy, obt. 1772.

Ferrerers: for Ferrers: see page 25.

Foluile; from Folleville, in Picardy. The town of Ashby-Folville and the (now depopulated) hamlet of Newbolt-Folville in Leicestershire owe their names to this family, whom we find seated at Ashby in the reign of Stephen. From Fulk de Folville, who was living there in 1137, the pedigree is regularly traced to Sir William, who sided with the revolted barons in 1216; and whose son Sir Eustace "was one of those who, after the battle of Evesham, so stoutly defended Kenilworth Castle against the King in 1265; notwithstanding all which he was suffered to compound for his estate and received the King's pardon." Three Folvilles served as knights of the shire for Leicester during the reign of Ed. II. In 1326, another Eustace, "with two of his brothers, having been threatened by Roger le Beler, one of the justices itinerant, they took the law into their own hands, and barbarously murdered the judge in a valley near Reresby. This Eustace died in 1347, and is traditionally supposed to be represented by a monumental figure in Ashby Church."—*Nichols.* He appears to have received no punishment: the King "gave pardon for this and other trespasses." The principal line ended with four brothers, sons of Sir John de Folville and his wife Mabel, daughter and sole heir of Sir Geoffrey De la Mare. The eldest, again Sir John, was childless, having "wedded an old ancyant lady of Yorkshire that was the wyfe of the Lorde Marmion; and he might dispende yearly by her vii C. marks. And they kept a worthy household and a greate at Ashby-Folville. And the said Sir John was a knight of the good Duke of Lancaster, and the said Duke would come and lie at Ashby many divers times when it pleased him; and he gave Sir John xx marks of fee yearly." Geoffrey, the second brother, died early in life, and left two daughters; Mabel, his heiress, who was in ward to

II.   C

John of Gaunt, and married to John de Woodford, and Alice, the wife of Edmund Kinvile of Norfolk. Sir Christopher, the third, also died before his time, leaving an only child, Margaret, married to Sir John Browe, a knight of Cheshire mentioned in the reign of Richard II., and Sir Matthew, the youngest, knight of the shire for Leicester 31 Ed. III., was never married. "After the decease of Sir Christopher, his widow Margaret" (her maiden name is omitted) "was in household with Sir John her husband's brother, and was mickel cherished with him, and was with him when he died; and there she imagined false deeds and let write them, and ensealed them with his hand when he was dead, for she had the seal of his arms, and all his deeds and evidences that belonged to all the lordships that Folville were ever enheryte in England." It was of course for her own daughter that she schemed to obtain the inheritance that rightfully belonged to her niece Mabel de Woodford; and her son-in-law Sir John Browe maintained the "false feoffment" she had made with such fraud and subtilty that "therefore," continues the family chronicler, "I verily suppose that she be in Hell. Nevertheless, she made confession, ere she died, to the Abbot of Croxton, kneeling on both her knees, asking mercy and forgiveness of all the wrongs and disherison, that lay on her." These Folvilles bore Party per fesse *Argent* and *Or* a cross moline *Gules.*

Fitz Water. Robert Fitz Walter was a subtenant in Bucks in 1086; and Ralph Fitz Walter held in Leicestershire. "As to these Fitzes," says Sir Egerton Brydges (there are twenty-nine of them on the Roll): "it is true William fil. Alan, &c., occur in Domesday Book, but by no means as exclusive or hereditary appropriations. Fitz Walter seems to have been appropriated exclusively by Robert Fitz Walter, a great Baron temp. King John, and great grandson of Richard de Tonbridge, fifth son of the Earl of Clare, to whom the Conqueror granted one hundred and seventy-five Lordships.

Fitz Marmaduke. John Fitz Marmaduke was one of the bravest knights at the siege of Carlaverock—

> "Ke tuit prisoient, prince e duc,
> E autre ke li conoissent."

"Le bon Bertram de Monboucher" led the first assault on the castle—a castle so placed and defended that it "did not fear siege;" next came Gerard de Gondrouville, "Bachelier legier e joli:" and after him

> "Lors vint le chastel assaillir
> Li Fiz Mermenduc à baniere,
> O um graunt route e pleniere
> De bons bacheliers esleus."

They won their way forward to the very brink of the fosse, amid a storm of missiles and stones showered from the battlements; and when there,

> "Li fiz Mermenduc cel affaire
> Tant entreprist à endurer,
> Cum li autre i porent durer,
> Car il estut cum une estache;
> Mès sa baniere ot meinte tache
> Et meint pertuis mal à recoustre."

But I am sorry to say that this gallant soldier's name can find no place here. He was the first born son of Marmaduke Fitz Geoffrey, Lord of Hordene in the Bishopric of Durham, and belonged to the Lumley family, whose fesse and popinjays he bore. He married Isabel de Bruce, and died in 1313 at St. John's Town (Perth) in Scotland, of which he had been appointed Governor. He has been called the "boiled baron." The country between the Border and the distant garrison in which he died being "harassed in every direction by the Scots, who owed the English no courtesy, it was impossible to comply in any usual manner with the Baron's dying request, of receiving sepulture in Durham Cathedral: yet, rather than leave their master's reliques in Scotland, his servants dismembered the body, boiled the flesh from the bones in a huge cauldron, and preserved the reliques till an opportunity offered of transmitting them across the Border."—*Surtees' Durham.*

Fleuez. At first sight this seemed an altogether hopeless name to identify; but a reference to Leland's roll shows it to be merely a mis-spelling of Fiennes. In his copy, this and the succeeding name are joined together as "Fenes et Felebert."

This was a baronial family, from Fiennes in the county of Guines. "Eustace, Baron of Fiennes, c. 1020, married Adela, Lady of Ardres, daughter of Everard de Furnes, and had Conon de Fiennes, who founded Beaulieu Abbey, Boulogne, and had issue Conon, father of Eustace, ancestor of the Barons de Fiennes (Des Bois). This family was seated in Kent at an early date, and held the office of hereditary Castellans of Dover."—*The Norman People.* Yet it is remarkable that Dugdale, in his enumeration of the family possessions, does not include a single Kentish manor. Ingelram de Fienes, the first mentioned by him, married a great niece of King Stephen, Sybil de Tingrie, daughter and heir of Faramus de Boulogne, the descendant, in the third generation, of the Count Eustace of the Conquest; and their son John, in 1216, held Mertoc in Somersetshire and Wendover in Buckinghamshire, that had been his mother's, and formed part of the Honour of Boulogne. The next heir, Ingelram II., possessed Hoyland and Tolleshunt in Essex, with lands in Northamptonshire, and purchased of Robert de Guisnes Gayton in Hampshire, where he obtained license to enclose his woods, within the bounds of Silchester Forest, and make a park. Both he and his brother Baldwin served in the Gascon wars of Henry III., and he was rewarded for his fidelity to the King during the Barons' War. His son William had been educated with Prince Edward, whom he attended to the Holy Land in 1269, and in 1281 on his campaign in Wales. At the first outbreak of the quarrel between France and England, he "favoured the French," and his lands were seized for treason ; but he made his peace, received them back, and died a loyal subject in 1301. He had evidently lived much abroad, for a difficulty arose as to the succession of his son Sir John, who had been born "beyond seas," and held land in Flanders. Sir John, again, suffered forfeiture "in respect of his residence within the power of France," and had to furnish satisfactory proof of his loyalty before he could recover his estates. His wife, Maud de Monceaux, brought him the beautiful domain of Hurstmonceux in Sussex ; and his son William married a still greater heiress, Joan, one of the three daughters of Geoffrey, third Lord Say, who became the co-heiresses of their brother William. The grandsons of this marriage, Roger and James, were the founders of the two branches of the family that bore the titles of Dacre and Say. The elder, one of the heroes of Agincourt, built the great castle of Hurstmonceux—the first brick castle ever seen in England—now only a majestic ruin, but still entire in the last century, when Horace Walpole walked up "a brave old avenue" (long since gone) to the gate, "with ships sailing on our left hand the whole way," and admired "the wings of the blue hills, covered with wood" beyond. The *alaune* or wolf-dog of the Fiennes' supports their shield on the great gateway, and once figured in most of the windows throughout the building.

Sir Roger was the father of Richard Fiennes, declared in 1459 Lord Dacre, in right of his wife Joan de Dacre, the grand-daughter and heir of the seventh and last Lord. She was dowered with all his magnificent possessions in the North ; but "great disputes" arose concerning this inheritance, which was hotly contested by her uncle, Sir Humphrey Dacre, the heir male of the family. The point was at length referred, by mutual agreement, to Edward IV. and the House of Lords, and virtually decided in Sir Humphrey's favour. The title and precedence of her father was confirmed to Lady Joan ; but Gillesland, the ancient seat of the De Vaux's, and the great bulk of the property, was adjudged to him, and he was created Lord Dacre; being styled Lord Dacre of the North for distinction's sake, as to the older title was assigned the designation of Lord Dacre of the South. This latter is still borne by a descendant in the female line (see *Brand*).

For three more generations it remained in the Fiennes family, till, when Gregory, the eleventh Baron, died without issue in 1594, it passed through his sister Margaret to the Lennards. Their father, Thomas, tenth Lord Dacre, had been executed at Tyburn for the murder of Sir Thomas Pelham's park-keeper. It was a harsh sentence; for the man died of a chance blow dealt by one of Lord Dacre's followers, when he himself was not present. It would seem that this madcap young lord (he was not more than twenty-four) with some other frolicksome Sussex gentlemen, organized a raid in humble imitation of Chevy

Chase, and sallied out to hunt the deer in Sir Thomas' park at Laughton. They encountered the keepers; a fray ensued, and the foolish prank ended in a tragedy: but Lord Dacre, being in a different part of the park, did not see Sir Thomas' servant receive the hurt that afterwards proved mortal. Yet not only he, but three of his poor retainers were put to death as murderers. The King's severity towards him was attributed to some courtiers who "gaped after the estate:" but it proved too strictly entailed to be touched.

James de Fiennes, the younger grandson of Sir William de Fiennes, was created Lord Say and Sele in 1446. He was at that time high in office and in favour at the Court of Henry VI., having in earlier life done good service to his father in the French wars; and from being Esquire of the Body to his young master, became Constable of Dover and Warden of the Cinque Ports,* Lord Chamberlain, Constable of the Tower, and in 1449 Lord Treasurer of England But the ruinous and humiliating issue of the hundred years' war with France had roused the country to fury against the King's advisers, "the enemies to his honour, suckers of his purse, and robbers of his subjects, for rewards corrupted and for indifferency nothing doing." In the following year, he and the Duke of Suffolk were impeached by the Commons for the surrender of Maine and Anjou; and the King not only sequestered Lord Say from his office, but, on hearing that twenty thousand of the men of Kent were in arms under Jack Cade, committed him to the Tower. Yet the popular outcry was far from being appeased, and when the victorious rebel, striking his sword against London stone, proclaimed himself lord of the city, his first act of authority was to fetch Say from his prison, and bring him to a mock trial at the Guildhall In vain he claimed his privilege to be tried by his peers, and passionately pleaded that he was no traitor:

> "I sold not Maine, I lost not Normandy;
> Yet, to recover them, would lose my life.
> Justice with favour I have always done;
> Prayers and tears have mov'd me, gifts could never.
> When have I aught exacted at your hands?
>
> * * * * * * *
>
> Have I affected wealth, or honour; speak?
> Are my chests filled up with extorted gold?
> Is my apparel sumptuous to behold?
> Whom have I injured, that you seek my death?
> These hands are free from guiltless blood-shedding:
> This breast from harbouring foul deceitful thoughts.
> O, let me live!"—*Henry VI., Part II., Act IV., Scene 7.*

He might have spared his eloquence, for when was remonstrance ever regarded by a raging multitude? He was dragged to the foot of the standard at Cheapside,

---

* He received a patent of these two offices to himself and his heirs-male, which was surrendered by the second lord in 1450 to Humphrey, Duke of Buckingham.

i

there heheaded before the priest could shrive him, with his half spoken confession still on his lips: and his head, pitched on a high pole, was borne before Cade, "as he rode, like a lordly captain, thro' every street." Not content with this, the mob leader, proceeding to Mile End, apprehended Sir John Cromer, Say's son-in-law, and then Sheriff of Kent, "and without confession or excuse heard, caused him likewise to be beheaded, and his head fixed on a pole, and with these two heads this bloody butcher entered into the city again, and in despite caused them in every street kiss together, to the great detestation of all the beholders." —*Holinshed.* Say's headless body was stripped, and dragged naked at a horse's tail to St. Thomas of Waterings, "so that the flesh clave to the stones all the way from Chepe to Southwark."

His son, too, fell upon evil times, for he lost his life, and the greater part·of his fortune, in the Wars of the rival Roses. "The last of the Lorde Sayes," writes Leland, "being in Renowme was twice taken Prisoner, wherby he was much punishid by the Purse. Wherapon he was fain to lay most part of his Land to ·Morgare, and sold clerely part of it. So that sins the name of the Barony of Say is extinctid, but the Heires Male of the Lord Say in Descent yet remainith caulled by the Name of Fines." "The fact is," explains Banks, " that Henry Fiennes, son of William, died in 1476, without having received summons to parliament; in consequence of the loss of property, as did his son Richard in 1486; though they were both called Lord Saye. But Edward, son and heir of Richard, did not even use that title; because his mother held the capital seat, and the greatest part of the estate; but his son and heir, Richard, was father of another Richard, who obtained from James I., on his accession, letters patent confirming to him the title of Saye and Sele."

In the next generation, William Fiennes was created a Viscount by James I. in 1624. " He was a man of a close and reserved temper, of a mean and narrow fortune, of great parts, and of the highest ambition. He had for many years been the oracle of those who were called Puritans in the worse sense, and steered all their counsels and designs."—*Clarendon.* Being poor, proud, and discontented, one strong motive of his violent opposition to the Court was the hope of extorting some preferment, for it was sagaciously observed by another contemporary that " the harshnesse of his humour was a little allayed by the sweet refreshments of Court favour." No promotion seems to have come in his way during the Commonwealth; and he died two years after the Restoration. The title that had been granted to him became extinct in 1781, on the death of the eighth Viscount, who was the last heir male of his house. The old barony of Say and Sele was then claimed by Thomas Twistleton,* as the representative of his

* He was the son of John Twistleton (who had put in an unsuccessful claim to the barony in 1733) and a woman of low origin named Anne Gardner; but this marriage rests on the faith of a· Fleet Register only, and ·no parochial register of his baptism could be produced.

great-great-grandmother, Elizabeth Fiennes (eldest daughter and coheir of the second Viscount), who had married John Twistleton; and with his descendants, who have assumed the name of Fiennes, it still remains.

Filberd: Fibert (Duchesne); Felebert (Leland); Seint Philbert in Brompton's list; a baronial family, whose name, derived from St. Philibert-sur-Rile, in the arrondissement of Pont Audemer, was abbreviated by the same process that converted the "nuces de S. Philiberto" into filberts. They bore *Argent*, three bendlets *Azure*, and were Lords of Bray, in Berkshire, and Beach amwell in Norfolk, at the end of the twelfth century. Nicholas de St. Philibert, in 1213, went with King John to Poitou. Hugh de St. Philibert (who, with his wife Albreda, is first mentioned in 1201) was in arms with the insurgent barons, but returned to his obedience on the accession of Henry III., had restitution of his lands in Norfolk and Cornwall, and was appointed Governor of Jersey in 1225. His son Roger, and another of the name, William de St. Philibert, were both actively engaged in the rebellion of 1262; and the former was taken prisoner at the rout of Northampton. The latter assisted in the defence of Dover Castle; but, "after the Battle of Evesham, submitting himself, had reception to the King's grace and favour, and restitution of his lands in Northants."—*Dugdale.* Roger's daughter and heiress, Beatrix, married Stephen de Scales; and his brother Hugh succeeded as next heir, and was summoned to parliament by Edward I. in 1298. He was a staunch soldier in the Scottish and Gascon wars, constantly employed in the King's service from 1296 till his death in 1304. He had obtained through his wife a large property in Norfolk and Suffolk that had been the inheritance of Benedict de Blakeham. It seems that this infatuated youth, within a few months after his coming of age, divested himself of the whole of his possessions, granting them, in consideration of a trifling annuity, to Lady St. Philibert in fee. Her husband survived her, and when he was on his death-bed, "in the presence of his household, acknowledged to Benedict in person that he had much wronged him, and begged his forgiveness." —*Gage's Suffolk.*

Sir John de St. Philibert, Hugh's son, performed his homage in 1313, and three years later had a charter of free warren in his lands at Rackheath Magna, &c., Norfolk, Thomson and Suthorp in Gloucestershire, Westwell and Adwell in Oxfordshire, Leghes Parva in Essex, and Lackford, &c., in Suffolk. He served in the wars of Edward II. and Edward III., and was appointed Governor of Bordeaux in 1331, "with an assignation of £100 for the expenses of his journey thither." In 1333 he died, leaving two sons; John, his heir, then but six years old, and Thomas, who had the manor of Sudham, but d. s. p.; with three daughters, Margery, Alice, and Maud, eventually the heirs general of the family. John, while yet an infant, was contracted in marriage to Joan de Ufford, daughter of the Earl of Suffolk; but she died early, and in 1347 he espoused the heiress of Basing, Margaret de St. John, elder sister and co-heir of Edmund, third Lord

St. John of Basing, in whose right he received a summons to parliament the following year. He fought under the Black Prince in the French wars, and five times crossed the Channel in his retinue, dying "beyond seas" in 1359. His only child, a son named St. John, was barely six months old at the time; and his widow followed him to the grave within the next two years. The little orphaned boy died the day after he had lost his mother; and his share of the great St. John inheritance merged in that of his aunt Isabel de Poynings. His paternal estates passed to his father's three sisters, Margery, wife of Sir Richard Plays; Alice, wife of Sir Brian Stapleton of Carleton and Wighill in the county of York, K.G.; and Maud, wife of Sir Waryn Trussel.

Blomfield also mentions a Pain de St. Philibert, who lived about the same time as John I., and with his wife Ysolda held some lands at Thorp at Norfolk; but gives no further account of him or his posterity.

Fitz Roger. Walter Fitz Roger held Barington and Cerney in Gloucestershire, and some manors in Hampshire, of the King in 1086 (Domesd.). He was the son and heir of Roger de Pistres, Viscount of Gloucester, and, on the death of his uncle Durand (see Vol. I. p. 345), succeeded to his father's office. He had the custody of the castles of Gloucester and Hereford, and has been styled "Constable of all England under Henry I.," though it is not quite clear whether this title actually belonged to him. But his son Milo, the famous Earl of Hereford, undoubtedly held the great hereditary office of *Constabularius Regis*, which passed through his eldest daughter to the Bohuns. Milo had succeeded in 1131; for Walter, some time before, renounced the world and its vanities, and became a canon of Llanthony Abbey, where he died.

I do not think that he can possibly be ranked among the combatants at Hastings, or that his name, for that reason, ought to be inserted here. There are good grounds for concluding that he was a minor when his father died about 1072, and he must therefore have been a mere child in 1066.

Fauecourt, for Fanecort (Duchesne). This name, derived from Vandelicourt, near Beauvais, appears twice again on the Roll, as Venecorde and Vancorde. It is also spelt Phanucourt or Pencurt, and dates from very early times in this country. Helias de Fanecourt held a fee of ancient enfeoffment from Deincourt in Lincolnshire.—*Liber Niger.* Robert Vancort was a tenant of William de Valence.—*Testa de Nevill.* Geoffrey de Fanecourt, in 1235, held three parts of a knight's fee under Robert de Buci at Hartley.—*Nichol's Leicestershire.* Elias de Fancourt, at about the same date, "mortgaged his share of the manor Little Ercall, Shropshire, to Combermere Abbey. His son Gerard was a tenant by knight's service under John L'Estrange."—*Eyton's Salop.* Elias held of the Archbishop of York at Bruneby, Yorkshire, and John de Fancourt both there and at Elvele, of the Honour of Vesci.—*Kirkby's Inquest.* Gerard de Fancourt succeeded to his father's fee at Bruneby.—*Nomina Villarum.* About 1272, Roger, Nicholas, and Egelina de Pencurt are found in Bedfordshire.—

Rotuli Hundredorum. "Sire Bertin de Fanecort" was pardoned as an adherent of the Earl of Lancaster in 1318, and summoned from York to the great Council at Westminster in 1324.—*Palgrave's Parl. Writs.* Lucia de Thweng, the frail heiress who was first married to William, second Lord Latimer of Danby, and eloped from his house during his absence in Scotland, was subsequently divorced by the Court of Rome, and had three other husbands, the last of whom was Bartholomew de Fanecourt. Of this lady, who died in 1346, an account, with some curious particulars, is to be found in *Fasti Eboracenses,* i. 377.

The name was still found in its original *habitat* up to the time of the Commonwealth, for John Fancourt of Manthorpe was among the Lincolnshire gentlemen who compounded for their estate under the Protectorate. His must have been inconsiderable, as the sum he paid was only £38.

I can meet with no account of any existing representatives of the family. A Lt.-Colonel Fancourt was elected M.P. for Barnstaple in 1835.

Ferrers : from Ferrières-St.-Hilaire, near Bernai, in Normandy, sometimes called St. Hilaire de Ferrières.* The site of their castle.is still to be seen. Walkelin or Vauquelin de Ferrers, about 1031, had a bitter feud with Hugh, Sire de Montfoit, and fought a duel with him in which both combatants lost their lives. (See *Montfort.*) Walkelin left two sons, William and Henry, who both distinguished themselves at the Conquest : but Henry only—and another of the name, Hermerus de Ferrers—are among the Domesday Barons. At the battle of Hastings, " Henri the Sire de Ferrières, and he who then held Tillières both brought large companies, and charged the English together. Dead or captive were all they who did not flee before them ; and the field quaked and trembled."
—*Wace.* Henry de Ferrers, as "a person of much eminency both for his knowledge and integrity," was one of the Conqueror's Commissioners for the formation of the Domesday Survey, where he is recorded as one of the principal land-owners of the country. He held two hundred and ten manors ; one hundred and fourteen of them in Derbyshire ; but his *caput baroniæ* was Tutbury Castle, in Staffordshire, near which he founded a Cluniac monastery. Two of his sons—Engenulph and William—died before him ; and the third, Robert, who commanded the men of Derbyshire at the Battle of the Standard, was the first Earl of Ferrers ; according to Dugdale the first Earl of Derby ; but

* " Henry de Ferrers assumed the surname he bore from Ferriers, a small town in the Gastinois, celebrated for its iron mines. Hence, too, originated the six horse-shoes, the armorial ensigns of the House of Ferrers, allusive to the seigneurie's staple commodity."—*Sir B. Burke.* The house of Groby adopted the arms of De Quinci, still borne by its descendants. Thus, at the siege of Carlaverock, we find the first Lord Ferrers of Groby :

> Guillemes de Ferieres bel
> E noblement i fu remez,
> De armes vermeilles ben armés,
> O mascles de or del champ voidiés.

Orderic says that this Earldom was only given to his successor, who was also Earl of Nottingham. This second Robert founded Derby Priory, and Merevale Abbey, where, wrapt in an ox-hide, he desired to be buried. His grandson, the fourth Earl, "raised the power of Leicestershire" against Henry II., and marching early in the morning to Nottingham (then held for the King by Reginald de Luci) surprised, sacked, and burnt the town, and put to the sword or imprisoned the townsmen. Soon after, however, he was reduced to submission, and forced to surrender his castles of Tutbury and Duffield, which were demolished by order of the King. William, the next Earl, was the partisan and favourite of King John, and received vast grants * of lands; amongst them the great Northamptonshire estates of William Peverel, whose daughter and heir Margaret had, says Dugdale, married his grandfather. Other genealogists have given her to two different Earls of Derby; but Mr. Planché maintains that she was the wife of none of the three, and questions the very existence of this "phantom Margaret." Earl William was among the powerful barons that helped to place Henry III. on the throne: took part with William Mareschal (then Governor of the young King and of the kingdom) both in the siege of Mountsorrel and the battle of Lincoln; and in 1230 was one of the "three chief Counsellors recommended to the King by the Barons, who made Oath, That they would not, for any respect, give him other than wholesome advice." He died in 1240; "his Countess dying also in the same Month, having been Man and Wife at least seventy-five years, if Matthew Paris mistaketh not, for he affirmeth that S. Thomas of Canterbury celebrated the marriage between them, who died in 18 Hen. II." But, according to another account, they were only married in 1192. This Countess Agnes was the sister and coheir of Ranulph de Meschines, Earl of Chester, dowered with all his lands between Ribble and Mersey, and the castle and manor of Chartley in Staffordshire; and her son, the seventh Earl, on whom such splendid heritages already centred, again married two great heiresses. Sybil, his first wife, one of the five rich sisters who shared the possessions of William Mareschal Earl of Pembroke, brought Kildare as her portion, and was the mother of seven daughters: Margaret de Quinci, the second wife, was the step-daughter of the youngest of them, and the eldest co-heir of her father, Roger, Earl of Winchester. She had two daughters and two sons: Robert, eighth Earl; and William, who received from her the Lordship of Groby, and founded the still existing line. The second Earl William was, as his father had been, all his life a martyr to the gout; therefore, contrary to the custom of the age, he could travel only in a wheeled carriage; and in 1254, he was thrown over the bridge at St. Neots through the heedlessness of his driver, broke all his limbs, and died of the fall. His eldest son, who succeeded while yet a minor,

---

* Amongst others he received a house in the parish of St. Margaret's, London, to be held by the service of waiting upon the King at all festivals yearly, without any cap, but with a garland of the breadth of his little finger upon his head.

"had," says Dugdale, "the hard hap to be the last of this great Family:" though in reality he was only the last Earl of Derby, and his posterity continued in the male line for six more generations. No sooner was he come to man's estate, than he embarked with heart and soul in the baronial war; entered Worcester "with a multitude of soldiers at his heels," plundered and partly destroyed the town, and suffered a severe reprisal at the hands of Prince Edward, who was sent to avenge the outrage by carrying fire and sword through his counties of Nottingham and Derby. After the final rout at Evesham, he was specially excepted from the benefit of the *Dictum de Kenilworth;* but, throwing himself on the King's mercy, he succeeded in obtaining his pardon for a sum of one thousand five hundred marks, and a gold cup set with precious stones, for which he had to mortgage one of his Northamptonshire manors to Michael de Toni. The one thousand five hundred marks were, however, not all forthcoming; and the very next spring found him again in revolt in North Derbyshire, defeated at Burton Bridge, and forced to hide himself in a church under some sacks of wool, where he was discovered through the treachery of a woman, and carried prisoner to London. He was then formally disinherited by act of Parliament; and his Earldom, "with all his goods, chattels, lands, and castles," given to Edmund Crouchback, the King's son. He remained in custody for three years; and after his release instituted a suit in the Court of King's Bench for the recovery of his property; but after various pleadings, it was dismissed by the court in the beginning of Edward I.'s reign. He must, however, have either retained or regained Chartley Castle, and the town of Holbrook in Derbyshire, which passed to his only son John, who was summoned to parliament as Lord Ferrers of Chartley in 1299. John inherited some of his father's turbulent spirit, and had joined the Earl of Hertford's rebellion only three years before; but later in life he did good service in the French wars, and was Seneschal of Acquitaine under Edward II. Five of his successors—all noted as gallant and approved soldiers—held the barony till 1450, when, at the death of the last heir male, it passed through his daughter Anne to the house of Devereux;* and is now in abeyance. A younger son of the second Lord had married Elizabeth, sole heir of Robert Lord Boteler of Wemme, and had summons in her title in 1375; but his son left only two daughters, Elizabeth,

* Chartley came to the Shirleys in 1615 through a co-heiress of Devereux (Lady Dorothy, the youngest daughter of the unfortunate Earl of Essex): and her grandson, Sir Robert, was created Lord Ferrers of Chartley in 1677, and Viscount Tamworth and Earl Ferrers in 1711. The beautiful chase of Chartley—a part of the old forest of Needwood—contains one of the rare herds of wild cattle still preserved in England. They are sand-white; and there is a popular belief that whenever a parti-coloured calf is born, it forebodes a death in the family. It is said that in the fatal year of the battle of Burton Bridge, where the power of the last Earl of Derby fell to rise no more, a black calf was for the first time seen; and that this ill omen, which has never been known to fail, has ever since pursued all the successive Lords of Chartley.

the wife of the sixth Lord Greystock; and Mary, married to Ralph Nevill, a younger son of the Earl of Westmorland.

. On the extinction of the elder line of Chartley, the representation of the house passed to the Ferrers of Groby, descended from the second son of the fourth Earl, who held his Leicestershire castle in right of his mother, Margaret de Quinci, and bore her arms. His son became Lord Ferrers of Groby in 1297; and his grandson and great-grandson married, the one the heiress of Verdon, the other the heiress of Ufford. Both were, like the rest of their kin, deeply engaged in all the wars of Edward III., and the former received large territorial grants from the crown for his services. The fifth and last Lord had two sons; 1. Henry, who died before him, and 2. Sir Thomas, who acquired the old castle of the Marmions at Tamworth through his wife Elizabeth de Freville. Henry left one daughter, who carried the barony of Groby to Sir Edward Grey, ancestor of the Duke of Suffolk, in whose attainder it perished in 1554.* Sir Thomas had two sons, who each founded a family. The elder line of Tamworth continued only till 1680: but the younger, seated at Baddesley-Clinton in the same county, flourishes to this day, the last off-set of the stately tree that once spread its branches far and wide over the Midland Counties.

There had been several others. Walcheline de Ferrers, a younger son of the Earl who fought at the battle of the Standard, was seated at Oakham in Rutland; and though his son died s. p. and the property passed away through his daughter Isabel, his ancestral horseshoes still keep their place in his castle. Of this the hall—an admirable and perfect specimen of the architecture of the twelfth century—alone remains, and is adorned with nearly seventy horseshoes of all sizes, varying from four feet eight to five inches in diameter, according to the generosity of the donors. "The Lord of the castle and manor of Okeham for the time being claims by prescription a Franchise or Royalty very rare and of singular note, viz.: That the first time any Peer of this Kingdom shall happen to pass through the precincts of this Lordship, he shall forfeit as a Homage a Shoe from the Horse on which he rideth unless he redeem it with money. The true Original of which custome I have not been able on my utmost endeavour to discover. But that such is, and time out of mind hath been, the Usage, appears by several Monumental Horseshoes (some gilded and of curious Workmanship) nail'd upon the Castle Hall Door."—*Wright's Rutlandshire.* Some are yet there; but although a proportion of the more ancient ones have disappeared, they have long ago outgrown their original destination. On each is inscribed the name and title of the peer who presented it. Many bear crests and coronets: and the so-called Golden Shoe (taken off Lord Willoughby de Eresby's favourite horse Clinker) was once abstracted by some ingenious thief who mistook the gilding for gold; but returned it in a railway parcel on discovering his error.

* It was revived in 1603, and is now held by his representative, the Earl of Stamford and Warrington.

Another Ferrers, Lord of Eggington in Derbyshire, is mentioned by Dugdale; and a branch, to which a curious tradition is affixed, remained at Market Cell, in Bedfordshire, until the last century. "On the Hertfordshire side of the parish of Caddington is Market Cell, the site of a nunnery of the Benedictine order, founded by Geoffrey Abbot of St. Albans, about the year 1145. We are told that Humphrey, a natural son of Lord Berners, bestowed much cost and art in building a house on this site, but did not live to finish it. It was after this, in 1548, granted to George Ferrers, whose descendant Sir John Ferrers died seised of it in 1640."—*Lysons' Bedfordshire.* The last heiress of this house, who had been early left an orphan and lived by herself at Market Cell, by some untoward chance became acquainted with the captain of a band of highwaymen which then infested the neighbourhood, and fell desperately in love with him. She used to ride out, disguised in men's clothes, night after night to meet him; shared all his dangers and adventures, and sat with him and his followers at their carousals and merry makings. None of her household ever suspected her absence; for she inhabited a tower somewhat detached from the rest of the house, from whence a postern reached by a secret stair, opened on the terrace; and thus she could go out, saddle her horse, bring him back to the stable, and return to bed unobserved. Only the grooms, now and again, grumbled, and declared the fairies must have ridden Mistress Ferrers' favourite black, when they had left him over-night cool and comfortable in his stall, and found him next morning covered with sweat and mire. At length, one day, Mistress Ferrers was missing from her chamber; and though the clothes she had taken off the night before lay by her bedside, the bed had not been slept in. She was sought for everywhere in vain, till some one remembered the door in her room that led to the secret staircase, generally believed by the servants to have been long since closed and disused. It was unlocked; but some obstacle from without hindered its opening; and when, with some trouble, they had forced their way through, the dead body of Mistress Ferrers, dressed in her highwayman's clothes, with the crape mask still on her face, was found lying across the threshold. She had been severely wounded in some desperate encounter the night before; but, with wonderful courage, had managed to keep her saddle, ride home, stable her horse, and struggle up the turret stair to her chamber door. Then, at the very moment that she thought she had gained her refuge, and saved herself from disgrace and exposure, her strength failed her, and she fell down dead. The place passed into other hands, and the greater part of the stately old manor house (including Mistress Ferrers' tower) has been either pulled down or burned; but it is affirmed that she still haunts her former domain, and may be seen pacing the terrace, peering in at the windows, standing in the doorway, or clapping her hands in furious glee as the flames curl and circle around its gables. The doom of fire, which has several times fallen on Market Cell, is popularly attributed to her curse, which rests on her successors for their demolition of her favourite tower, and ordains that the building should always be left incomplete. In fact, it remains unfinished at the present time, the final decoration of one of the rooms being purposely omitted.

The name continues affixed to many of their old manors. It is borne by Higham-Ferrers (part of the Peverel estate in Northamptonshire), Woodham Ferrers in Essex, Newton Ferrers, and Churston-Ferrers, in Devonshire.

. **Fitz Philip;** interpolated. "The name of Philip or Fitz-Philip is traced in successive generations in Norfolk (see Blomfield, ii. 194, xi. 28, vi. 415) to Philip de Mortimer, third son of Robert de Mortimer of Normandy, temp. Henry I., son of William de Mortimer, who held lands from De Warrenne in Norfolk 1086 (ancestor of the Lords Mortimer of Attelburgh, 1296)."—*The Norman People.*

Filiot, or Foliot: from the castle of Omonville-la-Foliot; in La Manche. "Hence," says Sir Francis Palgrave, "the great family of that name, amongst whose members Gilbert Foliot, the Bishop of London, is conspicuous: and Robert Foliot certified to fifteen knight's fees which his family had possessed since the Conquest." Gilbert Foliot—who had himself been the ancient opponent and rival of Thomas à Becket—was the Bishop officiating in Canterbury Cathedral when Henry II. did public penance for the murder of the Archbishop, and held in his hand the "balai," or monastic rod, with which the castigation was inflicted. The King, clad in hair-cloth, his feet bare and bleeding, in the guise of a penitential pilgrim, knelt before the shrine of Becket, and placing his head and shoulders in the tomb, "received five strokes from each bishop and abbot who was present, beginning with Foliot, and three from each of the eighty monks."—*Dean Stanley.* There were three bishops of this name; Gilbert, already mentioned, first Abbot of Gloucester, and successively Bishop of Hereford and London, who was excommunicated by Becket in 1169:* his

---

* Matthew Paris, tells us that "coming one night from the King after long conference had with him of the troubles with Archbishop Beckett; as he lay meditating and musing thereon in his bed, a terrible and unknown voice sounded in his ear—

> 'O Gilbert Foliot,
> While you compute what's to be got,
> Your God's the God of Astaroth.'

Which he, taking to come from the Devil, answered boldly—

> 'Devil or man, you lie, you sot,
> My God's the God of Sabaoth.'"

This is a translation; the original words are given in Latin.

"Gilbert Foliot," writes Fuller, "was observed when a Common Brother of his Covent, to inveigh against the Prior; when Prior, against the Abbot; when Abbot, against the pride and laziness of Bishops; but when he himself was Bishop, all was well, and Foliot's mouth, when full, was silent."

cousin Archdeacon Robert, Bishop of Hereford in 1174, and one of the four English bishops present at the Lateran Council in 1179 when Alexander III. excommunicated the Waldenses and Albigenses; and lastly, Hugh, also Archdeacon of Salop, who founded and endowed Ledbury Hospital, and became Bishop of Hereford in 1219. The Foliots were of note in Devonshire, where Tavy-Foliot still keeps the name; and were landowners in Hampshire in the twelfth century. Sampson Foliot witnessed a charter of Baldwin, second Earl of Devon, who died in 1155; Walter Foliot, thirteenth century, held some lands at Exbury "by forty days' service in England of a man-at-arms": and Geoffrey Foliot, fourteenth century, was a benefactor of Christ Church Priory. —*Woodward's Hampshire.* In Worcestershire Richard Foliot (grandson of John Foliot, who held Fenwick and Foliot's fee in Yorkshire in the time of the Conqueror) was Lord of Longdon and Richmarsh in the reign of Henry II. "Their first habitation was, I believe," says Nash, "at Morton Foliot, in the former parish." From this Richard a direct male descent leads us to Aylmer Foliot, "the first of nineteen generations who did not marry and have children"; and who, though he left his duties unfulfilled in that respect, found an heir in a nephew or cousin named Robert. A younger son of this house was Sir Thomas Folliott, governor of Ballyshannon, co. Sligo, under Queen Elizabeth, who was knighted by her Lord Lieutenant the Earl of Essex, and commanded a regiment at the victory of Kinsale. James I. created him Lord Folliott of Ballyshannon, in 1619; but the title expired, within one hundred years, with his grandson.

The most ancient and considerable of the possessions of the family were in Yorkshire. "An extensive sweep of country, beginning between Smeaton and Norton, lying along the S. bank of the Went, and extending to the lands which compose the parish of Fishlake, comprehending what are now the separate townships of Norton, Fenwick, and Moseley, was granted out, in the original distribution of the Pontefract fee, to a family who are known by the addition of Foliot, in whom, and in their descendants the Hastings, this tract continued for many centuries. Flat and open land, presenting scarcely anything which could be regarded as a natural boundary, and assimilated in all its natural characters to the lands which formed the chace of Hatfield, it was early a matter of question, whether Fenwick at least was not rather part of the Warren, than of the Laci fee.

"The Foliots and Hastings, however, uniformly attached themselves to the Lords of Pontefract, and were ever among the most considerable of their subinfeudatories. They had their mansion house at Fenwick, where are still some faint indications of its existence, while they had their chapel, a free chapel, called in early times, as at present, a priory, at Norton, where several of them, perhaps most of them, found interment as one by one they returned to the earth.

"The first Foliot known to Dodsworth was William, who in the time of

Rufus, was a benefactor to the monks of Pontefract. The termination of the line was in the early part of the reign of Edward III., when it ended in two coheirs, Margery and Margeret, aged respectively seventeen and sixteen in 1329. Margaret married John Camoys; and Margery, who had all these lands, married Hugh de Hastings."—*Hunter's South Yorkshire.*

Furnieueus, or Furneaux. Leland couples this and the succeeding name together, as "Forneus and Fournevous." This family came from Fourneaux, near Coutances, and settled in several different counties. Odo de Furnell held *in capite* in Somerset, 1086 (Exon. Domesday), and Galfrid de Furnell was Sheriff of Devon 1 Hen. II. His son Henry followed him in the office 25 Hen. II. and 7 Richard I. Alan Furneaux, in 1165, was one of the Justiciaries. (Mon. i. 999.) One of their seats was at Kentisbere. Another, Fenn Ottery, "was for many descents held by the Furneaux by sergeantry, and so continued unto the latter end of King Edward II.'s days." They had received it from Henry I. The last heir, Sir Matthew, died in 1315, the year of his shrievalty. The name is found in Northumberland, when Robert Fitz Roger and Ralph de Furnell were joint Sheriffs in 1200, 1201, and 1202: and is still borne by Pury or Perry Furneaux, in Somersetshire. In Norfolk and Cambridgeshire "the Furneaux held of the Earl of Richmond. Sir Jeffrey de Furneaux was Lord about 1180, and had his chief seat at Bergham in Cambridgeshire. Sir Simon de Furneaux, Lord of Pelham-Furneaux, in 1281, had a market and fair granted to him at Bergham:" and left an only daughter, with whom the elder line ended. A junior branch, seated at Herling in Norfolk continued till the middle of the fourteenth century. The last named, John, and his sister and heir Elizabeth, were both wards of John Duke of Lancaster and Earl of Richmond. John died a minor in 1361. The Furneaux bore *Sable*, a Pale Lozengee *Argent.*— *Blomfield's Norfolk.* John de Furneaux or Furness held Aynderby-Fourneaux (now Ainderby-Steeple) in Yorkshire in 1316, and in 1322 "was one of the Manucaptors for the good behaviour of John de Swynnerton, on his discharge from imprisonment as an adherent of the Earl of Lancaster." Richard de Furneaux received a pardon, for having joined the same cause, in 1318 at York.—*Palgrave's Parl. Writs.* He descended from Anchitel or Asquitell de Furnell, an under-tenant of the Earl of Richmond's in 1086, who held Ainderby and some other lands, and witnesses his suzerain's grant to the monk Yvo of Swavesey Priory.—*A. S. Ellis.* This Anchetil gave some of his land at Aynderby, Morton, and Thyrntoft to St. Martin's, Richmond (Mon. Angl.) His name is there written Forneys; and in the *Rotuli Hundredorum* of 1272 we again find a De Fornays in Yorkshire. Robert, son of Richard de Furneys, occurs in the *Testa de Nevill;* he was of Wellinghore in Lincolnshire, and at that time in the King's custody. During the reign of Edward III., Henry, eldest son of the first Lord Fitz Hugh, married Joan, daughter of Sir Richard Fourneys (obviously the same Richard who had been in arms for the Earl of

Lancaster), and sister and heir of William Fourneys, with whom ·he. had the Lordships of Carleton, Kingstone, Beghton, and Bothomsall.—*Dugdale.*

Furnivaus. See *Furnivale.*

Fitz Otes. *Otto Aurifaber* or *Aurifex* held a barony in Essex in 1806 (Domesday). "Morant and Kelham agree that this Otto the goldsmith was ancestor of Thomas Fitz Otho, mint-master or engraver for the King's mint; and that the last of the male line of his family died in 1282. Otto the younger, by a charter still remaining in the Tower, and directed to Maurice Bishop of London, in or before the seventh Hen. I., had 'the mystery of the dies' restored to him, which his father had held, together with all other his offices, and certain lands. The same privilege was afterwards conferred by the same King to William Fitz Otto the grandson. The office which these persons successively held appears to have been that of cuneator or manager of the dies. Madox, in his History of the Exchequer, says he claimed the old and broken dies as his fee; which claim was allowed to Thomas Fitz Otto in the 49th Hen. III. on his petition to the King in the Court of Exchequer, that they belonged to him of right and inheritance, and that his ancestors had been accustomed to have them. This, upon examination, was found to be true. The serjeanty continued in a female branch of Otto's family at least as late as the first of Edward III.

"In the Testa de Nevill, p. 362, it is said, 'Willelmus fil. Ote tenet in Lilleston, Midd. in serjean. unam carucatam terræ quæ valet xl⁴ per servicium signa R. monetæ et facit servitum per totum annum.'"—*Sir Henry Ellis.*

· "Otto Aurifaber" was employed to make the Conqueror's monument in the church of St. Stephen's, Caen; and "a mass of gold and silver and precious stones" was handed over to him for the work. "The coffin itself, wrought of a single stone, and supported by three columns of marble, was surmounted by a shrine of splendid workmanship, blazing with all the precious materials which had been entrusted to the cunning hand of Otto. On that shrine the epitaph of William was graven in letters of gold."—*Freeman.*

This famous goldsmith was succeeded in his Essex barony by his son William Fitz Otto and his grandson Otto Fitz William, who, according to Morant, was Sheriff of Essex and Hertfordshire the seven last years of Henry II., and the first two of Richard I., and gave his name to Belchamp Otton, or Otes, near Castle Hedingham, which he had acquired in the former reign. The next heir, another William, who, with his mother, paid scutage for two knight's fees in 1200, left his son Otto a minor, for in 1214 Robert de Vere, third Earl of Oxford, bought of the King "the wardship of the heir of William Fiz-Oates, to marry to his niece." This Otto was still living in 1256. William, his son, had no children, and the inheritance passed to a nephew, Thomas Fitz Otes, engraver to the King's mint, who married Beatrice de Beauchamp, one of the heiresses of the last Baron of Bedford, and died in 1274. He left a son and three

II.   D daughters. The son, who survived him eight years only, died s. p., and the three daughters, Johanna, Maud, and Beatrice, inherited; but the eldest and youngest were either spinsters, or childless wives, and both their shares accrued to Maud. She was married in 1302 to Sir John de Boutetourt of Mendlesham in Suffolk, summoned to parliament as Lord Boutetourt in 1307, by whom she had four sons, and a daughter named Beatrix, the wife of William Latimer.*

In addition to this baronial line, there were various junior branches of the family, and one of them undoubtedly gave birth to Robin Hood. "His true name," says Thoroton, "was Robert Fitzooth, or Fitz Othes, but agreeably to the custom of dropping the Norman addition Fitz, and the two last letters being turned into d, he was vulgarly called Ood or Hood." † His arms, given (on the same authority) as *Gules* two bends engrailed *Or*, were evidently derived from the coat of Fitz Otes of Essex, *Azure* 3 bends *Or:* a canton dexter *Argent*, and sometimes *Ermine*. There seems little doubt that Robin Hood was of gentle birth, and that Leland had good authority for calling him *nobilis ille exlex*. But Thoroton proceeds to assert that " it is probable he might claim the title of Earl of Huntingdon, by reason of John Scot, tenth Earl, dying s. p., as he was heir by the female line, as descended from Gilbert of Gaunt, Earl of Kyme and Lindsey. This title, it seems, lay dormant ninety years after Robert's death, and about ten of the last years of his life." In support of this popular fallacy, he gives the pedigree I have here inserted, and which I should have thought it impossible for the most credulous mind to accept. Gilbert of Gaunt's wife was Alice de Montfort; there is no record of any second marriage; and as he died in the reign of William Rufus, he could scarcely have been the son-in-law of the co-heiress of the Countess Judith, who survived till 1140. I may add that the Fitz Ooth brought up by the Earl of Oxford, and represented as Robert's father, might in reality have been his son or grandson, as he was still a minor in 1214, when Robert must have been at the very least fifty years old. · It was owing to the glamour of romance with which later generations have invested their favourite hero, "the gentlest thiefe that ever was," and the record of his "robberies, frolics, clemency, and charities," that this illustrious descent was invented, and he was credited with an Earldom.

---

* It was in right of this Beatrix that, at the coronation of Henry VI., Lord Latimer, jointly with Thomas de Moubray (coheir of Maud de Beauchamp, another of these heiresses) claimed the office and perquisites of Lord Almoner to the King, that had been held by the old Barons of Bedford. "The claim of Lord Latimer was allowed, and Sir Thomas Grey was appointed to represent Thomas de Moubray, whose lands were in the King's hands."—*Lysons.*

† The name became Ode, or Hode, in many instances. John Ode, or Hode, of Lynn, is mentioned by Blomfield; and John Ode, of Ode-Barton, in Oxfordshire, founded a chantry at Fitton Hall, in that county, in the time of Edward III.

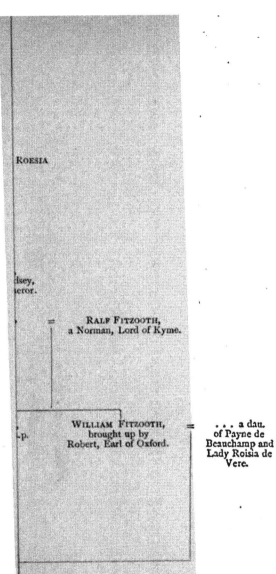

ROESIA

dsey,
eror.

=   RALF FITZOOTH,
a Norman, Lord of Kyme.

.p.   WILLIAM FITZOOTH,
brought up by
Robert, Earl of Oxford.   =   . . . a dau.
of Payne de
Beauchamp and
Lady Roisia de
Vere.

The place of his birth, which occurred between 1160–70, is uncertain, and has been claimed by various localities. All the old ballads unanimously pronounce in favour of "merry sweet Locksley town" in Notts, but unfortunately no such place exists·in the county. There is a Loxley in Staffordshire, a Locksley in Warwickshire, and Loxley Chase, traversed by the river Loxley, in Hallamshire, "which," says Hunter, "seems to have the fairest pretension to be the Locksley of our own ballads, where was born that redoubtable hero Robin Hood. The remains of a house in which it was pretended he was born was formerly pointed out in Bar-wood, and a well of fair clear water rising near the bed of the river has been called, from time immemorial, Robin Hood's well." Loxley in Staffordshire, where there is a similar tradition, belonged to the Ferrers, and "the family of Fitz Otho were subfeudatories of the Ferrers in the time of King John."—*Lipscomb's Bucks.* "This famed robber," continues Thoroton, "may have been driven to this course of life on account of the attainder of himself or relatives, or of the intestine troubles during the reign of Henry II., when the son of that King was in arms against his father. The Ferrers being Lords of Loxley, the birthplace of our hero, and Robert de Ferrers manning the castles of Tutbury and Duffield on behalf of that prince, William Fitz Ooth, Robert's father, might by his connection with that family be implicated in the guilt and consequences of that rebellion. Thus might it happen, that Robin Hood was possessed of no paternal estate and deprived of the title of Earl of Huntingdon, and driven to take refuge in the woods and forests to avoid the punishment of his own or his father's crimes against the State." But there is no evidence to show that the Fitz Otes family were undertenants of Loxley; whereas Dugdale tells us that Robert Fitz Otes was Lord of Westcote and Locksley in Warwickshire, holding of the Barons of Stafford, in the time of Henry II. He left three daughters his co-heirs : Basilia (mentioned in 1201), who married Peter de Mora, and was the mother of Ralph le Falconer; Agnes, the wife of William Trussell ; and Margerie, married to William Bagot. This is the family to which, in all likelihood, Robin Hood belonged, and, " being of a wild and extravagant disposition, so prodigiously exceeded in charges and expenses," that he ruined himself, and was cast adrift to make his living as best he could. It is just possible that he may have been the disowned brother of these three sisters. Little did they ever dream of the time to come, when the renown of having given him birth would be eagerly sought for and jealously contested, and the scapegrace of the family transformed into a disguised Earl !

Robin Hood, "the prince of thieves," who robbed the rich to feed the poor, was the darling of the common people, and lived in their memory for many centuries after his death. He has been called " the English ballad-maker's joy," for no theme was more welcome to the mediæval minstrel, or gave greater delight to the listeners ; and he and his merry men clad in Lincoln green have been the heroes of enough ballads and broadsides to fill several volumes. The story of his freaks and exploits was in every man's mouth; even Chaucer's ignorant and slothful priest is made to say—

> " I cannot parfitli my paternoster . . .
> But I can ryms of Roben Hode."

Most of these older ditties have perished. Those that survive are of subsequent date; but though some of the adventures they relate must be judged apocryphal, the greater part of the stories have evidently been handed down by tradition, and afford a vivid picture of the lusty outlaw and his doings. We see him brave and daring to a fault, yet a wary and adroit leader; loyal to his friends, and kind to the poor; fond of disguises, surprises, and every species of frolic; playing his pranks on all men, and chiefly on the "proud Sheriff of Nottingham"; yet clement and generous withall; "murdering none but the deer," and dispensing the venison among his neighbours with a free hand. There is a genial love of fun and good fellowship that runs like a key-note through the whole, showing that the life he led, if hard and hazardous, was none the less cheery.

> "Ye were merry lads, and those were merry days,"

says the old ballad-monger: and Shakespeare's outlaws in the Forest of Arden (*As you like it*) " live like the old Robin Hood of England, and fleet the time carelessly, as they did in the golden age." While summer lasted, the free camp-life in the wild greenwood, among the glorious oaks and brake-clad dells of old Sherwood, must have been delightful—all the more fascinating for its flavour of danger and adventure; and though it had its reverse in winter, the outlaws would be then less molested by the King's officers, and either sheltered in caves and huts, or (as has been suggested) quartered on friends living near the skirts of the forest.

Though Robin was as merciless to priests as he was to usurers, and bore a particular grudge to the dignitaries of the Church—

> " These byshoppes and these arch-byshoppes,
> Ye shall them bete and bynde:"

making one captive prelate dance a saraband in his heavy riding boots round one of the old oaks of Sherwood, he was scrupulous in his religious observances, and heard mass every day. Once he was surprised in "that most secret recess of the wood where he was at mass" by the Sheriff and the King's officers. His followers urged him to fly, and most of them set the example of making off at full speed; but Robin reverently refused to move till the service was over; and then, setting upon his enemies with the few men he had left, took several prisoners and put the rest to flight. He held the Blessed Virgin in great veneration, and respected all women for her sake.

> " Robyn loved Our dere Lady,
> For dout of dedely synne ;
> Wolde he never do company harme
> That ony woman was ynne."

His band numbered from one hundred to two hundred men, tried and chosen by himself, and esteemed the best archers in the country. Whenever he heard of "any that were of unusual strength and hardiness," he went, sometimes disguised as a beggar, to seek them out ; and "after he had tried them with fighting, would never give over tyl he had used means to draw them to lyve after his fashion." Once, while crossing a long narrow foot-bridge, he found himself face to face with a stalwart young giant* named John Little (John Nailor, according to others), who was armed with a staff, and would not make way for him to pass. Robin, who carried only his bow, went and cut a staff for himself in the thicket ; and the two men belaboured each other with hearty good will, till the giant dealt Robin a blow that sent him spinning into the water. Far from being angered or discomfited, Robin pronounced him to be

> " A jolly brisk blade, right fit for the trade ;"

enlisted him forthwith, and, equipping him with a bow and a suit of " the outlaw's colour " (the green livery of the forest) christened him Little John—a name that became almost as famous as his own.

> " Thou shalt be an archer as well as the best,
> And range in the greenwood with us ;
> Where we'll not want gold and silver, behold,
> While bishops have aught in their purse ;
>
> " We live here as squires or lords of renown,
> Without e'er a foot of free land ;
> We feast on good cheer, with wine, ale and beer,
> And everything at our command."

Robin was devoted to his followers, rescuing them at all risks—sometimes from the very hands of the hangman ; sharing the booty to all alike ; and standing by them even in their love affairs. He found his way, in the guise of a harper, to the church where Alan-a-Dale's true love, "a finikin lass that shone like the glistering gold," was being unwillingly married to a rich old knight, and swearing that "the bride should choose her own deare," put his horn to his mouth and summoned his men. Four-and-twenty came at his call ; and, stripping off the priest's vestments, he put them on Little John, made him

---

* Little John was, says the ballad, " Seven feet high, and an elle in the waist." He lies buried in Hattersage church-yard, in the Peak of Derbyshire, where, in 1652, part of his bow still hung in the church-chancel.

perform the marriage ceremony, and with his own hand gave away the bride to Alan-a-Dale. His own fortunes were shared by a disguised damsel who went by the name of Maid Marian, and is popularly believed to have been Lord Fitzwalter's daughter, "the chaste Matilda, poysoned at Dunmow by King John." But there is no possible ground for identifying her with Maud Fitzwalter, and I may add that she is not alluded to in the *Lytell Geste of Robyn Hode*, or the older ballads.

Though Sherwood was his usual haunt, Robin and his band ranged over a wide extent of country. He was often to be found in Barnesdale in Yorkshire, and Plompton Park, a forest in Cumberland; and when closely pressed, he was wont to cross the moors towards Whitby, strike the seacoast at a place, still called Robin Hood's Bay, about six miles beyond, where he always had some fishing boats in readiness, and "putting off to sea, hold the whole power of the English nation at defiance." ·Once (it was in 1188) when he and Little John were dining at Whitby Abbey, the Abbot asked them to show him a specimen of their skill with the long bow. "To oblige him, they went up to the top of the Abbey, whence each of them shot an arrow, which fell not far from Whitby Laths, a distance of more than a measured mile; but when we consider the advantage they must have from so great an elevation (the Abbey standing on a high cliff) the fact will not appear so very extraordinary. The Abbot set up a pillar where each arrow fell, and these were still standing in 1779, each pillar retaining the name of the owner of the arrow."—*Thoroton's Notts.* Robin lived for fifty-nine years after this, and must have been at least eighty when he died. The great Justiciary, Hubert de Burgh, had set a price upon his head, but he could be taken neither by force or stratagem, and fell a victim at last to foul play. "Being dystempered with could and age, he had great payne in his lymmes," and sought relief in the loss of blood, in those times a universal specific, but the last remedy we should now think of for rheumatism. He had a kinswoman "skilful in physique" who was Prioress of Kirklees, near Leeds; and to her he went to be bled; but the perfidious cousin, incited by her paramour Sir Roger of Doncaster, who owed Robin some grudge, opened the vein of his arm and left him, locked up in a narrow cell, to bleed to death. As he lay there, helpless and despairing, feeling his life ebb slowly away, he "bethought him of his bugle horn," and raising it for the last time to his lips, attempted to summon his comrades. The blast was faint and uncertain; and Little John, as he caught the sound "in the greenwood where he lay," was struck with dismay:

> "I feare my master is nigh dead,
> He blows so wearilie."

He sprung up on the instant, led his men to Kirklees, and, breaking open the convent gates, forced his way to his dying chief. ·He was too far gone for human aid; and Little John, thirsting for revenge, proposed to burn down "Kirklees Hall and all their nunnery." But Robin would not hear of it:

> "I never hurt fair maid in my time,
> Nor at my end shall it be:
> But give me my bent bow in my hand,
> And a broad arrow I'll let flee;
> And where this arrow is taken up,
> There shall my grave digg'd be."

His faithful henchman helped him to the casement, put the bow in his hand, and raised him in his arms as, with a last supreme effort, he struggled to his feet, and bent it once again. He shot two arrows; the first fell in the river Calder, but the second lighted in the park at Kirklees, where he was buried according to his desire, and a stone placed (it is said by the treacherous Prioress herself) to mark his grave. A tombstone bearing a very ancient cross remained in 1750; but is now replaced by one inscribed with the spurious epitaph that found a place in the collections of the late learned Dean of York, Dr. Gale:

> "Hear underneath dis laitl stean
> laiz robert earl of Huntingtun
> near arcir ber az hie sa geud,
> an pipl-kauld im robin heud
> sick utlauz az hi an iz men
> bil england nibr si agen.
> . obiit 24 (r. 14) kal. dekembris 1247."

But, though no one puts faith in the inscription, the site, at least, is believed to be genuine. "It is no small confirmation of this opinion," writes Thoresby, "that the spot pointed out for the place of his interment is beyond the precinct of the nunnery, and therefore not in consecrated ground. He was buried as a robber and outlaw, out of the peace of the church. Yet on the stone which was supposed to cover his remains, and was entire in the year 1750, there was a cross of the precise form which was in use at the beginning of the thirteenth century. But this difficulty will be removed by reflecting that at the dissolution of the nunnery many ancient gravestones would remain, and that, the place of the outlaw's interment being still notorious and popular, one of them might be removed hither to mark a place which perhaps an older memorial had ceased to recall. Moreover, this stone never had an inscription; therefore, either the epitaph first produced by Dr. Gale is spurious, or my hypothesis as to the gravestone is confirmed, or both. I think the last; for, 1st, a cross without a sword can have originally covered none other than an ecclesiastic; and secondly, the internal evidence is strongly against the genuineness of the epitaph. If it ever existed, it must have been the invention of some rhymer in long subsequent times. But the spelling, so far as it deviates from common old English, is not according to the dialect of the West Riding, but of the North. On the whole, I should think it a fabrication somewhere between the time of Henry VIII. and Elizabeth, when the terms archer and outlaw were become familiar."

His band dispersed after his death (though outlaws are still called " Roberds-men " in a statute of Ric. II. more than 200 years afterwards), but the affection felt for his memory was as remarkable as it was enduring. Not only in the counties that had been his favourite resort, but throughout the whole of England it was cherished and held dear, and it cannot even yet be said to have died out.* Fuller included him in his list of Worthies, "not for his thievery, but for his gentleness;" and Walter Scott has immortalised him in his 'Ivanhoe.' No mediæval masque was complete without him, Maid Marian, and the faithful Little John; and the celebration of Robin Hood's Day on the 1st of May, with its games and sports, and merry crew of mummers and morris-dancers, went on rejoicingly till it was put a stop to by the Puritans.† Indeed, no public servant that ever earned the thanks of the State has lived so long in popular estimation as the outlawed robber who loved and fed the poor.

Fitz William. "As to the time and occasion of assuming this surname, the greatest certainty I have found is that William, the son of William FitzGodric, in King Henry the Second's dayes, called himself William Fitz William."— *Dugdale.* It probably here stands for the *Robertus filius Willelmi* who held *de capite* both in Derby and Nottingham (Domesday), and became a very considerable landowner during the reign of Henry I., whose tutor he had been (see *Archer*).

Fitz Roand; or rather, as in Leland's list, Fitz Rohaut. "This family is Breton, deriving from Roald or Rouault, a Breton noble living c. 1000, whose son, Hasculph, Viscount of Nantes, c. 1050, had four sons who accompanied the Conqueror; viz. 1. Ruald; 2. Hasculph; 3. Hugh; 4. Enisaud (see *Musard*). Ruald, surnamed Adobé (*i.e.* dubbed knight), held three lord-ships in capite 1086 in Devon (Domesday, 114 b). His son Ruald was father of Alan Fitz Ruald, who married Lady Alis de Dodbrooke, and acquired estates by her. (Pole, Devon). Roald Fitz Alan, his son, had John Fitz Rohaut, father of Alan, whose grandson Sir Roger Fitz Rohault had a daughter, and heir (Pole)."—*The Norman People.* This daughter, Elizabeth by name,

---

* The old women in Nottinghamshire still bind up a wound, chanting the familiar rhyme :

> " Nine times round,
> Robin Hood's charm—
> If it does thee no good,
> It will do thee no harm."

† In 1561, "the rascal multitude," writes sour John Knox, "were stirred up to make a Robin Hude, whilk enormity was of many years left and damned by statute and act of parliament."

married Sir Roger Champernowne; her father died about 1346. He held Kimcote and Long Clauston, in Leicestershire, of the Bishop of Lincoln, and bore *Or*, 2 chevrons and a canton *Gules;* in the canton a lion passant guardant *Argent.* (Nichols' Leicestershire.)

Fitz Pain. "This name," says Sir Egerton Brydges, "was first taken by Robert Fitz Pain, son of Pain Fitz John, and brother of Eustace, ancestor of the Veseys; both sons of John de Burgo, surnamed Monoculus." This Pain, according to Dugdale, "was one of the Chief Counsellors" of Henry I.; and the name of his son must therefore be an interpolation here.

Fitz Auger: for Fitz-Alcher, Aher, or Aer. "William the Conqueror gave the Manor of Bosham in Sussex to William son of Augeri and his heirs in fee-farm, rendering therefore at the Exchequer yearly, forty-two pounds of silver in solid metal for all service &c."—*Blount's Tenures.* "William Fitz Auger holds his tenement in Epping and Waltham, Essex, by serjeantry to attend before the King."—*Lib. Rub. Scacc.* A family of Fitz Alchers or Fitz Aers existed in Shropshire till the fourteenth century. They descended from Alcher or Auger, a tenant of Rainald the Sheriff in 1086 (Domesday): and held Harcott *in capite* under the Crown, by the service of finding "one serving foot soldier with a bow and arrows to attend the King's army in Wales." Their other manors formed part of the barony of Fitz Alan. Robert Fitz Aer occurs in the *Liber Niger;* William Fitz Aer in 1240: Sir John Fitz Aer, in 1272, was Sub-Escheator of the county, "exercising his authority well and honestly;" Conservator of the peace in 1287; and Knight of the shire in 1290. His grandson Thomas, who died in 1316, was the last of the Fitz Aers, and left a daughter Marjory, married to the son of her guardian, Sir Alan de Charlton of Apley.

Fitz-Aleyn. The first bearers of this great historical name were the sons of Alan Fitz-Flaald, Baron of Oswaldestre in Shropshire and of Mileham in Norfolk, who received from Henry I. the shrievalty of Shropshire, and died about 1114. No one exactly knows who he was. Eyton, after a close and laborious investigation of the question, has adopted the legend found in the fanciful *Booke* of Hector Boece, who believed he had discovered in him the grandson of Banquo, the murdered Thane of Lochaber.[*] The names of Fleanchus and Flaaldus are, as he argues, easily convertible; and he states that when Fleance fled from Scotland about 1050, he took refuge at the court of Gruffyth-ap-Llewellyn, and fell in love with Gruffyth's daughter Guenta, who became his wife, and the mother of Alan. The author of *The Norman People* brings evidence to show that Flaald, his father, lived in

---

[*] Shakespere alludes to this story in *Macbeth*, when the witches foretell the future greatness of his race to Banquo:

"Thou shall get kings, though thou be none."

Brittany, and was a brother of Alan, Seneschal of Dol, descended from the old Armorican Counts of Dol and Dinan. At all events, whatever may have been the origin of Alan Fitz Flaald, he was

> "The mighty Father of our Kings to be,"

for, from his second son, Walter Fitz Alan, appointed Steward or Seneschal to David I. of Scotland, sprung the royal House of Stuart. The elder son, William Fitz Alan, was the progenitor of the Earls of Arundel, and received from Henry II. in second marriage Isabel de Say, Baroness of Clun, the greatest heiress in Shropshire. His name must have been a later addition to the Roll; for Alan Fitz Flaald, who survived the Conquest for nearly sixty years, must have been far too young a man when he fought at Hastings to have had a grown-up son by his side. Nor do either William or Walter occur in Domesday, where we find only *Ricardus filius Alann* entered as a sub-tenant in Norfolk.

Fitz-Rauff. This, as a surname, was first borne in the time of Henry II. by Hubert, the grandson of Ralph Fitz Hubert, "a fierce man and a great Plunderer," who held considerable estates in Notts and Derby in 1086 (Dugdale). It might here stand for Harold Fitz Ralph, who held a barony in Gloucestershire at that date. "He was the only son (as far as we know) of Ralph, Earl of Herefordshire, nephew of Edward the Confessor, and in all probability named after him, and a godson of King Harold. Earl Ralph was the elder son of the Countess Goda, sister of King Edward, by her first husband, Drogo, Count of French Vexin, who died of poison in Bithynia in 1035, on his way to the Holy Land with Robert Duke of Normandy. Ralph came to England when his uncle became King, and obtained the office of Earl of Herefordshire. This post was no sinecure, and having to lead the men of the shire against Earl Algar and the Welsh, 'the cowardly son of the King's sister,' says Florence of Worcester, 'suffered a defeat, the Earl, with his French and Normans, being the first to flee.' This took place near Hereford in 1055. The Earl died in 1057."—*A. S. Ellis.*

Harold must have been very young at the time: for in 1066 he was still a minor, under the guardianship of Queen Editha. Herein lies the difficulty I find in placing his name on the Roll. Even though his father was half Norman, it is inconceivable that a youth so situated should have been in the invading army. But it is evident he came to terms with the Conqueror, for he was suffered to retain a shred of his father's Earldom. Harold Ewyas in Herefordshire, where he had his castle, is named from him, and passed through his great-granddaughter Sybil to Robert de Tregoz.

Fitz Browne: (see *Browne*).

Fouke, or De Foucques; a Norman family that bore *Sable* a lion *Or* armed *Gules*, fronting a stork *Argent.* Thomas Fouque occurs on the Exchequer Rolls of the Duchy about 1198. Robert Fulco was one of the Justiciaries in 1267

(Roberts, Excerpt. II. 469). Peter, John, Richard, Robert, and Walter Folke all occur in Kent c. 1272 (Rotuli Hundred.). Sir Bartholomew Fouke, Master of the Household to Queen Elizabeth and James I., died in 1604. "The Baronets Folkes and Fouke are of this family."—*The Norman People*. The former, however, did not trace their descent further back than the reign of Queen Anne, when their ancestor, Martin Folkes, was Attorney-General, and are now extinct. The latter derive from the Fowkes of Brewood and Gunston in Staffordshire. Sir Frederick, created a baronet in 1814, was the son of one of the Grooms of the Bedchamber to Henry, Duke of Cumberland. Both families bore very similar arms, though entirely unlike those of the French house. The coat of the Folkes was Per pale, *Vert* and *Gules*, a fleur de lis *Ermine;* that of the Foukes is *Vert*, a fleur de lis *Argent*.

Freuil. I find four different branches of this family in Normandy; the "Sires de Tannières, Election de Lions;" the "Sires de la Haye, &c., Election de Pont Audemer;" another, also in Pont Audemer; and the "Sires de la Haye, Election d'Argentan." One of these was represented in the great assembly of Norman nobles in 1789. In England, "though but one of them had ever summons to parliament," the Frevilles were "of eminent note, some ages before that time, and afterwards." *—Dugdale.* They were seated in Cambridgeshire, where, as Lysons tells us, Little Shelford belonged to them and their representatives for over three hundred years. One of their monuments is still to be found in the church chancel. It represents Sir John de Freville, who died 6 Ed. II. : a cross-legged knight carved in stone, with a couchant lion at his feet; and bears on a tablet this inscription in Lombardic characters :

> "Ici gist sire Johan de Friville,
> Ke fust seigniour de ceste vile ;
> Vous ke par ici passet
> Par charite pur lalme priet.

This crusader is left out of Dugdale's pedigree, which commences with Baldwin de Freville, living in the reign of Henry III. He bought of the King, for the sum of two hundred marks, the wardship of Lucia de Escalers, and shortly afterwards made her his wife, thus acquiring her father's barony of fifteen knights' fees, of which the chief seat was at Caxton in Cambridgeshire. Their grandson, Sir Alexander, went four times to Scotland with Edward I., and followed his successor to the disastrous field of Bannockburn, where his son

* I am not clear whether the name of Fraelville, which is found among the earliest benefactors of Battle Abbey, is not in reality the same. Sir Anselm de Fraelville (whose father had been one of the Conqueror's knights) "offered for the souls of him and his" some lands for making salt pits, an acre of meadow, "and the whole tithe of his vill called *Glesi*. All these gifts Roger, his son, agreed to, on condition of receiving a dog which he demanded." The poor boy was done out of part of his inheritance at a very cheap rate.

Baldwin—then a young knight of twenty-one—was taken prisoner. He married Joan, daughter of Ralph de Cromwell, and Mazera, one of the co-heiresses of Sir Philip Marmion, and died in 1328, the year after he had been summoned to Edward III.'s first parliament. His barony, though asserted by Dugdale, is not included in the latter's List of Summons, and must be considered questionable; Sir Harris Nicolas maintains that he only received a writ of military summons; and it was at all events never repeated to any of the five Baldwins that succeeded him. Of these, the second was appointed Seneschal of Xaintonge, for life, by the Black Prince, under whose victorious banner he served in Gascony. The next contested the Championship of England with the Dymokes at the coronation of Richard II. He claimed by right of tenure, as Lord of Tamworth Castle, which had descended to him from his ancestress, Mazera de Marmion; but the Constable and Marshal of England, before whom the question was argued, decided that Scrivelsby in Lincolnshire was the manor held by this service, and adjudged it to Sir John Dymoke, the descendant of Joan de Marmion. (See *Marmion.*) The fifth and last Baldwin, who succeeded when but two years of age, died during his minority, and "a fair inheritance thus came to the Families" of his three sisters. Sir Thomas Ferrers, who had married the eldest, Elizabeth, had Tamworth Castle, with other estates in Hereford, Stafford, and Warwickshire: Sir Richard Bingham, the husband of Margaret, the second, had Newdigate in Surrey, and estates in Wilts and Warwickshire; while Roger Aston, whose wife Joice was the youngest sister, had Middleton and Whitnash in the latter county, and various manors in Notts and Herefordshire. Of him came the Scottish Lords Aston.

Front de Boef: see *Estouteville.*

Facunberge: Anglicized Falconbridge; "a great Yorkshire family, probably," says Sir Egerton Brydges, "of later date, at least as to the name." This was taken from Fauquemberg, near St. Omer (the family, in spelling the name, long preserved the m), and was imported into Holderness by *Franco homo Drogonis de Beurere,* an under-tenant in Domesday. "By the name of Franco de Falconberg de Rise, he is mentioned in the chronicle of Meaux Abbey, as one of the contemporaries and neighbours of Gamel de Melsa, on whose land the abbey was built. His family was one of the few received into favour by the Earls of Albemarle."—*A. S. Ellis.* They held their manor of Rise for four hundred years. Franco's son or grandson, Walter, married (according to the above authority) Agnes de Arches, but Poulson, in his *History of Holderness,* states that his wife was the sister and heiress of Anselmus de Stuteville. Here, however, we are met by a chronological difficulty, as this lady's son by her first husband, Sir Alexander St. Quintin of Harpham, lived in the thirteenth century. Peter de Fauconberg, temp. Stephen, was a benefactor to the monks of Pontefract. They "covenanted to celebrate his Obit and Anniversary, and likewise that of Beatrice his Wife, as solemnly as for any Monk of their own Convent."—*Dugdale.* He had five sons, Sir Walter, Sir Philip, Eustace, William, and Stephen. Sir Philip, who married the co-heiress of Scotney, is styled of Appleton, and mention is made of his two sons and two grandsons. Eustace, a man of some note in his generation, was one of the King's Justices Itinerant in 1200. "He was," says Fuller, "born in this county of York, where his name appeareth among the ancient Sheriffs thereof. He was chosen Bishop of London 1222, carrying it clearly from a company of able competitors, occasioning the following distich :

'Omnes hic Dignis, tu Dignior omnibus : omnes
Hic plene sapiunt, plenius ipse sapis.'

Others played on his name, Eustatius (one that stood well), both in respect of spiritual estate (yet 'let him that standeth take heed lest he fall') and temporal condition ; well fixed in the favour of prince and people ; being Chief Justice, then Chancellor of the chequer, and afterwards Treasurer of England, and twice ambassador to the King of France. He deserved right well of his own cathedral, and dying October 31st, 1228, was buried under a marble tomb on the South side of the presbytery."

The eldest son, Sir Walter, and his brother Stephen, married two sisters, Agnes and Petronel, the daughters and co-heirs of Simon Fitz Simon of Brikesworth in Northamptonshire, by Isabel his wife, daughter and heir of Thomas de Cukeney, founder of Welbeck Abbey, Notts. Sir Walter's son, Peter II., who rose in arms against King John, but returned to his allegiance on the accession of Henry III., was the father of another Walter, summoned to parliament (though, according to Nicholas, by a doubtful writ) in 1295. His wife was Agnes, one of the co-heiresses of Peter de Brus III. of Skelton, who brought him, with her father's castle, extensive lands in Yorkshire, and no less than seven sons, of whom two were friars preachers. He was followed by five successive bearers of the title, almost all of whom were, in common with most of their contemporaries, active soldiers under the three first Edwards. The third Lord, knighted on the same day as Edward I., went four times to the wars of Scotland ; the fourth Lord, Constable of York in 1341, and Governor of Berwick-upon-Tweed in 1342, fought both there and in Flanders ; the fifth Lord, a Banneret, also served constantly "beyond sea," and was appointed, with Lord Mowbray and others, to guard the Yorkshire coast against an expected French invasion. Thomas, the last Lord Fauconberg, who had estates in Northamptonshire in right of his mother, Maud de Pateshull, and was, again, in the French wars, left as his sole heiress a daughter named Joan, who had apparently survived both a brother and an elder sister. Poulson asserts that Joan was an idiot from her birth ; nor does Dugdale's quotation of one of her affidavits militate against his statement. "She made proof of her age 10 Hen. V., viz. : That being born at Skelton, and Baptized in the Church there, she was 15 years of age upon the Feast Day of St. Luke the Evangelist the same year ; also that she had a Sister

called Isabel, married to John de Wilton upon the day she was Baptized." Had
Joan been altogether in her right mind, she could scarcely have been asked to
bear testimony as to what occurred at her baptism.[*]

But, idiot or no idiot, Joan found a husband, and a husband of illustrious birth
and renowned valour, William Nevill, afterwards Earl of Kent, one of the younger
sons of Ralph, first Earl of Westmoreland, by his second wife, Joan Beaufort.
He was summoned to parliament *jure uxoris* as Lord Fauconberg in 1429, and the
barony fell into abeyance between his three co-heiresses in 1463. Joan, the eldest,
married Sir Edward Bethune; Elizabeth married Sir Richard Strangeways; and
Alice was the wife of Sir John Conyers, and the mother of the first Lord Conyers.

The fifth Lord Fauconberg left, by his second marriage with Isabella Bigot,
a younger son named Roger, whose posterity carried on the male line for two
additional descents. This Sir Roger, who was of Holme, on Spalding Moor,
took to wife the Lady of Flixburgh, Margaret Darcy, and in the following generation we find Sir Walter de Fauconberg transplanted into Lincolnshire, and
seated at Whitton. His childless son Roger was the last heir; and once again
three sisters shared the estate. Margaret carried Holme to John Constable, and
re-married William de Monceaux; Izabel was the wife of Edmund Percehay of
Park, Lincolnshire, and Constance remained unmarried.

There was likewise a Nottinghamshire branch, derived from Stephen (a
younger son of the first Peter) and Petronel Fitz Simon, who had inherited·
Cukeney from·his mother. According to an old Inquisition, it was held by the
service of shoeing the King's horses whenever he came to Mansfield, to hunt in
Sherwood Forest. Stephen's great-grandson William was, as Dugdale tells us
(though it is denied by Banks), summoned to parliament as Lord of Cukeney in
1299; but the summons, if any, was never repeated. John, the eldest of his two
sons, was an idiot. Sir Henry, the other, was living in 1329, and married Ellen
de Henford. Poulson gives him no posterity.

I can discover no historical authority for Shakespeare's jovial Bastard of·
Falconbridge, with his ready wit and sharp tongue; nor for his spindle-shanked
brother, the

> "·eldest son,
> As I suppose, of Robert Falconbridge,
> A soldier, by the honour-giving hand
> Of Cœur de Lion knighted in the field."

True, he is called a Northamptonshire gentleman. But then Sir Peter II., at
that time the representative of the family in the county, was, as we have seen, in
arms against King John.

About two hundred and fifty years later, however, we meet with a genuine

---

[*] It reminds me of an affidavit made not many years ago by a young lady then in
ward to the Scottish Court of Session, by which she was required solemnly to
asseverate—as it were f her own knowledge—that she was her mother's daughter !

Bastard of Fauconberg, known as the instigator of "the grievous insults made to the City of London," as Camden phrases it, in 1471, who was the natural son of William Nevill, Earl of Kent, Lord Fauconberg in right of his wife. Though his father had been a strong Yorkist, he himself was devoted to the House of Lancaster. "After the battle of Tewkesbury, Thomas Fauconberg, known as the Bastard of Fauconberg, who had been practising piracy, collected a number of mercenary supporters in Calais, and landed in Kent. He sailed up the Thames with seventeen thousand men, adherents of the House of Lancaster, (including some Kentish men) intending to surprise London, and release King Henry, who was then confined in the Tower, but was repulsed; and finding that Edward IV. was marching towards London, he retired in good order to Sandwich, where he fortified himself . . . having forty-seven ships under his control: but hearing of the death of Henry VI., he submitted to King Edward, who had marched to Canterbury. Fauconberg was soon afterwards beheaded."—Furley's *History of the Weald of Kent.*

Fort. There is a "venerable and almost uniform tradition" that the ancestor of the Fortescues was a certain Richard le Fort, Duke William's cup-bearer, "who fought by the side of his master at Senlac, and after the Duke had three horses killed under him, protected him with his shield, and thus saved his life. He was thenceforward known as Richard le Fort-escu (strong shield), and after the battle returned to Normandy, where his lineage still survives, whilst his son Sir Adam remained in England, received a grant of Wimpstone in Devonshire," and was the founder of the English house. Both William of Poitou and William of Malmesbury tell us that the Conqueror had three horses killed under him on the hard-fought field of Hastings, but of this rescue by Richard le Fort, termed by old Westcote "the posy of the family," they make no mention whatever. In any case the Fortescues cannot, I think, be the family here designated, as, in the Roll that recorded the combatants in the famous battle, so gloriously earned an addition to their name would never have been left out. It may be added that, according to Sir William Pole, Wimpston did not come into their possession till 1209. "John Fortescue was the firste of yᵗ famyly I finde toe inhabit Devonshire. Kinge John gave him in the tenth yeare of his raigne Wymondeston in the parish of Modbiry in Devonshire, wᶜʰ contynewed in yᵗ name and famyly unto these late tymes." I find that the Le Forts and Fortescues are treated as two perfectly distinct families in the Nobiliaire de Normandie. The former were Lords of Bonnebose, in the district of Pont-Audemer; and another branch held Montfort, Carneville, &c., in that of Valognes.

I first met with the name in a totally different part of England. Ranulph de le Forte, or de Forte, was a benefactor to Lanercost Priory, in Cumberland (Mon. ii., 130) giving some land in Beaumont, and "a free net in Eden." He probably held under the old Lords of Bowness, of whose barony Beaumont formed part, but I can find no further mention of him. Sampson Forte and

Adam Forte occur about 1272 in the *Rotuli Hundredorum.* Another Sampson le Fort, "in the year 1150, founded a priory at Harold, in honour of St. Peter, for canons and nuns of the order of St. Nicholas of Arrouasia, but it was afterwards occupied by a prioress and a few nuns of the order of St. Austin."— *Lyson's Bedfordshire.* According to a pedigree of the Mordaunts, quoted by Lipscomb in his *History of Bucks,* this "*Sampson Fortis,* of whom many fees were held by knight's service, was one of the most famous knights of his time ; and so called from his great strength and valour, being a great champion, and an associate in war with David of Scotland and Simon de St. Liz. He was lord of several towns and villages, among the rest of Chellington, which he gave to Osmund Mordaunt with his daughter Ellen." His foundation charter to Harold Priory is witnessed by Amalricus Fortis. Henry de Fort, with Philip de Branlasche, held at Brocton by the serjeanty of finding a man-at-arms to serve for fifteen days in the castle of Montgomery.—*Testa de Nevill.*

This family was wholly distinct from that of De Forts, Forz, or De Fortibus (see *Aumale*). "The name of Forz is French and local ; possibly from Fors, a village in Poitou, about four leagues south of Niort ; or from a seigneury of Fors in Poitou. Seeing the spelling of the name in this country was Forz, and occasionally Fortz, it is not improbable that it was here pronounced as if written Fortz, and this would account for its plural form in Latin, de Fortibus."—*Archæological Journal,* vol. xviii. See also *Vivonne.*

Frisell: or Frezel. "This name does not appear in Normandy ; it was of Touraine, where René Frezel, about 1030, was a benefactor to Notre Dame des Noyers. He had issue : 1. René, living 1084, who was ancestor of the house of Fréseau, Marquises of La Frezelière ; 2. Simon (Des Bois). The latter came to England at the Conquest. His descendants, bearing the name of Fresel, or Fressel, long continued in England, and temp. David I. Simon Fresel settled in Scotland, and about 1150 granted the church of Keith to Kelso (Chart. Kelso)." —*The Norman People.* The Peerage genealogy, being much puzzled with this name, has no better hypothesis to offer than a legend that one Julius de Berri presented a dish of strawberries to Charles the Simple, King of France, and had his name changed from De Berri to Fraisier, *fraises,* or strawberry flowers, being assigned to him as his coat of arms ! But this punning derivation is simply the invention of some sixteenth or seventeenth century herald, who chose to convert the silver roses or cinquefoils of the Frasers into strawberry flowers. That they were never so interpreted in earlier times is evident from the Roll of Carlaverock, where, among the knights present at that famous siege in 1300 we find

> "Symon Fresel, de cele gent,
> Le ot noire à rosettes de argent :"

and they are still locally known as "Lochaber roses." The badge of the Lords Saltoun—a strawberry—is, however, clearly allusive to the name.

Sir Simon Fresel, or Fraser, under David I., "enjoyed half the territory of Keith in East Lothian, called after him Keith-Symon," but left only a daughter, Eda, married to Hervey, the King's mareschal, from whom came the great house of the Earls Marischal of Scotland. Another branch of the Frasers had settled in the same county as vassals of the Earls of March; and in the reign of Alexander II., Bernard Fraser, the chief of this family, "raised himself by his talents, from being a vassal of a subject, to be tenant-in-chief of the King." He is a frequent witness to the Royal charters of the time, and was made Sheriff of Stirling in 1234. Richard Fraser, in 1292, was one of the nominees on the part of Baliol in the competition for the throne of Scotland, and twice swore fealty to Edward I. On the other hand, Simon Fraser, though he served at Carlaverock, was in arms against him as early as 1303, and after the defeat of Robert Bruce, was taken prisoner, carried to London, and there executed by order of the King in 1306; his head being "placed on the point of a lance, near the head of William Wallace." His brother and heir, Sir Alexander, more fortunate, fought by Bruce's side at the victory of Bannockburn, and received from him large grants of lands in Stirling and Kincardine, with the hand of his widowed sister, Lady Mary. He was Great Chamberlain of Scotland from 1325 till the death of his Royal brother-in-law, and "died fighting valiantly" at the battle of Duplin in 1332. His grandson and namesake married a co-heiress of the Earl of Ross, and through her acquired a share—which would seem to have been considerable—of that Earldom. "The whole of these lands went under the name of the barony of Philorth:" which, according to the words of Thomas the Rhymer:

"While there is a thistle in the North,
  There shall be a Frazer at Philorth,"

is still the seat of his descendant, Lord Saltoun. This title was brought into the family eight generations later by another Sir Alexander, whose wife, Margaret, was the eldest daughter of George, seventh Lord Abernethy of Saltoun. Their son succeeded his cousin, Alexander, 9th Lord, as "heir of line" in 1669; and the title and dignity of Lord Saltoun was confirmed to him by Charles II. in the following year. During the Civil War he had done and suffered much in the Royal cause; advancing large sums of money to the King, and raising a regiment at his own expense for the expedition into England. From him the present and eighteenth Lord is directly derived.

The Lords Lovat descend from Simon Fraser, slain at Halidon Hill in 1333, whose exact relationship to the elder line is not known. "The received opinion is, that he and James Fraser (who also fell at Halidon Hill) were sons of Sir Alexander Fraser, slain at Duplin, and the nephews of Robert I. by their mother, Mary Bruce. But this," adds Sir Charles Douglas, "is contrary to chronology:" and they were more probably brothers of Sir Alexander. He married Margaret, one of the heirs of the Earl of Caithness, and thus obtained a great territory in the Highlands, and became the chief of a powerful clan that took its name from him. Simon's son, Hugh, who was left an orphan in the cradle, is styled Dominus de Lovat as early as 1367; but it was not till the following century that another Hugh Fraser was created a "lord of parliament" by James I. of Scotland, with whom he was high in favour. On the death of the tenth Lord (who left no son) in 1696, his daughter Amelia assumed the title of Baroness of Lovat and inherited the estate. The heir male of the family, at that time, was the notorious Simon Fraser of Beaufort, who paid assiduous court to the young lady, and persuaded her to elope from her mother's house of Castledownie, under the conduct of Fraser of Tenechiel, "their mutual confidant." But Tenechiel, either dreading the consequences, or hoping for a reward from her relatives, refused to proceed with the abduction of the heiress, disclosed the plot to her mother, and forcibly carried back the unwilling damsel to her home. She made no further attempt to wed her kinsman, and gave her hand in due time to Mr. Mackenzie, of Prestonhall. Thus foiled with the daughter, Simon seized upon the mother—this time dispensing with any preliminary formality of courtship—carried her off by open violence, forced the unhappy Dowager to marry him, and took possession of the Lovat property. It speaks volumes as to the difficulty of meddling with a great Highland chieftain at that period, that though the Edinburgh courts fulminated edict after edict against Simon Fraser—sentencing him to execution, forfeiture, and outlawry—he actually underwent no punishment of any sort, except a few months' banishment, for any of his misdeeds. His subsequent career need scarcely be recapitulated here. Every one has read of the crafty traitor, who, by alternately selling the secrets of either party, obtained all that he wanted from both : the Lovat lands and his acknowledgment as Lord Lovat from King George, and the Dukedom of Fraser from King James ; who sent his son to head his clan in the battlefield whilst he kept himself out of danger, and at last died on the scaffold—fearlessly enough—a hated and unpitied old man, of whom "nobody ever knew any good." Chambers tells a characteristic story of his second marriage to Miss Primrose Campbell, a sister of the fourth Duke of Argyll. She was staying with her sister, Lady Rosebery, at Barnbougle Castle (a few miles from Edinburgh), when Lord Lovat first paid his addresses to her. Knowing his bad character, and how he had treated his first wife, she rejected him with abhorrence. He then forged a letter, as from her mother, announcing that she had arrived at Edinburgh, and entreating Primrose to come at once to a lodging in the Lawnmarket, which was particularly described, where she was lying dangerously ill. Lady Rosebery hurriedly desired the carriage to be got ready for her, and the poor girl drove to the place appointed, and finding the house lay down a close, and could only be reached on foot, she alighted at the entrance to this wynd, where she found a servant ready to receive her luggage, and dismissed her sister's coach. But no sooner had she set foot in the house where she was to meet her sick mother, than she found herself a prisoner in the hands of Lord Lovat, who coolly told her she had no alternative but to become his wife, "as she was now in a house of bad fame, from which, after it should be known in whose company she had been, it would be impossible again to go forth into decent society." She pleaded and protested, with many tears, and held out bravely for a while, " till a hopeless confinement of several days reduced her to despair, and she at last consented to the match." She brought him a son, in addition to the two sickly boys he had by his first marriage; and whenever he went away to the Lowlands, he used to tell her " that, if he found either of the boys dead when he returned, he would shoot her through the head." She herself was never allowed to leave the Highlands, but was kept in strict durance within his castle walls, unable to communicate with any one, and it was only by a stratagem that she finally succeeded in making her pitiable case known. She rolled up a letter in a clew of yarn, and managed to drop it from her window into the hands of a trusty messenger, who conveyed it to her family. A separation was then arranged, and she lived in peace to a great age, honoured and beloved for her goodness, and a Lady Bountiful on her meagre jointure of £190 a year.

Lord Lovat's eldest son, Simon, who had been unwillingly forced into rebellion by his father, received a free pardon in 1750, "and every act of his future life justified the favour of government." He refused a commission under the King of France, and after having served long and honourably in the English army, his forfeited estates were restored to him in 1774. The barony was given back in 1837 to Thomas Alexander Fraser, the grandfather of the present and seventeenth Lord.

It is believed that the family still exists in France. While the grandfather of the present Lord Saltoun was serving in the army of occupation at Paris (after Waterloo) he was struck by seeing a carriage drive by on which he recognised his own coat of arms, and found, on inquiry, that it belonged to the Baron de Frezel.

There were Frezels remaining in England for at least three centuries after the Conquest. Walter Frezel, of Great Saxham, in Suffolk, held Frezel's manor 14 Edward I. Sir Robert Frezel was knight of the shire 24 Edward III. and bore *Gules* fretty *Or*, on a chief *Argent* two mullets *Sable*, as appears by his seal. His daughter and heiress Agnes was the wife of Simon Saxham, from whom the estate passed by another heiress to the Drurys.—*Gage's Suffolk.*

Fitz Simon: interpolated. "The first who bore the name was Robert Fitz Simon, son of Simon Fitz Robert, Baron of Daventry, a scion of the great house of Clare. This Robert was ancestor of the Fitz Walters of Daventry, Barons by writ in 1292."—*Sir Egerton Brydges.* But he lived three generations after the Conquest.

Fitz Fouk. Robert, Geoffrey, Theobald, and William Fitz Fulco occur in the *Rotuli Curiæ Regis* of 1190. See *Fouke.*

Filioll. This name is found in the muniments of Battle Abbey. Ralph de Fillel or Filliol confirmed a grant made by his ancestor (who came over with the Conqueror) of some land in Pevensey Marsh to La Battayle, about the beginning of the thirteenth century. Bernard Filloyel, at nearly the same date, witnessed a deed of Hugh Baliol: and in 1270 Richard Filliol went with Prince Edward to the Holy Land. Their Sussex seat was at Old·Court in Worthing; and in the time of Edward I., Sybilla Filiol inherited it, and married Sir John Fiennes. They were from very early times seated in Essex. "This family took its name from Filioles, in French *Filleul*, or Godson, as appears by a seal appended to a grant of William Filiol to Cogeshall Abbey in Essex, which has a representation of a font, a king on one side and a bishop on the other, holding a child as in the ceremony of baptism; so that the surname seems given by some King of England" (or Duke of Normandy) "to one of their ancestors at the time of baptism. A branch of them held Filiol's (vulgarly Felix) Hall in Essex; in which county they held lands in the time of King Stephen; also the manor of Kelvedon, or Keldon, there: but this branch was extinct about 1345. William, second son of Sir John Filiol, who died 1332, married a daughter of Welsh, or Wallis, of Langton, and became the founder of the family of Filiol in Dorset, and of Old Hall in Rayne, co.˙ Essex, which continued till 1720. They had very early a concern in Dorset—before the reign of Edward I. There was another branch seated at Knight Street in Marnhull, lately extinct."— *Hutchins' Dorset.* William Filiol was knight of the shire 40 Edward III.; and William Filiol 15, 20, 28, 29, and 33 Hen. VI. Their estate in Dorset appears to have been very considerable, and at the death of the last male heir (a lad of sixteen) in 1509, it passed to his two sisters. The.younger of these, Katherine, was the divorced wife * of Sir Edward Seymour, afterwards Duke of Somerset and Lord Protector of the realm. The Essex family ended with Sir

---

* Not only was she herself divorced, but by a special limitation of the patent, her two sons were debarred from succeeding to the Dukedom till after the failure of all descendants of their father's children by his second marriage. This extraordinary disposition was evidently connected with the terrible domestic calamity that had forced the Duke to repudiate Katherine Filiol. To her name in 'Vincent's Baronage' at the Heralds' College is appended this note, "repudiata, quia pater ejus post nuptis eam cognovit." Some tradition of this ghastly story lingered on in the last century at Berry Pomeroy. The apparition of a young and very beautiful woman, wailing and wringing her hands in frenzied distress, was believed to haunt the old castle—long since deserted by the Seymours—whenever the death of one of its inmates was at hand. She always showed herself hurrying towards a staircase that led to one of the upper chambers, and as she disappeared on the last step, turned round with a look that, once seen, no one ever forgot. Such mingled hate, rage, horror, and despair, as it might have been supposed the human countenance was powerless to convey, were written on her fair young face. The local explanation given was that she had been the daughter of a former Baron of Berry Pomeroy, who bore a child to her own father, and strangled it in the upper chamber to which she is ever seen wending her way.

John Filiol, obt. 1381, whose daughter and sole heir, Cecilia, married John de Bohun of Midhurst, a baron by writ in 1363.

The name is common in Normandy, and I find it mentioned there in 1830. Six families of Filleul, all bearing different arms, are included in the authenticated list of "Gentilshommes Normands"; and Le Filleul d'Amertol, Le Filleul, Baron de Montreuil, Du Filleul des Chênets, and Filleul de Verseuil appear among the assembled nobility of the province in 1789.

Fitz Thomas. Several of this name are to be found in the *Monasticon.* William Fitz Thomas, of Scostorn, Lincolnshire, a benefactor of Barling Abbey; Peter Fitz Thomas, who gave lands to Ellerton Priory, Yorkshire, &c., &c., but I cannot find that these were hereditary appellations. Maurice Fitz Thomas, one of the greatest Irish magnates, who was created Earl of Desmond in 1329, and his brother, Sir John Fitz Thomas, were so named from their father, Thomas Fitz Maurice, Lord Justiciar of Ireland, and the chief of the mighty Geraldines. (See below.)

Fitz Morice. No more illustrious name than Fitz Maurice is to be found in the annals of Ireland, for it was borne during several generations by the descendants of Maurice Fitz Gerald, the founder of the great historical house of Geraldine. He was a companion-in-arms of the redoubtable Earl Strongbow, and by his gift Baron of Naas and Wicklow. One of his sons was the ancestor of the Earls of Kildare and Dukes of Leinster—Premier Dukes of Ireland; from another sprung the princely Desmonds, and a line of seventeen powerful Earls. But, having been adopted only in the middle of the twelfth century, I am sorry to say the name must not be included here.

Fitz Hugh: "These great Yorkshire barons descended from Bardolph, Lord of Ravenswath and other manors in Richmondshire at the time of the Conquest; but they certainly did not assume this surname till temp. Edward III."— *Sir Egerton Brydges.* (See *Bodin.*) As here given, it must refer to Robert Fitz Hugh, Baron of Malpas, one of the barons of Hugh Lupus, Earl Palatine of Chester, and generally believed to be his illegitimate son. He was among the most powerful of "the cruel potentates that spilt the Welshmen's blood" with the never-sheathed swords of Lords-Marcher, in the ruthless battles of the Border. His castle of Malpas commanded the important and difficult pass that formed one of the gates of Wales: and two other frontier-fortresses, Oldcastle and Shocklack, were included within his great domain. In his descendants, and probably in him, was vested the office of *Serjeant of the Peace* for all Cheshire, except the hundreds of Wirrall and Macclesfield. "Some would have the Baron of Malpas to be the prime baron, forasmuch as Robert Fitz Hugh hath for the most part the pre-eminence in the subscription of old charts in those ancient times, as also in the record of Domesday Book, where among all the rest of the barons he is put down first next after the Earl, and by which it appears also that he held more land in the county than any one of the rest except

William Malbedenge."—*Ormerod's Cheshire.* But this point of precedence is admitted to be exceedingly dubious; and it is certain that when the Baron of Halton was constituted Hereditary High Constable of Chester, he ranked in right of his office as Premier Baron.

"It is agreed by all parties that Robert Fitz Hugh died without male issue; and by the best authorities he had two daughters, Letitia, the wife of Richard Patric" (see *De La Laund*), and Mabilia, the wife of William Belward (see *Belevers*). "The representation of the Patrics passed through the Suttons and Dudleys to the Wards, and that of the latter through the Egertons and Breretons to the Holts."—*Ibid.* William Belward is the Cheshire knight mentioned by Camden, "each of whose sons took different surnames, while their sons, in turn, also took different names from their fathers. They altered their names in respect to habitation, to Egerton, Cotgrave, and Overton: in respect to colour, to Gough, which is red: in respect to learning, to Ken-clarke (a knowing clerk or learned man): in respect to quality, to Goodman; in respect to stature, to Little: and in respect to the Christian name of one of them, to Richardson, though all were descended from William Belward."—*Remaines,* p. 141. "Who would conceive, without good proof," asks Sir Edward Dering, "that Malpas, Gough, Golborne, Egerton, Goodman, Cotgrave, Weston, Little, Kenclerke, and Richardson, were all in short time the issue of William Belward?"—Lower's *Curiosities of Heraldry,* App. p. 305. And yet one name—Cholmondeley—is omitted from the list.

Fitz Henrie. No Fitz Henry is to be found in Domesday, and I am unable to identify this name. It may have been inserted. Robert Fitz Henry founded Burscough Priory, temp. Henry II. (Mon. ii. 393), and was the ancestor of the Lathams. Two Fitz Henrys were summoned to parliament during the reigns of the first two Edwards; *Hugo filius Henrici Dominus de Ravensworth,* the father of the first Lord Fitz Hugh; and Aucher Fitz Henry, who married Joan, one of the daughters of John de Bellew and Laderina the Bruce co-heiress. His parentage is unnoticed by Dugdale; Banks suggests that "he would rather seem to be a brother of the before-named Hugh Fitz Henry; but for so being, there is no authority whatever."

Fitz Waren: "Taken not earlier than Hen. I. by Fulk, son of Guarine de Metz, sometimes called Guarine Vicecomes."—*Sir Egerton Brydges.* This Guarine, or Warine, surnamed the Bald, was of the House of Lorraine, and is described by Ordericus as "a man of small stature but great courage, who bravely encountered the Earl's enemies, and maintained tranquillity throughout the district entrusted to his government." His Earl was Roger de Montgomeri, who selected him from among his barons as his chief counsellor, and Viscount or Sheriff of Shropshire (then an hereditary office): attaching to his sheriff's-fief seventy manors in that and other counties, and giving him his niece Amieria in marriage. Warine thus "stood the second man in Shropshire," and maintained a state and magnificence unusual even in those hospitable times. Such was his passion for entertaining his guests, that he caused the King's highway to be turned through the hall of his manor at Alleston, in order that no traveller might have an excuse for passing by without stopping to receive some food and drink. He died the year before the compilation of Domesday, leaving his son a minor.

Fitz Rainold. William Fitz Rainold, who in 1086 held of William de Warrenne "Poninges" in Sussex (Domesday), was the son of Rainold de Pierrepont, and the nephew of Robert, Lord of Hurst-Pierrepont in the same county. (See *Pierrepont.*) He was the founder of a renowned house, that took its name from this South Down manor, and held it for three centuries.* Adam, a benefactor of Lewes Priory, living in the reigns of Stephen and Henry II., was the first who was called De Poynings. His grandson Michael, who in 1202 gave the King "a good Norway Goshawk" to have a Wednesday market at Crawley, and was afterwards in arms against him, held ten knight's fees in Sussex and other counties.

His descendants—all of them soldiers—have borne their banner to the front on so many a well-fought field, that its very blazonry has become historical.† Sir Michael, a baron by writ in 1293, served eight times in France between 1296 and 1313: Sir Thomas, who married one of the heiresses of the great baronial house of Criol, was slain in the famous sea-fight off Sluys; and the third Lord Poynings followed Edward III.'s standard for nearly thirty years as a Knight Banneret, fought at Cressy and Poitiers, and was one of the appointed guardians of the Sussex coast when a French invasion was impending in 1352. Richard, fifth Lord, who succeeded his elder brother in 1375, lost his life in John of Gaunt's expedition to Spain. When summoned to attend it, and part from his wife and yet unborn child, he seems to have left his pleasant home in

---

* There is a curious bequest in the will of the third Lord Poynings relating to this estate: "I demise to him who may be my heir a ruby ring which is the charter of my heritage of Poynings, together with the helmet and armour which my father demised to me."

† "Fix upon the escutcheon of any knightly family, and enumerate the scenes it has visited, among what glories it has shone! Take that of Poynings, Barry of 6, *Or* and *Vert*, a bend *Gules*, and track its presence. It probably waved on the ramparts of Acre, and witnessed feats of arms against the Saracens: it was certainly seen in the ranks of the insurgent barons under Simon de Montfort: its bearer was conspicuous in the retinue of Earl Warrenne in Scotland: Sir Nicholas Poynings, in 20 Edward III., at the head of eight knights, twenty esquires, and thirty-five archers, bore it at the siege of Calais: it was with Sir Thomas and Sir Richard Poynings both at Cressy and Poitiers: with another Richard, who accompanied John of Gaunt to Spain, and there died: with Robert, the last Lord Poynings in the French wars under Henry V. and VI., and with Sir Edward Poynings, Henry VII.'s Viceroy in Ireland."
—*Sussex Archaeologia.*

the South Downs with a foreboding that he should see it no more. The night before he embarked at Plymouth, he made his will, enjoining that "if it so happen that I depart this life in such a place that my body cannot be buried at Poynings, to the end that my friends afar off may take notice thereof, I will that a stone of marble be provided, with an escutcheon of my arms, and an helmet under my head, and an inscription declaring my name and the time of my death." Three months afterwards, he died of fever at Villalpando, in Leon. He was only twenty-nine. His wife Isabel was a great heiress, the daughter of Robert Lord Fitz Payne by Elizabeth, daughter and coheir of Sir Guy de Bryan ; and it was through her that the Poynings became entitled to a share in the Bryan estates in 1489. Their son Robert was the last Baron of this line. He, too, showed that "his blood was fetched from fathers of war-proof," for he attended four successive Kings, Richard II., and the fourth, fifth, and sixth Henries, in all their French wars ; in 1423, with a following of sixty men-at-arms and one hundred and eighty archers, assisted at the taking of Yvry and the battle of Vernoil, and was killed at the siege of Orleans in 1446. Alianor, his grand-daughter, succeeded to the barony, and married Sir Henry Percy, summoned as Baron Poynings during his father's lifetime, and afterwards third Earl of Northumberland.

Her father (who never lived to be Lord Poynings) had, however, a twin brother who carried on the line, and whose son, Sir Edward, "being," says Dugdale, "an active person in his time, became an expert Souldier," and according to Lloyd, "the best camp-master in Christendom." He served all his life ; first with Henry VII. at Bosworth ; next as one of the chief commanders of the forces sent in aid of the Emperor Maximilian ; was employed "to conjure down the last walking spirit of the House of York which haunted the King—Perkin Warbeck ; " and appointed Lord Deputy of Ireland in 1495. His government was judicious and successful ; and the code he enacted, known as "Poynings' Law," remained in force till the end of the last century. Henry VIII. on his accession, made him Comptroller of his Household, and gave him the command of the English contingent in the wars of the Low Countries ; in 1509 he was Warden of the Cinque Ports ; in 1514 with the King at the siege of Therouenne ; and upon the taking of Tournay in the same year, was left in charge with a strong garrison. In 1521, as Constable of Dover, he received Charles V. on his landing in England : and died two years afterwards, leaving no legitimate children. But he had three sons born out of wedlock, of whom the eldest, Sir Thomas, like himself an excellent soldier, gained distinction by his services in the field. Henry VIII. created him Baron Poynings in 1545 ; appointed him Marshal of Calais, and gave him the command of the army then besieging Boulogne. Nothing more is known of him, except that he married the co-heiress of Lord Marney, and left no issue. Neither did his brother Edward, slain at the siege of Boulogne : and the remaining son, Sir Adrian, who was Governor of Portsmouth in 1561, had only daughters. They were the last that bore the time-honoured name of Poynings.

Another branch there had been, which did not outlast the third generation. Lucas, a younger brother of Michael, third Lord Poynings, married Isabel, the sister and eventually the sole heiress of the last Lord St. John of Basing, and then the childless widow of Henry de Burghersh. In her right, Lucas de Poynings was summoned to parliament as Lord St. John in 1368. His son Thomas, in 1400, obtained license to go on pilgrimage to Jerusalem, and to remain absent three years. Later in life he was engaged in the French wars. In 1422 he was with the Earl of Salisbury at the siege of Pont-Meulan ; and the next year appointed, with Robert de Willoughby, to take over four hundred men-at-arms and twelve hundred archers to the Duke of Bedford, then Regent of France. He died in 1428, having survived his only son, and his daughter Constance conveyed the barony to her husband Sir John Paulet, the grandfather of the first Marquess of Winchester.

" Blomfield, in his History of Norfolk, makes mention of a Lucas de Poynings, who married Isabel, one of the four daughters and co-heirs of Robert de Aguillon, by Agatha his wife, one of the daughters, and co-heirs of Fulk de Beaufo, and thereby acquired Poynings manor in that county. This rather intimates some great discrepance in the early account of the Poynings family given by Dugdale." —*Banks.* I have—I must confess with some misgivings—followed the latter in calling Michael the first Lord Poynings; though Dugdale states that the first writ of summons was issued to his son Thomas.

Flamuile : "from Flamanville, near Yvetot, Normandy. Roger de Flamville witnessed a charter of Walter Esper for Rievaulx, York, temp. Hen. I., being one of his tenants (Mon. i. 729). He is mentioned in 1130; also Hugh de Flamville in York, and in 1165 Roger de Flamville, York, held eight and a half fees of Mowbray (Liber Niger). The family long flourished in great eminence in England."—*The Norman People.* William de Flamville was of Northumberland, temp. Edward I.—*Rotuli Hundredorum.* The sisters and heiresses of this William are mentioned in the *Testa de Nevill*, and held of the King at Wytingham, in Northumberland. Elias de Flamville, holding Stokesby of Peter de Brus in Yorkshire ; John de Flamville, holding *de veteri feoffamento* of the Honour of Bedford : appear in the same record. Elias also held in North Cave, of the fee of Percy of Kildale.—*Kirkby's Inquest.* Dugdale tells us that " Hugh de Hastings, by gift of King Henry I., obtained all the Lands of Robert de Flamenville, with Erneburgh, Niece of the said Robert." These lands had been granted by Robert de Limesi, Bishop of Coventry, and comprised " Burbache, Barewell, and Birdingburte with their Appurtenances, viz. Scatescleve (now Sketchley) and Eston (now Aston Flamville) and Stapelton." Aston-Flamville is in Leicestershire. In 1130 Hugh accounted for ninety marks and two *Destriers*, being the whole of the balance of a Fine he had given the King for 'having the land and the niece of Robert de Flamville.'"—*Eyton's Salop.* Erneburgh's father was Hugh de Flamenville.

. **Formay:** perhaps Forney, "the Norman French pronunciation of Fornet. Sylvester Fornet of Normandy, 1195: Nicholas and Sylvester de Fornet, 1198 (Magn. Rotul. Scaccarii Normanniæ). Fornet was in the Côtentin."—*The Norman People.* It still survives in England as Furney. But the only Forneys I have met with in old records invariably stand for Furneaux.

Fitz-Eustach. I can find mention of no Fitz Eustace of earlier date than Richard, Baron of Halton, son of Eustace Fitz John, "one of the first peers of England, and of infinite familiarity with King Henry I., as also a person of great wisdom and judgment in counsel."—*Dugdale.* This must be an interpolated name.

Fitz Laurence. Hugh Fitz Laurence held at Napton half a knight's fee of the Prior of Coventry.—*Testa de Nevill.*

Formibaud: or rather Fermebaud—(Leland). "The Firmbauds," says Lysons, "are among the earliest extinct families which are known, by records subsequent to the Norman survey, to have possessed property in Bedfordshire, and twice represented the county in parliament in the reign of Edward III." They also held Bow-Brickhill, in Buckinghamshire, which passed from them to the Staffords. "Nicholas Frembaud was Constable of Bristol Castle in the reign of Edward III. He had also the custody of the see of Bath and Wells and other great estates, which yet were occasionally seized into the King's hands. His son Thomas succeeded him in his Bedfordshire estates; and afterwards, Sir John Frembaud (probably Thomas's son) exercised the patronage of the church of Bow-Brickhill between 1336 and 1349."—*Lipscomb's Buckinghamshire.* In the latter year Henry Fermbaud served as knight of the shire for Bucks. Geoffrey Frumbaud held sixty acres of land at Wingfeud in Suffolk, by the service of paying the King two white doves yearly.—*Plac. Coron. 4 Ed. I.*

Frisound; in Duchesne's list, Frisoun. "Walonus de Frisc" or "de Frise" occurs in the *Rotulus Cancellarii*, 3 John. William de Frisa held two knight's fees of the King's gift at Martlegh in Worcestershire.—*Testa de Nevill.* Robson gives the coat of arms of Frise, Fris, or Frys, as *Or* 3 bars *Vert.* I have been very unsuccessful in my search for some account of this family. I find that in 1333 Robert de Frison was Prior of Cogges, Oxfordshire; but the Priors of this house were generally chosen by the Abbey of Fescamp, in Normandy, of which it was a cell. It may therefore be presumed that he was a foreigner. In Gloucestershire, there was a Robert Frize of Pucklechurch, whose daughter and heiress married William Llewellyn. This must have been about the end of the sixteenth century, as the marriage of William's grandfather Humphrey with Isabel Berkeley took place in 1511.—*Berkeley MSS.*

Finere. According to Sir William Pole, Sir Gilbert Finemer or Finemore held half a knight's fee in Devonshire of the Honour of Clare, temp. Henry II.; and bore the red chevrons of his suzerain on a field ermine. The name is also found at Hinksey in Berkshire; and in the church of St. Lawrence at Reading there is a monument to the memory of one of this family, with the following quaint inscription: " Under thy feet, reader, lie the remains of Richard Fyne-more, his father's Benjamin, and his brother's Joseph ; who, coming from Oxon to the burial of a friend, found here his own grave, 1664." The manor of Tingewick in Buckinghamshire was given in 1210 by this family to the monastery *de Monte Rothomago* in Normandy.—*Lysons.* It had passed to them from the Lacys before the reign of Henry III.—*Lipscomb's Bucks.* They probably gave their name to the neighbouring village of Finmore in Oxfordshire. Hugh de Finemer was Vicar of Shabbington, Bucks, in 1348. They had been seated in that county from very early times ; for Gilbert de Finemere is mentioned there in 1207.—Hunter's *Fines.* William de Finnore served as knight of the shire for Middlesex in 1322.—*Palgrave's Parliamentary Writs.* William Fimner gave some land at Esthorpe, in the East Riding, to Walton Priory.—*Burton's Mon. Ebor.* Richard and Roger de Vinemer, Kent, c. 1272.—*Rotuli Hundredorum.* According to Foxe, the Church historian, Henry Finmore, Filmer, or Finnemore —for he spells the name in each way—was Churchwarden of Windsor, and burnt to death under the Act of the Six Articles on July 3rd, 1543. At about the same date some Fynemores were seated at Cam in Gloucestershire, where they are first mentioned in a Crown lease of 1522, and many of their tombstones remain in the church and church-yard. The name constantly occurs in the parish register between the years 1571 and 1825, variously spelt Fynamore, Fynymore, Fynemore, Phinnymore, Fyllimore, and Fylymore. " It is first spelt Phillimore in 1640, and from that time both forms of the name occur during thirty or forty years, the later one alone being used after about 1680 in the Cam register, though the early one is still common in Gloucestershire and elsewhere." —*Blunt's Dursley.* At one of their former residences in the neighbourhood, Nash'Hall, now called The Knapp, " there is a grim tradition that a body lies buried under the stone steps which lead down from the hall to the cellar, and that the spirit of the deceased rises whenever grass grows on the steps. Boiling water used to be poured upon them to prevent the grass from growing."—*Ibid.* The last of the family that remained in the old locality died in 1826. One of the younger brothers, early in the preceding century, migrated to London, where his son Robert married the heiress of Kendalls in Hertfordshire, and was the ancestor of " the Phillimores of Kendalls, the eminent ecclesiastical judges, Dr. Joseph Phillimore and his son Sir Robert Joseph Phillimore, and Sir John Phil-limore, a naval officer of high repute in the last century."—*Ibid.* An anecdote of this family is preserved in the Berkeley MSS. Among the " Proverbs peculiar to the Hundred " is this: *He hath offered his candle to the divell.* " It thus arose : Old ffilimore of Cam, going in Anno 1584 to p'sent S' Tho. Throgm. of Tortworth with a sugar lofe, met by the way with his neighbour S. M. who demanded whither and upon what busines hee was goinge, answered, ' To offer my candle to the Divill;' which cominge to the eares of S' Tho. at the next muster he sent two of ffilimores sonnes soldiers into the Low countries, where the one was slayne and the other at a deere rate redeemed his return."

The ancient Kentish family of Filmer is clearly of the same stock : for their coat of arms is almost identical. They bear *Sable* three bars and in chief as many trefoils *Or ;* and the only difference perceptible in the Phillimore coat is that their bars and cinquefoils are *Argent.* Most probably the Filmers are descended either from Roger or Richard de Vinemer of Kent, living in 1272 (see p. 59) ; but Wotton only begins their pedigree in the following century, temp. Edward III., when they "wrote their name Finmere, Fylmere, Filmour, and Filmer, and were seated at Ottringden, at a place called Finmore." Robert Filmer, in the time of Elizabeth, purchased their present seat, East Sutton ; and another Robert, his descendant, received a baronetcy in 1674 from Charles II.

Fitz Robert. Ralph Fitz Robert, and William Fitz Robert, both holding in Kent, appear as under tenants in Domesday. It seems likely that they were brothers. William held West-Selve of Bishop Odo ; but I have no further means of identifying them. A Turstin Fitz Robert is found in Dorsetshire ; but "all we know of him is that he held Gillingham."—*Hutchins' Dorset.*

Numerous Fitz Roberts occur at a later date. "John Fitz Robert was a powerful Soldier in the days of Henry I., and held Dagworth of the Bishop of Norwich : and his brother William held of the old feoffment in 1165. This William married Sibil, sister and coheir of John, son of Ralph de Caineto or Cheney, and left three coheiresses."—*Blomfield's Norfolk.* But he elsewhere describes Sibil de Cheney's husband as Robert Fitz Walter, son of Walter de Caen or de Cadomo. Again, "Ralph and John Fitz Robert were Barons in King John's time, and bore *Or,* two chevrons *Gules.*"—*Ibid.* A family of the name " early acquired prominence " in Shropshire—v. *Eyton.* Sir Geoffrey Fitz-Robert (who died before 1211) was a Baron in Ireland.

Furniuale : interpolated. The first of this family in England was Sir Gerard de Furnival, who went with Cœur de Lion to the Holy Land.

Fitz Geffrey. This may very probably stand for Hervé Fitz Geffrey, who was of the illustrious house of Montmorency. "Hervey, the eldest son of Geoffrey de Montmorency, came to England in 1066, and was father of Geoffrey Fitz Hervey (Duchesne, 67). He held several manors in Essex, of which his descendant Hervey de Montmorency, Constable of Ireland, was possessor a century later. He married Adelaide de Clermont, whose name appears with his in charters (Perkin, Hist. King's Lynn, 171). He had Burchard de Montmorency, who was a benefactor of Thetford (Mon. i. 667), and Robert Fitz Geffrey, who was a baron 1165. He is mentioned in Lincoln in that year as Robert Maurenciacus (Liber Nig.). He had Hervey, Constable of Ireland, whose nephew Geoffrey was Deputy of Ireland temp. Hen. III., and from

whom descended the Barons de Marisco, and the Viscounts Mountmorres and
Frankfort in Ireland. The spelling of this name varies greatly, as Mont-
morentii, Montemarisco, Montemoraci, Montemorentino, &c."—*The Norman
People.* In Ireland it had long been simplified to Morres, and the two
Viscounts had to obtain the Royal license, in 1815, to exchange it for Montmorency. Mr. Freeman calls it "a singular fact that a family named Morres
in Ireland, dissatisfied with a very respectable name which might have reminded
them of the Theban legion, thought proper in the present century to change
it to Montmorency, and to give out that a branch of the house of the first
Christian Baron followed the banner of the Norman." He throws discredit
upon the pedigree, because the name of Montmorency is not found in
Domesday: evidently believing that the present rule by which every member
of a family bears the father's surname, existed at that period. This was so far
from being the case, that the Norman archæologists expressly state that no son
was permitted to bear the surname of the family till after his father's death.
Till then he was known only by their joint Christian names: as, Alan Fitz-
Flaald, William Fitz-Alan (Recherches sur le Domesday).

Fitz Herbert. *Herbertus Regis Camerarius,* the ancestor of all the
Herberts, was Chamberlain in fee to Henry I., two of whose charters he attests
at Windsor in 1101. There are only conjectures as to his lineage, of which
in reality nothing whatever is known. He died "not long before 1130," and
left, according to Eyton, three sons: 1. Herbert Fitz Herbert; 2. Stephen Fitz
Herbert; and 3. William Fitz Herbert, Archbishop of York in 1143, who was
canonized by Pope Honorius III. in the succeeding century. Herbert filled
his father's place at Court, and married one of the numerous mistresses of
Henry I., Sibil (or Adela) Corbet, mother of Reginald de Dunstanville, Earl of
Cornwall, and daughter and co-heir of the Domesday baron, Robert Corbet,
on whom the King had bestowed the Royal manor of Alcester in Worcestershire.
They, again, had three sons: 1. Robert; 2. Herbert; and 3. Henry. Robert
Fitz Herbert, "the third lineal Chamberlain of his family, succeeded to the
office and estate of his father, ere Henry II. had been three months on the
throne of England," and had d. s. p. before 1165. His heir was his brother
Herbert, whose wife Lucia was a daughter, and eventually a co-heiress of
Milo de Gloucester, Earl of Hereford, Lord High Constable of England. For
some reason or other, that remains unexplained, this Herbert was out of favour
with Henry II. "It is evident that he was admitted to far less than a full share
of the inheritance which should have come to him by his wife and mother; and
there is some proof that at one period he was under total forfeiture. . . . Before
King Richard had reigned a year, he recovered part of his wife's inheritance,
and later on the moiety of Alcester."—*Eyton.* His sons were: 1. Reginald,
who left no children; 2. Peter, his successor; and 3. Matthew, the reputed
ancestor of Vincent Fitz Herbert surnamed Le Finch, of Netherfield in East

Sussex, from whom the Earls of Winchilsea claim descent. But, according to Eyton's pedigree, Matthew's grandson and last male representative, Matthew Fitz John, who was summoned to parliament in 1296, died s. p. in 1309–10.

Peter Fitz Herbert, "being," as Dugdale informs us, "very obsequious to King John at the time of his differences with his Barons, was reputed one of his Evil Counsellors" (though he afterwards fell off in his allegiance); and took an active part in affairs during his reign. He is credited with three wives; one of whom, Isabel, daughter and co-heir of the William de Braose who was hanged by Llewellyn in 1229–30, brought him the Welsh lands of Blaynthelevenny and Thalegard.* Accordingly, in the next generation, Reginald Fitz Peter is enrolled in the ranks of the truculent Barons-Marcher, summoned in 1257 "to fit himself with Horse and Arms and attend the King at Chester to resist the Incursions of the Welch;" and two years later commanded "to reside in those Parts, with all his Power, to prevent their further hostilities." His son, John Fitz Reginald, was a baron by writ in 1294; but the summons was never repeated to any of his successors, nor can I find any further notice of them.

John's younger brother, Peter, is believed to be the ancestor of the Earls of Pembroke. But, as all his descendants were settled in Wales, we have to search for them in the mysterious mazes of Welsh genealogy, in which hereditary surnames are apparently unknown. Sir Bernard Burke, who intrepidly threads his way through this formidable labyrinth, derives from him no fewer than seven other families: the Prodgerses of Gwarrindhû; the Morgans of Arxton; the Joneses of Llanarth;† the Gwynns and Raglans of Glamorganshire; the Hughes of Coelwch or Killough; and the Powells of Perthyr. I have not the power— nor indeed the ambition—of tracing out any of these. If the posterity of John Lord Fitz Herbert was even approximately numerous, the two brothers together may be said to have founded a colony.

William, Lord of Raglan Castle, in right of his grandmother Maud de Morley, with whom Dugdale commences the pedigree, was the eldest son of Sir William-ap-Thomas, knighted by Henry V. for his valour in the French wars. He was an excellent soldier and a staunch Yorkist, whose exploits in the Wars of the Roses had been of such signal service to the cause, that no reward seemed too great for him when Edward IV. came to the throne. He was summoned to parliament, magnificently endowed with the spoils of the attainted Lancastrians, and appointed Justiciar and Chamberlain of South Wales, and Chief Forester in all those counties for life. Nor was this all. Year by year he seemed to grow in favour with the King, as fresh grants and fresh honours poured in upon him. In 1463 he received Dunster Castle and all the lands of Sir James Luttrel; in 1466

---

* She was then (according to Dugdale) the widow of David-ap-Llewellyn, the son of her father's executioner!

† John Jones of Llanarth assumed the name of Herbert not many years ago.

the offices of Justiciar of North Wales, Forester of Snowdon, and Constable of Conway ; in 1468 was created Earl of Pembroke—taking his title from one of his newly acquired possessions* : and in 1469 was made a Knight of the Garter " for having won the Castle of Harlow by assault, it being one of the strongest Forts throughout all Wales." But his career terminated in disaster during the following year. He and his Welshmen were outnumbered and routed at Danes-moor near Edgcote, having been sent to put down the Lancastrian rising under Sir John Conyers and " Robin of Riddesdale." Humphrey Stafford, Earl of Devonshire, had joined him at Banbury with " 6000 good Archers to assist" ; but upon some paltry quarrel about lodgings, forsook him in face of the enemy, and left him to fight the battle against formidable odds. He was taken prisoner, and with his brother, Lord Rivers, and others, beheaded the next day by order of the Duke of Clarence and Warwick the King-maker. By his wife, Anne Devereux, he left, besides six daughters, three sons : 1. William, his successor ; 2. Sir Walter ; and 3. Sir George, of St. Julian's-upon-Usk.

William, the heir, surrendered his Earldom to the King, who wished to give it to his own eldest son ; and was instead created Earl of Huntingdon in 1479. Richard III. named him Justiciar of South Wales, and betrothed him to his daughter, the Lady Katherine Plantagenet ; but the little princess " died in her tender years," and his wife was Mary Widvile, a daughter of the Lord Rivers who had been beheaded with his father at Northampton. Their only child, Elizabeth, married Sir Charles Somerset, the illegitimate son of Henry Beaufort, Duke of Somerset, who was created Earl of Worcester in 1514, and is the ancestor of the present Dukes of Beaufort. She brought him Raglan Castle and a great Welsh inheritance : but some share in her father's estates passed to her uncle, Sir George, whose descendant and representative married Lord Herbert of Cherbury in 1595.

In addition to this numerous family born in wedlock, Lord Pembroke left two bastard sons that bore his name : Sir Richard Herbert of Ewyas, and Sir George Herbert of Swansea. Sir Richard married a Glamorganshire heiress, and had, with other children, a son known as Black Will Herbert, who, beginning life under very poor auspices, successfully achieved a brilliant position at Court. " He was," writes old John Aubrey, " borne in Monmouthshire. He was (I take it) a younger brother, a mad fighting young fellow. 'Tis certain he was a servant to the house of Worcester, and wore their blue coate and badge. My co. Whitney's great aunt gave him a golden angel when he went to London.

---

* It was on the occasion of his receiving this Earldom that he and his brother Sir Richard were desired "to take their surnames after their first progenitor, Herbert Fitz Roy, and to forego the British manner, whose usage is to call every man by his Father, Grandfather, or Great Grandfather's name." It appears that his descent had been made out by the Welsh authorities, from " Herbert, Son Natural to King Henry I."

One time being at Bristowe, he was arrested, and killed one of the sheriffes of the city. He made his escape through Back Street, through the then great gate in the Marsh, and gott into France. In France he betook himself into the army, where he showed so much courage and readinesse of wit in conduct, that in a short time he became eminent, and was favoured by the King, who afterwards recommended him to Henry VIII. of England, who much valued him, and heaped favours and honours upon him. Upon the dissolution of the Abbeys, he gave him the Abbey of Wilton, and a country of lands and manours thereabout belonging to it. He gave him also the Abbey of Ramesbury in Wilts, with much land belonging to it: Cardiff Castle, in Glamorganshire, with the ancient crown lands belonging to it. He married Anne Parr, sister of Queen Katherine Parr, daughter and co-heir of Thomas Parr, I thinke, Marquesse of Northampton, by whom he had two sons, Henry, Earl of Pembroke, and Edward, the ancestor of the Lords Powys. He was made conservator of King Henry 8. He could neither read nor write, but had a stamp for his name. He was of good naturall parts, but very colericque. In Queen Mary's time, upon the return of the Catholique religion, the nunnes came again to Wilton Abbey; and this William, Earl of Pembroke, came to the gate which lookes towards the court by the street, but now is walled up, with his cappe in his hand, and fell upon his knees to the Lady Abbess and nunnes, crying *peccavi*. Upon Queen Mary's death, the Earl came to Wilton (like a tigre) and turned them out crying, ' Out, ye jades ! to worke, to worke—ye jades, goe spinne ! ' "

He received the Earldom of Pembroke from Edward VI. in 1551. Camden calls him " an extraordinary man," who obtained favour and employments at the courts of four successive and very different sovereigns; and Sir Robert Naunton attempts to explain how this was done. " This Earl and the old Marquess of Winchester were ever of the King's Religion, and over-zealous Professors. Being younger Brothers* (yet of Noble Houses) they spent what was left them, and came on Trust to the Court: where, upon the bare stock of their wits, they began to traffick for themselves, and prospered so well, that they got, spent, and left more than any Subjects from the Norman Conquest to their own times. Whereunto hath been prettily replyed, ' that they lived in time of dissolution.' "

Lord Pembroke's marriage with the Queen's sister materially advanced his interests under Henry VIII.; and he sought an even more ambitious alliance for his eldest son, whom he married to Lady Katherine Grey. But, " finding that great mischief had like to have befallen him" through this match with the blood royal, he actually caused Lord Herbert to repudiate the poor lady, and found him another wife, whose father, Lord Shrewsbury, was then high in favour with Queen Mary. This Lady Anne Talbot shortly after died; and the third

---

* Lord Winchester was the eldest son of a noble house in the legitimate line, and heir to a considerable estate in Hampshire.

Lady Herbert (afterwards Countess of Pembroke) was the Mary Sidney immortalized in Ben Jonson's epitaph :

> " Underneath this marble hearse
> Lies the subject of all verse,
> Sidney's sister, Pembroke's mother :
> Death, ere thou hast slaine another
> Wise, and fair, and good as she,
> Time shall throwe a darte at thee."

It was to her that Sir Philip Sidney dedicated the "Arcadia" he had written in her house at Wilton. Her eldest son, William, "the most universally beloved and esteemed of any man in that age," succeeded the Earl of Somerset as Chamberlain to James I.; and "having a great office at court, made the court itself better esteemed and more reverenced in the country. And as he had a great number of friends of the best men, so no man had ever the confidence to avow himself to be his enemy. He was a man very well bred, and of excellent parts, and a graceful speaker upon any subject, having a good proportion of learning, and a ready wit to apply it, and enlarge upon it : of a pleasant and facetious humour, and a disposition affable, generous, and magnificent."—*Lord Clarendon.* His marriage with Lady Mary Talbot, daughter and coheir of Gilbert Earl of Shrewsbury, was "most unhappy, for he paid much too dear for his wife's fortune by taking her person into the bargain," and both his children died young. A book of his poems (addressed to Christiana, Countess of Devonshire under another name) was published in 1660. He died in 1630 "of an apoplexy after a full and cheerful supper," and the title passed to his brother Philip, who "by the comeliness of his person, his skill and indefatigable industry in hunting," had become a favourite courtier of James I.'s, and been created Earl of Montgomery in 1605. Philip's second wife was one of the most remarkable women of her day, the celebrated heiress, Anne Clifford, sole daughter of George third Earl of Cumberland, and at that time the young widow of the Earl of Dorset. She brought him no children, and the present Earl of Pembroke and Montgomery—the thirteenth bearer of the title—descends from her husband's first marriage with Lady Susan Vere. A grandson of the eighth Earl was created Baron Porchester of Highclere in Hampshire in 1780, and Earl of Carnarvon in 1793.

All the other titles of honour granted to the house of Herbert are extinct. The only three legitimate lines descended from a brother of the first Earl of Pembroke (of Edward IV.'s creation) Sir Richard Herbert of Colebrooke in Monmouthshire, "that incomparable hero, who (in the history of Hall and Grafton as it appears) twice passed through a great army of Northern men with his pole-axe in his hand, and returned without any mortal hurt." He had been sent with his brother and some Welsh levies against the Lancastrians under Sir John Conyers and "Robin of Riddesdale," shared his defeat at Danesmoor, and was beheaded with him at Northampton. His son and namesake, Steward of the Marches of North and East Wales and Cardiganshire under Hen. VIII., was the father of Edward Herbert, who, having in early life spent most of his means at Court, "became a soldier, and made his fortune by his sword." He bought a considerable estate, and built a house at Blackhall,* where he kept up such lavish hospitality, that "it was an ordinary saying in the county at that time, when they saw any fowl rise, 'Fly where thou wilt, thou wilt light at Blackhall.'" This open-handed Welshman had four sons: 1. Richard, of whom came the Lords Herbert of Cherbury; 2. Matthew, ancestor of the Earls of Powis; 3. Charles, father of the Earl of Torrington, and 4. George, of New College, Oxford.

Richard, the eldest, could boast of two sons whose names were famous in their generation, and are unforgotten in our own—Edward, Lord Herbert of Cherbury, and George Herbert, the poet and divine.† Edward was a soldier, a scholar, and a courtier:—a brilliant cavalier, brave to a fault in the field, and keenly sensitive on the point of honor, yet withal a deep and original thinker, whose philosophical writings are in advance of his age. His biography is best told in his own words. He early went to reside in France; served under the Prince of Orange in 1610: then travelled in Italy; and in 1616 was sent as Ambassador to the Court of Louis XIII. He received his first peerage (an Irish one, for he had a "fair estate" in Ireland) for his diplomatic services from James I.; and "having approved himself likewise a most faithful servant to King Charles I. as well in Council as in Arms," was created Lord Herbert of Cherbury in Shropshire in 1629. Yet, on the breaking out of the Civil War, he, in the first instance—though but for a short time—sided with the Parliament. He died in 1648. When not yet fifteen, he had married a kinswoman six or seven years his senior, the heiress of Sir William Herbert of St. Julian's in Monmouthshire (enjoined by her father's will to wed none but a Herbert,) by whom he left three children. His eldest son, an enthusiastic loyalist, who is computed to have raised in all two thousand eight hundred men at his own cost for the King's service, succeeded as second Lord Herbert of Cherbury, but the title expired with the last of his two grandsons in 1691. It was twice revived by fresh creations; first, three years afterwards, in favour of his nephew, with whose only son it again came to an end in 1738: then, in 1743, it was granted to a grandson of Matthew, already mentioned (see above), Henry Herbert of

---

* It was afterwards burnt down. Montgomery Castle had been the original seat of the family.

† "George Herbert's tender and poetic spirit started back from the bare, intense spiritualism of the Puritan to find nourishment for his devotion in the outer associations that the piety of ages had grouped around it, in holy places and holy things, in the stillness of church and altar, in the pathos and exultation of prayer and praise, and the awful mystery of sacraments."—*Green's History of the English People.*

Oakley Hall, who, having married Barbara, only daughter of Lord Edward Herbert, and niece and heiress of the last Marquess of Powis, further received the Earldom of Powis in 1748. But it seemed fated never to endure. His son died s. p. in 1801; and the husband of his daughter Henrietta, Edward Lord Clive, eventually obtained the Earldom, and took the name and arms of Herbert.

The title of Earl of Torrington had been granted in 1689 by William III. to Arthur Herbert, an officer in the navy, who, deprived of his commission by James II., had crossed over to Holland and joined him while still Prince of Orange. He went disguised in the garb of a common sailor, having undertaken the perilous task of conveying the treasonable paper that invited William to the throne. For this service he received the command of the fleet, and was placed at the head of the Admiralty. " But both as Admiral and First Lord he was utterly inefficient. Month after month the fleet which should have been the terror of the seas lay in harbour while he was diverting himself in London. The sailors, punning upon his new title, gave him the name of Lord Tarry-in-town. When he came on shipboard he was accompanied by a bevy of courtesans. There was scarcely an hour of the day or night that he was not under the influence of claret. Being insatiable of pleasure, he necessarily became insatiable of wealth. Yet he loved flattery almost as much as either wealth or pleasure. He had long been in the habit of exacting the most abject homage from those who were under his command. His flag-ship was a little Versailles. He expected his captains to attend him to his cabin when he went to bed, and to assemble every morning at his levee. He even suffered them to dress him. One of them combed his flowing wig, another stood ready with his embroidered coat. Under such a chief there could be no discipline."—*Macaulay*. Yet, during the very next year, he took command of the united Dutch and English fleets, and disgraced our flag by retreating before the French under M. de Tourville, and abandoning to them the coast of the Isle of Wight. Positive orders were dispatched to him to fight; Lord Devonshire—alone of all his colleagues—urged his instant dismissal. " It is my duty, Madam," he said to the Queen, "to tell your Majesty exactly what I think on a matter of this importance; and I think that my Lord Torrington is not a man to be trusted with the fate of three kingdoms." His words fell on unheeding ears. On the following day Torrington engaged the French off Beachy Head, placing the Dutch ships in the van, and leaving them to bear the brunt of an unequal contest for many successive hours, while he himself held aloof. They fought with great gallantry, but the result could only be a crushing defeat. Torrington was at once sent to the Tower, where he remained for six months. He was then tried by court-martial, and though acquitted, dismissed the service. He died in 1716.

He, again, left no posterity. But the lineage of the old Yorkist captain has not altogether passed away. Some descendants of the first Sir Richard are still to be met with in Ireland, the Herberts who own the beautiful domain of Muckross on the romantic shores of Killarney.

One other branch there was, derived from a younger son of the first Earl of Pembroke of the existing creation, Sir Edward Herbert of Poole-Castle (as it was then called) "the fair red castle on the hill" now known as Powis, which either he, or his father, had purchased from the Greys. His son William, Lord Powis, received a peerage from James I: and his successor in the second generation become Earl of Powis in 1674, and Marquess of Powis in 1687. James II. had no more faithful and devoted adherent. "He was," says Macaulay, "generally regarded as the chief of the Roman Catholic aristocracy, and, according to Oates, was to have been prime minister if the Popish plot had succeeded." He loyally followed the fallen fortunes of his master, and shared his exile at St. Germains, where he bore the titles—never recognized in his own country—of Marquess of Montgomery and Duke of Powis. One of his five daughters was the brave Lady Nithsdale that saved her husband's life.—*See Herries.* He died outlawed, for refusing to make his submission to the new government; but his son was restored in blood, and to the dignities of Earl and Marquess of Powis. Both titles became extinct in 1748, for this son never married, and devised Powis Castle and the whole of his estate to the kinsman who had married his niece, and was created Earl of Powis (as already stated) in the course of the same year.

The title of Lord Herbert of Lea was borne by a statesman and politician of our own day, Sidney, second son of the eleventh Earl of Pembroke; but was merged in the higher title when his son succeeded to the Earldom in 1862.

Fitz Peres: interpolated. I can find mention of no other Fitz Piers but Geoffrey, who succeeded Hubert de Burgh as Justiciary of England, and was girt with the sword as Earl of Essex at the coronation of King John.

Fichet. "After the Conquest the Manor of Spaxton was held of the Castle of Stowey, for many successive generations, by the family of Fichet. In the time of Henry II., Robert the son of Hugh, the son of another Hugh Fichet, is certified to hold it of Philip de Columbers, by the service of one knight's fee. (Lib. Nig. v. i. 97)."—*Collinson's Somerset.* The last of the race, Sir Thomas Fichet, died 19 Richard II. Pury-Fitchet recalls their name. Hugh Malet, the eldest son of William Lord Malet (expelled by Henry I.) and the ancestor of the Malets of Wilbury, took the name of Fitchet, and bore *Gules* a lion rampant *Or,* a bend *Ermine.* His son was Sir Hugh Fitchet of Enmore, but the grandson, Sir Baldwin, resumed the name of Malet, and we are not informed why it had ever been changed.—*Hoare's Wilts.* There were Fitchetts in Leicestershire, who bore the same arms: and "Dominus Hugone Fychet de Pakst." witnesses a deed of Hugh de Craucumb's in Oxfordshire about 1230.

Ralph Fichet held a knight's fee of the old feoffment of the Bishop of Chichester in Sussex in 1165.—*Liber Niger.*

Fitz Rewes, or Fitz Rou, the Norman equivalent for the Scandinavian Rolffssen. Toustain Fitz Rou—in Norse parlance Tostig Rolfssen—was the standard-bearer at Hastings. When Raoul de Conches, to whom this honour belonged by hereditary right, and old Walter Giffard, to whom it had been offered, both excused themselves, electing rather to fight "in the fore-front of the battle," the Duke looked round for a worthy substitute. "Then he called out a knight, whom he had heard much praised, Tostain Fitz Rou le Blanc by name, whose abode was at Bec-en-Caux. To him he delivered the gonfanon; and Tostain took it right cheerfully, and bowed low to him in thanks, and bore it gallantly and with good heart, high aloft in the breeze, and rode by the Duke, going wherever he went. Wherever the Duke turned, he turned also, and wheresoever he stayed his course, there he rested also. His kindred still have quittance of all service for their inheritance on that account, and their heirs are entitled so to hold their inheritance for ever."—*Wace.* This privilege must have applied only to their Norman barony. "Toustain afterwards became the name of a noble house in Upper Normandy, who, in memory of the office performed at Hastings, took for supporters of their arms, two angels, each bearing a banner." —*Taylor.*

Toustain Fitz Rou le Blanc* was, says Wace, "a brave and renowned knight, born at Bec near Fescamp." He belonged to the great baronial house of that name, but there are different and conflicting accounts of his genealogy, into which I do not propose to enter. He was richly rewarded for his service, for his barony at Domesday included lands in ten different counties. "In Monmouthshire he had possessions of considerable extent between the Usk and the Wye. These lands were probably wrested from the Welsh rather than granted to him, the Survey stating that part was claimed by the King's Bailiff, saying that Turstin had taken them without gift. He had probably assisted at the subjugation of this district under William Fitz Osbern."—*A. S. Ellis.* "Besides Thurstin, there is a Robert Fitz Rou in Domesday, possibly his brother." —*Taylor.*

It is very doubtful whether he left descendants. In any case, "his fief was not transmitted intact to heirs-male. In 1166 it was in the possession of Henry Newmarch, but in what way it came to him is not apparent."—*A. S. Ellis.*

Fitz Fitz: Fitz or Le Fils occurs as a surname in the *Rot. Hundred,* about 1272. The descents given by Gale (from a MS. in the Cotton Library) prove Thoresby, Marmion, and Fitz to be of one common stock. The family was of ancient date and "respected estimation" in the West of England; and gave

---

* "It is clear that in 1066 there was another Toustain Fitz Rou, from his being styled Le Blanc."—*A. S. Ellis.*

their name to their seat at Fitz-ford, near Tavistock, " where they long dwelt in great reputation. But the male line ended in these our days in a most unfortunate gentleman, Sir John, whose sole daughter and heir was, according to her worth, highly married into honourable houses."—*Westcote's Devon.* The father of this unfortunate Sir John was, according to Prince a "very eminent counsellor in law," who served as Sheriff of the county in the time of Queen Elizabeth. He was much given to astrology, and when his wife was travailing in the pains of child-birth, "he would needs be enquiring into the fortune of her burthen before she was delivered;" and proceeded to cast the horoscope of his yet unborn son. But the planets were adverse and threatening, boding a terrible doom; and trembling lest his child should first see the light under so hostile and sinister a conjunction, "he desired the midwife, if possible, to hinder the birth but for one hour. This not being to be done, he declared that the child would come to an unhappy end, and undo the family. And it fell out accordingly." This astrologer gave his name to Fitz's Well, a spring of "marvellous virtue" on Dartmoor, to which young folks in former times used to resort at the first dawn of Easter Day. He chanced to discover it one summer's day, when, riding with his wife, they were, in the country phrase "pixy-led," and lost their way on the moor. Tired and thirsty, they rejoiced at the sight of the water, and alighted from their horses to drink; and as they drank, the fairy spell was broken, and their eyes opened; they recognized the path they had so long sought in vain, and quickly found their way home. This simple miracle is commemorated by two rude granite slabs that still enclose the well, bearing the initials of John Fitz, and the date 1568.

His son Sir John, the doomed heir whose evil destiny had been read in the stars before his birth, died by his own hand in the flower of his youth, having thrice before incurred the penalty of blood-guiltiness. His first quarrel was with Sir Nicholas Slanning, whom he slew near Tavistock. "The matter, it seems, was likely to have been composed, but the villain, Fitz's man, twitting his master with a 'What, play child's play! Come to fight, and now put up your sword!' made him draw again, and Slanning's foot in stepping back (having his spurs on) hitching in the ground, he was then unfortunately and foully killed: whereupon Sir John Fitz, by the interest of his friends, sued out his pardon soon after this happened, which was in 1599. But," continues Prince, "as one sin became (as oftentime it doth) the punishment of another, Sir John was so unhappy as to be guilty of a second murder;" and once more posted away to London to obtain pardon. He was possessed by the idea that the sheriff's officers were on his track, and in constant dread of being taken; and at every stage of his journey, was careful to make the door of his lodging secure. When he had got as far as Salisbury, or thereabouts, he was roused in the early morning by a violent knocking at his chamber door; and "he, not well awaked from his sleep, and not well understanding his servant's voice in the dark," leaped from his bed, drew his sword, flung open the door, and made a deadly thrust at the unseen intruder. When lights were brought, he found that it was his own servant, come to summon him betimes for the journey, whom he had killed ; and overwhelmed with remorse and despair, he fell upon his own sword, and was pierced to the heart. He had married Gertrude Courtenay, and left behind him a baby daughter, who grew up to be "a lady of extraordinary beauty, and was looked upon," says Clarendon, "as the richest match in the West." She had no lack of suitors, and was four times married. Her first husband was Sir Alan Percy, sixth son of the eighth Earl of Northumberland : the second Thomas Darcy, eldest son of the Earl of Rivers : the third Sir Charles Howard, fourth son of the Earl of Suffolk : and her last, Sir Richard Grenville : but it is as Lady Howard that she is still remembered in local tradition.

Many are the legends and hob-goblin stories told about her in the neighbourhood. She was of very evil report in her generation ; for some dire mystery attached to the "unknown means" by which she had disposed of her first three husbands.* With the fourth she had a bitter and life-long quarrel. The match had been made by the Duke of Buckingham ; but the bridegroom was disappointed in his expectations, and "by not being enough pleased with her fortune, grew less pleased with his wife ;" while she "quickly resented the disrespect she received from him." Sir Richard was a man of violent and tyrannical temper, "indulging to himself all those licenses in his own house which to women are most grievous," and withal took complete possession of her property. After a few miserable years of discord, she left him to take up her abode with the Howards, settling her whole estate on the Earl of Suffolk : and thus suddenly bereft of all he had to live on, he engaged in a Chancery suit with the Earl, challenged him to single combat, and vented his wrath in such opprobrious language that he was fined 6000*l.* by the Star Chamber, and committed to the Fleet. Later in life he retrieved his reputation by his valour during the Civil War, and commanded for the King in the West.

His wife, however, never forgave nor forgot. She resolutely refused to bear his name, and visited his sins upon his children with relentless and vindictive cruelty. Her two first marriages were barren : but by Sir Charles Howard she had two daughters, besides a son that died s. p. ; and by Sir Richard "she hath," says old Westcote, "fair issue, which she cast off, refusing to own them, so unconstant and irregular are some women's affections." One little daughter she especially disliked, and so savagely maltreated that a lady who was staying in her house as a guest was struck with compassion at the child's sufferings, and privately took her away to her own home. Lady Howard, who had made no secret of her wish to be rid of the child, was far from displeased at hearing that

* "There is a story about one of her husbands (I do not know which) being drowned whilst riding in his coach on the day of his marriage, in the deep pool still called Fice's or Fitz's Pool, in the river Tavy."—*Mrs. Bray.*

she was missing, and some months later received the tidings of her death with equal complacency. But it was a false rumour, intended to mislead and divert enquiry, for the little girl was in reality alive and well. She was brought up under the roof of her kind protectress, and in due time became a beautiful young woman, gifted with a charm and grace of manner that won all hearts. The lady who had adopted her then judged it right to reveal to her the secret of her birth, and to take her to see her mother, introducing her under a strange name as the orphan of a former friend. Lady Howard took a singular fancy to the girl, who, on her part, did her utmost to please and win her; and succeeded so well, that she seemed, day by day, to be gaining ground in her affections. At length, on one occasion when Lady Howard was loud in her praise, the lady thought her opportunity had come, and with some trepidation informed her that the girl of whom she spoke so warmly was no other than her own long-lost daughter. Lady Howard started back with horror at this unlooked-for announcement, and for the moment was struck dumb; then, in a sudden frenzy of passion, she turned upon her unhappy daughter, abused and threatened her with frightful violence, and peremptorily ordered her out of the house.

The poor girl accepted her dismissal, and for many long years never ventured into her presence again. But in the end her gentle heart began to yearn towards this unnatural mother, who was now an old woman, with but a short span of life before her; and she determined to go and make one last effort to obtain a kind word from her before she died. Thus it came to pass that Lady Howard (then living in her house of Walreddon) as she was one day coming down the broad oak stairs that led to the state-rooms on the first floor, perceived her hated daughter ascending the lower flight from the hall, and coming towards her. They met on the landing-place; and the daughter, throwing herself at her mother's feet, implored her compassion and endeavoured to kiss her hand. Lady Howard snatched it angrily away, and rushed towards the state-room; but the poor girl caught hold of her .gown, and clinging to her in piteous entreaty, was dragged along on her knees, still praying and beseeching to be heard. But Lady Howard was obdurate; and as she passed into the room, slammed the door behind her with such violence that it closed upon the outstretched and imploring arm that was striving to clasp her knees. The arm was crushed and fractured, and the unfortunate sufferer, half dead with grief and pain, was for the second time turned out of her mother's house, and never saw her more.

By her will she gave the whole of her property to the Courtenays (her mother's relations), with one trifling reservation—a small pittance to be doled out "to any person who could prove herself to be the daughter of Mary, sole heiress of the late Sir John Fitz, and widow of Sir Richard Grenville." This legacy was never claimed. She is said to have ended her days in great tribulation and anguish of mind at a house she had near Oakhampton, and there, according to popular belief, she is still doing penance for her sins. Every night, as the clock strikes twelve, she issues forth from the old gate of Fitzford, in the form of a black hound with glowing eyes and fiery tongue, and runs to Oakhampton Park, where she picks a blade of grass and brings it back in her mouth, always returning before cock-crow; and this she is to do till every blade of grass in the park is picked. She has also been seen ("scores of time") driving in a coach of bones up the West Street of Tavistock in the direction of the moor. Men still living remember that it was a common saying among the gentry of the county, when a party was breaking up—"Come, it is growing late; let us begone, or we shall meet Lady Howard as she starts from Fitzford!"

These Fitzes have a very singular coat; *Argent:* a cross engrailed between twelve *guttes de Sang.* The name is found in several other parts of England.

Fitz Iohn. "This surname was taken by John Fitz John Fitz Geffrey, temp. Henry III.: he was one of the Mandeville family."—*Sir Egerton Brydges.* With this entry we need not therefore concern ourselves.

Fleschampe. Remigius, Almoner of Fecamp, "a man of small stature but of lofty soul," was the first Norman ever appointed to an English see; and succeeded Wlfin of Dorchester in 1067, "in the great Bishopric of Mid England, a large part of whose diocese was not yet in William's power." He had furnished one ship and twenty knights to the Conqueror's expedition, and "it was in after times brought up as a charge against the new prelate that, before the fleet had sailed from St. Valery, an English Bishopric had been promised as the price of his contribution."—*Freeman.* He translated the see to Lincoln, and was one of the five Commissioners appointed for the compilation of Domesday. It can scarcely, however, be this churchman who is here designated. The name must stand for "Pierre de Bailleul, Seigneur de Fescampe," who is on Tailleur's list, or "Guillaume de Fécamp"* (Dives Roll.) Gilbert de Feschaump witnesses a deed of Hugh Pudsey (consecrated Bishop of Durham in 1153); and Richard de Fescamp, of Hampshire, occurs four times in the *Rotuli Curiæ Regis* of 1199; probably the same Richard who held in Kent in 1202 (Rotuli Cancellarii). William de Fiscamp is mentioned in the same record. They probably descended from Hugo de Fiscampe, who, in the time of Henry I., was of Surrey and Hants (Rotuli Magnus Pipæ); contemporary with whom we find William de Fiscampo, in Gloucestershire and Hampshire. Walter de Fescamp, of Worcestershire, is

---

* A William of Fécamp (probably another monk) is mentioned by Freeman as having devised a new mode of singing, which, in 1082, the monks of Glastonbury were commanded by their Bishop to use, instead of the immemorial Gregorian chants. They refused obedience; and when Bishop Thurstan called in his Norman archers, locked themselves up in the minster; but the soldiers, breaking in, "shot sorely" at the terrified fugitives, slaying some and wounding others, so that the blood came from the altar upon the grees, and from the grees upon the floor."

found in the Great Roll of the Pipe, 1180–90. William de Fiscamp, the King's physician, was Prebendary of Bridgenorth in 1263.—*Eyton's Salop.* Alberic de Fescamp was one of the clerks and keepers of Henry III.'s wardrobe; and in November 1260 the King issued a writ to his Treasurer and Chamberlain, for payment to Alberic de Fescamp and Peter de Winton " of £100 to buy jewels, to be presented to Alexander, King of Scotland, and his retinue, as the King has enjoined on the said Albric and Peter." (Calendar of documents relating to Scotland.)

Gurnay. This is a name of note in the history of the Conquest, and belonged to one of the first baronial families of Normandy. They occupied the frontier district called the Pays de Brai, an essart of the ancient Forest of Lyons, and an important post in the defence of the Duchy, that had been allotted to their ancestor by Rollo himself, and bore the name of Gournay, the head of their barony. They continued to hold this great fief till the time of King John, when it was seized by Philip Augustus. One remaining tower of their castle—" La Tour Hue"—was still standing at the beginning of the seventeenth century. It was surrounded by a triple wall and fosse, and considered so strong a place that one boastful chronicler maintained that it could guard itself, and might resist an attack without a single man to defend it. This marvellous fortress is supposed to have been built by the father or grandfather of the Hugh de Gournay who was one of the chief commanders at the victory of Mortemar in 1054, and is mentioned by Wace at Hastings:

> " I vint li viel Hue de Gornai,
> Ensemble o li sa gent de Brai."

He might well be called old Hue, " when we see Jehan de Flagy—or whoever wrote the old romance of Garin le Loherain—boldly introducing " Hues qui Gornay tient' as meeting 'la pucelle Blanchefors au cler vis' at the court of Pepin."—*Taylor.* He had first invaded England more than thirty years before, as one of the Norman leaders of the fleet with which the Saxon prince Edward, the son of Ethelbert, made an attempt to recover the kingdom after the death of Canute. On this second occasion he brought with him his son Hugh and the Sire de Brai—evidently a kinsman; with " numerous forces" that did great execution among the English. The Gournays were distinguished by a plain black shield; for they bore " pure sable;" a singular bearing, not unsuited to the descendants of one of the followers of the great *Dux Piratarum,* which was only exchanged for their present coat, *Argent,* a cross engrailed *Gules,* by Sir John de Gurney in the time of Henry III. " Hue le vieil " is said by the Norman chroniclers to have been mortally wounded at the battle of Cardiff in 1074, and thence brought home to Normandy to die. But the Welsh accounts fix the date of this battle nearly twenty years later, and he is believed to have been dead before 1086, as it was probably his son who appears as a great Essex baron in Domesday. Little more is known of the time when this second Hugh died, but he cannot have survived his father long. It is at least certain that he ended his days as a monk at Bec, and that in 1089 we find his son Gerard de Gournay Baron of Yarmouth, "a person of great power, stoutly adhering to King William Rufus against Robert Curthose Duke of Normandy, giving up his Castle of Gurnay, and other strongholds into his hands; and endeavouring to reduce all the adjacent parts to his obedience. Howbeit, after this, in An. 1096, Duke Robert, for ten thousand marks of Silver, delivering up Normandy unto Rufus, and thereupon travelling into the Holy Land; this Girard, with Edith his Wife (Sister to Earl Warren) accompanied him: But in this journey he died, his Wife surviving him, who afterwards married to Dru de Monceaux."—*Dugdale.* Edith or Editha de Warrenne was the Conqueror's grand-daughter (her mother had been the Princess Gundreda) and brought him three children; Hugh, his heir; " Gundreda the Fair," the wife of Nigel de Albini; and another daughter whose name is lost, married to Richard Talbot, ancestor both of the Talbots of Bashall and the Earls of Shrewsbury. Her second husband, Dru de Monceaux, possessed himself of the honour of Gournay, probably as the guardian of his step-children during their minority; but it was only restored to Hugh de Gournay. by the express mandate of Henry I. The King was very fond of this young kinsman, with whom he had grown up: (*educatus cum Henrico I., et ab illo multum honoratus et dilectus*, says the Latin pedigree) and " advanced him among his chief Nobles; " yet we find him ranked among the rebels who joined Stephen in 1134. Three years later, he deserted the new King, who took him prisoner at Pont Audemare, and " partly by good words and partly by threats, endeavoured to reconcile" him, with some show of success. His famous Norman castle was burnt down during Prince Henry's rebellion in 1173; and he died in 1185, leaving a son of the same name, who was at the siege of Acre with Cœur de Lion : and lost a great part of his estates by taking part with the Barons against King John. They were restored to the next Hugh de Gournay by Henry III.; but he again " highly incurred the King's displeasure," for he appeared at a tournament in Nottinghamshire from which he had been ordered to keep away; and, worse still, " boldly presumed to hunt with Hound and Horn for the space of three days, in the King's Chase at Bristoll, without leave, and contrary to the command of the Foresters. Whereupon the Constable of the Castle of Bristoll was required to seize all his Lands, Goods, and Chattles, within his Liberty." He married Lucy de Berkeley, and left an only daughter, Julian, who became the wife of William Bardolph. With him ended the principal line of the house of Gournay; but two junior branches remained, the one seated in Somersetshire, the other in Norfolk.

The former—by far the most distinguished of them—has been conjectured by some to belong to a different family, and certainly bore different arms, Paly of 6, *Or* and *Gules.* It had been seated at Inglishcombe and Barew-Gurnay (then Berve) at the date of Domesday; for we there find both manors described as part of the great domain of Geffrey, Bishop of Coutances, and held under him by Nigel de Gournay. Barew reverted to the Crown, and was granted by William Rufus to Robert Fitz Harding (from whom it descended to his grand-daughter Eva); but Hawise de Gournay is mentioned at Inglishcombe in the beginning of King John's reign, when she gave the church there to the monastery of Bermondsey in Surrey. Thomas, Baron of East Harptree at the same time "gave sixty marks for his lands at Inglishcombe, which he had by the grant of Hawise de Gournay." She must have been either the heiress of the Gournays, or a widow dowered with their possessions, but how she was related to Thomas de Harptree does not appear. He was descended from a younger son of Ascelin Lupellus (see *Lovel*) who adopted the name of his manor, and founded a line of great feudal lords in the West of England, who in the time of Henry II. held a barony of thirteen knight's fees in Dorset, Gloucester, and Devon. Thomas' mother had been an heiress, Alice de Orescuilz or Orcas; and his wife Eva doubled his possessions by bringing him another barony nearly equal to his own. Collinson calls her Eva de Gorniaco or de Gournay, the heiress of the Gournays; but upon what grounds he does not attempt to explain, nor can I find that she had in her veins one drop of Gournay blood. She was the daughter of Robert Fitz Hardinge, or de Berkeley, and sister and heir of Maurice de Gant, who had taken the name of their mother Alice, sole child of Robert de Gant, Lord Chancellor of England in 1153, by his wife Alice, da. and h. of William Paganel and of Julian de Bahantune, a great Devonshire heiress. Eva's paternal grandmother (after whom she was probably named) had been Eva de Esmond. Thus, though she undoubtedly represented four of the greatest families in the country, Berkeley, Gant, Paganel, and Dowai (Bahantune), she had nothing whatever to do with the Gournays; and yet it was this latter name, instead of one of the former, that was adopted by her son Robert.* This Robert de Gournay, who held in all no fewer than twenty-two and a half knight's fees, was several times summoned to serve against the Welsh; and built the hospital of Gaunt, near Bristol, for the health of the soul of his uncle Maurice. By his wife, Hawise de Longchamp, he left Anselm his heir, the husband of Sybil de Vivonne, and the father of John de Gournay, with whom the elder line terminated. The latter left only a daughter, Elizabeth, the wife of John ap-Adam, who is said to have "profusely squandered away" much of the great inheritance that came to her in 1291.

* Dugdale, in his pedigree of the Earls of Lincoln calls her "Emma uxor . . . . Gurnai:" and in his account of the Gurneys, by some strange confusion, marries her, as Eve, sister of Maurice de Gant, to a namesake of her own grandson, Anselm de Gournay, whom he makes out to have been a younger brother of the last Hugh de Gournay of the elder line.

Elizabeth's uncle, Thomas, who was seated at Farringdon-Gournay, carried on the line as heir male, and was father to Sir Thomas, of unenviable notoriety as one of the murderers of Edward II. To him and to Lord Maltravers had been committed the custody of the unhappy King at Berkeley Castle; and for the foul deed there done, he had to "fly into foreign parts on the change of times." But he fled across seas in vain, for a price had been put upon his head, and he was captured at Burgos, and delivered up by the Spaniards to the emissaries of Edward III., who commanded him to be brought over to England. Whether, however, from some misunderstanding, or "secret practices" against him, he was executed at sea, during his voyage home. All his lands were confiscated to the King, who annexed them to the Duchy of Cornwall for ever, and to this day Faringdon-Gournay, Harptree, and several other Somersetshire manors (all parcel of the Gournay estate) belong to the Prince of Wales, as Duke of Cornwall. Some favour was, however, shown to the children of the attainted Sir Thomas, who appear to have retained at least some part of his estates, till they reverted to the crown on the death of Sir Matthew de Gournay, the last of his family, in 1405. The name of this Sir Matthew constantly appears in the pages of Froissart. He was a famous knight, of "consummate skill and reputation" in arms, who served in all the great battles of that glorious time, at Benamazin, Sluys, Cressy, Ingenny, Poictiers, and Nazaron in Spain, and fought the Saracens at the siege of Algezira. He long outlived all his contemporaries in the wars, and died at the great age of ninety-six, having nobly retrieved the ancient lustre of his name. It is still borne by several places in Somersetshire; Faringdon-Gurnay, Harptree-Gournay, Barew-Gurnay, and the hamlet of Gourney-Slade.

The Norfolk Gurneys, who alone continue in the male line, were originally mesne-lords under their baronial cousins, and first appear in Norfolk temp. Hen. II. Unlike most families of so ancient a date, they have been faithful to their early home, and never migrated from the county in which they had settled. Sir John de Gournay was in arms against Hen. III. both at Lewes and Evesham, but obtained his pardon, and went with Prince Edward to the Holy Land in 1270. One of their manors, Harpley, had come to his grandfather Matthew through his marriage with Rose de Burnham or de Warrenne; another, West Barsham—long their residence—was brought by the heiress of the De Wauncys to Edmund Gourney, who lived in the reigns of Edward III. and Richard II., and was recorder, or, as it was then termed, standing counsel, of Norwich. On the failure of the direct line in 1661, the estates were divided among different co-heiresses; but there remained a descendant of one of the younger sons, John Gurney, an eminent silk merchant at Norwich about 1679, who may be said to have re-founded the present family. He made his fortune, adopted the tenets of the Quakers, and was the immediate ancestor of the Gurneys of Keswick, who derive from his second son Joseph.

Gressy. In Leland's copy this name corresponds with Cressy, and may here, I think, be accepted as a slightly disguised duplicate. (See *Cressy.*) It is to be met with in a variety of forms. "Le Seigneur de Grissey" is entered among the *Conquérants d'Angleterre* in Tailleur's Norman Chronicle; and a Richard de Grisey occurs about 1180 in the Exchequer Rolls of the Duchy. "Magistro Alano de Greycy," in the same century, witnesses a deed of Henry Pudsey, bastard son of the Prince-Bishop of Durham; and Roger de Gruszi is found in London and Middlesex 1189–90 (Rot. Pip.). Gilbert de Gressy, in the time of Henry III., was a benefactor of the Templars (Mon. Angl.). Hamo de Gruscy, in the following reign, sold some land to the Black Friars of York.—*Yorkshire Archæologia*, vol. vi. p. 399.

Graunson, Anglicized Grandison. The French Grandsons have the punning motto: "A petite cloche grand son." Stretton Gransham or Grandison keeps the name in Herefordshire. "William de Grandison, the son of a Burgundian noble (the ruins of whose castle on the lake of Neufchatel are familiar to the Swiss tourist), obtained a grant of land in Herefordshire from Edward I., and added largely to it by his marriage with the wealthy heiress of John de Tregoz. In the year 1292 he had license from the King 'to crenellate his mansion at Asperton' (Ashperton), and was summoned to Parliament from the twenty-seventh year of Edward I. to the nineteenth year of Edward II., inclusive. The date of his death is unknown, but Leland states that both he and his wife Sibil were buried at Dore Abbey. Three of the children of William de Grandison achieved considerable distinction in their day. The best known of them, John de Grandison, is said to have been born at Ashperton, which was presumably the birth-place of his brothers also.

"John de Grandison * probably owed some of his success in life to his great-uncle Bishop Cantilupe, 'St. Thomas of Hereford,' or rather to his venerated memory. He was made Bishop of Exeter in 1327, and has been compared to the present occupant of the see" (this was written before 1869) "in respect of the extraordinary duration of his episcopate (forty-two years), the extent of his acquirements, and what Fuller calls his 'Stout Stomach,' shown especially in resisting Archbishop Meopham, *vi et armis*, when he came to visit his diocese. He founded the Collegiate Church of St. Mary Ottery in Devonshire, and contributed largely to the embellishment of his own Cathedral. (*Fuller's Worthies.*)

"The Bishop's elder brother Sir Peter was summoned to the first three Parliaments of Edward III., and died in the thirtieth year of that reign. He lies

---

* "John de Grandison, a Burgundian, Bishop of Exeter, foreseeing what might happen in after-times, built a very fine house at Bishop's Teignmouth (upon account of a sanctuary in it), that his successors might have where to lay their heads, in case their Temporalities were at any time seiz'd into the King's hands. Yet so far was this from answering his design, that his successors are now depriv'd of this house, and almost all the rest."—*Camden's Britannia.*

buried in Hereford Cathedral, and his monument, long supposed to commemorate one of the Bohuns, is a beautiful piece of sculpture, and will be found on the north side of the Lady Chapel. Four of the figures with which it is enriched, viz. St. Ethelbert, St. John the Baptist, and the two English St. Thomases, were recovered by Mr. Cottingham, the architect, from behind the choir-screen where they were concealed among rubbish and fragments of stone.

"Sir Otho Grandison, a younger brother, was a statesman as well as a warrior, and was sent by Edward II., in the first year of his reign, as ambassador to the Pope. He died in 1359, and in his will 'entreats that no armed horse nor armed men be allowed to go before his body on his burial day, nor that his body be covered with any cloth painted in gilt or signed with his arms; but that it be only of white cloth marked with a cross.' "—(*Nicolas Test. Vetusta.*)

"The Castle of the Grandisons has wholly disappeared. The site on which it stood was planted about the close of the last century, when the foundations were grubbed up, but the moat still exists and is full of water."—*Castles of Herefordshire and their Lords*, by C. J. Robinson.

It will be seen that this account omits all mention of William de Grandison's elder brother, Otho, beyond all question the foremost man of the family. He had gone to the Holy Land in 1270 with Prince Edward, who, soon after his accession to the throne, appointed him Governor of the Channel Islands, and later on his secretary. It is clear that he was much in the King's confidence, and benefited very largely by his munificence. He was sent Ambassador to Rome in 1288; in 1295 employed to negotiate for peace with France; the next year again in treaty with the Envoys sent over by the King of the Romans and King of France; and in 1298 summoned to parliament among the barons of the realm. Besides his Kentish estates he had vast grants in Ireland, including the towns of Tipperary and Clomme, and the castle, cantred, and territory of Hokenath; all of which he made over to his brother in 1289. The coveted feudal privilege of a weekly market and yearly fair was accorded to him in no fewer than four of his manors; namely, De La Sele, near Kemsing, Farnborough, and Chelsfield in Kent, and Attonach in Ireland. "When he died," says Dugdale, "I cannot certainly find; but in 12 Edw. II., all those Castles, Manors, and Lands, which he had in Ireland, for life, were given by the King to Prince Edward (his eldest Son) and to his Heires Kings of England." There is no record of his ever having been married.

His brother William, who was summoned to parliament within a few months of the same time, had served three times in the wars of Gascony, and four times in Scotland. Dugdale calls him "a menial servant to Edmund, Earl of Lancaster," by which I suppose it is meant that he was of the prince's household; and in 1281 he received for "his faithful service" two manors in Gloucestershire. Besides these, he had (as we have seen) grants from Edw. I., and his heiress wife, Sibill de Tregoz, brought him Lydiard-Tregoz and Norton-Scudamore, in Wiltshire, Burnham, in Somersetshire, and Eton, in Herefordshire. They had six children; Peter, John, Otho, Mabel, Katherine, and Agnes; yet these three sons only carried on the line for one generation more.

Peter, Lord Grandison, the eldest of them, a banneret in the French wars, had been heavily fined for taking part with the Earl of Lancaster, and died in 1358, leaving no issue by his wife, Blanche de Mortimer, daughter of the Earl of March.

John, Bishop of Exeter, the second son, succeeded him at the age of sixty, and survived his younger, as well as his elder, brother.

Otho, the third, was a soldier of some distinction, who was sent by Edward II. as Ambassador to the Pope, and followed Edward III. to France and Flanders. He died in the same year as Peter, seized of the Kentish manors of Chelsfield, Kemsing, and La Sele, which had belonged to his uncle, Otho I. He had married Beatrix, daughter and co-heir of Nicholas de Malmains, and left besides a daughter Elizabeth (mentioned in his will), an only son, Sir Thomas, who succeeeded as fourth Lord Grandison, but died s. p. in 1375.

The three daughters of the first Lord Grandison had, on the other hand, no lack of descendants. Mabel married Sir John Pateshull; Katherine, William de Montacute, Earl of Salisbury, and Agnes, Sir John de Northwood. So numerous. was their progeny, that when the late Sir Henry Paxton Bedingfield claimed the barony of Grandison in right of his descent from Mabel, it was adjudged to be in abeyance between thirteen different families. No aspirant has since been intrepid enough to enter the list.

This long extinct name is still borne by the manors of Stretton-Grandison, in Herefordshire, and Okeley-Grandison, in Gloucestershire.

Gracy: or Grancey; repeated further on as Grensey. Grancey is on the confines of Champagne and Burgundy, and gave its name to a great Burgundian family, several times Constables of the province, that ended in the fourteenth century with Eudo de Grancey. He married Beatrix de Bourbon, the widow of the heroic King of Bohemia who fell at Cressy; and being almost blind, had "caused his men to fasten the reines of the bridels of their horses ech to other, and so being himself amongst them in the foremost ranke, they ran at their enemies."—*Holinshed.* The feudal castle of Grancey, dating from his time, was only pulled down at the beginning of the last century.

The first trace I could find of the family in England was at Warford in Cheshire; the seat of the Grascys, Grasties, or Greestys, for many successive generations. Randle Greesty occurs among the "Knights, Gentlemen, and Freeholders of Cheshire" in 1445 (Macclesfield Hundred) : and William Grascy in 1548. They "entered a pedigree of five descents in the last Visitation of Cheshire, taken in 1664, when they claimed the following arms:—*Argent* on a fess engrailed *Sable*, three martlets of the first; and for crest a martlet *Argent*, round the neck an engrailed collar *Sable.* Randle Grastie, of Warford, had by a daughter of Robert Sidebotham of Alderley, a son and heir-apparent, Henry

Grastie, who died s. p.; and a second son, Thomas, who succeeded him. This Thomas Grastie, who was living when the pedigree was taken in 1664, was then eighty years of age. By his wife Alice Ellis he had eight sons and eight daughters, of whom Thomas, his son and heir-apparent, had died in his life-time, leaving one son, Thomas Grastie, described as of Warford and Withington, who was heir to his grandfather. The Grasties subsequently went to live at Warrington in Lancashire, where they appear to have engaged in trade. Thomas Grastie, the above-named grandson, was buried at Alderley in 1698–9, his wife having been buried there in 1676. The name is now almost unknown in the district."—*Earwaker's East Cheshire.*

Again, there are traces of the family both in Scotland and Ireland. Lancelot Gracy was "among the Presbyterian landowners of Ulster proposed to be transplanted into Leinster and Munster in 1653, on account of their attachment to monarchical and Presbyterian principles;" and we are told that "the Graceys still exist in the barony of Lecale."—*Ulster Archæologia,* vol. i. Robson has preserved the arms of Gracie (of Scotland), *Ermine,* three lions' heads erased. He also gives the coat of Grasay; *Azure* a lion rampant *Argent;* and that of Grance or Grancey, *Gules* a lion rampant *Argent* crowned *Or,* within a bordure engrailed of the third:—both of them entirely unlike the bearing of the Cheshire family.

Georges: (Gorgeise in Leland's list) from Gaurges in the Côtentin. This family originally bore a whirlpool or *gurges* (as may be seen in their sepulchral chapel at Cliefden): but adopted the Lozengy *Or* and *Azure* of Morville on the marriage of Ralph de Gorges with the heiress of John de Morville, temp. Hen. III. This Ralph, the son of Ivo, seated at Tamworth in Warwickshire, "was a knight, and a great warrior, being one of those who in 1263 were blocked up with King Henry III. in the city of Bristol by the disaffected citizens. Soon after which he was appointed Constable of Sherborne and Exeter; and 50, 51 Hen. III. was Sheriff of Devonshire. 54 Hen. III. he attended Prince Edward to the Holy Land, and died soon after his return."—*Collinson's Somerset.* His son and namesake was Marshal of Edward I.'s army in Gascony in 1293, and the next year was taken prisoner and carried to Paris; but must have been speedily ransomed, for not long after we find him engaged in the Scottish wars. He was a baron by writ in 1309; but his son*

---

* This son must have been the newly-dubbed knight "of haughty spirit" at Carlaverock:

> . " Ilucques vi-je Rauf de Gorges,
> Chevalier nouvel adoubé,
> De peres à tere tumbé,
> Et defoulé plus de une foiz:
> Car tant estoit de grant bufoiz,
> Ke il ne s'en deignoit departir.
> Tout son harnois e son atire
> Avoit masclé de or e de asur."

never was summoned to parliament, and left no children. Eleanor, his daughter, thus became his heir, and married Sir Theobald Russell of Kingston Russell in Dorsetshire (direct ancestor, by his second marriage with the heiress of John de la Tour, of the Dukes of Bedford). Their descendants all bore the name of Gorges.

One of them, Sir Thomas (the fifth son of Sir Edward Gorges of Wraxall), who was seated at Longford in Wiltshire in the time of Queen Elizabeth, married one of her maids of honour, Helena, daughter of Wolfangus, "a noble Swede." She had first come to England in the train of King Eric, who courted the Queen; and became a great favourite, for Elizabeth treated her with "all the intimacy of a friend, and often made her a bed-fellow:" and when her first husband, the Earl of Northampton, died, leaving her a young widow, it is believed that the Queen herself furthered Sir Thomas' suit. She proved an expensive wife. She had a fancy to have his house rebuilt on the plan of Tycho Brahe's Castle of Uraniberg, in Sweden; and Sir Thomas accordingly pulled down the old mansion of the Cervingtons at Longford, and constructed the singular triangular house, crossing the river Avon, that is now the residence of the Earl of Radnor.* "So great was the expense of driving piles, &c., that Sir Thomas nearly sunk his fortune in the foundation. During the threat of the Spanish Armada, he was made Governor of Hurst Castle; and a Spanish galleon having been wrecked near it, his wife begged the hull of the Queen, in which were found bars of silver and other treasure to an immense amount, which not only served to complete their pile at Longford, but also to enrich their steward Richard Grobham, who chiefly managed their business, procured a knighthood, and left a fortune almost equal to his master's. Their son Edward was created Baron of Dundalk in 1620."—*Hoare's Wills*. The second Lord died s. p. in 1712: having involved himself in great debts, and been obliged to sell Longford to Lord Coleraine. It was bought by the Bouveries in 1717.

Samuel Georges, the last heir-male of the family of Wraxall, died in 1699: but a branch remains in Ireland. Braunton-Gorges retains the name in Devonshire.

Gower, as Leland also gives it; in Duchesne's copy, Gouer. Sir Bernard Burke classes this among the monkish additions, as a Saxon origin has always been assigned to the old house now represented by the Dukes of Sutherland, Earls Granville, and Earls of Ellesmere. Their Yorkshire manor of Stittenham is believed to have been transmitted through a line of ancestors that held it at the Conquest; though Sir Egerton Brydges derives them first "from one Guhyer, whose son, called William Fitz Guhyer, of Stittenham, was charged with half a

---

* The architect employed was the same Thomas Thorpe who built Holland House. Longford is the "Castle of Amphialeus" of Sir Philip Sidney's *Arcadia*.

mark (or rather a mark) for his lands in the sheriff's accounts, 1167." The name (which began to be written Gower about the time of Edward I.) is, however, incontestably to be found in Normandy, and is said to have been imported from Scandinavia. It is borne by a place still called Goher; and Thomas and Osmond Goher, at Caen, Ralph Goher at Bayeux, and Thomas Goher at Coutances are all mentioned in the Norman Exchequer Rolls during the last years of the twelfth century. Two De Guers—one of them Marquis de Pontcalé, were among the Norman nobles convoked for the election of the States-General in 1789 : they belonged to the Côtentin. "In England it appears in 1130, when Walter de Guher paid scutage for his lands at Carmarthen (Rot. Pip.). He had probably been one of the Norman knights who accompanied Arnulph de Montgomery. Adelard de Guer witnessed a charter of Geoffrey de Mandeville, Earl of Essex, 1136, (Mon. i. 460) from which family Roger de Guer held a fief in 1165, (Liber Niger) when also Hugh de Goher held a fee from the Earl of Warwick (Ib.) William Guhier obtained a pardon in Oxford 1158 (Rot. Pip.) being also of Essex, for after 1152 the Abbey of Tilteney, Essex, acquired lands of the fief of William Goer (Mon. i. 889). This William Guhier or Goer was Lord of Stittenham in Yorkshire, and was dead A.D. 1200 (Rotuli Curiæ Regis). He confirmed the grant of Godfrey Fitz Richard of Stitnam to Rievaulx Abbey (Burton, Mon. Ebor, 363). Walter Goher, his son or grandson, (Mon. ii. 822) had issue William, 'son of Walter Goher,' who in 1270 paid a fine to the Crown (Roberts, Excerpt. ii. 513). This William had a park in Dorset, temp. Henry III. (Placit. Abbrev. 281). His son John was summoned in 1300 for military service in Scotland ; and in the same year Robert Gouer (probably his brother) was commissioner of array in Yorkshire, according to Palgrave's Parliamentary Writs. From this family descend the Dukes of Sutherland, &c."— *The Norman People.* Still, it should be noted that the arms of the Gowers of Essex, a chevron between three wolves' heads erased, are entirely different from those borne by the Duke, and more nearly resemble the coat of the poet Gower and the Kentish family to which he belonged. "They bore the chevron charged with three heads, whether of lions, leopards, or wolves, it were hard to say." Gower's lineage has been carefully investigated by Sir Harris Nicolas. He was probably nephew and heir male of Sir Robert Gower, who resided in Kent, and from whose daughter he acquired by purchase the manor of Aldington in Kent about 1365 : also that of Kentwell, Suffolk, and another in Essex. He was born c. 1325, as it is supposed, in Wales, and lived into the reign of Henry IV., having lost his sight a few years before his death. It is conjectured that he was a knight, and even a judge ; a rich man he certainly was. He graduated at Oxford, was on terms of friendship with most of the great men of his day, and, attaching himself to Thomas of Woodstock, became as zealous a Lancastrian as was his contemporary Chaucer. But here the resemblance between them ends. In Gower's stiff, pedantic, frigid verses—aptly described as "heavy platitudes," there is none of the beauty, brilliancy, and humour that brightens every page of Chaucer's writing.

Gaugy: from Gauchi, Gaucy, or Gaacy, near L'Aigle, in Normandy. The Barony of Gaugy was in Northumberland, and one of the twelve that paid " Castleward and Cornage " towards the support of the " New Castle upon Tyne." " Ellington was an ancient barony of this family, who possessed it from the time of King Henry I., as appears by the Testa de Nevill. The church was founded by Ralph de Gaugy, in the pontificate of Hugh Pudsey, Bishop of Durham."— *Hutchinson's Northumberland.* At about the same date, Robert de Gaugy held the barony of Slesmouth by the service of three knight's fees. (Lib. Niger.) His descendant of the same name was in high favour with King John, being, says Dugdale, " reckoned to be one of that King's Evil Counsellors ; " and an old manor-house of the Gaugys, Heaton, is traditionally believed to have been the habitation of King John, when he came into Northumberland. The ruins of the building still go by the name of King John's Palace. It is at all events certain that Robert de Gaugy had special trust reposed in him by his sovereign, who made him Constable of the castles of Lafford in Lincolnshire and Newark in Notts, and obtained for him the hand of an heiress, Isold Lovel, who brought him a considerable estate in the Bishopric of Durham. The line ended with Adam, who succeeded to the barony of Slesmouth, 7 Ed. I., and " being then a Leper, could not come to the King to do him Homage, but died within few years."—*Dugdale.* Roger de Clifford, his cousin, was found to be his heir.

The Gaugys were, however, far from being extinct. Dugdale mentions two brothers of Robert's, who, like him, " stood stoutly to King John," Roger and Sampson de Gaugy, both of whom obtained considerable grants of land in recompense of their services. In 1203, the King committed to Roger the custody of the castle and forest of Argentan. (Hardy, Rot. Norm.) " William de Gaugi, his son, of Northampton, was father of John de Gaugi, who in 1260, with Petronilla his wife, paid a fine in Essex, (Roberts, Excerpta) and in 1269 he occurs in Suffolk (Hunter, Rot. Select. 221). Roger Gaugi, 1324, was returned from Suffolk to a great Council at Westminster (Palgrave's Parliamentary Writs). John Gage, of this family, settled in Gloucestershire, from whom descended the Viscounts and Baronets Gage."—*The Norman People.*

The direct ancestor of Lord Gage was John Gage, living 9 Hen. IV., whose grandson, a zealous adherent of the House of York, was knighted by Edward IV., and acquired Firle, the present seat of the family, through his marriage with a co-heiress of St. Clere of Heighton-St.-Clere in Sussex. From his elder son descended the Gages of Firle ; from the younger the Gages of Raunds in Northamptonshire, who flourished there till 1675. In the next generation, Sir John Gage, of Firle, was a favourite at the court of Henry VIII., and (in the words of his son Robert Gage) served him and the two very different sovereigns who succeeded him "truly and paynfully, untouched with any reproach or unfaithfull service" till his own death in 1556. He was at different times Captain of Guisnes Castle, Vice Chamberlain and Captain of the Guard, Chancellor of the Duchy of Lancaster, Comptroller of the Household, and Constable of the Tower. Henry made him a Knight of the Garter, and had him painted by Holbein in the robes of the Order: he was also one of the Royal Commissioners appointed to take possession of the monasteries at the time of their dissolution; and at the surrender of Battle Abbey on May 27, 1538, received the manor of Alciston as his share of the spoils. This was by no means the only property he acquired from the Church: yet he was apparently none the less acceptable to Queen Mary, for at her accession he was re-instated in his office of Constable of the Tower and Lord Chamberlain, of which he had been deprived by the Protector. He had for some time the custody of Princess Elizabeth, the future Queen: and was "the iron-hearted Lieutenant of the Tower" who attended Lady Jane Grey to the block, and received from her, as a memorial, her tablets with some lines in Latin, Greek and English, written in her own hand. His descendant, another Sir John, received a baronetcy in 1622, and married Penelope, third daughter and eventually co-heiress of Thomas Darcy, Earl Rivers, by Mary his wife, daughter and co-heiress of Sir Thomas Kitson, of Hengrave Hall, in Suffolk. "Penelope, like her classical namesake, was accounted a great beauty, although her portraits at Hengrave and at Firle, according to modern ideas, hardly warrant such a claim. While yet in her early teens, she had three suitors at once, Sir George Trenchard, Sir John Gage, and Sir William Hervey, who were constantly quarrelling over her. In order to end their disputes, she told them that the first aggressor should be visited with her everlasting displeasure, and then humorously added, that if they kept the peace and waited with patience, she would have them all in their turn! These, though spoken in jest, proved to be true words, and she married the three in succession. Sir George Trenchard, the first so favoured, left her a widow of seventeen, and she became the wife of Sir John Gage, and by him mother of nine children. The third suitor, a collateral ancestor of the Marquess of Bristol, had a long time to wait. Sir John's eldest son, Sir Thomas, succeeded him in the baronetcy and the Sussex estate, and the third son, Sir Edward, of Hengrave Hall, inherited the maternal estate, and was created a baronet in 1662; from him descends the present Sir Thomas-Rokewood Gage, the eighth baronet of the Hengrave branch."—*Lower's Worthies of Sussex.* Penelope's great grandson, Thomas Gage, was created Viscount Gage of the kingdom of Ireland in 1720; and his son received an English peerage in 1780. This elder line now alone survives, for the Hengrave baronetcy is extinct; and the Suffolk estate, with its rarely beautiful old mansion, lately passed, on the death of the widow of its last owner, to the Earl of Kenmare.

The brother of the first Viscount, Joseph Gage, was "concerned in the

Mississippi Scheme in France, and is said to have acquired the immense wealth of twelve or thirteen millions sterling, which so intoxicated him, that he made an offer to Augustus King of Poland of three millions for that crown, which being refused, he proposed to the King of Sardinia the purchase of that island, who rejected the offer. But the next year (1720), by the fall of that famous bubble, he became so much distressed, that he was necessitated to seek for new adventures in Spain, where he was, however, well received into favour, and advanced to many high posts, and honoured with the title of Grandee in Spain in 1743; being also presented by the King of Naples with the order of San Gennaro, and a pension of 4000 ducats a year."—*Banks.* He was General of the Spanish army in Sicily, and afterwards Commander-in-chief in Lombardy. He married Lady Lucy Herbert, daughter of the first Marquess of Powis, but left no posterity.

Another cadet of this house was Colonel Henry Gage, who was Governor of Oxford under Charles I., and twice fought his way to Basing, to relieve " Loyalty House." For this service he was knighted by the King: but, scarcely two months afterwards, in January 1645, he was shot through the heart in a skirmish at Culham Bridge, while marching at the head of his men. " The King," says Lord Clarendon, " sustained a wonderful loss at his death, he being a man of great wisdom and temper, and one among the very few soldiers who made himself to be universally loved and esteemed." He had " scarce been in England for twenty years before," and had lived much at the Archduke's Court at Brussels, being " a great master in the Spanish and Italian tongues, besides the French and Dutch, which he spoke in great perfection."

Goband, for Gobaud. " Baldwin Wac granted to Robert Fitz Gubold, temp. Henry I., one fee, held of the Barony of Brunne, Lincoln (Lib. Niger): from whom descended John Gobaud, thirteenth century, who held of the same barony (Testa de Nevill). Robert Goebald occurs in 1158 (Rot. Pip.), and Henry Gobaud in Devon (Testa)."—*The Norman People.* Guy Gobaud, Gubaut, or Gubout, and Galfrid Gubaut occur in Lincolnshire temp. Ed. I.; and John Gubaud both in that county and Huntingdonshire. — *Rotuli Hundredorum.* Probably the same John who was one of the Conservators of the peace for Lincolnshire in 1307. Sir John Gobaud was summoned from Warwick to the great Council held at Westminster in 1324; and married Annabel, daughter and heiress of Simon Basset of Sapcote in Leicestershire.—*Dugdale's Warwickshire.* Their son and heir was again John. William Gumbaud, or Gobaud, held Thorne juxta Hedon in Holderness (*Kirkby's Inquest*), and died 33 Ed. I., leaving as his heirs his sisters, Lora de Fletwyth, Margaret de Hollebeck, and two others, Christiana and Joanna, both of them nuns. Lora re-married Thomas de Newmarch (*Poulson's Holderness*), who was certified joint Lord of " Thornegombaud " with Laurence de Hollebeck and Edward Wasteneys in 1316.

Gray. Anchitel * de Gray only appears in Domesday as a small sub-tenant of William Fitz Osborne's in Oxfordshire, and "the first mention of this family in public records is temp. Ric. I."—*Sir Egerton Brydges*. Yet, when it became great and illustrious, genealogists busied themselves in devising for it a magniloquent descent from a maternal uncle of the Conqueror's, who received from Duke Robert the castle of Croy in Picardy, and assumed its name, which was afterwards converted into Gray. Dugdale wisely ignores this pedigree, and we learn from the *Recherches sur le Domesday*, that Anchitel in reality belonged to a family of considerable note in the Bessin, who were Sires of Luc (a village near Caen) and inhabited a parish in the arrondissement of Bayeux, to which they either gave its name of Gray, or whence they perhaps themselves derived it. In 1082, Gisla, daughter of Turstin de Gray, Sire de Luc, entered the convent of the Holy Trinity at Caen, of which she was a benefactress: and four years later, her brother Robert Fitz Turstin occurs in Domesday (fo. 160). Their father was one of the two sons of Turgis, Sire de Luc and de Gray. Hugh, the other son, and apparently the elder brother, was the father of another Turstin, and of Anchitel, the founder of the English house. This second Turstin remained in Normandy, and though his descendants cannot be very distinctly traced, they were certainly to be found there till the end of the thirteenth century. Their names occasionally appear as benefactors of religious houses; and among the last mentioned are Richard and Roger, who, in 1260, granted lands to the same convent where, nearly two hundred years before, Gisla de Gray had taken the veil.

The first few descents from Anchitel de Gray are variously given. M. de Ste. Marie believes that he had a son, grandson, and great-grandson who all bore the name of John. On the other hand, "Columbanus de Grae, the son of Anchitel, witnessed a charter of Ralph de Limesi in the time of Henry I. (Mon. i. 331). He had issue, 1. Robert; 2. Roger, a tenant of the See of London in 1165, father of Henry de Grey, first Baron of Codnor, ancestor of the Lords Grey of Ruthyn, Wilton, Codnor, and Walsingham, the Earls of Kent and Stamford, Marquesses of Dorset, and Duke of Suffolk.

" Robert, the elder brother, was of Rotherfield in Oxfordshire" (the *Redrefeld* held by Anchitel in Domesday), "and in 1165 held lands of the barony of Windsor (Liber Niger). His son Robert was the father of 1. Walter; 2. Robert.

" Walter was Chancellor 1205, Archbishop of York 1216, and in 1245 resigned his barony of Rotherfield to his brother Robert, who had issue; 1. Walter, ancestor of the Lords Grey of Rotherfield, Barons by writ 1296: 2. Richard; 3. William, of Langley, Northumberland (Testa de Nevill, 388); 4. Hugh, ancestor of the Barons Grey of Scotland.

---

* Anchitel, according to M. de Ste. Marie, signifies in the Northern tongue Petit Jean, or Johnnie.

"Richard, the second brother, was Viscount of Northumberland in 1236: and from him descended the Greys Earls of Tankerville, and the Earls Grey."—*The Norman People.* Dugdale's account is, however, altogether different; for he asserts that both the Archbishop and his brother Robert were the younger sons of Henry de Grey.

With this Henry he commences the long and superb pedigree which it is my ungracious task to endeavour to compress into a few short pages. The glories of the great historic house that stood so near the throne, with all its multiplicity of branches and centuries of splendour, can hardly be summarily dealt with, and I will attempt no more than a glance at its history.

Henry de Grey received from Coeur de Lion in 1195 a grant of Thurrock in Essex—since known as Thurrock-Grey—which was confirmed to him by King John; and married Ysolda, one of the co-heirs of Robert Bardolfe, who brought him the honour of Codnor in Derbyshire. Richard, his eldest son, was Baron of Codnor; and John, the second, Justice of Chester, was the father of the first Lord Grey de Wilton, to whose descendants the principal illustrations of the family belonged.

Richard "stood firm" to King John, from whom he obtained various grants; and was Governor of the Channel Islands, Constable of Dover, and Lord Warden of the Cinque Ports under Henry III. But he fell into disgrace in 1257, for allowing an obnoxious emissary of the Pope's to come on shore at Dover: and Hugh Bigot the Justiciar took from him the custody of the castle and ports, with the bitter words, "Have you been trusted by the People of England, as a faithful Warden of the Ports, and suffered this Person to Land, without our knowledge, to the manifest violation of your Oath?" His grandson Henry had summons to parliament in 1299; and, like most of his contemporaries and his three immediate successors, was a sturdy soldier diligently employed in the French and Scottish wars. One of these Lords Grey of Codnor was Seneschal of Gascony and Steward of Acquitaine: another, Admiral of the Fleet from the mouth of the Thames northwards; while a third—the hardest fighter of them all—was "in such great Esteem" with Edward III., that he received at his hands the extraordinary gift of "a Hood of White Cloth, embroidered with Blue Men, dancing, button'd before with great Pearls." The seventh Lord, with whom the line expired in 1495, was a chemist, who obtained from Edward IV. "a Licence to practise the Transmutation of Metals, by his Philosophical Skill. How he sped therein," cautiously adds Dugdale, "I cannot say." He left only two base born sons, and his aunts, Elizabeth, wife of Sir John Zouche, Eleanor, married to Thomas Newport, and Lucy, wife of Sir Rowland Lenthall, were his heirs. "These three," says Leland, "had the Lord Greyes Londes in copartion, whereof the lordship of Ailesford, in Kent, and How Hundred, was parte. There were some of the Lord Greyes of Codnor byried at Ailesford Freres." The castle and manor of Codnor fell to the share of Elizabeth.

The next in order of succession was John, Justice of Chester and Steward of all Gascony, a knight " much esteemed for his civility and valour, as also Chief of the King's Council," whose son Reginald married Maud, daughter and heir of William Fitz Hugh, by Hawyse, the heiress of Hugh (or Henry) de Longchamp, a great Herefordshire baron seated at Wilton Castle, and was summoned to parliament as Lord Grey de Wilton in 1295. He succeeded his father as Justice of Chester, and "merited so well" that he received, among other rewards, the castle and barony of Ruthyn, in the marches of Wales, from which one of his grandsons took his title as a baron of the realm. His line was of far longer continuance than his elder brother's, for he was the first of fifteen Lords Grey de Wilton, of whom the second was Justiciary of North Wales. Their records are uniformly military; a succession of writs of summons to attend the King "well fitted with horse and arms," and due retinue of men-at-arms and archers; and they played their part gallantly in most of the home and foreign wars. One above the rest, William, thirteenth Lord, who joined the Duke of Northumberland in his attempt to place Lady Jane Grey on the throne, was renowned for his services, and esteemed "the greatest soldier of the nobility." He commanded the victorious army that invaded Scotland in 1547; and though thrown into the Tower as an adherent of the Protector in 1551, "yet," says Dugdale, "this Storm, when the Duke of Somerset's head was off, lasted not long:" and in the following year we find him Deputy of Calais, and Governor of Gisnes in Picardy. Here he was besieged by the Duc de Guise, and after a long and stout defence, forced to yield himself prisoner, and pay a ransom of twenty-four thousand crowns, "which did much weaken his Estate." His grandson Sir Thomas was involved in what has been called "Raleigh's conspiracy," and tried for his life with Lord Cobham in 1603. Cobham made an abject defence, but Grey spoke boldly and fearlessly, and when sentenced to die, refused to plead for mercy. "I have," he declared, "nothing to say, yet a word of Tacitus comes in my mouth:
"'Non eadem omnibus decora.'

The house of Wilton have spent many lives in their prince's service, and Grey cannot ask his." He was not, however, executed, and died in the Tower eleven years afterwards. His barony had expired under attainder, and he left no children. But he had two sisters; Elizabeth, born of his father's first marriage, and the wife of Sir Francis Goodwin; and Bridget, married to Sir Rowland Egerton, who, as his sister of the whole blood, became his heiress. Five generations afterwards, her descendant, Sir Thomas Egerton, received, first the barony, and then the Earldom of Wilton, with remainder to Thomas Grosvenor, the son of his daughter Eleanor.

Roger, the founder of the house of Grey de Ruthyn, was the second son of the second Lord Grey de Wilton, and was summoned to parliament in his grandfather's barony in 1325. He married Elizabeth, daughter of John Lord Hastings of Abergavenny, by his wife Isabel, one of the sisters and co-heirs of Adomare de Valence Earl of Pembroke; and his son and successor Reginald was, on the premature death of John Hastings, the last Earl of Pembroke (killed at seventeen by an accidental lance-thrust in the tilting-yard), found to be his heir of the whole blood. This decision was disputed by his heir of the half blood, Sir Edward de Hastings; but after a contest carried on for twenty years in the Court of Chivalry, "the right and title to the name and arms of Hastings was adjudged to him and his heirs for ever, as Lord Hastings;" and in 1425 he is styled, in the Rolls of Parliament, Lord Hastings, Weysford, and of Ruthyn. It was a quarrel of his about a common lying between Ruthyn and Glendower that led to Owen Glendower's formidable insurrection in 1401. At the accession of Henry IV., "as better Friended than Owen," who had adhered to the dethroned King, he seized upon the disputed land, and Owen vainly sought redress from Parliament; some of the barons declaring "That they did not at all fear those rascally bare-footed People." The Welsh prince then resorted to arms; and his countrymen, believing their deliverance from the English yoke to be at hand, flocked round him from far and near. He met and routed Grey in the field, took him prisoner, and exacted a ransom of ten thousand marks, "handling him strictly" until it was paid.

This Lord Grey was twice married. By his first wife, Margaret de Ros, he was the ancestor of the Earls of Kent; by the second, Joan, daughter and heir of Sir William de Astley, son and heir of Thomas, seventh Lord Astley, of the Marquesses of Dorset, Duke of Suffolk, and Earls of Stamford.

The first wife, Margaret, brought him an only son who died in his life-time, leaving issue Edmund and Thomas. Thomas was created Baron of Rougemont-Grey by Henry VI., with various grants conferred for special services in the Wars of the Roses; "but for this his Fidelity to the House of Lancaster he paid dear," being attainted on the accession of Edward IV. Edmund, on the other hand, was never likely to suffer from any changes of dynasty; for he is said "to have reposed with equal security on a bed of white and red roses." He was high in favour with the new Yorkist King; became Lord Treasurer in 1464, Earl of Kent in 1465; and was confirmed in his new title alike by Richard III. and Henry VII. In point of fact, if we may credit Leland's account, he had begun life, as he ended it, a Lancastrian. "In the time of the Civil War betwixt King Henry the Sixth and King Edward the Fourth, there was a Battel fought without the South Suburbs of Northampton. The Lord-Fanhope took totally King Henry's part. The Lord Grey de Ruthyn did the same in countenance; but a little afore the field, he practised with King Edward. Others saying, that he had a Title to Lord Fanhope's Lands at Antehille, or thereabout, or depraving him with false Accusations, so wrought with King Edward, that he, with all his strong Band of Walschemen, fell to King Edward's part, upon promise, that if Edward won the Field, he should have Antchille, and such Lands as Fanhope had there. Edward won the Field, and Grey obtained Antehille, *cum perti-nentiis.*"

His house continued for nearly two hundred and eighty years. There should have been in all twelve Earls of Kent, but one of them declined to take the title, his predecessor having "much wasted his Estate by gaming, and died in poverty at the sign of the 'George' in Lombard Street." However, it was "much recovered by the wise Frugality" of the next Earl, with whose nephew Henry the direct line terminated in 1639. The barony of Grey de Ruthyn then passed to the sister of this eighth Earl, Susan Lady Longueville; and the Earldom devolved on Anthony Grey, a Puritan divine,[*] who was "parson and patron" of Burbach. He refused to take his seat in Parliament "by reason of age and infirmities, but did not abate the constancy of his preaching, so long as he was able to be led up into the pulpit. Such his humility, that honours did not change manners in him. Thus a mortified mind is not more affected with additions of titles, than a corpse with a gay coffin."—*Fuller.* Yet this "mortified" Earl had a long struggle with Charles Longueville for the barony of Grey de Ruthyn. His great grandson, Henry, who had inherited from his mother the title of Baron Lucas, was created in 1706, Marquess of Kent, Earl of Harold, and Viscount Goderich; and three years afterwards Duke of Kent. But the line ended, as its honours had culminated, with him. He survived both his sons, and both died childless; the elder choked by an ear of barley that he had inadvertently put into his mouth; the second before he had completed his twenty-first year; and his grand-daughter Lady Jemima Campbell, the only child of his eldest daughter, Amabel, Viscountess Glenorchy, became his heir. The Duke arranged her marriage with Philip, second Earl of Hardwicke; and in 1740—the year before he died—obtained a fresh creation as Marquess de Grey, with remainder to her and her heirs male. But a strange fatality seemed to pursue the family. She left none, and the new title died with her. Her eldest daughter, Lady Amabel Yorke, who inherited the barony of Lucas, and was created in 1816 Countess de Grey, married Lord Polwarth, but had no children; and it was her second daughter, Lady Jemima, who became the mother of the long expected heir. She was the wife of Thomas Robinson, Lord Grantham, and brought him two sons; of whom the younger was created Viscount Goderich and Earl of Ripon, and the elder succeeded his aunt as Earl de Grey. But here again the line failed, with two sons who died in their first youth; leaving their eldest sister, Anne, Countess Cowper, to succeed to the barony of Lucas, and the ancestral seat of the Earls of Kent, Wrest in Bedfordshire (mentioned by Dugdale among the possessions of the first Lord Grey de Ruthyn); while the Earldom devolved on their cousin, the present Marquess of Ripon.

* The names of his twelve children are cited among the 'Curiosities of Puritan Nomenclature:' one of them (a daughter) was christened " Faith-my-Joy."

I now come to the illustrious house that has not passed away like the rest, and for which was reserved the loftiest fortune among them all—that of Grey of Groby. It was founded by Sir Edward Grey, the eldest son of Reginald Lord Grey de Ruthyn and the Astley heiress who was his second wife. He married Elizabeth, grand-daughter and heir of William Lord Ferrers of Groby, and was summoned to parliament in her barony by Henry VI. It was their son, Sir John, killed in 1460 at the battle of St. Albans, who made the match that led to such momentous results. His wife, one of the twelve children of a poor Northamptonshire knight, could bring with her no inheritance; but she was dowered with the subtler gifts of beauty and fascination. The charms of Elizabeth Widvile, and her lovely hair "that shoan like the gold wire," have been lauded more than enough; and her powers of fascination were in after days solemnly denounced by Act of Parliament as sorcery and witchcraft. Her husband had fought and died under the Red banner of Lancaster; and at the accession of Edward IV. she found herself deprived of some lands that had been given to her in jointure. She took her two young sons to meet the new King, who was hunting near her father's house;* and throwing herself on her knees before him, humbly made her petition on their behalf and her own. The King fell in love with her; and the fair suppliant who had pleaded only for her slender jointure won for herself the crown of England, and was the first subject that ever shared the throne.

The new Queen was keenly intent on the advancement of every one that belonged to her, but above all of her sons, Thomas and Richard Grey. For Thomas she procured in 1466 the hand of the King's niece Anne, daughter and heiress of Henry Holland, the last Duke of Exeter (having, it is said, paid four thousand marks for the consent of the bride's mother); but the poor little girl died in her minority. Another wealthy heiress was found to take her place, Cecily de Bonvile, who brought him the two baronies of Harrington and Bonvile; and he received in 1471 the Earldom of Huntingdon, which he resigned four years afterwards on being created Marquess of Dorset. As the half-brother of the poor young King murdered in the Tower, he was attainted when Richard III. came to the throne; but took sanctuary, escaped thence to Brittany to join the Earl of Richmond, and was restored to his lands and honours after the battle of Bosworth. He had fifteen children, seven of whom were sons; and one of them, Lord Leonard, who was Lord Deputy of Ireland, was created in 1535 Viscount Graney, but accused of treason and beheaded four years afterwards.

The eldest, Thomas, second Marquess, figures in the reign of Henry VIII. as "the best general of those times for embattling an army," of speech "soldier-

---

* The oak is still shown in Whittlebury Forest under which the golden-haired Elizabeth watched for the King's coming—not knowing him even by sight. She is said to have asked a young knight riding by for tidings of him, and found that she was speaking to the King himself.

like, plain, short, smart, and material"; and esteemed by the King "an honest and good man." He commanded the troops sent to Spain in 1511; carried the sword of Estate at the Field of the Cloth of Gold; and attended Charles V. on his visit to England. He left four sons: 1. Henry, his successor; 2. Edward, d. s. p.; 3. Thomas, beheaded in 1554; and 4. John, of Pirgo in Essex, ancestor of the Earls of Stamford.

Henry, third Marquess, married Lady Frances, the elder of the two co-heirs of Charles Brandon, Duke of Suffolk, by his marriage with the King's sister, the Lady Mary Tudor, Queen Dowager of France. Her two half-brothers, Henry, third Duke, and Lord Charles Brandon, died of the sweating sickness on the same day in 1551, both of them under age; and Lady Frances' husband "was, in favour to her, though otherwise for his harmless simplicity neither misliked nor much regarded, created Duke of Suffolk." They had three daughters, Lady Jane, Lady Katherine, and Lady Mary; to whom, for their misfortune, Henry VIII., on failure of his own posterity, left the Crown by his will. Lady Jane, as reversionary heiress, then became, in the eyes of her father and mother, nothing more than a trump card to be played to the best advantage. The Duke and Duchess trafficked shamelessly for her guardianship and disposal in marriage; compelled her, by blows and violence, to take a husband whom she did not like, when troth-plighted and "engaged in conscience" to another: forced her to live with the two people she most dreaded and detested in the world, her father and mother-in-law; and finally proclaimed her Queen against her will. When told of her new dignity, she "swooned and lay as dead." She reigned for ten days, and then laid her gentle head on the block in expiation of the crimes of others.

Few episodes in history are so pathetic as the fate of the "fair and incomparable" Lady Jane. We see her first at Court, a little child of eight years old, waiting upon Queen Katherine Parr whenever she visited the King, and walking backwards before her with a candle in each hand. Next, growing up as the destined bride of Edward VI. in the dissolute household of the Lord Admiral; thence transferred, after his execution, to her own father's house—"to her, in very truth, a House of Correction "—and affianced to the Earl of Hertford; but ever the same serious and studious girl of whom Roger Ascham has left so charming a picture.

One summer's afternoon, in 1550 (when she was not yet fifteen), he found her sitting in her chamber at Bradgate reading *Phædo Platonis*, while the Duke and Duchess, with all their household, were out hunting, and a joyous "blast of venery" was ringing through the park. She had not cared to go with them. No cry of hounds or hunter's horn could lure her away from her book; for their sport, she said, was but a shadow of the pleasure she found in Plato. "Alack, good folk!" added she, with a pretty air of superiority, "they never felt what true pleasure meant." She told him she took refuge in her books from the petty miseries of her daily life; and "fell a-weeping" when called away from them to attend upon her father and mother. They were "sharp and severe parents. When I am in their presence, whether I speak, keep silence—sit, stand, or go—eat, drink—be merry or sad, be sewing, playing, dancing, or doing anything else —I must do it even so perfectly as God made the world; or else I am so sharply taunted, so cruelly threatened — yea, presently sometimes with pinches, nips, and bobs, and other ways which I will not name, for the honour I bear them.—so without measure misordered, that I think myself in hell till I go to Master Aylmer, who teacheth me so gently, so pleasantly, with such fair allurements to learning, that I think all the time nothing while I am with him."

Her brief and joyless life had been twice attempted before its tragical end. "Once," she tells us, "I was poisoned in my mother-in-law's house, and once in the Tower. So powerful was the venom, that all the skin came off my back." Yet she had hardly completed her seventeenth year when she was beheaded on Tower Hill :—

> "Seventeen—and knew eight languages—in music
> Peerless—her needle perfect, and her learning
> Beyond the churchmen; yet so meek, so modest,
> So wife-life humble to the trivial boy
> Mismatch'd with her for policy! I have heard
> She would not take a last farewell of him,
> She fear'd it might unman him for his end.
> She could not be unmann'd—no, nor outwoman'd—
> Seventeen—a rose of grace!
> Girl never breathed to rival such a rose ;
> Rose never blew that equall'd such a bud."—*Tennyson.*

The story of her two younger sisters, now so perilously near the throne, is only one degree less melancholy. On her own infelicitous wedding day, Lady Katherine had been married to Lord Herbert, son of the Earl of Pembroke ; and Lady Mary—then only eight years old—betrothed to their kinsman, Lord Grey de Wilton. But, after her execution, "when what was the Highway of Honour turned," in Fuller's phrase, "into the ready Road to Ruin," Lady Mary was cast off by Lord Grey, and Lord Pembroke procured a divorce for his son, and turned poor Lady Katherine out of his house. Their mother, within a fortnight of her widowhood, re-married an equerry almost young enough to have been her son ; and the two forlorn girls were taken into Queen Mary's household, and continued maids of honour after the accession of Elizabeth. But the new Queen "could not well abide the sight of Lady Katherine, who lived in great despair," and at last resolved, at all risks, to marry. She had formed a passionate attachment to Lord Hertford ; and one day that the Queen went to Greenwich, complained of a terrible toothache, tied up her face, and, having thus contrived to be left behind, stole out with his sister, Lady Jane Seymour, to his house in

Cannon Row, where they were married. No one gave her away, and no one was present but Lady Jane, who died shortly afterwards, and the priest, who took good care never to be forthcoming. She concealed her marriage till, finding herself with child, she was driven to confess it to the Queen, who forthwith sent her and Lord Hertford to the Tower. At first, by the connivance of the Lieutenant, she was allowed to see her husband; but when, in 1562, a second son was born to them in their captivity, Elizabeth's wrath literally knew no bounds. "She committed her own Lieutenant prisoner in his own Tower," and sent Lady Katherine to her uncle's house at Pirgo, where she remained till his death in 1564. She was then transferred to the unwilling custody of strangers, each in turn receiving her under protest; and so passed on from house to house, a burden and incumbrance wherever she went, helpless, sickly, and very poor. In vain, with sad insistence, she constantly implored the Queen's mercy; in vain she conjured and coaxed Cecil; in vain the old Duchess of Somerset pleaded for "this young couple, waxing old in prison"—Death alone was to break her bonds, "This Heraclita, Lady of Lamentation, was seldom seen with dry Eyes for many years together, sighing out her sorrowful Condition." At last, in 1567, she died of atrophy at Sir Owen Hopton's house in Suffolk. On her death-bed. she desired that her wedding ring and "ring of assurance" (betrothal) should be sent to her husband; and taking out another on which was enamelled a death's head, with the legend, "While I lyve yours;" "This," said she, "shall be the last token to my lord that ever I shall send him: it is the picture of myself." As she looked down at her hands, she perceived that her nails were purple, and cried with a sudden smile, "Lo, He comes! Yea, even so come, Lord Jesus!" adding—as well she might—"Welcome, death!" Then, closing her eyes with her own hands, she passed away while the words "Oh Lord, into Thy Hands I commend my spirit," were still on her lips.

The last sister, Lady Mary, warned by the example of her elders, chose a husband "whom she could love, and none need fear," and was secretly married to Martin Keyes, Sergeant Porter of the Watergate at Westminster Palace, a burly Kentishman known as the "biggest gentleman of the court." * He was, according to Fuller, "a Judge at Court (but only of doubtful Casts at Dice)," who had held his office for twenty-two years, and was then a widower of forty or fifty, with several children. Yet even this humble happiness was denied to Lady Mary. No sooner was the marriage discovered, than Martin Keyes was consigned to a noisome prison at the Fleet, whence he vainly sought release by offering to renounce his unlucky bride, and permit his marriage to be annulled. Lady Mary was despatched on a pillion to Mr. Hawtrey's house in Buckinghamshire, and was kept in confinement there and elsewhere till her husband died

* They were ill-matched, for Lady Mary, "the least of the court," was a dwarf. Lady Jane, too, was very short, and wore gilt *chopines* (a sort of cork shoe, four inches high) to appear taller.

seven years afterwards. She was then set free; and the heiress of the Greys and
Bonviles passed the remainder of her life in poverty and obscurity, subsisting on
a pittance of £80 a year.

The father of these three ill-fated princesses perished on the scaffold five
days after his daughter's execution; having been sentenced to death for high
treason by his peers in Westminster Hall. He had sought to save his life by
hiding himself in a hollow oak in his park of Astley, but was betrayed by a faith-
less keeper. All his honours expired under attainder; but the barony of Grey
of Groby was revived in 1603 in favour of the son of his only surviving brother
Lord John, Sir Henry Grey of Pirgo. Twenty-five years afterwards, the grandson
and successor was created Earl of Stamford by Charles I. Nevertheless, he
commanded the Parliamentary Army in the West during the Civil War; and his
son sat in judgment on the unhappy King, and signed his death-warrant. The
fifth Earl, whose mother, Lady Mary Booth, had been the sole heiress of the last
Earl of Warrington, received his grandfather's title in 1796; but it expired with
the seventh Earl in 1883. By the will of this last Lord Stamford, the great
heritage of the Greys was divided; for their beautiful ancestral domain of Bradgate was left to Mrs. Arthur Duncombe, the surviving daughter of his only sister,
Lady Margaret Milbank: Enville, with its princely gardens and treasures of
silver plate, to an utter stranger in blood, who was his wife's niece; and Dunham-
Massey, the Booth estate in Cheshire, and the only one to which his successor
could have no possible claim—to the very distant kinsman on whom the older
Earldom devolved.

I have left myself little or no space to deal with the other titles pertaining to
the name of Grey. That of Viscount Lisle, granted in 1483, lasted for less than
thirty years; that of Grey of Rotherfield, dating from 1297, had passed to the
D'Eyncourts in 1387; while the more modern barony of Walsingham, bestowed
in 1780 on Sir William de Grey, Chief Justice of the Common Pleas, still
continues.

The Northumbrian Greys, whose arms are wholly different, and similar to
those borne by the Scottish house, are represented both in the male and female
line. Their common ancestor, Sir John de Grey, a famous soldier in Henry V.'s
wars, received in 1418 a grant of the French Earldom of Tankerville, and
married the eldest coheir of Edward de Cherlton, Lord Powis. The third Earl
was attainted as a Yorkist under Henry VI.; but his son had summons to Parliament in 1482 as Lord Grey of Powis, and left two successors in the title.
The last died without legitimate issue in 1552.

From Sir Thomas, a younger son of the first Earl of Tankerville (according
to Burke, for Dugdale makes no mention of any relationship), descended William
Grey, created by James I. Lord Grey of Werke; whose grandson Ford became
Earl of Tankerville in 1695. But he died s. p.; and his brother Ralph, the
fourth and last baron of Werke, left only a daughter, Lady Mary Bennet, whose

husband received the Earldom of Tankerville in 1714, and was the ancestor of the present Earl.

An uncle of the first Lord Grey of Werke, Sir Edward Grey of Howick, had, however, descendants in the male line, and one of them was created Earl Grey in 1806. Between these two families the great Northumberland estate was equally divided.

The Scottish Grays—still represented in the female line—have held their barony since 1445.

Gaunson: obviously Graunson, as it stands in Leland's list: "Gray et Graunson;" and therefore a duplicate. Leland likewise repeats the name.

Golofre: Galofer (Leland): "Guillaume Goulaffre" (Dives Roll). "Roger Gulafre claimed property from St. Evroult, Normandy (Ordericus Vitalis, 483). He was Lord of Mesnil Bernard (Ib. 466). William Gulafre had great estates in Suffolk in 1086 (Domesday) and gave tithes to Eye Abbey (Mon. i. 356). Roger Gulafre was of Suffolk 1130 (Rot. Pip.), and Philip Gulafre held four fees in barony in the same county (Liber Niger). The name occurs afterwards in Oxford and other parts of England."—*The Norman People.* "Fyfield in Berkshire was formerly the property and seat of the family of Golafre. John Golafre was knight of the shire in 1337. Sir John Golafre was employed in an embassy to France, in 1389. Either this Sir John, or a son of the same name, died seised of the manor of Fyfield, in 1442. The same year a licence was granted by the Crown, for the foundation of a chantry, at the altar of St. John the Baptist, pursuant to the will of Sir John Golafre, who is styled in the charter servant to King Henry V. and King Henry VI. Francis Little, in his MS. History of Abingdon, says that the daughter and heir' of the last mentioned Sir John married John de la Pole, Earl of Lincoln, who lost his life at the battle of Stoke, and was attainted of treason. In the N. aisle of the parish church is the monument of this Sir John, who died in 1442. His effigies in armour lies on an open altar tomb, beneath which is the figure of·a skeleton in a shroud. The common people call it Gulliver's tomb, and say that the figure on the top represents him in the vigour of youth; the skeleton in his old age; the arms of Golafre are on the· tomb, and in the windows of the church."— *Lysons.* He descended from a younger son of Sir Roger Golafre, *dominus de Cereedene* (Sarsden), co. Oxon, in the reign of King John; who, with some of his posterity, was buried in the chapter house of Bruern Abbey, of which he was probably a benefactor. Fourth in succession from Sir Roger was the Sir John who married the heiress of Fyfield, and first settled in Berkshire. The last Sir John was illegitimate, the son of "a leman called Johanet Pulham;" but nevertheless inherited the estates, and married one of the co-heiresses of Dunster, Philippa de Mohun.

Sir Roger's eldest son bore his name, and was seated at Norton in Northamptonshire, when William, his heir, acquired Heyford by marriage.

"William was appointed deputy Chamberlain of the Exchequer 1 or 2 Edward I. by William de Beauchamp, Earl of Worcester. His son 'Master John de Golafre' afterwards executed the same office on the nomination of Guy de Beauchamp, Earl of Warwick, Chamberlain in fee, and retained it till his death, for in 1315 John de Aston, clerk of John de Golafre, deceased, surrendered two great keys and twenty-three lesser keys of the doors of the treasury and coffers of the Exchequer."—*Baker's Northamptonshire.* There was one other John de Golafre, and then the estate passed to the Mantells.

Gobion; "from Bretagne, where Guido Gobio witnessed a charter of Geoffrey de Dinan, c. 1070, as one of his knights. (Morice, Hist. Bret. Preuves, i. 430). Hugh Gubion was of Northants 1130 (Rot. Pip.) and in 1165 Richard Gubiun, or Gobio, held fiefs in Bedford and Derby from Beauchamp, and Ferrers Earl of Derby (Liber Niger)."—*The Norman People.* In Bedfordshire, "Higham-Gobion, a small village about nine miles from Luton, derived its additional name from the family of Gobion, to whom the manor belonged from an early period till the year 1301; when it passed by marriage to the Botelers."—*Lysons.* Gobions in Herts was another of their manors. Richard Gobion, of that place, and of Knaptoft in Leicestershire, was the last male heir, and died in 1300, leaving two daughters: Hawise, married to Ralph le Boteler of Norbury in Staffordshire; and Elizabeth, married to Sir Robert Paynel, of Boothby-Paynel, Lincolnshire.—*Nichol's Leicestershire.* I also find Yardley-Gobion in Northamptonshire, where Hugh Gubiun served as Sheriff in 1161 and 1163. Woodhall, in Herts, "heretofore the estate of the Butlers, by marriage, came to the estate of the Gobions: (as this estate, by the same way, passed to Francis Shallcross of Digginsworth)."— *Camden's Britannia.* Gobions in the parish of Up-Havering, and Gobions in Toppesfield, retain their name in Essex, where they had a considerable estate. "Sir Thomas Gobyon was High-Sheriff of Essex and Hertfordshire in 1323. John Gobyon is on the list of the Gentry of this country in 1433."—*Morant's Essex.* Another John Gobion (perhaps his father), who died in 1422, held the estate of Ashwell Hall by the service of finding one spit of wood in the King's kitchen on his Coronation Day, "Gebon, or Gibbon, is a corruption of Gobion, a very considerable family, which held the estate of Le Gibbon's Fee in Bumsted, one at Toppesfield, and others in divers parts of the county."—*Ibid.* Gobions in Great Lees, Essex, was another of Sir Thomas' manors, as well as Gobions in East Tilbury, held under the Bohuns. He founded a chantry in the latter parish about 1328.

"Sir Hugh Gobyun, of York, occurs about 1300 in *Palgrave's Parliamentary Writs.* The name was corrupted to Gubbins."—*The Norman People.*

Grensy, a duplicate: see *Gracy.*

Graunt: We are accustomed to look upon this merely as the familiar name of a Scottish clan. But in reality the Grantes or Grentes were resident in Normandy from the earliest times, and held their heads high among their contemporaries. According to William de Jumièges, Gilbert Grente married, about 985, a daughter of Hugh de Montfort-sur-Rille, who was the niece of Richard Sans Peur; and in 1010, La Chesnaye (vol. 7) tells us that * * * de Marguerie allied himself to the Dukes of Normandy by taking to wife a daughter of this house, evidently Gilbert's child. Further, it is to be noted that "Hugh de Grente-maisnil is said to have been so called from his seat in Normandy, built by Grento (*Grentonis Maisnel*, in Latin *Mensis*)."—*Sir Henry Ellis.* His coat of arms was, however, wholly different from that of the Grentes, who, in open defiance of the laws of blazonry, bear *Argent* on a fesse *Azure*, a cross moline *Gules.* They are still represented in Normandy, where they claim to have held the estate of Saint-Pierre-Azis, or Azise, in the bailifry of Coutances, "from time immemorial." Charles de Grente, Comte de Grécourt, was the first President and King's Advocate of the Parliament of Normandy.

Robert Grante is among the additions made by M. de Magny to the Dives Roll; but I have not succeeded in finding any trace of him in Domesday. Hugo Grando, de Scoca,* who is there entered as an under-tenant in Berkshire, can scarcely have been of the same family; but we may rightfully claim Grento, who held both in Devonshire and Shropshire; in the latter county of Roger Fitz Corbet at Worthin. Roger Grente witnesses a deed of John Le Strange in 1161.—*Eyton's Salop.* "Grento de Everwic" is found in the *Rotulus Magnus Pipæ* of 31 Hen. I.—the earliest record that we possess after the date of Domesday; and Peter Fitz Grente, perhaps his son, held half a fee of William de Percy in Yorkshire.—*Liber Niger.* William Grent was of Buckinghamshire in the reign of John.—*Rotuli Curiæ Regis.* For a family that could boast of kinship with the Conqueror, it is obvious that their position in his new kingdom was very far from brilliant.

The subsequent notices are difficult to identify, for "Grant," as often as not, stands for Le Grand, a name very frequently found in Normandy. On the earliest of the Spencer tombs in their burial place at Brington Church, Northants, lies the elaborate effigy of a Graunt heiress, married to Sir John Spencer, whose coat of arms, as blazoned on the heraldic mantle looped across her breast, almost exactly corresponds with that of one of the Norman Le Grands. She bore *Ermine*, on a chevron *gules*, three bezants; while he, styled Sieur de Sainte-Marie-d'Herbetot and various other manors in the district of Pont-Audemer, bore *D'hermine au chevron de gueules chargé de trois molettes d'éperon.*

The Scottish families of this name are Celtic. The first of the Grants is

---

* This name is hard to explain. I subjoin a communication on the subject with which I have been favoured by one of our first antiquarian authorities: "His name was probably mangled by the Italian clerks of the Exchequer, who compiled the Survey of Berkshire from the local returns, but there can be little doubt that his name is written Hugo-de-Grando-de-Scoca, and that it was taken from some place on the other side of the Channel."—*R. E. Chester Waters.*

said to have been Gregory, Sheriff of Inverness in the days of Alexander II., who reigned 1214–49. This would give them a very respectable antiquity of nearly six centuries and a half; but there is an old joke current in Scotland respecting a former Lord Seafield, who was not disposed to rest content with it. He aimed at establishing a far loftier and more remote origin; and this seemed to him easy of accomplishment. All that was required to rest it on incontestable authority was the alteration of one little letter in the family Bible. Accordingly, under his manipulation, "Giant" became "Grant," and he could read with perfect complacency in the sixth chapter of Genesis how "there were Grants on the earth in those days," born of angels and the daughters of men.

Greile, or Greilly, as Leland spells it, from Gresillé, Anjou. "Albert Greslet, Baron of Manchester under Roger de Poitou, occurs in Domesday (270). The name was often written Gredley, Gridley, and Gresley, but was altogether different from that of Gresley" (see *Toesni*).—*The Norman People.* Dugdale begins their pedigree with Robert de Greslei, who founded a Cistercian Abbey at Swineshead in Lincolnshire in 1134, and bestowed upon it his mill at Manchester. The next in succession, Albert II., married the sister and co-heir of the Baron of Halton in Cheshire; and was the father of Robert, who in King John's time forfeited all his lands in Lincoln, Norfolk, Suffolk, Oxfordshire and Lancashire (twelve knight's fees in all) by taking part with the rebellious barons. However, he made his peace with Henry III., received them back, and in 1218 "gave five Marks and one Palfrey, for Licence to have a Fair at his Lordship of Manchester." His wife was a niece of Cœur de Lion's famous Chancellor, Longchamp. Their son Thomas, 27 Hen. III., "being in the King's Service beyond Sea, was quit of his Service of Castle-gard to the Castle of Lancaster:" and named Warden of the King's Forests South of Trent some years later. Second in descent from him was another Thomas, summoned to parliament in 1307, who died s. p., leaving as his heir his sister Joan, "who, taking to Husband John the Son of Roger de la Warre, brought a fair Inheritance to that Noble Family."

Ralph de Gresli—evidently a younger son of this house, was among those who took arms against Henry III., and married Isabel, daughter of Robert de Muschamp of Muschamp and Elkesdon in Notts, who brought him three knight's fees held of the Honour of Peverel. He, too, had no son; and his daughter and heiress, Agnes, married Hugh Fitz Ralph.

But the name survived; for temp. Edw. III. Thomas and Avicia de Greyle held part of a fee at Addington, in Kent, of the Archbishop of Canterbury.

Greuet; no doubt for Gernet,* a well known Lancashire house. The name

---

* This transposition of the letter "r" is by no means uncommon. Gernon, for instance, is several times given as Grenon in Domesday.

appears in the Norman Exchequer Rolls of the twelfth century. "Guillaume de Carnet" is entered on the Dives Roll, and as William de Chernet, a Hampshire tenant, in Domesday. Hugo de Chernet—evidently his descendant—in 1165 held three knight's fees in the county of John de Port.—*Liber Niger.* At the same date, William Gernet was of Bedford, and Alexander and Geoffrey of Essex.—*Ibid.* In the latter county, at least, the family must have continued nearly two hundred years longer, for we find a Henry Gernet serving as Sheriff of Essex and Herts in 1341. They were chiefly, however, settled in Lancashire, where they are believed to have been first enfeoffed by Roger de Poitou. Several of them are named in the *Testa de Nevill.* " Roger Gernet held as being chief forester : William Gernet, by the service of meeting the King on the borders of the county with his horse and white rod, and conducting him into and out of the county ; and Thomas Gernet, by sounding the horn on meeting the King on his arrival in those parts."—*Bain's Lancashire.* This Roger, Chief Forester of Lancashire, had a grant of Leylandshire, and further increased his estate by his marriage with Quenilda, fourth daughter and co-heir of Richard Fitz Roger, the founder of the priory of St. Cuthbert at Lytham. " He died 36 Hen. II., leaving a son, Benedict Gernet, who had 3 John been fined ten marks to have the serjeanty of the forests of Lancashire, and to have the King's favour. His daughter and heiress married William de Dacre, son and heir of Ranulph de Dacre, Governor of Carlisle 54 Hen. III. Halton was the original seat of the Gernets. It was held by the service of being Chief Forester of the whole county, and they are presumed to have been the first grantees under Roger de Poitou."—*Ibid.* The descendants of William Gernet became De Lydiates and De Halsalls, having adopted the names of their manors.

Gurry. William de Gueri 1165 held lands in *capite* in Passy, Normandy.[*] (Feod. Norm. Duchesne). In Domesday "Gueri, a canon of St. Paul's," held in Twyford, Middlesex. Alured Geri, of Shropshire, is mentioned in the *Rotulis Cancellarii* of 1202, and Hugo Gery paid a fine in Berkshire in 1213.—*Hunter.* In Yorkshire " Guerri " witnessed the deed of gift by which Robert de Brus (who died in 1141) conferred the manor of Elwick on his daughter Agatha as her marriage portion.—*Gale's Richmondshire.* William Gurry, of Wiltshire, occurs in the time of Edward I.—*Rotuli Hundredorum.* The Lincolnshire estates of Adam Lord Newmarch, taken prisoner at the battle of Northampton in 1263, were granted by Henry III. to William de Gery—perhaps the same William. Many of the name are found at about the same date in Shropshire. Henri Geri and Geoffrey Geri of Mose are mentioned there in 1262 : Roger Gery two years before that : and in 1272 Walter de Geri was arrested for the murder of John de Gatacre. Herbert de Gerys was a land-owner in the county : and Richard Gery

[*] " Mont-guerré was the designation of one of the component *terres* of the Marquisate of Châtillon, derived apparently from the tenure of William Geré."— *T. Stapleton.*

of Acton-Reynald witnesses a number of deeds in that neighbourhood between 1299 and 1330. The last of them named by Eyton, Thomas Geri, was Vicar of Moreton-Corbett in 1371. " The Gerys of Beds, and a younger branch seated at Swebston, bore *Gules* two bars *Argent*, charged with three mascles of the field. The first mentioned is Thomas Gery of Royston, Sheriff of Cambridge-shire in 1509."—*Nichol's Leicestershire.* His descendants still remain in Bedford-shire, seated at Bushmead Priory. In the last century there was likewise a Sir Thomas Gery of Great Ealing, Middlesex (who does not appear in their pedigree), one of whose co-heiresses married Sir John Cullum, Bt.

Gurley. This is another of the Norman families domiciled in Scotland at a very early date. Ingelram de Gourlay is believed to have accompanied William the Lion from England in 1174, and witnesses one of his charters about 1200. Fourth in descent from him was William de Gourlay, who made his submission to Ed. I. in 1296, being then styled *Willielmus de Gourlay de Balgally in vicecomitatu de Fife.* His son Simon first settled at Kincraig in the same county, which has ever since continued the home of his descendants. The last heir · male only died in 1833.

"In 1361, John de Gourley died seised of the manor of Ponthorp and half the manor of Shepmanstede in the county of Durham, leaving Richard his son and heir aged fifteen. In 1395 this same Richard died seised of the manor, held by offering one bezant at the feretory of St. Cuthbert on his feast day in March, and one bezant to the Bishop."—*Surtees' Durham.*

Grammori. "Rannulf, a vassal of Ilbert de Laci, who held Knottingley of him in 1086, is afterwards mentioned as 'Ranulfus Grammaticus,' and as having held lands there, given by Ilbert de Laci towards the endowment of St. Clement's chapel in Pontefract Castle. (Old Mon. i. 659.)

" The name of ' the Grammarian' had no doubt been given to him from the more than usual amount of learning he had acquired, not then considered an honourable distinction in a layman. The name was continued to his descendants, and was probably in their case meaningless enough, except as pointing to their descent from him. Next after Rannulf occurs Richard Grammaticus, who held a knight's fee of Henry de Laci in 1166 (Liber Niger). The name afterwards assumed, in common parlance, the form of Grammary."—*A. S. Ellis.* Ralph Grammaticus is mentioned in Henry I.'s confirmation charter to Nostel Priory ; and William Grammaticus witnesses the same King's charter to Tywardreth Priory, Cornwall. (Mon. Angl.) John and William Grammaticus of Middleton, Yorkshire, appear on the Pipe Roll of 1189. The latter was probably the William Grammaticus or Grammary who, about 1202, had a fierce dispute with his neighbour Adam de Beeston concerning the boundary of their adjacent manors. " In the same year, William Grammary, Lord of Middleton, gives to the King one hundred marks and a palfrey for having an inquisition concerning the appeal which Adam de Beeston made against him. The matter in dispute was the ownership of the wood between Beeston and Middleton. It had been adjudged to Beeston, but one day Grammary caught one of the Beeston foresters in this wood, seized him, and carried him to his house at Middleton, where he put him in the stocks as a trespasser. Irritated by the tediousness of the suit, this last act resolved both the disputants to bring matters to a crisis. They determined to settle their difference by an appeal to arms. A duel was fought in 1209, but what were its consequences we do not know, other than that the wood seems to have been ceded to Beeston."—*History of Sherburn and Cawood. W. Wheater.* Another of the name, Sir William Grammary, "Lord of Bickerton, near Wetherby, of Becca, and of Middleton near Leeds," was one of the Commissioners of Array in the wapentake of the Ainsty in 1318, and in the county of Cambridge, when he had considerable estates, in 1325. He had been summoned to the great Council at Westminster in the previous year. He conducted the West Riding men from Sherburn to Newcastle-on-Tyne, where they were to meet their leaders, in 1334; and five years afterwards "led his own service from Bickerton, five men-at-arms and twenty archers, into Scotland."

The family has long since passed away. Sir Henry Grammary occurs in 1362: and was followed by a Sir William, whose son Richard—clearly the last of his race—in 1439 released to Robert Stokes, the son and heir of his sister Alice, Bickerton, Beckhaugh, and other lands in Salley and Ripon.—*Wheater.* Their principal estate in Yorkshire lay about Aberford and Becca: and their arms, carved in stone, are still to be seen in the wall of Aberford Church.

Herbert Grammaticus, "the Wise Clerk," was Archdeacon of Salop about 1083–86. "He is mentioned by Ordericus as one of three learned clerks whose society Earl Roger much affected, and by whose counsels he was advantageously guided."—*Eyton's Shropshire.*

Gernoun, or whisker (some say, moustache): an appellation given to a branch of the Barons of Montfichet or Montfiquet (see p. 266). "About 1050 Robert surnamed Guernon, Baron of Montfiquet, witnessed a charter of Duke William (Gall. Christ. xi., Instr. 229). He had issue, 1. William de Montfichet, who died s. p. when the barony descended on the son of his brother: 2. Robert Guernon, or Gernon, who held a great barony in Essex, &c. in 1086. From his eldest son, William de Montfichet, descended the Barons Montfichet; the younger branches retained the name of Gernon. Alured Gernon, the brother of William de Montfichet, had estates in Essex and Middlesex 1130 (Rot. Pip.) Matthew, his son, witnessed a charter of William de Montfichet five years later (Mon. i. 803). Ralph, his son, in 1165, held a fief from Montfichet, Essex, and was granted Bakewell, Derbyshire, by Richard I. (Testa de Nevill). He had Ralph Gernon, founder of Lees Priory, Essex; father of William Gernon, who had two sons: 1. Ralph, ancestor of a line of Gernons frequently mentioned in Essex, Suffolk, and Derby, and which long continued; 2. Geoffrey, surnamed de Cavendish, from his residence at Cavendish in Suffolk. This Geoffrey was grandfather to Sir John Cavendish, Chief Justice temp. Richard II., and ancestor to the Dukes of Newcastle, Devonshire, &c. The identity of the family of Cavendish with that of Gernon in the Eastern Counties appears in all the old heralds' visitations, where the two names bear indiscriminately the same arms, and the account of the descent of this family given by Collins, which has been disputed, appears to be perfectly authentic."—*The Norman People.* There is, however, some difficulty in explaining why the name of Cavendish (or, as it was then called, Candish) was originally assumed ; for it is certain that the manor of Cavendish-Overhall only came into the possession of the Chief Justice through his marriage with the heiress of John de Odingseles. Yet it seems equally proved that his younger brother, who was seated at Grimston in the same county, always bore the name of Cavendish. Grimston appears to have been the seat of their father Roger, and Geoffrey, the grandfather, " was wrote of Moor-hall in the Peak in co. Derby."

Chief Justice Cavendish had a tragic end. He was beheaded in the market place of Bury, during an insurrection in 1382, the rebels "being the more incensed against him, for that his son John, an esquire of the King's house, had killed Wat Tyler at Smithfield." * The sixth in descent from him, William, a London mercer, sold Cavendish Overhall in 1569. But long before this, another William Cavendish (uncle to the last) had built up the greatness of this house, that, like so many others, rose on the ruins of the monasteries. He was a younger brother, who obtained an appointment as Gentleman Usher of the Chamber to Cardinal Wolsey, and became one of his favourite and best-trusted servants ;—a faithful servant, too, who did not desert his fallen master, but abode with him loyally to the very end. The King, "pleased with his honesty and truth," then took him into his own household, and in 1546 named him Treasurer of his Chamber. He had been one of the Royal Commissioners

---

* There are several claimants for this distinction, which has been generally accorded to Sir William Walworth, under whose statue in Fishmongers' Hall an inscription still proclaims that it was

> " Brave Walworth, Knight, Lord Mayor, yᵗ slew
> Rebellious Tyler in his alarmes ;
> The King therefore did give in lieu
> The dagger to the City arms."

But the sword on the shield of the Corporation of London—the ensign of the patron saint of the City, St. Paul—was not added at that time ; and though the old Corporation seal was broken up during the mayoralty of Sir William, the new one was provided on April 17th, 1381, whereas the Wat Tyler incident only took place on June 15th of the same year. The Phillpots of Porthgwidden in Cornwall claim the deed for their ancestor, Sir John Philipot, who was one of the knights made on that occasion. Fuller and Stowe, however, both affirm that the blow was struck by John Candish or Cavendish, one of the esquires in attendance on Richard II. : and Froissart (who transforms Candish into Sandwich) adds that he was dubbed for the feat.

appointed to receive the surrenders of the religious houses, and was loaded with their spoils; yet, as regarded his fortunes, by far the most successful venture of his life was his marriage with the famous Bess of Hardwick. He was a mature widower with six surviving daughters, and she, a beautiful young widow and the heiress of Hardwick, when she became his third wife. She brought him "a hopeful number of sons and daughters," whose advancement and . aggrandizement became the great object of her existence. From the very first she had set her mind steadily on money-getting; and the story of her success affords another instructive proof—if more were needed—of the irresistible power of a dominant will. All around her bowed to its sovereign ascendancy. According to the custom of the time, she had been a mere child—barely fourteen—when she was first married, and her husband died soon after; yet he had lived long enough to secure to her and her heirs all his worldly possessions, She induced her second husband, Sir William Cavendish, to sell all his lands in the Southern counties, in order to buy property in Derbyshire, where her own friends and kindred lived, and to commence a great manor house at Chatsworth, which he did not live to finish. She next married Sir William St. Lo, of Tormarton in Gloucestershire, Captain of the Guard to Queen Elizabeth, and Grand Butler of England, first stipulating that the whole of his estates should be settled on her, to the exclusion, not only of his brothers, but of his own daughters; and when she was for the third time left a widow, she captivated George Earl of Shrewsbury, "whom she brought to terms of the greatest honour and advantage to herself and children." Not only did she require a large jointure, but she insisted that her daughter Mary should be married to his eldest son, and her own son Henry to his daughter Lady Grace. Thus, each successive marriage brought greater wealth and higher honours to this grasping and intriguing woman; yet her lot as Countess of Shrewsbury was not without its thorns. She and her husband had the charge of Mary Queen of Scots during seventeen years; and though for a long time she was on friendly and familiar terms with the unhappy prisoner who was called her guest, entertaining her with Court gossip and various scandalous tales of Queen Elizabeth, yet in the end the license of her tongue took a different direction. She became jealous of Mary's influence over her husband; and the domestic peace at Sheffield came to a violent end. "The children took part with their mother, the father stood by his duty to the lady in his charge; and, as a final touch to family dissensions, the Countess informed the world that Mary Stuart had admitted her husband to too close an intimacy, and was about to become a mother.

"The fury of the Queen of Scots at a false accusation, the fiery peremptoriness with which she insisted that the Countess should either prove her charge or do penance for slander, contrasts curiously with her anxiety to prevent too close a scrutiny into the murder of Darnley. The offending Countess was examined before the Privy Council, and was made to acknowledge upon her knees that she had lied."—*Froude.* Lord Shrewsbury was finally separated from her in 1585,[*] and perhaps it was owing to these disagreeable reminiscences that, on his death in 1590, she refrained from taking a fifth husband, but lived a widow for the remaining seventeen years of her life, "in absolute power and plenty," occupied in building three great houses at Chatsworth, Hardwick, and Oldcotes.[†] Her eldest son left no children by Lady Grace Talbot, but each of the two others became the founder of a Dukedom. One of her daughters, married to the Earl of Lennox, was the mother of the ill-fated Lady Arabella Stuart; and in honour of this royal connection, her second son William was created Lord Cavendish of Hardwick by James I., 1605. She had given him, as her favourite child, a greater fortune than had fallen to his elder brother's share; and on the death of the latter he united both in 1616. Two years afterwards, he was advanced to the Earldom of Devonshire. It is remarkable that he should have taken the old Courtenay title, for I cannot find that either he or any of his belongings ever had the slightest connection with the co. of Devon. The second Earl, a courtier and a prodigal, whose house "appeared like a prince's court rather than a subject's," left at his death his son a minor, and his widow burdened with the care of an estate that was "loaded with debt, and charged and complicated with near thirty law-suits." But she extricated herself gallantly from her difficulties; for she managed to pay off the debt, and prosper in all her law business, so that Charles I. once said to her in jest, "Madam, you have all my judges at your disposal." She was in every way a remarkable woman; distinguished not only as an able and active politician who worked hard for the Restoration, but as the patroness of the wits and poets of the age, who used to congregate at her house. "Waller read his verses there, and William Earl of Pembroke wrote a volume of poems in her praise, published afterwards, and dedicated to her by Donne."—*Lysons.* "She never affected the title, of a wit; carried no snares in her tongue; and as she was never known to speak evil of any, so neither would she endure to hear of it, from any, of others." Her grandson was the first of seven successive

---

[*] In one of his letters, the Earl speaks of her as "so bad and wicked a woman, that no curse or plague in the earth could be more grievous to me." The Bishop of Lichfield attempted conciliation in a fashion of his own; though he admits "the Countess is a sharpe and bitter shrewe, and therefore like enough to shorten your life if she should keep you company. Indeed, my good Lord, I have heard some say so; but if shrewdnesse or sharpenesse may be a just cause of separacion between a man and wife, I think few men in England would keep their wives long; for it is a common jest, yet true in some sense, that there is but one shrewe in all the worlde, and every man hath her; and so everie man might be ridd of his wife, that would be ridd of a shrewe."

[†] She had a superstitious belief in a prophecy that she would die whenever she ceased to build; and her death did actually take place during a long frost that interrupted her works at Hardwick.

Dukes of Devonshire. He had taken part vehemently with Lord Russell in opposing Charles II.'s government, gave evidence at his trial in his behalf, and was among the first to declare himself for the Prince of Orange. He officiated as Lord High Steward at the coronation of William and Mary, received the Garter in the same year, and was created a Duke in 1694.

The other Cavendish Dukedom, which had become extinct three years before, was granted for military service. Bess of Hardwick's third son, Sir Charles Cavendish, of Welbeck Abbey in Notts,* had married Catherine, sole heir of Cuthbert,ʼseventh and last Lord Ogle, who brought him her father's barony and great Northumbrian estate : and their eldest son successively bore the titles of Baron Ogle of Bothal, Viscount Mansfield, Baron Cavendish of Bolsover, Earl of Ogle, and Earl, Marquess, and Duke of Newcastle-upon-Tyne. He was the dashing Cavalier commander who first raised the Royal standard in the North, and, planting it on the battlements of Tynemouth Castle, manned and fortified Newcastle. Thence—in the very depth of winter—he fought his way to York at the head of his new levies, routing the rebels in every direction. He fully maintained the reputation thus gained, most of all by his splendid defence of York against three several armies of English and Scots. But after the fatal day of Marston Moor, he sheathed his sword and went abroad ; men said, in consequence of a misunderstanding with Prince Rupert. He had lost nearly three parts of a million sterling during the Civil War; and after the Restoration received a Dukedom as some compensation for his sufferings in the Royal cause. Though so intrepid and successful a soldier, the natural bent of his mind was towards literature ; and he wrote a Book of Horsemanship, that, as Horace Walpole tells us, made him familiar as an author " to those who scarce knew any other." But he adds, that though "he was a man extremely well known from the course of life into which he was forced, yet he would soon have been forgotten in ʼthe walk of fame he chose for himself. Though amorous in poetry and music, as Lord Clarendon says, he was fitter to break Pegasus for a manege, than to mount him on the steeps of Parnassus. Of all the riders of that steed, perhaps there have not been a more fantastic couple than his Grace and his faithful Duchess, who was never off her pillion." This was his second wife, Margaret Lucas, " the authoress of thirteen folios, of whom he is reported to have said, in answer to a compliment on her wisdom, ' Sir, a very wise woman is a very foolish thing.' She was surrounded night and day with young ladies, who were to wake up at moment's·notice to take down her Grace's conceptions."—*Dean Stanley*.

---

* He had first selected another residence. " Sir Charles Cavendish had begun to build a great House in the Lordship of Kirkby Woodhouse, on a hill by the Forest side near Annesley Woodhouse, where he was assaulted and wounded by Sir John Stanhope and his men as he was viewing the work, which was therefore thought fit to be left off, some blood being spilt in the quarrel, then very hot betwixt these two families."—*Thoroton's Notts.*

Her husband died in 1676, having reached the good old age of eighty-four, and lies buried in Westminster Abbey, where a costly monument commemorates " the loyal Duke of Newcastle." His first wife had been an heiress, by whom he left one surviving son, Henry, second Duke ; who, again, had (besides five daughters) an only son, the last heir of his house. This young Earl of Ogle, on whom rested so many hopes and expectations, was matched very early in life with the greatest heiress in England, Lady Elizabeth Percy, dowered with six ancient baronies, and the whole of the territory that had been held by the Earls of Northumberland. The estate that was his by birthright was one of the largest in the country ; and with two such inheritances merged into one, the prospect of earthly grandeur opened before him would have gladdened the covetous heart of old Bess of Hardwick. But this fair promise was blighted almost as soon as it dawned. The poor boy destined to so exceptional a lot died the year after his marriage, leaving a child-widow of fifteen ; and when his father followed him to the grave in 1691, every one of the new-born honours of the family expired, and the old barony of Ogle fell into abeyance between five sisters. The two elder ones, Elizabeth, first Duchess of Albemarle and then Duchess of Montagu, and Frances, Countess of Breadalbane, were both childless ; and the third, Margaret, the wife of John Holles, Earl of Clare, was thus constituted sole heir. Her husband, created in 1694 Marquess of Clare and Duke of Newcastle, was " considered the richest subject that had been in the kingdom for some ages." But here again the male line failed. Their only child was Henrietta Countess of Oxford ; and she, in her turn, had but one daughter, Lady Margaret Harley, celebrated by Prior as " My noble, lovely little Peggy," on whom the whole splendid heritage ultimately devolved. She brought it to William Bentinck, second Duke of Portland, whom she married in 1734.

Three other still existing titles have been granted to the Cavendishes. The elder brother of the first Earl of Devonshire left an illegitimate son, to whom he gave Doveridge Hall "with a suitable estate" in Derbyshire. One of his descendants, Sir Henry Cavendish, married an Irish heiress, who was created in 1792 Baroness Waterpark, in the co. of Cork, with remainder to her heirs male. Again, Lord George Cavendish, second son of the fourth Duke and his richly-endowed wife Lady Charlotte Boyle (see vol. iii. p. 18) received her father's title of Earl of Burlington in 1831. He had himself married a lady of great wealth, and —to judge from her portrait—of even greater beauty, the only child of Charles Compton, seventh Earl of Northampton, and devised a part of her possessions, and the superb mansion of Burlington House (now pulled down) to their fourth son, Charles Compton Cavendish, created Lord Chesham in 1858. The title of Burlington was merged in the same year, when Lord George's grandson, the second Earl, succeeded to the Dukedom of Devonshire.

Grendon : apparently the Graundyn of Leland's list. This spelling gives the name a French aspect ; but there seems no reason to doubt Dugdale's assertion that it was assumed from Grendon in Warwickshire. " Roger de Grendon first took his sirname from thence in King Stephen's time. Which Roger of his Father was originally enfeoft thereof in Henry the First's Time, by Camville, who (it seems) had the first grant of it from the said Henry, or his son." This family was baronial, and lasted till the end of Edward III.'s reign. But it has no claim to be included here.

Gurdon : from the Seigneurie of Gurdon near Cahors, on the border of Perigord : a Gothic race, very early seated in Hampshire. Adam de Gurdon " the King's servant," received from Cœur de Lion half a knight's fee in Selborne and Ostede, and a grant of the lordship of Tisted from his successor. Henry III. gave by charter " free chase. of hares and foxes in and without the forest," to another Adam de Gurdon (the name continued in the family for many descents), who took part with the rebel barons, and was outlawed. " Somewhere between Alton and Farnham, in a wooded dell, not far from the high road which lies a few miles off on our left beyond Long Sutton, was the scene of the fight between Prince Edward and Adam de Gurdon, one of the outlawed followers of Simon de Montfort, who had to shift for themselves as they best might. The Prince, then attending the Parliament at Winchester, heard of the fame of the outlaw, and fired with the desire of measuring swords with so brave a soldier, sought him out among the thickets of his retreat, and challenged him to fight. So nearly were they matched that for some time the fortune of the contest seemed doubtful. In a pause of the fight, the Prince offered Adam his life and advancement, if he would give up his arms. The offer was accepted. Adam was sent that same night under safe escort to the Queen at Guilford. The Prince restored to him his inheritance, and ever after cherished him as his faithful follower."—*Woodward's Hampshire.* On his accession in 1272 the new K'ng accordingly appointed Sir Adam Keeper of Woolner Forest, and we subsequently find him a great landowner in Somerset, Dorset, Sussex, and Cambridge. His residence was in Hampshire, at a house called The Temple, that overlooked the forest. He was three times married. By his first wife he had no children ; by the second two sons ; and by the third a daughter, Joan, the wife of Richard Achard, to whom he bequeathed Selborne * and his Hampshire property. Her two brothers were, it is said, passed over on account of their mother's misconduct (the pedigree declares she was divorced), and virtually disinherited. Of the elder, who removed into Wiltshire, there is no further account ; but the second, Robert, settled in London, where he died in 1343, and his son engaged in trade. Eighth in descent from him was John Gurdon, Sheriff of Suffolk in 1585, who married Amy Brampton, the heiress of Letton in Norfolk, which from that time forth has been the seat of the family. A younger branch is seated at

* This estate still bears the name of Gurdon Manor, and now belongs to Magdalen College, Oxford.

Assington in Suffolk. They bear *Sable* three leopards' faces, jessant fleurs de lis *Or*.

The Scottish Gordons have no connection with this house, as (according to Douglas) they derive their name from Gordon in Berwickshire, granted about 1130 to a family of Anglo-Norman origin. Nevertheless, there is a curious coincidence in the Christian names as well as the surname; for in the time of Edward I. we find Sir Adam de Gordoun, "a knight of great renown," among the last to resist the bond of fealty and submission to the English King, although his estates lay close to the Border. The arms are entirely different.

Gines, or Guisnes, probably derived from the town of Guisnes, near Calais, and of very early occurrence in England. We find in the *Liber Niger* that Richard de Guinnes held eleven fees of Earl Patric in Wiltshire, William de Giñs three fees of the Honour of Clare in Suffolk, and Ralph de Guines one fee of Earl Alberic de Vere in Essex. In Norfolk, "the family of De Gisneto, Gisne, or Gyney, was enfeoffed of Haverland soon after the Conquest. Sir William and Roger lived in the time of Henry II. They remained Lords of Haverland till Edward Gisnes sold it 20 Hen. V. William de Gyney founded Mountjoy Priory in the reign of Richard I."—*Blomfield's Norfolk*. One of these Guisnes married Joan, the sister and co-heir of Peter de Peleville, Lord of Bodney, who died 56 Hen. III. Another, Sir John—the last of whom I can find mention—bequeathed the manors of Dilham and Pauncefotes in 1413 to Sir Henry Inglos, K. G. They bore Paly of six, *Or* and *Gules*, a chief *Ermine*.

But these Norfolk squires were far from being the principal representatives of the name. It belonged to one of the illustrious houses of history, the Counts of Guisnes, ancestors of the famous De Coucys, one of whom, during the minority of Louis XI., refused an offer of the Crown of France, adopting the proud *devise* which he handed down to his posterity—

> "Ne suys ny Roy, ny Prince aussi,
> Je suys le Seigneur de Coucy."

Alberic de Vere, the first Earl of Oxford, bore the title of Earl of Guisnes in right of his wife Beatrice; and Ralph de Guisnes, who in 1165 was his tenant in Essex, was probably one of her kinsmen. Ingelram de Guisnes, a witness of Ivo Tailbois' charter to Cockersand Abbey in Lancashire, may, both from his Christian name and some similarity in the coat of arms borne by the Gynes or Geines of that county, be presumed to have been another. In the reign of King John, Arnold Count of Guisnes (who had succeeded the childless Countess Beatrice) held twelve knight's fees in Kent, Essex, and Bedfordshire, which formed part of the Honour of Boulogne, and "had the reputation of a Baron of this Realm." To these estates his son and heir Baldwin succeeded in 1218 : and another son, Robert de Guisnes, held the Honour of Cioches in Northamptonshire, and in 1248 sold the whole of his English inheritance to Ingelram Lord Fiennes. He had married Amicia de Clare, the widowed Countess of Devon, with the King's consent, in the previous year.

Contemporary with these two brothers was "a noble Baron of France," Ingelram de Guisnes or de Coucy, "how related to these before-mentioned," Dugdale "cannot say;" whose son and namesake made a great English alliance. He married Christian, the only child of William de Lindsay (one of the heirs of William de Lancaster) by his wife Ada, sister and coheir of John Baliol, sometime King of Scotland. He did homage for her lands in 1282; followed Edward I., as his liegeman, three times to the Scottish wars, and was summoned to parliament by him in 1295. His eldest son William died s. p., and the second, Ingelram III., was the husband of an Archduchess of Austria, and the father of Ingelram IV., Count of Soissons, created Earl of Bedford in 1366. This was not the first mark of favour, and by no means the greatest, that he had received from Edward III., to whom, as a powerful noble of acknowledged ability, he had been of signal service from the beginning of the peace with France. So highly did the King esteem him, that he not only bestowed upon him all the lands and lordships in Yorkshire, Lancashire, Cumberland, and Westmorland, that had been William de Coucy's, and on his death, for "certain reasons" (not specified) had come to the Crown, but gave him his daughter Isabel in marriage, with a yearly grant of one thousand marks for her maintenance. Furthermore, when he took his bride over to France in 1365, the King decreed that all the children born to them beyond sea should enjoy their inheritance in the realm as freely as if they had been English-born. The year following, he, with the Dukes of Bourbon and Burgundy, attended the King of France at the festive reception given to Lionel Duke of Clarence as he passed through Paris on his way to his ill-starred wedding at Milan. His next visit to France was in 1372, when he came as an enemy in his father-in-law's train; and he was there once again in 1377. He died in 1397, having survived Isabel Plantagenet, by whom he left two daughters his co-heiresses. Mary, the eldest, was. the wife of Henri de Barr, Seigneur d'Oisy; and Philippa, the second, married Richard II.'s notorious favourite, the Duke of Ireland, and was divorced by her unworthy husband to make room for a low-born Portuguese with whom he had fallen in love. Mary alone left children, and through her descendant, Mary of Luxemburg, the great-grandmother of Henry IV., the representation of the House of Coucy was vested in the Bourbons, and descended to the Comte de Chambord, the last heir of the elder line.

Griuil, or Greville, from the castle of that name in the Côtentin. "There is another Greville or Graville, in Normandy, but this is the original habitat." [*]

---

[*] "Some people believe Greville and Graville to be the same; but their perplexity would be at an end if they knew that there is a parish of Greville in Normandy, and would remember that Graville was the Seigneurie of Malet, who bore no surname."— *M. de Gerville.* There is no vestige of a castle at Greville.

—*Sir Francis Palgrave.* This cannot be intended for the·existing family of Greville, Earls of Warwick, who would appear to be a branch of the Grenvilles. Dugdale speaks of their name as "Greyvill or Greynvil (for both ways it is written)," and the arms of Greville are those of Grenville with the tinctures changed and a border added for a difference. They were seated at Drayton in Oxfordshire (the adjoining county to Bucks) which Leland calls "the veri ancient house of the Gravilles": and their ancestor, "John Greville (or Grenville) appears to be the same who is mentioned by Collins as of Wotton in 1308, and whose father John, son of John de Grenville, was living in 1305. There can be little doubt that the present branch sprang from the Grenvilles at about this date, both from the arms and the recurrence of the same contemporary Christian names."—*The Norman People.* Once only have I succeeded in meeting with a Greville who did not bear the cross and roundels of the Grenvilles. This was Sir Adam de Greyville, whose daughter and heir, Elizabeth, married Sir Humphery Stafford of Hooke, one of the retinue of the Black Prince. His coat was *Argent*, six lionels rampant *Gules*, three, two, and one; armed *Azure*. But in this case even, it may have been adopted through some previous intermarriage with an heiress. The name is spelt "Gravale" in the *Rotuli Curiæ Regis* of 1194–99; and "Grovil"·in Poulson's *History of Holderness.* In the former case I believe it refers to a different family; for I find in Robson's *British Herald* that Gravell or Gravill bore *Gules* three buckles *Or*, and Grauell *Argent* a lion rampant *Azure* crowned *Or* a chief *Gules*.

Greneuile : from ˌGrenneville in the Côtentin, a fief of the Barons of St. Denis-le-Gaste : "not to be confounded with Granville, and unquestionably," says Sir Francis Palgrave, "the cradle of the Grenvilles." * The name continued to be written Grenville until the Earls ˙of Bath, in the seventeenth century, adopted the form of Granville. In Dugdale's Baronage it is given "Grenevil;" and without adducing a shred of evidence, he proceeds to derive the family from Hamon Dentatus Earl of Corboil, "lineally descended from the Warlike Rollo." The "Norman People" furnishes them with a different ancestor : "Meurdrac, a Scandinavian Viking, who was seated at St. Denis le Gaste c. 930. It is believed that the families of Meurdrac, Trailly, Grenville, Beauchamp, and Montagu, whose ˙arms were·closely related, and whose fiefs formed part of the barony of St. Denis, were of the same origin." There was clearly a close connection between the Grenvilles and the Giffards ; for William de Grenville, with Robert his son, witnessed Walter Giffard's charter to Bolbec Abbey in 1061 (Neustria Pia, 402) ;

---

* "The late Marquess of Buckingham," writes M. de Gerville, in his *Anciens Châteaux de la Manche,* "used often to visit the ecclesiastics residing at Winchester Castle" (during the first French Revolution), "and constantly spoke to them of the Norman origin of his family, regretting that *son curé de Grenneville* was not among· them. He was well acquainted with the site of the old castle, and described it accurately."

and the latter, who accompanied the Conqueror, received of the said Walter three knights' fees in his county of Buckingham. Robert's son, Richard de Grenville, married Isabel Giffard, the second daughter and eventual co-heir of this same Earl of Buckingham. Her elder sister, Rohais, was the wife of Richard de Bienfaite, Lord of Clare and Tonbridge ; and Richard de Grenville, very soon after the Conquest, was enfeoffed by his brother-in-law of three and a-half knight's fees at Bideford in Devonshire, where he took up his residence. His descendants continued to hold of the De Clares, and adopted the three clarions of their suzerains in lieu of the cross, charged with five roundels, that had been their original coat, and is still borne by the Duke of Buckingham and Chandos, the last remaining Grenville.[*] In the time of William Rufus, Richard de Grenville went with Robert Fitz Hamon to the conquest of Glamorgan, and was one of his " Douze Peres," among whom the territory was divided. " But our bounteous and noble-minded knight, having Neath in Glamorgan allotted to his part, builded there a monastery dedicated to the Virgin Mary, gave all his conquered lands to the perpetual maintenance thereof, and returned back again to his house here at Bideford."—*Westcote's Devon.* Dugdale says that he settled in the course of the same reign at Kilkhampton in Cornwall, which is believed to have belonged to the Grenvilles from the time of the Conquest, and is at all events mentioned in a *quo warranto* roll of Henry II. as having at that time been long in the family. Here, for many successive generations, they dwelt in their old manor-house of Stowe, ever true to its kindly motto—

"An open door and a greeting hand :"

in honour and renown, and are still remembered to the present day. Here, too, the first Lord Bath built "by far the noblest house in the West of England," which was pulled down soon after the death of his grandson in 1711, and its contents dispersed. " It used to be said that almost every gentleman's seat in Cornwall had received embellishments from Stowe. The cedar wainscot, which had been brought out of a Spanish prize, and used by the Earl of Bath in fitting up a chapel in this mansion, was purchased by Lord Cobham at the time of its demolition (the house being then sold piece-meal), and applied to the same purpose at Stowe, the magnificent seat of the Grenvilles in Buckinghamshire."— *Gilbert's Cornwall.*

There would appear also to have been a Somersetshire branch, for Sir Thomas Grenville was of that county temp. Henry II., and gave his name to his manor of Grenevyleswick.

---

[*] " These clarions, organ-rests, or sufflues, as they have been variously called, were a rebus of the De Clares, Earls of Gloucester, and probably their badge. The earliest example of them is to be found on the seal and encaustic tiles of Neath Abbey, Glamorgan."—*The Norman People.*

Two of the Grenvilles are memorable in their country's annals—Queen Elizabeth's gallant Admiral, Sir Richard, and his chivalrous grandson, Sir Bevill. Sir Richard was one of the daring and dauntless spirits that have made the navy of England what it is, and won for her triumphant flag the dominion of the seas. To him strife and adventure were as the breath of his nostrils, and danger the fairest mistress that ever lover wooed and won. A born sea-farer, thirsting for fresh fields of enterprise and eager for the fray, he was ill at ease on shore, and spent most of his years on active service.

> "Home is very calm—
> But Honour rides upon the crested wave."

He was the kinsman and companion of Sir Walter Raleigh; had carried out his earliest colonists to Virginia; and was entrusted with the defence of Cornwall on the approach of the Armada. He lost his life in the crowning exploit of his career, the famous sea-fight in the Azores, "admirable even beyond credit and to the very height of some heroical fable," that has been nobly sung by Tennyson. In 1591, he commanded the Revenge in the English squadron under Lord Thomas Howard, then lying off Flores, when a fleet of fifty-three Spanish ships of war was reported to be bearing down upon them. The English had only six sail of the line, all told: and Lord Thomas, seeing the hopeless disproportion of his forces, weighed anchor and put to sea. But Sir Richard Grenville, who had ninety of his men sick on shore, swore that he would not leave them to "the thumb-screw and the stake" of the Spaniard, and refused to follow till they were all safe on board. Being "last to weigh, he lost his wind: whereupon some of his officers advised him to cut his main sail and cast about, and trust to the sailing of his ship, as the Spanish squadron had already got on his weather-bow. This Sir Richard peremptorily refused, saying, ' He would much rather die than leave such a mark of dishonour on himself, his country, and the Queen's ship.'" The little Revenge carried no more than one hundred fighters, and they knew they could only fight to die, but they cheered his brave words, and steered straight into the enemy's fleet. Several of their ships he forced to luff, and fall under his lee: but at three o'clock of the sultry tropical afternoon the conflict began in bitter earnest. The Spanish Admiral, in his huge sea-castle, the San Felipe, "principall of the twelve sea-apostles, that carried three tiers of ordnance on each side," took the wind out of his sails and immediately boarded, no doubt counting on a speedy surrender. He had to learn that the Englishmen were of far other mettle; for the San Felipe, "having receiv'd the lower tier of the Revenge, discharged with cross-bow shafts, shifted herself with all diligence from her side, utterly disliking her entertainment." Then four more heavily armed vessels, two on the starboard, and two on the larboard, closed in round the devoted English ship. But she met her assailants undismayed, and fought them as they came, one with the other, hour after hour, till the day turned to night, and the night again to day, shaking them off

> "As a dog that shakes his ears
> When he leaps from the water to the land.
> And the sun went down, and the stars came out far over the summer sea,
> But never a moment ceased the fight of the one and the fifty-three:
> Ship after ship, the whole night long, their high-built galleons came;
> Ship after ship, the whole night long, with her battle-thunder and flame;
> Ship after ship, the whole night long, drew back with her dead and her shame;
> For some were sunk, and many were shattered, and so could fight no more—
> God of battles! was ever a battle like this in the world before?"

By daybreak the next morning, Sir Richard had repulsed the enemy no less than fifteen times, two of their vessels had gone down alongside, two more had taken refuge on shore in a sinking state, and little more than a hulk was left of the gallant Revenge. She had endured, according to Raleigh's computation, "eight hundred shot of great artillery, besides many assaults and entries;" her masts were shot overboard, and her rigging cut to pieces: "nothing left overhead either for flight or defence:" she had six feet of water in her hold, and "resembled a slaughter-house rather than a ship." Two-thirds of her crew were dead or disabled. Sir Richard had been hit early in the action, but kept the deck notwithstanding till eleven at night, when he received a shot in the body, and was carried down to have his wound dressed. While this was being done, he received another dangerous wound in the head, and the surgeon was killed by his side. The battle only ended when the English wanted powder, and their pikes were all broken: then "Sir Richard exhorted his men to yield themselves to the mercy of Heaven rather than to the Spaniard, and gave orders to his gunner, a resolute and bold fellow, to split and sink the ship." The other officers, however, interposed, locked the master gunner into his cabin, and made terms with the enemy, surrendering the blood-stained ship that had kept the whole Spanish fleet at bay, and the wounded lion, who only survived his capture three days. His last words were spoken in Spanish: "Here die I, Richard Grenville, with a joyful and quiet mind, for that I have ended my life as a true soldier ought to do, fighting for his country, Queen, religion, and honour: my soul willingly departing from this my body, leaving behind the lasting fame of having behaved as a valiant soldier is in duty bound to do." Even his enemies mourned him; and John Evelyn, recording the action, cries out, "Than this, what have we more? What can be greater?"

Sir Bevill, the "Bayard of England," was not unworthy of such an ancestor. "Where," asks Martin Llewellyn

> "shall the next fam'd Grenvill's ashes stand?
> Thy grandsire fills the sea, and thou the land."

"A brighter courage and a gentler disposition," says Clarendon, "were never married together." When the troubles of the great Civil War began, he raised a troop of horse at his own expense. "I cannot," he wrote to Sir John Trelawny, "contain myself within my doors when the King of England's standard waves in the field upon such just occasion. The cause being such as must make all that die in it martyrs. And for my own part I desire to acquire an honest name or an honourable grave." Both his prayers were granted. He was one of the boldest and most successful of the Cavalier leaders, triumphantly cleared his own county of rebels, and led his stout Cornishmen from victory to victory, till he fell in his last and most brilliant field at Lansdowne Hill.* His intrepidity alone assured the wavering fortunes of the day. When the rebels seemed to be carrying all before them—

> "Grenville stood,
> And with himself oppos'd and check'd the flood.
> His courage work'd like flame, cast heat about,
> Here, there, on this, on that side, none gave out.
> Not any pike in that renowned stand
> But took new force from his inspiring hand;
> Soldier encourag'd soldier, man urged man,
> And he urged all, so far example can.
> Hurt upon hurt, wound upon wound, did call,
> He was the butt, the mark, the aim of all."

It was at the third charge of the enemy's troopers that "his horse failing and giving ground, he received, after other wounds, a blow on the head from a pole-axe, with which he fell." His loss would have clouded any victory.

He left a large family—six daughters and seven sons. The eldest, Sir John, was not more than sixteen when he took his father's place in the command of his regiment, and fought in all the considerable battles of the West of England. He was afterwards one of the negotiators of the Restoration, and in acknowledgment of his own and his family's services, created Earl of Bath, Viscount Lansdowne, and Baron Granville of Bideford and Kilkhampton in 1661. His son Charles, who served under Sobieski at the siege of Vienna, and was made a Count of the Holy Roman Empire by the Emperor Leopold, only bore the title for a few days, being killed by the accidental discharge of a pistol while the

---

* "In 1643, a little band of Cornishmen gathered round the chivalrous Sir Bevill Grenville, 'so destitute of provisions that the best officers had but a biscuit a day,' and with only a handful of powder for the whole force: but, starving and outnumbered as they were, they scaled the steep rise of Stratton Hill, sword in hand, and drove Stamford back on Exeter with a loss of 2,000 men, his ordnance and baggage train. Essex despatched a picked force under Sir William Waller to check their advance: but Somerset was already lost ere he reached Bath, and the Cornishmen stormed his strong position at Lansdowne Hill in the teeth of his guns."—*Green's History of the English People.*

preparations for his father's funeral were going on, in August 1701. The third and last Earl died of the small-pox ten years later, unmarried : and the inheritance reverted to three aunts, Lady Jane, married to Sir William Leveson Gower (ancestor of the Duke of Sutherland) : Lady Catherine, married to Craven Peyton : and Lady Grace, married to Lord Carteret, who was created Countess Granville in her own right in 1714. This title has been revived in our own time in favour of a descendant of Lady Jane's, Lord Granville Leveson Gower.

A brother of the second Earl of Bath's had been created Lord Granville of Petheridge by Queen Anne in 1702, but died childless ; and a similar failure attended a second peerage, granted a few years afterwards. Bernard, third surviving son of the renowned Sir Bevill, who was a mere child when he lost his father, and ran away from school to join his brother John in the defence of the Scilly Isles, had been very active in the King's service at home and abroad, and received an appointment in the Royal household after the Restoration. His son George became in 1712 Baron Lansdowne. But the title expired with him in 1734, for he left only daughters behind him ; and the last heir male of this famous Cornish house was his nephew Bernard, who, dying unmarried in 1775, bequeathed his property to the son of his sister Anne, John D'Ewes, thenceforward known as John Granville. His other sister was Queen Charlotte's favourite, Mrs. Delany.

But the lineage of the Grenvilles was far from having died out in its original *habitat.* They had never removed from Buckinghamshire, but were still seated at Wotton, one of the manors dependent on the great Honour of Giffard, of which their ancestor had been enfeoffed at the Conquest. They descended from a brother of the Richard de Grenville who sought and found his fortune in the West; an elder brother, it may fairly be assumed, holding this fief as the head of the family. Gerard de Grenville, his brother Robert, and Ralph de Grenville, all appear in various charters of the time of Henry II. One of these, witnessed by Gerard, is a grant by his suzerain Walter III., Earl of Buckingham, of the tithes of Wotton, and several other places in the county, to the Cluniac Abbey, founded by his father at Newton-Longueville. To this day—seven hundred years and more after that grant was made—"there are tythes at Wotton called Longeville tythes."—*Collins.* Gerard is mentioned in the Pipe Rolls of 1130 and 1158, and held three fees *de veteri feoffamento* of the Honour of Giffard in 1165.—*Liber Niger.* The next in succession, Eustace, "in 32 Hen. II. gave 100 marks to obtain the lands that were Gerard de Grenville's, his uncle, then in the hands of the King, which debt was not discharged till 2 Ric. I."—*Collins.* He was Constable of the Town and Seneschal to King John in 1214, and did homage as a baron in 1230, having married the daughter and co-heir of Robert Arsic, Baron of Coges (Roberts, Excerpt. i. 193). His line terminated with his great-grandson, and the progenitor of the present family was his uncle Richard

From this Richard fifteen descents, in unbroken succession, are counted to another Richard Grenville of Wotton, born in 1677, who married Hester Temple, the heiress of Stowe. This auspicious match first inaugurated the brilliant political career of the Grenvilles, who, till then plain Buckinghamshire squires, rapidly rose to be a power in the State. " A writer of our own day has computed that, within the space of fifty years, three First Lords of the Treasury, three Secretaries of State, two Keepers of the Privy Seal, and four First Lords of the Admiralty were appointed from among the sons and grandsons of the first Countess Temple."—*Earl Stanhope's History of England.*

Hester Temple represented an illustrious Saxon house. Her father, Sir Richard Temple of Stowe,* bore the black eagle of Mercia by right of descent from Earl Leofric himself (the same Leofric who, as the story goes, "set Coventry toll-free" for the love of Godiva †); and her only surviving brother being childless, obtained, when he was created Viscount Cobham in 1718, a remainder to her and her heirs male. Accordingly, at his death in 1749, the title, as well as the great Buckinghamshire estate, devolved upon her, and, in the following month, she was created Countess Temple. She had then been for many years a widow, and died in 1752, leaving one daughter and four of her seven sons surviving: 1. Richard, Earl Temple ; 2. George, of whom presently; 3. James, whose son of the same name was created Baron Glastonbury in 1797, but died s. p. ; and 4. Henry, Governor of Barbadoes and Ambassador to the Porte, who left an only child, Louisa, the wife of Charles, third Earl Stanhope. Their sister Lady Hester, Baroness Chatham in 1761, will ever be held in honoured remembrance as the wife and mother of two of England's greatest statesmen. She was the youngest of the family, and married William Pitt in 1754, "a marriage which, while securing his domestic happiness, strengthened his political connexion."— *Ibid.*

The eldest son, Richard, second Earl, a man of considerable ability, who was a prominent member of Pitt's great administration, left no children ; and the inheritance passed to the son of his next brother George, the well-known minister of George III. George Grenville had early entered political life under the auspices of his uncle, Lord Cobham, and successively passed through the different gradations of office till he became First Lord of the Treasury in 1763. He was,

---

* Sir Richard's grandmother, Dame Hester Temple, was the mother of four sons and nine daughters, who all married but one, and multiplied so exceedingly that she lived to see—and she is believed to be the only woman on record that ever did so— 700 of her descendants !

† This familiar legend is stigmatized by Freeman as a disgrace to English history. The town of Coventry, we are now told, was not then in existence : there was only a *vill* so named, chosen by Earl Leofric and his wife, as the site of their projected monastery ; and Godiva stripped herself, not actually of her clothes, but allegorically of all her earthly possessions, for its endowment.

however, "virtually no more than a tool of Bute's and the King's:" and his name is unhappily associated with the ill-starred Stamp Act that led to the American war. He married Elizabeth Wyndham (a grand-daughter of the Percy heiress), who brought him, besides four daughters, three sons, who all took a prominent part in political life: 1. George, third Earl Temple; 2. Thomas, an eminent classical scholar, and most accomplished and amiable man, who, having attained the great age of ninety-one, is still affectionately remembered by a few surviving friends and relations; and 3. William Wyndham, created Lord Grenville in 1790, the distinguished statesman who, after being Mr. Pitt's principal colleague, was himself named Premier when, on the death of the great minister, "All the Talents" came into office in 1806. This was the last post he would ever accept under the Crown; and he ended his life in complete retirement among the beautiful gardens and groves he had planted at Dropmore. His wife Anne, the sister and heir of Lord Camelford, lived to be the last survivor of all who had borne the illustrious name of Pitt. She died in extreme old age in 1864.

George, third Earl Temple, married the daughter and heir of Robert Earl Nugent, whose Irish Earldom he received in 1776; and his wife was created Baroness Nugent in 1800, with remainder to their second son, Lord George, who bore the title for thirty-six years, but died s. p. in 1848. Lord Temple had further sought to obtain a Dukedom; but only succeeded in becoming Marquess of Buckingham in 1784. His son Richard was more fortunate. He, too, had married an heiress, and a far greater one than his mother had been, for his wife was Lady Anna Eliza Brydges, daughter and sole heir of the last Duke of Chandos, by which alliance the Grenvilles became the representatives of Mary, Duchess of Suffolk, the youngest sister of Henry VIII., and added two more to their already numerous patronymics. The Marquess thenceforward bore the names of Temple-Nugent-Brydges-Chandos-Grenville, and the long-coveted Dukedom fell to his share in 1822, when he was created Duke of Buckingham and Chandos. At the same date, he received not only the Marquessate of Chandos, but a fresh grant of the Earldom of Temple of Stowe, with remainder (failing heirs male) to his grand-daughter, Lady Anna, afterwards married to William Gore Langton, of Newton Park, Somerset. These last additions made up the astounding sum of eleven different titles of honour granted to the descendants of Hester Countess Temple within seventy years of her death. But not long after they had reached the culminating point of their prosperity, the scales slowly began to turn, and the shadow of a boding cloud to appear on the horizon. There had been profuse expenditure, and there were soon formidable debts. The vast and continually enlarged palace of Stowe, with its 500 acres of pleasure ground and their galaxy of emblematical temples; the splendid household and grand receptions—especially a most magnificent entertainment given to the exiled King of France—and, above all, the enormous election expenses, had already obliged the first Duke to practise economy by going abroad, and the second Duke completed his ruin by reckless purchases of land upon borrowed money. Then came the still-remembered catastrophe, with the great sale at Stowe, and the dispersion of all its far-famed collections. The young Marquess of Chandos, disdaining to take advantage of the entail, nobly relinquished to his father's creditors the greater part of his inheritance. Since his accession to the Dukedom, he has in some measure retrieved the disaster, and Stowe is once more tenanted by the descendant of its ancient lords, now their last living representative in the male line.

Glateuile. The only hypothesis I can form of this name is, that the second letter is wrong, and that, as in the case of Grancy (vide *Gracy*) an *n* has been left out. This gives us Granteville or Grenteville; and Thurold de Grenteville appears on the Dives Roll as one of the Conqueror's companions. According to the *Monasticon*, William de Granteville held land near Skelton in Yorkshire, and Hawise de Grenteville gave one bovate at Skelton, and a toft at Wyhill to the Knights Hospitallers of St. John of Jerusalem.

They derived their name from Granville, in the arrondissement of Mont St. Michel. "Those," writes M. de Gerville, "who have undertaken to speak of this family, have perceived no difference between the names of *Magnavilla* and *De Grandisvilla*, and yet the difference is a very real one. Nor should the Granvilles be confounded with the Grennevilles from the other end of La Manche, as has been done by the most accredited Peerages of Great Britain, in assigning to both a common origin.

"In the chartulary of Mont St. Michel, we find, on a deed of 1054, the signature of Duke William and Rainald de Grandevilla; and the following charter bears that of William de Grandevilla. Roger de Grandivilla, about 1180, was one of the knights of Mont St. Michel. Sir Thomas de Granville, in 1252, owned the site on which the castle of Granville was afterwards built, and his fief, named the fief of Lihou, passed through Jeanne de Granville to the family of Argouges." In 1440, Lord Scales, then Seneschal of Normandy, bought of Jean d'Argouges the rock and mountain of Granville *pour un chapel de roses vermeilles*, and erected the great fortress that was to hold in check the hostile garrison of Mont St. Michel, at the same time removing and re-building the town in its present position.

Gurney: a duplicate.

Giffard. Three brothers of this name, Walter, Berenger, and Osberne, are entered in Domesday as holding English baronies from the time of the Conquest. Walter, the eldest, who received as many as 107 manors in different counties, had his largest domain in Buckinghamshire, and was Earl of that county; Berenger held the barony of Fonthill, called from him Fonthill-Giffard, in Wilts; and Osberne that of Brimsfield in Gloucestershire. They were the sons of Osberne, Baron of Bolbec, who descended from Avelina, one of the sisters of

Gunnor Duchess of Normandy,* and thus the kinsmen of their sovereign, " both
owning a common ancestor in the forester of Equiqueville, the father of Gunnor
and her sisters." The name—one of the greatest written in the records of the
Conquest—is certainly not territorial, and as a *sobriquet* has been variously and
ingeniously interpreted. The reading of " Liberal" or " Free-Giver" seems
merely to rest on an atrocious mis-spelling of Giffard, and is inadmissible from
its being English—a tongue wholly unknown to the Normans.† In M. Métivier's
new ' Dictionnaire Franco-Normand,' there is a better-grounded explanation.
" Giffair; rire comme un joufflou; Giffe, Giffle, Joue. Telle est l'origine de
l'illustre famille Normande de Giffard." Giffarde signified fat-cheeked, and was
so commonly applied to women employed in the kitchen, that it became a usual
term for a cook or a scullery wench. Thus, Ducange gives "Giffardus," rendered *ancilla coquina;* and in Roquefort's ' Dictionnaire de la langue Romane,'
we find " Giffarde : Joufloue, qui a de grosses joues—servante de cuisine." But
it is not conceivable that such a nickname should have been given to a powerful
noble of the blood royal of Normandy. " Giffle," in Romance, also means
soufflet (blow on the cheek), and it is more likely the Giffards earned their name
by their reputation as hard hitters.

Walter Giffard, as Count of Longueville and Baron of Bolbec, held a great fief
in Normandy, and contributed thirty ships and one hundred men to the Duke's
expedition ; himself commanding his contingent at Hastings. It was not for the
first time that he invaded England. More than thirty years before, he had
come over with King Ethelred's son Edward, when, after the death of Canute,
he made his ill-starred attempt to recover the crown. Since that time, he had
gained the reputation of a famous soldier; had fought amongst the foremost
at Mortemer, commanded at the siege of Arques, and been entrusted with the
defence of the frontier district of Caux (which included his own Comté of
Longueville) against Henry King of France. He next went on a pilgrimage
to the shrine of St. Jago de Compostella, combined, it may well be, with a
private mission to Don Alfonso of Galicia, whom William afterwards affianced
to his daughter Agatha. From thence he brought back to the Duke the
beautiful Spanish charger that he rode at Hastings—the first of the three
horses that day killed under him, and " the gift of a King that had a great
friendship for him." When William was fully armed, and ready to mount,
Walter Giffard himself led out this highly prized horse ; and when Ralph de
Toeni had claimed quittance of his service as hereditary gonfanonier of
Normandy, it was to him the Duke first offered this post of honour. " Then,"
says Wace, " the Duke called to him Galtier Giffart. ' Do thou take · this

* William de Jumièges calls her their mother, but as her sister Gunnor was the
great-grandmother of the Conqueror, this seems a chronological impossibility.

† " The Normans knew not what the English said ; their language seemed like
the barking of dogs, which they could not understand."—*Wace.*

gonfanon,' said he, 'and bear it in the battle.' But Galtier Giffart answered: 'Sire, for God's mercy look at my white and bald head; my strength has fallen away, and my breath become shorter. The standard should be borne by one who can endure long labour. I shall be in the battle, and you have no man who will serve you more truly; I will strike with my sword till it is dyed in your enemies' blood.'

"Then the Duke said fiercely, 'By the splendour of God! my lord, I think you mean to betray and fail me in this great need.' 'Sire,' said Giffart, 'not so! We have done no treason, nor do I refuse from any felony towards you; but I have to lead a great chivalry, both soldiers' (soldéiers, mercenaries) 'and the men of my fief. Never had I such good means of serving you as now; and if God please, I will serve you; if need be, I will die for you, and give my own heart for yours.'

"'By my faith,' quoth the Duke, 'I always loved thee, and now I love thee more; if I survive this day, thou shalt be the better for it all thy days.'" On both sides was this pledge most faithfully redeemed. When, during the battle, Giffard was struck down in the *mêlée*, he was rescued by the Duke himself; and when the day was won, and the Conqueror, after kneeling down on the field to give thanks to God, was unbuckling his armour and preparing for rest, his old comrade was still watchful for his safety. He had ordered his tent to be pitched by his gonfanon, where the English standard had stood, and the struggle had been fiercest; and his supper to be served—a dark picture of the savage temper of the times—amid the heaps of slain that cumbered the ground; when, "behold, up galloped Galtier Giffart. 'Sire,' said he, 'what are you about? you are surely not fitly placed here among the dead. Many an Englishman lies bloody and mingled with the dead, but yet sound or only wounded, tarrying of his own accord, and meaning to rise at night and escape in the darkness. They would delight to take their revenge; and would sell their lives dearly; none of them caring who killed him, if he but slew a Norman first. You should lodge elsewhere, and let a careful watch be set this night, for we know not what snares may be laid for us. You have made a noble day of it, but I like to see the end of the work.' 'Giffart,' said the Duke, 'I thank God we have done well hitherto; and if such be God's will, we will go on and do well henceforward. Let us trust God for all.'"—*Ibid.*

Walter Giffard survived that memorable day by nearly twenty years, dying about the time that the compilation of Domesday, for which he had been appointed one of the Commissioners, was brought to a close. In 1079 he had founded the Priory of St. Michel de Bolbec in Normandy. He left at least two sons and two daughters; Walter, his successor; William, who was Chancellor to William Rufus, and afterwards Bishop of Winchester: Rohais, the wife of Richard de Clare, and the great-grandmother of the renowned Earl Strongbow, and Isabel, married to Richard de Grenville.

Walter, the eldest son, having been confounded with his father by Dugdale and others, is generally considered to have received, rather than inherited, the Earldom granted by the Conqueror. But of this there is no evidence. "I can," says Mr. Planché, "find no ground whatever for the ordinary assertion that this second Walter, and not his father, was the first Earl of Buckingham."—*The Conqueror and his Companions.* There is no mention of him in England, but he was actively employed in Rufus' service in Normandy, where he fortified his castles against Robert Court-heuse. He died in 1103, and was buried in the church of an Abbey that he had founded for Cluniac monks at Longueville, leaving a son of his own name, who proved the last heir male. Walter III., a stout soldier in Henry I.'s French wars, died s. p. in 1164, having in his latter years founded Nutley Abbey in his park at Crendon, Bucks. His great barony of ninety-six knights' fees passed to the representatives of his aunt Rohais, Richard de Clare, Earl of Hertford, and William Mareschal, Earl of Pembroke.

But if Walter Giffard's Earldom was short lived, the posterity of his two brothers was numerous and enduring. Osberne had, as I have said, his *caput baroniæ* at Brimsfield, where the castle he built remained till 1322, when it was destroyed by Edward II.'s soldiers; but for more than one hundred years before that time, the head of the honour had been transferred to Winterborne-Giffard, in Wilts. His son Helias was the father of another Helias, who became a monk of St. Peter's Abbey at Gloucester, and of Gilbert, ancestor of the Giffards of Chillington. "To Helias II. succeeded Helias III., who in 1165 held nine knights' fees, and gave one hundred marks fine for livery of his inheritance. His successor was Thomas Giffard, who had lived in the time of Richard I., and was father of another Helias, who joined with the rebel barons against King John, and thus lost many of his estates."—*Collinson's Somerset.* The next heir, Sir John, a baron by writ in 1295, successfully recouped himself by the abduction of a wealthy widow. In 1270, Maude, Countess of Salisbury (the heiress of Walter de Clifford and his wife the Welsh Princess Margaret), wrote to complain to the King that she had been forcibly carried off by Sir John Giffard to his castle at Brimsfield, and was there detained against her will. He received a summons to appear before the King, but it came too late for the poor prisoner; as, though he denied the charge of violence; he admitted that he had married the Countess, and only paid the usual fine for having dispensed with the King's consent. This unfortunate heiress was the mother of two daughters, Katherine, Lady Audley, and Alianor, Lady Strange, who eventually became his representatives; for, though he married two other wives, and had a son by the last, the second Lord Giffard left no children. He had joined the Earl of Lancaster in his revolt against the tyranny of the Despencers, and was hanged for high treason at Gloucester in 1322.

The descendants of Osberne Giffard's younger grandson, Gilbert, are still to be found in Staffordshire. Gilbert's son William first adopted the present bearing of the house, *Azure*, three stirrups *Or*, in lieu of the arms of the Earls of Buckingham, *Gules*, three lions passant in pale *Argent*, that were borne by his elder brother.* Peter, the next heir, who went to Ireland with his kinsman Earl Strongbow, and received for his services the grant of an Irish manor, first acquired the present seat of the family.

"Giffard of Staffordshire cam to Landes by this meanes.

"The Lord Corpessun that was Founder of Studley Abbay in Warwickeshire, and that had a fair Maner Place half a Myle thens gave a Lordship of his yn Stafordshire, caullid Chillingtoun, in Frank Mariage with the one of his Doughtters to one of the Giffardes. After one of the Doughters and Heirs of Whitston of Whightston a Knight in Staffordshire was maried to one of the Giffardes; and of late tyme one of the Doughters of Montgomery of Careswell was maried to young Giffard Heire of Chillingtoun."—*Leland.* The son of this "young heire" received a visit from Queen Elizabeth at Chillington. In the following century, another Peter Giffard lived to witness both the downfall and restoration of his house. As a zealous loyalist, who had garrisoned Chillington for the King, he had been thrown into prison, and his estates put up for sale by the Drury House Commissioners. Several of his kinsfolk were with Charles II. at the fatal field of Worcester; and one of these—his nephew Charles—was among the few gentlemen that remained with the King after the battle, when, closely pressed by Cromwell's troopers, he was, in pursuance of Lord Derby's advice, endeavouring to reach Boscobel. They lost their way in the night on Kinfare Heath, and young Giffard, taking the place of their bewildered guide, conducted the King in safety to the appointed place. Boscobel then belonged to the Giffards, and was inhabited by one of their dependants, a poor wood cutter, named William Penderel. It was a solitary house, standing in a tract of the ancient Forest of Brewood; and had a cunningly contrived secret chamber, into which many a Jesuit priest—for the Penderels, like their masters, were staunch Catholics—and distressed Cavalier had crept during the Civil War. Lord Derby knew the place from having himself taken refuge there during a hot pursuit. But the King dared not linger under any roof; for a troop of rebel horse was quartered in the neighbourhood, and no time was to be lost. Dismissing his attendants, he disguised himself in a coarse suit, cutting off his hair, and blackening his hands against the chimney, and followed William Penderel into the inner fastnesses of the forest, while Penderel's brother Richard acted as scout. "The heavens wept bitterly at these calamities;" no dry place was to be found among the dripping trees; and Richard went to borrow a blanket from his sister-in-law, and folded it for the King to sit on. The good woman also brought him a mess of milk and eggs. When night fell, Richard

* Their motto, "Prenez haleine et tirez fort" (addressed to an archer) connects these stirrups with the cross-bow or arbalest, "which had what is called a stirrup at the end of the stock, into which the foot was put in stretching it."—*Planché.*

guided him towards the Severn, hoping that they might be able to cross into Wales, but they found all the fords and passes strictly guarded, and after a weary tramp, returned to Boscobel at three in the morning. As the day dawned, the King discerned another fugitive descending from an oak-tree, who proved to be one of his own officers, Captain Carless, a Staffordshire gentleman who had served under Lord Loughborough. He persuaded the King to climb up into his hiding-place, telling him the wood would be searched in all directions as soon as it was fully light; and there, ensconced together within its friendly boughs, they spent the entire day. The troopers passed and re-passed on their vain quest below; their voices sounded close at hand; but the King, who had not slept for two nights, "slumbered away some part of the time" with his head resting on the trusty Captain's lap. When the search ended after dark, he was permitted to remove to the house; and the good wife brought him a piece of bread and a pot of buttermilk—all she had to offer, which he thought "the best food he had ever eaten." He remained for several days under the charge of the honest Penderels, who, at the greatest personal risk, harboured and guarded him with a devotion and fidelity that have been rarely equalled and never surpassed. Boscobel House, "the scene of such romance, heroism and loyalty," though much altered, is still standing; and a hole in the garret, reached by a ladder through a trap door, is shown as the King's hiding-place.

Old Peter Giffard lived to see the wandering fugitive again on the throne, and to receive from him a grant of his estreated possessions. He died, "full of days," three years after the Restoration.

The third Domesday Baron, Berenger, Lord of Fonthill-Giffard, Wilts, has left his name to two other manors in the county, Morris-Giffard, and Ashton-Giffard. His son Osbern occurs in Devon 1130; a second Osbern held fiefs there in 1165; and another descendant, Andrew, in the time of King John, resigned his Wiltshire barony to Robert Mandeville. See *Hoare's Wilts.* Thenceforward the family solely belonged to the county of Devon, and divided into several branches; one seated at Buckton, which terminated in 1372; one at Brightlegh, one at Tiverton, and one at Weare-Giffard, where their old manor house remains. Compton-Giffard, Aveton-Giffard, &c., still bear their name. They changed their arms, as their kinsmen of Chillington had done, adopting *Sable* three fusils in fesse *Ermine;* and like them, were zealous loyalists. One of the Giffards of Brightlegh, who was "decimated, sequestrated and imprisoned" during the Rebellion, "brought great reputation," says Prince, "to the Royal cause in these parts where he lived;" for "such was his deportment towards men in all his actions, as if he were conscious the eye of God was upon him." According to Sir Bernard Burke, this branch is still represented at Kilcorral, in Ireland. Lord Chief Justice Giffard, who was raised to the peerage in 1824, was a Devonshire man, born at Exeter, and took the title of Lord Giffard of St. Leonard's in his native county. Nevertheless, he bore, as his grandson now bears, the golden stirrups of Chillington with the addition of a chevron and border.

The Giffards were a widely spread family. In the time of Henry VIII., Leland enumerates two more branches besides those I have mentioned. "There be at this tyme 4 notable Housis of the Giffardes; one in Devonshire, a nother yn Hamptonshire, the thirde yn Staffordshire, the fourth in Buckinghamshire." And he incidentally alludes to a fifth. "Ther was one of the Giffardes of Shropeshire Companion to Syr Robert Knolles in the Batelles of Fraunce that was a Waster of his Lande." In Essex, Sir John Giffard of Giffard's Hall, who died in 1348, the last heir male, gave his name to Bower's Giffard. The Giffards of Burstall in Leicestershire (also extinct) received a baronetcy in 1660. I also find Norton Giffard in Gloucestershire.

Two of this race, Hugh and William Giffard, came into Scotland temp. David I. The latter was probably the "Brother William Giffard" of the monastery of Dunfermline, who witnessed one of the Scottish king's charters to the monks of May. Hugh had a considerable grant of lands in East Lothian, and his son further received from William the Lion in 1174 the barony of Yester. Another Hugh was one of the Regents of the Kingdom appointed by the treaty of Roxburghe in 1255, and died in 1267. He was popularly believed to be a wizard, and "must," as Sir David Dalrymple quaintly conjectures, "have been either a very wise man, or a great oppressor." In his castle at Yester there was a capacious cavern, called in the country Bo-Hall (Hobgoblin Hall) that was attributed to magical art :—

> To hew the living rock profound,
> The floor to pave, the arch to round,
> There never toil'd a mortal arm—
> It all was wrought by word and charm :
> And I have heard my grandsire say
> That the wild clamour and affray
> Of these dread artizans of hell
> Who labour'd under Hugo's spell,
> Sounded as loud as ocean's war
> Among the caverns of Dunbar.

" A stair of twenty-four steps (now fallen in) led down to this large and spacious hall, which hath an arched roof, and is still as firm and entire as if it had only stood a few years. From the floor of this hall, another stair of thirty-six steps leads down to a pit which hath a communication with Hopes-water." Sir Walter Scott makes this the scene of "The Host's Tale" in Marmion, where Alexander II., anxious to learn his fate, visits and consults the wizard knight, and is sent out to an enchanted encampment at midnight, where he breaks a lance with " an elfin foe, in guise of his worst enemy." A traditional curse still clings to the old castle, and it was noted by the country people, that the heir of the last

Marquess of Tweeddale received the hurt of which he died while superintending some repairs that were going on there.

The last male heir of the Giffords—also Hugh—founded the collegiate church of Botham, or Yester, and died in 1409, leaving four co-heiresses. The eldest of these, Joan, brought the barony to her husband, Sir William Hay. The village of Gifford, about four miles from Haddington, retains the name, and gives their title to the eldest sons of the house of Tweeddale.

Gouerges, or Guierche. Geoffroi de la Guierche is on the Dives Roll, and appears as a great landowner in Domesday, under the Anglicized form of Geoffrey Wirce, or Lawirce. " He was a young Breton of rank, who probably had a command in the contingent of Alan Fergaunt, Count of Brittany. His name was derived from the seigneury of 'La Guerche,' a town near Rennes, on the borders of Brittany, called so from an ancient chapel of 'la guerche' (Gallic for La Vierge, the Virgin, or Our Lady). There is an account of the seigneurs of this place and Pouencé (which they also held) in the rare work of Père du Paz (' Hist. Généalogique de plusieurs Maisons illustres de Bretagne') : from which we learn that Geoffrey was son of Silvester, lord of those places, Chancellor of Brittany, who, becoming a churchman after his wife's death, was in 1075 consecrated Bishop of Rennes, and died such in 1096. When he entered the church, his son and heir, Geoffrey, succeeded to his estates."—*A. S. Ellis.*

Long before this date, however, Geoffrey had been established in the barony he had won by his sword at the Conquest—a very considerable one. He obtained Medelton (Melton Mowbray) and twenty-six other manors in Leicestershire, twelve in Warwickshire, the entire Isle of Axholme, with the manors of Gainsborough, Somerby, and Blyborough, in Lincolnshire, and Adlingfleet in Yorkshire. At the time of the Survey he had also the custody of Count Alberic's Warwickshire land. His principal residence is believed to have been at Melton, where he had a market. He was a benefactor to Selby Abbey, and St. Mary's, York ; and " bestowed no mean share of his lands and tithes on the monastery of St. Nicholas at Angiers, particularly the church of Kirkby in Warwickshire, which, being decayed, he had re-built in honour of the Holy Virgin and St. Denys. The monks then established a priory or cell there, and the place is still known as Monk's Kirby."—*Ibid.* One of these charters makes it clear that he had no family ; as the grant is made " for his own soul, Alueve his wife's, and his friends" omitting all mention of children. " He was back in Brittany in 1093, for, as ' Galfridus de Guirchiâ,' we find him witnessing a deed of ' Hervey, son of Goranton' (Lobineau, Hist. Bretagne, vol. ii. 217a), and died soon after, for next year his heir founded the Priory at Pouencé. Whether he left England of his own accord, or was banished for implication in the rebellion in favour of Duke Robert, does not appear : but certain it is in the next reign Nigel de Albini was in possession of all his lands, except Adlingfleet (which Lovetot got), and confirmed his predecessor's grant to Selby Abbey."—*Ibid.* The heir who succeeded him as Lord of La Guerche and Pouencé was Walter, surnamed Hay. "Walter had a son Geoffrey, but his daughter Emma inherited these two places, and her descendants adopted the name of La Guerche, and bore *Gules* three leopards passant *Or*, which may have been the coat of the old stock."—*Ibid.* A Josbert de la Guircht is mentioned at Dover in 1189–90 (Rotul. Pip.).

Gamages. " The castle and *vill* of Gamaches* were situated in the Norman Vexin, and gave name to a Deanery in the Archdiocese of Rouen. Godfrey de Gamaches, who doubtless derived his name from this *vill*, inherited two knight's fees of old feoffment in the Honour of Lacy. The English interests of his family were therefore established before the reign of Henry I."—*Eyton's Salop.* This Godfrey received from Henry II. a grant of Stottesden in Shropshire, where his posterity remained seated till about 1254, when the line terminated in co-heiresses. He also obtained Marshall, in the same county, by grant of Richard I., and died before 1176. His second son, William, inherited Mansel-Gamage, Herefordshire, Gamage Hall in Dimock, and other lands in Gloucester-shire, and was Constable of Ludlow. From him descended Sir Pain de Gamages, Lord of Rogiad in Monmouthshire, and Sir Robert, of the same place, whose eldest son, Sir William, Sheriff of Gloucester in 1325, married Assar, daughter of Sir Pain de Turberville (fourth of the name) of Coyty Castle, Glamorgan. When the heir of the last Turberville was murdered by his wife in 1412, this Sir William's grandson and namesake succeeded to Coyty, and his posterity held it for about one hundred and seventy years. The line ended with John Gamage, whose only daughter Barbara was a beauty as well as an heiress. She had no lack of suitors ; but the Earl of Pembroke, at that time "the most influential man in North Wales," succeeded in obtaining her hand for his brother-in-law, Sir Robert Sidney, afterwards Earl of Leicester. They were married in 1584, at her guardian Sir Edward Stradley's house in Wales. Two hours after the ceremony, there arrived an imperious mandate from Sir Walter Raleigh to Sir Edward, desiring, in the Queen's name, "that you suffer not my kinswoman to be bought and sold in Wales without Her Majesty's privilege to the consent, and advice of my Lord Chamberlain and myselfe, her father's cozen-Germayne, considering she hath not any nearer kyn nor better." But the knot was already tied; and though Lord Burghley threatened legal action, the young couple remained unmolested. She was the grandmother of Algernon Sidney ; and "Gamage's Bower" is still shown in Penshurst Park.

"One of the daughters of this house of Gamages married Sir Richard de la Bere, of Weobley and Molton in Gower, who received for services at Cressy 'five ostriches feathers issuing from a ducal coronet' as his crest. Another married Lord Howard of Effingham, and was the mother of Queen Elizabeth's famous

* The Lords of Gamaches in the French Vexin were said to be descended from Protadius, Mayor of the Palace to Theodoric, King of Orleans, 604 (Des Bois)."— *The Norman People.*

Lord Admiral. Some of the family migrated to America with their kinsman Lord Effingham, when he was Governor of Virginia, and are still represented there. The house in which they lived at Cambridge is yet called Gamage's House."—Nichols' *Counties and County Families of Wales.*

Haunteny: in Leland's list, Hauteyn. Godwin Haldein held in Norfolk in 1086 (Domesday). Blomefield contends that this is a Danish name, but it appears as Alden in the Norman Exchequer Rolls of 1180–95. He had held his lordship of Gratyngton in the time of Edward the Confessor, and was not only permitted to retain it, but received a grant of three other manors at the Conquest. "How he came to be in such favour and to merit so much from the Conqueror, is not known; it is, however, worthy of remark and notice, that if he was an English Saxon, he is the only one I have yet found in Norfolk that was allowed to keep his land at the Conquest, and held it at the Survey."—*Blomefield.* Two Hauteyns are mentioned in the time of Henry II.; both resident in the parish of Haylesdon: Walter, who held two fees of the Honour of Clare; and Theobald, who gave his name to Hauteyn's Manor, which, together with Oxnead, he had obtained through his wife Agnes, daughter of Albert de Greslei. She re-married an Amundeville, and in 1183 held Hauteyn's Manor in dower; John, the eldest of her three sons, being then a minor in the King's custody. He died s. p., but from one or other of his brothers descended Sir Hamo de Hauteyn, a man of some note and importance in the county under Henry III. He was "one of the justices appointed to look after the Jews' affairs; and there was a mandate to the barons of the realm to deliver to them the keys of the chest of the Jews, with the rolls, &c. belonging to that office"; from which, however, he was suspended for "certain misdemeanours" in 1228. In 1218 he claimed "frank pledge, free warren, gallows, and assize of bread and beer" at Oxnead; and in 1226 was summoned to meet the King in Parliament at Shrewsbury. He afterwards sided with the barons, and lost his estate, which was granted to Patrick de Chaworth; but it was given back to him in 1268, when Sir Bartholomew de Hauteyn (perhaps his brother?) likewise recovered his lands, forfeited for the same cause to Ernisius de Stuteville. Sir Hamo served as Sheriff of Norfolk in 1258. His son Sir John, who held two knight's fees of Humphrey de Bohun, Earl of Essex, is "said to have incurred the displeasure of Edward I., and to have paid a fine of £569 6s. 8d. This Sir John was probably the same person who was receiver of the King's customs of wool, and citizen of London in 1322, and sealed with *Argent* a bend *Sable.* Some of the Hauteyns sealed with Bendy of 8, *Argent* and *Sable.*"—*Ibid.* The next heir, William, conveyed Oxnead to his brother John, rector of Oxnead, "who with his feoffees sold it to Sir Richard de Salle, Henry Hauteyn, another brother, and Jeffrey de Smalbergh, his brother-in-law releasing their rights." In 1368 Sir Robert accordingly entered into possession, "but was much disturbed in suits about it," another younger brother who had not been consulted, with his two sons (one of them "a professed fryar at Blackeney")

II. K

and a grand-daughter, each in their turn suing for the estate. In the end the priest carried the day, but not till seventy-five years afterwards, unless—as seems most likely—Blomefield has made an error in his dates. He says that "in 1443, John Hauteyn, then a Carmelite friar at Blakeney, had license from Pope Eugenius (on proving that, before he was fourteen years of age, his parents forced him to enter among the fryers and become a religious) to leave his house, habit, and Order, and proceeding in his claim, recovered his inheritance." This is all I can find respecting the Hauteyns in Norfolk.

In Yorkshire, Peter Halden held one knight's fee, temp. Henry III. "pro Warda Castri de Richmond."—*Gale's Richmondshire.* Stephen Hauteyn was summoned from Holderness for military service 4 Ed. III.: and John Hautayn of Ald-Ravensor, was among those rated in Aid for Knighting the Black Prince in 1346.—*Poulson's Holderness.*

The Heraldic Visitation of Oxfordshire of 1634 (printed in Vol. 5 of the Harleian Society's publications) contains a pedigree of five generations of the Hawtayn or Hawten family. The name, now Hawtin, is still to be found in and near Banbury.

Haunsard: Barons of Evenwood, in the county of Durham. Hutchinson commences their pedigree with Sir Gilbert Haunsard, or Hansard, whose grandson, Gilbert 2, was one of the most powerful barons of the Palatinate about the middle of the twelfth century, and a benefactor to Kepyer Hospital. He married a sister of Robert Fitz Maldred Lord of Raby, the ancestor of the Nevills, who brought him as her portion the lordship of Walworth, in that neighbourhood, which thenceforward became the seat of the family. Their new home in the rich and beautiful valley of the Tees must have formed a happy contrast to the bleak and wind-swept moorland they had hitherto inhabited, called in an old rhyme

" Evenwood,
Where straight tree never stood."

In the following century—about 1279—they parted with it altogether, John Hansard conveying it to Bishop Beke, and receiving the manor of Werkensale in exchange. As late as Bishop Hatfield's Survey, however, we find Thomas Hansard still "held the barony tofts, rendering three arrows." They subsequently acquired by marriage South Kelsey in Lincolnshire, and came to an end temp. Henry VIII., when " Cardinal Wolsey granted the wardship of Elizabeth, the heiress of the last William Hansard, to Sir William Ayscough" (or Aske) " who married her to his own son, Sir Francis." A younger branch, seated at Whittingham in Suffolk, died out a little later in the same century.

One of these Barons of Evenwood is mentioned at Carlaverock :

" Robert de Hamsart tout apresté
I vi venir, o bele gent,
Rouge o trois estoiles de argent,
Tenant le escu par les enarmes."

This Robert is believed to have been the son of Sir John Haunsard mentioned in the time of Anthony Beke, and who held a manor at Caterham, in Surrey, about 1275.—*Manning's Surrey.* "Dominus Gilb. Hansard" occurs in Lincolnshire about the same date.—*Rotuli Hundredorum.* Camden calls the Hansards "a very eminent family in this County."

In Scotland, "Johan de Haunsard, probably of the Haunsards of England," performed homage to Ed. I. at Berwick-upon-Tweed in 1296.—*Ragman Rolls,* p. 126.

Hastings. Sir Egerton Brydges pronounces this name to be inadmissible, as "of palpable local English origin." Further on in the list we come to that borne by the family in Normandy—De Venoix; but Robert, the founder of the English house, certainly did not use it at the date of Domesday. He is there styled either *Marescallus* or De Hastings, as the first Norman Port-reeve of that town; and I shall therefore treat of this famous lineage under the name by which it has been always known; reserving some account of the descendants of his younger brother for *Venoix.* "The Barons of Venoix, near Caen, held their fief as hereditary Marshalls of the Stable (Masters of the Horse) whence they bore the name of 'Le Mareschal,' or 'Mareschal of Venoix'" (*Mémoires de la Société des Antiquaires de Normandie,* xii. 15). Milo le Mareschal, born probably about 980, and Lescelina his wife, were living 1050, when the Duchess Matilda purchased lands at Vaucelles from them for Holy Trinity, Caen.—(*Ibid.*) He had issue Ralph le Mareschal and other sons, who came to England 1066. Ralph was living 1086; and had 1. Robert; 2. Roger le Mareschal, who, 1086, held lands in Essex; 3. Gerold, owner of estates in Suffolk, 1086; 4. Gosfried, owner of estates in Hants and Wilts, 1086, father of Gilbert, ancestor of the Mareschals, Earls of Pembroke.

"Robert, the elder son, is sometimes styled Fitz Ralph, elsewhere 'De Hastings,' and 'Le Mareschal' (Domesd. 17, 73, 74 b. 160 b.; Essex, 107 b.). He was Lord of Venoix, and was the King's viscount or seneschal at Hastings, where and at Rye his descendants long held the revenues in farm from the Crown. He had William de Hastings, who, c. 1100, married Juliana, granddaughter and heir of Waleran, a great baron of Essex, and was living 1130 (Rot. Pip.) He, with Robert de Venoix his brother, instituted a suit against his cousin Gilbert Mareschal and his son to recover the office of hereditary marshal, which Gilbert, or perhaps Goisfrid, his father, had obtained to the prejudice of the elder line. The suit failed, but in compensation William de Hastings was created Dapifer."—*The Norman People.* With this William, Steward to Henry I., who held Ashele in Norfolk by the service of taking charge of the "Naperie" (or table-cloths and linen) at the King's coronation, Dugdale commences the pedigree. His grandson and namesake was the father of 1. William, ancestor of the Earls of Pembroke; and 2. Thomas, ancestor of the Earls of Huntingdon.

The elder line was carried on by William's son Henry, who made the first of

K 2

the successive Royal alliances by which it was illustrated. He married a niece of William the Lion, King of Scotland, Ada, the daughter of David Earl of Huntingdon, through whose two elder sisters the Scottish crown was conveyed to Edward Baliol and Robert Bruce. Their mother Maud, the sister and coheir of Ralph Earl of Chester, had brought that Earldom to her only son, John le Scot; and on his death in 1237, the whole of this great inheritance was divided between Ada and her sisters. The next Henry de Hastings joined the rebel barons, and was knighted by Montfort's own hand on the field of Lewes. "No man," says Dugdale, "was more active against the King than he;" and after the rout of Evesham, he shut himself up in Kenilworth Castle, and held it for six whole months against the victorious army. The King's messenger, inviting him to surrender "with gracious Offers, he most inhumanly maimed; not being at all daunted with the sentence of Ottobon, the Pope's Legate, then there, and thundred out against him; nor all the Power wherewith he was begirt." At last he had to yield on honourable terms; but as a punishment for his obstinate bravery was excluded from the benefits of the *Dictum*, and condemned to seven years' imprisonment, though the sentence was only partially carried out. His son Henry, whose wife, Eve de Cantilupe, bought him the castle and honour of Bergavenny, was summoned to parliament in 1268, and was the father of John de Hastings, who followed Edward I. in all his campaigns, and was one of the claimants for the crown of Scotland in 1290. He is called on the roll of Carlaverock "the most intimate and best beloved of all those the King had there; reckless and daring in the field, but gentle and debonnair in the hall." * He was named Lieutenant of Acquitaine in the following year, and in 1305 received as his guerdon the entire county of Menteith, with the Isles, forfeited by its Scottish Earl. He had first married a near kinswoman of the King's, Isabel de Valence, daughter of William de Valence or de Lusignan, Earl of Pembroke, the halfbrother of Henry III.; † and when her brother Aymer de Valence was murdered in France in 1323, she became one of the famous " Pembroke heiresses." She was the second of them; but her elder sister Anne had no children; thus the succession centred on her and the third daughter Joan Comyn; and her grand-

---

*   "... Il estoit
Li plus privez, li plus amez
De kanques il en i avoit.
E voir bien estre le devoit;
Car conneus estoit de touz
An fair des armes feris e estous,
En ostel douz e debonnaires;
Ne onques ne fu justice en aires
Plus volentris de droit jugier."

† Through his mother, Isabel of Angoulême, King John's widow, who re-married Hugh de Lusignan, Count de la Marche.

son Lawrence de Hastings was declared Earl of Pembroke in her right in 1339. Lord Hastings had a second wife—another Isabel, the daughter of Hugh Earl of Winchester (the elder of the two favourite Despensers) : and his eldest son by her, Sir Hugh, of Gressing Hall in Norfolk, was the grandfather of another Hugh, summoned to parliament as Lord Hastings of Gressing in 1342.

A curse was believed to rest on all the lineage of Aymer de Valence, who had sat in judgment on his cousin Thomas Plantagenet, Earl of Lancaster, at Pontefract, and condemned him to die unheard ; and his own violent death, two years after, was held to be a retribution for this "mercenary and time-serving act of infamy." But the fatality did not end with him; for " it was observ'd, that after that Judgment so given, none of the succeeding Earls of Pembroke ever saw his Father, nor any Father of them took delight in seeing his Child." Family tradition accordingly asserts that both the second and third Earls of this house were posthumous children ; but it is impossible to reconcile this statement with the dates, though I have diligently endeavoured to do so. Lawrence, the first who bore the title, was bred up in the soldier-court of Edward III. ; followed him to the wars with a princely train, and died early in life (though not in battle) leaving an only son of about a year old. This second Earl was a singularly unfortunate man. He began his career brilliantly by marrying the King's daughter, Lady Margaret Plantagenet ; and when she left him a childless widower, paid 1000 golden florins to the Pope for dispensation to espouse her cousin in the third and fourth degree, Anne, the heiress of the renowned Sir Walter de Manny. In 1372, he was named Lieutenant of Acquitaine, and went, with a great force, to the relief of Rochelle, then beleaguered by the French; but " was attended," says Dugdale, " with very unhappy success. For no sooner was he got with his Ships into that Haven, but the Spanish Fleet fell suddenly upon him, before he could put his Men in Order to fight ; so that few of them escaped Death, Wounds, or Imprisonment: and the Enemy forthwith set fire on all the English Ships, carrying away this Earl, with many other gallant Men, with no less than 20,000 Marks in Money, sent over by King Edward to maintain the War." After this dire catastrophe, he underwent four years' imprisonment in Spain, with "most inhuman Usage;" and when he was at length released, died on his way home—probably from its evil effects, but as was currently believed, of a slow poison administered by the Spaniards. His little son—at that time not five years old—who succeeded in 1376 as third Earl of Pembroke, was judged too young to carry the Golden Spurs at the coronation of Richard II. in the following year, according to his hereditary right. But he was not too young to be married ; for his deputy on that occasion was his father-in-law : his wife being a young princess of the House of York, Philippa de Mortimer, the daughter of Edmund Earl of March and his wife Philippa Plantagenet. He was a youth of excellent promise; " of so Noble a Disposition, that in Bountie and Courtesie he exceeded most of his Degree :" but he died in his boyhood, the last of his doomed race ; and men discerned in his untimely fate the working of "the curse that weighed upon the blood of Aymer de Valence." In 1389, "the King keeping his Christmass at Woodstock, and there holding a Tournament, he (being then but seventeen years of age) adventured to Tilt with Sir John de St. John ;" and by an unlucky slip of Sir John's lance, he was run through the body, and killed on the spot. He was an only child, without any near relative ; and his heirs were declared to be Reginald Lord Grey de Ruthyn (descended from Elizabeth, daughter of John, third Lord Hastings, and the Valence heiress) in the whole blood ; and Edward Hastings (descended from her half-brother Sir Hugh) in the half blood. But the father of this last Earl " did so little regard his next Heir male, and so much dislike Reginald Grey (Father to this last Reginald) that he Entail'd the Castle and honour of Bergavenny, and the greatest part of his Lands upon William de Beauchamp (his Mother's Sister's Son) provided he should bear his Arms, and endeavour to obtain the Title of Earl of Pembroke." Thus little was left for the heirs to claim, beyond the right to bear the arms of Hastings, *Or*, a Maunch *Gules;* but this they held in such high esteem, that they con-tended for it during little less than twenty years in the Court Military, before the Constable and Marshal of England. Edward Hastings' right to his paternal coat seemed indisputable ; but so powerful was the house of Grey, that in the end it was adjudged to Reginald, and he was not only condemned to pay nearly £1000 costs (then a very great sum) but imprisoned for sixteen years for disobeying the sentence. This was hard measure, but there was more yet to come. He questioned Beauchamp's right to the estates ; and " Beauchamp invited his Learned Counsel to his House in Pater-noster-row ; and after Dinner, coming out of his Chappel, in an angry mood, threw to each of them a Piece of Gold, and said, ' Sirs, I desire you forthwith to tell me, whether I have any Right or Title to Hastings' Lordships and Lands ?' Whereupon William Pinchebek stood up (the rest being silent, fearing that he suspected them) and said, ' No man here, nor in England, dare say, that you have any Right in them, except Hastings do quit his Claim therein ; and should he do it, being now under Age, it would be of no validite.' Perhaps," continued Dugdale, "there had been some former Entail, to settle them upon the heir male of the Family : But what-ever it was, Hastings apprehended the Injury thereby done him, to be so great, that with extreme anguish of mind, at his latter end, he left God's curse, and his own, upon his Descendants, if they did not attempt the Vindication thereof." This injunction they certainly left unfulfilled ; nor did they ever attempt to take the titles of Lord Hastings and Stoteville, which, though never summoned to parliament, he had chosen to assume. The last of them, Sir Francis Hastings, died about the time of Elizabeth, and his estates went among his four sisters. But in 1841 the ancient barony was called out of abeyance in favour of Sir Jacob Astley, who traced his descent from one of them ; and his grandson, counting up all the intervening heirs and heiresses, is now styled the twelfth Baron Hastings, though the title has been actually borne by no more than five of them.

The kindred house of Huntingdon is derived from Thomas de Hastings (see p. 131), whose son Hugh married a Yorkshire heiress, and settled at Allerstan in the North Riding. Towards the middle of the fourteenth century his posterity migrated to Kirby in Leicestershire, which Sir Ralph Hastings had acquired through his wife Margaret de Herle. They were zealous Yorkists throughout the Wars of the Roses; and when Ed. IV. came to the throne, no man was more honoured and rewarded for "his good and faithful service" to the King and the King's father than was Sir William Hastings. He was literally loaded with the estates of the attainted Lancastrians, the honours of Peverel, Boloin, Hagenet, and Huntingdon, the lands of Viscount Beaumont, Belvoir Castle, with a great part of the possessions of Lord Ros, Ashby-de-la-Zouch, which had been the Earl of Wiltshire's, and the Castle and Rape of Hastings, all falling to his share; and was summoned to parliament as Lord Hastings-de-la-Zouch in 1461. Nor were the offices of trust that he held less numerous or less important; he was twice Captain of Calais, once Ambassador to France, Chamberlain of North Wales, Keeper of several of the King's forests and Constable of six of his castles, with many other preferments too numerous to detail. Two Barons, nine knights, fifty-eight esquires, and twenty gentlemen were retained by indenture to serve him in peace and war. He commenced a magnificent castle at Ashby, and unroofed and dismantled Belvoir Castle and Stoke Daubeney (another house of the Lord Ros) to furnish lead and materials for his building. As Lord Chamberlain, he was in constant attendance on the King, and according to Comines (who knew him well), "in great authority with his master, and not without cause, having ever served him faithfully." Yet he was the pensioner both of the Duke of Burgundy and the King of France, receiving from the latter (besides a present of plate to the value of 10,000 marks) a yearly income of 2000 crowns, for which he refused to give either receipt or acknowledgment, saying, "Put it here" (being in Gold) "into my Sleeve: for no Man shall say, that King Edward's Lord Chamberlain hath been Pensioner to the French King; nor that my Acquittances be found in his Chamber of Accompts."

But with the death of the King came the sudden collapse of his greatness. The new Protector, Richard Duke of Gloucester, found this powerful baron a stumbling-block in his path, and resolved to get rid of him. So craftily did he conceal his purpose, that Hastings, when summoned to attend a council at the Tower, followed Sir Thomas Howard thither without suspicion; and being in a merry mood, stopped to chat with his pursuivant and a priest whom he met on the way, telling them the good news that his old enemies, Rivers and Vaughan, were that day to be beheaded at Pomfret. "I pray you come on," quoth Sir Thomas, who was in the secret of his impending doom: "wherefore talk you so long with a priest?" adding ominously, "You have no need of a priest as yet." Hastings entered the council chamber without a shadow of foreboding; in the full confidence that he was on the most friendly and familiar terms with the Protector. Then followed the scene of violence and reproaches so admirably dramatized by Shakespeare, which was to prepare the way for his arrest as a traitor. The Protector seized him with his own hand, crying, "Make speed, and shrive him apace; for by St. Paul, I will not dine till I see his head off!" "It booted him not," adds the chronicler, "to ask why; but taking a priest at a venture, he made a short shrift, for no longer would be suffered, the Protector made so much haste to his dinner;" and was then led out to the Tower green, and beheaded on a log of wood that lay there for the rebuilding of the chapel.

He had married the sister of the King Maker, Katherine Nevill, daughter of Richard Earl of Salisbury, and widow of Lord Bonville and Harrington; and their son Edward had been summoned to parliament the year before his father's execution as Lord Hungerford; one of the four baronies brought to him by his wife, Mary, the sole heir of Walter, last Baron Hungerford, Botreaux, Molins, and Moels. The attainder was reversed and his lands restored on the accession of Henry VII.; and George, the next heir, who was with Henry VIII. at the taking of Therouenne and Tournay in 1512, was created Earl of Huntingdon in 1529. He was the first of ten Earls of the name that followed each other in uneventful succession up to the end of the last century. The second Earl and his brother Thomas married two sisters, Mary and Winifred Pole, the daughters and coheirs of Henry Lord Montacute, eldest son of the unhappy Margaret, Countess of Salisbury, who, after the execution of her brother, the last male Plantagenet, became his sole heiress and representative, and herself perished on the scaffold. Winifred, the wife of the younger brother, had no children by him, and married again; but Mary, Countess of Huntingdon, was the mother of a large family, and has transmitted her Plantagenet blood to a considerable number of descendants. Francis, tenth Earl, died in 1790, unmarried, leaving two sisters as his heirs; the younger of these, Lady Selina, also never married; and thus the baronies of Hastings, Hungerford, Molines, Botreaux, &c., devolved upon her elder sister Lady Elizabeth, who was the wife of John Rawdon Earl of Moira. Her son the second Earl was created Marquess of Hastings in 1816; but this title ended with the fourth Marquess in 1868: and the old baronies, again passing in the female line, are now vested in the son of his sister, Edith Countess of Loudoun.

For twenty-eight years after the death of this last Earl, the Earldom remained unclaimed, and was believed to be extinct. At length, in 1817, it was found that the old name had not altogether passed away; for an unsuspected claimant to its honours was brought to light. In August of that year Captain Hans Hastings, a retired naval officer, who was then ordnance store-keeper to the garrison of Enniskillen, was electrified by receiving a letter from a local attorney, named Bell, asking permission to claim for him the Earldom of

Huntingdon. As Mr. Bell was, in the first instance, to take upon himself the entire cost and responsibility of the proceedings, the astounded Captain made no difficulty in sending the required authorization, but added in a postscript, "By all things good, you are mad!" Mr. Bell at once set about collecting information, and procured his first valuable cue through a chance acquaintance he picked up on the road, a talkative old crone who offered him a seat in her market cart, and proved to be a former servant of the Hastings family. He followed it up with indefatigable assiduity; succeeded in making out his case; and within a year and a half had obtained a writ of summons for his client, and triumphantly seated him in the House of Lords. The Captain's great-grandson is the present and fifteenth Earl of Huntingdon.

This junior branch of the house of Hastings bears *Argent* a maunch *Sable* in contradistinction of the elder. It has held three other peerages. A brother of William, first Lord Hastings, married Joan, the sister and heir of the brave Lancastrian commander, Lord Willoughby and Welles; and by the favour of Edward IV. obtained the restoration of her forfeited estates, and a summons to parliament as *Richardo Hastings de Welles, Chl'r*, in 1482: but his only son died before him. Another cadet, Sir Edward, son of the first Earl of Huntingdon, "a very eminent person in the time of Queen Mary," and Lord Chamberlain of her household, was created in 1558 Lord Hastings of Loughborough in Leicestershire, and also left no male heir. His title was revived in 1643, and granted to Henry Hastings, a brother of the sixth Earl, in reward for his gallantry during the Civil War. He died unmarried in 1665.

Hanley: Duchesne gives it Hauley, and Leland, Haulley. This family took its name from La Haulle, in Normandy. Warin de Haulla is mentioned in Somerset, 1154, and 1165 he held a barony of eight fees in Devon (Lib. Nig.). De Aulo or De Halla held St. Lawrence, Stenbury and Yavesland in the Isle of Wight about the same time: several of the name occur.—*Worsly's Isle of Wight.* "The family of De Aula, called also Durandesthorp or Duranthorpe, are described as lords of Donesthorpe during the twelfth, thirteenth, and fourteenth centuries. It is probable they held under the Gresley family."—*Lysons' Derby.* In Worcestershire the name also occurs; and the arms are given by Nash: *Gules*, five Lioncels rampant in cross *Or.* Peter and Ralph de Haulay were of Lincolnshire in the time of Edward I.—*Rotuli Hundredorum.*

Haurell: or Harel. This name is found several times in the Norman Exchequer Rolls of 1180–95; and subsequently appears enrolled among the nobility as Sires de Bretteville. Two Harels, both belonging to the bailiwick of Falaise, took their place in the Church of St. Stephen at Caen in 1789, as members of the *Ordre de la Noblesse* of Normandy. I found this name, in the first instance, in the chartulary of Vale Royal, Cheshire, where Alexander Harel occurs, temp. Hen. III., as a witness, and the mesne-Lord of Bruggestreet, in that county. (Mon. Angl.) William Hurel, in 1166, held land of Havering-Bower, by the serjeancy of keeping the park.—*Morant's Essex*. Either he, or another William Hurel, occurs in Berkshire 1189–90 (Rot. Pip.) John, and Richard Haurel, circa 1272 (Rot. Hundred.) Reginald Hurel represented Canterbury in the Parliament held at Westminster 23 Ed. I. (*Hasted's Kent*) : and Adam Hurel, with Gerarda his wife, are found there in the ensuing reign (*Kent Fines*, 13 Ed. II.). Roger Hurel witnesses the Archbishop of York's charter to Marrick Priory, Yorkshire, in the time of Henry II. v. *Marrick Chartulary*.

Husee, Hoese, or Hussey. Sir Richard Hoare, in his History of Wilts, gives the following pedigree of this family, taken from an ancient MS. said to have been found among the muniments of Glastonbury Abbey. It derives them (in the female line) from Duke Rollo, fantastically described as " un Sarazin " (then probably the generic term for all heathens) " qi vient hors de Denemarche en ffrance."

" Richard le tierce, Duke de Normandie fuist le filz Richard le quinte Duke, q'l Richard avoit issue Robt le sisme Duke et Elene, Countasse Husees. William Bastard fuist le filz Robt, et le septisme Duke de Normandie, et cest William Bastard fuist conquer' d' Englete'. La dite Elene file Richard le quint' Duke et frere Robt le sisme Duke avoit issue Hubert Husee, qi fuist le premer q'vient en Englete' avec le Conquer' soun cosyn germayn, et icestuy Hubert fuist counstable del hoste le Roy William Conquer' et mult ayda et soverayment p'sta en la conquest al Roy soun dit cosyn, et icestuy Hubert le premier engendra William Husee. William engendra William Husee. William engendra Geffrey Husee, q' mult avea, et sovaynement p'fita a soun cosyn Emprice Maude, et a Henry filz Maude en lour querele encountre le Roy Stevene. Geffrey Husee engendra Henry et Hubert Husee, Roy d'Aubegeys, et eisne frere Saintz William le bon moigne, et X autres fils qi totent fuerunt chivalers, prus et errantz en armes. Henry, eisne frere Roy Hubert, engendra James Husee. James engendra Hubert, q' fuist marie a la file le Counte de Warwyk, qi avoit issue James Husee et III autrez filz et II files. James engendra Renaud Husee. Renaud engendra Edmund Husee. Edmund engendra Johane q' fuit mariez a Thomas Hungerford, chivaler, et Maude, q' fuist mariez a Philip de la Mare.

" Icestuy Hubert Husee Roy d'Aubegeys, fuist tre noble chivaler, et vaillant. Icestuy Hubert al temps qil fuist en jeouene chivaler, a une tornament a arne blanc tornea al Roy de Ffraunce et sakka le Roy de Ffraunce hors de son chival ; le graunt feraunt enporta le Roy entre ces bras hors del tornement a son estaundard, et la conq'st se dit Hubert p' covenant p' entre le Roy de Ffraunce, et luy p' devaunt fait le bon cheval le graunt feraunt qi le Roy de Ffraunce fuist montes, et cink mil florenes d'or, et puis icestuy Hubert p' bataille et champestre conquest, et tua le Duke haine de Antioche a Antioche, et illoq 's conquist le goupyl d'or pour quoi il fuist appelle Sr Hubert Husee le goupil. Et puis icestuy Hubert conquist le isle d'Aubegeys s' les Sarazins, et c'y p' g'unt fortz, et g'unt batailles, oue graunte ayde de les vaillantz chivalers ses ffrere, et de soun frere William le bon moigne, le dit Hubert devaunt son departez fuist coronez Roy d'Aubegeys, et plusours auns apres le Roy Hubert vient en Engletere, et oue gunt noblesse p' estre venu en la pais dont il estoit ne, et come fortune luy voudroit mourust en Engletere, et fuist enterez a Baa (Bath); et icestuy Roy Hubert fist mult des autres preves, et quientises en armes dyvers pais passaunt totes altres chivalers en son temps. Et dauntz William, le bon moigne de Glastonbirie, frere a Roy Hubert, fuist fort et vaillant, et de honeste conversacion, et combata al Soudan de Babyloyne corps a corps a un graunt bataille, q' fuist entre eux assiz, et le bon moigne occis le Soudan et les Sarazins ove graunt prees et noumbre de peple fauusement encountre lour pinysse, environnerent le bon moigne, et luy tuerent et martizirent, et les oos de luy p' graunt raunson donez a les Sarazyns de part les freres, et altres del sanke le bon moigne, fuerent emportez a Glastonbiri, et alleq's enterez," &c. &c. &c.

I fear we must admit that the element of romance is predominant in this composition. The Lord Constable of England under the Conqueror was, according to Dugdale, not Hubert Hussey, but Walter, the father of Milo, Earl of Hereford;[*] no daughter of any Earl of Warwick is mentioned as having married a Hussey; nor can I even suggest what island in the Mediterranean is disguised under the name of Aubegeys. The Norman princess Ellen, Countess Hussey, sounds equally apocryphal. But the story of the gallant knight-errant crowned King of an unknown kingdom; and the valiant monk, who fought the Soldan single-handed and slew him; with their ten brave brothers, "all of them knights;" has the true ring of the chivalrous age in which it was written.

"The Husseys came from a place a mile North of Rouen, which is now called 'le Houssel.' La Houssaie is still a common name in Normandy."—*Lower's Sussex.* They certainly date from the time of the Conquest in this country. Gautier Heusé is on the Dives Roll, and was either the same "Walterius Hosatus" who witnessed a charter of John Bishop of Bath in 1106, or his father. In Domesday, William Hosed or Hosatus held Charlcomb, in Somersetshire, of Bath Abbey, as well as other manors in the county: and the first lords of Bath-Eaton were of this family. They had afterwards estates in Wiltshire and in Sussex, where Harting appears to have been their principal residence; though "one of these lords built much at Shockerwicke, in Somersetshire, and the manor from thence was in succeeding times called the manor of Husei's Court."—*Collinson's Somerset.* Standen-Huse retains their name in Wiltshire. Later in the twelfth century, we find two brothers, Henry and Geoffrey, the

---

[*] This Milo of Gloucester had succeeded to the office in the time of Henry I.: and his eldest co-heiress, Margery, conveyed it, with the Earldom of Hereford, to the Bohuns.

sons of Henry de Hoese. Geoffrey was Sheriff of Oxfordshire in 1181, and one of the Justices Itinerant in 1182. He held under Adam de Port in Berkshire, with several manors in Wiltshire, and died in 1200, probably leaving no son, as 1 Ric. I. he had paid a fine of £23 16s. "that he might enjoy his Lands in Peace during his own Life, and dispose of them afterwards to whom he should think fit." The eldest brother, Henry, held four knight's fees at Harting and Chithurst, Sussex; and founded a hospital for lepers at Harting, and Dureford Abbey, also in Sussex, in 1163. Henry his son succeeded in 1214. "After him," says Dugdale, "came another Henry, but not his son;" probably his nephew, who also inherited Geoffrey de Hoese's property, and was the grandfather of Henry de Hoese, who took part in the Barons' War, and "had license to enclose, fortify, and crenellate with a wall of stone and lime, his place of Harting." In the next generation, "Henrico Husee" attended Ed. I. in his wars, and was a baron by writ in 1295. His son succeeded, and died in 1349, leaving a grandson his heir, but "neither he, nor any of his descendants, were ever summoned to parliament." The year before this last baron died, another of the family—but how nearly related we are not told—Roger de Hoese or Husee of Beechworth in Surrey, who also served with distinction in the Scottish wars, had summons as Lord Hoese of Beechworth. This second barony became extinct at his death in 1361. A third followed in 1534, when Sir John Hussey, Chief Butler of England, received the title of Lord Hussey of Sleford. Again we are left in the dark as respects his genealogy. He was the son of Sir William Hussey, Lord Chief Justice of England in 1478, whose coat of arms, with his name "William House" may still be seen in the circular or bay window in Grays' Inn Hall. Lord Hussey had ample estates in Lincolnshire, and built a grand house at Sleford; but forfeited the whole of his possessions after the celebrated Pilgrimage of Grace. "At that time," says Froude, "the nobleman who had to answer for the peace of Lincolnshire was Lord Hussey." At first "he sat still at Sleford: he would give no orders—he would remain passive—waiting to see how events would turn:" and sending messengers to enquire the intentions of the rebels. "He had not the manliness to join the rising—he had not the loyalty to assist in repressing it. He stole away and left the county to its fate." For thus deserting his post, he was tried by his peers, found guilty of high treason, and beheaded at Lincoln in 1537. In his dying confession he declared he "was never traitor, nor of none counsel of treason against his Grace:" but he admitted that he had spoken against the new religion. Three years before when he, Lord Darcy, and Sir Robert Constable "sate at the board, Lord Darcy said, in good sooth I will be none heretic; and so said I, and likewise Sir Robert Constable; for we would die Christian men." Though his children were restored in blood by Elizabeth, neither the estate nor honour were granted to his heir. From one of Lord Hussey's brothers descended the Husseys of Yorkshire; from another Sir Edward Hussey, who received a baronetcy (now extinct) from James I. The arms they bore were not those of the baronial Husseys.

There were many more collateral branches. One of these—claimed by the Glastonbury pedigree as the elder line—ended in the fourteenth century with Reginald Hussey, one of whose daughters became the wife of Philip De La Mare, and the mother of the great De La Mare heiress married to William Paulet, ancestor of the Marquess of Winchester. Another—the Husseys of Shapwick and Tedworth—ended in the seventeenth century. A third was established in Ireland as early as the time of Henry II. About 1171, Sir Hugh Husee there married the daughter of. Theobald Fitz Walter, the first Butler of the kingdom, and obtained large grants in Meath from Hugh de Lacy, whose heiress became his son Walter's wife. From him descended Sir John Husee, one of the King's council, summoned to parliament as Baron of Galtrim in 1374; and, more remotely, James Hussey, the younger son of one of these barons (living in the seventeenth century) and the ancestor of Edward Hussey of Westown, who achieved his fortune in 1743 by marrying the widowed Duchess of Manchester. She was the eldest of the co-heirs of John, Duke of Montague; and on the death of his father-in-law, Edward Hussey assumed the name and arms of Montague, and was created, first Baron Beaulieu in 1762, and then Earl Beaulieu in 1784. The heiress brought him a son and a daughter; but both of them died unmarried; and his brother Richard—the last heir male—who succeeded to Westown, did the same.

Sir Bernard Burke tells us that two branches of the family still continue; the Husseys of Lyme and Marnhull, in Dorset, and the Husseys of Scotney Castle, in Kent.

Hercy, from Héricy, Normandy. "D'Héricy" is included in the Abbé De La Rue's list of the earliest Norman settlers in England. Pillerton Hercy, in Warwickshire, was named from Hugh de Hercy, to whom it was granted by King John. "Gilbert de Waseville possess'd Nether Pillerton in Richard I.'s time, and by committing felony forfeited his whole estate, which the King bestowed upon Hugh de Hercy, who gave for his Armes only a label of five points, and left John his son and heir in ward of Thomas Basset in 13 John. From which John descended John de Hercy (I suppose his grandson) who in 7 Ed. I. held this manor of the Earl of Warwick by the service of one knight's fee, but this John had no issue· as I guesse; for in 35 Ed. I., he settled it after the decease of himself and Lettice his wife upon Thomas Wandak and Alice his wife."—*Dugdale.* Yet the name survived in the neighbouring counties: for Hugo de Hercy was Sheriff of Derby and Notts 15 Ed. III.; Humphrey Hercy 15 Hen. VII., and John Hercy 2 Edward VI. Richard and Robert Hercy, Norfolk; and Hugo and Mauveisin Hercy, Notts; occur in the *Rotuli Hundredorum* of the time of Edward I. This Mauveisin had, in the previous reign, been appointed Constable of Tickhill. A brother of his, named Baldwin is also mentioned. William Hercy of Northampton, 4 Henry V., and his son of the same name, citizen and haberdasher of London, 6 Henry VI., are incidentally alluded to in Bridge's *History of Northamptonshire.*

Herioun; from Heron, near Rouen. "Tihel de Herioun was of Essex, 1086. Odonel Heron, temp. William Rufus, witnessed a charter in Durham (Raine, North Durham, App. 3). In 1165 Alban de Hairun held in Hertford, Richard in Essex, Dru in York, and Jordan in York and Northumberland."— *The Norman People.* In the latter county they were of great note, and held a barony from the time of Henry I., "who enfeoffed them thereof." Sir William de Heron, Governor of the castles of Bamborough, Pickering, and Scarborough, Lord Warden of the Forests North of Trent, and Sheriff of Northumberland for eleven consecutive years under Henry III., married the heiress of Odonel de Ford, and built Ford Castle in 1227. Another Sir William was summoned to parliament by Edward III. in 1371, and was Ambassador to France and Steward of the King's Household, but left no posterity; and his grand-nephew and namesake, "a gallant soldier and eminent diplomatist," who married the heiress of Lord Say, and was a baron by writ in 1404, also d. s. p. The last of the line, Sir William Heron, Sheriff of Northumberland 17 Hen. VIII., was the father of the beautiful Elizabeth, who detained James IV. at Ford, so as to give the Earl of Surrey time and opportunity for advancing towards the Borders with a large army: From its strong position, commanding the bridge over the river Till, the castle had been a constant bone of contention between the English and Scots; and was entirely demolished by the latter in 1385: but its most memorable capture was by King James in 1513, for it thus became for ever associated with "the tale of Flodden, that is written in blood on every Scottish heart." Close beyond

> "the dim-light glen
> Where flows the sullen Till,"

rises the bleak hill side where perished the whole chivalry of Scotland, and the devoted circle of dead nobles was found lying around their dead King, in the same rank and order in which they had guarded him while living. Only less disastrous were the losses sustained by our own Northern counties. The "white harvest" that succeeded Flodden Field—when none but grey-haired men were the reapers—lived in the memory of the people for many a long year; and many an Englishwoman could say, with her Scottish neighbour,

> "Now I ride single in my saddle,
> For the Flowers o' the Forest are a'wede away."

Hutchinson goes so far as to assign to that "sweetest of sweet songs" an English origin.

Sir Walter Scott, who tells the story in "Marmion," asserts that it was Lady Heron, the wife of the Castellan of Ford, whose witcheries cost the Scottish

King so dear. " He saw her for the first time on his march into England, fell desperately in love with her, and was detained at her Border castle while she came and went between the Scottish and English armies, causing the delays that led to the fatal defeat of Flodden. Sir William Heron was at that time a prisoner at Fast Castle in Scotland, having been delivered up by King Henry as an accessory to the slaughter of Sir Robert Kerr of Cessford, Warden of the Middle Marches,* and part of the pretence of Lady Heron's negotiation with King James was the liberty of her husband." But Hutchinson, the historian of the county—a far higher authority—is positive that it was the daughter, and not the mother, that fascinated the King. Nor was she by any means a new acquaintance. "There is a tradition that King James, returning from a visit to Mistress Heron at Ford Castle, found himself in danger of drowning in his passage through the Tweed, near Norham, at the West Ford, which is pretty dead on the Scotch side. Upon which he made a vow to the Virgin Mary, that if she would carry him safe to land, he would erect and dedicate a church to her upon the banks of the Tweed : which he performed in the jubilee year, A.D. 1500, according to an old inscription upon the church, mostly now defaced." The date given—thirteen years before Flodden—would make it a very ancient love-affair, and must be either a mistake or a misprint.

Elizabeth Heron inherited Ford, and married Thomas Carr of Etal. Their granddaughter Mary conveyed it to the Delavals, from whom it passed to the Marquesses of Waterford.

Mackenzie, in his *History of Northumberland*, speaks of a Cuthbert Heron, then (in 1825) living at South Shields, and " a lineal descendant of the famed knightly family of the Herons; but as it cannot be satisfactorily ascertained whether or no an elder brother of his grandfather left issue, the Heralds' College refuse to acknowledge his right to the title, which, however, he continues to receive from courtesy." What title can be here meant? surely neither of the two baronies by writ; for both the Sir Williams, as has been already shown, died s. p.

It is at least certain that there were several collateral branches of the Herons of Ford Castle. Cecilia de Lisle brought Chipchase (a member of the barony of Prudhoe) to a younger son of that house in 1366 : and their descendant claimed Ford on the extinction of the elder line. This led to a blood-feud with the Carrs, and an affray near the castle, in which Giles Heron, the claimant's brother, lost

---

* It was Sir William's bastard brother John, "a famous soldier in those days," who had slain the Warden in a fray at a Border meeting, and been thereupon outlawed in both kingdoms. He did good service at Flodden ; for when, in the first onset, the right wing of the English host gave way, and Sir Edmund Howard was sore beset, he threw himself between the armies with a troop of horse he had raised in the Cheviots, and gave his countrymen time to rally. He fell, not long afterwards, in a Border skirmish.

his life; till at length, "for quietness' sake," one of the manors was ceded to them. Cuthbert Heron, one of the many suffering loyalists in the Civil War, was created a baronet in 1662; and his posterity "continued the possessors of Chipchase until Sir Harry Heron sold it in 1737. On the death of Sir Harry without issue in 1759, Thomas Heron, his first cousin, who had taken his mother's name of Myddleton in addition to his own, succeeded to the title of Baronet."—*Betham's Baronetage.* Then there were the Herons of Bokenfield, also in Northumberland, who settled at Newark in the seventeenth century, and received a baronetcy in 1778; and the Herons of Cressy in Lincolnshire, which, according to the Visitation of the county of 1562, "came from Ford Castle" in the fifteenth century.

But Morant tells us that they were seated in Essex as far back as 1165, when Hayron's manor in High Estre was held of Geoffrey de Mandeville by Ralph de Heron; and Richard de Heron had an interest in that of Heyron in Danesbury. (Liber Niger). Two other manors—Heron in East Hornden, and Herons in Fifield, retain the name. John Heyroun, who died in 1343, "held in Lackingdon of the King *in capite* of the Honour of Hagenet." Their principal seat was at Cressy, where Margaret, the mother of Henry VII., was entertained by Sir John Heron, and the bedstead on which she lay is still preserved in a farm-house by the fen side.* He was one of her son's Privy Councillors, and later in life Treasurer of the Household to Henry VIII. :—the first ever appointed, for he is named in the Act of 1512, by which the office was created. His son Sir Giles married a daughter of the famous Chancellor Sir Thomas More, and forfeited his estate for refusing to acknowledge the King's supremacy. The last heir, Henry Heron, died in 1730. He was very desirous that his estate should continue in the old name, and failing the issue of his sister and nephew, sought out a successor who bore it. He at first inclined towards Mr. Heron of Newark; but they differed so widely in politics, the one being a Jacobite, and the other a Hanoverian, that he went further afield, and placed a Scotsman, Patrick Heron of Kirouchtree, whose ancestor was said to have migrated from Northumberland during the thirteenth century, in the entail. Patrick's grandson inherited Cressy Hall in 1769. It yet retains the vast heronry established by the family in allusion to the herons on their coat of arms.

Herne: apparently only a repetition of the same name. But I believe it here stands for Herice, as in Leland's list it appears joined to the succeeding name as "Heryce et Harecourt." The family of Herice is said to descend from a son of the Count of Vendome, and bore his allusive arms, three urcheons (*hérissons*) or hedgehogs, which still appear on the coats of the Earls of Malmesbury and Lord Herries. "Ivo de Heriz was Viscount of Notts before 1130:

* "It is very large, shut up on all sides with wainscot, and two holes left at the bottom end, each large enough to admit a grown person."

and had issue five sons: 1. Ralph, who held the Barony of Notts in 1165: 2. Robert Fitz Herice, mentioned in a charter of Barberie Abbey, executed by Henry II.: 3. Josceline, mentioned in Hunts, 1156 (Rot. Pip.): 4. William, who held, 1165, two fees in Notts and four in Lincoln: 5. Humphrey, who was of Berks, 1158 (Rot. Pip.). William Herez, thirteenth century, possessed estates in Wilts. From him descended William Harrys, one of the principal inhabitants of Salisbury in 1469 (Hoare), ancestor of the Earls of Malmesbury."—*The Norman People.* Collins, however, traces their genealogy no further back than William Harris, who married in 1561.

The family is first mentioned in Derbyshire. "South Winfield was held at Domesday by one Robert, under Alan, Earl of Brittany, who held under William Peverel. The baronial family of Heriz held this manor under the superior lords at a very early period, and are supposed to have descended from Robert, mentioned in Domesday. The heiress of Heriz married De la Rivière about 1330: a co-heiress of Rivière married Belers, and a co-heiress of Belers married Swillington. In the reign of Henry VI. Ralph, Lord Cromwell, Lord Treasurer, as nearest of kin to Margaret Swillington, acquired this manor by compromise, after a long law-suit with Sir Henry Pierrepont, the heir-at-law of John de Heriz, who died 1330."—*Lysons.* Robert's son Gaufrid held Stapleford in Notts, also of William Peverel, at the foundation of Lenton Priory in the time of Henry I., and it continued with his descendants for six more generations, till Idonea de Heriz conveyed it to John Furmery. They had a considerable estate in Nottinghamshire, where their principal seat was at Wyverton. One of the younger sons took the name of Stapleford, and founded a separate branch, which ended with Sampson de Stapleford, who died s. p. 42 Edward III.—See *Thoroton's Notts.* Another cadet of the house of Wyverton, William Heriz, who built Withcock Church, and died in 1512, assumed the name of Smith on acquiring Withcock by grant of his father-in-law William Ashby of Loseby, but why he did so we are not informed. He retained, however, his paternal coat. His descendants were seated at Somerby, Husband's Bosworth, Frolesworth, and Edmondthorpe: the last male heir, Hugh, died in 1755, and his daughter Lucy married Lord Strange, eldest son of the eleventh Earl of Derby. In honour of the inheritance she brought, the two next Earls added her name to their own, and it was said of the last that "he was the only nobleman left in England who had the courage to bear the name of Smith." The present Lord Derby discarded it when he sold the estate.

A branch of this house came into Scotland during the first half of the twelfth century, and settled in Nithsdale. William de Heriz witnessed several charters of David I.; and the names of Thomas, Henry, Ivon, and Nigel de Heriz appear on other deeds and charters of somewhat later date. Nigel was Forester, in the Southern districts, to Alexander II. William de Heriz was one of the barons who swore fealty to the King of England in 1296. Robert de Herris, in an original charter of Robert Bruce, is designated *Dominus de Nithisdale;* and Sir John Herice was "of great consequence" in the reign of his successor David. Another Sir John—probably the son of the last—is first styled of Terregles, co. Dumfries, still the seat of one of his descendants in the female line. Fourth in descent from him was Herbert de Heriz, created a "Lord of Parliament" by James IV. soon after his accession in 1488, by the title of Baron Herries of Terregles. It was either he or his father that built Hoddam Castle in Annandale, and according to some accounts, pulled down a neighbouring church or chapel at Trailtrow, to use the stone for his new building. On a small hill near, stands a curious square tower, that "was anciently used as a beacon, and the Border laws direct a watch to be maintained there, with a fire-pan and bell, to give the alarm when the English crossed, or approached, the river Annan."—*Sir W. Scott.* Over the door are the sculptured figures of a dove and a serpent with the word "Repentance" between them; and thus the building, though its proper name is Trailtrow, is more generally called the Tower of Repentance. Some say that it was erected in memory of the sacrilegious destruction of the church; others, that it was the work of a Lord Herries, notorious as a marauder even among the Border freebooters, who went by the expressive name of John the Reif. Even as he was crossing the Solway Firth on his way home from England, with a great store of booty, and a good many captives that he had "unlawfully enthralled," his heavily laden boat was overtaken by a storm, and to relieve it of part of its freight, he cut the throats of his prisoners, and threw them overboard. For this, it is further said, he afterwards felt many qualms of conscience, and built this tower, carving over its entrance the emblems of remorse and grace, with the motto "Repentance" by which he wished to be remembered.

The line of these fierce Border chieftains failed with the fourth Lord Herries, and the barony was re-granted in 1566 to his daughter Agnes and her husband Sir John Maxwell, a cadet of the great house of Carlaverock, who, as Lord Herries, is often honourably mentioned in contemporary Scottish history. As a "man of unshaken loyalty and approved worth," he was throughout the faithful follower of Queen Mary, and twice in his life, at least, found bold enough to give her honest advice, that was, each time, disregarded. On the first occasion, he told her she must "remember her honour and dignity" and not marry a man so "loaded with infamy" as was Bothwell; and on the second, after the defeat of Langside, when the Queen announced her sudden intention of crossing the Solway, Herries again knelt at her feet, and implored her not to put her trust in Elizabeth. He was afterwards nominated as one of her Commissioners, and made a celebrated speech in her behalf at York in 1568. John, eighth Lord Herries, who fought under Montrose, and was in consequence excommunicated by the General Assembly, succeeded a distant cousin as Earl of Nithsdale on the extinction of the senior branch in 1667, and was grandfather to the unhappy

Earl engaged in the Jacobite rebellion of 1715, and commemorated in the Border Lament,

"Make mane, my ain Nithsdale, thy leaf's i' the fa'."

He was thrown into the Tower, and condemned to death; but on the very eve of his execution, his brave Countess, Winifred Herbert, planned and effected his escape. She dressed him in "all her petticoats, excepting one," covered him with a long cloak, and with his head muffled in a riding hood, and a handker-chief held to his eyes, "the better to pass for the lady [Mrs. Mills] who came in crying and affected," herself led him by the hand through the guard-room. She feigned to be in great anxiety and distress, and spoke to him "in the most piteous and afflicted voice," entreating him to send her tiring-woman to her immediately. "She forgets that I have to present a petition to-night; and if I let slip this opportunity, I am undone—My dear Mrs. Betty, for the love of God run quickly, and bring her to me!" Everyone, she adds, "seemed to compassionate me exceedingly, and the sentinel officiously opened the door." The brown camlet cloak worn by Lord Nithsdale on that eventful night is retained as a valued relic by the family, and while the story of his escape was still fresh in men's minds, similar cloaks, named "Nithsdales," were extensively worn, and became the fashion of the day. The rescued Earl and his Countess betook themselves to the mock court of the exiled Stuarts, and ended their lives in Italy, steeped to the very lips in poverty, of which her selfish and ungrateful husband made his wife bear the chief brunt. He had secured his estate by transferring it to his son, Lord Maxwell, and his life-interest only was declared forfeited. His honours were of course extinguished by his attainder; but on his death, Lord Maxwell assumed the title of Earl of Nithsdale, and the granddaughter that proved to be his heiress was styled Lady Winifred Maxwell. She married in 1758 William Haggerston Constable, of Everingham, co. York, who took her name; and—exactly one hundred years afterwards—the ancient barony of Herries was restored to their grandson.

Another cadet of the Herizs of Notts settled at Claxton, co. Durham, about the time of Henry II.; and his descendants, after a few generations, assumed the local name. They retained, however, the three *hérissons* of their paternal coat, varying only the tincture; and continued to be one of the leading families of the Bishopric for more than five hundred years. One of them fell at Bosworth, bearing the standard of Richard III. Another—Sir William Claxton—succeeded in 1416 to the barony of Devylstoune (Dilston) in Northumberland, as heir to Emma de Tyndale, in right of his great-grandmother, who had been one of that family. But it soon passed away through another heiress, married to John Cartington, whose only daughter, Lady of Dilston, Cartington, &c. conveyed it to the Radcliffes. At length, in 1596, Robert Claxton, of Old Hall, co. Durham, wrought the downfall of his house by joining—hesitatingly and unwillingly—in the fatal Rising of the North. A pathetic old ballad, named 'Claxton's Lament,' records how he pondered and wavered when he received the Earl of Westmorland's peremptory summons:

> "I charge thee, Claxton, ride with me."

His family, in all its branches, had always been zealously attached to the Nevills; the Claxtons of Holywell were Constables of their Castle of Brancepeth; and he owed to them a portion at least of his lands. He could not choose but go; and yet he shrank from the doom he was bringing on his two hopeful sons:

> "To Wetherby I needs must ride,
>   No better chance since I may see:
> My eldest son is full of pride—
>   My second goes for love of me.

> "Now bide at home, my eldest son!
>   Thou art the heir of all my land."
> "If I stay at home for land or fee,
>   May I be branded on forehead and hand!

> "The Percies are rising in the north,
>   The Nevills are gathering in the west:
> And Claxton's heir may bide at home,
>   And hide him in the cushat's nest?"

> "Now rest at home, my youngest son!
>   Thy limbs are lithe, thy age is green."
> "Nay, father, we'll to Wetherby,
>   And never more at home be seen.

> "We'll keep our bond to our noble Lord—
>   We'll tyne our faith to the Southern Queen:
> And when all is lost, we'll cross the sea,
>   And bid farewell to bow'r and green."

And so it was to be. They were pardoned, and one of the sons was knighted by James I.; but their fair inheritance was gone from them for ever, and the old home knew them no more.

Harecourt: This is one of the families that derived their descent from Bernard the Dane, Regent of Normandy, c. 940. Anguerrand or Errand de Harcourt was in the Conqueror's army, and is said to have commanded the archers of Val de Ruel at the battle of Hastings; but he returned to his own country after the new king's coronation; and it was his younger brother Robert, who had accompanied him to England, that was the ancestor of this illustrious house. This Robert who was surnamed Le Fort, and built the castle of Harcourt in Normandy, was the father of seven sons, of whom the first born,

William, having taken part with Henry I. against Robert Curthose, was rewarded with large estates in England, which he bequeathed to his second son Ivo, who became permanently settled in this country. The elder brother remained in France, where he was the progenitor of a long list of great houses. From him descended Jean d'Harcourt, Vicomte de Châtelherault, in whose favour the barony of Harcourt was erected into a Comté by Philip de Valois in 1338: the Harcourts, Barons Bonestable and Montgomery; the Harcourts, Barons d'Ollande; the Harcourts, Counts of Harcourt and Aumale, the Marquises of Montmorency 1578, and Pierre d'Harcourt, Baron de Beuvron, Beauffou, etc., " in recompense of whose services the baronies of La Motte, Mery, Cleville, and Vareville were by letters mandatory of Henry IV. in 1593 erected into a marquisate called La Motte Harcourt." This Pierre was the ancestor of Henri d'Harcourt, Marshal of France, whose two marquisates of Thury and La Motte Harcourt were united into a dukedom by Louis XIV. In spite of the many wars and revolutions that have since swept over France, the Ducs d'Harcourt retain, as I am informed, the Château d'Harcourt, near the old Norman stronghold that has borne their name for eight hundred years; and the adjacent village of Harcourt-Thury, which gives them one of their titles, recalls a memory of still more ancient date, their Scandinavian *cri de guerre* of Tur-aie (Thor aide).

The English Harcourts were seated at Stanton Harcourt in Oxfordshire, acquired through the heiress of the Camvilles, whose mother received it as a marriage gift from her cousin, Queen Adeliza of Brabant, the second wife of Henry I. Here the ruins of the castle they built attest its former magnificence, and their effigies, for many successive generations, remain in the parish church. One of these, that of Dame Margaret Harcourt, the wife of a Sir Richard who fought for the House of York in the wars of the Roses, and received the Garter from Edward IV., shows the Order worn immediately above the elbow of the left arm, with the motto *Honi soit qui mal y pense.* It is an almost unique instance of a woman's effigy so decorated :* and shows that she belonged to the few rarely-honoured ladies who, in early times, were affiliated to the Order.†

* There are only two other known examples; that of Constance Holland, wife of Thomas Mowbray, Duke of Norfolk, whose monument (now much defaced) is in St. Catherine's Church, near the Tower of London; and that of Alice Chaucer, wife of William de la Pole, Duke of Suffolk, in Ewelme Church, Oxfordshire.

† They were " Ladies of the Fraternity of St. George and of the Society of the Garter," for whom robes and hoods were duly provided, as they were for the knights. " The Robes were lined with fur, but the hoods with scarlet, and both embroidered over with little Garters; and the proportion of cloth, fur, and Garters, were allowed according to their several degrees."—*Sir Harris Nicolas.* Dame Harcourt would receive " five ells of cloth and half an ell of scarlett, and one fur, consisting of two hundred bellies of pure miniver." The first two ladies who wore " Saint George's livere " were Isabel Plantagenet, the daughter of Edward III. and the wife of John, Sire de Coucy and Earl of Bedford, who received robes in 1375 : and the Fair Maid of Kent, wife of

The Stanton-Harcourt line were far from emulating the blaze of titles of honour that surrounded their French cousins. Though they made great alliances, acquired great possessions, and did their duty manfully in the wars, no Harcourt was ever summoned as a baron in the feudal times; and it was not till the reign of Queen Anne that Sir Simon Harcourt, on being appointed Lord Keeper of the Great Seal, received a peerage. He was created Baron Harcourt of Stanton-Harcourt in 1711 : and declared Lord High Chancellor of England in the course of the following year. He was considered the ablest of the Tory lawyers; and when, in 1701, he impeached Lord Somers before the House of Lords, it was confidently predicted that he would one day sit in Somers' chair. The next year he was appointed Solicitor General, and in 1707 Attorney General, but resigned with Harley in 1708. The preamble to his patent of peerage, previous to the usual panegyric of his virtues and abilities, makes honourable mention of the "warlike action" of his ancestors; more particularly of his grandfather Sir Simon, who raised the siege of Dublin in 1641, and, "fighting courageously against the Irish rebels, was the first Englishman that fell a sacrifice to their fury."

Lord Harcourt retained the office of Lord Keeper till the accession of George I., who transferred the Great Seal to Lord Cowper. He received, how-ever, a Viscountcy in 1721 ; and his grandson and successor was advanced in 1740 to an Earldom, with the second title of Viscount Harcourt of Nuneham-Courtenay, taken from his seat in Oxfordshire. All these honours expired with the third Earl in 1830, but the grand old Norman name did not perish with them. Counting from Bernard Le Danois, their first recorded ancestor in the far-off Scandinavian time, it had then been handed down through twenty-eight generations ; nearly two more have since passed away, and it lives among us yet. Its present representative is the descendant of Philip Harcourt, a younger brother of the Lord Chancellor's, who acquired through his wife Ankerwyke in Buckinghamshire, the present seat of the family.

Earl Harcourt's estates passed through an heiress to the Vernons, with one notable exception. During the emigration of the French nobles at the close of the last century, the Marquis d'Harcourt and his family took refuge in England, and became intimate with Lord and Lady Harcourt. Both parties were equally proud of the name they bore, no less than of the remote ancestry they had in common, and equally disposed to claim the tie of kindred, though it had to be sought for in the dim twilight of past ages, after a severance of seven hundred years. The French cousins spent much of their time at Nuneham, and the

---

the Black Prince, three years later. The two last were the little daughters of Henry VII., in 1495 ; Lady Margaret (afterwards Queen of Scotland), who was then not yet five years old ; and Lady Elizabeth, only three. These tiny princesses must have been nearly buried under their burden of miniver. .

childless Earl grew so fond of the sons, that he proposed to leave his only unentailed estate, St. Leonards, near Windsor, to one of them, on condition that he was bred up as an Englishman and a member of the Church of England. The eldest boy was accordingly sent to Eton, educated as a Protestant, and, dropping his foreign title to become a plain English esquire, inherited St. Leonards under Lord Harcourt's will. But he left only daughters; and the estate, after some litigation (for a clause in the will, providing that it should never belong either to a Frenchman or a Roman Catholic, had first to be set aside), passed to his nephew in France, by whom it was sold.

Henoure. Robert de Henouere, in 1324, was summoned from Derbyshire to attend the great Council at Westminster.—*Palgrave's Parl. Writs.* John de Henoue held land at Horsley in that county, temp. Ed. I.—*Rotuli Hundredorum.* At the same date, "Mag. Will. de Hanouere" was incumbent of Potter's Pery in Northamptonshire.—v. *Bridges.* Nicholas, son of John de Henoure, held part of a knight's fee at Shipley, Nottinghamshire, of Gilbert de Gant.—*Testa de Nevill.*

Houell. "The name of Houël or Hoël is of Breton origin, and was at first, like Conan, Mériadec, and others of the same kind, a personal denomination.

"During the reigns of Rollo's successors, a considerable intercourse was established between Normandy and Brittany. A certain number of younger sons from Brittany entered the service of the Dukes of Normandy, and acquired fiefs and lordships, generally in the parts adjoining their own country. The different branches of the family of Houël, whose cradle was in the parish of Tourneur, near the town of Vire, probably had for their ancestor one of these Breton emigrants, who established himself in this fief, of which his first descendants bore the name. In fact, we find in some of the lists of the Conquest the name of Houel, replaced in others by that of Sire du Tourneur. 'E li sires de Vaacie, del Torneor, e de Praeres:' (Wace): 'De la Huse et Howel' (Leland). What confirms us in this opinion is, that an ancient pedigree of the house, dated 1596, declares the Houëls to be descendants of the race and *estres* of the Sires du Tourneur."—*Nobiliaire de Normandie.* The existing family of Houël du Tourneur bear Paly of six *Or* and *Azure*, but this cannot have been the original coat, for the seal of "Thomæ Hoel," affixed to a deed of 1216, shows an estoile of eight prints. Another Thomas Houel was one of the one hundred and nineteen knights that defended Mont St. Michel against the English in 1423.

The Celtic Hoele or Howell is familiar to us in Wales, and widely diffused throughout England. In some cases the name is surmised to be a corruption of Hautville, which "became in Norfolk Auville, Haville, Hovel, and Dunton."—*The Norman People.* Yet Leland gives both, as distinct names; and the Hovels that were seated in Suffolk bore arms entirely different from any of the coats used by the Hautvilles. They dated from the time of the Conqueror, when Richard Hovel held a lordship at Wigvereston in that county of Baldwin,

Abbot of Bury. "Sir Hugh Hovel was Lord of Hovel's Manor, Chediston, in 1287. He was the ancestor of Sir Richard Hovel, Esquire of the Body to Henry V., and is now represented by Lord Thurlow. Sir Hugh was evidently a knight of great consequence in this county. In a list of knights, made in the reign of Ed. II., his name stands first among the Suffolk families, and his arms are thus emblazoned: 𝔖𝔦𝔯 𝔥𝔲𝔤𝔢 𝔥𝔬𝔟𝔢𝔩, 𝔡𝔢 𝔰𝔞𝔟𝔩𝔢, 𝔢𝔱 𝔲𝔫𝔢 𝔠𝔯𝔬𝔦𝔰 𝔡𝔢 𝔬𝔯. The family seem to have been rather contumacious subjects at this period of almost universal anarchy; for Robert Hovel is returned in the Hundred Rolls as prohibiting the proclamation of the King's command in this village."—*Suckling's Suffolk.* Sir John Hovel of Wretting Parva, Suffolk, was living in 1370: and a William Hovel of Rishanger died in 1433: but their chief seat was at Ashfield, near Ixworth, where they were still to be found at the beginning of the last century. They had, it appears, adopted the name of Smith; and in 1730 Elizabeth Smith, their heiress, married the Rev. Thomas Thurlow, clergyman of the parish, and was the mother of Lord Chancellor Thurlow. The next Lord Thurlow added the name of Hovel to his own.

A branch seated during four generations at Hillington in Norfolk had ended with William Hovel in 1671, when his three sisters, Clementia, Dorothy, and Etheldreda, divided his estates.

Hamelin. Three of this name are entered as under-tenants in Domesday: Hamelin *homo Hugonis filii Baldrici* in Lincolnshire; Hamelin holding of Roger de Montgomery in Sussex, and also mentioned in Devonshire, and Hamelin of Cornwall. "Whether Hamelin of Devonshire and Hamelin of Cornwall were the same person, does not appear. In the latter county Hamelin held twenty-two manors under the Earl of Mortaine. He is supposed to have been the ancestor of the Trelawny family, and to have resided at Treloen, one of the manors described in the Survey as his property."—*Sir Henry Ellis.* According to Lysons (Cornwall) this Hamelin was of unknown origin. His descendants bore the name of their residence. The pedigree begins with Richard; from whom John (living 9 Ed. I.) was fourth in descent, and the father of William, who served as one of the burgesses for Launceston in the parliament held at Westminster 19 Ed. II. He was the first of the long list of Trelawnys who succeeded each other as burgesses, High Sheriffs, and knights of the shire; and "he, Sir Reginald de Botreaux and Sir John Arundell, were Commissioners to return the names of such as held £100 yearly in the county of Cornwall." Sir John Trelawny was the companion at arms of Henry V., and shared in all the glories of his wars in France, where he "so eminently signalized himself that the King granted him twenty Pounds yearly for Life." The King honoured him with a higher reward; for, as if in illustration of the words that Shakespeare puts into his mouth before the battle of Agincourt:—

> ". . . He this day that sheds his blood with me
> Shall be my brother . . ."

a memorial of his friendship for his gallant knight long remained at Launceston. There, over the great gate of the town, formerly stood the effigy of Henry V., with this rhyme written underneath :—

> " Hee that will do oughte for mee,
> ·Let hym love well Sir John Tirlawnee."

Henry VI. continued the pension, and granted him an augmentation to his arms, ".the Coat of the three oaken or Laurel leaves, the Symbol of Conquest," ever since borne by the family. The direct line ended with his eldest son, and the manor of Trelawny (the original Treloen held by Hamelin at the time of the Survey) passed away through an heiress; but there remained a younger son, also named John, who held of the Courtenays. There is still extant a curious agreement between him and Thomas Earl of Devonshire, made in 1455, by which the Earl, "in consideration of an Annuity of ten Marks, yearly, covenants to be a firm and sure Lord to him in all Things that appertain to his Lands, as far as the Law shall permit." In the next generation another John Trelawny married Florence, fourth daughter of Sir Hugh Courtenay of Boconnoc, and sister to Edward, Earl of Devonshire, who, upon the extinction of the line with the last unfortunate Marquess of Exeter in 1556, became with her sisters, the co-heirs of the family. Thus a great part of the inheritance of the Courtenays was acquired by the Trelawnys; and we find the widowed Countess of Devonshire (Lady Katherine Plantagenet, the youngest daughter of Edward IV.) granting to Walter Trelawny the Constableship and Bailiwick of the Honour and hundred of Plympton for life 1 Hen. VIII., and two years later, the Bailiwick of Exitond and the West Gate of the City of Exeter to his younger brother Alneth. In 1600, "Sir Jonathan Trelawny, a knight well spoken, staid in his cariage, and of thrifty providence" purchased of Queen Elizabeth another manor of his name (there are two Trelawnys in Cornwall, one in the parish of Alternon, the other in Pelynt): and thus became once more Trelawny of Trelawny, as his forefathers had been during four hundred years, and his descendants have continued to be for nearly three hundred more. It was this Sir Jonathan, who, while serving in parliament as knight of the shire for Cornwall in 1604, died so suddenly that he was said "to be found sick and dead within a quarter of an hour," and was followed to his grave by the whole House of Commons. His son, Sir John, received a baronetcy from Charles I. in 1629. Sir Jonathan, the third baronet, Bishop of Bristol in 1685, was one of the seven prelates who signed the memorable petition to James II., pleading for the rights of the Church, that led to their subsequent trial for libel. The Bishops were admitted to the Royal Closet, and themselves presented it to the King. " James read the petition," says Macaulay; " he folded it up; and his countenance grew dark. 'This,' he said, 'is a great surprise to me. I did not expect this from your Church, especially from some of you. This is a standard of rebellion.' The Bishops broke out into passionate protestations of loyalty; but the King, as usual, repeated the same words over and over. 'I tell you, this is a standard of rebellion.' 'Rebellion!' cried Trelawny, falling on his knees. 'For God's sake, Sir, do not say so hard a thing of us. No Trelawny can be a rebel. Remember how my family has fought for the Crown. Remember how I served your Majesty when Monmouth was in the West.'" Nevertheless, the King dismissed them from his presence, in great wrath, as "trumpeters of sedition;" and within three weeks they were summoned before the Council, and committed to the Tower. The storm of indignation called forth by this arbitrary act spread like wildfire through the kingdom, and nowhere raged more violently than in the "farthest corner of the island," the remote county of Cornwall. The stout Cornish miners, "a fierce, bold, and athletic race, among whom there was a stronger provincial feeling than in any other part of the realm, were greatly moved at the danger of Trelawny," and ready to march up to London to his rescue. The old name had been held in honour among them from generation to generation, and the burden of the rousing song which then rung, like a challenge, from one end to the other of the county, still keeps its place as a popular favourite :—

> "Trelawny is in keep and hold,
> Trelawny he may die—
> But thirty thousand Cornishmen
> Will know the reason why!"

The present Trelawny of Trelawny is the ninth baronet of the name : but he does not derive from the Bishop, whose male descendants all died out in the second generation.

The seventh baronet, Sir Harry, so far departed from the family traditions as to become a Roman Catholic. He lost his father when he was a boy at school; and even at that age showed a disposition to preach, which developed itself as time went on. His first discourses were delivered at Westminster (we are not informed how his school fellows received them) : and when he went from thence to Oxford, he was unable, as a professed Nonconformist, to take his degree. He began life by taking orders in the Church of Scotland, and preached at various meeting houses in his own neighbourhood—one of them built by himself at West Looe; then entered the Church of England, and obtained a Cornish living which he resigned on joining the Church of Rome. This was his last conversion; he changed no more, but died at Rome, in 1834, a Bishop *in Partibus Infidelium.* Soon after, several priests arrived from the Continent, bearing with them an empty coffin, and masses were said and requiems sung for the peace of his soul at Trelawny.

.Harewell: Hareville in Leland's list. "The name of Harivel," says M. de Gerville, "is very common in Normandy. It is synonymous with *Haridelle,* still found in our modern dictionaries. ' Harivels,' or ' harivilliers,' are frequently seen at our fairs; they are persons dealing only in ' harins ' or ' haridelles,' small or inferior horses, leaving the trade in riding horses and animals of a superior quality to the regular horse dealers." There exists, however, an aristocratic family named Le Harivel, that is found in Normandy as early as the fifteenth century, and once possessed several important fiefs, such as Sourdeval, Beaumanoir, Maizet, Gonneville, Flagy, &c. It furnished proofs of its nobility in 1463, and in 1671 was again declared *Estre noble par charte de franc-fiefs.* The Le Harivels bear *Gules,* three roses *Or,* two and one ; and may have derived their name from Hareville, Arnouville, or Harunville, which is mentioned in the Norman Exchequer Rolls of the twelfth century.

In England, John de Harewell was chaplain to Edward the Black Prince, Chancellor of Gascony, and Bishop of Wells. He lies buried before the altar of St. Calix in Wells Cathedral. Dugdale tells us that he was the son of another John de Harewell, and brother to Roger, who "towards the latter end of Ed. III. and beginning of Ric. II.'s time married Maud de Standford of Wotton in Warwickshire. Which Maud became her brother's heir, and possesst all those his lands; whereunto by marriage of severall heirs, and otherwise, her descendants made so fair an addition, as that they were rankt amongst the superior gentry of this Shire." Her great-grandson, William de Harewell " was a trusty friend of the House of Lancaster (as it seems) for, upon the re-gaining of the Kingdom by King Henry VI., he had the custody of this county and Leicestershire; and before the end of that his Shirivealtie, fought stoutly on King Henry's part at Barnet field : in which battail being taken prisoner, he was thence carried to Windsor Castle, whereupon also his lands were seized by the King, and bestowed on Humphrey Stafford. But after a while, through the solicitation of his kinsman John Leighton, made with John Talbot, then Earl of Shrewsbury, he was released from his imprisonment and restored to his lands : for which favour the said Earl had first XI li that the same John Leighton promised to give for obtaining his enlargement and lands, and XL marks more which he exacted over and above." William's two grandsons were the last heirs-male. Thomas, the elder, died s. p. before 1511 : and William was a priest. Their four sisters thus became coheirs; and Wotton-Waven fell to the share of Agnes, who was the wife of John Smyth, one of the Barons of the Exchequer, and great-great-grandmother of Sir Charles Smith, created in 1643 Baron of Wootton-Waven and Viscount Carrington "in consideration of his fidelity to King Charles I."

William de Hareville, a cadet of this house, was Lord of Besford in Worcestershire 15 Hen. VI., and his descendants continued there for five generations. One of them served as High Sheriff of the county, and Sir Edmund Harewell, who sold the place in the sixteenth century, is called "an excellent justice and a learned gentleman." The line ended at about the same time as the parent house: Roger Harewell being the last male heir. The Harewells bore *Argent* on a fesse wavy *Sable* three hares' heads *Or.—Nash's Worcestershire.*

A Cecilia de Harewell, and her son Robert are mentioned in 1202 in Oxfordshire (Rotuli Cancellarii) : but I cannot find that the name occurs there again.

Hardell. If we are to credit M. de Gerville, who gives a similar meaning to *Harivel* and *haridelles*, this name is but a synonym of the last. I first met with it in Norfolk, where Robert de Hardele witnesses one of the grants to Normansburgh Priory. Roger de Hardel is a witness of Edward II.'s confirmation charter to Tichfield Abbey, Hants; and John de Hardele to Robert de Vipont's grant to Heppe Priory, Westmorland. (Mon. Angl.) In Suffolk, according to an Inquisition taken at Dunwich 21 Hen. III., it was found that " William Hardyll takes Wrec of the Sea in the Town of Westleton, from the aforesaid Limits unto the Port of Menesmeer."—*Davy's Suffolk Collections.* Was this the same William Hardell whose widow, Katherine, received from Henry III. a grant of twenty feet of land in length and breadth in Smithfield, next to the chapel of St. Bartholomew, "to build her a Recluse or Ankerage"?—*Stowe.* A hermitage at Smithfield—of all places in the world! is very suggestive of the lapse of time! Robert Ardell witnesses a convention made between Ralph, Abbot of Battle, and the citizens of London, in 1243. In 1249, Richard Hardell was joint-sheriff of London and Middlesex : and from 1254 to 1257 Lord Mayor. William Hardel had preceded him in the civic chair in 1215 The latter bore *Vert* a fesse flory counterflory *Or.—Robson.* Galfrid de Ardel held by Castleguard of the Honour of Richmond in Hertfordshire.—*Gale's Richmondshire.* William Hardell was of Kent, and Robert Hardell of Buckinghamshire, in the reign of Ed. I.—*Rotuli Hundredorum.* At nearly the same date we find in Essex a Sir John Hardel, the husband of Lady Alice Beaumont, who had two daughters and coheirs: Helen, married to Sir William de Hareburgh : and Alice, the wife of William Fitz Warin, then *Valectus*, or gentleman of the Bedchamber, to Edward I. To the latter he gave in free marriage the manor of Whatley, that had been granted to him by John de Burgh.—*Morant's Essex.* Laurence de Hardell, who inherited from John de Kokeham (who lived in 1274), and his son Nicolas, are also mentioned. The Hardells of Essex bore a chevron between three molets of six points *Gules—Ibid.*

Robert Hardell occurs in the Norman Exchequer Rolls between 1198 and 1203.

Haket, or Achet. Walter Achet held of Walter Gifford in Buckinghamshire. (Domesd.) There are two parishes of this name in the department of the Pas-de-Calais; and the name appears in 1040 in the list of the household of Thibaut III. Count de Chartres; but nothing is really known of this family, which as Haget, Hachett or Hackett, spread into all parts of England and Ireland. Ralf Haget was Sheriff of Durham 1159–1181 : and in the previous century a Haget was seated at Helagh in Yorkshire, whose two sons, Farice and Bertram, are mentioned in 1147. Bertram's four daughters became his heirs; for one of his sons was Abbot of Fountains, and the other, Geoffrey, died s. p. Agnes married Brian Fitz Alan of Bedale, Alice John de Friston; and Lucia Peter Fitz Toret; Gundred died single. See *Eyton's Salop.* The elder son's descendants continued at Helagh, where Bertram Haget founded an Abbey in 1200. Leland mentions "Geoffrey Haget, owner of Helagh Lordship, and beside a great owner in Ainste." Walter Haket, of Weshull and Eggarton in Shropshire, served as knight of the shire for Worcester in 1313, was Commissioner of Array and Leader of the levies in the counties of Salop and Stafford in 1317, and the following year received a pardon as an adherent of the Earl of Lancaster. —*Palgrave's Parliamentary Writs.* William Haket, living at the same date, and one of the "Nobiles" of Ireland, was summoned to serve against the Scots.*— *Ibid.* In Worcestershire William Haket held in Claines in the time of Henry I.; and his descendants have left their name to Broughton-Hacket and Cofton-Hacket—the latter held of the Bishop of Worcester. Their heiress, Matilda Haket, married Robert de Leycestre temp. Ed. III.—*Nash.* Ralph Haket, Buckinghamshire; Robert Haket, Norfolk; Thomas Haket, Kent; Bertram and Nicholas Haket, Oxfordshire; are mentioned in the *Rotuli Hundredorum* temp. Ed. I. Burke speaks of some Hakets seated at Niton in the Isle of Wight; and others still established in Ireland. The name is, in fact, found in every part of the country.

"At Oundle, where he some time followed the trade of a maltster, of low extraction, was born William Hacket, an impious blasphemer in the time of Queen Elizabeth. He was of so savage a disposition, that he is reported, when at school, to have bitten off and swallowed the nose of his master. He was first an informer against Popish recusants, afterwards a violent partizan for the Geneva discipline, and a pretender to revelations, and immediate communications with God: asserting, that he was commissioned from Heaven to reform the State and the Church, and by extraordinary means to make a new settlement of both. He pretended to be invulnerable, and defied any one that would to kill him. Afterwards giving out, that the Spirit of the Messias rested in him, he had two attendants : Edward Coppinger, a person of good descent, whom he named his prophet of mercy; and Henry Arthington, a Yorkshire gentleman, whom he named his prophet of judgment. These, among other impieties, proclaimed from a cart in Cheapside, that Christ was come in Hacket, with his fan in his hand, to purge the godly from the wicked. Being all three apprehended, they were sent to Bridewell, where Coppinger, it is said, starved himself to death:

* A previous William Hacket, in the time of Henry III., founded a Franciscan abbey near Cashel, commonly called Hacket's Abbey; amongst the ruins of which, three effigies, presumed to be his and some of his descendants', were discovered some years ago.

Hacket was tried before the Judges at Westminster, found guilty, and in 1591 executed on a gibbet near the Cross in Cheapside. Arthington on his repentance was pardoned."—*Bridge's Northamptonshire.*

Hamound. In this form the name can be only an interpolation. Hamo or Haimo is, indeed, several times entered in Domesday, but only as the Christian name of Hamon de Crevecoeur, Viscount of Kent, who was a son of the great Hamon Dentatus. "Hamo Dapifer, and Hamo the Sheriff, were the same person. Hasted says his family name was Crevecoeur. He was one of the Judges of the County Court when the great cause was tried between Archbishop Lanfranc and. Odo. He died some time in the reign of Henry I., without issue."—*Sir Henry Ellis.* (See also *Crevecoeur.*)

Yet the name appears in Normandy during the following century as a surname, for Geoffrey, Ranulph, Waleran, Richard, and Stephen Hamon or Hammon are found on the Exchequer Rolls of the Duchy in 1180–98; and, as Hammond, became common in England. The last Abbot of Battle was a Hammond.

The Heymans, of Somerfield, in Kent, extinct baronets, claimed descent from the Crevecoeurs; and are said to have anciently borne their coat, *Or* three chevronels *Gules*, though it was subsequently changed. Their pedigree, however, only commences with Peter Heyman, one of the Gentlemen of the Bedchamber to Edward VI. Somerfield was sold, at the latter end of Charles II.'s reign, by the second baronet, who wasted his substance and ruined the family. His son, Sir Bartholomew, found an asylum among the Poor Knights of Windsor; but the next heir, Sir Peter, pleading that his grandfather had dissipated his inheritance, was compelled to appeal to the public for assistance. Thus was fulfilled the old Kentish prophecy

> " Somerfield
> Shall quickly yield :
>   Scott's Hall *
> Shall have a fall ;
>   Ostenhanger †
> Was built in anger ;
>   Merstham Hatch ‡
> Shall win the match."

A branch of this house remains in Somersetshire.

The Baronets Hamound (now Hamond-Græme) also originated in Kent: their first recorded ancestor being Samuel Hamound of Blackheath, who died in 1715 : and their arms bear a strong family resemblance to those of the Haymans.

---

* The Scotts.

† Ostenhanger—now Westenhanger—is said to have been built by Bertram de Criol, temp. Henry III. ; it afterwards belonged to the Poynings and Smythes.

‡ The Knatchbulls.

Harcord: for Harcourt: a duplicate.

Iarden; or, as Anglicized, Garden. Des Jardens, Sieur de Saint Rémy, and Vicomte de Lions, was enrolled in 1668 among the Norman nobles, and bore *De gueules, à un écot, de 6 branches d'or posées en pal, chaque branche chargée d'une merlette de sable.* In England, Walter de Garden occurs in 1199 (Rot. Curiæ Regis): Nicholas de Gardin about 1272 (Rot. Hundred.): and Sir Thomas de Gardyn of Cambridge nearly thirty years later (Palgrave's Parl. Writs). They were of even earlier date in Scotland. "The Jardines held lands in the parish of Applegarth in Annandale before the Celtic element in the population was overlaid by that of the Saxons. Winfredus de Jardine, the first of the name on record, flourished prior to 1153; he having been a witness to various grants conferred during the reign of David I., on the Abbeys of Aberbrothwick and Kelso. Members of this old house have at various times intermarried with the Charterises, Douglasses, and other patrician families of the district. Sir William Jardine, Bart., the eminent naturalist, is the present head of the family." —*McDowall's Dumfries.* To this house probably belonged Sir Humphrey del Gardino, or Cardino, who witnesses several charters 1214–1218: and Sir William de Gardino, a witness to one of Robert Bruce in 1215. (Calendar of Documents relating to Scotland.)

A branch of these Jardines settled in Kent, where they gave their name to their residence, Jardines, in the parish of Leybourne. The last owner, Thomas de Gardinis, died 2 Ed. III., and left no sons.—*Hasted's Kent.* Another was seated in Somersetshire from the time of Henry III., when Emeric de Gardino or Gordain acquired through his marriage with a granddaughter of Geoffrey de Marisco some estates there, and made it his principal residence. The places where he held property still go by the names of Easton-in-Gordano, Weston-in-Gordano, Clapton-in-Gordano, &c.—*v. Collinson's Somerset.* William de Gardinis, in 1251, received from the Crown the lands of William Burnell the Outlaw, comprising Langley, a tenure *in capite.* In 1266 they were sold by his son William back to the Burnells.—*Eyton's Salop.* The Sir Thomas mentioned in Sir Francis Palgrave's work was Sheriff of Gloucester from 1287 to 1302, and of Cambridge and Huntingdon in 1299 and 1300.

Iay, or Gai. "Before 1135 the ancestor of Helias de Jay had been enfeoffed in the Shropshire manor of Bedston; and in 1165 the said Helias held it as a knight's fee under Geoffrey de Vere, then (*jure uxoris*) Baron of Clun. Helias seems to have married Margery, sister of Gilbert de Buckenhull. She was probably his second wife, and very much younger than himself."—*Eyton's Salop.* His line was extinguished in the fourth generation, ending with Thomas de Jay, who had died before 1349; but two of the manors dependent upon his Lordship of Bedston, Jay and Beckjay, are still called after him. A cadet of this house, "Brian de Jay, was the last Master of the English Knights Templars: at least he occurs in that office just before the dissolution of the Order in the reign of

Edward II." [*]—*Ibid.* He was the only Englishman of note slain at the battle of Falkirk in 1298: and Trivet tells us that "his fellow Master of the Order in Scotland, fighting along with Jay, was also killed."

In this, as in almost all other cases, the name was far from being confined to one county, or perchance even to one family. Philip Gai is mentioned in 1138 as a kinsman of the Earl of Gloucester (Flor. Wigorn. ii. 109): and may have left descendants in Gloucestershire; for a brass in the church of St. Mary Radcliffe, Bristol, commemorates John Jay, Sheriff of the county in 1472, with his six sons and eight daughters. Robert de Gay was a benefactor of Oseney, Oxford (Mon. ii. 142): the same Sir Robert, of Hampton-Gay in Oxfordshire, who, in the time of Stephen, founded a Cistercian house at Ottley; the fourth monastery of that Order in England. The foundation charter is witnessed by Robert D'Oyly, the King's Constable, and Ralph de Salcey, and D'Oyly's frail wife, Edith Forne, was among the benefactresses. "Before the buildings were, however, complete, the monks deserted Ottley on account of the unwholesomeness of the low, damp situation; and fixed themselves near the Bishop of Lincoln's park at Thame."—*Lupton's Thame.* The new foundation was thence named Thame Abbey. The monks obtained a confirmation charter from Sir Robert's heirs; of whom three generations are given. His grandson and namesake married Edith D'Oyley. Adam de Gay, no doubt his descendant, held lands in Oxford and Wilts 9 Ed. II.—*Testa de Nevill.* According to Sir Bernard Burke, the family migrated into Devonshire, and married the heiress of Goldsworthy, where they settled in 1420. "John Gay, the poet, was of the Goldsworthy family, the heir male of which, when Lysons wrote, was Mr. Lawrence Gay, of South Molton." Dr. Johnson, in his *Life of Gay*, alludes to his descent "from an old family that had been long in possession of the manor of Goldsworthy;" but adds that "Goldsworthy does not appear in the *Villare:*" and Chalmers suggests that Holdsworthy is probably meant. His parents were in poor circumstances; and "being born without prospect of hereditary riches, he was sent to London in his youth, and apprenticed to a silk mercer."

Ieniels, Juels, or Joels. Helias and Robert Juels are mentioned in the Norman Exchequer Rolls of 1180–95. Galfrid, William, and Richard Juel or Joel occur in Huntingdonshire, about 1272. (Rot. Hundred.) "This family derived probably from Juel or Judael de Mayenne, Baron of Totness and Barnstaple, temp. William I.: a Breton noble (see *Maine*). He held lands from the Earl of Mortaine, besides his own barony; and a portion of the former, as well as a fief created in the Barony of Totness, seems to have passed to the younger branch named Fitz Juel. Warin Fitz Juel, in 1242, held a knight's fee,

---

[*] This is an error. The last Grand Master of the Temple in England was Brother William de la More, who in 1312 "died of a broken heart in his solitary dungeon in the Tower, persisting with his last breath in the maintenance of the innocence of his Order."—*Addison's Knights Templars.*

which had been granted by the Earl of Mortaine at the Conquest (Testa de Neville, 184). Thomas Fitz Juel, at the same time, held lands from the Barony of Totness (*Ibid.* 176). A Juel occurs c. 1450 (Pole, Devon, 375). John Jewell, Bishop of Salisbury, the famous divine, was born at Bowdon in Devonshire, where the family of Juel or Fitz Joel had been long resident."—*The Norman People.* Froissart mentions a Sir John Joel, who, with Sir Jacques Planchyn, "went to serve the captall of Buch with two hundred spears," and were both slain when he was taken prisoner.

But the chief illustration of the family was the Bishop, "a perfect rich gem and true jewel indeed, whose life is written in fair sunshine."—*Westcote.* "So devout," says Fuller, "in the pew where he prayed, diligent in the pulpit where he preached, grave on the bench where he assisted, mild in the consistory where he judged, pleasant at the table where he fed, patient in the bed where he died, that well it were if, in relation to him, 'secundum usum Sarum,' were made precedential to all posterity." By Queen Elizabeth's special command, his 'Apology for the Church of England' was read in every church throughout the realm; and "his 'Sermons,' in black letter, may yet be seen chained up, as of yore, in some of the churches of the West."—*Worth's Devon.* Bowden Farm, the little house among the hills where he was born—a small, poor place where his ancestors had lived for many generations—is still standing.

Polwhele tells us that " John Jewell of Northcot (in right of his wife, Agnes Cutcliff) left five co-heiresses." The Bowden family had been extinct previous to 1600. They bore *Or*, on a chevron *Azure* between three July flowers, a demi-maiden *Gules* crined *Or*: on a chief *Sable* a lure between two falcons *Argent*, legged and beaked *Or:* a most remarkable coat, that probably refers to some now forgotten legend.

Ierconuise. Here, as in the case of Vasderoll, I believe an *s* has crept into the place of an *l*, and that we should read Jerconville. "Andreâ de Jarcumvyle and Simone de Jarcumvyle" witness a grant made to Chartley Priory by William de Ferrers (obt. 1288), the second son of the Earl of Derby. Nicholas de Jarcumvyle was of Oxfordshire, temp. Ed. I.—*Rotuli Hundredorum.* About the end of the previous reign, Sir David de Jargonuile was among the persons suggested as fit gaol-deliverers for the counties of Sussex and Surrey. — *Public Record Office, no.* 4692. In the Camden *Roll of Arms,* " Jerkavile " bears Quarterly *Or* and *Azure*, in the first quarter a Lion rampant *Gules.*

Ianuile, for Joinville or Geneville. "Thomas de Joannisvilla and his fief occur in Normandy 1180–95 : Ralph de Jehanville 1198 (Magn. Rotul. Scaccarii Normanniæ). Of this family, Roger de Geneville gave the church of Pictariville about 1000 to St. Taurin Abbey, near Evreux (Gall. Christ. xi. 139 Inst.). His descendants came to England 1066; and temp. Henry I. Hugh de Janville witnessed the charter of Lenton Priory 1100–1108 (Mon. i. 654). He was

Viscount of Leicester 1130, and Seneschal to Matilda de Senlis (Rot. Pip. and
Mon. i. 672). Ivo de Leicester, his son, was living 1130 (Rot. Pip.)."—*The
Norman People.* Nicholls gives their coat *Azure* 3 barnacles *Or,* on a chief
Ermine a lion naissant *Gules.* William Jaunville was knight of the shire for
Leicester in 1322. Nicholas de Janville was of Oxfordshire, and Galfrid de
Ganville of Devonshire temp. Ed. I.—*Rotuli Hundredorum.* He must have been
the Geoffrey de Geyneville, sometimes called Joinville de Vaucouleurs and
Dominus de Valli Coloris, who is mentioned at Ludlow in 1277, and was the
brother of Sir John de Joinville, Grand Seneschal of Champagne, the biographer
and companion-at-arms of St. Louis, whom he accompanied to the Holy Land in
1248. He was of an altogether different race from the Jehanvilles or Genevilles
of Normandy. The house to which he belonged was one of the noblest of
Champagne, and had been seated at Joinville, a small town on the river Marne
from whence it derived its name, as early as the 11th century. The elder
brother, on his return from Palestine, spent his time chiefly at the court of his
suzerain the King of Navarre, Count of Champagne; but Geoffrey became the
second husband of a wealthy Englishwoman, Maud, the eldest of the two grand-
daughters and coheiresses of the great Walter de Lacy. She brought him a
moiety of Meath in Ireland, afterwards called the Lordship of Trim, and the
castle of Ludlow in Wales, with the privileges and duties of a Baron Marcher;
and he was twice summoned for military service against the Welsh. He also
fought in Gascony, and had summons to parliament as a baron of the realm in
1298. Eyton mentions him among the chief benefactors of the Black Friars of
Shrewsbury. According to Dugdale, he had four sons, Geoffrey, Peter, Simon,
and William. Geoffrey died before him, leaving no posterity; and Peter
succeeded to his possessions, though not to his barony by writ. Peter's wife was
Joan de Lusignan, daughter of Hugh XII., surnamed Le Brun, Count de la
Marche, by whom he had three daughters, Joan, Isabel, and Beatrix; the two
youngest took the veil at Aconbury, and Joan remained sole heiress. She was
married to Roger Mortimer Earl of March, the notorious favourite of Edward II.,
" whereby the whole inheritance of Genevill, and half the lands of Lacy came to
that family, and by its heiress eventually to the Crown, in the person of King
Edward IV."—*Banks.*

Simon de Genevill, the next brother, married Joan de Fitz Leons, Lady of
Culmullen, and, as one of the " Fideles " of Ireland, several times occurs in
Palgrave's *Parliamentary Writs.* . He was three times called upon to serve
against the Scots : thanked for " his good service against the Scottish and Irish
rebels " in 1315 : and " commanded to attack and pursue Roger de Mortimer "
(his niece's husband) " in the event of his taking refuge in Ireland " in 1323.
He had one son, Nicholas; and five daughters; the eldest married to John
Hussey, Lord of Galtrim ; the second to William de Loundres of Athboy ; the
third to the Baron of Slane ; the fourth to Walter de la Hyde, and the fifth to

John Cruce, or Cruys. Nicholas left no heir male ; and his only daughter Joan conveyed Culmullen to John Cusack of Beaurepaire.

The youngest son of Geoffrey, William de Geneville, received from Edward I., " in consideration of the valuable services performed by them both, the marriage of the younger Daughter of John Giffard of Brimsfield, and Maud Longespe his Wife, one of the Co-heirs of the said Maud."—*Dugdale.* It must have been through this, his last born son, that Geoffrey became, as the Père Anselme styles him, " tige des Seigneurs de Vaucouleurs," but I have met with no account of his posterity.

Iasperuile. Can this be intended for Jarpenville? In 1316, Andrew of Jarpenville was Lord of Mentmore, and William de Jarpenville Lord of Woughton, both in Buckinghamshire, where William de Gerpounvill had witnessed Henry II.'s grant to Nutley Abbey. Roger de Jarpenville, in 1325, was summoned from Surrey to pass into Guyenne under the command of the Earl of Warrenne, and served as knight of the shire in the same year.—*Palgrave's Parl. Writs.* The name was taken from Jarpenville, near Yvetot, and occurs at a very early date in Essex, where Geoffrey de Jarpenvill held of the Earl in 1165 (Lib. Niger) : and it is retained by Totham Jarpenvill, and Gerbervill, or Jerpins, in the parish of Rainham. " The earliest possessors, after the General Survey, that we have there are the Jarpenvill family. John de Jarpenvill, who died in 1259, held of the King *in capite.* Roger was his next heir. At the time of his decease, in 1287, he was found to hold, *in capite,* in Totham and Goldangre, by the service of five knights' fees, and 40*s.* yearly to the ward of Dover castle. Maud, wife of Philip de Heveningham, was his daughter and heir."—*Morant.* David de Jarpunvill was of Hertfordshire, temp. Ed. I. (Rotul. Hundred.) In the reign of King John, " Albritha de Rumenel, who was *Marshall of the King's birds* by inheritance, married William de Jarpenvile : their daughter and heir Alice married Thomas Fitzbernard, to whom and their heirs for ever, on the petition of their mother, the King granted that office after her death."—*Hasted's Kent.* David de Jarpenvile held a knight's fee at Albury in Surrey of the Honour of Clare : and Galfrid de Jarpenville another at Abingworth in the same county of Roger de Someri. The latter was likewise a tenant of the Earl of Essex in Essex, where Dom' Matilda de Jarponville is further mentioned.—*Testa de Nevill.*

Kaunt. This family is mentioned as early as 1153-1194 in the Durham *Bolden Buke* (a survey of his diocese ordered by Bishop Hugh Pudsey) where it is said that " Gilbert the Chamberlain held the service of Ralfe Caunt, of Bursebred, in exchange for the Isle of Bradbere." In Bishop Hatfield's time (1345-1381) Henry de Kaunt held lands in Kyo. The name is found up to the middle of the 17th century. I am, however, doubtful whether it is the one really intended ; as Leland, in his list, gives this and the next as Gaunt et Garre. (See *Gaunt.*)

Karre: Two brothers, of Anglo-Norman descent, who bore this name, are said to have settled in Scotland during the 13th century. No one knows which was the elder of the two, for "neither house would yield the superiority to the other,* forming two distinct races of war-like Border chieftains." The Kers of Fernihirst are represented by the Marquesses of Lothian, the Kers of Cessford by the Dukes of Roxburghe; but the first only of these families now continues in the male line.

The Kers of Cessford descend from "Johanni Ker de foresta de Selkirk," mentioned in 1307. The barony of "Auld Roxburghe" was in their possession as early as 1451: and Andrew Ker "of Cessford" was one of the conservators of a truce with the English in 1457. In the latter end of that century, Sir Robert Ker, "a favourite with James IV., and his chief cup-bearer," was Warden of the Middle Marches, and ruled with such exasperating severity, that he was set upon and slain (about 1500) by three Englishmen, Lilburn, Starked, and "the bastard Heron." Andrew, the son, retaliated by sending two of his retainers to bring him Starked's head, which was triumphantly "exposed in one of the most public places in Edinburgh." Another Sir Robert, tenth in descent from the founder of the family, also a march-warden, and "a brave active young man, though somewhat haughty and resolute," was created a baron about 1600 (the exact date is not known), and Earl of Roxburghe in 1616. Both his sons died before him, leaving no heirs-male; and the Earldom was inherited by Sir William Drummond, the fourth son of his eldest daughter, Jean, Countess of Perth; the liberal terms of his charter of creation having empowered him to select whatever heir he chose to "call to the succession." Four of Sir William's descendants bore the title: and Robert, fifth Earl, one of the Secretaries of State in 1704, "having heartily promoted the Union and the Protestant succession,' was created Duke of Roxburghe in 1707, with remainder to "other heirs destined to succeed to the title and dignity of Earl of Roxburghe." When the third Duke died s. p. in 1804, the Dukedom consequently devolved on a remote kinsman, William, sixth Lord Bellenden, then a childless old man of seventy-six, who only survived till the following year. He was descended from John Lord Bellenden the fourth son of the second Earl (Sir W. Drummond,) and with him, the whole male line of the latter failed, and a long litigation ensued. After a "tedious investigation" that lasted seven years, the House of Lords decreed the titles to Sir James Innes, as the representative of Margaret Ker, third daughter of Harry, Lord Ker, and granddaughter of the first Earl. He, too, had reached the age of seventy-six, but lived to be eighty-seven, and in his eighty-first year his second wife brought him a son, who succeeded as sixth Duke in 1823.

One of this family, named Mark, the second son of Sir Andrew Ker of

---

* So savage did this quarrel become, that William Ker of Ancrum was actually assassinated by Robert Ker of Cessford, "when the disputes about the seniority of the families of Fernihirst and Cessford ran high" in 1590.

Cessford, had been elected Abbot of Newbottle in 1546 : but, at the Reformation " renounced the profession of popery," took to himself a wife, and obtained a charter as " commendator " of Newbottle : thus, by a strange metamorphosis, ruling as a lay lord where he had ruled as a monk. His eldest son Mark had the lands erected into a barony, with the title of a baron, in 1587 ; and was created Earl of Lothian in 1609. The second Earl left only two daughters, of whom the elder, Lady Anne, in her own right Countess of Lothian, married William, eldest son of Robert, first Earl of Ancrum, " and thus carried the title into the house of Fernihirst, of whom we have now to treat."

The first of this house was Ralph Ker, who settled in Teviotdale about 1330, and " got possession of the lands lying betwixt the water of Jed and the lands of Straseburgh " (thence called Kersheugh), which he held of the Douglases. Towards the end of the following century, Thomas Ker " built a house in Jedburgh Forest, to which he gave the name of Fernihirst," and erected his lands into a barony, under the charter of his feudal superior, the Earl of Angus. The next in succession, Sir Andrew, who " made a great figure in the reigns of James IV. and V.," received, on the forfeiture of the House of Angus in 1528, a charter of Fernihirst from the Crown. He had two sons : 1. Sir John, ancestor of the Lords Jedburgh : 2. Robert, ancestor of the Earls of Ancrum.

Of the elder line was Sir Thomas Ker, " a stout and able warrior, and a steady friend and most loyal servant to Queen Mary," who sheltered and protected her adherent, the Earl of Westmorland, in his castle of Fernihirst after the Rising of the North. He was ill repaid, for the gallant Earl disturbed the peace of the household by amusing himself with " the Laird's new wanton lady." Fernihirst was destroyed by the English in the following year, to revenge a foray made only a few months before, when he, and Sir Walter Scott of Buccleuch, entered England with fire and sword. In 1671 he suffered forfeiture as one of " the Queen's party," and wandered about France, Spain, and Holland, till the accession of James VI. enabled him to return home and recover his estates. His third son was the notorious Robert Ker, who attended King James to England as one of his pages, and soon shone forth like " a comet " among the crowd of competitors, as the first favourite at court. On the death of Dunbar, he was named Lord Treasurer of Scotland ; then, in 1611, he became Viscount Rochester and a Knight of the Garter : in 1613 Lord Carr of Brancepeth, with a grant of the Castles and honours of Raby, Brancepeth, and Barnard, forfeited by the Nevills, in the Bishopric of Durham, Earl of Somerset, and Lord Chamberlain of the Household. But, unhappily for himself, he fell in love with the most profligate woman of her time, Lady Frances Howard, Countess of Essex, who divorced her husband in order to marry him. He had " received into his intimate familiarity a Knight of excellent parts, called Sir Thomas Overburie," who very sensibly " disswaded him from her company : " but, " finding that, notwithstanding what had been said, he had a purpose to marry her, he so far presumed upon the friendly freedom which he had otherwise given him, to press him more earnestly to forbear her. And one night, dealing more plainly with him, said, ' My Lorde, I perceive you are proceeding in this Match, from which I have often disswaded you, as your true servant, and friend; I now again, advise you not to marry that woman: for if you do, you shall ruine your Honor: and yourself.' Adding, 'that if he went on in that business, he should do well to looke to his standing.'

"Which free Speech of his, this Earl, taking impatiently, because he had touch't the Lady in her Honor; replyed in Passion : 'That his Legs were strong enough to bear him up: and that he should make him repent those Speeches.' But Overburie, interpreting this to be only a sudden passion, thought not that their long continu'd Friendship would break off by this occasion; and therefore continued his wonted attendance; neither did this Earl wholly abandon him. Howbeit, having discovered his words to the Lady, she never ceased; but by all means sought his overthrow. It hapning therefore about this time, that Overburie being design'd for Embassador into Russia, this Earl (whose Counsel he askt) advised him to refuse the service, but to make some fair excuse. Which advice he followed, supposing that it did proceed of kindness; but, for his refusal, was committed to the Tower.

"The Lady thus having him where she wished; and resolving to dispatch him by Poyson, wrought so with Sir Gervase Elways, then Lieutenant of the Tower, as that he admitted one Richard Weston, upon her recommendation, to be his Keeper; by whom (the very evening after he was so committed) a yellow Poyson was ministered to him in a Broth at Supper."—*Dugdale.* This first dose was a failure : and six different poisons—whatever was reputed most deadly, "to be sure to hit his complexion"—were tried upon him. One Mistress Turner, well skilled in their use, prepared them, with the help of a man named Franklin. Everything he tasted was poisoned; arsenic was mixed with his salt, cantharides used instead of pepper, and diamond powder sprinkled as a seasoning: yet, in spite of this fiendish perseverance, they were a long time in killing him. When he was at last dead, they hurried him into his grave, pretending that he had died of "the French Pox" to explain the state of his body. Yet rumours of foul play presently got abroad; and though the known "greatness of the promoters" sealed men's lips for awhile, the truth was not very long in leaking out, and the whole detestable story was brought to light. The poisoners confessed their guilt: the conscience-stricken Lieutenant of the Tower admitted that he had "winked at their doings;" and all four suffered on the gallows at Tyburn. Mistress Turner, who was a milliner and clear-starcher, was "order'd to be hanged in her yellow Tiffiny Ruff and Cuff, being she was the first inventor and wearer of that horrid garb. Never since which," it is added, "was ever any seen to wear the like." Yet the foul instigators of the crime escaped with their lives. After great efforts to avoid being brought to justice, the Earl and his wicked Countess were tried, found guilty, and sentenced to death. "With the Lady," says Dugdale, "there was not much ado; she, with many teares, confessing the fact; but the Earl made some show of defence," and the King chose to reprieve them both. Somerset was confined for a few years in the Tower, and then received a full pardon. He died in 1645, leaving one daughter, Anne, married to the first Duke of Bedford,* and the mother of the celebrated Lord Russell.

Some share in the sunshine of Royal favour fell to the lot of Lord Somerset's elder brother, Sir Andrew Ker, who was created Lord Jedburgh in 1622. His nephew, the third Lord, having no children of his own, in 1670 made an entail of his estate and honours in favour of his nearest heir-male, William, Lord Newbottle, son of Robert, then Earl, and afterwards Marquess of Lothian.

Lord Newbottle descended from a younger son of their joint ancestor Sir Andrew (see p. 164), Robert Ker of Ancrum, whose grandson had been created Earl of Ancrum by Charles I., and sacrificed his whole fortune in the Royal cause. He died during the Commonwealth, in exile and deep poverty, embittered by the knowledge that his favourite son, Lord Lothian, had been serving in the enemy's camp. This son was the husband of Anne, Countess of Lothian (see p. 165), and obtained a fresh charter of her Earldom in 1634, though he is always styled the third Earl of that name. After the death of his father and younger brother, he was also Earl of Ancrum. From the first a zealous adherent of the Covenant, he was in the Scottish army that invaded England in 1640; imprisoned in Bristol as a traitor in 1643, and the following year again in arms against Montrose. But he was also one of the Scottish Commissioners who

---

* The Earl, his father, who had sat upon their trial, was "horrified when his son proposed to marry the child of so ominous a pair. But Lady Anne was not touched by the crimes of her parents. Her loveliness shone perhaps the more attractively against so dark a background. Her character must have been singularly innocent, for she grew up in entire ignorance that her ņother had been tried for murder." It was not till after the execution of her son that, "in the midst of her wretchedness she found accidentally in a room at Woburn a pamphlet with an account of the Overbury murder. For the first time she learned the dreadful story. She was found senseless, with her hand upon the open page, and she never rallied from the blow."—*Froude.* One more anecdote of this fair Lady Anne. The old Earl had said to his son, "Marry whom ye will, so that it be not Lady Anne Carr:" and when it was found that Lady Anne Carr was the only woman in the world whom the young man cared to marry, there was a long and direful struggle before he would give his consent. But Lady Anne, though ignorant of the real cause of his opposition, bore no malice. When he sickened of the small-pox, and every one around him shrank away from the dreaded contagion, his daughter-in-law, alone of all his family, remained faithfully by his side to nurse him. She took the infection; and though she recovered from the cruel malady, paid the penalty of her devotion by the entire loss of her beauty. How radiant that beauty was, is avouched by the golden-haired portrait by Van Dyck that remains of her at Petworth.

protested against the execution of the King, and so out-spoken in his honest indignation, that he was put under arrest, and sent back to Scotland with a guard. It would, in fact, appear to have wrought a complete change in his sentiments, for he afterwards went to Breda on an embassy to invite Charles II. to Scotland. His son Robert, fourth Earl, created Marquess of Lothian in 1700, was the father of Lord Newbottle, to whom Lord Jedburgh left his title and property, and is now represented by the ninth Marquess.

The lineage of the founders of the family, the two brothers of Anglo-Norman blood, has never been traced; but the author of the 'Norman People' believes them to have belonged to the house of Espec. "Walter Espec, in the time of Henry I., possessed estates in York and Northumberland, and on the death of his son he founded Kirkham Abbey, to which he gave the church of Carr-on-Tweed (Burton, Mon. Ebor.). The lordship, however, appears to have been to another Walter Espec, brother of William, whose sons Robert and William de Carrum held it t. Henry II.; for the former in 1165 returned his barony as one fee held by him and his brother t. Henry I. (Lib. Nig.). Walter de Carum, his son, was deceased before 1207 (Hardy, Obl. et Fin.). Thomas de Carro, his son, was father of William, whose son Richard Fitz William, with Michael Ker and John Ker (his kinsman) paid scutage together in Northumberland. This Richard Fitz William Carr or Ker was seated in Scotland before 1249, as appears by the Chartulary of Melrose (i. 232). His son was father of 1. Ralph, living 1330: 2. John Ker of Selkirk Forest, living 1357," the progenitors of the two rival races. But if we admit the original form of the name to be Cairune or Cairum, it is at least equally probable that the Kers descend from the "Guillaume de Cairon" on the Dives Roll. This family was certainly established in the North, for it appears, as Charron, in the earlier records of the Bishopric of Durham.

Karrowe. Here again we come upon a disputed etymology. Mr. Carew, in his 'Survey of Cornwall,' tells us that "his first ancestor came out of France with William the Conqueror by the name of Karrow.

> " Carew of ancient Carru was; and Carru is a plow ;
> Romans the Trade, Frenchmen the Worde; I do the name avow."

Karo, or Caro, is a Cornish word signifying hart or deer. Dugdale, and most other authorities, believe that the family is denominated from Carew Castle in Pembrokeshire. Sir Egerton Brydges declares that " Kari (or Carey) and Karrowe (or Carew) are derived from the castles of Kari and Carew in Somersetshire." Well may our puzzled county historian piteously cry out— "Thus God, in his providence, to check our presumptuous inquisitions and pretensions, hath wrapped all things in uncertainty, and bars us from long antiquity."

Prince, in his 'Worthies of Devon,' asserts that the name was first assumed by William de Windsor or de Carew, to whom King John, "by deed dated 1212, made a further grant of Molesford in Berkshire, reciting the former deed of King Henry I to his grandfather Gerald." This Gerald, Castellan of the Welsh castle of Carew, was the second son of Walter Fitz Other, Castellan of Windsor under the Conqueror, and ancestor of the great Irish house of Fitz Gerald. But the name was certainly borne before the thirteenth century, for, as early as 1189, Peter de Carow held a knight's fee in Oveton and Seaton—from him still named Seaton-Carew—on the coast of Durham. Leland's account, given on the authority of one of the family, is probably the most trustworthy. "The very name of Sir George Carow in the Weste Cuntrey and of his Familie, ys Mont-gomerick; and Carow is a Name of Hônour taken upon the Name of a Barony so caullid." It is an unquestioned fact that Arnulph de Montgomery, one of the younger sons of Roger, first Earl of Shrewsbury, was the builder of Carew Castle; and it is quite in accordance with the usual practice of those times, that his descendants should have borne the name of his barony; though Camden, in his 'Remains,' gives a different explanation. "The same," he says, "holds by tradition, I know not how truly, that Arnold, or rather Adam, alias Montgomery, marrying the daughter of Carew of Molesford, his son, relin-quishing his own name, left to his posterity his mother's name of Carew, from whom the Carews of Surrey, Devon, and Cornwall, are descended." At all events, as a local English name, adopted after the Conquest, it should have no place here.

Koine; synonymous with Cahaignes, and denoting one of the most numerous and powerful families of the realm. The name is derived from the fief of Cahaignes in the arrondissement of Vire (Latinized *Chaineis* in the Norman Infeudation Roll of 1172), which was held of the Comté of Mortaine. William de Cahaignes—the "Sire de Chaignes" of the Roman de Rou—came over in the train of the Earl his suzerain, and was one of his principal feudatories in England as in Normandy, holding lands in Sussex, Bucks, Cambridge, and Northants. As he was also a tenant-in-chief in the two latter counties, he is counted among the Domesday barons, and had his seat at Dodford in Northamptonshire. His son Ralph, who, as "Radulfus de Caisned," also appears in Domesday, holding Horsted-Keynes in Sussex, was a benefactor of Lewes Priory. On its consecration (between 1091 and '97), he "offered, on the altar of St. Pancras, the churches of Brighton, Balcombe, Hoathley, Kymer and Barncombe; his son Ralph also offered a hide of land; both subscribed the charter which recites these gifts."—*Sussex Archæologia.* This second Ralph married a Kentish heiress, Alice, daughter of Hugh, and sister of Walkelin Maminot,* with whom he had "in Frank Marriage" by gift of

---

* Most authorities make her out to have been his father's wife; but the elder Ralph's gifts to Lewes Priory were bestowed "for the Soul of Emme his Wife."

Henry I., Tarent and Combe (both of which still retain his name) in Dorsetshire, and Somerford in Somersetshire. He founded a nunnery at Tarent-Keynes (now Tarent-Keyneston), which was held of the King in chief by the service of three knights. He also gave Dodford Church to the monks of Luffield in Northamptonshire; and those of Combe Keynes and Cahaignes to Merton Priory, where his wife had been buried. It further appears, that before the close of Henry I.'s reign, the barony held by his grandfather in 1086, with the Norman fiefs, had been parted between him and his brother Hugh; and "on this patrimonial division, Dodford was constituted the *caput baroniæ.* There were then fourteen mesne manors dependent upon it."—*Baker's Northamptonshire.* Hugh had Gretworth and the Sussex estates, and his son William was Sheriff of the county for nine years under King John. But the line expired with the following generation, and the lands passed, through an heiress, to Roger de Lewkenor.

Ralph, the Baron of Dodford, who possessed the Northamptonshire and Dorsetshire property, had also a son named William, "succeeded by another Ralph de Cahaignes, Sheriff of the counties of Dorset and Somerset from 3 to 6 Ric. I.; in which last year he was deceased, for then his son William paid relief for his lands, and became his successor in the shrievalty, which he held till the end of the reign of Richard I. On the accession of King John he fell under the royal displeasure, and both his lands in Normandy were seized and his chattels in England sold by the officers of the crown: but, having made proffer of one hundred marks for having the good will of the King, he had restitution of his lands, for which he paid scutage in 1202."—*T. Stapleton.* He died in 1221. The succession continued uninterrupted for five generations more;—till the death, in his boyhood, of the last male heir in 1337. His sister Wentiliana, who "never had Child," and his aunt Elizabeth, likewise unmarried, died within a few months of each other in the succeeding year; but another aunt, Hawise, the wife of Sir John Daventry, had left a granddaughter, Alice, then married to Lewis Carroll, in whom "the right of inheritance clearly vested."[*] Yet, through the "artful chicaneries" of Sir William Brantingham,[†] who had been the guardian of the young heir and his sister Wentiliana,

---

[*] Not only were Hawise de Keyne's descendants disinherited, but her very existence was denied in the following century; when a letter, dated 1404, was produced, "under the seals of many worshipful men at Tarent Keynes, and another, under the seals of many gentlemen of Northants, declaring that Sir William de Keynes (her father) never had a daughter Hawise."—*Baker's Northants.*

[†] Of this Sir William's "collusions and 'contell'" it was proved: That after the death of Wentiliana, he excited (incited) a woman to present herself before persons unknown, and personate Elizabeth Keynes, as late coming from the Holy Land, 'in white clothyn as it were in an estate of innocencye;' when on discreet examination she was found to be 'a beest envenymed through the covetyc of the said Brantingham.'"—*Ibid.*

Dodford passed to a descendant of their great-aunt Lettice Ayote, John Cressy, whose son and grandson successively held it. When the latter died s. p. in 1452, it apparently reverted to the representatives of Hugh de Keynes, a cadet of the house, who, in the time of Henry II. had married Amabel de Bereville, the heiress of Milton (since Milton-Keynes) in Buckinghamshire. The male heir of his posterity failed in the first part of the fourteenth century, when Margaret, the heiress, married Sir Philip de Ailesbury. In 1462 Dodford belonged to Dame Eleanor Stafford, "to whom it had been assigned on the partition of the Ailesbury property;" and was claimed by the King's ever greedy brother-in-law, Sir Edward Widville, on the ground of a pretended descent, through the Purefoys, from Lettice Ayote; though "the Purefoys came never of the blood of Keynes or of Ayote." However, Edward IV., to whom the dispute was referred, decided in favour of the Staffords.

Another younger brother, William de Cahaignes, called by Dugdale the son, but more probably the grandson of the Domesday Baron, "being in the Battle of Lincoln (in 6 Stephen) on the behalf of Maud the Empress, had a vigilant Eye on King Stephen, and observed where he was, who fought most courageously, first with his Pole-Ax till it broke, and afterwards with his Sword, so long as it held. Which when he discerned, he rushed in upon him, and took him by the Helmet, crying out, 'Come hither, come hither, I have hold of the King,' and so took him prisoner." Stephen, deserted as he was by his army, had held his ground to the very end: and when "left almost alone on the field, no Man dared approach him, while grinding his Teeth and foaming like a mad Boar, he drove back with his Battel-axe whole Troops that came to assail him," and felled the Earl of Chester from his horse with a single blow. Even in the last extremity, when both his weapons had broken in his hands, and William de Cahaignes' grasp was on his crest, it was to none other but his cousin, the Earl of Gloucester, that he would deign to surrender.

The seat of this gallant Sir William was in Devonshire. "The Fee of Winkley, now called the Fee of Gloucester," writes old Westcott, "belonged to Keyns, from whom both castle and parish had addition, and were called Keyns Castle and Winkley Keyns; they were powerful in the country; and Sir William Keyns, a stout and valiant knight fighting under Robert Earl of Gloucester, took King Stephen prisoner at the battle of Lincoln. John Keyns was Sheriff of this county 4 Hen. IV. Another of them was £60 on the subsidy book 14 Hen. VI. Divers of them lie interred in the church, one especially noted for being donor and patron of the church." Lysons asserts that they remained for fifteen generations at Winkley-Keynes. One of them, John de Keynes, acquired a large estate in Dorset and Somerset in the time of Edward III. through Isabel Wake his wife. Her father John Wake, held Candel Wake, and Stoke-Wake in the former county; and "became possessed of Compton Martin in Somersetshire by seizin, because Alice his mother, who held the manor in her demesne as of fee, of William de Martin, knt., forfeited it by contriving the death of Ralph her husband, for which she was burnt, according to her sentence, after fair trial. He also held the lands of East and West Dowlish, co. Somerset, of which, fifteen days before his death (in 1350) he feoffed Isabel, wife of John de Keynes, Margery Tyrel, and Elizabeth Wake, his daughters."—*Hutchins' Dorset.* The heiress of the elder branch of this house, Joan Keynes, married John Speke in the reign of Henry V.; but the Keynes continued seated at Wake Court till 1594; not long after (as Hutchins tells us), one of the family alienated it to the Mores, and, according to Lysons, removed into Somersetshire.

Hitherto there has been no difficulty in affiliating the various branches of the house of Cahaignes to the parent stock; but we now enter upon the knotty question of distinguishing from each other the different families merged in the common name of Cheney. (See *Cheney.*) Here the coats of arms alone can help us. The Cheneys of Norfolk and Suffolk, representing the De Quesnais, bore *Or* two chevrons *Gules:* the De Chenduits ("falsely called Cheney") *Gules* on five lozenges in fesse *Argent* as many escallop shells *Sable;* while the De Cahaignes had two distinct bearings. The Barons of Horsford and Tarent-Keynes bore Vaire *Argent* and *Azure,* two bars *Gules* (v. *Baker's Northants*): and the house of Winkley-Keynes *Azure* a bend undée cotised *Argent,* which is also attributed to Tarent-Keynes, though, as the Northamptonshire and Dorsetshire estates were never separated, it is hard to conceive how the same man could possibly bear a different coat in each county. This bend and these bars, amalgamated into a fesse, re-appear, in an infinite variety of tinctures, on most of the Cheney coats, indicating that their bearers were of the blood of Cahaignes. Thus, the Cheneys of Chesham-Boys, Viscounts Newhaven, bore Chequy *Or* and *Azure* a fesse *Gules,* fretted *Argent;* in other cases the fesse was fretted *Ermine,* or, as borne by the Cheneys or Chanus of Willaston in Cheshire, fretted *Or.* Again, the Cheneys of Fen Ditton, Cambridgeshire, whose heiress married Lord Vaux of Harrowden in the sixteenth century, bore Quarterly *Or* and *Sable,* over all a bend lozengy *Gules;* while the Kentish Cheneys bore *Ermine* on a bend *Sable* three martlets *Or.* It would require far more time and patience than I have to spare to recapitulate all the changes rung upon this bend and fesse, which the multiplied sub-divisions of the family rendered necessary.

Of all these—and their name was Legion—the greatest was incontestably the Kentish house, that at one time held its place among the foremost in the county. Its first recorded ancestor, Sir Alexander, was seated at Patricksbourne-Cheney, and went with Coeur de Lion to the Holy Land: but it was not till about one hundred years afterwards that William de Cheney founded the great fortune of the family by his marriage with the heiress of Shurland. Her father, Sir Robert de Shurland, "a man of eminent authority in the reign of Edward I., under whom he was Lord Warden of the Five Ports," was the hero of the curious tradition,

commemorated on his monument,[*] that forms the subject of one of the
'Ingoldsby Legends.' Shurland, where "a very grand and spacious mansion"
was afterwards built, from this time forth became the residence of the Cheneys;
they adopted the coat of Shurland, *Azure* six lions rampant *Argent*, a canton
Ermine, for their own, and are constantly found on the roll of Sheriffs and
knights of the shire. One of their manors, Cheney's Court, in Chart Sutton,
recalls their name in the neighbourhood. Sir William's descendant, Sir John
Cheney, was "in arms for Henry Earl of Richmond at Bosworth Field, when
King Richard himself encountering with him (after he had overthrown Sir
William Brandon, the Earl of Richmond's Standard-Bearer) though this Sir John
was a person of very great strength, fell'd him to the ground."—*Dugdale.* Sir
John had pressed forward to raise the royal standard as it dropped from the
dying hand of Brandon; and to shield the Earl from the deadly arm of the
King. But, giant though he was in strength and stature, he had met with more
than his match.

> "With scorn he throws the standard to the ground,
> When Cheney, for his height and strength renown'd,
> Steps forth to cover Richmond now exposed
> To Richard's sword: the King with Cheney closed,
> And to the earth the mighty giant fell'd."—*Sir John Beaumont.*

The blow sundered his helmet and laid his head bare, but only stunned him;
and when, after a while, he recovered his senses, his first thought was to fit

---

[*] His effigy, clad in the chain-mail of the thirteenth century, remains on his tomb
in Minster Church, his hands clasped on his breast, and his legs crossed, to show that
he had fought in the Holy Land. Immediately above it, from the wall of the recess in
which the tomb stands, projects the head of a horse, which "seems to be emerging
from stony waves," as if in the act of swimming. "This figure," says Hasted, "has
given rise to a tale, which has been reported among the common people for many
years, viz.: That Sir Robert, having upon some disgust at a priest, buried him alive,
swam on his horse two miles through the sea to the King, who was then on ship-board
near this island" (of Sheppey), "and, having obtained his pardon, swam back to the
shore, where, being told his horse had performed this by magic art, he cut off his head.
About a twelvemonth after which, riding a-hunting near the same place, the horse he
was then upon, stumbled, and threw him upon the skull of his former horse, by which
he was so much bruised, that it caused his death: in memory of which, the figure of a
horse's head was placed by him on his tomb. The foundation of which story is by
others supposed to have arisen from Sir Robert Shurland's having obtained the grant
of wreck of the sea, which privilege is always esteemed to reach as far into the water,
as upon the lowest ebb, a man can ride in and touch anything with the point of his
lance; and on this account the horse's head was placed by him." To my thinking
this is a very lame explanation. Why should the horse's head appear above cloven
waves, as if swimming? The right of wreck was one of the accustomed feudal
privileges of lords of manors on the sea-coast; yet I have never heard of the existence
of any similar tomb.

himself again for the fray. He looked about him for the means of replacing his cloven helmet, and finding the hide of a slaughtered ox, cut off the scalp and horns, placed them on his head, and fought for the rest of the day in this eccentric head-piece. The family adopted it as their crest, and ever after bore the bull's scalp in memory of the field of Bosworth.

The new King was not slow in recompensing so intrepid and devoted a follower: he was sworn of the Privy Council, received the Order of the Garter, and was summoned to parliament in 1488 among the barons of the realm. But he left no posterity, and his well-earned honours expired with him. His nephew and heir, Sir Thomas, "lived under the sunshine and favour of four sovereigns, Henry VIII., Edward VI., Queen Mary and Queen Elizabeth, and acquired possessions in Kent almost as large as Odo's. He was a Knight of the Garter, Sheriff of Kent, Lord Warden of the Cinque Ports, Constable of Dover, Queenborough and Saltwood, High Steward of the Manors of Aldington and Chilham, Keeper of the parks of Ostenhanger (Westenhanger), Saltwood, Aldington, &c., and Treasurer of the Household to Henry VIII., who appointed him Governor over the seven Hundreds and adjoining districts, in case of war, for the term of his life."—Furley's *History of the Weald of Kent.* He was one of the knights-challengers at the Field of the Cloth of Gold, pledged to "exercise feats of arms against all comers, on horseback or on foot, for the space of thirty days."

But the full-blown prosperity of his house was doomed to collapse in the succeeding generation. He was cursed with a spendthrift son, aptly termed "the extravagant Lord Cheney," who dissipated the whole of his possessions. This reckless heir was created by Queen Elizabeth Baron Cheney of Tuddington in Bedfordshire, where he built a magnificent house on his mother's inheritance.* "In his youth," says Fuller, "he was very wild and venturous; witness his playing at dice with Henry II. King of France, from whom he won a Diamond of great worth at a Cast: and being demanded by the King, what shift he would have made to repair himself in case he had lost the cast: 'I have,' said young Cheney (in a hyperbolical brave) 'Sheep's Tails enough in Kent, with their Wool to buy a better Diamond than this.' His reduced Age afforded the befitting fruits of Gravity and Wisdom, and this Lord deceased without issue." Thus this second title again became extinct with its first bearer, who died in 1587. One of this house, Sir Robert Cheney (born in 1353) was the ancestor of the Cheneys of Cralle, who held lands in several parts of Sussex.

Another important family has left its name to Iselhampsted Cheneys (now abbreviated to Chenies), which had once been a royal residence, and was granted

* She was the representative of Paulin Peyvere, Sewer to Henry III., who had there built a "seat with such palace-like grandeur, such a chapel, such lodgings, with other houses of stone covered with lead, and surrounded it with such avenues and parks, that it raised an astonishment in the beholders."—*Matthew Paris.*

by Ed. III. to his shield-bearer, Thomas Cheyne. "From the Cheynes it passed to the Sapcotes, pursuant to the will of Agnes Lady Cheyne, who died in 1494; it is now the property of the Duke of Bedford, whose ancestor married the heiress of Sir Guy Sapcote."—*Lysons' Buckinghamshire.* The church, now the burial place of the Russells, retains many brass and two stone effigies of the Cheneys, the latter much defaced.* "The olde House of the Cheyneis," writes Leland, "is so translated by my Lorde Russel that lytle or nothing of it yn a maner remaynith ontranslatid: . . . it is within divers Places richly painted with antique Workes of White and Blak. And there be about the House two Parkes, as I remembre."

Another seat of the Cheneys, in the neighbouring parish of Chesham, was "a place of great strength," with a chapel adjoining; part of the great hall was still standing in 1750.—*Lysons.*

From this Buckinghamshire house sprung Sir John Cheney, who acquired Cogenhoe in Northamptonshire through his wife, and died in 1468, nearly a hundred years old. His descendant, Charles, sold it in 1657 to buy Chelsea from the Duke of Hamilton, and was created in 1681 Viscount Newhaven in Scotland. Unlike most Scottish peerages, it descended to none but heirs male, and expired with his son William in 1738. Cheyne Walk, Chelsea, takes its name from them.

On all this imposing array of local magnates, time and oblivion have done their remorseless work; slowly and surely rooting up each venerable stock, and scattering its memorials to the winds. I only know of two gentlemen that now bear the lions of Shurland by right of male descent—Edward Cheney of Badger Hall in Shropshire, and Edward Cheney of Goddesby in Leicestershire. They are first cousins; the grandsons of Robert Cheney of Meynell Langley, who was High Sheriff of Derby in 1765. But neither of them is married; and both are now well advanced in years.†

Kimaronne: one of the names I have had to give up in despair. Leland gives it rather differently—in his list it is Kymarays, and in this latter form bears some resemblance to the Breton name Kermarec.

* In 1837, they held their own under difficulties. "There lie the ancient lords of the soil—but see the changes and chances of this mortal life! Its vicissitudes are not ended with the grave—men, honoured in their generation, 'who loved the church so well, and gave so largely to it, it should have canopied their bones till doomsday,' have been shoved away into any hole or corner to make way for their powerful successors. One figure is built into the wall; and another is cut in two by the weight of a huge Russell monument, his clasped hands raised in prayer, as if appealing against this degradation."—*Archæological Journal,* vol. x. These effigies have been restored and replaced by the present Duke.

† Since writing the above, I have lost one of the oldest and best-esteemed of my friends in Edward Cheney of Badger, who died April 16th, 1884, in the eighty-second year of his age.

Kiriell: the Anglicized form of Criol, already given.

Kancey: for Cancey, or De Canci, a name that appears in all parts of England as Chancey, Chancy, &c. Godfrey de Chansy appears in the *Rotuli Curiæ Regis* of 1194.—*The Norman People.* (See *Chauncy.*)

Kenelre, for Kevelers. Leland gives this and the preceding name as "Kanceis et Kevelers." It is retained by the manor of Chevelers, in the parish of Chelsham, Surrey (Manning), and appears to have been common in Normandy, both as Cavalier and Le Chevalier. Seven different families named Le Chevalier proved their nobility in the seventeenth century; four of them were represented in the Assembly of Nobles in 1789; where we also find Cavelier de Mocomble, Cavelier d'Esclavelles, and Cavelier de Piscal.

Seven of this name occur about 1272 in the Hundred Rolls; Stephen Chivaler or Chevaler in Norfolk; Walter le Chivaler in Buckinghamshire and Wiltshire; Richard le Chivaler again in Bucks; William Chivaler in Yorkshire and Oxfordshire; Jordan le Chivaler in Northamptonshire: and Roger le Chivaler, with Agnes his wife, in Huntingdonshire. Ralph Chivalers, in 1333, was Vicar of Hemel Hempstead.

Loueney: for Louvigny, a well-known Norman house, that bore *Argent*, a chevron *Sable*, between three wolves' heads of the last. The De Louvignys were Sires de la Martinière and Marette, in the district of Bernay; and De Louvigny de la Marette sat in the great assembly of the "Ordre de la Noblesse" convoked in 1789 at Rouen for the election of the States General.

In England Walter de Louveney was Sheriff of Dorset and Somerset in 1292 and 1293; and at that time one of the principal landowners in Somersetshire. But I can find no account of his descendants. William Louveney, in 1408, served as Sheriff for Essex and Hertfordshire. Louveney's Manor, in the parish of Thurston, Norfolk, and Great and Little Loveney Hall, in the parish of Colne Wakes, Essex, speak of their possessions in the Eastern counties. William de Loveney, who appears in the list of Essex gentry in 1433, was probably the same William that was Lord of Stratton, in Suffolk, in 1417; and received from Henry IV. Worton, in the parish of Isleworth, for life.—*Lysons' Middlesex.* According to Morant, he was succeeded by John de Loveney, living in 1440, and probably the last of the family, as his next heir was Thomas Cavendish. Domina Mabil de Luveny held Thoresby, Lincolnshire, of Segrave.—*Testa de Nevill.* John Loveney was Archdeacon of Hereford in 1404. They bore *Argent* a fesse between three cocks *Gules.* In the Norman Exchequer Rolls of 1198, "Juhel de Louvigny rendered accompt for a hearing of the gift, which Ranulph Earl of Chester had made to him of land at St. Martin and other places, as the charter of the Earl testified."

Lacy: from Lasci (now called Lassy) on the road from Vire to Auvray. "The branches of this house were so numerous that Robson furnishes above forty coats of arms of different houses. Walter de Lacy is mentioned by Wace at the battle of Hastings, and witnessed a charter of Walter Fitz Osborne; and from him descended the barons of Evias, Earls of Ulster and Lincoln, Barons of Pontefract, and Palatines of Meath."—*The Norman People.* Four of the name are on the Dives Roll—Ibert, Roger, Gautier, and Hugues; but the two former only are to be found in Domesday. The Walter de Lacy who, with some others brave as himself, "forming one troop, fell on the English offhand, fearing neither fence nor fosse" (*Roman de Rou*), had died in the previous year. His lands had been assigned to him in the West, where he held territory—to what exact extent is not known—under William Fitz Osbern, the first Norman Earl of Hereford; and upon the rebellion of William's son, Earl Roger de Britolio, the whole vast fief was conferred upon him by the Conqueror. He waged war successfully with the Welsh, defeating three of their princes with great slaughter in Brecon; and was killed in 1085 by a fall from a ladder while inspecting a new church he had founded at Hereford. Roger his son, the Domesday Baron, held, besides his Norman fief of Lasci, one hundred different manors in Shropshire, Hereford-shire, Worcestershire, Gloucestershire, and Berkshire; but forfeited them by his rebellion against William Rufus, and was exiled in 1095. His brother Hugh, on whom the King then conferred the barony, and "whose loyalty and recti-tude Ordericus contrasts with his own conduct," had already conquered for himself the territory of Ewias in Wales, which became one of the Baronies-Marcher, instituted to guard the frontier, and defend "these lands thus acquired with the sword." It was a perilous honour, but it conferred a kind of Palatine jurisdiction. With him ended the male line, for his only brother was a churchman who became Abbot of Gloucester, and he himself died s. p., leaving two sisters, who neither of them inherited, as his lands escheated to the crown. One only had children, and her son Gilbert assumed the name of De Lacy. He was "an approved soldier, a prudent man, and one of great foresight and activity in any military undertaking," and living, as he did, "in a time when all law and kingly authority were in abeyance, he could readily turn his sword to good account." For some time he was at the Court of the Empress Maud, and fought stoutly on her behalf; then, opportunely shifting his allegiance, he went over to Stephen, and received his uncle's great barony as his reward. He assumed the habit of a Templar some time before his death in 1163. His son, Hugh II., accompanied Henry II. to Ireland in 1171, received the whole province of Meath, to be held by the service of one hundred knights, and on the King's departure, was left in charge of the country as Justiciar, and *custos* of the city of Dublin. But when Prince Henry's rebellion broke out in 1173, he was summoned in all haste to the King's aid in Normandy; and did signal and gallant service in the war. He then returned to Ireland—though no longer as Viceroy; and married a daughter of the King of Connaught without license, thus incurring the dire displeasure of the King, who, in spite of his tried and devoted loyalty, suspected him of designing to rule Ireland independently, and when he was murdered by one of his Irish vassals in 1185, heard of the event "with vast delight." He left four sons, Walter, Hugh, Gilbert, and William. Of the two last I can find no further account, but both the elder brothers were pre-eminent among the nobles that subdued and governed Ireland. Hugh, styled by Matthew Paris "this famous soldier," who had been the conqueror of a great part of the country, was appointed Constable of Ireland by King John, and obtained the Earldom of Ulster by a foul act of treachery. John de Courcy, the Norman lord of Ulster, was then in open revolt; and De Lacy, pretending to be his friend, invited him to his castle with a promise of protection and safe-conduct.* But when he had got the unfortunate Earl into his power, he broke his plighted word, and delivered him up to the King, receiving in return his lands and honours. He left no son· to succeed to them, and the Earldom passed through his only daughter Maud to her husband Walter de Burgh, Lord of Connaught.

Walter de Lacy, as the eldest brother, inherited the three great fiefs in England, Ireland, and Normandy, but lost the latter when the Duchy was ceded to France. He was confederated with his father-in-law De Braose in his rebellion; and he and Hugh together arrayed Meath, Ulster, and Munster against King John. But in 1210 the King came over in person to Ireland, and carried on a successful campaign against the rebels, which ended in the banishment and outlawry of De Braose and both the De Lacys. The two brothers, in humble disguise, found shelter in the Abbey of St. Taurin at Evreux, where they lived for some time as servants before the Abbot discovered who they were. He then interceded for them with the King; and in token of their gratitude, they founded in after years Foure Abbey in Ireland as a cell to St. Taurin. Walter obtained the restoration of his estates only by payment of an exorbitant fine; and seems to have remained ever after on fair terms with the King. When Hugh and the men of Meath rose in rebellion against .Henry III., he was sent over to subdue his own brother and his own vassals. He died, blind and infirm from old age, in 1241; having survived his only son and an infant grandson; and his grand-daughters Maud and Margery were his heirs. Maud was first married to Peter de Geneva, a low-born Provençal favourite of Henry III., and then to Geoffrey de Genevill or Joinville. Margery was the wife of John de Verdon.

The other Domesday baron, Ilbert de Lacy, was an even greater land-owner

---

* Banks gives a rather different account. "Lacy, Lord Justice of Ireland, offered a large reward to any one who should bring in this Earl John (denounced as a traitor) dead or alive; but this proving ineffectual, he prevailed, by great promises, on some of the Earl's retainers to betray their master to· him. Accordingly, on Good Friday, 1203, when the Earl, for penance, was walking barefoot and unarmed five times round the churchyard of Down Patrick, he was attacked unawares, and having nothing to defend him but the pole of a cross, he was overpowered and forced to yield; but not until he had killed thirteen of Lacy's men with his own hand."

than his brother or kinsman Roger. His fief comprised the whole district of Blackburnshire in the county of Lancaster, with nearly one hundred and fifty manors in Yorkshire, ten in Nottingham, and four in Lincolnshire. He was seated in the West Riding; and there, near the town then called Kirkby, he built the famous Castle of Pontefract (so named from a broken bridge over the Aire) which was the great stronghold of South Yorkshire, commanding the passes of the river as effectually as a former Roman station had done. Within this new fortress he founded a collegiate chapel dedicated to St. Clement; and he likewise laid the foundation of Nostell Abbey, which was completed and endowed by his successor. He left two sons; Robert, and Hugh. Robert, also called de Pontefract, took part with Robert Curthose against Henry I., and "was forced to buy his peace at a dear rate." Yet after this he obtained from the King a grant of Bowland,* that had been Roger de Poitou's, with other lands in Yorkshire; and next, by a sudden transition of fortune left unexplained by Dugdale, he and his son Ilbert were expelled the realm. He was never allowed to return, and must have died in exile; but Ilbert obtained from Stephen the restoration of his barony, and "calling to mind the misery of his banishment by King Henry I., approved himself the more cordial to King Stephen." He was one of the chief commanders at the Battle of the Standard, and a powerful magnate in the Northern counties. Henry his brother succeeded him; and Henry's son Robert proved the last of his race.† He did not live to complete the great castle he began to build at Clitheroe, but d. s. p. in 1193, and was buried in Kirkstall Abbey.

The great Lacy inheritance then definitively passed away from the Lacy blood. It was arbitrarily appropriated by the half sister of the last heir, Albreda de Lisours, who was his mother's daughter by her second husband, Eudo de Lisours. This was an outrageous assumption, for she had not even the shadow of a claim, and could only make some pretence of a grant or deed of gift obtained from Henry de Lacy by her mother before he died. But she was the wife of a powerful and ambitious noble, Richard Fitz Eustace, Baron of Halton and Constable of Chester, whose will might not be gainsaid; and her son John took

---

* A relic of the ancient supremacy of the Lacys in Lancashire—the "dog-gauge" —is still preserved at Bowsholme, "the depository of Forest lore, on the Yorkshire side of the boundary. They held the forests in the Clitheroe fee, Bowland and Blackburnshire; and the tenants of the Forest of Bowland engaged 'to suffer the deere to go unmolested into their several grounds;' they are also fined, 'if anie without licens keep any dogg bigger than will go through a stirupe, to hunt the deere.' Herds of wild deer continued to range the forest of Bowland till the year 1805, when the last vestige of feudal superiority in the domains of the Lacies was destroyed."—*Baines' Lancashire.* The dog-gauge is a large round stirrup.

† "The true line of Lacy terminated with the above Robert, and the Constables of Chester and the Earls of Lincoln, who assumed the name, inherited the lands and honours, but not a drop of the Lacy blood, as it would be inferred from the polite peerages in which the reader would naturally look for information."—*Planché.*

the name and place of De Lacy, and transmitted the united baronies of Ponte-fract and Halton to four generations of his descendants. His grandson and namesake, John, Constable of Chester, was one of the twenty-five great barons appointed to enforce the observance of Magna Charta, with the custody of the counties of York and Nottingham; and married Margaret de Quincy, through whom he obtained the Earldom of Lincoln, that had belonged to her uncle, Ralph de Meschines, Earl of Chester. Henry, the last Earl, was a man of great ability, eminent both as a soldier and statesman. · He attended Edward I. in his wars, and stood high in his esteem, was sent by him to treat with the French King, and appointed his Chief Commissioner for reforming the administration of justice in the realm. There had been great complaints made in parliament of the venality of the judges; and the Earl swept away four—the Chief Justice of the Common Pleas among them—that were convicted of receiving bribes. After the conquest of Wales, the King, who "much studied the fortifying of that country, especially North Wales and the Marches, for that respect gave him the land of Denbigh; whereupon he began the town of Denbigh, walling it, and making a Castle there, in Front whereof was his Statue in long Robes: And every Sunday (antiently) Prayers were made in Saint Hillaries Chapel there for Lacy and Percy." This castle, however, was never finished: for his only son was drowned in a deep well belonging to the so-called Red Tower, and the Earl lost all heart in the work. His wife was the sole heiress of William de Longespee, who brought him her grandfather's Earldom of Salisbury. They were long married without children; but at length she brought forth this long expected and early lost heir, and one other child, Alice, who succeeded as Countess of Lincoln and Salisbury.

. When the great King lay on his death-bed at Burgh-upon-Sands, this Earl was one of the chosen friends and comrades to whom he made his last appeal, desiring them "to be good to his son, and not to permit Piers de Gaveston to return to England." Edward II. left him in charge of the realm during his absence in Scotland in 1307. But he was unable to stem the rising tide of abuses and misgovernment that his dead master had foreseen; and as he felt his own death drawing near in 1312, he called his son-in-law, the Earl of Lancaster, to his bed-side, and reminding him "how highly God had honoured him, and inriched him above others, told him, 'That he was obliged to love and honour God above all things. Seest thou (quoth he) the Church of England heretofore honourable and free, enslaved by Romish oppressions, and the King's unjust exactions! Seest thou the Common People impoverished by Tributes and Taxes, and from the condition of Freemen reduced to a servitude! Seest thou the Nobility, formerly venerable through Christendom, vilified by Aliens in their own Native Country! I therefore charge thee by the name of Christ, to stand up like a Man: for the Honour of God, and his Church, and Redemption of thy Countrey; associating thyself to that valiant, noble, and prudent Person, Guy,

Earl of Warwick, when it shall be most ·proper to discourse of the Publick Affairs of the Kingdom; who.is so judicious in Counsel, and mature in Judgment. Fear not thy Opposers, who shall contest against thee in thy' truth. And if thou pursuest this my Advice, thou shalt gain eternal honour.'"[*] —*Dugdale.*

He could not have committed this great charge to abler hands. Alice de Lacy's husband, Thomas Plantagenet, Earl of Lancaster, the elder son of Edmund Crouchback, a younger brother of Edward I., was the most powerful baron of the time; and held the several Earldoms of Lancaster, Leicester, Derby, Lincoln and Salisbury:—the two latter brought to him by his wife. He accepted and loyally fulfilled the duty imposed upon him, and placed himself at the head of the barons who revolted against the rule of Edward II.'s worthless favourites. The tragic sequel is well known. He was utterly defeated at Boroughbridge, and not choosing to yield to mortal man, knelt in the chapel, and turning to the crucifix, said, "Good Lord, I render myself to thee, and put myself at thy mercy." He was sentenced to death without even the form of a trial, asking, "'Shall I die without answer?' A certain Gascoyne took him away, and put a pill'd broken Hood on his Head, and set him on a lean white Jade, without a Bridle, and thus he was led away to die, crying, 'King of Heaven have mercy on me, for the King of Earth *nous ad guerthi.*'"

His widow was twice again married, but never had children.[†]

The Lacys took as their badge the *lacet*, or Lacy knot; a rebus on their name. "No less than one hundred parishes in the Welsh marches bear the suffix Lacy" (Taylor); as, Stanton-Lacy in Shropshire; Holme-Lacy and Mansel-Lacy in Worcestershire, &c.

Linnebey. Leland here once more comes to our assistance, for he gives this and the following name as "Lymesay et Latymer." It appears in another part of Duchesne's copy under its Scottish form of Lindsay. Lord Lindsay tells us that "the names Lindesay and Limesay are identical, both of them implying 'Isle of Lime-trees,' and are frequently interchanged, and applied to the same individuals, not merely in the heraldic MSS. of two hundred years ago, but in ancient public records, and in the early transcripts of Battle Abbey Roll.

[*] This great Earl died in the new mansion house—then called "Inne"—that he had built in the suburbs of London, on some ground formerly occupied by the Dominicans. Lincoln's Inn Fields, now tenanted by a colony of astute lawyers, was then partly a coney-garth, harbouring, in addition to the "feeble folk," several kinds of game; and partly a garden, to which they must have been nibbling and vexatious neighbours. There were no flowers but roses: the vegetables grown were beans, garlic, onions, and leeks; and, after supplying the Earl's table, enough apples, pears, nuts, and cherries remained for sale to yield an annual income of £9 2s. 6d. (about £135 of our currency).

[†] She was the Countess of Lancaster who was carried off by the hunch-backed knight, Richard de St. Martin (see Vol. III.).

" The original Norman Sires de Limesay were seated at the place so called in the Pays de Caux, near Pavilly, fives leagues N.W. of Rouen. They flourished for many generations after the Conquest, and failed apparently shortly after the middle of the thirteenth century, when the Sires de Frontebosc, a younger branch, succeeded to the property. Their descendants in the female line, Comtes de Frontebosc and Marquesses de Limesay, flourished till the French Revolution, and still, I believe, exist. Randolph de Limesay, said to have been sister's son to the Conqueror, was the first of the Anglo-Norman stock who settled in England. He obtained above forty lordships in different counties of England, including Wolverley in Warwickshire, the chief seat of his posterity, and from which they took their style as barons. There was but little of the castle remaining in Dugdale's time, save the moat, and certain ' great banks, whereon ancient trees do grow,' coeval probably with the first arrival of the Normans. Randolph died towards the close of William the Conqueror's reign, after founding the Priory of Hertford, in dependency of the Abbey of St. Albans, within whose hallowed precincts he and his wife Hadewisia were admitted as brother and sister before their decease. Alan de Limesay, his son, and Gerard, his grandson, succeeded him, and were similarly bountiful, but the son of Gerard dying without issue, the property went to his two daughters, Basilia, wife of Sir Hugh de Odingsels, and Aleonora, wife of Sir David de Lindsay of Crawford."

The husband selected for the younger co-heiress of the barony of Wolverley was of her own blood, being the descendant of Walter de Lindesay, who first settled in Scotland under the banner of David I. He figures repeatedly in the charters of the latter while Prince of Cumberland; and " is a witness and juror in the celebrated *Inquisitio* or inquest of Prince David into the possessions and rights of the see of Glasgow within his territories, in 1116." His exact relationship to the English Limesays is not known; but it is certain that for many generations his posterity bore the same arms—*Gules*, an eagle displayed *Or*. They resided at Ercildoune in Roxburghshire—in after times the home of Thomas the Rhymer; but from the latter part of the twelfth century we find them associated with the great mountain territory of Crawford—commonly called Crawford-Lindsay—in Clydesdale, " so inseparably connected with their later history." Sir David, High Justiciary of Scotland, who married his English kinswoman in 1201, was the son of a Scottish princess, Marjory, sister of King William the Lion and David Earl of Huntingdon; and as all his four sons died without issue, the descendant of his only daughter, Alice de Pinkeney, claimed the Crown of Scotland at the competition in 1292. Sir David himself was the elder of three brothers. Sir Walter, the second, founded the house of Lamberton, of which four successive generations married heiresses, till Christiana de Lindesay, representing the last of the line, carried its accumulated riches to her husband Ingelram de Guisnes, Sire de Coucy. Thus the descendants of the third brother, William, who had the barony of Luffness, in East Lothian, as his appanage, became the heads of the house, and eventually recovered the hereditary estates. "Even before the death of Sir Henry Pinkeney in 1301, Crawford and its dependencies had been seized and declared forfeit by the Scottish authorities, and bestowed on Sir Alexander Lindsay of Luffness, who sat as one of the great barons in the Parliament of 1308–9, which acknowledged Robert Bruce as lawful King of Scotland." From his son, David, also a faithful adherent of Bruce, and the

> "Schir Daẅy the Lyndyssay,
> That was true and of stedfast fay—"

descend the greater part of the twenty distinct branches of the family—one of them settled in the United States of America—that are enumerated in the pedigree given in the *Lives of the Lindsays*,* and were for the most part extinguished during the great civil war. His grandson and namesake was created Earl of Crawford in 1398: "the Earldom of Crawford being the third created since the extinction of the Celtic dynasty; that of Douglas having been the second, and that of Moray the first." Another branch were Lords Lindsay of the Byres, and Earls of Lindsay, the most powerful cadet of the house; a third Earls of Balcarres; a fourth Lords Spynie; and a fifth gave birth to the famous poet and herald, who was sent as ambassador to the Emperor Charles V. by James V.

> "Still is thy name of high account,
> And still thy verse has charms,
> Sir David Lindsay of the Mount,
> Lord Lion-King-at-Arms."

It would be idle for me to attempt to trace out the varied and romantic fortunes of this renowned family, whose annals, written by a former head of the house, fill three interesting volumes; the briefest summary is all my space admits of. There have been in all twenty-six Earls of Crawford of this name. They had their castle at Finhaven in Angus, and held their great fief with rights of regality that ensured them "at least as many of the privileges of an independent prince as a Margrave or Pfalzgrave." For many successive generations they were hereditary Sheriffs of Aberdeen and Forfar. One of them was the fierce Tiger Earl—Earl Beardie—whom tradition believes to be still playing at "the de'il's buiks" in the secret chamber at Glamis Castle; "doomed to play there till the end of time;" and nightly issuing forth, as each month of November comes round, to prowl about the house, and bend over the beds of its inmates, startled from their sleep as his long beard sweeps across their faces. Another, the fifth Earl, "under whom the Lindsays rose to their highest power in Scotland," was created

---

* These formed, however, but an insignificant portion of the clan. "Within three or four centuries of their settlement in the North, above one hundred different minor Houses or families of Lindsays were flourishing in Scotland, many of them powerful independent Barons, holding *in capite* of the Crown."—*Ibid.*

Duke of Montrose by James III. in 1488, having " deserved nobly of him " for loyalty and devotion : but at his death the Dukedom sank into dormancy, and was unsuccessfully claimed only a few years ago by the late Earl.   Another had to appeal to the Crown in 1526 for protection against his own son, who laid violent hands upon him, and imprisoned him in his own dungeon at Finhaven, pillaging his writs and appropriating his rents.   By the Scottish law the " Wicked Master " (as he was justly called) thus incurred the guilt of parricide, and entailed a curse on all his descendants, who seemed " hereditarily doomed to prodigality and crime."   Accordingly, one of them, the *Comes Incarceratus*, died in duresse in Edinburgh Castle, leaving his only child, Lady Jean, literally a beggar for her daily bread.   During the Thirty Years' War, " six young Crawford cousins," Earl George, with his brothers and kinsmen, took service under Gustavus Adolphus ; and the younger of these brothers, Ludovic, the " Loyal Earl," was among the first to join Charles I. at the rearing of the standard at Nottingham, and died an exile for his sake.   His Earldom was declared forfeit, and granted by the Covenanters to John, first Earl of Lindsay, and tenth Lord Lindsay of the Byres, who had espoused their cause, and was at the same time appointed High Treasurer ; and with his posterity it remained till the line failed with the twenty-second Earl in 1808.   It then passed to Alexander, sixth Earl of Balcarres (descended from a second son of the ninth Earl) ; but " he was," says his grandson, " unwilling to assume the title or advance his pretensions, owing to the difficulty of dealing with such a mass of intermediate pedigree and extinctions, and to the uncertainty which existed as to the ultimate remainder or limitation in the patent of 1642 :" by which Charles I. had reconferred the title on Earl Ludovic.   He consequently never bore it ; but the discovery of that document in the charter-room at Crawford Priory, in 1833, enabled his successor to make good his claim, which was confirmed in 1848 by the decision of the House of Lords.

Latomer, or Latimer : for Le Latinier,* or interpreter.   Four of these are among the barons mentioned in Domesday : David *interpres*, who held in Dorset ;

---

* " A latinier, or latimer, was literally a speaker or writer of Latin, that language being then the vehicle of all record or transcript.   Latin, indeed, for centuries was the common ground on which all European ecclesiastics met.   Thus it became looked upon as the language of interpretation.   The term I am speaking of, however, seems to have become general at an early stage.   An old lyric says—

> " ' Lyare was mi latymer,
>   Sloth & sleep mi bedyner.'

Sir John Maundeville, describing an eastern route, says (I am quoting Mr. Lower) : ' And men allweys fynden Latyneres to go with them in the contrees and ferther beyonde in to tyme that men conne the language.' "—*Bardsley's English Surnames.* " The word *Latimarius* (whence the proper name Latimer) was first applied to one who understood Latin.   Then it came to signify one who had acquired a knowledge of any other than his native language."—*Eyton's Shropshire.*

Hugo *latinarius* (elsewhere called Hugolinus *interpres*) who held in Hants and Somerset; Ralph *Latimarus*, who held in Essex; and Lewin *Latinarius*, who held in Herefordshire.

It is only with the third of these, Ralph, Secretary to the Conqueror, that we have here to do. Of him derived William le Latimer, who in 1165 held a knight's fee of Vesci in Yorkshire (Liber Niger): and another William, most likely the son of the first, who paid 100ˢ· in 1190 to have a trial at law with Geoffrey de Valoins, who had taken possession of part of his park at Billenges. A third William was Sheriff of York and Constable of York Castle in 1254, and had at different times also the custody of Pickering, Cockermouth and Scarborough. He did "laudable service" to Henry III. during the Barons' War, and followed Edward I. throughout his martial career; first, in 1269, to the Holy Land, and then in all his campaigns in Wales, Scotland, and Gascony. The King rewarded him with a grant of Danby in Yorkshire, and a summons to parliament in 1299. He and his brother John married two sisters, the co-heirs of Walter Ledet, or de Braibroc, who divided his great Northamptonshire barony between them. His wife, Alice, was the elder, and brought with her, besides half the Honour of Warden, one moiety of the town, and the whole hundred of Corby. William IV., their son, took to wife another heiress, Lucia de Thweng, who, during one of his absences in the Scottish wars, was carried off from his Yorkshire manor house of Brunne, "with divers other goods, by certain unknown persons. Whereupon, the King sent his Precept to the Sheriff, to make strict search for her, throughout all that County; commanding him, that in case he did find her out, he should, if need were, raise the power of the County, and carry her back to Brunne." But the hue and cry was of no avail; the lady, having gone away of her own accord, could not be recovered; and the next we hear of her is her divorce, by sentence of the Court of Rome—a notable instance of the early disregard of the sacrament of marriage in a church that now pronounces it indissoluble. Lord Latimer married again: and had the "ill hap" of being taken prisoner at Bannockburn. He was followed by two more Williams, his son and his grandson: the latter being only six years old when he succeeded to the barony. This fourth Lord Latimer proved the last of the line. He was a soldier from his very boyhood, and passed his life almost uninterruptedly in the French wars, in which various gallant feats of arms are recorded of him. In 1364, "being with John de Montfort at the Siege of Doveroy, with scarce one thousand six hundred Men, he encountered with Charles de Bloys, who came to raise the Siege with no less than three thousand six hundred; And in a sharp Battle, slew him, with almost one thousand Knights and Esquires; taking Prisoners two Earls, twenty-seven Lords, and one thousand five hundred Men at Arms." He served as Constable of Becherel in Brittany, Lt. and Captain General to John Duke of Brittany and Captain and Governor of the town, castle and Viscountcy of St. Sauveur, and was successively Steward of the Household and the King's Chamberlain. But in 1376 he was "removed from all his trusts," and impeached by the House of Commons. He was accused of squandering and appropriating the King's treasure; the loss of the town of St. Sauveur and the castle of Becherel was laid to his charge, and he was sentenced to pay a fine of 20,000 marks. This, however, the King mercifully remitted, and soon after, the Lords and Commons both representing that he had been erased from the Privy Council and deprived of his offices by "untrue suggestions," he was reinstated—partly, it was said, by the favour of the Duke of Lancaster. Richard II. appointed him Captain of Calais, and sent him to treat of peace with Scotland. His last campaign was under Thomas of Woodstock, with whom he went to the siege of Nantes in 1380 as Constable of the host. He died the same year, leaving by his wife Lady Elizabeth Fitz Alan an only child, Elizabeth Latimer, his sole heiress. She was twice married—each time to a widower; for she became the second wife of John, Lord Nevill of Raby, and then of Robert, Lord Willoughby de Eresby; and by her first husband was the mother of three children, John, Elizabeth, and Margaret. John Nevill, who in her right was Lord Latimer, died childless in 1430; his sister Margaret likewise died s. p.; and thus Elizabeth, who had married her stepson Sir Thomas Willoughby, remained the only heir. But, within two years, the barony was granted, through the great power and predominance of the Nevills, to a grandson of Lord Nevill's by his first wife, Sir George Nevill, on whom a part of the estates had been settled, and though an utter stranger to the blood of Latimer, he held it without dispute or cavil till his death. However, in the time of his grandson and successor Richard, it was claimed by the great-grandson and heir of Sir Thomas Willoughby, Robert Lord Broke; when it was declared that Sir George had been created Lord Latimer by a new title; and Lord Broke "having a title of his own, was contented to conclude a match between their children; and Richard suffered a recovery on certain manors and lordships demanded by the Lord Broke."—*Banks.*

The second brother of the first Lord Latimer, John de Latimer, who had married the younger Ledet heiress, left at his death, in 1283, a son known as Thomas le Latimer Bochard, and summoned to parliament in 1299 as Lord Latimer of Braybrooke, to distinguish him from his uncle, who at the same time had summons as Lord Latimer of Danby. He built a castle on his mother's inheritance at Braybrooke, and founded a line of Northamptonshire barons, that ended with his three childless grandsons, who each in turn succeeded to the title. Sir Thomas, the second of these, was eminent among the leaders of the Lollards, but recanted before his death, and like Sir Lewis Clifford, expressed his deep penitence in his will. He declared himself, "a false Knyghte to God;" praying that He "would take so poore a present as my wrecchid Soule ys, into his merci, through the beseching of his blessed Modyr, and his holy Seynts." Edward, the last Lord, who died in 1411, bequeathed Braybrooke and all his other property to his sister's son, John Griffin.

Some descendants of the first Lord Latimer of Danby, survived till 1505 in Dorsetshire, where John, his younger son, had acquired the manor of Duntish through its heiress Joan de Gouis. Sir Nicholas, the last heir, was attainted in the reign of Edward IV., though the attainder was afterwards reversed. Edith Latimer, the wife of Sir John Mordaunt, was his only child.

The martyred Bishop Latimer was probably derived from a younger branch of this house, of which, as it had lapsed into obscurity, the pedigree is lost. His parents lived in Leicestershire, but had inherited none of the property held there during the fourteenth century by the Latimers of Braybrooke. "My father," he tells us, "was a yeoman, and had no lands of his own; only he had a farm of 3 or 4 pounds a year at the uttermost, and hereupon he tilled as much as kept half a dozen men. He had walk for 100 sheep, and my mother milked 30 kine; he was able and did find the King a harness with himself and his horse while he came to the place that he should receive the King's wages. I can remember that I buckled his harness when he went to Blackheath Field. He kept me to school; he married my sisters with five pounds a piece, so that he brought them up in godliness and in the fear of God. He kept hospitality to his poor neighbours, and some alms he gave to the poor: and all this he did of the same farm, where he that now hath it payeth 16 pounds a year or more, and is not able to do anything for his prince, for himself, nor for his children, or give a cup of drink to the poor."

Loueday; from Loveday or Louday, Toulouse. Several of this name occur in the thirteenth century; Alexander, Walter, Nicolas, and Roger de Loveday held in Kent; Roger also in Lincolnshire; John in Lincolnshire; and Richard in Huntingdonshire.—*Rotuli Hundredorum.* This Richard witnessed a charter of Almaric Peché (Mon. Angl. ii. 84). William de Loveday was a benefactor of the Knights Templars (Ibid. i. 545): and probably the same William, seated in Oxfordshire, who received a writ of military summons in 1297.—*Palgrave's Parliamentary Writs.* About the same time, Katherine, one of the sisters and co-heiresses of Richard Loveday, and youngest daughter of Roger Loveday and Sibilla his wife, married Roger de Tichborne, and brought him various manors in Suffolk and Cambridgeshire. Another and elder sister married Richard Hakoun. Their armorial bearings were *Azure*, 3 bars dancettée *Or.—Archæological Journal*, 1855. Roger Loveday was a Justice Itinerant in Gloucester in 1286. The Lovedays now seated in Oxfordshire do not trace their descent further back than the first years of the last century, and acquired Williamscote, near Banbury, through an heiress in 1777.

It was probably the William Loveday already mentioned, who held in Great Wilburgham, Cambridgeshire, of the King *in capite*, "by the serjeanty of finding a soar sparhawk, and carrying it to the King's court, and there staying 12 days, with 2 horses, 2 pages, and 2 greyhounds, at the cost of the King."—*Plac. Coron. Ed. I. Cant.*

In addition to that already given, three other coats are attributed to this family. The Lovedays of Essex have *Azure* three fleurs de lis *Or;* those of Norfolk, and Cheston in Suffolk, Per pale, *Argent* and *Sable*, an eagle displayed with two necks counterchanged, gorged with a ducal coronet *Or:* and another branch, *Sable* guttée de sang, on a chief *Argent* three greyhounds' heads erased of the first, collared *Or.* In Essex the name still existed in the early part of the seventeenth century. John Loveday, of Dudinghurst, occurs there about 1610.

Lovell. "Asceline, Seigneur of Breherval, and Lord of Castle Cary in England, was a vassal of William de Breteuil. Goello or Goel was the surname which Asceline usually assumed, derived from a noble Breton barony,* but the designation of Lupellus, or young Wolf, had been bestowed upon him in consequence of his savage temper, common to the whole family. Through his son William, softened into Lovell, the name became hereditary. 'Lovell, our dog,' was his lineal descendant. Lovells of Castle-Cary, Lovells of Tichmarsh, Percevals, Egmonts, Beaumonts, and Somersetshire Gurneys, the second line of Barewe Gournay (where the walls of the old manor-house are partly standing)— all come from Asceline. By ill usage and torture, he compelled his liege lord to grant him his daughter Isabel, with £3,000 of Dreux currency. During three months Breteuil was kept in duresse, ironed, chained, plagued, and starved, without yielding: till at length the livres and the lady were extorted by an ingenious mode of torture. In the depth of winter, Asceline fastened him to the grating at the bleak top of a tower, unclothed, save by a poor, thin shirt: he was thus exposed to the whistling, biting, bitter winds, while water was poured upon him abundantly and continually, till he was sheeted with ice. This anguish Breteuil could not resist: he consented to the terms proposed, endowed Isabel in the church-porch, and gave her away."—*Sir Francis Palgrave.*

The father of Asceline was Robert de Breherval, one of the eight sons of Eudo, Count of Brittany, who held the castle and barony of Ivery, in Normandy, by the service of three knights' fees. He came to England with the Conqueror, and fought at Senlac; but soon after returned home and died a monk in the Abbey of Bec. Ascelin, surnamed Gouel, and Gouel de Percheval, appears in Domesday as a large landowner in Somerset, where he held the barony of Castle-Cary. He had three sons: the eldest, Robert, died s. p. in 1121: William, the second, succeeded him; and John, the youngest, was portioned in the manor of Harptree, and in consequence took that name, but afterwards changed it to Gournay. From him descended the Barons of Harptree Gournay.

William Gouel de Percheval had both the Norman and English estates; and inherited, with his father's turbulent and ungovernable temper, his nick-name

---

* Here authorities differ. "Goël, or Goule, by which name Asceline, as well as his son, was known, is clearly Guelph, or Whelp, the wolf-cub, of which Louvel or Lupus is the Norman-French equivalent."—*A. S. Ellis.*

of Lupellus, or Louvel, which was ever after used by his posterity. His life is one long record of different rebellions. First, he took up arms, with his father-in-law, Waleran of Mellent, against Henry I.; "and fighting stoutly on his part in that notable skirmish, near the Borough of Turold, where Waleran was utterly vanquished and made prisoner: being taken in his flight by a Peasant, gave him his Armour for liberty to escape; and having so done, cut all his Hair according to the mode of an Esquire; by which means he passed unknown to a Ferry upon the River of Sene, where he gave his Shoes to the Boatman to carry him over, and so at length got bare-foot to his own house."—*Dugdale.* Next, with other Somersetshire barons, he espoused the cause of the Empress Maud, and was twice besieged in his castle of Cary: first in 1138, when it was taken by King Stephen: and again—but on that occasion unsuccessfully—by William de Tracy in 1153. "It is probable that from this time the castle fell to ruin and decay; for little more is heard of it in the succeeding reigns, and at present the spot wherein it stood is hardly known to the inhabitants of the town; being marked only by an intrenched area of about two acres, called the Camp, in which implements of war and bolts of iron have frequently been dug up."— *Collinson's Somerset.* He left five sons: 1. Waleran, Lord of Yvery in Normandy; 2. Ralph, and 3. Henry, who were successively Lords of Castle-Cary; 4. William, ancestor of the Lovels of Tichmarsh; and 5. Richard, who retained the original surname of Percheval or Perceval, and was the ancestor of the Earls of Egmont. See *Perceval.*

The barony of Castle-Cary descended in regular succession to Richard, third of the name and last of the line, who had the custody of the Dorsetshire castles of Corfe and Purbeck, and was summoned to parliament as a baron by Edward III. in 1348: but, as both his son and grandson died before him, left no heir save his granddaughter Muriel, who carried his title and estate to her husband, Nicholas Lord St. Maur.

The younger branch of the Lovels (the posterity of William) were of longer continuance and greater account in the world. They were seated at Minster-Lovel in Oxfordshire, and exchanged their paternal coat for that of the Bassets, with whom they had intermarried. Tichmarsh was acquired through Maud Sydenham, a great Northamptonshire heiress, in the time of Henry III. One of the family, Philip Lovel, was Treasurer of England during the same reign: but was accused and brought to trial by the barons for having taken bribes from the Jews to exempt them from tallage, and being "put from that high trust," and heavily fined, died of grief and vexation in 1258. His nephew John, who served in the Scottish wars, and first had license to castellate Tichmarsh, was summoned to parliament as Lord Lovel of Tichmarsh in 1299; and his descendant, the fifth Lord, acquired a second barony through his wife Maud, granddaughter and heir of Robert de Holland, Lord Holland. To these, the next but one in succession, Sir William, added a third and fourth, by his marriage with

Alice, in her own right Baroness D'Eyncourt and Baroness Grey de Rother-field; and both his sons followed their father's example. John, the elder, eighth Lord Lovel, married Joane, only sister and heir of William, second Viscount Beaumont, who brought him her brother's barony of Beaumont: and William, the second, married Alianor, only child of Robert Lord Morley, and was summoned to parliament as Lord Morley. (See *Morlei*.) John's son, Francis, in addition to the accumulated baronies he thus inherited, received the title of Viscount Lovel on the accession of Richard III. Though his father had been throughout a staunch Lancastrian, rewarded for his services to Henry VI., and forced to fly for his life on the landing of the Duke of York, the son became the bosom friend and counsellor of the Yorkist king, and was one of the hated favourites denounced in the old distich:

"The Rat, the Cat, and Lovell our Dog,
    Govern all England under the Hog."

He was appointed Constable of Wallingford, Lord Chamberlain of the Household, and Chief Butler of England: but all these evanescent dignities passed away with his master's brief reign; and his after fate was strange and pitiable. After the rout of Bosworth, he fled for sanctuary to St. John's, Col-chester; and thence, hunted from place to place, he at last made his way to Flanders, and betook himself to the court of Margaret, Duchess of Burgundy, the late King's sister. She greeted him kindly, and employed him on the expedition sent over to Ireland to uphold the counterfeit Duke of York, Lambert Simnel; from whence he came back to England with John de la Pole, Earl of Lincoln, and fought under him at the disastrous battle of Stoke. From this point a certain mystery hangs over his fate. He was last seen, after the battle, swimming his horse across the Trent; but it was said he could not gain the further side, on account of the steepness of the banks, and that both he and his horse were swept away by the current. There was always, however, a report in the country that he was not drowned, but had succeeded in making good his landing, and sought refuge in some hiding-place, where he lived for a long time, but in the end was left to starve to death. This tradition, which is alluded to by Lord Bacon, was curiously confirmed by a discovery made in the first years of the last century. "On the 6th of May, 1728," writes Mr. William Cowper, Clerk of the Parliament in 1737, "the present Duke of Rutland related in my hearing, that about twenty years before, viz. in 1708, upon occasion of new laying a chimney at Minster Luvel, there was discovered a large vault under-ground, in which was the entire skeleton of a man, as having been sitting at a table, which was before him, with a book, paper, pen, &c.: in another part of the room lay a cap, all much mouldered and decayed. Which the family and others judged to be this Lord Lovel, whose exit has hitherto been so uncertain." It would thus appear that he had gone straight to his own house, and shut himself up in a hidden chamber probably contrived for some such emergency, trusting his secret to a confidential servant who had either forgotten or betrayed him and there, mewed up like a rat in a hole, he had been suffered to die by inches, in all the lingering agonies of starvation.

He had no children, and all his honours fell under attainder. One only—the barony of Beaumont—was restored in 1840 to a descendant of his elder sister, Joan, the wife of Sir Brian Stapleton of Carlton in Yorkshire.

"Benham-Lovell, in Berkshire, took its name from this family; it was held by the service of keeping a pack of dogs (*canum deynectorum*) at the King's expense for the Royal use."—*Lysons.*

The Lovells are also found in Scotland, and had crossed the Border at an early date, for in 1183 Henry Lovell granted some of his land at Hawick to the prior and canons of St. Andrew's. Hawick in Roxburghshire was their ancient residence; thence they removed to Ballumbie, in Angus, which they held till about the middle of the sixteenth century. Thomas Lovel witnesses the foundation charter of the *Maison Dieu* at Brechin in 1267. "*Eva, quae fuit uxor Roberti Lovel,*" did homage for lands in the counties of Aberdeen, Forfar, and Roxburgh in 1296 : and, much about the same time, "*Agneys, qu fu la femme Henry Lovel,*" performed the same service for lands in Roxburghshire. James Lovel is recorded as one of the Angus barons who fell at Harlaw in 1411. Alexander, the son of Richard Lovel of Ballumbie, is said to have married Catherine Douglas, who was in the Convent of the Black Friars at Perth, when King James I. and "Walter Straton, the kyng's chalmer chyld," were murdered by the Earl of Athole and his associates. This lady was maid of honour to Queen Joanna, and it is said by an old writer that, on hearing the approach of the regicides, and with a view of allowing the king time to escape, she "put hir arme in the hole where the bolt suld have bene for haste, bot the upstriking of it brak hir arme." *—*Memorials of Angus and the Mearns.* Andrew Lovell, in 1572, "was denunceit rebell and thairfor put in ward." After this, but few traces remain of the family. Ballumbie had passed into the possession of Sir Thomas Lyon of Aldbar. "Some of the family became burgesses in the neighbouring town of Dundee : and the last notice of them, as landed proprietors, occurs in 1607, when Sibylla and Mariota were served heiresses-portioners of their father, James Lovell, in the lands and fishings of Westferry and 'the Vastcruik, *alias* Kilcraig,' on the north of the Tay, which probably goes to show that the family failed in co-heiresses."—*Ibid.*

Lemare: or, more correctly, as Leland has it, De La Mare : from the

* "Tradition says, that Catherine Douglas, in honour of her heroic act when she barred the door with her arm against the murderers of James I. of Scotland, received popularly the name of 'Barlass.' This name remains to her descendants, the Barlas family in Scotland, who have for their crest a broken arm."—Notes to *The King's Tragedy.*

great fief of La Mare, near St. Opportune, in the *commune* of Autretot, Normandy; where their castle was built upon piles on the margin of the lake still called Grande-mare. The Sire de La Mare is one of the Norman nobles enumerated by Wace at the battle of Hastings; and the family became very numerous both in Normandy and England. Sir William de la Mare, and his lands in the valley of La Mare, are mentioned in a charter of St. Louis, dated 1259; and as many as nine Sires de La Mare (almost all of them bearing different arms) are entered on the roll of "Gentilshommes de la Normandie" given in the *Nobiliaire.* De La Marre de Longueville, of the bailifry of Bayeux, and the Sieur de La Mare, of that of Carentan, sat in the Assembly of Norman nobles convened in 1789.

The ancestor of the English families, "Norman de La Mare, lived c. 1030. Hugo de La Mare, 1070, occurs in a Breton charter (Morice, Hist. Bret. Preuves, i. 434)."—*The Norman People.* This was one of his sons, of whom four came to England at the Conquest, though in all probability not the eldest of them. William Fitz Norman, who in 1086 held of the King in chief in Gloucester and Hereford, and as William de Mare, appears as an undertenant in Wiltshire and Hertfordshire (Domesday), must have been the head of the house. Hugh, also called Fitz Norman (Hugo de Mare in Domesday), held of Hugh Lupus in Cheshire. Ralph, the third, was the Earl's Dapifer or Seneschal, and the ancestor of the Palatinate Barons of Montalt. He and Roger, a fourth brother, are mentioned in a charter of Hugh Fitz Norman's to St. Werburgh's Abbey, Chester, between 1107–20.

William is said to have married a daughter of Hugh Lupus (it must have been a bastard daughter), and had a son, named after his grandfather, Hugh, "ancestor of the Barons of Kilpec, and censor of the Forest of Dean, 1131."— *A. S. Ellis.* The custody of this forest "had been attached to the holding of some of Fitz Norman's lands in the time of Edward the Confessor."—*Sir Henry Ellis.* Hugh gave the church of Kilpec, with the chapel of Our Lady within the Castle, in 1124 to the monks of St. Peter's at Gloucester; and his son Henry assumed the name of this Herefordshire castle, which was the head of his barony. This Henry, in 1175, was fined one hundred marks for trespassing in the King's forests; and his successor John, obtained a charter from King John, the year after his accession, "That neither himself nor any of his Heirs, should be abridg'd of the Bailiwick of his Forest of Herefordshire."—*Dugdale.* He died four years afterwards, leaving a son who proved the last heir male, and had two daughters who inherited. Isabel, the eldest, carried the barony to William Waleran; and Joan, the second, married Philip Marmion.

The three other sons of Norman de La Mare were, as I have already said, settled in Cheshire. Hugh Fitz Norman, Lord of Lea, held a considerable estate that had been allotted to him by the Earl in his county palatine; but his line failed with his grandson, and the whole reverted to the Barons of Montalt, descended from his next brother Ralph, Seneschal of Chester.

Ralph's son Robert had adopted the name of the head of his barony, " a little Hill," says Dugdale, " in Flintshire, then called Montalt, whereon he built a castle, but of late time (vulgarly) Moulde " :* and ruled his territory with the iron hand of a Baron Marcher. In the time of his successor Roger it was over-run by Llewellyn's son David ; and one of the articles in the treaty of peace concluded in 1243 between Henry III. stipulated that the Baron of Montalt should enjoy his own again. In 1249, "being reputed one of the greatest Barons of this Realm, and signed with the Cross in order to an Expedition to the Holy Land " with Prince Edward, he sold to the Monks of Coventry " a great part of his Woods and Revenues " there, to raise money for his outfit. This property had come to him through Cecily his wife, one of the coheirs of Hugh de Albini, Earl of Arundel, by whom he left two sons ; John, twice married, but childless : and Robert, styled the " Black Steward of Chester," who was the father of the two last Lords of Montalt, Roger, and Robert. Roger was in arms against Hen. III., but twice followed Edward I. to the Gascon wars, and was rewarded by a summons to parliament in 1294. He died s. p. three years afterwards ; and his brother Robert, again a soldier and again a baron by writ, being likewise childless, settled his whole vast estate, with the castles of Monthalt, Hawarden, &c., on Queen Isabel, the mother of Edward III. for her life, and afterwards on her younger son, John of Eltham, and his heirs. He died in 1329.

But, according to Ormerod, he had another brother and heir-at-law, Hugh de Montalt, whom he thus defrauded of his rights ; and Hugh was succeeded by a son and a grandson. Judith, the daughter of the grandson, married—Glegg ; and "her descendants claimed the town, castle, lordship, and manor of Mohaute and Mohautesdale." But what they obtained is a widely different question.

The name of Monhalt or Monhaut was transmuted to Moulde or Maude ; and a branch of the house—vaguely described as " cousins "—was long seated at Riddlesden in Yorkshire. Robert Maude, of Riddlesden and Ripon, living in the seventeenth century, sold his English estates to buy land in Ireland, and settled at Dundrum, co. Tipperary. His grandson, who married a Cornwallis heiress, received a baronetcy in 1705, and was the father of Sir Thomas Maude, created Baron of Montalt in 1776, whose title expired with him in the following year. It was revived in favour of his brother, Sir Cornwallis, in 1785 ; and the Viscountcy of Hawarden followed in 1793. Both titles are still borne by his descendant ; and another—the Earldom De Montalt—was added in 1886.

The collateral branches that retained the original name of De La Mare, which, by a curious fatality, had been discarded by the principal families—were

---

* It is called by the Welsh " Wyddgrug," the conspicuous hill, translated Montalt by the Normans.

extremely numerous. Nearly twenty different bearings are assigned to the name in Burke's Armoury, exclusive of the coat of the Barons of Kilpec, *Argent* a sword in bend *Sable;* or that of the Barons of Montalt, *Azure,* a lion rampant *Argent.* The unravelling of their respective pedigrees would be a task over which a conscientious genealogist might grow grey. Robert de La Mare (no doubt belonging to the house of Kilpec), who in 1165 held ten knight's fees of the Earl of Gloucester, is credited with being the ancestor of the Gloucester, Worcester, and Herefordshire branches. " By the White Book of Worcester it appears that Thomas de La Mare held in Ordewicke, in the parish of Eldersfield of the gift of William Earl of Gloucester, about 1182: and 20 Ed. III. John Delamare held lands in Eldersfield. This family extended themselves into the county of Hereford, and gave name to the parish of Tedstone Delamare. In 7 Hen. VI. the Delamares of Tedstone were returned into the Exchequer in rank next to the knights, and before the esquires, to attend the King's person with horse and arms to France. About the same time John Delamare of Hardwicke was returned into the same court as an esquire to serve the King. Delamare having sold this estate to Sir Thomas Coventry, soon after left the country."— *Nash's Worcestershire.* Sir Peter de La Mare of Yatton, knight of the shire for Herefordshire, was chosen Speaker of the House of Commons at the accession of Richard II. He had been nominated for the office in the last Parliament of the previous reign, but rejected through the influence of the Court party, and imprisoned in Nottingham Castle for speaking his mind too freely respecting Alice Perers, " the Abishaig of King Edward III." He continued none the less independent and " bold of speech ; " for his first act as Speaker was to make several important regulations for the government of the country during the young King's minority. At his death, Yatton passed to his great nephew Roger Seymour, ancestor of the Dukes of Somerset. Richard De la Mare was Sheriff of Hereford 1 Henry VI. Their arms, Barry of six, dancetté *Or* and *Gules,* remain in Hereford Cathedral.

In Oxfordshire, Henry de la Mare, on the death of his father in 1139, paid a fine "that he might enjoy his office of *Veltrare* (Vaultrer, or Huntsman), holding it by petty Serjeanty." His successor, Robert, Sheriff of Oxon 34 Hen. II., and of Oxon and Berks in the first two years of Cœur de Lion's reign, was the father of Geoffrey, who held Dudcote in Berkshire. From him (I am still quoting the *Baronage*) descended John de la Mare of Gersynden (Garsington) in Oxfordshire, who served in Edward I.'s foreign wars in 1293 and 1297, and was summoned to Parliament by him in 1299. None of the name ever received a second summons ; and with him Dugdale consequently closes the pedigree. Even the portion he has given must be far from complete. There was a Henry de la Mare in the reign of Henry III., who " held £12 of land at Elwescot in Oxfordshire by the serjeanty of keeping the door of the King's hall, and providing brushwood and litter for the use of the King's household ; and two marks of land at Eston by the serjeanty of keeping the *meretrices** following the King's Court" (Testa de Nevill). His wife Gunnor has left her name to Winterborne-Gunnor in Wiltshire, also called (in the Pipe-Roll of 1254) Winterborne de la Mare. They had "a son named Henry, who was slain in 1267, *fugiens de pace.* He was a robber of churches and monasteries, and was imprisoned at Bampton in Oxfordshire, where, breaking his prison, he was pursued and cut down with an axe. According to one account he left Alicia his sister and heiress; but his lands, as those of a felon, were seized into the King's hands."—*Hoare's Wilts.*

Contemporary with him was Nicholas de la Mare, Lord of Nunney-de-la-Mare in Somersetshire, of which the family had been "very early possessed. He was succeeded by another Nicholas, who lived there in the time of Edward I., and had several children, of whom Elias de la Mare was a great warrior, and was the first projector of the castle there, which was finished by his successors. John de la Mare was Sheriff of Wilts" (where he has left his name to Fisherton-de-la-Mare) "in 1377, and then bore on his shield two lions passant. This John and his younger brother Jaques finished the castle, embellishing it with spoils brought from abroad, which had been won in the wars of France. Philip de la Mare succeeded to the manor of Nunney-de-la-Mare, and was father of several children, of whom Sir Elias de la Mare was Sheriff of Wilts 2 Hen. V., but died without issue; and Eleanor his eldest sister became heir to the whole estate lying in Somersetshire. This Eleanor was married to William Paulet, second son of Sir John Paulet of Melcombe in this county."—*Collinson's Somerset.* He was the ancestor of the Marquesses of Winchester and Dukes of Bolton. Leland describes Nunney as "a praty castle at the weste end of the paroche churche, havynge at eche end by northe and southe 2 praty rownd towres gatheryd by cumpace to joyne into one. The waulls be very stronge and thykke, and the stayres narrow; the lodgynge within somewhat darke. It standith on the lefte ripe of the ryver devidethe" (dividing) "it from the churcheyarde. The castell is motyd about, and this mote is servid by water conveyed into it owte of the ryver. There is a stronge waulle withe owte the mote rounde about, saving at the est parte of the castell where it is defendyd by the brooke." It was held by the Paulets till the time of Henry VIII.

"Ther was," continues Leland, "a younger Brother of this House of the Delamares; and he by Præferrement of Mariage had about the tyme of Edwarde the 3, the Doughter and Heyre of one Achard, a Man of fayre Landes in Barkshire. Syr Thomas Delamare, Knight of the Sepulchre, the last of this House had a Sun callid John; and he dying afore Thomas his Father left two Doughters; whereof one was maried to Humfre Foster, Father to Syr Humfre that now lyvith; the other to Morton of Dorcetshire, Kinsman to Cardinal Morton; but

---

* It should be borne in mind that in mediæval times this word was used for *latrices* or laundresses.

she had no Children, and so the Landes of this Delamer cam totally to Foster."
Her sister, however, amply atoned for this deficiency: for, adds Leland, "Syr
Humfre Foster's Father had twenty Children."

There were probably other ramifications of this ubiquitous race that I have
left unnoticed. But at least one family, bearing the same name, may be discarded
from the list. The De la Mares or De la Meres of Cheshire were a younger
branch of the Venables, seated at Mere in that county; a town originally held by
Gilbert de Venables, and so called from the adjoining lake or mere. Their coat
of arms—an ancient three-masted ship; and their crest—a mermaid with a green
tail holding a golden comb or mirror—betoken this origin.

Leuetot; from Lovetot in Lower Normandy. "The earliest person in this
splendid line is William de Luvetot, founder of the priory of Worksop. His
appearance in the North is subsequent to the date of Domesday, but it could not
be long after that time. In Hallamshire, at the castle of Sheffield, placed at the
junction of the Sheaf with the Don, the Lovetots, Furnivalls, and their successors,
had their principal seat, the caput baroniæ; though they had other houses
dispersed throughout their fee, particularly Sheffield Manor, a house in the centre
of their extensive park, the hall at Hansworth, and the manor of Worksop, to
which has succeeded the present magnificent home of the Duke of Norfolk, the
illustrious representative of this splendid line."—*Hunter's South Yorkshire.* Since
then, Worksop has been sold to the Duke of Newcastle; but the feudal
seignorality of Hallamshire, whose lords may be traced to within thirty years of
the Conquest, is still vested in their descendant by right of inheritance; "no
sale, and what is more extraordinary, no forfeiture, having ever happened to this
great domain." It forms part of the high and mountainous tract compared by
Dodsworth to the Apennines, "because the rain-water that there falleth sheddeth
from sea to sea:" a wild untrodden upland of wood and moor, which when
Hunter wrote (in 1819) comprised "no less than twenty thousand acres over
which no plough has yet passed, and where scarcely a human habitation is to be
found." * Who first raised the axe in its forests, or fixed their abode in the
romantic valley where

> "Five rivers, like the fingers of a hand,
> Flung from black mountains, mingle and are one,"

---

* One of these "cloud-kissing mountains" is "so high that on a cleere day a man
may from the top thereof see both the minsters of York and Lincolne, neare sixty
miles off us; and it is to be supposed that when the Devil did look over Lincolne as
the proverb is, he stood upon that mountaine or neare it." In the "woody, rocky,
stony wildernesse" of Wharncliffe Chase the Dragon of Wantley had his home;—a
cleft in the rocks is still shown as the Dragon's den; and old Sir Thomas Wortley
"causyd a lodge to be made for his plesor to heare the hartes bell." The first man
who ever shot grouse on the wing died in 1687.

is not known ; but at the time of the Conquest Earl Waltheoff had an *aula* (hall, court) at Hallam, near the present town of Sheffield. His treacherous wife, Countess Judith, was allowed to retain his lands after his execution, and held them at Domesday. " She sub-infeuded Roger de Busli ; ten years afterwards Dominus William de Louvetot appears in the place of De Busli, and it continued to be held of the heirs of the Countess."—*Hunter's Hallamshire.*

It is not explained how De Louvetot, who had been a Huntingdonshire baron, acquired his interest in Yorkshire ; nor is there any certainty as to his genealogy ; but he is conjectured to have been the son of the Ricardus Surdus of Domesday, who was one of the two great sub-feudatories of the Earl of Mortaine (Nigel Fossard being the other) in this part of England. His coat of arms, *Argent* a lion rampant parti per fesse *Gules* and *Sable*, was allusive to his name, *Luve* (cognate to the German *Loewe*) being Danish for lion.

He found his new domain—thenceforward styled, from the caput baroniæ, the Honour of Sheffield—suffering from " the skirt of the storm" of the Conqueror's wrath, that had swept across the contumacious North in ruin and devastation. But he and his successors proved wise and humane rulers. They made the castle they had built at Sheffield their chief residence ; and the new town—then a rude collection of huts and smithies—grew and prospered under its protection. One of their first cares had been to plant churches throughout their territory, where in Saxon times there were none ; and they built a hospital, a corn-mill, and a bridge "where one was most wanted" over the Don. Unfortunately their reign was brief ; for the line ended with William de Louvetot's grandson and namesake, who died between 1175-80. He had married a De Clare, and left a daughter named Maud, then " of very tender years," to be the Lady of Hallamshire. She was first in ward to Henry II., and then to Cœur de Lion, who bestowed her hand on Gerard de Furnival, the son of one of his companions in arms at the siege of Acre. The homage-fine agreed upon by the fortunate bridegroom was 400 marks of silver ; but " this sum was never paid ; for not long after happened the great fight under the walls of Mirabel. To the success of that day the valour of De Furnival contributed ; and in the battle and pursuit two hundred knights were made prisoners. One of them, whose name was Conan de Leon, fell into the hands of De Furnival : and this prisoner he rendered to the King, having in return a remission of his homage fine."—*Ibid.*

Maud, who like other great heiresses, constantly used her family name, not only survived her husband for many years, but saw all her three sons go down to the grave before her. The eldest, Thomas, fell in Palestine, " probably in the great slaughter of the Christian host at Damietta :" and his mother, in her bereavement, dwelt with bitterness on " the shameful fact that he whose life had been sacrificed to Christian zeal should lie in ground that was cursed by the step of the infidel." Her younger son Gerard, with true filial piety, undertook a second pilgrimage to the East to bring back his brother's remains ; and she had them solemnly interred in the Abbey founded by her great grandfather at Worksop.*

The Furnivals continued in possession for five generations; till the last Lord Furnival died in 1383, leaving an heiress married to Sir Thomas Nevill, who in her right was Lord Furnival. Their only child, Maud Lady Furnival, was the wife of the great Earl of Shrewsbury, first summoned to parliament as " John Talbot of Hallamshire." The inheritance she brought remained with the Talbots for two hundred years. At last, in 1623, the seventh Earl left three coheiresses; Mary, Countess of Pembroke, Elizabeth, Countess of Kent, and Alethea,† Countess of Arundel and Surrey; and as neither of the two elder sisters had children, the whole succession devolved on the last born. Lady Alethea Talbot thus conveyed Sheffield, Worksop, and the three baronies of Talbot, Furnival, and Strange of Blackmere to the head of the great house of Howard; and her grandson Thomas, soon after the return of Charles II., was restored to the forfeited title of Duke of Norfolk.

There had been another branch of the Louvetots, derived from a second son of the first Baron of Hallamshire, named Nigel, who remained in their old home in Huntingdon, and made Southoe, " on the land of Eustace the Sheriff, the seat of that Seignory, on which, in this Shire, thirteen and a-half knight's fees were dependent. But from this line, by gift of Verdon and Vesey, drowned were these in the Honour of Gloucester."—*Cotton MS.* He had five sons; one of whom, named like himself Nigel, held the Honour of Tickhill in 1201; and, as heir male, had a great contest with Gerard de Furnival, which lasted six years. At length Gerard " gave one thousand Marks and fifteen Palfreys to the King that he might quietly enjoy those lands." Roger, the next, Constable of Bolsover and Sheriff of Derby and Notts in 39, 40, and 41 Hen. III., fell on the Baron's side at the battle of Evesham, and the inheritance was shared by his three sisters, one married to Amundeville, one to Braunford, and the third to Patric. One of the first Nigel's younger sons was, however, still represented in Nottinghamshire till the following reign, when Oliver de Louvetot, of Carcolston in that county, left only female heirs.

Lucy: from Lucy, near Rouen. The Lucys performed the office of Castle Guard at Dover for seven knight's fees, lying in the counties of Kent, Norfolk and Suffolk. Richard de Lucy (the first of the family mentioned by Dugdale) was Constable of Falaise in Normandy for King Stephen, and held it so stoutly

---

* " The nameless and mutilated effigies in an obscure corner of this church," supposed to represent some of the De Louvetots, are all that is now left of the once splendid monuments that commemorated these great barons.

† " Queen Elizabeth was her godmother, and gave her a name till then unknown to the baptismal vocabulary of England; and Vincent informs us, ' out of her majestic's true consideration and judgment of that worthy family, which was ever true to the state : . . . Αληθεια signifying in our English, veritie or truth.' "—*Ibid.*

against Geoffrey Earl of Anjou that he was rewarded with thirteen additional knight's fees in Essex, including the town of Grinstead. He fought on the King's side throughout his contest with the Empress Maud, and routed the forces of the latter in a pitched battle near Wallingford. When the agreement between Stephen and Henry Duke of Normandy was entered upon in 1153, by which Henry was named as successor to the throne, " for the better securing of that Accord, the Tower of London, and Castle of Winchester, by the advice of the whole Clergy, were then given into the hands of this Richard de Lucie, he (by his solemn Oath) promising that upon the death of King Stephen he would faithfully deliver them to Henry; and for his more effectual performance of that Trust, gave up his own Son as a Hostage."—*Dugdale.* The new King, on his. accession, rewarded and employed him. He had a grant of the whole hundred of Angre with other manors in Essex; and in 1162 was appointed Lord Justiciary of England, the highest post of honour that could be held by a subject. When the quarrel between Henry II. and Beckett first arose in 1166, " Beckett fleeing into Normandy, and coming to Viceliac to celebrate the Feast of the Ascension of our Lord (the King being then also in those parts) discerning various persons who then repaired to this Festival, and amongst them this Richard de Lucie, he stept into the Pulpit, and then with lighted Candles pronounced the sentence of Excommunication against them all, as publick Incendiaries between the King and him. But being neither Convicted, nor called to answer, with the rest he appealed, and entered the Church."—*Ibid.* Five years previously, he had been sent over to England by the King to procure the election of this same Beckett.

In 1173 he was for the second time High Justiciary, and marching into Scotland with Humphrey de Bohun, Constable of England, wasted the country and burned Berwick-upon-Tweed; then aided the King's uncle, Reginald Earl of Cornwall, in putting down the rebellion of the Earl of Leicester; stormed and sacked Huntingdon, took the town of Leicester, and laid it in ashes. But as advancing years began to press upon him, he turned from this savage warfare to the "deeds of piety" that were to ransom his soul; and founded two priories in Kent, Westwood and Lesnes, taking "the habit of a Canon Regular" in the latter only a few months before his death in 1179.

This powerful baron had two sons, Geoffrey and Herbert; and two daughters, Maude, married to Walter Fitz Robert (ancestors of the Fitz Walters) and Rohais, married to Fulbert de Dover, Lord of Chilham in Kent. Geoffrey, the heir, did not survive his father, and left an only son who died s. p. : Herbert, the younger, also had no issue; and their sister Rohais had livery of the whole barony, though Maude appears to have inherited Angre and the Essex property.*

* He seems also to have had considerable possessions on the other side of the Channel. " Richard de Lucy, Lord of Gouviz and Baron of Crétot in Normandy," is mentioned in the MSS. of the Cotton Libr. Tib. D. II., among the nobility of France.

But the Lucys did not become extinct with the male line of the great Justiciar. He had certainly one brother, named Walter, and Reginald de Lucy, whose parentage Dugdale "could not discover," is generally supposed to have been another, and this "is the more probable, as he gave a moiety of the church at Godstone in Surrey to the Abbey of Lesnes, founded by Richard (Mon. ii. 302)."—*Manning's Surrey.* Walter de Lucy was the fifth Abbot of Battle; and according to the Abbey Chronicle, ruled wisely and energetically for thirty-three years. He is specially lauded for his zealous zeal in upholding the numerous "liberties and dignities" of his House, which involved him in a constant succession of lawsuits. On one occasion, as lord of the soil of Dengemarsh, he enforced the cruel law of "wreck" against the King himself with these bold words, " If thou, O king, but destroy ever so small a right of our Abbey, conferred and observed by King William and others, thy predecessors, may God grant that thou no longer wear the crown of England !" The greatest contest in which he ever engaged was with the Bishop of Chichester, who claimed spiritual jurisdiction over the Abbey, and had obtained from Pope Adrian IV. a letter formally admonishing Abbot Walter to "obey faithfully his bishop and master." The cause was brought before Henry II. immediately after his coronation, and the long account of it given in the "Chronicle" abounds with characteristic touches. We read how the Bishop taunted the Abbot with having unsuccessfully tried to obtain the See of London, and told the King roundly he had no right to interfere in spiritual matters; how the King, provoked past all bearing, rapped out some words—carefully erased in the MS.—conjectured to have been "gross Norman oaths;" how the Chancellor, Thomas à Beckett, interfered to check the prelate with the words: "Your Prudence must be careful;" and how the latter finally told one falsehood so astounding, that the Archbishop of Canterbury, "knowing how matters really stood, marked himself with the sign of the cross, in token of astonishment." The Abbot pleaded eloquently in his own behalf, and his brother Richard de Lucy stood by him manfully, saying to the King, " This Abbey ought to be held in high account, by you, and by all us Normans, inasmuch as in that place the most noble King William, by God's grace and the aid of our ancestors, acquired that whereby you, my Lord King, at this time, hold the crown of England by hereditary right, and whereby we have all been enriched with great wealth." In the end the Bishop had to disclaim all authority over the Abbot, and all parties gave each other the "kiss of peace" at the Archbishop's request, the King declaring that he was ready to kiss the Bishop "not only once, but a hundred times," possibly as some compensation to the latter for his defeat.

In most cases, as in this one, the Abbot seems to have triumphantly carried his point, though sometimes—apparently greatly to the disgust of the brethren— he consented to a compromise. But though litigious and troublesome as a neighbour, to his own people he was the kindest of masters. " With great pity towards the poor, he allayed their hunger with food, and covered their nakedness with raiment;" and like St. Elizabeth of Hungary, tended and cherished the loathsome lepers—shunned by all else—for whom he founded a lazar house at Battle. He annually provided his monks with a little treat, consisting of one gallon of white wine, a "pepper-cake" (gingerbread is still so called in Germany) and two good dishes in addition to their ordinary fare, "one of which, if circumstances will possibly admit, shall be of fresh salmon." This "benefaction" was to be continued on every anniversary of his death, and lest any of his successors should neglect it, he put on his stole, took a lighted candle, and went with all his priests and deacons to the chapter-house, there solemnly to pronounce a " perpetual and inexorable anathema upon all who should violate this institution." He died in 1171.

Reginald de Lucy, the third brother, acquired by marriage a very large property in Cumberland. This was the great Saxon barony of Coupland or Kopeland, lying between the rivers Dudden and Darwent and the sea, granted by Ranulph de Meschines (the first Norman lord of Cumberland) to his younger brother William, who built his castle on a steep sharp-topped hill which he called Aigre-mont. Kopeland thus became Egremont in the new tongue. William married Cecilia de Roumeli, the heiress of Skipton-in-Craven, and left an only child, Aaliza, or Alice, who bore her mother's name of Roumeli, and brought the united baronies of Skipton and Egremont to her husband William Fitz Duncan, a prince of the blood royal of Scotland, and the grandson of Malcolm Canmore. They had issue a son, commonly called the Boy of Egremont, from his grand-father's barony (where he was probably born), who, surviving an elder brother, became the last hope of the family. One day that he had been out coursing, and was returning home through the deep solitude of the woods lying between Bolton and Barden Tower, he had to cross the narrow channel—little more than four feet wide—in which the imprisoned Wharfe boils along in wrath, forcing its way through a tremendous fissure in the rock. The place was then, as it is yet, called the Strid :—either from the Anglo-Saxon *stryth* (turmoil, tumult), or from the familiar feat of the dalesmen, who show their agility by striding or bounding across this fearful chasm, " regardless of the destruction which awaits a faltering footstep." The young heir of Craven took the leap—as he had probably done a hundred times before—without a thought of danger ; but at the critical moment, a grey hound that he held in leash (some say fastened to his girdle) hung back and checked him. He was baulked in his leap, missed his footing, and in another instant had fallen headlong between the cruel gates of rock, to be swept away in the whirl of the raging torrent below. There was no one to witness his fate but a forester in attendance, who went back with a stricken heart, to break the tidings to the Lady Aaliza. He stood before her troubled and woebegone, and with bent head and lowered eyes, asked " What is good for a bootless Bene?"* The wretched mother read her sentence in his face, and knew, without being told, that her son was dead. She answered at once " Endless sorrow:" and, true to her word, from that evil day to the last day of her life, never ceased to mourn for this lost heir. According to tradition, she desired that perpetual prayer should be offered up near the spot where he was drowned; and accordingly, the Cistercian priory founded in 1121 by her father and mother at Embsey was transferred to Bolton, and there re-built and re-endowed by her.

> " In darkness long the mother sat,
> And her first words were—' Let there be
> At Bolton, on the field of Wharfe,
> A stately Priory.'
> That stately Priory was reared,
> And Wharfe, as he moved along,
> To matins joined a mournful voice,
> Nor failed at even-song."

The latter part of this story is an undoubted fact. Aaliza de Roumeli was the foundress, or rather the second foundress, of Bolton; but it is no less certain, that " her drowned son is himself a party and witness to the charter of translation. Yet," adds Whitaker, " I have little doubt that the story is true in the main, but that it refers to one of the sons of Cecilia de Roumeli, the first foundress, both of whom died young." Lord Lindsay tells us that the " Boy of Egremont was alive in 1160, and a partaker of the rebellion of the Scotch-Pictish Celts of Scotland, of which the object apparently was to set him on the throne as the rightful heir." This much at least is evident, that he left no posterity; and his great inheritance fell to his three sisters. Cecily, the eldest, had Skipton; Amabel, Egremont; and Alice, Cockermouth. Cecily was married by Henry II. to William le Gros, Earl of Albemarle; Amabel became the wife of Reginald de Lucy; and Alice had two husbands, Gilbert Pipard, and Robert Courtenay; but her children all died young, and thus the whole of her share, comprising, in addition to the honour of Cockermouth, Aspatric, and the barony of Allerdale, eventually came to the Lucys.

Reginald and Amabel had an only son, Richard, whose wife, Ada de Morville, was another great heiress (see *Morville*): but male issue failing in him, the lands were once more partitioned between his two daughters. By a convenient family arrangement not uncommon in those days, they were married to two brothers, Lambert and Alan de Multon, while their widowed mother espoused the father of her two sons-in-law. Amabel, the elder sister, brought to Lambert the barony

---

* " Bootless Bene signifies unavailing prayer: thus the meaning of the words would be, What remains when prayer is useless? The language of this question, almost unintelligible at present, proves the antiquity of this story, which nearly amounts to proving its truth."—*Whitaker's Craven.*

of Egremont, retained by their descendants for several generations, while the son of Alice and of Alan was seated at Cockermouth, bore his mother's name of De Lucy, and transmitted it to his posterity. His grandson, Anthony, was a man of considerable note as a soldier, who followed Edward I. through his Scottish wars, was twice appointed guardian of his native county against the Scots, Governor of Carlisle, Berwick-upon-Tweed, Justice of Ireland, &c., and was summoned to parliament as Lord Lucy 16 Ed. II. The second Lord greatly added to his estate by marrying his kinswoman, Margaret de Multon, one of the co-heirs of John de Multon, with whom the elder line terminated; but the younger was not destined to survive it long. Neither of his sons left an heir; and the barony passed to their sister Maud, the last of the name of Lucy, who was first Countess of Angus (see *Umfreville*) and then Countess of Northumberland. She, too, left no children, for an only son by Lord Angus died before his father; and it was agreed on her second marriage with Lord Northumberland, that, on failure of their issue, her great possessions, and her castle and honour of Cockermouth, should be settled on the Earl's eldest son by a former wife (the renowned Hotspur) on the sole condition that he and all his posterity should quarter with their own Brabant lion, the three silver lucies * that she bore as her coat of arms. This stipulation was so faithfully carried out, that the Duke of Northumberland, as representative of the old Percies, still bears this coat of the Lucies, with whom, as we have seen, they could claim no relationship; and Hotspur's descendants were even sometimes styled Barons Lucy; "their pretensions to that dignity," says Sir Bernard Burke, "being manifestly without a shadow of foundation." In 1557, however, the brother of the sixth Earl, received, among other honours, the title of Baron Lucy, which only expired at the death of the last heir male in 1670.

Leland enumerates several branches of the family, existing in his time:

"Lucy of Warwikeshire, that dwellith at Charcote, by Avon, bytwixt Warwicke, and Stratford upon Avon, came oute of the house of Cokermuth.

"Syr Edmund Lucy, that lately lyvid and dwellid at * * * * yn Bedfordshire, came oute of the house of Lucy of Charcote.

"There hath been other Lucies, men of meane Landes, that hath descendid out of the aforesaid housis of Lucies."—*Itin., vol. vi.*

The Lucys of Charlecote flourished up to the end of the last century. Charlecote had been granted to their ancestor by Henry de Montford in the reign of Richard I., who confirmed the grant; and for a time they called themselves De Charlecote, but soon resumed their original Norman name. Sir Thomas Lucy was in the retinue of John of Gaunt; another Lucy was a soldier

---

* Lucie, or luce, was the old name for pike:

> "Full many a fair partrich had he in mewe,
> And many a breme and many a luce in stewe."

of repute in the Wars of the Roses, and commanded a division of the Royal army at Stoke. The great grandson of this latter, Sir Thomas, who built the existing manor house of Charlecote, prosecuted Shakespere for stealing deer in his park of Fulbrooke, and was in consequence immortalized as "Justice Shallow." Second in descent from him was another Sir Thomas, knight of the shire for Warwick in six successive parliaments, of whom it was said, that "his tables were ever opened to the learned, and his gates never fast to the poor." The last of the family was George Lucy, who died unmarried in 1786, leaving Charlecote to his great nephew, the Rev. John Hammond, who thereupon took the name and arms of Lucy, still borne by his descendants.

One of the "other Lucies" was Robert de Lucy, who died 47 Ed. III., seated at Upton-Lucy, in Wiltshire, and whose name does not appear in the pedigree of the baronial Lucys. His son died in his minority, s. p. Yet some collateral descendants must have remained, for William Lucy was Escheator of the King in the co. of Wilts 6 Ed. IV. Sutton-Lucy and Lucyhays in Devonshire belonged temp. Hen. II. to Maurice de Lucy (*Pole*).

Luny: Lownay in Leland's list: from Launai in Normandy, where Walter, Joscelin, and Hugo de Launay occur in the Exchequer Rolls of 1198. There were four noble families of this name; and three De Launays are found in the assembly of Norman nobles in 1789. In England, Sir John de Launay witnesses John de Herlyng's grant of the manor of Corton, &c., 49 Ed. III.—*Suckling's Suffolk.* "Wendon-Loughts, the chief manor of the parish, is one of the two knight's fees that were holden by Maud Launey, and Alice de Bottiller, under Robert Fitz Walter, who died in 1328. And under Walter Fitz Walter, who died in 1386, Thomas Lawney, and his partners, held it as one fee."—*Morant's Essex.* John Louney held of the Fee of Mowbray at East Heslardton, in the East Riding of Yorkshire.—*Kirkby's Inquest.* Robert de Launay, in 1270, was a member of the Inquisition appointed by Royal writ to divide the lands of Roger, Earl of Winchester. John de Launay, at the same date, held of Richard de Buslingthorpe in Lincolnshire.—*Calendar of Documents relating to Scotland.*

Logeuile, for Longueville, a branch of the house of Giffard, Barons of Longueville and Bolbec, near Dieppe. Henry de Longavilla, in 1165, held of Lovetot Overton (now called Orton) Longueville in Huntingdonshire.—*Liber Niger.* Roger de Longueville is mentioned in the same county about 1200. *Rot. Curiæ Regis:* William, in Herts, and Richard, in Bucks, 1190–98.—*Ibid.* In the early part of the fourteenth century, the existing church of Overton-Longueville was built by one of this family, supposed to be commemorated by the mutilated effigy of a knight placed between the chancel and the North chantry. Some have, however, assigned to it a much earlier date. The knight lies cross legged, with a heater shield on his right arm, and a couchant lion at his feet. In any case it is clear that he was a soldier of the Cross, and the ghastly legend attached to him, and preserved by Bishop Kennet, must be based on some desperate encounter with a Paynim in the Holy Land. "According to local tradition, the figure represents a Lord Longueville, who in fighting with the Danes near this place, received a wound in his belly, so that his entrails fell out, but wrapping them round the wrist of his left hand, continued the combat with his right hand till he had killed the Danish King, and soon after fell himself." In early times Dane and Saracen were convertible terms, being classed together under the common name of Infidels. As an instance in point, I may quote the monkish genealogy of the Husseys, where the Danish invaders are called Saracens.

We next find the family in Northamptonshire, where Henry de Longueville, "deduced from Walter Lord of Overton, co. Hunts, &c., in Domesday," sat in parliament for Northampton in 1310 and 1311. His son Sir John was knight of the shire in 1314, 1315, and 1319; and one of the Justices, Conservators of the peace, and Commissioners of array for the county. He founded a house for Augustine Friars at Northampton, which became the burial place of the family, and "was seated at Little Billing, as were his successors for eight generations." He also held Weston-Turville in Buckinghamshire. Another John Longueville, who was Sheriff of Bedfordshire and Buckinghamshire in 1394, and died in 1430, acquired through his wife Wolverton, in the latter county, which had been the seat of the Domesday barony of Maigno Brito, and was held by his descendants for three hundred years. "This marriage with the heiress of Wolverton not only furnished the family with a residence in Buckinghamshire, but greatly augmented their wealth and influence in this county. Sir George Longueville, son and heir of John, gained a still further accession of honour with his first wife Elizabeth Roche, whose grandson and heir, Richard Longueville, enjoyed the barony of Roche, and jointly with Ferrers of Chartley, that of Birmingham, of her inheritance."—*Baker's Northamptonshire.* Richard's son, Sir John, whose years far exceeded the term allotted by modern theorists to human life, left no legitimate children, and was the last of the line. Leland, whose contemporary he was, speaks of him in his Itinerary: "Langeville an 1c3 Yeyres old made his Landes from his Heires general to his Bastard Sunne Arture." This Arthur bore the name and arms of Longueville; and "Sir Edward, his great grandson, in reward for pecuniary assistance rendered to King Charles at Edinburgh, was created a baronet of Nova Scotia in 1638. He lived to see the Restoration, and dying in 1661, was succeeded by his son and heir Sir Thomas, who was killed by a fall from his horse near Wolverton in 1685, and left an only son Sir Edward, third baronet, who was a zealous Catholic, and sold Billing to support the cause of James II., the very day the army declared for the Prince of Orange at Blackheath. Within a few months, his necessities compelled him also to dispose of Wolverton. He met with a similar fate to his father, being thrown from his horse and killed at Bicester races in 1718; and leaving no issue, the title devolved on his cousin and brother in law Sir Thomas, the fourth and last baronet; and he, too, dying without issue, the baronetcy became extinct."—*Ibid.* Wolverton was sold to "the celebrated physician Dr. Radcliffe, who bequeathed it, with other large estates in trust for the University of Oxford."—*Lysons.* The seat of the Longuevilles, rebuilt in 1586, and described by Browne Willis as "a magnificent mansion," has been pulled down; but the keep of Maigno Brito's castle still remains near the vicarage.

Sir Michael Longueville, the fourth son of Sir Henry, married Lady Susan Grey, daughter of Charles, seventh Earl of Kent, and sister and heiress of Henry, eighth Earl. Their only son, Charles, "claimed, and was allowed, the barony of Grey de Ruthyn, in 1640, and was introduced into the House of Lords the 10th of February, 1640: but he did not enjoy the peerage long, deceasing in 1643, in the King's garrison at Oxford. He married Frances, one of the daughters and co-heirs of Edward Neville, and left an only daughter, Susan, who married Sir Henry Yelverton, Bt."—*Banks.* Her grandson Henry was created Viscount Longueville in 1690; but this title became extinct in 1799, at the death of his descendant Henry, third Earl of Sussex.

It was revived no later than the following year in favour of an Irishman, Richard Longfield of Longueville, Governor of the county of Cork, who had been created Baron Longueville in 1795. He left no posterity, but the family is still represented at Longueville. Though its pedigree, as given by Burke, claims for it nothing beyond "ancient descent," it may possibly be derived from the same stock as the house of Wolverton. The arms, *Gules* a chevron *Ermine* between seven cross-crosslets fitchée, favour this supposition, for they are very nearly the same as these used by the English Longuevilles, viz.: *Gules* a fesse dancettée *Ermine* between six cross-crosslets *Argent.*

Longespes. "Rogerus Lungus Ensis" held in Norfolk 1086 (Domesday). But there is no mention of him (at least by this name) in the county history; and I have in consequence no means of identifying him. This is one of the numerous cases in which a continuation of the *Recherches sur le Domesday* would have been invaluable in helping to decide the question.

Moreover, it is possible that this entry may be an interpolation, referring to the famous bastard son of Henry II. and Fair Rosamond. (See *Devereux.*)

Louerace. This name is retained by a Wiltshire manor, Cowsfield Loveraz (now corrupted to Loveries). "Loveraz appears among the Norman holders in Wiltshire at the time of the great Survey, and possibly one of the same house may have received this portion of Cowsfield, when the rebellion of Brictric was followed by its forfeiture to the Crown."—*Hoare's Wilts.* William de Luveraz, 12 Henry II. held two knight's fees of the great barony of Waleran. Galfrid de Luveraz occurs 3 John: Odo de Luveraz 9 John. William de Luveraz, 10 Hen. III., married Matilda, a kinswoman of Ela de Longespee, Countess of Salisbury, who gave to him and his wife, and their heirs, the manor of East

Morden in Dorsetshire, which was held "of the King in chief, by service of paying yearly to the Exchequer 8*s.* by the hand of the Sheriff of Dorset." (See *Hutchins.*) Their son, Walter, was Forester of Buckholt 54 Hen. III. John, his eldest son, is mentioned as being then twenty-eight years of age ; and succeeded to East Morden : while his second son, Stephen, was Lord of Cowsfield Loveraz. The Dorsetshire branch ended with John's son Richard, who died s.p. 25 Ed. I., but Stephen had two descendants of his own name, of whom the last was probably childless, as he disposed of Cowsfield, which passed by fine to Roger Normaunde.

 Longechampe. This great baronial name is not written in Domesday ; but appears in England within the next twenty years. Henry I. granted to Hugh de Longchamp the castle and manor of Wilton in Herefordshire, to hold by the service of two men-at-arms in the Welsh wars : and the gift was confirmed to his son, Hugh II., by Henry II., the year after his accession. The next heir, Henry de Longchamp, Sheriff of Hereford in 1190, and of Worcester in 1195, married Maud, sister of William de Cantilupe, and died in 1211. "Whereupon," continues Dugdale, " the said William gave 500 Marks and five Palfreys for the Wardship and Marriage of his heir, viz., Henry ; of whom I can say no more, than that he took to Wife Joane, the Widow of Thomas Birkin, and had Issue by her one sole Daughter and Heire, call'd Maude, married to Reginald Grey, Justice of Chester, by which means the Lordship of Wilton came first to that Family."

 There was another Henry de Longchamp, seated in Hampshire, who "answered for his relief as a Baron" in the time of Henry III. ; but the line ended with his son of the same name ; and his grand-daughter Alice, the wife of Roger de Pedwardine, succeeded.

 William de Longchamp, Bishop of Ely, Cœur de Lion's famous Chancellor and Justiciar, and his brother Osbert, who, in the time of his power was for some years Sheriff of York, Norfolk and Suffolk, claimed no kinship to the baronial house. They were of humble origin, the grandsons of a serf in the diocese of Beauvais. But "Longchamp possessed great worldly wisdom and talent for business, and his low birth was, in truth, a proud commendation."—*Sir Francis Palgrave.* He had gained the absolute confidence of the King, who, on leaving England for the Crusade of 1189, appointed him and Hugh Pudsey, Bishop of Durham, joint regents of the Kingdom. He was to govern the South, while Pudsey was to bear rule over "as much of the ancient kingdom of North-umbria as remained to England." It was a breach of good faith as regarded the latter, who had been appointed sole Justiciar in succession to Ralph de Glan-ville, and had bought his promotion by the sacrifice of a vast sum of money. "Richard's Presence Chamber was a market overt, in which all that the King could bestow, all that could be derived from the bounty of the Crown, or im-parted by the royal prerogative, was disposed of to the best chapman. Hugh

Pudsey purchased the Earldom of Northumberland, together with the Lordship of Sadberge. For the Chief Justiciarship he paid, at the same time, the sum of 1,000 marks."—*Ibid.* Longchamp, for his part, gave 3,000 marks for the Chancellorship, was entrusted with the custody of the Tower of London, and appointed Legate by Pope Clement. Being thus all-powerful in Church and State, he assumed the government of the entire kingdom; and when Pudsey, armed with a fresh Royal mandate, sought to re-establish his usurped authority, feigned concession, and courteously invited his brother Bishop to meet him at Tickhill Castle. Pudsey came without suspicion, and was instantly seized by Longchamp, who exclaimed, "As sure as my Lord the King liveth, thou shalt not depart until thou hast surrendered all the castles which thou dost hold." Nor was he set at liberty till he had unconditionally given up the whole of his new possessions. Longchamp's rival was thus disposed of; and all the royal castles—"the bones of the kingdom," as they are termed by the chronicler—placed in his keeping. He ruled unopposed, but his rule proved arbitrary rapacious, and unpopular. "He is represented as tyrannizing equally over clergy and laity. ' Had he continued in office,' said his enemies, " the kingdom would have been wholly exhausted, not a girdle would have remained to the man, nor a bracelet to the woman, nor a gem to the Jew.'" He steadily opposed Prince John and his party, and it was through their influence that he was at last disgraced and deposed from his high place, and compelled to surrender the keys of the Treasury and the Tower. Furthermore, he had to cast down his legate's cross in Canterbury Cathedral, and was thrown into prison until he had taken a vow to go on pilgrimage to Jerusalem. From thence he made his way to the coast, and endeavoured to obtain a passage to France, shielding himself from the hatred of the populace in the disguise of a woman. Nor did this avail him ; for as he walked along the shore thus attired, carrying a web of cloth on his arm, he was detected and very roughly handled by the Dover fish-wives. He was, however, rescued from their hands, and permitted to embark and return to his native country.

A brother of the Bishop, Osbert de Longchamp, was, "in the time of his power," for some years Sheriff of Norfolk, York, and Suffolk ; but Dugdale tells us nothing of his posterity.

Lascales. "Of this ancient family, seated in the county of York, were divers persons," says Dugdale, "of great note many ages since." They had apparently come over with the Breton contingent of the Conqueror's army. Their ancestor, "Picot," an important vassal of Earl Alan of Richmond's in Yorkshire and Lincolnshire (Domesday), is identified by means of an early Survey of the fiefs of the latter county, made about the year 1108. He is there entered as " Picotus de Laceles," holding some land of Roger Marmion, "whose sister or daughter he may have married, as Roger de Laceles was his successor and son. We probably have a brother of Picot in William de Loceles, who occurs in the

Survey as holding Strailley, in Bedfordshire, of Hugo de Belcamp."—*A. S. Ellis.*
They were Barons of Messie in Normandy, and " derived their name from
Lacella, near Falaise, which, with its church, belonged in 1154 to the Abbey of
St. Sauveur, Evreux (Gall. Christ. IX.). William de Lacelles, who in 1165 held
two fees in Yorkshire, was plaintiff in a suit against his uncle Ralph for Lacelle
and the barony of Messie, which Ralph yielded to him as his inheritance.
(Mémoires de la Société des Antiquaires de la Normandie, XV., 92.)"—*The
Norman People.*

Picot probably died soon after 1108. His son Roger de Lacelles is mentioned
in 1131 as one of the " men" of Earl Stephen of Richmond, and held Scruton
and Kirkby in the North Riding. After him we hear of Picot, Roger and Robert
Fitz Picot, and, lastly, of another Roger, who was summoned to parliament as a
baron in 1294 and the two following years. He died shortly after his last writ
of summons, leaving by his wife Isabel, the heiress of Thomas Fitz Thomas,
four daughters his co-heirs: 1. Matilda, married first Robert de Hilton, of
Swine in Holderness, and secondly, Sir Peter Tilliol; 2. Théophania, the wife
of Ralph Fitz Randolph; 3. Johanna, the first wife of Thomas de Culwen;
4. Avicia, married to Sir Robert le Constable of Hailsham. His brother Richard
was seated at Escrick, where his posterity continued for one hundred and twenty-
seven years longer; but to none of his lineage was the writ of summons ever
again repeated.

The collateral branches were numerous. Duncan de Lascells, in the reign
of Cœur de Lion, acquired Bolton in Cumberland through Christian de
Bastingthwaite; and their descendants held it for three generations.—*Hutchinson's
Cumberland.* John de Lascells, mentioned in the Pipe Roll of 1131, " was
probably ancestor of the Lascelles of Otterington in Holderness, and settled
there by the Earl of Albemarle."—*A. S. Ellis.* Jordan and his brother Turgis
are found in the same record. Jordan's grants to Nostel Priory were confirmed
by Henry II. in 1154; and about the year 1146, his sons Gerard and Alan were
benefactors to Byland Abbey (Mon. Angl. i. 1032). Alan's son Simon in 1165
held three fees of De Lacy, and " may have been the same Simon who had a duel
with Adam Fitz Peter about land at Birkin, which he recovered by overcoming
him (Pipe Roll, 5 Ric. I.). Branches of the family remained at Escrick, until
1424, and in Notts, until after 1700: and another branch is now represented by
Robert Morley Lascelles, Esquire, of Slingsby. This time-honoured name is also
now associated with the Yorkshire Earldom of Harewood."—*Ibid.*

In this latter case, however, there is considerable doubt and difficulty in
determining the descent.* Lord Harewood's pedigree begins with John Lascelles,

* " Yet how far those genealogists may be correct, who have consimilitated the
descent of the Lascels family of the present day, with the blood of the illustrious
baron in the time of Edward I., is not for controversy here; although the assertion is
a pretty evident proof, that these *gentle historians* had never read the epitaph made by

II.   P seated at Hinderskelfe (now called Castle Howard) in the time of Ed. II.), and "thought (by Collins) to be a younger son of the house of Sowerby and Brackenbury, who bore the arms without the bordure." This coat, *Sable* a cross flory within a bordure *Or*, is not that of Roger Lord Lascelles, which was *Argent* three chaplets of roses *vermaux*, within a border engrailed *Sable.* The author of ' The Norman People' declares their ancestor to have been the Simon de Lacelles mentioned in the *Liber Niger*, " from whose son John descend lineally the Earls of Harewood." Here we are at once met by a formidable hiatus in the line of descent; for a blank of no less than one hundred and twenty-five years intervenes between these two Johns—John the son of Simon and John of Hinderskelfe.

The latter, at all events, is the recognized and undoubted progenitor of the present house. His son was called *filius Johannis*, or Jackson, and for the next seven generations his descendants successively bore this name. About the end of the fifteenth century, they removed to Gawthorpe, also in the North Riding, where Harewood House was afterwards built, and thence to Stank and Northallerton. Daniel, the sixteenth child born to Francis Lascelles of Stank and Northallerton, served as High Sheriff in 1719, and was the father of two sons who settled in Barbadoes, where the younger, Henry, became Collector of the Customs. This Henry, who had married a West Indian, eventually inherited the estates, including Harewood, bought a few years before: and his son Edwin was created Baron Harewood of Harewood Castle in 1790. But he died childless in 1795; and his cousin Edward, who became the head of the family, received first the barony, in· the following year, and a Viscountcy and Earldom in 1812. Both these peers had been born at St. Michael's in Barbadoes.

Lacy: a repetition.

Louan. William de Loven is mentioned in Normandy 1180–95 (Magna Rotul. Scaccarii Normanniæ): Robert de Lovent, John his son, and Henry de Lovent, in Buckinghamshire; William de Lovent in Bedfordshire, during the reign of Edward I.—*Rotuli Hundredorum.* Unless this be an interpolation, it cannot refer to the noble family of Lovaine of Estains in Essex, who descended from Henry IV., Duke of Brabant, by Maud, daughter of Matthew, Earl of Flanders, and bore *Gules*, a fesse *Argent* between ten billets *Or*. Their ancestor Godfrey was this Duke's younger son, and held in 1200 the Honour of Eye in Suffolk, which had been given to the Duchess of Lovaine in Richard I.'s time.—*Dugdale.*

Leded; originally Laidet. Guiscard Laidet and N. Laidet are to be met with in the Norman Exchequer Rolls of 1180–95: and we find the same

---

Henry Lascels, Esq., the collector of the Crown revenues at Barbadoes, who departed out of this transitory world anno 1753; for had that celebrated epitaph ever met their eye it is to be imagined their ideas of the noble lineage of the Baron of Harewood would have been confined to a more recent and a more humble extraction."—*Banks.*

Christian name, as Wischard, repeated in England at about that date. This Wischard Ledet, in 1204, had a suit with Elias Foliot for West Warden in Northamptonshire, which he held in right of his wife Margery, daughter and heir of Richard Foliot, and of another Margery, who had inherited Ramerick from her father Richard de Reinbudecourt or Reincourt. It was a great barony of thirteen and a-half knight's fees, for which he paid scutage in 1211, and passed, on his death in 1221, to his only child, Christiana. She was twice married: first to Henry de Braibroc, and secondly to Gerald de Furnival. By Henry de Braibroc she had two sons, of whom the elder, named after his grandfather, Wischard, took the name of Ledet, and transmitted it to his son Walter. But in the latter it again became extinct; for he left only two co-heiresses, Alice, the wife of William Latimer, summoned to parliament by Edward I. (see *Latimer*); and the other married to his brother John. The Barons of Wardon bore (according to Burke) *Or* a bend within a bordure *Gules* bezantée.

The name is three times entered in the *Testa de Nevill*. We there find Robert Ledet holding three parts of a knight's fee of Warin Fitz Gerald's Berkshire barony: Joan Ledet, a tenant of Richard de Montfichet in Essex: and Cecily Ledet, who held a knight's fee of old feoffment in Beckingham and Sutton, Lincolnshire, of Gilbert de Gaunt. There is a John de Leddrede who witnesses the foundation charter of Bisham Priory in the time of Ed. III. (Mon. Angl.), but I think he must have belonged to a Somersetshire family whose coat, a chevron between three talbots' heads erased, was entirely different from that of the Northamptonshire house.

Luse. Walter and William Luz appear in the Norman Exchequer Rolls of 1198, and are conjectured to have belonged to the same family as Robert de Los, to whom Philip Augustus in 1219 granted lands in Normandy (*Mémoires de la Société des Antiquaires de Normandie*). There exists a place called Los in the Duchy, from which the name was probably taken. John de Los is named in the same *Magni Rotuli Scaccarii Normanniæ* of the twelfth century. Julianus de Losa was of Kent 1189–90 (Rot. Pip.): John and William de Lose of Norfolk, circa 1272 (Rot. Hundred.). Three generations of the Kentish family, holding the vill of Lose (Loose) of the Prior of St. Trinity, Canterbury, are mentioned in the *Pedes Finium*; the last of them, William de Lose, was living in 1204. In Norfolk, Goscelin de Lose paid a fine 34 Hen. III.; and Ralph de Lose (infirm) another in 41 Hen. III., for not attending the hundred court (Crown Pleas Roll). A branch was evidently settled in Ireland; for Jordan de Luse witnesses the foundation charter of Woney Abbey, Limerick, by Theobald Fitz Walter Pincerna (Mon. Angl.).

Loterell. Robert Lotrel and Hugh his son were benefactors to the Abbey of Barbarie, Normandy, at its foundation (Gall. Christ. xi. 85 Instr.). In England the Luttrells were first seated in Nottinghamshire. Geoffrey Loterel, who held

Gamston, &c., in that county, and some other manors in Derbyshire, obtained a great Lincolnshire barony, with Hoton-Paganel in Yorkshire, through his wife Trethesenta, daughter of William Paganel, and in the end his sole heir. "All these lands, 6 Rich. I., were seized into the King's hands for his adherence to the Earl of Morton, afterwards King John; but upon that Earl's coming to the Crown he had a ratification under the Great Seal of his title to those manors, and all other lands which he had purchased of Gerbod de Scaud, and Gerard de Rodes. 5 Joh. he had a grant of £10 per annum out of the King's treasury for his life. 16 Joh. he was sent into Ireland, and a direction given to the Bishops and great men of that country to treat him as one much trusted by the King. The year following he was, with some others, appointed to represent to the Pope the state of that kingdom, and the difference between the King and his barons, and had also a particular commission of adjusting the disputes between King John and Berengaria, the Queen Dowager, at that time referred to the Pope's arbitration."—*Collinson's Somerset.* He was seated at Irnham in Lincolnshire, which he held by barony, and died 2 Hen. III., leaving Andrew his son and heir; who in 1230 accounted for fifteen knight's fees and a half (being the whole barony of Paganel), attended the King "with horse and arms in France" in 1242, and served as Sheriff of Lincolnshire in 1251. This Andrew had two sons; Geoffrey, the father of the first Baron Luterel, and Alexander, who received as his portion the manor of East Quantock's Head in Somersetshire, where his descendants continued till the reign of Henry IV. Geoffrey was insane, and in the custody of his brother, till the latter followed Prince Edward on his crusade to Palestine, from whence he never returned home. The next in succession, Robert, was a baron by writ in 1295; but none other of the family ever appear to have been summoned to parliament. One of his grandsons, Sir Geoffrey, is mentioned in 1355 among the chief knights serving in Edward III.'s army in Scotland. The line ended with another Geoffrey, the eighth Baron of Irnham, on whose death in 1417 the inheritance devolved on his sister Hawise.

The Somersetshire Luttrells still remained. They, again, had divided into two branches, of whom the elder, seated at East Quantock's Head, had died out a few years previously, but the younger was established in the beautiful domain of Dunster Castle, and then represented by Sir Hugh Luttrell. He was the grandson of John Luttrell, of Chilton in Devonshire (the second son of Sir Alexander, who first settled at East Quantock's Head); and his mother, Lady Elizabeth Courtenay, a daughter of the Earl of Devonshire, was of the blood royal of England. Her mother was the daughter of Humphrey de Bohun, Earl of Hereford, by a daughter of Edward I.: and as the kinswoman of the King, she had a grant of £200 a year in 1360. "Besides this pension from the Crown, which in those days was very considerable, it appears that she had a great dower in several manors lying in the counties of Bucks, Oxford, and Bedford, being the possessions of Sir John Vere, her first husband. This enabled her to execute the great things she did for her family, the honour and prosperity of which she greatly advanced. Her husband being dead, 48 Ed. III., she purchased the manors of Stonehall and Woodhall, with lands in Debenham, in the counties of Norfolk and Suffolk: and soon after the barony, honour and manor of Dunster, reversional after the life of Lady Mohun."—*Collinson's Somerset.* Her son, who succeeded to this fair patrimony, rebuilt a great part of Dunster Castle, where he " kept great hospitality ": and had a further grant of lands in Buckinghamshire from Richard II. as kinsman to the King. He attended Henry V. to the French wars, was present at the taking of Honfleur, etc.; and at different times held the offices of Lieutenant of Calais, Constable of Bristol, Warden of Kingswood Forest, and Steward of the Household to two successive Queens. The barony was forfeited by his grandson, who fell at the second battle of St. Albans, fighting manfully for the Red Rose; and Edward IV. granted Dunster to William Herbert, who, when he was soon after created Earl of Pembroke, took his second title from it. But the accession of Henry VII. changed the scene, and at once restored it to its rightful owner. In the next reign, Sir John Luttrell served at the siege of Boulogne, and afterwards had a command at Musselburgh :. he is praised as a " complete captain," and " complete and worthy courtier," but he was a spendthrift as well, who sold a great part of his demesne, and mortgaged the plate and furniture belonging to Dunster Castle. His wife was a Welsh woman named Mary Griffiths, and the county history affords us a glimpse of some romance connected with this marriage. " There is an ancient picture in the castle, done by a tolerable hand, of a man swimming in the sea, and looking up to a certain figure in the clouds; to which is added, by a later and very indifferent painter, the figure of a lady floating by his side. This is traditionally said to have been the picture of Sir John Luttrell, and refers to his having saved a certain lady from drowning, whom he was then in love with, and afterwards married."

The last Luttrell died in the middle of the last century, and his daughter Margaret was the heiress of Dunster, which still belongs to her descendants. She married Henry Fownes of Nethaway, co. Devon, who took her name.

Another branch of the family, that had settled in Ireland, survived till 1829. They bore the same punning arms, three otters or *loutres* for Loutrel; but their connection with the parent stock is not satisfactorily made out. Sir Bernard Burke derives them from Robert, second son of the Sir Hugh Luttrell that first possessed Dunster: but Collinson distinctly states that Sir Hugh had no second son. It probably dated considerably further back, as there is mention made of a grant from King John of some Irish lands to Sir Geoffrey Loterel, the patriarch of the house. Be this as it may, they certainly had, from very early times, a property in the co. Dublin, where they gave their name to Luttrellstown. They first became of note as zealous loyalists in the Civil War: and Simon Luttrell was Governor of the town and castle of Dublin for James II., as well as colonel of a regiment of dragoons in his service. He faithfully followed his master into exile, and was killed at the battle of Landen in 1693, while commanding an Irish regiment in foreign service. His brother and heir, Henry, was also an officer of rank in King James's army, but deserted his colours in 1691. "He had served long in France, and had brought back to his native Ireland a sharpened intellect and polished manners, a flattering tongue, some skill in war, and much more skill in intrigue."—*Macaulay.* Being, according to the same authority, "the least scrupulous of men, always fond of dark and crooked ways," he had opened a secret negotiation with the English some time before, and when, after the capitulation of Limerick, the Irish troops were called upon to make their election between their old allegiance and the new Sovereign, "Henry Luttrell was one of those who turned off. He was rewarded for his desertion, and perhaps for other services, with a grant of the large estate of his elder brother Simon, who firmly adhered to the cause of James, with a pension of £500 a year from the Crown, and with the abhorrence of the Roman Catholic population. After living in wealth, luxury, and infamy, during a quarter of a century, Henry Luttrell was murdered while going through Dublin in his sedan-chair; and the Irish House of Commons declared that there was reason to suspect that he had fallen by the revenge of the Papists. Eighty years after his death his grave near Luttrellstown was violated by the descendants of those whom he had betrayed, and his skull was broken to pieces with a pickaxe. The deadly hatred of which he was the object descended to his son and to his grandson; and, unhappily, nothing in the character either of his son or of his grandson tended to mitigate the feeling which the name of Luttrell excited."—*Ibid.*

About forty years after his assassination in 1717, the son received an Irish peerage as Baron Irnham (a reminiscence of his Lincolnshire ancestry), and in 1785 was created Earl of Carhampton. The third Earl took the name of Olmius, having married Elizabeth Olmius, sister and heir of the last Lord Waltham, and left only two daughters as his representatives.

Loruge: for Loring. In Leland's list this is joined to the name that here precedes it, as " Loring et Loterel." We find it in Bedfordshire and Devonshire. "A manor in Chalgrave was held under the Beauchamps, in the twelfth century, by the family of Loring. Sir Nigel or Neale Loring, who was knighted by King Edward III. for his bravery in a sea-fight at Sluys in 1340, who attended that monarch in his glorious campaign in France, in the year 1359, and was one of the Knights Companion of the Garter at the original institution of that Order, retired to spend his latter days at Chalgrave, where, in 1365, he had the royal license to enclose a park. This Sir Neale Loring was founder of a chantry in Chalgrave church. Two ancient altar tombs (one on each side the nave) with effigies in stone of knights in armour with mail gorgets, have been supposed to belong to some of this family; but it must be observed, that none of the shields, of which there are several on the tombs, exhibit the arms of Loring."—*Lysons'*

Bedfordshire. Leland tells us that Sir Neale was buried in the church of the Black Canons at Dunstable. "Ther lay buried also in this Priory one Nigellus Loring, a Noble Man of Bedfordshire, and a great Benefactor to this Priory."

"This Nigellus made 3. Cantuaries in the Paroch Chirch of Tuddington" (Toddington) "in Bedfordshire a 2. miles from Dunestaple, and there, as I hear say, ly buried sum of that Stokke." He was the same "Nele Loring of Knowston-Beaupell, Landekey," in Devonshire, mentioned temp. Ed. III.; who, "under Richard II., wrote himself of Kingston."—*Westcote's Devon.* The manor of Landkey was the original seat of the family of Beauple or Beaple, and had come to him through his wife Margaret, daughter and heir of Sir Ralph Beauple of Cnubeston (Knowston), and Elizabeth, daughter and heir of Alan Bloyho. By her he had two daughters and heirs; Isabel, the wife of Robert Lord Harington; and Margaret, married to John Peyvre of Tuddington (now Toddington) in Bedfordshire. He died in 1386. "The earliest existing representation of one of the first Knights Founders in the Habit of the Order of the Garter," writes Sir Harris Nicolas, "is that of Sir Nigel Loring, which occurs in the list of Benefactors to St. Albans Abbey." The grateful monks preserved not only the names, but the portraits, of those who contributed to their revenues, and Sir Nigel is introduced as the donor of 10 marks. He appears as an old man with a red cap or hood on his head, and red shoes on his feet, covered with a white robe powdered with Garters, and holds a purse in his left hand. He bore Quarterly, *Gules* and *Argent*, a bend *Or.*

The name is still kept by Ingelby-Loringe, in Yorkshire. Its original form was Le Lorrain; and in the last years of the twelfth century we find it entered in the *Rotuli Curiæ Regis* as Le Loherain, Le Lohereng, Le Lohereg, and Le Loereng. In the *Liber Niger* it is Loerene.

It remained in Gloucestershire till the last century. "Haymes, a manor within the tything of Southam, continued in the name and family of Lorrange for 400 years, from the time of Ed. II."—*Rudder's Gloucestershire.* Lorrenge Farm is near Cam. An epitaph in Oundle Church informs us of their descent. "Here lyeth the body of William Loring, died 1628, 2nd son of William Loringe of Haymes in the co. of Gloucester, lineally descended from the brother of the Honble. Sir Neele Loring."

Longueuale: see Logeville or Longueville.

Loy. Anselme, in his *Histoire Généalogique de la France*, mentions a Pierre Loys, living in the seventeenth century, who was Seigneur de-la-Grange-le-Roy, and Baron of Muravaux. This is the old French form of *Louis*. Robert Loys of Oxfordshire, is mentioned in the *Rotuli Hundredorum*, c. 1272. There is also a Loys Hall, in the parish of Terling, Essex, but no other trace of the family in that county.

Lorancourt: perhaps Louvencort, a name also given by Anselme, and in the same century. Louis de Hangest-Argenlieu was Seigneur of Louvencort and

Quarty. But in England I have met with nothing that even resembles it, unless it be Nonancourt. Were it admissible (which I think it is not) to transform L into N, I could furnish three De Nonancourts: Oliver, a Northamptonshire baron, whose fee of Nonancourt was at Branteston; and two others in the same county, Robert and William, both holding of the Honour of Peverell at Gildsburg.—*Testa de Nevill.* I might also produce a Bovancourt. "Henry Fitz Hugh" (obt. 1262) "married Alice, daughter of Randolf Fitz Walter, with whom he had the Lordship of Mickelton" (Middleton-in-Teesdale) "and service of Guy de Bovencourt, for certain lands there and in Northumberland."— *Dugdale.*

Loions, for Lions, a name derived from the castle and forest of Lions, in Normandy. "Ingelram de Lions came to England 1066, and held Corsham and Culington from the King (Mon. Angl. ii. 604). He had Ranulph, whose brother William de Lions had a grant in Norfolk from Earl Walter Giffard, and left descendants there. Ranulph had Ingelram de Lions, named Parcar, as being forester of Croxton, Leicester, by exchange with the King (Mon. Angl.). William Parcarius de Lions was a benefactor to Croxton Abbey, t. Henry II., and was brother of Hugh de Lyons, who was deprived of his estates 1203 (Nicholls, Leicester). From him descended the family of Parcar, or Parker, and the Earl of Macclesfield."—*The Norman People.* The Earl's pedigree, however, is only traced back to Thomas Le Parker, his first certain ancestor, who lived in the reign of Edward III; and his coat of arms, *Gules* a chevron between three leopards' heads *Or,* bears no analogy to the allusive lions or lioncels of the De Lions: though it resembles one of the coats borne by the family in Normandy. Des Lions, Seigneur de Theuville, gives *D'azur à trois têtes de leopard d'or.*

The posterity of William de Lyons flourished at Lyons' Manor in Weston, Norfolk, till the reign of Edward II. Roger de Lyons held Melton Constable of William de Beaufoe, Bishop of Thetford, jointly with Anchitel de Melton or de Constable. The last heir was William de Lyons, whose two daughters inherited. —*Blomfield's Norfolk.* Meanwhile, the family had spread into the adjoining counties; for I find that John Lyons of Framlingham in Suffolk attended the array and muster of the Hundred of Loose in 1316 (Palgrave's Parliamentary Writs): and Lyon or Lions Hall, in Essex, as well as Lyons Manor in the parish of Bocking, were named "from an ancient family that flourished there in the reigns of Edward II. and Edward III."—*Morant's Essex.*

In Oxfordshire, John de Lyons of Begbrooke received a writ of military summons in 1322 (Palgrave's Parliamentary Writs). This was Sir John de Lyons, Lord of Warkworth in Northamptonshire, whose genealogy is furnished by the county histories. He was sixth in descent from Nicholas de Lyons, and the son of another Sir John, who had married the co-heiress of Great Oakley and Preston Capes. His own wife, Alice, had a share in the inheritance of her father, Sir William de St. Liz; and in 1319 he made over to her "all his goods moveable and immoveable in his manor of Beckbrok, with investiture or livery of his lands." Their only son, a third Sir John, died s. p. in 1385; and their daughter and sole heiress, Elizabeth, married first Sir Nicholas (others say Sir John) Chetwode, and secondly Richard Widville. "The tomb of this last Sir John Lyons is in the parish church. He is in plate armour; each elbow gusset is decorated with a lion's face; his shield, charged with a lion rampant, is on his left arm: and the upper part of it is sustained by a small lion seated on his breast: his feet rest on a couchant lion. He reposes on his helmet, surmounted by his crest, a talbot's head issuing out of a ducal coronet."—*Baker's Northamptonshire.* A younger son of the co-heiress of Oakley, Richard de Lyons, inherited her moiety of the manor, which he held of the Honour of Huntingdon; but in 1371 his descendants in the male line failed with another Richard; and three sisters, Isabella, Cecilia, and Christina, shared the property.

Another Nicholas de Lions (from a comparison of the dates it cannot possibly have been the one already mentioned), in 1252 held the office of reeve of the city of Bristol, and held lands at Long Ashton, Somersetshire. His posterity continued there till the end of the fourteenth century; the last of the name was Thomas de Lions, "who 15 Ric. II. obtained a charter of free warren, and liberty to make a park in his manor of Long Ashton, which from this family was henceforward named Ashton-Lyons."—*Collinson's Somerset.* The mansion house of Ashton Court, a noble old structure, partly erected by the family of Lyons, still retains their devices and coat of arms. They also built the church of Long-Ashton, where some of their tombstones are to be seen. Their arms, differenced in tinctures, are nearly the same as those borne by the late Lord Lyons, who descended from a branch seated in Hampshire, where William de Lyons, in the thirteenth century, witnessed a charter of William de Redvers to Christ Church Priory. His immediate ancestor, John Lyons, of Lyons in the island of Antigua, was father of another John, seated at St. Austin's, Hants, whose two elder sons both entered the navy. The second, Sir Edmund, was the gallant admiral who received a peerage in 1856 for his services during the Crimean War. He had lost his younger son—a young officer of the greatest promise—in the previous year at the siege of Sebastopol. Richard, the eldest, succeeded in 1858 as second Lord Lyons, and was the eminent diplomatist that for nearly half a century so ably represented his country abroad, and by his judgment, tact, and incomparable discretion, more than once warded off the threat of impending war. He was Minister at Washington in 1861, when the exasperation caused by the 'Trent' affair, and the seizure of Mason and Slidell, seemed to render a conflict between the two great Anglo-Saxon nationalities imminent if not inevitable. It was due to his coolness, prudence, and admirable temper, that the crisis was averted, and the danger passed over. His last post was at Paris, where he remained for twenty years, again rendering important services to the cause of peace, and gaining the respect and good-will of all. The Parisians never forgot that, when the siege was raised in 1871, he was one of the first to procure provisions for the famished capital. He, was created a Viscount in 1881, and on his retirement from the Embassy in 1887, the Queen announced her intention of conferring upon him the further reward of an Earldom. He died shortly after, lamented by many attached friends, and not leaving behind him a single enemy.

Limers. No such name is to be found in the *Nobiliaire de Normandie;* yet Dugdale tells us that Henry V., in 1418, granted to Sir James de Fiennes (afterwards Lord Say) "the Lordship of De la Court le Compte, within the Bayliwick of Caux, in Normandy, part of the possessions of the Lord of Lymers." William de Lymars, of Leicestershire, fought in the Baronial army temp. Henry III. Stanton-Lymar, by Keworth, Notts, took its name from John de Lymare, who, held it 30 Ed. I., apparently in right of his wife Cecily. Dom. John de Lymar occurs in the Register of Selby.—*Burton's Monas. Ebor.* In 1257, on the death of John de St. Amand, it was found that his sister Lucy, then the wife of Sir John de Lymare, was his next heir.—*Archæologia Cantiana.* In the previous reign, William de Limeres held some land at Comelessend, Hampshire, of the King *in capite*, by the service of hunting the wolf with the King's dogs.—*Harl. MS. No. 708, p. 8.*

Longepay: a duplicate.

Laumale. "Guillaume d'Aubellamare, Seigneur de Fougères," is on Tailleur's list of those who came over with the Conqueror; and "at the battle of Hastings, "Cil de Felgières," as Wace calls him, "also won great renown with many very brave men he brought with him from Brittany." This is believed to have been Raoul or Ralph, the third but only surviving son of Maine II., who, as well as William, is entered in Domesday; but their exact relationship has not been ascertained. They came of a very ancient Breton stock, for the ancestry of the Barons of Fougères or Filgères reaches back to the year 900: and bore branches of fern (*fougère*) in allusion to their name. These *armes parlantes,* "may be seen on the seal of William de Fougères, engraved in Lobineau's *Histoire de Bretagne,* and are also those of the town of Fougères to the present day."—*J. R. Planché.*

William was only a sub-tenant in Buckinghamshire; but Ralph held by barony, and possessed land in six different counties. He was a great benefactor of the Church. In 1112 he founded the Abbey of Savigny * in Normandy; "he confirmed the foundation of the Priory of the Holy Trinity by his mother Adelaide, and gave it, as well as the church of St. Sulpice at Fougères, to the Abbey of Marmoutier. Subsequently he travelled to Rome, and passing by

---

* The Cistercian Abbey of Savigny was "originally a hermitage situated in the woods which terminated the southern frontier of the diocese of Avranches. It soon established itself as the leader of a separate Order, called Savigniac or Tironensian, but in 1147 was re-united to the Cistercian body."—*R. W. Eyton.*

Marmoutier, confirmed all his previous gifts to it. He died in 1124, leaving by his wife Avoyse or Avicia, daughter of Richard de Bienfaite, seven children—Meen, Henri, Gauthier, Robert, Guillaume, Avelon, and Beatrice."—*Ibid.*

His eldest son died s. p. in 1137; and the second, who married Olive de Bretagne, was probably the Henry de Fulgeres entered in the *Liber Niger* as a sub-tenant of Walter Maminot in Kent. His line ended with his great grandson, whose sister Clemencia was the wife first of Alan de Dinant, and secondly of Ralph Blundeville, Earl of Chester. Alan de Fulgeres, in 1165 held of Henry de Scaliers in Cambridgeshire, and William by barony in Yorkshire.—*Ibid.* It is believed that many branches of this old Breton family existed in England. The Barons Bohun of Midhurst derived from Frangualo [*] de Fougeres, the first husband of Cana, daughter of Gelduin II., Lord of Chaumont-sur-Loire, who "transmitted to his heirs a considerable interest in the barony of Fougères."—*E. Chester Waters.* See *Bohun.* He was an uncle of the Raoul that fought at Hastings.

Another Domesday baron, Robert de Albemarle, left a numerous posterity in Devonshire, where he held twenty manors in 1086. He belonged to quite another family. "From the silence observed by historians concerning this Robert, we may presume that he was either a descendant of the ancient Seigneurs d'Aumale, or a simple knight residing in that town, who had adopted its name. There existed, in fact, a very old family of this name in the province of Picardy, which probably had the same origin, and continues there undoubtedly to the present day. The first we meet with is Jean d'Aumale, Seigneur of Herselines (near Gamaches), who, with his squire, Aliaume de Boucret, repaired to Lisle in 1339 to serve under the Constable of France, Raoul de Brienne, Count of Eu and of Guisnes, one of the barons that defended Tournay against the English. This house was divided into several branches, comprising the Seigneurs of Balastre, of Bugny, of Ivrencheux, of Hancourt, of La Horgue, of Gondreville, and of Nampfel. They bore *Argent* a bend *Gules* charged with four besants. It is evident that this family of Albemarle or Aumale still existed in England at the beginning of the 15th century. We find, in the archives of La Manche, a charter of the date of 1206, by which Reginald de Albemarle, *miles et dominus* de Wodbery, gives to the Abbey of St. Michael his domain of Blakedon; and, later on, we likewise find a William de Albemarle, father of another William, and of a daughter named Elizabeth, coheiress to her brother, defunct in 1361. Elizabeth was then only seventeen. She was twice married; first to John de Maltravers, obt. 1386; and secondly to Humphrey de Stafford, the elder. She died at the age of sixty-nine, in 1413, leaving issue only by her first marriage.

" Finally, whatever may have been the alterations undergone by the name of

---

[*] This name is peculiar to the house of Fougères; and "was originally a sobriquet, for the bearer of it in 1112 is styled in a charter of Marmoutier 'Maino cognomento Fransgualo.' "—*Ibid.*

Albemarle or Aumale either in France or in England, we cannot discern in it the least affinity to the English family of Damarell, which, according to Lysons, derived from Robert de Albemarle, and gave their name to the manors of Milton-Damarell and Stoke-Damarell in Devonshire."—*Recherches sur le Domesday.*

This conclusion is palpably erroneous; for, in point of fact, both the Sir Reginald and the Sir William above quoted were Damarells of Woodbury. Their coat of arms differed altogether from that of the Aumales of Picardy, for they bore Per fesse *Gules* and *Azure*, three crescents *Argent.*

Peter de Lameil—perhaps one of the grandsons of Robert—held of the Honour of Exeter in 1165 (*Liber Niger*): and for the next two hundred years the family grew and prospered in the county, with increased possessions and extending influence. Sir William de Albemarle or Damarell had a writ of summons to parliament in 1367 with other barons and prelates; and Sir John served as Sheriff in 1374. Five different branches, the Damarells of Milton-Damarell, North Huish, Woodbury, Gidley, and Aveton-Giffard—distinguished from each other by some slight variations of blazonry—are enumerated by Lysons: but all simultaneously disappear from the scene in the time of Edward III. Milton-Damarell—one of the Domesday manors—had been sold to the Courtenays during the previous reign. Woodbury, which had come to them from the Carbonells through a succession of female heirs, passed away again with two co-heiresses married to Maltravers and Bonville. Gidley Castle and Aveton Giffard (both of them brought by the heiress of Prouz to Roger de Mules, and by their daughter Alice to John Damarell) were similarly transferred ; the former through William Damarell's daughter to Walter Code of Morvall in Cornwall, the latter to the Durnfords and Berrys. Fleet-Damarell, which had been inherited from the time of the Conquest, went to the Hills and the Prideaux. All these families appear to have collapsed in the male line at about the same date: yet a branch of the Damarells survived "in a mean condition" in Sir William Pole's time. They resided at Stone, a manor that had once been theirs "for many descents." A John Damarel of Ilton was living when the *Magna Britannia* was written (1822).

Another of Robert de Albemarle's Domesday manors, Stoke-Damarell, is now the site of the town of Devonport. It passed successively to the Courtenays, Keniells, Branscombes, Britts, and Wises, and was sold to Sir William Morice in 1667 for £11,000. About twenty years afterwards, a project that is said to have been first conceived by Charles II. was carried out by William of Orange, and the Royal dockyard commenced that was to transform it into the great arsenal of the West of England. In the last census, Devonport numbered sixty-three thousand nine hundred and eighty inhabitants: and "the ancient village of Stoke has developed into a very handsome residential suburb."—*Worth's Devon.*

Lane: or L'Asne, a baronial name. "Hugh l'Asne or *Asinus*, seems to have been only known by his opprobrious nickname. How he came by it does not appear; it might have already become a meaningless surname distinguishing his family. But the Normans seem to have had a propensity for giving most undignified epithets to persons who appear to have not only been exclusively known by such, but were obliged, for the sake of identity, to use these themselves in documents. As early as 1046, twenty years before the Conquest, William Fitz Osbern had founded an abbey at Lire, and we find "Hugo Asino" witnessing the charter of William, when Earl of Hereford, granting the monks their lands in England. (Gallia Christ. xi., Instr., p. 123.) He was also one of the witnesses to the charter of William confirming to the abbey of St. Evroult the gifts of Fulk, late Dean of Evreux (Ord. Vital. v. xii). He was, in all probability, a feudatory of that baron in Normandy, and a man advanced in years at the date of the Survey. He was surviving 1095–1101, as his name occurs among those who had tenants in the towns of Gloucester and Winchcombe. He evidently came over with William Fitz-Osbern, and settled in the West under him; and on the Welsh marches was actively employed in the defence of the border under his lord, now Earl of Hereford. In the county of Hereford he held, *in capite*, Kentchester and some twenty other manors: and at the time of the Survey was claiming the great lordship of Radnor. Hugh also held Knighton and Norton in Shropshire, Brockworth and the lands of Wluuard, in Shipton, Salperton, and Bagendon, Gloucestershire. He probably did not become a tenant *in capite* until the forfeiture of Roger, the second Earl of Hereford, in 1074.

"All we know about his family is that he had a daughter, who seems to have been a nun at the Abbey of St. Mary at Winchester, for that church held land of him at Kennet, in Wilts, pro filiâ eius."—*A. S. Ellis.*

There is every reason to conclude that L'Asne was a *sobriquet*, for as "Hugh never occurs as De L'Asne, he could not have derived his name from Lasne, near Argentan, as suggested." Yet the authors of the *Recherches sur le Domesday* incline to think it was taken from a hamlet in Brittany, still named L'Asne, in the arrondissement of Vannes. It several times occurs in the chartulary of Mont St. Michel during the thirteenth century; and a family of L'Asne—"famille fort honorable et vivant noblement"—is to be found at Bailleul-la-Vallée in the département of the Eure. "It is really extraordinary," add they, "that so powerful a tenant-in-chief as Hugh L'Asne should have left no trace of his family in England. The compilers of the extinct Peerages do not mention it, and do not even inform us what became of his domain." According to *The Norman People*, the barony was lost temp. Henry I.; but the family continued. Dudo de l'Ane in 1165 had a barony in Essex (Lib. Niger)." Burke calls the "Lane" of Battle Abbey Roll the ancestor of the Staffordshire Lanes. Their pedigree, however, only begins with Adam de Lone, living in 1315.

These Lanes were enthusiastic loyalists during the Great Rebellion; and at their house of Bentley the fugitive King "remained in peace and blessed security for many days" during his wanderings after the fatal field of Worcester. His host, recommended to him by Lord Wilmot as "an honest gentleman with an excellent reputation for fidelity," had a son who was a Colonel in the Royal army; and with these two trusty friends Charles conferred as to the best means of getting to the sea coast, where he hoped to be taken on board some outward bound vessel. It was agreed that he should go to Bristol. But how was he to get there? it was a four or five days' journey, and the country swarmed with rebel soldiery. The daughter of the house, Mistress Jane, a young woman "of very good wit and discretion," offered to undertake the adventure, and herself bring the King to Bristol. She had a cousin married to Mr. Norton of Leigh, who lived near there; and she set forth to pay a visit to this cousin. She rode on a pillion behind the disguised King, who, "fitted with clothes and boots for such a service," passed for William Jackson : and was attended by a servant in her father's livery. "And in this equipage the king began his journey : the colonel keeping him company at a distance, with a hawk upon his fist, and two or three spaniels; which, where there were any fields at hand, warranted him to ride out of the way, keeping his company still in his eye, and not seeming to be of it." Lord Wilmot, too, hovered about their route, though he did not approach them, and took care never to lodge in the same house. When, however, they were within a day's journey of Leigh, "the Colonel gave his hawk to Wilmot," who took his place as escort. It was late in October, and the days were short ; but they pressed on as fast as they could. Wherever they stopped for the night, Mistress Joan asked for a good bed and a separate room for "her neighbour's son, whom his father had lent her to ride before her," and who had been "miserably afflicted with quartan ague." When they arrived at Mr. Norton's, they found a number of people assembled on the bowling-green before his door : and the first man the King saw was one of his own chaplains, sitting upon the rails to watch the bowlers. They dismounted, and William Jackson took the horse to the stable : but Mistress Lane presently sent for him to a "pretty chamber" where a fire was prepared for him ; and when dinner was brought, she filled a little dish, and bade the butler carry it up to "the good youth, who was very sick." The butler went, "and spoke kindly to the young man," but, on scanning his face more narrowly, he fell on his knees, and with tears told him he was glad to see His Majesty. He had been falconer to Sir Thomas Jermyn, and knew the King perfectly by sight ; but he promised to hold his tongue, and faithfully kept his word. After supper, Dr. Gorges, the chaplain, went, out of good-nature, to visit the sick man ; sat by his bedside, felt his pulse, and asked many questions. The King withdrew to the farthest corner, screened himself as far as possible from the light, and answered briefly, and in a muffled voice, that he was drowsy, and wished to sleep. The good man went away unsuspecting, and told Mistress Jane that "William was doing well."

Thus, though twice within a hair's-breadth of discovery, brave Mistress Joan had kept her word, and brought him in safety to his journey's end.[*] She was not (like too many others) forgotten at the Restoration, but received a pension of £1000 a year. Her brother was, it is said, offered a peerage; but would only accept an augmentation to his paternal coat; the arms of England in a canton "as a special badge of honour:" and for his crest, a strawberry roan horse (in memory of the one that had carried the King) bearing between his fore-legs a Royal crown, with the motto " Garde le Roy."

Louvetot: a duplicate.

Mohant, for Monhaut, as it appears further on in the list, or Montalt: a name assumed by Robert, Dapifer of Chester, "from the chief place of his residence, which was at a little Hill in Flintshire, then called Montalt, whereon he built a Castle."—*Dugdale.* See *La Mare.*

Mowne: (Leland spells it Mooun), for Mohun, Mohon, or Moion, from Moion, near St. Lo, Normandy, where the site of their castle is still to be seen. Wace tells us that "old William de Moion had with him many companions" at the battle of Hastings, and one of Leland's rolls of the Norman conquerors is nothing but a long list of those who came in the train of " Monseir William de Moion le Veil, le plus noble de tout l'oste." It gives him a following worthy of an Emperor, comprising all the noblest names of Normandy, and numbering at least ninety-four knights, but it is evidently, as Mr. Planché points out, a mistake of the copyists.[†] Sir Francis Palgrave, though he calls him "one of the greatest Barons of the Côtentin," says he was only accompanied by "five knights who held of him." Dugdale, however, gives him " forty-seven stout Knights of name and note," and he was rewarded for his services by the grant of no less than fifty-five manors in Somerset, besides two in Wilts and Dorset. He chose Dunster—a place of some note in Saxon times—and built his castle where a former fortress of the West Saxon kings had stood, in a situation unsurpassed in beauty by any in England. From a regally commanding height, it looks across the broad expanse of the Bristol Channel to the distant mountains of South

---

[*] " To escape from the vengeance of the dominant rogues, Jane Lane and her brother crossed to France, where they were received with great honour at the French Court. King Charles, with all the Stuart grace, took her hand, and said, 'Welcome, my life!' Jane Lane had walked, disguised as a country wench, from Bentley to the sea-side."—*Notes and Queries*, 6th S. x.

[†] " It is nothing more nor less than a copy of all the names mentioned in the Roman de Rou, from line 13,621 to line 13,761, just as they follow each other in the poem ; and the assertion that all these noble Normans were 'à la retennaunce de Monseir Moion' resulted from a curious blunder of the copyist, who considered the lines

> "' Le Viel Willame de Moion
> Ont avec li maint compagnie,'

had reference to the knights and barons named immediately afterwards, all of whom he pressed into the service."—*The Conqueror and his Companions.*

Wales, and down upon the lovely valley that nestles at its feet; while on every
other side it is encircled by a grand amphitheatre of lofty hills.   Here, too, on
the N.W. side of his dwelling, he built a Benedictine priory dedicated to
St. George, which he made a cell to Bath Abbey, and where he is generally
believed to have been buried.   His grandson William, third of the name, was a
devoted adherent of the Empress Maud, in whose behalf he fortified his castle,
laid waste the country around, and besieged Henry de Blois at Winchester.   For
these services she bestowed upon him the title of Earl of Somerset and Dorset,
which he bore till his death, about 1165.   The next but one in succession,
Reginald, married in 1205 Alice, one of the sisters and co-heiresses of William
Bruer, of Torre (since called Torre-Mohun) in Devonshire, who brought him a
great estate, and " is set down among the benefactors to the new Cathedral
Church of Salisbury, having contributed thereto all the marble necessary for the
building thereof for twelve years."   From her younger son John descended the
Mohuns of Ham-Mohun in Dorsetshire.   The first of this family who had
summons to Parliament was John de Mohun, who fought under Edward I. in the
wars of Scotland and Gascony, and was a baron by writ in 1299.   His name
appears on the Roll of Carlaverock :

> " Jaune o crois noire engreelie
>   Là portrait Johans de Mooun."

He survived his son, and his grandson, another John, became the second Lord
Mohun, who " 16 Edward III. served in the expedition then made into France, in
the retinue of Bartholomew de Burghersh, with whom, during his minority, he
had been in ward, and whose daughter Joan he afterwards married.   Of this John
it is recorded, that upon a petition of the inhabitants of Dunster for certain lands
adjoining to the town, whereon to depasture their cattle freely and in common,
he allowed his lady, Joan Mohun, who supplicated on the townsmen's behalf, as
much soil as she could go round in one day barefoot for the purpose above-
mentioned."—*Collinson's Somerset.*   He was one of the Founder Knights of the
Garter, and from 1348 to 1370 served five several times in the French wars, first
under the Black Prince, and then in the train of John of Gaunt.   He died about
1375, leaving three daughters his co-heiresses ; Philippa, married to Edward
Duke of York, Elizabeth, to William de Montacute, Earl of Salisbury, and Maud,
to John Lord Strange of Knocking, " which three daughters should have
jointly inherited the patrimonial estates; but it seems that a deed and fine
had been levied and made by the said John Lord Mohun their father some
time before his death, of the barony, honour, and manor of Dunster, together
with the manors of Minehead and Kilton, and the hundred of Carhampton,
which he thereby vested in the Archbishop of Canterbury, and other trustees
for such uses as his wife should, in case she survived him, declare.   In pursuance of which deed the said Lady Mohun 50 Ed. III. sold the reversion

of the said premises to Lady Elizabeth Luttrell, relict of Sir Andrew Luttrell of Chilton, co. Devon, and daughter of Hugh Courtnai, Earl of Devonshire."—*Ibid.* See *Luttrell.* ˙ This great barony of Dunster was held by the service of forty knights (Testa de Nevill, 162): and in 1165 the Norman barony of the De Mohuns consisted of sixteen fees. (Feod. Norm. Duchesne.)

Of these despoiled sisters, the two elder were childless, and the title passed to Lady Strange's son, and through her granddaughter to George Stanley, Earl of Derby. It is now in abeyance.

Sir Reginald de Mohun, the fourth son of the first Lord Mohun, settled in Cornwall temp. Edward III. "They say that this Sir Reginald, coming into Fowey harbour with a company of soldiers bound for Ireland, and landing there, let fly a hawk at some game, which killed it in the garden of Hall, where Sir Reginald going for his hawk, and being a very handsome personable young gentleman (qualities which his descendants retained to the last), the young lady fell in love with him, and having a great fortune, the match was soon made up." —*Gilbert's Cornwall.* This young lady was Elizabeth, the heiress of Sir John Fitzwilliam of Lanteglos, which remained the chief seat of his posterity till they removed to Boconnoc. In the fifteenth century William Mohun married Isabel, daughter of Sir Hugh Courtenay of Boconnoc, and sister of Edward Earl of Devon, who eventually became one of the four co-heiresses of her great-nephew Edward Marquess of Exeter. Their grandson, Reginald, purchased Boconnoc in 1566; and the next in descent, John, one of the chief Cavalier commanders in the West of England, was created Baron Mohun of Okehampton, in right of his ancestress Isabel Courtenay, whose brother had been "lord of the manor, honour, and borough of Okehampton," the ancient Devonshire barony of Richard de Redvers. He received it in 1628, and married Cordell, daughter of Sir John Stanhope of Shelford, by whom he had two sons who successively inherited it, and a third, killed fighting under the royal banner at Dartmouth. The line ended with Charles, fifth Lord; "a nobleman of very bright parts and great natural endowments both of body and mind; but having the misfortune to lose his father while he was yet in the cradle—and the estate being left to him much involved in law suits between his nearest relations and with a considerable debt—he had not an education bestowed on him suitable to his birth; and happening to fall into ill company, he was drawn into several extravagancies."—*Gilbert's Cornwall.* A less indulgent term might more fitly describe them, for he was twice arraigned for murder, though each time honourably acquitted. At length his passionate and vehement temper led him to fight a duel with the Duke of Hamilton, in which both combatants were killed. It took place in Hyde Park in 1712. "This morning at eight," writes Swift to Stella on the day of the catastrophe, "my man brought me word that Duke Hamilton had fought with Lord Mohun and killed him, and was brought home wounded. I immediately sent him to the Duke's house in St. James's Square; but the porter would hardly answer for tears, and a great rabble was about the house. In short, they fought at seven this morning. The dog Mohun was killed on the spot; and while the Duke was over him, Mohun shortened his sword, and stabbed him in the shoulder to the heart. The Duke was helped towards the Cake House, by the Ring in Hyde Park, where they fought, and died on the grass before he could reach the house, and was brought home in his coach at eight, while the poor Duchess was asleep. Macartney and one Hamilton were the seconds, who fought likewise, and are both fled. I am told that a footman of Lord Mohun's stabbed Duke Hamilton, and some say Macartney did so too. Mohun gave the affront, and yet sent the challenge." Both the seconds were tried for murder, and acquitted: Hamilton swore positively that Macartney was the person who had given the Duke his death-wound, but the jury did not believe him, and he had to fly to the Continent to avoid a prosecution for perjury.

The fifth son of the first Lord Mohun, Robert, had a descendant of the same name who married a Dorsetshire heiress, and first settled in that county. His son, Maximilian, was very active in the service of Charles I., and had his estate sequestrated for his loyalty. The last heir male, another Robert, died unmarried in 1758. A second (very short-lived) branch, gave their name to Mohun's Ottery in Devonshire.

Mandeuile; or "Magnaville, one of the proudest honours of the Côtentin; altered by habit of speech into Mandeville." So says Sir Francis Palgrave; but opinions are divided as to the place from whence the name of this great house was derived. M. le Prévost also considers it to have been Magneville, near Valonges; "while M. Delisle reports that it was Mandeville le Trevières: the Norman estates of the Magnavilles, Mandevilles, or Mannevilles, as they were indifferently called, lying partly in the neighbourhood of Creuilli, and the rest round Argentan, where, at a later period, they held the honour of Chamboi."—*Planché.* They were, it is said, derived from Manno, or Magnus, a Northern Viking, who gave his name to the fief in the tenth century. Geoffrey, the "Sire de Magnavile" mentioned by Wace as rendering great aid in the battle of Hastings, was one of the chief grantees after the Conquest, and held lands in ten different counties. Walden, in Essex, was the head of his barony, and remained the principal seat of his descendants. This "famous Souldier" was one of the great potentates of his day. The Conqueror appointed him Constable of the Tower of London, and he held the Shrievalties of London, Middlesex, and Hertford. He founded a Benedictine monastery at Hurley in Berkshire, as a cell of Westminster Abbey, and desired to be laid in the Abbey, "giving, in return for his burial, the manor of Eye, then a waste morass, which gave its name to the Eye Brook, and under the names of Hyde, Eyebury (Ebury) and Neate, contained Hyde Park, Belgravia, and Chelsea."—*Dean Stanley.* William de Mandeville, his successor, married Margaret de Rie, heiress of the great Eudo Dapifer, and their son Geoffrey was in her right Hereditary Steward of Normandy. This second Geoffrey received from King Stephen the Earldom of the county of Essex, but was bribed to desert his service by two other more ample charters from the Empress Maud, of which the second, dated from Westminster and re-conferring the Earldom, "is," says Dugdale, "the most antient Creation Charter which hath been ever known." Both are remarkable for the privileges and concessions they contain. She granted him all the lands, forts and castles that his father and grandfather had held; the Tower of London, "with the little Castle under it," to strengthen and fortify at his pleasure; the Hereditary Shrievalties of London, Middlesex, and Hertfordshire, with the trial of all causes in those counties; all the lands granted to him by Stephen, with twenty additional knight's fees; the whole of Eudo Dapifer's Norman estates, with his office of Steward, and covenanted that "neither the Earl of Anjou (her Husband) nor herself, nor her children, would ever make peace with the Burgesses of London, but with the consent of the said Geoffrey, because they were his mortal Enemies." She constituted him Earl of Essex, with the third penny of the pleas of the Shrievalty, "as an Earl ought to enjoy in his Earldom," gave him the Hereditary Shrievalty of the county, and made him and his heirs Chief Justices of Essex for ever. His adherence had been valued at no contemptible price; but, great as were the powers and dignities conferred upon him, he did not long enjoy them. No sooner was Stephen firmly established on the throne, than he had his recreant liegeman seized at the Court of St. Albans. The Earl, a violent and headstrong man, did not submit without a sharp struggle; "they had a bloody fight, in which the Earl of Arundel (though a stout Soldier), being thrown into the Water with his Horse, escaped drowning very narrowly." He was securely lodged in prison, and only set free after surrendering the Tower of London, with his own castles of Walden and Plessey; and thus bereft of his strongholds, and maddened by rage and disappointment, he betook himself to the savage life of an outlaw.

> "He was to weete, a stoute and sturdie theefe,
> Wont to robbe churches of their ornaments."

He collected a band of determined followers, and foraged the country in every direction for spoil; first invading the King's own demesne lands, and "wasting them miserably. Likewise, having married his sister Beatrix to Hugh Talbot of Normandy, he caused her to be divorced, and wedded to William de Say, a stout and warlike Man; and with his aid, he went on in Plunder and Rapine everywhere, without mercy; making use of divers cunning Spies, whom he sent from door to door, as Beggars, to discover where any rich men dwelt; to the end he might surprise them in their Beds; and then keep them in hold, till they had with large sums of Money purchased their liberty. And being highly transported with wrath, he at length grew so savage, that by the help of this William de Say, and one Daniel, a counterfeit Monk, he got by

Water to Ramsey; and entring the Abbey very early in the morning, surprised the Monks (then asleep, after their nocturnal offices) and expelling them thence, made a Fort of the Church; taking away their Plate, Copes, and other Ornaments, and selling them for Money to reward his Soldiers." For this last outrage he was publicly excommunicated in 1144, and not long after, while besieging the castle of Burwell, "he put off his helmet (it being Summer), on account of the heat," and going bare-headed with shield and lance, he was shot in the head with an arrow, and mortally wounded. "Whereupon, with great contrition for his sins, and making what satisfaction he could, there came at last some of the Knights Templars to him; and putting on him the habit of their Order, with a Red Cross, carried his dead Corps into their Orchard, at the Old Temple in London; and Coffining it in Lead, hanged it on a crooked Tree. Likewise, that after some time, by the industry and expences of the Prior of Walden, his Absolution was obtained from Pope Alexander the Third, so that his Body was received amongst Christians, and Divine Offices celebrated for him; But, that when the Prior endeavoured to take down the Coffin, and carry it to Walden; the Templars being aware of the design, buried it privately in the Porch before the West door of the New Temple." This is a striking story; all the more striking, perhaps, because it reminds us that this spoliator and outcast had been in his younger days a benefactor of the Church. The Prior who interceded for his absolution was the Superior of the Abbey that he had founded near his Essex castle; "placing it upon a meeting of four Road-ways, and in angle of two Waters, that the Monks should of necessity be charitable to Poor-people and hospitable to Passengers." It had been conse-crated in 1136, but apparently not over richly endowed; for his successor Geoffrey III.—evidently himself unwilling to increase its income, "advised the Prior to be content with a small Church, and little Buildings."

Geoffrey III., the second of his three sons by Rohese de Vere (the elder, Ernulph, had died in banishment), was again created Earl of Essex by Henry II., and received back his forfeited lands, certifying to one hundred and three knight's fees. He was "an elegant man of speech, much noted for his abilities in secular affairs," and was sent with the Justiciary Richard de Lucy against the Welsh in 1167; but, falling sick at Chester, "it hapned that his servants being all gone to dinner, and nobody left with him, he died." He left no children, having been early divorced from his wife Eustachia—a kinswoman of the King's; and his brother William, who succeeded him, proved the last of his race. This third Earl, "of sharp wit, prudent in council and a stout Soldier, did not much verse himself amongst his own relations, but spent his youthful time, for the most part, with Philip Earl of Flanders," and only came home after his brother's death. He was much employed in military service, chiefly in Normandy, where he had the custody of several castles; and joined with Hugh Pudsey, Bishop of Durham, as Justiciary of England during Cœur de Lion's absence in the Holy

Land. He was twice married; first to Hawise, the heiress of William le Gros, Earl of Albemarle, with whom, by the King's gift, he had the whole county of Albemarle, "antiently assigned to guard the Borders of Normandy;" and secondly to Christian, daughter of Robert Lord Fitzwalter, but had no heirs, and his Earldom expired with him. He died in 1190 at Rouen, and when "drawing near his end, called together his Kindred and Servants; and gave them charge (with his hands lifted up on high) to convey his Body to Walden in England, there to be buried. But Henry de Vere, his Kinsman, standing by, told him, That the difficulty of the passage was such, that it could not be done. To whom he replied, 'If you cannot, it is because you have no mind to effect, what I, a dying man, desire; then take my Heart, and carry it thither.'"

The great Mandeville inheritance reverted to his father's sister Beatrix, the wife of the same William de Say who had helped the outlawed Earl to surprise Ramsey Abbey. She was the mother of two sons and two daughters; William, who died in his father's life-time; Geoffrey; Beatrix, married to Geoffrey Fitz Piers; and Maud, married to William de Boeland. Though then very aged and decrepit, she lost no time in establishing her claim; and despatched her surviving son Geoffrey, whose right to the barony seemed beyond dispute, to the King, "to transact the Business, for Livery, of that great heritage." But the younger Beatrix had married one of the most potent nobles in the kingdom, an able and ambitious man, "skilful in the Laws," who insisted that it belonged to his wife; and hotly and persistently contested it. Geoffrey de Say, however, had friends at court, and obtained an instrument under the King's seal for the whole barony, on promising to pay 7,000 marks into the Treasury. But this, at the time appointed, he neglected to do; and Fitz Piers, "rich in money and everything else," seized upon the opportunity, proffered the sum demanded in his stead, and procured the King's confirmation of his title. At the coronation of John, he was girt by the King with the sword as Earl of Essex. He had been appointed by Cœur de Lion Justiciary of England in 1197; and "ruled the reins of government," says Matthew Paris, "so that after his death, the Realm was like a Ship in a Tempest, without a Pilot." Dugdale adds that "he was allied to all the Great Men of England, either in Blood or Friendship, so that the King feared him above all Mortals."

His children by Beatrix de Say (he had afterwards another wife) all took the name of Mandeville, which ended with them. There were, besides a daughter, three sons; the youngest was a clerk in holy orders, and Dean of Wolverhampton; and the two others were successively Earls of Essex, and died s. p. Both were men of mark amongst the barons who wrested Magna Charta from King John; and the elder, who was also Earl of Gloucester in right of his wife, was one of the twenty-five lords chosen to enforce its observance. The second died in the flower of his age in 1227; and the Earldom devolved on their sister

Mary, the wife of Robert de Bohun, Earl of Hereford; while the lands passed to their half-brother, John Fitz Piers, the son born of the great Justiciary's second marriage. His grandson, John Fitz John, was summoned to parliament in the time of Henry III.

There was a branch of this house seated in Dorsetshire, where they held the honour ,of Merstwood, consisting of 14½ knight's fees, which Robert de Mandeville recovered from Henry de Tilly in the first years of King John's reign. It was an old suit, begun in his grandfather's time, and in 1211 "he accounted to the King £183 6s. and 8d., 5 Palfreys, and 3 Norway Goshawks for it." His brother Geoffrey succeeded, and the line ended with Geoffrey's son.

Several manors continue to bear this long defunct name; such as Kenton-Mandeville and Hardington-Mandeville in Somersetshire; Sutton-Mandeville in Wiltshire; Stoke-Mandeville in Buckinghamshire, &c.

Marmilon, or Marmion: the hereditary Champions of England. "They appear to have been a branch of the Tessons. Ralph Tesson, who brought 120 knights of his dependence to the aid of Duke William at the battle of Val des Dunes in 1047, founded c. 1055 the Abbey of Fontenay, near Caen (Gall. Christ. xi. 413). A charter of his was witnessed by William Marmion or Marmilon, probably his brother, c. 1070 (*Ibid.*), who, with his family possessed part of Fontenay. Robert Marmion, his son, Viscount of Fontenay-le-Tesson, passed into England with the Conqueror, and had extensive grants, his descendants a century later holding 17 fees in England and 5 in Normandy (Lib. Niger: Feoda Norm. Duchesne). The Tessons of Normandy bore *Gules* a fesse *Ermine;* the Marmions *Vair* a fesse *Gules.*"—*The Norman People.* They were, it is said, the hereditary Champions of Normandy; and after the Conquest, Robert de Marmion held the castle and manor of Tamworth * in Warwickshire and Scrivelsby in Lincolnshire by the tenure of performing that office at the King's coronation; being bound "to ride completely armed upon a barbed horse into Westminster Hall, and there to challenge the combat with whomsoever should dare to oppose the King's title to the crown." His seat was at Tamworth Castle, the head of his Warwickshire barony; and with the land-hunger common to the Norman invaders, he sought to enlarge its boundary by appropriating the neighbouring Abbey of Polesworth, and expelling the nuns. But "within the compass of a twelvemonth," writes Dugdale, when his castle was crowded with festive guests, among whom was "his sworn brother," Sir Walter de Somerville of Whichnour, his revelry was rudely interrupted by a visit from the offended saint as he lay on his bed. In this case it was St. Edith, habited as a veiled nun, and holding a crosier in her hand, who, not content with threatening him with eternal

---

* That he received Tamworth from the Conqueror "is verified," says Dugdale, by an antient window in this church, where the said King, being depicted in his Robes of State, and crowned, stretcheth forth his hand to him, holding a Charter therein, neer the Gate of a faire Castle."

perdition, emphasized her words with so sharp a blow on the side from her crosier, that he "cryed out loud;" and "being extremely tormented with the pain of his wound," could find no ease till he had confessed his sin, and restored Polesworth to the nuns. He went in person to crave their pardon, "desiring that himself, and his friend Sir Walter, might be reputed their patrons, and have burial for themselves and their heirs in the Abbey—the Marmions in the chapter-house, the Somervilles in the cloister." Robert his son, unwarned by his example, again meddled with Church property; for, having a bitter feud with the Earl of Chester (who possessed a castle at Coventry), he forcibly entered the Priory there and driving out the monks, proceeded to fortify the place on his own account. In order to defend its approaches, he dug deep ditches in the adjoining fields, which, being cunningly disguised and lightly covered over, were to become pitfalls to the enemy. But it so happened that while riding out to reconnoitre, the Earl's forces then drawing near, he fell into one of his own ditches, broke his thigh, and was killed by a passing soldier. His grandson Philip, who throughout the Barons' War remained the devoted adherent of Henry III., was the last Marmion. Though twice married, he had only four daughters; and of these, not more than two—Mazera de Cromwell, who had the barony of Tamworth, and Joan de Ludlow, who inherited Scrivelsby—left descendants. Mazera's sole daughter married Lord Freville; and Joan's son had also an only child, Margaret de Ludlow, who was the wife of Sir John Dymoke. At the coronation of Richard II. the office of Champion was claimed by the representatives of these two heiresses, Sir Baldwin de Freville, as Lord of the manor of Tamworth, and Sir John Dymoke, as Lord of the manor of Scrivelsby : and the dispute was referred to the Constable and Marshal of England, who adjudged the right to the latter. It was therefore Sir John who appeared in 1377 as the young King's Champion, and from that distant time to our own, there has always been a Dymoke at Scrivelsby to claim the honourable service by which he held his manor, and to ride into Westminster Hall armed *cap-à-pie* as the challenger. In 1814, Lewis Dymoke further sought to establish his right to the barony of Marmion; but the House of Lords decided that, even if a barony by tenure were admitted, it must have belonged to the elder daughter of the last baron, who was the heiress of Tamworth.

The last appearance of the Champion of England was at the coronation of George IV., when Westminster Hall was fitted up for the grand feudal display of a Royal banquet. At the further end, raised on a dais, stood the King's table, where he sat, between the five Royal Dukes, on a throne facing the great entrance; and on either hand three tables, each of fifty-six covers, extended down the whole length of the hall. On the one side these were reserved for the peers and great officers of State; on the other were placed the Bishops, the Barons of the Cinque Ports—whose privilege it was to bear the canopy of cloth of gold over the King's head, and sit on his right hand at his banquet—the Lord Mayor and

Sheriffs of London, the Kings-of-Arms and heralds, and the law officers and Masters in Chancery. The centre space was thus left open for the gorgeous procession of the officers of the Royal Household—by all accounts a curious and striking pageant—who, summoned to their duties by Garter King-of-Arms, were to serve the two courses of meat with all the traditional honours of mediæval ceremony. As they came in, every man in the hall rose from his seat. They walked in their order of precedence, in fanciful and splendid attire (even one of the lowest officials, the Clerk Comptroller, wore a velvet gown decked with silver lace), marshalled by the three principal officers of State on horseback, and attended by a glittering bevy of pages, squires, and serjeants-at-arms, followed by the twenty Gentlemen Pensioners who bore the covered gold dishes containing the first course. These being duly delivered to the clerks of the kitchen for the King's table, all retreated in the same order, stepping reverently back from the Royal presence; the horsemen, who had halted at the foot of the dais, reining back their chargers "with great precision." Then the King, preparing for the banquet, delivered the sceptre to the Lord of the manor of Worksop, who stood on his right hand, and the orb to the Duke of Devonshire on his left; while behind were ranged the lords with the four Swords of State—three of them unsheathed—that had been borne before him, the Lord Great Chamberlain of England with his white wand of office, and the Duke of Rutland, holding the Sceptre with the Dove. The Cup-bearer next brought a gold ewer and bason, and poured water over the King's hands; the Lord of the manor of Heyden offered the towel; and the dinner began. The Duke of Norfolk, who, as representing his ancestor William de Albini, should have officiated as Chief Butler of England, was not present; but the Lord of the manor of Wymondley, and the Hereditary Master of the Household in Scotland (the Duke of Argyll) each served the King with wine in a gold cup, which they retained as their fee.

When the first course was over, the trumpets sounded three times for the challenge; the passage to the King's table was again cleared by the Knight Marshall; and Henry Dymoke the Champion, accoutred in bright armour, and mounted on a superbly-caparisoned horse, rode into the hall. Before him went his two Trumpeters, bearing his coat of arms on their banners, the Serjeant Trumpeter and two serjeants-at-arms with their maces on their shoulders, and a herald with a paper containing the challenge. Two Esquires, in half-armour, bore his shield and lance; and four pages followed him. At his right hand, on a beautiful white charger, rode the Duke of Wellington, Lord High Constable of England, holding his Constable's staff; at his left, the Marquess of Anglesea, officiating as Lord High Steward, with his white rod, riding a golden dun. Both wore their full peer's robes and coronets; both were attended by a page; and both their horses had, like the Champion's, plumes of feathers nodding on their heads, and were resplendent in the shining trappings that dated from the period

—"dont memorie ne court"—of the bygone glories of chivalry.* On his entrance, the herald gave out the challenge, proclaiming in a loud voice that "if any person of what degree soever, high or low, shall deny or gainsay" the King's .title, "here stands the King's Champion, who saith that he lieth, and is a false traitor, being ready in person to combat with him: and in this quarrel will adventure his life against him, on what day soever he shall be appointed." Thereupon the Champion flung down his gauntlet on the floor of the hall, where, during a brief pause—as if in expectation of its being taken up †—it was suffered to lie, till the herald raised it, and returned it to the challenger, crying, "Long live the King!" This ceremonial was again gone through in the centre of the hall, and repeated for the third and last time at the foot of the dais: after which, the Champion, resuming his gauntlet, made a low obeisance to the King, and the King pledged him in a covered gold cup full of wine. The.Cup-bearer then brought this cup to the Champion, who, with three more profound "reverences," drank "Long life to His Majesty King George the Fourth": and, reining back his horse, retired, step by step, to the door through which he had entered, accompanied, as before, by the Constable and Lord Steward, and carrying the

* During the banquet at Richard II.'s coronation, the Lord Steward, the Constable, and Earl Marshal, with some other knights deputed by them, rode about the Hall on great coursers to keep order among the people. In the 14th century, when the floor was strewn with rushes and herbs, this might be easily done; but in after times, on the bare pavement, amid the blare of trumpets and blaze of colours, it became a more difficult matter to manage a horse properly. There is a lamentable story told of one poor Champion, who had taken such pains in accustoming his horse to back, that, when he came to the door of the Hall, the highly-trained animal wheeled suddenly round, and insisted on entering backwards.

† "It was always said, though with very little appearance of truth, that upon the coronation of George III., when the Champion of England appeared in Westminster Hall, and in the language of chivalry, solemnly wagered his body to defend in single combat the right of the young King to the crown of these realms, at the moment when he flung down his gauntlet as the gage of battle, an unknown female stepped from the crowd and lifted the pledge, leaving another gage in room of it, with a paper expressing that if a fair field of combat should be allowed, a champion of rank and birth would appear with equal arms to dispute the claim of King George III. to the British kingdoms."—*Sir Walter Scott.* This story has been improved upon by the suggestion that the gauntlet was taken up by Prince Charles Edward himself, who was then visiting London in disguise. The fact of his presence at the Coronation was related to Hume the historian by the Earl Marischal, only a few days after the ceremony. "I asked my lord," says Hume, "the reason for this strange fact? 'Why,' says he, 'a gentleman told me that he saw him there, and that he even spoke to him, and whispered in his ear these words, Your Royal Highness is the last of all mortals whom I should expect to meet here. It was curiosity that led me, said the other; but I assure you, that the person who is the object of all this pomp and magnificence is the man I envy the least.' What if the Pretender has taken up Dymoke's gauntlet?" Let us hope not in the disguise of an old woman.

gold cup and cover with him as his fee. As soon as he had left the hall, the five Kings of Arms, with their pursuivants, in all "the pomp of heraldry," proclaimed the King's Styles in Latin, French, and English, three several times; first on the steps of the throne, then in the middle of the hall, and finally at the lower end, with the customary cry of "Largesse!" but I can find no intimation of any Largesse having been bestowed upon them. In the Middle Ages, the Champion had license to furnish himself with the best suit of armour, save one, in the King's armoury, and the best steed, save one, in the King's stables; and thus, in addition to the coronation cups, some goodly ancient armour was to be found at Scrivelsby Court. But the whole collection was sold and dispersed on the death of the last Champion, a few years ago.

There was a younger branch of the Marmions that survived till 1355. Robert, the second son of the third Baron of Tamworth, had lands in Lincolnshire, Gloucestershire, and Suffolk granted to him by his father; and was in arms, first again King John, and then against Henry III., holding out with the barons to the very last. Both he and his son married great heiresses: and his grandson John was summoned to parliament in 1294 as Lord Marmion of Wetrington in Lincolnshire. Another John, who fought in the Scottish wars under Edward I., and John's son Robert, succeeded to the barony; but Robert, being childless and "of infirm constitution," made his sister Avise his heir, and married her to John, Lord Grey of Rotherfield, on condition that their children should bear the name of Marmion. They had two sons, who both assumed it; but John, the eldest, died s. p., and Robert, the younger (whose wife was a co-heiress of the St. Quintins), left only one daughter, married to Henry, Lord Fitzhugh.

Leland tells us the following picturesque story of the father of the first Lord Marmion of Wetrington.

"About this tyme there was a great feste made yn Lincolnshire, to which came many Gentlemen and Ladies; and among them a Lady brought a heaulme for a man of were, with a very rich creste of gold, to William Marmion, Knight, with a letter of commandment of her Lady, that he should go into the daungerest place in England, and there to let the heaulme to be seene and knowne as famous. So he went to Norham: whither within four dayes of cumming, cam Philip Moubray, Guardian of Berwicke, having in his band one hundred and forty men of armes, the very flour of men of the Scottish Marches.

"Thomas Gray, Capitayne of Norham, seying this, brought his garison afore the barriers of the castel, behynde whom cam William richly arrayed, as al glittering in gold, and wearing the heaulme as his Lady's present.

"Then sayd Thomas Gray to Marmion, 'Sir Knight, ye be cum hither to fame your heaulme, mount upon your horse, and ryde like a valiant man, to yown even here at hand, and I forsake God, if I rescue not thy body deade or alyve, or I myself will dye for it.'

"Whereupon he took his cursore, and rode among the throng of enemyes; the which layd sore stripes on him, and pulled hym at the last oute of his sadel to the grounde.

"Then Thomas Gray with all the hole garison lette pryk yn among the Scottes, and so wondid them and their horses, that they were overthrowen, and Marmion sore beten was horsid agayn, and with Gray persewed the Scottes in chase. There were taken fifty horses of price: and the women of Norham brought them to the foote men to follow the chase." Was the Lady in question the same rich Lora de Dovor, who brought him as her dowry the town of Ludington in Northamptonshire?

Moribray: or rather, as in Leland's copy, Moubray, from the castle of Molbrai or Moubrai, near St. Lo, in the Côtentin. Dugdale, following Ordericus, often spells the name Molbrai.* "It probably includes in its first syllable the name of the Scandinavian grantee c. 930, which is also preserved by Molbec, another place in the Côtentin."—*The Norman People.* In the Dives Roll, however, it is given "Montbrai."

Three of this name—afterwards so illustrious in English history—Geoffrey, Bishop of Coutances, his brother Roger, and his nephew Robert, came over in the Conqueror's train. "This Geffrey, being of a Noble Norman extraction, and more skilful in Arms than Divinity, knowing better to train up Soldiers, than to instruct his Clergy," did good service at the battle of Hastings, though Ordericus does not tell us that he held any command in the army. In those days, when "the old Danish leaven was still at work," no one thought the worse of a priest who could fight as well as pray; for churchmen held lay fees by military service, and bore arms without scruple. He had spent the vigil of St. Celict in exhorting and preparing the troops for the great issues of the morrow; and with Bishop Odo, "received confessions, and gave benedictions, and imposed penances on many."—*Wace.* On Christmas Day following, he assisted at the coronation of the Conqueror in Westminster Abbey. When, according to ancient custom, the consent of the commons was asked before proceeding to the rite of consecration, the question, first put in English by Archbishop, Eldred, was repeated by him in French; and the voices which, at the Epiphany, had shouted, "Yea, yea, King Harold," shouted at Christmas with equal apparent zeal, "Yea, yea, King William."—*Freeman.* He received one of the largest grants of English lands, "an endless list of lordships in Somerset," besides many in other counties,—two hundred and eighty manors in all; and dedicated his immense wealth to the building of Coutances Cathedral. In 1069 he marched against the Western insurgents and raised the siege of Montacute; and three years later presided, as Justiciary of England, at the Kentish

* The Mowbrays used the mulberry as their *rebus.* Thos. Duke of Norfolk, at his famous duel with the Duke of Hereford at Coventry, rode "a horse barded with crimson velvet embroydered with Lions of silver and mulberry trees."

Scirgemót held on Penendon Heath to decide the suit between Bishop Odo and Lanfranc. He was in the successful campaign against Ralph Earl of Norfolk: and appointed Earl of Northumberland; but he soon relinquished the ungrateful task of ruling that disaffected and turbulent province to his nephew Robert, who, on his death in 1093, became heir to all his temporal possessions.

Robert, Earl of Northumberland, was the son of the "Sire de Moubrai" mentioned by Wace at Hastings, Roger de Moubray, of whom, singularly enough, there is no further trace in history. Robert's portrait has been minutely painted by Ordericus. "He was a person of large stature, strong, black, hairy, bold, and subtile; of a stern countenance, few words, and so reserved, that he was seldom seen to smile; stout in arms, disdainful to his equals, and so haughty-minded, that he thought it below him to obey his superiors." No description could surely less enlist our sympathies; and yet it is impossible to read of his horrible fate unmoved. He had successfully governed Northumberland during several years, and had taken prisoner at Alnwick the Scottish King who invaded his territory, when, in an evil hour, he, with the Earl of Eu and others—for some variously explained cause—rose in arms against William Rufus. He was summoned to court to answer for his conduct; but "being not a little puft up with pride, in regard he had not long before subdued Malcolme, he scorned to obey the King's commands." William at once took the field in person, and marching into Northumberland, besieged and reduced Newcastle-on-Tyne, and took Tynemouth by storm.* Both the Earl and the Earl's brother were in the fortress, but the latter only was captured, for the Earl escaped to Bamborough Castle, then considered impregnable, and held by one of his kinsmen, John Morrel (see p. 305). The King, pursuing him, beleaguered the place; and Mowbray, feeling himself insecure, again shifted his quarters, and getting out of the Castle by night with thirty of his followers, took sanctuary in his own collegiate church of Tynemouth. But he was dragged away from the very steps of the altar, grievously wounded, and paraded in triumph before his castle gate, with the threat that, if it were not surrendered, his eyes should be then and there put out. The gallant castellan, who had made a most obstinate defence, hereupon yielded up his trust; and the Earl's eyes were spared. But they never saw the light again. He was thrust into the dungeon pit of Windsor Castle, and there, for thirty-four dreadful years, lived in the dumb darkness of a noisome vault, as if he were already in his grave. He was actually dead in the eye of the law; for his newly-wedded wife, Maud de Aquilâ, who had "had little

* "In 1090, Earl Mowbray re-founded Tynemouth Priory, and filled it with Black Canons; and out of enmity to the Bishop of Durham, made it a cell of St. Albans, in Hertfordshire. In his unsuccessful conspiracy to dethrone William Rufus, he converted the place into a fortress, which after a siege of two months was taken by storm."—*Mackenzie's Northumberland.*

joy of her marriage," obtained the Pope's license to marry again, and chose for her next husband Nigel de Albini, the founder of the great English house. (See *Albeny.*)

Nigel's eldest son Roger, who by King Henry's desire bore the name of Moubray, was "the infant Earl of Northumberland" described in 1138 at North-allerton, as placed, with the more aged of the barons, upon the car on which was erected the famous mast or standard that gave its name to the battle, and bore the cross with the consecrated host in a silver pyx, and the three banners of St. Peter, St. Wilfrid of Ripon, and St. John of Beverley. Yet there is no evidence that either he or his posterity ever held the Earldom, though he certified in 1165 to a great barony of 99 knight's fees. He was not the famous soldier that his father had been; but he gained renown in the crusade under St. Louis in 1148, and assumed the cross a second time, when he and Guy de Lusignan were together captured by Saladin. He was redeemed by the Templars, to whom he had been a great benefactor; so great, in fact, that they covenanted to protect, release, and serve him and his heirs for ever, and to make them partakers of all their prayers and penances. On his journey home, "finding a fierce Dragon fighting with a Lion, he mortally wounded the Dragon; whereby he so gained the love of the King of Beasts, that he followed him into England, to his Castle at Hode." This fable was evidently suggested by the silver lion on his shield— a bearing far too renowned both then and thereafter on the battle-field to need any such fanciful illustration:

> "For who, in fight or foray slack,
> Saw the blanch lion e'er fall back?" *

Besides many grants of land to the Church, he founded two religious houses in Yorkshire; Byland Abbey, for the Cistercians, at the instance of the Lady Gundred, his mother, and Newburgh Priory. Part of his great possessions, the lands of Frontdeboef, conferred upon his father by William Rufus, were hotly contested by the Stutevilles; and the struggle was renewed in the time of his grandson William, and proved of long continuance. This William was one of the twenty-five illustrious conservators of Magna Charta. He was succeeded by two sons; of whom the last, Roger, married the eldest co-heiress of the Baron of Bedford, Maud de Beauchamp, and was the father of another Roger, summoned to parliament in 1295, and an active soldier in the Welsh and Gascon wars. The next Lord Mowbray served in Scotland from his boyhood, and was appointed Warden of the Marches, and Constable of Scarborough and Malton, by Edward II.

---

* "The field, (saith he) in which the lion stands
  Is blood, and blood I offer to the hands
  Of daring foes; but never shall my flight
  Dye black my lion, which as yet is white."

But in 1320 he joined the discontented nobles that rose in rebellion under the Earl of Lancaster, having, as the defrauded son-in-law of De Braose (see Vol. I., p. 54) a strong personal ground of quarrel with the Despensers; and after the rout at Borough Bridge, was taken prisoner and hung in chains at York. "So great,' adds Dugdale, "was the indignation of the King and the Spencers, that they would not suffer his dead body to be taken down from the gallows." His widow, the unhappy heiress of Gower, was committed to the Tower with her son; and so "grievously oppressed," that she was forced to give up great part of her patrimony to the favourite. The son, however, John, third Lord Mowbray, was restored at the accession of Edward III., and is styled in his charters *Dominus Insulæ de Haxiholme, et de Honoribus de Gowher et de Brember.* He had for some time the charge of "the Gibraltar of Scotland," Berwick-upon-Tweed; followed the King in his French campaigns with a train of forty men-at-arms and forty archers, married the King's cousin Joan Plantagenet, daughter of Henry Earl of Lancaster, and died of the plague at York in 1360. His successor, endowed with "the high blood's royalty" which came to him from the mother's side, made the most splendid alliance in the kingdom; for his wife, Elizabeth Segrave, was the daughter and heir of Lord Segrave by Lady Margaret Plantagenet, daughter and eventually sole heiress of Thomas de Brotherton, the eldest son of Edward I. by his second marriage with Margaret of France, who was Earl of Norfolk and Earl Marshal of England. With the honours of the Bigods, he had received the whole of their domains; and his granddaughter brought "a great inheritance in Lands with addition of much honour" to her husband. He did not long live to enjoy them; for, in 1367, when his eldest son was little more than four years old, he was attacked and slain by the Turks as he passed near Constantinople on his journey to the Holy Land. His young heir, John, fifth Lord Mowbray, received the Earldom of Nottingham on the day of Richard II.'s coronation in 1377, but dying the following year, unmarried, his only brother Thomas succeeded him, and in 1383 was created Earl of Nottingham, as he had been. Two years afterwards, in right of his descent from Thomas of Brotherton, he was constituted Earl Marshal of England.

The new Earl, who soon gave proof of rare power and energy, was looked upon with jealous hatred by the ignoble favourites that then had the King's ear; most of all by the Duke of Ireland, who is said to have designed to take his life. He was one of the great lords that solicited the Duke's dismissal from the Royal council, and banded themselves together against him at the battle of Radcote Bridge, where he was defeated and forced to fly the country. Mowbray was apparently none the less in favour with the King, who appointed him Captain of Calais, his Lieutenant in Picardy, Flanders, and Artois; then his Justiciary in Flintshire, Cheshire, and North Wales; and further, "acknowledging his just and hereditary title to bear for his Crest a golden Leopard, with a white Label; which of right did belong to the King's eldest son (if he had any) granted to him and his heirs, authority to bear the golden Leopard for his Crest, with a Coronet of Silver, about his neck, instead of the Labell."* He also confirmed the Earl Marshalship to him and his heirs male, directing that, "by reason of this their Office, they should bear a Golden Truncheon, enamelled with black at each end, having at the upper end of it the King's arms graven thereon, and at the lower end their own Arms." This was, according to Dugdale, in 1397. Yet, no later than the ensuing year, in the seeming height of his glory and success, his old enemies, "the Parasites by whom the King was governed," caused him to be arrested for high treason, and prepared to impeach him in Parliament. Finding himself in their power, and moved either by a pressing sense of danger or by flattering promises of future favour, he made terms with his captors, and joined them heart and hand. Thenceforward he cast in his lot with the men that he had all his life opposed and condemned, and acted with them unhesitatingly, even "in the destruction of that honourable person Richard Earl of Arundel, whose Daughter he had Married; and was one of the cheif that guarded him to his Execution. Nay it is said by some, that he bound up his Eyes, and beheaded him himself. And soon after that, had a principal hand in that execrable Murther of Thomas of Woodstock Duke of Gloucester (the King's Uncle), causing him to be smothered with a Feather-bed at Calais." —*Dugdale.* The recompence of his infamy followed on the instant. He received not only all the lands of his unfortunate father-in-law, but the forfeited estates of Thomas de Beauchamp, Earl of Warwick—two principalities—by a grant dated Sept. 28, 1398; and the day following was created Duke of Norfolk; his grandmother Margaret Plantagenet, who was still alive, being at the same time created Duchess of Norfolk. But the Nemesis that dogs the steps of the "slippery greatness whose foundation is laid in blood" was close upon his heels. On the very day twelvemonth that he had caused the Duke of Gloucester to be murdered at Calais, he was banished the realm for ever.

The story of his quarrel with the Duke of Hereford, as told by Shakespeare in the opening chapter of his Richard II., is taken from Holinshed; Froissart gives it rather differently. But the facts remain the same. Hereford denounced him as a traitor in the presence of the King at the parliament held at Shrewsbury, and, flinging down his gage, declared:—

> "What I do speak,
> My body shall make good upon this earth,
> Or my divine soul answer it in heaven."

---

* It is to this Shakespeare makes allusion :

> *King Richard :* Lions make leopards tame.
> *Norfolk :* Yea, but not change their spots.

Norfolk, retorting the accusation, gave the Duke the lie ; then, raising the gauntlet in token that he accepted the challenge, threw down his own :—

> " I interchangeably hurl down my gage
> Upon this overweening traitor's foot,
> To prove myself a loyal gentleman
> Even in the best blood chamber'd in his bosom."

The King appointed that the trial by battle should be held át Coventry, upon Gosford Green, where the lists were accordingly set up. Holinshed's minute account brings before us in " imaginary puissance " the splendid pageant that led to such momentous results. He tells us how the Duke of Aumerle, High Constable, and the Duke of Surrey, officiating as Earl Marshal, guarded the lists with " a great company apparelled in silk sendall embroidered with silver, every man having a tipped staff to keep order ;" and how the King, with a retinue of more than 10,000 men in armour, entered the field " with great triumph," attended by all the peers of the realm, and took his seat under a richly adorned canopy. The challenger, armed at all points, was the first to appear, mounted on a white courser barded with green and blue velvet, bearing the badges of the House of Lancaster, swans and antelopes in goldsmiths' work ; and proclaimed that he came to do his devoir against Thomas Mowbray, Duke of Norfolk, " as a traitor untrue to God, the King, his realm, and me." Then, swearing by the Holy Evangelists that his quarrel was just and true, he put down his visor, made a cross on his horse, and took his appointed place. The Duke of Norfolk, on a horse barded with crimson velvet embroidered with silver lions and mulberry trees, next made his oath before the Constable and Marshal, and " entered the field manfully, saying aloud, ' God aid him that hath the right.' Each champion, dismounting, seated himself on a canopied chair of state, while the heralds proclaimed the challenge, and the Earl Marshal viewed their spears to see that they were of equal length. Then the traverses and chairs were removed, and the herald commanded them " on the King's behalf to mount on horse back, and address themselves to the combat." The Duke of Hereford was quickly horsed, and closed his beaver, and cast his spear into the rest, and when the trumpet sounded, set forwards courageously towards his enemy six or seven paces. The Duke of Norfolk was not fully set forward, when the King cast down his warder, and the heralds cried, " Ho, ho !" Then the King caused their spears to be taken from them, and commanded them to repair again to their chairs, where they remained two long hours, while the King and his council deliberately consulted " what order was best to be had in so weighty a cause." The sentence finally pronounced was banishment from the realm. The Duke of Hereford was exiled for a term of ten years, and the Duke of Norfolk for life.

Hereford returned home the following year to reign as the first Lancastrian

King of England; but Norfolk never saw his native land again. He died in 1399 at Venice, on his return from a pilgrimage to Jerusalem, either of the pestilence, or, as others assert, of a broken heart. "The shield placed over his remains in St. Mark's Church remained in Venice when the Duke's ashes were removed thence to England in the spring of the year 1533."—*Rawdon Browne.*

He left by his wife, Lady Elizabeth Fitz Alan, two sons, and two daughters; Thomas, his successor; John; Isabel, married first to Henry, son of William Lord Grey of Groby, and secondly to James, sixth Lord Berkeley; and Margaret, the wife of Sir Robert Howard.

Thomas, the eldest son, who simply bore the title of Earl Marshal, was beheaded for conspiring against Henry IV. in 1405, and left no posterity. His brother John was restored as Duke of Norfolk by Henry VI. in 1424, and was succeeded in the title by a son and grandson, with whom this princely line expired. The last Duke married a daughter of the great Earl of Shrewsbury, and died in 1475, leaving a little child of two years old, Lady Anne Mowbray (sometimes styled Duchess of Norfolk), to inherit the immense estates—one great tract in Yorkshire is still known as the Vale of Mowbray—that had been handed down from the time of the Conquest. Edward IV. at once marked the prize as his own. His baby son, Richard Duke of York, was invested with the titles and dignities of Lady Anne's father, and in 1477, when both were about four years old, was married to Lady Anne herself. She did not long survive; for six years afterwards, when the little Prince was murdered in the Tower, he was already a widower.

The representation of the great house of Mowbray then reverted to the Berkeleys and Howards, as descendants of the two daughters of the first Duke, Isabel and Margaret. By her first husband, Lady Isabel had only a daughter, the heiress of Groby; but by Lord Berkeley she had two more daughters and four sons, of whom William, the eldest, died s. p. in 1492, having been successively created Viscount Berkeley, Earl of Nottingham, and Marquess of Berkeley; and Maurice, the next, eighth Lord Berkeley (the ancestor of the existing family), divided the great Mowbray inheritance with the second Duke of Norfolk in 1499. Lady Margaret was the mother of "Jock of Norfolk,"

> "the true knight to whom no costly grave
> Can give due homage,"

who died fighting for Richard III. on the field of Bosworth, and was the first of fifteen successive Dukes of his name and blood, who have been Earls Marshal of England in her right.

The two thirteenth-century baronies of Mowbray and Segrave remained in abeyance between the descendants of these two great heiresses, till Henry Howard, father of the fifth Duke, was summoned to parliament as Baron Mowbray in 1639. Then again the direct line failed with the eleventh Duke;

and in 1777 they once more lapsed between his two nieces Winifred Lady Stourton, and Anne Lady Petre, continuing dormant for more than a century. They are now vested in the nineteenth Lord Stourton.

A very ancient offset of the English Mowbrays still bears the name in Fifeshire. Nigel de Mowbray, the grandson of Nigel de Albini, had a younger son named Robert; "Of which Robert," says Dugdale, "I finde that he took to wife a Countess in Scotland, who had a faire Inheritance there; from whom descend the Mowbrays of that Kingdom." It was, however, not Robert, but Nigel's second son, Philip, that came to Scotland, presumably on a visit to his kinswoman Ermengarde de Beaumont, the Queen of William the Lion; and married Galiena, the daughter of the potent Earl of Dunbar. Though not a "Countess," she brought him great possessions; amongst them the baronies of Inverkeithing in Fife, and Barnbougle and Dunmanyne (Dalmeny) in West Lothian; and the office of Standard Bearer of Scotland, with the "hostilages thereunto belonging" (an obsolete word, signifying a house in every town where the King resided). He built his castle at Barnbougle, a rocky promontory on the S. side of the Forth, so named from some forgotten battle (in the Gaelic *Bar-na-buai-gàll*, the point of the victory of Strangers) where fell a Celtic chief whose cairn remains hard by. His grandson Galfrid had a writ of military summons as an English Baron in 1287, though he was conspicuous among the *Magnates Scotiæ* 1292–94, and one of the nominees of John Baliol. He married a daughter of the Red Comyn, and had four sons; William; John, the handsomest man in Scotland—

> "In all Scotland was nowcht than
> As this Jhon so fayre a man,"

(says *Wynton's Chronicle*); Roger, and Philip. All the three eldest died s. p. Roger, though he was Standard Bearer to the Bruce, and received the augmentation of a golden crown to his blanch lion for his services at Bannockburn, entered into a conspiracy against his sovereign in 1320, and was sentenced to death and forfeiture as a traitor. His last brother, Sir Philip, a gallant soldier, who unhorsed the King himself at the battle of Methven, had been killed at Dundalk two years before, leaving a son John, and a daughter of his own name. Sir John also fell in battle, in the service of Edward Baliol; and Philippa his sister, through the interest of her powerful relatives, received back her uncle Roger's forfeited baronies in 1346. Three kinsmen, Alexander, Galfrid, and William de Moubray, vainly preferred their claims as heirs-male. She married a foreign knight, Sir Bertold de Loen, and from her only son David, who bore her name, and married Lady Janet Stewart, a daughter of the Regent Duke of Albany, the present family descends. The principal line, seated at Barnbougle, ended with another heiress *

* One of her descendants—who again all took the name of Moubray—sold the three baronies of Inverkeithing, Barnbougle, and Dalmeny in 1615 to the first Earl of Haddington. They were afterwards acquired by the ancestor of the Earls of Rosebery.

in 1519, and the representation of the house passed to her great-uncle, William Moubray of Cockairny in Fife, with whose posterity it remains.

Moruile: from the castle of Morville, in the Côtentin. "Flourished in England, in Normandy, and in Scotland."—*Sir Francis Palgrave.* Hugo de Morville, the founder of the English house, is first mentioned in a Tynemouth charter of 1138; and Simon (probably his brother) acquired the great barony of Burgh-upon-Sands, through his wife Ada de Engaine. It had come to her, with the Hereditary Forestership of Cumberland, from her grandmother, Ebria de Trivers (see *Travers*). Ada left two sons, of whom the eldest, Sir Hugh, married another Cumberland heiress, Helewise de Stuteville, who brought him Kirkoswald and Lazenby as her dower.* Kirkoswald became his favourite residence; and the great castle standing on the river Eden, "once the fairest fabric that eyes ever looked upon," was built or at least castellated by him. In 1170, he was one of the four courtier-knights that hurried over from Normandy to fulfil what they conceived to be the express will and pleasure of the King in ridding him of Thomas à Beckett (see *Fitz Urse*). Morville, however, throughout the dreadful tragedy "retained the gentler disposition for which he was distinguished." He, alone, struck no blow; for, while his accomplices were massacring the defenceless Archbishop on the pavement of his own church, and one of them, plunging his sword into the dead man's skull, vindictively "stirred his brains," he "contented himself with holding back at the entrance of the transept the crowds who were pouring in through the nave." After the deed was done, he harboured the assassins for a whole twelvemonth at Knaresborough Castle, where they remained unmolested and unpursued; since it is clear that the arm of the civil law was never brought to bear upon them. "The general fate of the murderers," says Dean Stanley, "was far less terrible than the popular tradition delighted to believe. It would seem that by a singular reciprocity, the principle for which Becket had contended—that priests should not be subjected to secular courts—prevented the trial of a layman for the murder of a priest by any other than a clerical tribunal. The consequence was, that the perpetrators of what was thought the most heinous crime since the Crucifixion could be visited with no other penalty than excommunication. That they should have performed a pilgrimage to Palestine is in itself not improbable, and one of them" (see *Tray*) "certainly attempted it. But they seem before long to have recovered their position. Within the first two years of the murder, they were living at court on familiar terms with the King, and constantly joined him in the pleasures of the chase." Hugh de Morville, Forester of Cumberland, a man of high rank and great power, who was Justice Itinerant of the counties of Northumberland and Cumberland at the very time of the murder, suffered no punishment beyond that

---

* "The great mountain in Cumberland, Hugh-Seat-Morvill, was named after him."—*Hutchinson.*

of being discontinued in his office the following year. Yet, if free from the guilt of actual bloodshed, he was none the less an acknowledged accessory to the crime. His position in his native county was obviously never damaged. In the first year of King John's reign, he is recorded as paying twenty-five marks and three good palfreys for holding his court as long as Helewise his wife should continue in a secular habit. About the same period, he procured a charter for a fair and market at Kirkoswald, and died shortly after, leaving two daughters: Ada, the eldest, who inherited Kirkoswald, married first Richard de Lucy of Egremont, and secondly Thomas de Multon; and Joan was the wife of Richard Gernun. The sword he had worn on the day of the Archbishop's murder was long preserved in Kirkoswald Castle; afterwards transferred to Isell (a manor that belonged to the Morvilles, as heirs of Engaine), and is now said to be attached to his statue at Brayton Castle.

His younger brother had likewise no male heir, and with him the baronial line terminated. Yet it is clear that some of his kin remained. "Of this family doubtless was Eudo de Morville, who left issue two daughters, his heirs; of whom Maud married Matthew de Columbers, which Matthew, 22 & 23 Hen. III., paid a fine for the livery of the lands of Isabel, mother of the said Maud."—*Banks.*

The family had been of even greater account North of the Tweed. Hugo de Morville, the contemporary of his English namesake, was the first Constable of Scotland, and, according to the *Chronica de Mailros*, founded Dryburgh, one of the earliest Præmonstratentian Abbeys, in 1150. But David I., in his foundation charter (printed in the *Liber de Dryburgh*) to which Hugh's own name is affixed as a witness, distinctly states that he was himself the founder, having imported from Alnwick a colony of Præmonstratents for this purpose. It is, however, certain that Hugh and his successors were the chief benefactors of the Abbey; and "in those times when," in Chalmers' phrase, "the monks had much to ask, and the knights and barons much to give," few among them had ampler means of liberality. The Morvilles ranked among the most powerful Scottish barons, and held nearly the whole of Lauderdale, one of the three great divisions of Berwickshire.

Hugh died in 1162, and was followed by his son Richard, who was Constable of Scotland for twenty-seven years, and the father of William de Morville, with whom he witnesses King Malcolm's confirmation charter to Kelso. William died s. p. in 1196, the last heir male of his house. His only sister Elena was the wife of Uchtred, Lord of Galloway; and their son, the famous Alan of Galloway, was made Constable of Scotland in right of his grandfather by William the Lion.

Yet, as in England, the name appears to have survived; for, about the middle of the next century, Sir Ingram de Morville married the widow of Sir Thomas Bruce, one of the brothers of Robert I.

Miriell: spelt Myriet by Leland. There was a family of De Meriet, that took its name from a Somersetshire manor, and, according to Mr. Ellis,[*] claimed to be the elder branch of the illustrious house of Fitz Hardinge, " the only baronial family of the Middle Ages which has preserved its direct male line down to the present day without one instance of reversion to a distant collateral." But, as an English name, not borne till a century after the Conquest, it can have no place here. We must therefore revert to Miriell.

I find "Godricas Mirieldus" of Lincoln mentioned in 1189–90 (Rot. Pip.); John and Richard Miriel, Norfolk; Adam de Miriel, Suffolk; and Matilda de Miriel, with her daughter Margaret, Kent, in the time of Ed. I.—*Rotuli Hundredorum.* Nicholas de Meriel was of Yorkshire at the same date. Roger de Muriel held a knight's fee at Thorp-Bussel, Lancashire.—*Testa de Nevill.*

Maulay: *de malo lacu;* a baronial name. The first who came to England was Peter de Maulay, a Poitevin, brought over by King John, and distinctly accused by Ralph Niger and Henry Knighton of being the tool he employed for ridding himself of his nephew Arthur. Peter's reward was the heiress of Doncaster, Isabella de Turnham, who brought him the barony of Mulgrave. " This Peter de Malo-lacu, commonly called Mauley, built a castle, which, from its grace and beauty, he named, in French, Moultgrace; but because it became a grievance to the neighbours, the people, by changing one letter, named it Moultgrave; by which name it ever after remained known."—*Banks.* Peter de Maulay is obviously an interpolation; but it must be observed, that a " Seigneur de Meulay " is to be found on the list given in Tailleur's Chronicle of Normandy.

Malebraunch. This is one of the names added by M. de Magny to the Dives Roll. Of the French family I can only find mention of Guillaume de Crevant, Seigneur de Maubranches, living in the first years of the fifteenth century (Anselme, *Histoire de la Noblesse de France*). This proves that, like many other *sobriquets*, it had become territorial, some manor having received its designation from its former owners. Nicholas Malebranche, " eminent among the metaphysicians of France in the most illustrious age of French philosophy " as the author of *Recherche de la Verité*, was the son of a secretary of the King's, and his only claim to gentle blood was on his mother's side.

It is—as far as my experience goes—of rare occurrence in England. Richard Malebeench was Grand Master of the Temple about 1170, and Roger de Malebraunch, Abbot of Burton from 1177 to 1182.—*Nichol's Leicestershire.* Two of the name—both belonging to Lincolnshire—appear as benefactors of the Knights Templars, to whom John Malbraunche gave land at Appleby, and Roger de Malebraunche at Ouseby. Another (if not the same) Roger Malebraunch, with his wife Basilia, and their daughter Cecilia are found in Northamptonshire temp. Ed. I.—*Rotul. Hundred.* John Malebraunche was of Kent, at the same date. William de Malebraunch held at Farnley, in Yorkshire, during the previous reign.—*Archbishop Gray's Register.* The wardship and marriage of Agnes, daughter and heir of John Malebrank of Farnley, was granted in 1325 by William Melton, Archbishop of York, to John de Brantingham, Vicar of Otley.

Malemaine : evil-handed : a redoubtable nickname, akin to the talons of the ferocious Malegriffe (John Malegreffe, 9 Ed. II., held North Okendon, in Essex) : and boding no good to the peace of the neighbourhood. This family became powerful in East Kent ; and their allusive coat, *Ermine* on a chief *Gules*, three sinister hands coupled at the wrist *Argent*, is several times carved on the roof of the cloisters of Canterbury Cathedral. Le Malesmains, or *Maliis Manibus*, occurs more than once in the Norman Exchequer Rolls of 1180–95 ; and a Sieur de Mallemains, bearing the same three silver hands in their scarlet field, was to be found in Normandy during the present century. (Nobiliaire de Normandie.)

In England the name has long since perished, and is only retained by some of their former possessions ; Alkham Malemains, Pluckley Malmains, Stoke Malmains, and Waldershare-Malmains, in Kent. It is not written in Domesday ; but Hasted retails a family tradition—for which no authority is given, nor probably could be furnished—that "John de Malmains was standard-bearer to the Norman foot soldiers at the battle of Hastings."

Their principal seat, Waldershare, was originally held of the Mamimots, and then of their descendants the Sayes ; and their ancient manor house, Malmains Hall—the name has in course of time degenerated to Maaman's Hall—is now one of Lord Guilford's farmhouses. "Near it an open unenclosed down is called Maimage Down, corruptly for Malmains Down."—*Hasted.* They were, he tells us, "of eminent account in those parts." Gilbert Malesmains, in the latter years of the 12th century, married the widowed Countess of Salisbury, Alianor de Vitré. "She married, first William Paynell (obt. 1184), by whom she had a son who died young ; secondly Gilbert de Tillières (obt. 1190), by whom she had a son, Gilbert, under age at his father's death, and two daughters, Juliana and Joanna ; and thirdly William Fitz Patric Earl of Salisbury (obt. 1196), by whom she had a daughter Ela, Countess of Salisbury in her own right. A fourth husband, Gilbert Malesmains, in 1198 held Cooling in right of his wife, together with the lands in England of her dower, viz. Westcote in Surrey, Kingsbury and Edgeware, Middlesex, Wooton, in Oxon, and Gatesden in Herts, and held them to the year of the conquest of Normandy by Philip Augustus, when they were in the King's hands as an escheat of the land of the Normans."—*T. Stapleton.* It does not appear that she had children by this last marriage ; but Gilbert's son by a former wife, Thomas Malesmains, married one of her daughters by her second husband, Joanna de Tillières. With her "he is recorded to have had, of the gift of King John, Hadlegh in Surrey, which same vill is entered as *terra*

Thome Málesmains, in the *Rotulus de valore terrorum Normanorum inceptis a° regni Regis Johannis sexto.*[*] At the date of this seizure by the King of the lands of the Normans in England, Malesmains was absent in the Holy Land, having had leave, in contemplation of the journey, to mortgage his lands for two years. Upon his return he embraced the side of King John, and in 1206 obtained his precept to have such seizin of his land as he had on the day he took his journey. In 1209 he accompanied William Earl of Salisbury, the King's brother and the husband of Ela, his wife's half sister, into Germany on the King's service, and subsequently in the wars of the Barons we find him firmly adhering to the Royal party. By his Letters Patent, given at Corfe in 1216, King John makes known that he has retained in his service Thomas Malesmains, and that he will reckon him as one of his bachelors, and restores to him his rights, viz. " the land which Fulk de Cantelupe holds in Burton " (Northants), " and the land which Ralph Gernon holds in Cumtum " (Compton, in Berkshire).—*Ibid.*

Sir Thomas' son, Sir Nicholas, is mentioned in 1233 as dividing with Ela Countess of Salisbury their grandmother's manor of Cooling. He can scarcely, I think, have been the same Nicholas Malesmains who, as Hasted tells us, was knighted sixty-seven years afterwards at the siege of Carlaverock. Nor can this second Sir Nicholas have been his heir, for he left only co-heiresses, of whom one married Robert de Plessis, a younger brother of John de Plessis, Earl of Warwick *jure uxoris:* and another—Petronella—firstly, Ralph de Toeni, and secondly, Sir Thomas de St. Omer.

One of this family, Henry Malesmains, " joining with Simon, Earl of Leicester, in rebellion against Hen. III., would have forfeited all his lands, had not the abbot of the adjoining monastery of Langdon interceded for him and gained his pardon ; for which service his descendant Sir John Malmains through gratitude gave the two manors of Apleton and Southwold, by his will, to the aforesaid monastery."—*Hasted.* Henry Malesmains was Sheriff of Kent at the death of Henry III.; and Sir John Malesmains and his son of the same name several times served as knights of the shire in the reigns of Edward II. and Edward III. The wife of the latter, Elizabeth Countess of Atholl, the daughter of Henry Lord Ferrers of Groby, is commemorated by a fine brass in Ashford Church. She died in 1375. The last Lord of Waldershare had passed away three years before, leaving an only daughter married to Henry Holland of Solton, near Dover ; and I can find no further mention of the name after 1440, when one of the family was still resident at Malmaines-in-Pluckley. Several of them lie buried in the Grey Friar's church in London.

" Malmains-Alkham formed part of the barony of Avranches, held as one

---

[*] " Gilbert de Tillières the elder held of the Honour of Clare the vills of Headley and Westcote, co. Surrey, and also inherited some land in Compton, co. Berks, which Henry II. had given to his father Gislebert Crispin, all of which inheritance vested in the descendants of the marriage with Alianor de Vitré."—*Ibid.*

knight's fee as of Dover Castle, by the performance of ward to it."—*Ibid.* One of the Malesmains was Constable of Dover under Richard II. There is a manor of Malmaines in Beacontree Hundred, Essex.—*Morant.*

Mortimere: de Mortus Mari; from Mortemer in the Pays de Caux, at the source of the river Eaulne; the Castle of Saint-Victor-en Caux was the *caput baroniæ.* The progenitor of this illustrious house was "Walter, Lord of St. Martin in Normandy, who about 920 married a niece of the Duchess Gunnora, the great-grandmother of the Conqueror. William de St. Martin, his son, was father of Roger, Lord of Mortimer, and of Ralph, Sire de Garenne, and of the Sire de St. Martin, from whom came the family of St. Martin in Normandy and England."—*The Norman People.* This pedigree is furnished by William de Jumièges, but has, like most pedigrees, been disputed. Roger, Sire de Mortemer, commanded the Norman army sent in 1054 to oppose the French under Count Eudo, who had seized and pillaged his own town of Mortemer. They "devoted the night to revelry, searching out the wine and drinking their fill;" but before daybreak the Normans had surrounded and fired the town, and the revellers awoke from their drunken sleep to find themselves penned in between burning walls. The Normans guarded the barriers, letting no one pass, and the Frenchmen, though they fought desperately "from the rising of the sun till three in the afternoon," were utterly discomfited and routed. "There was no varlet, be he ever so mean, but took some Frenchman prisoner, and seized two or three horses with their harness; nor was there a prison in all Normandy that was not full of Frenchmen."—*Wace.* The Duke sent a messenger with the tidings to the King of France; and the man, finding the whole camp asleep, climbed a tree, and "all night cried aloud"—

> "Franceiz ! Franceiz ! levez ! levez !
> Tenez vos veies, trop dormez !
> Alez vos amiz enterrer
> Ki sunt occis a Mortemer !"

Notwithstanding this signal victory, Roger de Mortemer was disgraced and banished for having sheltered in his castle one of the leaders of the French army, his own father-in-law the Count de Montdidier, but was pardoned before the Conquest, for he furnished sixty vessels to the invading fleet. He was himself too old to follow the Duke; but his son Ralph, according to Ordericus, held a command in the army.

Ralph de Mortemer, the founder of the splendid English lineage that conveyed to the House of York its title to the Crown, had inherited his father's renown, and was one of "the most puissant captains" of the Conqueror. Wace (who calls him Hue de Mortemer *) tells us how, with the Sires d'Auvilliers,

---

* Eyton says there is some evidence that old Roger had two other sons, Hugh and William; and they may probably have been in the battle. But Ralph was certainly the heir.

Onebec, and St. Clair, he stormed one of the Saxon outposts at Senlac, and " overthrew many." He was afterwards selected to take the field against Edric Sylvaticus, the Saxon thane who had obtained the aid of Griffith King of Wales, and proved himself the King's ablest lieutenant in the West. After a toilsome campaign, and a protracted siege of the castle of Wigmore, he brought Edric captive to the King in 1074; and received all Edric's lands in Shropshire and Herefordshire as his reward, as well as a large share of the forfeited estates of William Fitz Osbern, Earl of Hereford. Wigmore Castle, built by Fitz Osbern, was the head of his Herefordshire barony; and in Shropshire Cleobury (which had also been Fitz Osbern's) became Cleobury Mortimer, and was held by him as Seneschal of Salop. In Domesday one hundred and thirty-one manors are recorded as his property. Dugdale tells us that he commanded Henry I.'s forces at Tinchebray, and captured Courteheuse; but Ordericus gives a different account, and the story apparently originated with the canons of Wigmore. This Priory was founded in 1179 by his son Hugh, who ended his days there in 1185; and on the anniversary of his death, Roger, who succeeded him, endowed it "with a fruitful and spacious pasture, lying near the Abbey, called *The Treasure of Mortimer*," saying, "I have laid up my Treasure in that field, where Thieves cannot steal or dig, or moth corrupt."

Wigmore was the chief residence of the Mortimers, who were styled Lords of Wigmore, and as Barons Marcher, guarded a long line of castles on the Welsh frontier. They lived the turbulent and quarrelsome life of Border chieftains on debateable ground, engaged in unrelenting warfare with the Welsh, in feuds with their neighbours, and sometimes in rebellion against the King, though they remained unalterably loyal during both the baronial wars. Ralph II., in the time of Henry III., made himself so obnoxious to Llewellyn of Wales, that the Prince bestowed upon him as a peace-offering the hand of his daughter Gladuse Duy, with a great dowry. She was the widow of Reginald de Braose, and their son Roger married the heiress of her step-son, Maud de Braose, who brought him a share in the vast English and Irish inheritance of the Earls Mareschal, and a third part of the Honour of Braose,— " proper fuel for the future ambition of the House of Mortimer." To this Roger belongs the credit of having planned and carried out Prince Edward's escape from Hereford Castle. " Seeing his sovereign in such distress, he took no rest till he had contrived some way for their deliverance," and sent a swift horse to the Prince, bidding him get leave to ride out for recreation in the direction of Widmarsh "and that upon sight of a person mounted on a White Horse, at the foot of Tulington Hill and waving his Bonnet (which was the Lord of Croft, as it was said) he should hast towards him with all possible speed." The Prince obtained Montfort's permission " to try if the Horse were of use for the great Saddle," and having effectually wearied out the other horses, mounted a fresh one held in readiness by a boy bringing two swords sent to meet him by Mortimer, "and so turning himself to Robert de Ros, then his Keeper, and other by-standers, said, 'I have been in your custody for a while, but now I bid you farewell;' and so rode away" to Tulington. Roger met him with his banner displayed, and five hundred armed men at his back, turned back his pursuers, with great slaughter, to the very gates of Hereford; and brought him home to supper at Wigmore Castle. From thence was gathered together the army with which he fought and won the battle of Evesham, and replaced his father on the throne. After the victory of that day, on which Roger commanded the third division of the forces, "no privilege, reward, or honour was too great for him to ask, or the King to grant." Amongst other gifts, he received the forfeited Honour and Earldom of Oxford; but Robert de Vere resumed them after the *Dictum de Kenilworth*, though the indignant Mortimer, with the other Barons Marcher, fiercely opposed and denounced the injustice of taking away "what for their pains and fidelity had been given to them by the King." On the day that all his three sons were knighted by Edward I., he held a tournament at Kenilworth, "the like whereof was never before seen in England:"—a foretaste of the ostentatious splendour of his grandson the "King of Folly." He "sumptuously entertained one hundred Knights, and as many Ladies, for three days; and there began the Round Table" (so called because the enclosure in which they practised their feats of arms was round). "And, upon the Fourth Day, the Golden Lion, in sign of triumph, being yielded to him, he carried it (with all that company) to Warwick. The fame whereof being spred into Foreign Countreys, occasioned the Queen of Navarre to send unto him certain Wooden Bottles, bound with Golden Bars and Wax, under the pretence of Wine; which (in truth) were all filled with Gold; and for many ages after, kept in the Abbey of Wigmore. Whereupon, for the love of that Queen, he added a Carbuncle to his Arms." *

His son Edmund, summoned to parliament in 1294, was the first baron by writ in the family; and married a Spanish kinswoman of the Queen's. It was he who commanded the detachment that encountered and slew the heroic Llewellyn at Builth in 1282, and caused the unfortunate prince's head to be cut off and sent to the King. The next in succession was the Roger de Mortimer who became notorious as the insolent paramour of Queen Isabel. "He seems," says Eyton, "to have inherited and combined the worst qualities of the three races whose blood mingled in his veins, the Norman, the Castilian, and the Cambro-Briton;" and his career, "a mixture of violence and ambition, of pride and folly, of intrigue and treachery," fills an ignoble page in our annals. It is too well known to need recounting here: nor will I attempt to reckon up the sum of the favours, honours, and grants that he coveted and obtained. The task would be heavy; for "the

---

* The "carbuncle" of Navarre, a cross and saltire of chains, affixed to an annulet in the fess point, was a canting coat; such a chain being called in Navarre *una varra*, and in the patois of the country, the "u" being dropped, *na varra*.

truth is," says Dugdale, "this Mortimer bore such sway, that he got what he had a mind to;" and the grasp of his ambition seemed measureless. As the declared enemy of the Spencers, he had been sent to the Tower by Edward II., but contrived to administer a sleeping potion at a banquet to Sir Stephen de Segrave, the Constable, "escaped with a Cord," and joined the Queen in France. Sentence of banishment was pronounced against him; and £1,000 was offered to whoever would bring his body to the King, alive or dead. But when, not long after, he returned to England with the Queen, the Prince of Wales, and their triumphant party, the scene changed as by enchantment. His three sons received knighthood at the coronation of Edward III.; his youngest daughter Beatrix (the six others were already splendidly allied) was married to Edward Plantagenet, the eldest son of Thomas de Brotherton, Earl Marshal of England; and he himself became Justice of Wales, and Earl of March; a new title suggested by his great power on the Border. There, during a progress that the young King made in Wales, he entertained him magnificently in his castles of Ludlow and Wigmore, with hunting, tilting, and other pastimes. His arrogance and presumption grew with his advancement, and passed all bounds; "he waxed proud beyond measure," and aped Royalty, "so that his own son Geoffrey called him the King of Folly. He kept the Round Table of Knights in Wales, for a pride in imitation of King Arthur." At length his insolence became altogether unbearable, and all men were unanimous in their determination to get rid of him. The nobles of the Council, to whom he was specially odious, warned the King of the impending mischief, urging him "to take into account his own dishonour and damage;" and Edward commanded Sir William de Montacute to seize him in the castle of Nottingham, where he was then staying with the Queen-Mother. Montacute took with him two of the Bohuns, Sir Ralph de Stafford, Sir John de Nevill, and others, and demanded admission in the King's name of the Constable, Sir William Eland, who told them that the keys of the Castle gates were every night brought to Queen Isabel, who laid them under the pillow of her bed until the morning. But he showed them an underground passage through the rock (said to have been made by a Saxon king in the Danish times) that led by some stairs up to the Keep; and by this secret sallyport (since known as Mortimer's Hole) the barons entered the castle "in the dead time of the night," and surprised Mortimer in a room adjoining the Queen's chamber. Some say that his capture was effected with little noise and no resistance; according to others, his attendants fought desperately, and two of them were slain. The Queen, roused from her sleep, cried piteously "Bel Fitz, Bel Fitz, ayes Pitie du Gentil Mortimer!" but the King reserved him for a public and more shameful death. He was brought to trial for complicity in Edward II.'s murder at Berkeley Castle and on five other counts, and sentence was passed upon him (as it had been on the Spencers) without his even being heard in defence. He was executed on the common gallows at Smithfield, when his body was suffered to hang for two days and two nights, stark naked, before it received burial. No end could have been more utterly ignominious; yet " his descendants and lineal representatives in the seventh degree were two sceptred Kings."

The Earldom was never restored to his son; but it was held by his grandson and the three following generations, and with it were given back nearly all the forfeited estates, which had been granted to Montacute, the new Earl of Salisbury.

Edmund, third Earl of March, through whose famous match with a grand-daughter of Edward III., the House of the White Rose, as "next in blood and parentage," inherited its undoubted right to the throne, was the great grandson of Roger. He must have been, as Dugdale represents him, a youth "of singular knowledge and parts;" for at the age of eighteen he was employed to negotiate a peace with France, and succeeded so well, that he was sent to Scotland on a similar occasion. Before he was of age, he had achieved the highest fortune of his day, and become the husband of Philippa Plantagenet, the only child of Lionel of Antwerp, Duke of Clarence, by his wife Elizabeth de Burgh, the heiress of Ulster, whose own mother had inherited a third part of the Earldom of Gloucester as one of the last daughters of the famous house of De Clare. In her right he bore the titles of Earl of Ulster, and Lord of Clare and Connaught; and he was also Marshal of England. Richard II. appointed him in 1378 his Lieutenant in Ireland, and he "so tamed the Barbarousness of that rude people by destroying ten or eleven of their petty Kings, within the space of half a year," that he regained the whole of her lost territory of Ulster, and even enlarged it. He ruled Ireland for three years, and well-nigh solved the impossible problem of "reducing that Realme to quiet," not solely by the cogent argument of the sword, but by kindness, prudence, and affability. Unfortunately, he caught a chill while crossing a river, and died at Cork in 1381, when he was only twenty-nine years old. His will, enumerating his legacies, is a curious record of some of his possessions; the "Saltseller in the form of a Dogg," bequeathed to his daughter Elizabeth; his "Cup of a Tortois;" another little cup "made like the Body of a Hart with the head of an Eagle," given to his son-in-law Hotspur; and "his Sword adorned with Gold, which was the good King Edward's," with "the great Horn of Gold," left, "together with God's Blessing and his own," to his eldest son Roger. He had two other sons and two daughters by Philippa Plantagenet; Sir Edmund, married to Owen Glendower's daughter; Sir John, executed by Henry VI.; Elizabeth, Lady Percy, and afterwards Lady Camoys; and Philippa, who was successively Countess of Pembroke, Countess of Arundel, and Lady St. John.

Roger, fourth Earl, though then but eleven years of age, was appointed Lieutenant of Ireland shortly after his father's death; and in 1385 declared "heir presumptive to the Crown of this Realm." He, again, spent the better half of his life in his Irish government, and most often sword in hand, "till at last, too much relying on his own valour, he adventured himself before his Army in an Irish habit, and was unhappily slain at Kenlis," in 1398. He was in the very flower of his age—a year younger than his father had been at the time of his death; and left another child-heir, not more than six years old. He had married Alianor Holland, daughter of Thomas, second Earl of Kent, and sister of Thomas Duke of Surrey and of Edmund, the last Earl, whose co-heir she became; and was the father of four children; Edmund; Roger, who died early, s. p.; Anne; and Alianor.

The eldest son, Edmund, the fifth and last Earl of his name, was in ward to Henry Prince of Wales, and as "the rightful heir, by just descent, to the Crown of England," was so jealously watched and guarded, that all his early years were spent in captivity. According to Dugdale, Lady Le Despencer (his kinswoman through the De Clares) made a successful attempt to rescue him from the Prince's custody: but he was soon brought back to his prison-house. We are next told that he headed the Herefordshire men against Owen Glendower, and being defeated, "became his prisoner; soon after which, by allurement or terror he contracted marriage with the Daughter of Owen; and being thus in the hands of that great Rebell, was with him at the battle of Shrewsbury, where the King obtained a happy victory, and this Earl was then released. But upon St. Valentine's Day, 7 Hen. IV., by means of a false Key, he and his brother were both taken out of Windsor Castle and carried again to Owen, but yet shortly after recovered again." Dugdale here follows Holinshed, as both Shakespeare and Hume have done; but it seems likely that he has confounded the two Edmund Mortimers, and that it was the uncle who led the men of Hereford against Glendower, and not the young heir of the realm, then barely ten years old, and a State prisoner. Even if he was present at the battle, no child of that age could have confronted the formidable Glendower in the single combat described in "King Henry IV.":—

> "When on the gentle Severn's sedgy bank,
> In single opposition, hand to hand,
> He did confound the best part of an hour
> In changing hardiment with great Glendower."

The young Earl's wife was Anne, daughter of the Earl of Stafford, and it was, beyond all doubt, Sir Edmund Mortimer (Hotspur's brother-in-law) who married Glendower's daughter.[*] The escape from Windsor can, however, only refer to the former.

[*] Shakespeare's Lady Mortimer, of whom her husband says,

> "This is the deadly spite that angers me—
> My wife can speak no English—I no Welsh."

They are said to have settled in Scotland, and to have left descendants.

He was released from durance on the accession of Henry V. ; went with the King to the French wars, where he served under the renowned Earl of Salisbury, and was Lieutenant of Normandy in 1418. Henry VI., as soon as he came to the throne, appointed him Lieutenant of Ireland, as his father and grandfather had been ; and he died in 1424, when he was about twenty-four—the youngest of all his short-lived race. Yet Shakespeare, in his pathetic death-scene, represents him as an aged captive :

> " Even like a man new haléd from the rack,
> So fare my limbs with long imprisonment ;
> And these grey locks, the pursuivants of death,
> Nestor-like aged, in an age of care
> Argue the end of Edmund Mortimer."

This is dramatised from the following passage in Hall : " The last Earl of March of that name was long time restrained of his liberty, and finally waxed lame ;" which obviously refers to his imprisonment in childhood. It had probably affected his health—when he went to France for the first time with Henry V. he had to return home invalided—and may have tended to shorten his life ; but he certainly did not " in prison spend his pilgrimage."

His brother was already dead, and no children had been born of his marriage ; thus the representation of the house of Mortimer passed to his two sisters. Alianor, who had married a Courtenay, was childless ; and the entire inheritance —a vast aggregate of manors and castles in England, Ireland, and Wales— reverted to Anne, who, as the eldest born, became, in succession, to her brother, the heiress of the throne. She was the wife of Richard Plantagenet, Earl of Cambridge (a younger son of Edmund Duke of York), or rather, at that time, his widow, as he had been beheaded at Southampton in 1415 for conspiring against Henry V. Within thirty years of his death, their son Richard (who had succeeded his uncle as Duke of York) in open parliament claimed the crown, and commenced the long contention that was to cost so many lives, and all but exterminate the nobility of England.

No less than five other branches of the family attained baronial rank. Robert (son or brother of the first Hugh of Wigmore) obtained the great Honour of Richard's Castle through his wife Margery de Say, and held twenty-three knight's fees in Herefordshire and six in Worcestershire. His great grandson Hugh was summoned to parliament as Baron Mortimer of Richard's Castle in 1229, but left no male heir ; and Joan, his eldest daughter, carried Richard's Castle to Sir Richard Talbot, whose posterity held it for two generations. A younger brother of this Lord Mortimer, named William, became Lord Zouche of Mortimer (see *Souche*).

The Barons of Attilbergh in Norfolk descended from Robert de Mortimer, whose Lincolnshire estates were forfeited for rebellion against King John, and bestowed upon his kinsman of Richard's Castle. The first summoned to parliament was William, 25 Ed. I., who was taken prisoner in the French wars, and died at Paris. Constantine his son had license to castellate his house at Sculton, and also received a writ of summons; but it was not repeated to any of the descendants. The last spoken of by Dugdale is another Constantine, living in the reign of Henry IV.

The Mortimers of Chirke acquired their barony by a flagrant breach of faith. Griffith ap Madoc, who had taken part with Henry III. and Edward I. against his own countrymen, left his children under age at his death. Edward I. gave the wardship of Madoc, the eldest son, to John Earl Warren; and of Llewellyn, the younger, "to whose part the Lordships of Chirke and Nanheydwy fell, to Roger Mortimer, a younger Son to Roger Lord of Wigmore. Which Guardians forgetting the Service done by Griffith ap Madoc, so guarded these their Wards, that they never returned to their Possessions; and shortly after obtained these Lands to themselves by Charter." Thus ignobly enriched, Roger became a man of note and importance in his generation. He built a castle at Chirke; fought with Edward I. in Scotland and Gascony, and was a baron by writ in 1299. Edward II. loaded him with favours. He was made first Justice of North Wales; then Justice of all Wales; most of the Welsh castles were committed to his charge; and two of them—Blaynleveny and Dinas—were granted to him as a free gift in 1311. But ruin overtook him at last. He was one of the lords who passed sentence of banishment on the Spencers, and was sent to the Tower, where he remained till his death. His grandson John sold Chirke to the Earl of Arundel.

Dugdale tells us very little of the Barons of Chelmarsh. The first, Hugh, was a younger son of Ralph Lord Mortimer and the Welsh princess Gladuse Duy; and the husband of his father's ward, Agatha de Ferrers, who at length became one of the co-heirs of Walter Mareschal, Earl of Pembroke. "This line ended in the fourth generation in Females."

Mortimer is among the many great names that are now merged in the Royal family of England; but it still clings to some of the ancient manors of the family. Besides Cleobury Mortimer, we find Streatfield Mortimer in Berkshire, Worthy Mortimer in Hampshire, Woodham Mortimer in Essex, and Luton Mortimer in Bedfordshire.

Mortimaine: this evidently stands for Mortaine, as it appears in Leland's copy, joined to the preceding name, "Mortaine et Mortimer." See *Morton.*

Muse. Roger Muse occurs in the Norman Exchequer Rolls 1198–1203; and Godfridus de la Mosca held a fief from Philip Augustus of the honour of Malherbe (Mém. Soc. Ant. Nor. v. 176). In England, Isabel Mus is found in the Hundred Rolls, about 1272; John le Mous, or Mows, of Wiltshire, in Palgrave's Parliamentary Writs 1307-25, and Roger Mus, and John de Muse,

Essex, circa 1272.—*Rotuli Hundredorum.* In 1309, Thomas Mus de Arkilgarth, chaplain, was, with several others, prosecuted by Eve de Faggardgill of Arkilgarth in Richmondshire, for the murder of her husband.—*Harrison's Yorkshire.* William Peverel of Dover's charter to Shrewsbury Abbey is witnessed by William de Musca.—*Mon. Angli.* Another William de Musca (or the same?) held half a knight's fee of William de Ros in Northamptonshire.— *Testa de Nevill.* One of the persecuted Templars in 1309 was Brother Philip de Mewes, who, "being advised and earnestly exhorted to abandon his religious profession, replied that he would rather die than do so."—*Addison's Knight Templars.*

Marteine. Martin, Sire of Tour (four miles from Bayeux, not Tours, as ·Dugdale gives it), came over with William of Normandy in 1066; and conquered the territory of Kemeys in Pembrokeshire. It was erected into a Palatine Barony, which he governed as Lord Marcher, having his castle at Newport, where its ruins still exist. He was a great benefactor to religious houses, and began the foundation of a Benedictine Abbey at St. Dogmael's, annexing it as a cell to the Monastery of Tyrone in France. The endowment was given by his son Robert Fitz Martin, whose charter is witnessed by Henry I., who afterwards granted a further confirmation charter. In the next generation, William Fitz Martin married a Welsh princess, the daughter of Rhys-ap-Griffith, sovereign of South Wales, "from whom he received great injury, for by force of arms he took from him his strong castle of Llanhever, in Kemeys-Land, contrary to his oath and solemn promise of peace and friendship." William's grandson acquired the honour of Barnstaple by his marriage with Maud, the daughter of Guy de Brian and Eva his wife, heiress of Henry de Tracy, Baron of Barnstaple. She brought him numerous estates in Devonshire, where he already had great possessions; for "shortly after Domesday, Robert Fitz Martin, enjoyed the honour of Dertington, and other lands, once William de Falaise's."—*Pole's Devon.* They had three sons; Nicholas, who left only a daughter; Colinetus; and Robert. Colinetus, who thus became the heir, was the father of Sir William Martin, engaged in the Scottish wars, and "constantly summoned to every parliament as Baron of Kemeys from 17 Ed. I. to 16 Ed. II., in which year he died." His son followed him to the grave in the ensuing year, dying s. p.; and two sister-heiresses, Eleanor de Columbers and Joan de Audley, divided his lands. " But the name of Martin was still kept up by Robert, the younger son, from whom are lineally descended the Martins of Seaborough, and those of Athelhampton in Dorsetshire."—*Collinson's Somerset.* They had a considerable estate in Somerset-shire, where Compton-Martin retains their name; and in Devonshire " Comb-Martin and another Martin will inform you of their antiquity."

Of the Martins of Seaborough I can find no account. Those of Athelhampton had their seat at Admiston Hall, and ended with Nicholas Martin, who died on the road to London, whither he had been persuaded to go—much against his will—to re-settle his estates. He left two daughters and co-heiresses, and lies buried in Piddlestown Church; with this inscription:

> "Here lies Nicholas, the first, and Martin, the last,
> Good-night, Nicholas."

But it was not good-night, Martin: for a younger son of this house, who had settled at Long Melford in Suffolk as far back as the early part of the fifteenth century, is yet represented in the male line. One of his descendants, Roger Martin, who in Queen. Mary's time lived to be nearly one hundred, was so remarkable for his charity that, "when he declined with age, and was not able to go far from home, he had a whistle to his cane by which he called the poor to him." In this changed world of the nineteenth century—the age of universal begging—it is hard to recognize the necessity of such a mode of summons. A subsequent Roger suffered grievously for his loyalty during the Civil War, and presented a petition for redress to both Houses of Parliament, setting forth that "he and his ancestors had quietly lived amongst their neighbours for nigh upon three hundred years." He died before the Restoration; but his son received a baronetcy in 1667, which is now extinct. Another, however, still survives, granted in 1791 to Henry Martin, belonging to a junior branch of the family.

Mountbother; or Mountbocher; Duchesne preserves the correct version; though in Normandy (where the name remained up to the present century), it is spelt Montbourcher. Henriette de Montbourcher, born 1672, was the heiress of the Marquisates of De la Moussaye and Du Bordage, and married François, first Duc de Coigny, Marshal of France. They bore *D'or à trois marmites de gueules* in Normandy; and these same red pitchers are shown on the shield of Sir Bertram de Montboucher, who led the assault at the siege of Carlaverock in 1300.

> "La vi-je tout primer venir
> Le bon Bertram de Montbouchier,
> De goules furent trois pichier
> En son escu de argent luisant,
> En le ourle noire li besant."

He is computed to have been then about thirty-six years of age, and was the second of six Bertrams de Montboucher that followed each other in direct lineal succession. It is stated that he belonged to Sussex; but on receiving from Edward II. the Northumbrian manor of Syhal, there took up his abode, and about 1309 married a great North-country heiress, Joan, the daughter of Guiscard de Charron. She endowed him with Beamish (Beaumeys) Tanfield, &c., in the county of Durham, and Sutton-on-Trent in Nottinghamshire. This latter estate, brought to her grandfather by one of the five coheirs of Sir Richard de Sutton, had by him been settled on Guiscard, his son by a second wife; and thus Joan, although representing the blood of the Charrons, found no place in the lineage of the Suttons. She and her husband rendered £20 a year for the manor, with a red, rose at Midsummer.*—v. *Thoroton's Notts.* Their son, Bertram III., was a leading man in Northumberland, serving three times as knight of the shire, and four times as Sheriff in 1374, 1377, 1379. and 1380; and built one of the towers—still known as Mont Boucher Tower—of the town wall of the New Castle on Tyne, that was to become the great emporium of the North. He married Isabel de Willoughby, and died in 1388, leaving, besides a son, Bertram IV., a daughter, named after her mother, and twice married, first to Sir Henry Heton, and secondly to Robert Harbottle, who survived to be the last representative of the family. For, though Bertram IV. was duly succeeded by Bertram V., and Bertram V. by Bertram VI., the line failed with the latter, who died s. p. in 1425. His great aunt Isabel then inherited the estate; and dying herself in the following year, transmitted it to her great-grandson, Robert Harbottle.

Leland speaks of this family in his *Itinerary*: "Mounbowcher was a Man of fair Landes in Northumbrelande; and Doctor Davelle told me that the Hospitale yn Newcastle hath yet Landes of his gifte." Other incidental notices of it are to be met with. Collins mentions a Sir Bartholomew de Mont Boucher, of very early date, whose daughter Philippa was the wife of Sir Robert de Maners, from whom he derives the Dukes of Rutland. Sir Edmund Pierrepont, in the time of Edward III., married Joan, sole daughter and heir of Sir George de Montboucher. John Monboucher, in 1408, died seized of the manor of Skipwith-cum-Menthorpe, which he held in right of Elizabeth his wife.—*Burton's Mon. Ebor.*

Mountsoler; for Montsorel, as Leland gives it in his list. This name is familiar to us as belonging to a place in Leicestershire, which "though now only famous as a market town, once boasted a strong and stately castle on its steep and craggy hill overhanging the river Soar."—*Nichols.* This castle, built probably by Hugh Lupus, was one of the strongholds of the Earls of Chester, who afterwards granted it to the Earls of Leicester; and Robert Blanchemains, third Earl, surrendered it to the King in 1174. Saer de Quincy was appointed Castellan by King John in 1213, but having joined the rebellious barons against Henry III., and been taken prisoner at the battle of Lincoln, Montsorrell was besieged and captured by the Royal troops, and "by the King's command, and the ready help of the neighbourhood, entirely razed to the ground, as a nest of the Devil and den of thieves and robbers." Not a single vestige of it now remains. The etymology of the name has given rise to a variety of fanciful conjectures, such as Mount Sore-hill (*difficile, fâcheux*), &c.; and the suggestion adopted by the historian of the county—Mount-Soar-Hill—can scarcely, I think, be accepted as satisfactory.

There is no evidence that the family of Montsorel took their name from this place any more than the Arundells derived theirs from the famous castle on the

---

* Her grandson, in 1390, held Pokerley, co. Durham, by one clove gilliflower, due on St. Cuthbert's Day.

Arun. They had apparently no connection with it at all; [*] and were no doubt a French family brought over in the Conqueror's train. "Dominus de Montesorel" is among the nobles of Touraine included in Duchesne's *Nomina militum ferentium bannerias*, and probably derived his name from Montsoreau, on the Loire (not far from Saumur), afterwards the seat of that cruel Comte de Montsoreau who carried out' the sanguinary decrees of Charles IX. against the Protestants of Anjou.

The name first occurs in the *Liber Niger.* Alured de Montsorell, in 1165, held three knight's fees of old feoffment in Dorset of Gerbert de Perci; and Robert de Montsorell part of one of Cerne Abbey, in the same county. In the following century, Thomas de Musorel held of the fee of Robert de Newburgh in the Hundred of Poorstock, Dorset.—*Testa de Nevill.* This is the last notice of them there. Jacob and William Mûsorel are found in Oxfordshire about 1272, and Henry Monsorel in Wiltshire (Rotuli Hundredorum), where Mount Sorrel —now abbreviated to Mouse Hill—recalls the name. Philip Montsorel was seated at White-Lackington, Somersetshire, in 1316: and Richard de Montsorel, in 1325, having been pressed to serve as a foot-soldier in Gascony, deserted thence after receiving his pay. "The Sheriff of the City of London was commanded to take him into custody."—*Palgrave's Parl. Writs.* Thomas de Montsorel of Somersetshire was one of the manucaptors (sureties) for the good behaviour of John de Raleigh of Nettlecomb, on his discharge from imprisonment as an adherent of the Earl of Lancaster, and also for the payment of the fine imposed upon him. This Thomas was summoned to the great Council at Westminster held in 1324 on the Wednesday next after Ascension Day.—*Ibid.* In a perambulation of the forests of Somersetshire, made in 1297, mention is made of "a certain hermitage, with its appurtenances, in the tenure of Thomas de Montsorell and John de Asselonde."—*Collinson's Somerset.* John de Muntsorel held of William de Sifrewast at Ewelme in Oxfordshire.—*Testa de Nevill.* Adam de Mont Sorel also appears as a former tenant in Berkshire.

Maleuile: from Esmaleville or Malaville, a barony in the Pays de Caux. "Guillaume de Malleville" is on the Dives Roll, and appears in Domesday as William de Smalavilla, holding lands in Suffolk. "Robert de Malavilla, temp. Henry I., witnessed a charter in Yorkshire (Mon. Angl. i. 660), and one of Roger de Poitou (Ibid.). Roger de Malavilla held a fief 1165 from William de Ros: and other branches were seated in Bucks and Scotland."—*The Norman People.* Galfrid de Maleville settled under David I. on some lands near Edinburgh to which he gave his name; and was the first Justiciary of Scotland on record. In the following reign, he founded the church of Maleville, and in

[*] Once only I find the name of Robert Fitz de Monte Sorello as witness to a deed of Margaret de Quincy, Countess of Winton, the sister of Robert Fitz-Parnel, who died in 1204. This Robert Fitz would seem to have been a resident in the town : and is elsewhere styled Rob' Phis.

grateful memory of his dead master, granted it to the monks of Dunfermline for the salvation of the souls, not only of himself and his ancestors, but of David I. and his son Malcolm IV., stipulating that "the monks should uphold a perpetual light before the sepulchres of the said kings." He left three sons: 1. Gregory, who founded a line that ended in the latter part of the fourteenth century, when the lands of Melville devolved upon Agnes, the wife of Sir John Ross; 2. Philip, whose posterity survived in the male line till 1468; 3. Walter, ancestor of the Earls of Melville. Walter's descendants were settled at Raith, in the co. of Fife, for many successive generations. Sir James Melville, who held the barony of Hallhill in that county, was ambassador from Mary Queen of Scots to Elizabeth, and afterwards in the household of her son, an accomplished statesman and courtier, who wrote the 'Memoirs' so often quoted in the histories of that time. His brother, Sir Robert, was also sent ambassador to England on two several occasions; the second time to endeavour to prevent the execution of the Scottish Queen; and spoke in her behalf with "such brave and stout language before the Council that Elizabeth threatened his life." In 1616, at the ripe age of eighty-nine, he was created Lord Melville of Monymaill, and survived to wear his new honours for five years. George, fourth Lord, was a zealous presbyterian, and had to fly to Holland on the discovery of the Rye-house plot, in which he had been implicated, thereby forfeiting the whole of his estates. He accompanied the Duke of Monmouth on his disastrous expedition in 1685, and had the good fortune again to escape abroad, and to return with the Prince of Orange three years later. His forfeiture was at once rescinded; and in 1690 he received the title of Earl of Melville from the new King, whom he subsequently served as Secretary of State, Keeper of the Privy Seal, and President of the Council. His wife, Catherine Leslie, was the grand-daughter of the famous Puritan General trained under Gustavus Adolphus (in whose service he attained the rank of Field Marshal), who commanded the Scottish army that invaded England in 1640, and routed the Royalists at Newbury. He was a cadet of the house of Rothes, and is described as "an unlettered soldier of fortune, of an advanced age, a diminutive size, and a distorted person." His soldiers bore on their colours the crown and covenant of Christ; and, true to his Swedish traditions, were "summoned by drums to sermon, and their tents resounded at dawn and sunset with psalms and prayers." On the conclusion of the treaty of Ripon in 1641, he was created by the parliament Lord Balgonie, and Earl of Leven. He was succeeded by a grandson and two great grand-daughters, but on the death of the last Countess in 1706, the title reverted to the son of his grand-daughter Catherine, David, second Earl of Melville, who thus united the two Earldoms that remain the heritage of his descendants.

Sir Walter Scott tells a ghastly story respecting one of this family, Melville of Glenbervie, who was Sheriff of the Mearns in the reign of James I. (of Scotland). "He bore his faculties so harshly, that he became detested by the barons of the country. Reiterated complaints of his conduct having been made to James I. (or, as others say, to the Duke of Albany), the monarch answered, in a moment of unguarded impatience, 'Sorrow gin the Sheriff were sodden and supped in broo!' The complainers retired perfectly satisfied. Shortly after, the Lairds of Arbuthnot, Mather, Laureston and Pittaraw, decoyed Melville to the top of the hill of Garvoch, above Laurencekirk, under pretence of a great hunting party. Upon this place (still called the Sheriff's Pot) the barons had prepared a fire and a boiling cauldron, into which they plunged the unlucky sheriff. After he was *sodden* (as the King termed it) for a sufficient time, the savages, that they might literally observe the royal mandate, concluded the scene of abomination by actually partaking of this hell-broth.

" The lairds were all outlawed for this offence : and Barclay, one of their number, to screen himself from justice, erected the kaim (fortress) of Mather, which stands upon a rocky and almost inaccessible peninsula, overhanging the German Ocean. The Laird of Arbuthnot is said to have eluded the royal vengeance by claiming the benefit of the law of clan Macduff,* and a pardon, or perhaps a deed of replegiation, founded upon that law, is said to be still extant among the records of the Viscount of Arbuthnot."

Malet. No figure stands out more vividly in the great battle of the Conquest than does " Guillame whom they call Malet," as Wace suggests for his bravery. But his name was in fact derived from a Norse ancestor. He was Baron of Gerardivilla or Graville, near Havre, and probably descended from " Gerard, a Scandinavian prince, one of the companions of Rollo, who gave his name to his fief, as his son (or grandson) Maleth, did to his posterity. Robert, the son of Maleth, about 990 united with Osbern de Longueville, William de Breteuil, Gilbert de Menill, and others, in giving the church of Pictariville to religious uses. The gift was confirmed by his family (Gall. Christ. xi. Instr. 139). William Maleth witnessed a charter before the Conquest (Ibid. xi. 328)."—*The Norman People.* The family was of great account in the Duchy :

> "Les Malets et les Marteaux
> Sont les plus nobles de Caux."

---

* " When the revolution was accomplished, in which Macbeth was dethroned and slain, Malcolm, sensible of the high services of the Thane of Fife, is said to have promised to grant the first three requests he should make. Macduff accordingly demanded (and obtained), 1st, that he and his successors, Lords of Fife, should place the crown on the King's head at the coronation (see Vol. i., p. 215) ; 2ndly, that they should lead the vanguard of the army whenever the royal banner was displayed ; and lastly, this privilege of the clan Macduff, whereby any person, being related to Macduff within the ninth degree, and having committed homicide in *chaude mêlé* (without premeditation) should, upon flying to Macduff's Cross, and paying a certain fine, obtain remission of their guilt." This cross, which was near Lindores (on the march dividing Fife from Stratherne), was destroyed by John Knox.

It is proved beyond doubt that William Malet had English·blood in his veins: His mother, it is believed, was an Englishwoman, though no one exactly knows who she was. It has been suggested that she was a daughter of Earl Leofric and the famous Godiva, "for it was doubtless through William Malet the Earls of Chester had their descent from the old Earls of Mercia, of which they boasted, but it seems they never knew correctly how, nor has any genealogist since entirely explained the mystery."—*A. S. Ellis.*

But if Malet's name was not given him in honour of his courage, he was none the less emphatically the "chevalliers durs e vaillanz" that Benoît de S. More terms him, and his feats of arms at Senlac are eulogized in the Roman de Rou. "He threw himself boldly in the midst : with his flaming sword he terrified the English. But they pierced his shield and killed his horse, and he would have been slain himself, when the Sire de Montfort and William de Vez Pont came up with a strong force, and gallantly rescued him, though with the loss of many of their men, and mounted him on a fresh horse." It was to him that, at the close of the hard-fought day, the Conqueror gave in charge the dead body of Harold, "to provide for its decent interment :" and he accordingly escorted the remains of the fallen King to the unconsecrated burial place on the cliffs of Hastings, where, according to the cruel irony of his epitaph, he was to watch the shore and sea he had so lately guarded. William Malet was probably selected for this melancholy office because, as Guy de Poitiers tells us, he was "partly English and partly Norman," and *Compater Haraldi :* that is, joint sponsor or *compère* with the English King. According to Saxon custom, they had thus become "God-syb," or relations in God.*

He followed the Conqueror on his expedition to the North; was present at the surrender of York : and with Gilbert de Gand and Robert Fitz Richard, took charge of the conquered city with its new Norman garrison. We next find him Sheriff of the county, with extensive grants of land; and Constable of the newly-built castle of York, where, in the autumn of 1068, he was besieged by the Northumbrians under the Saxon prince Edgar. The townsmen were disaffected, and he was threatened from within as well as from without. He sent word to the King that "he must surrender unless help came quickly :" and the King himself hastened to his rescue, defeated the insurgents, and fortified York with a second fortress. In the following year, when the Danes landed in England, William Malet and Gilbert de Gand were still in command of the city; but this time either strangely over-rated their own strength, or under-valued their opponents. Far from asking for aid, they told the King they could hold out for a year as they were : and "this message, it appears, was actually sent after Waltheoff, Edgar, and the rest had joined the Danish fleet in the Humber."—*Freeman.*

---

* In Brazil, to this day, the godfather and godmother of the same child, called "Compadre" and "Comadre," cannot marry without violating public opinion.

They prepared for a fresh leaguer: and lest the enemy should use the materials of the adjoining houses to fill up the Castle ditch, fired those that were nearest at hand. The flames spread till the whole city was ablaze and the greater part of it destroyed. When, two days later, the Danes drew nigh, the garrison sallied forth to meet them in the burning streets, and fought desperately to cut their way out. But Earl Waltheoff held York gate with his terrible battle-axe, and no man might pass through·alive. One hundred Normans are said to have fallen by his single hand, and three thousand were slain in all. Gilbert de Gand, and William Malet —with whom were his wife and two of his children—alone were spared for the· sake of their ransoms.

Two years after this great disaster, William Malet, as appears from a passage in Domesday, "died while in the King's service in the Marshes" of Ely, during the beleaguering of Hereward, as Mr. Freeman infers. By his wife Hesilia, daughter of Gilbert Crispin, he left three sons: 1. Robert, his successor: 2. William, who held the Norman barony, and died a monk at Bec: and 3. Gilbert, ancestor of the Malets of Somersetshire. His daughter Beatrix married William de Arches; and it is suggested by Mr. Ellis, that the famous Countess Lucy, who was three times married, first to Ivo Taillebois; secondly to Roger Fitz Gerald; and thirdly to Ranulph Earl of Chester, was another daughter of his. But in 1152, her son Earl Ranulph, "obtained the Honour of Eia as Robert·Malet his mother's uncle held it." Had she been William's daughter, she must have been Robert's sister: unless, indeed, as Mr. Stapleton and others have supposed, there were two Countesses Lucy, mother and daughter.

Robert succeeded to his father's barony,* and appears in Domesday as one of the greatest landed proprietors in England. With the Honour of Eye, he held two hundred and twenty-one manors in the county of Suffolk alone; and founded a Priory near his castle as a cell to the Norman Abbey of Bernai. He was Lord Great Chamberlain to Henry I., and for some short time high in favour at Court, but having taken part with Duke Robert lost his life and fortune in his cause. He was killed in 1106 at Tinchebrai: the honour of Eye escheated to the Crown, and the office of Great Chamberlain was granted to Alberic de Vere.

The Somersetshire estates, however, appear to have been restored either by Stephen or Henry II., and in 1168 William Malet of Shepton Malet held twenty-two knight's fees in the county, twelve of them of the Abbot of Glastonbury. Collinson derives him from Gilbert Malet, and he is, through his second son Hugh, the direct ancestor of the present house.

The eldest, William, whose *caput baroniæ* was Cury-Malet, was, as Lord Lytton informs us, "one of the twenty-five illustrious conservators of Magna

* According to Dugdale, William Malet bore a much higher title, though it appears not to have been hereditary. "This William was a witness to the Charter of King William the Conqueror, made to the Dean and Canons of St. Martins le Grand, in London, and subscribed next to the Earles, having then the title of Princeps."

Charta," and suffered excommunication in addition to forfeiture. "A short time before his death, he made his peace with the King, who, on his decease, compelled the husbands of his daughters, Hugh de Vivonne, who had married Mabel, and Robert de Mucegros, who had married Helewise, to pay a fine of two thousand marks! This Helewise afterwards married Sir Hugh Poyntz, and between these two coheirs the Barony of Malet was divided, Shepton going to Hugh de Vivonne and Cury to Sir Hugh Poyntz."—*Phelps' Somerset.*

Hugh, the younger son, took the name of Fitchett, "during the disgrace of his family," says Collinson; but more probably from his marriage with an heiress, as the coat of Fitchett appears among the family quarterings. Moreover, his son continued to bear it, and it was his grandson Baldwin who resumed the name of Malet. For a long series of generations they were seated at Enmore in Somersetshire, which passed away through Elizabeth Malet to Wilmot Earl of Rochester in 1680. The representation of the house then reverted to the posterity of Baldwin Malet, solicitor to Henry VIII., who, having married two Devonshire heiresses in succession, settled in that county. His great grandson Sir Thomas, of Poyntington in Somerset, received a patent of baronetage from Charles II., but suffered it to lie dormant; and the existing title dates only from 1791. Their present seat, Wilbury in Wiltshire, was bought in 1803. Their coat of arms, *Azure* three escallops *Or*, is, according to Sir W. Pole, that of the Deandoms of Devonshire, derived through an heiress. The ancient bearing of the Malets, three buckles, fibulæ or *fermails*, was no doubt allusive, as the diminutive of *fermails* would be *fermaillets.* Robert Malet, temp. Ed. I., bore *Argent* three fermeaux *Sable* (Harl. MS. 6137): and the coat of the Malets of Lincolnshire (formerly to be seen in a stained glass window in Irby Church) *Gules*, three buckles *Or*, two and one, was the same as that of the Norman Sires de Graville. These Malets descended from Durand Malet, who appears in Domesday as a tenant in chief in Lincolnshire, and is believed to have been the first Lord Malet's brother. They continued at Irby for many generations.

In Normandy, as in England, this long descended house is still represented by heirs male; though the elder line, holding the old Scandinavian fief of which it was wont to be said—

> " Syre en Graville premier
> Que roy en France : "

ended in 1516 with Louis Malet, Admiral of France and Governor of Normandy.

Mounteney, or Montigny, from a place of that name near Falaise, in Normandy. " Roger de Montigny gave lands to St. Vigor's, Cerisy, temp. William I. (Mon. i. 961) : and in Henry I.'s reign William de Montigny married a daughter and co-heir of Jordan Briset, a great baron of Essex (Mon. ii. 505)."—*The Norman People.* Sir Arnold Mounteney witnesses John Fitz Matthew

Brito's grant to Worksop Abbey. We find the family from an early date in Yorkshire. "Bartholomew de Sancta Maria, grandson of Pagan" (a contemporary of the Conqueror's) "left three sisters as his coheirs. Sibil, the second, married Jordan de Reneville, one of the subinfeudatories of the Baron of Hallamshire, and holding under him Cowley, and the part of the parish of Ecclesfield abutting upon Kimberworth. She had two daughters and coheirs,. Margaret, who married Thomas Mounteney, by which marriage the Mounteneys acquired Cowley; and Alice who married Thomas de Bella Acquâ."—*Hunter's South Yorkshire.* Alice (sometimes called Aliena) de Bellew, was childless, and Margaret became sole heir. The name of her husband is wrongly given. He was Sir Robert, the son of Arnold de Monteney, who had married a daughter of Gerard de Furnival and the Louvetot heiress, and held the estate of Shiercliffe of the castle and manor of Sheffield. The Monteneys obtained the King's license to make a park round their house at Shiercliffe, and enjoyed certain manorial privileges. At their other manor of Cowley they had "great woods and abundance of redd deare, and a stately castle-like house moated about, pulled down not long since by the Earl of Salop after he had purchased the land."—*Dodsworth.*

Sir Robert and Margaret de Reneville had two sons, Robert, and Thomas; but in neither case did their line continue for more than another generation. Robert's son left a daughter called Constance, the wife of John de Bosvile; and Thomas's son, another daughter, Joan—apparently the heiress of the family—married to Thomas, Lord Furnival, surnamed the Hasty.[*] "In her widowhood she resumed her maiden name. It is presumed that she entered into second nuptials. This is certain, that Thomas Lord Furnival, her husband, died without issue; yet in a deed preserved by Dugdale and dated 15 Ric. II. she acknowledges a son John de Mounteney, afterwards a knight, and her successor at Cowley and Shiercliffe."—*Hunter's Hallamshire.* The posterity of this John remained in Yorkshire till late in the seventeenth century. The elder line expired in the time of Henry VIII., when Barbara Mounteney, at length sole heiress, brought Cowley and Shiercliffe to Thomas Thwaites, who sold them to George, Earl of Shrewsbury. But some descendants of one of her great uncles were to be found at Wheatley and Rotherham for more than one hundred years after this.

The family were of higher antiquity and no less importance, in the Eastern Counties, where they had originally settled. Robert de Mounteney, of Norfolk, held three fees in 1161 from Richard de Lucy, whose daughter Dionysia he had married; and one fee of old feoffment as Lord of Beeston. His son Sir Arnold sealed with a bend between six martlets.—*Blomefield.* This was the coat of the

---

[*] A missal with many heraldic decorations, executed by one of the illuminators of the day for this Joan, is made the subject of a particular bequest by her descendant Thomas Mounteney of Wheatley in 1499 :—*unum primarium cum armis meis pictis.*

knight who settled in Hallamshire, who I have no doubt must have been the same Sir Arnold; all the more as he is followed by his son Robert. But in the succeeding descents the Christian names do not tally; and I conclude that it was a younger brother of Robert that inherited the Norfolk property. His line ended in 1313: and the heiress—another Dionysia—married Hugh de Vere.

In Essex they were seated at Ging-Mounteney, or Mountney's-ing (from Ing, a Saxon word signifying meadow or pasture, vulgarly Munnassing) from about the time of Stephen, when Robert de Mounteney witnessed the foundation charter of Thobie Priory. " He is supposed to have been the son of Læcia, eldest daughter of Jordan de Briesete, founder of the Hospital of St. John of Jerusalem near West Smithfield, London. His son was Eustace."—*Morant's Essex.* Dugdale thus recounts the death of one of his descendants.

"In 1252, there was a notable Tournament at Walden, wherein Roger de Leiburne encountered with Ernauld de Mountenei, a valiant Knight, and unhappily ran his lance into his throat under his helmet, it wanting a collar; whereupon Mountenei fell from his horse and died instantly, insomuch, as it was then supposed by some, that in regard his lance had not a socket upon the point, he did it purposely in revenge of a broken leg he had received from Mountenei, tilting with him in a former tournament." Another of them, Robert de Mounteny, "was presented at Chelmsford in 1254 or 1255 for not taking upon him the order of knighthood. Either he or his son, Sir Robert de Mounteney, died 15 Ed. I., holding Ging Mounteney of the Earl of Gloucester and also Mountney's in Elmdon. Ernulph, or Arnulph, afterwards created a Knight Banneret, was his son and heir," and gave his name to Arnold's manor, where his seat is said to have been. Sir John, who founded a chantry in Chelmsford churchyard, is the next mentioned; a Sir Robert held in 1375; and in 1417 William de Mounteney obtained of Henry V. free warren in "Yenge Mountenay." "In this family," continues Morant, "it continued till after Henry VIII.'s reign. John Mounteney, who died 1528, left a son and heir William, then thirty years old. About the beginning of Queen Elizabeth's reign the manor of Ging-Mounteney had changed hands."

Monfichet; from Montfiquet, in the arrondissement of Bayeux, said to be so named from their Scandinavian ancestor. "The castle of Monfiquet long remained, as well as the church of St. Catherine in the castle, a foundation of this family. Robert, surnamed Guernon, Baron of Montfichet, about 1050 witnessed a charter of Duke William (Gall. Christ. XI. Instr. 229). He had issue, first, William de Monfichet, who died s. p. when the barony devolved on William, the son of his brother; secondly, Robert Guernon or Gernon, who held a great barony in Essex, &c., 1086. From his elder son, William de Montfichet descended the Barons Montfichet of that name, whose seats were at Stansted Montfichet, Essex, and Montfichet Tower, London, of which city they were hereditary standard bearers and military chiefs in time of war." *—*The Norman People.* Dugdale, quoting the *Monasticon,* furnishes us with another and altogether fantastic genealogy. "It is reported of Gilbert de Monfichet, a Roman by birth, and Kinsman to William, Duke of Normandy, that he ever entertained that Duke in his House, when he came to the Court of Rome.† And, being privy to all his Councils, especially to that design of King Edward, to make him his Successor in the Realm of England, he brought with him a great strength, and fought stoutly on his behalf in that famous Battle against King Harold; as also afterwards against those who did not submit." For these services he obtained large grants, and "gave to one David, a Priest (but a Scot by birth, whom he specially loved) a certain place called Tremhale, whereon to build a Church, and other Edifices for a Monastery: and having so done, returned to Rome, leaving what he had so got in England, to his son Richard.

"Which Richard, when he attained to Man's Estate, travelled to Rome; and being a person of extraordinary strength, obtained much fame in casting a stone, no Man being able to do the like: In memory whereof certain Pillars of Brass were set up to show the distance."

M. le Prevost calls Gilbert de Montfichet "one of the most authentic personages that can be named as assisting at the battle of Hastings"; but I can find no other mention of him, and, contrary to practice, the Christian name of "De Monfiquet" is left out on the Dives Roll. As regards the Priory for Benedictine canons at Thremhall, Morant asserts that it was only founded in the thirteenth century by the last Baron of Stansted.

Counting the Robert Guernon or Greno of Domesday there were in all five generations of this house: William, who in 1135 founded Stratford-Langthorne Abbey in his lordship of West Ham; Gilbert, the founder of another Abbey in Buckinghamshire, who held forty-eight knight's fees in 1165; and two Richards, father and son. The first was Forester of Essex, with the custody of Havering, and all the King's other houses in the Forest, Constable of Hertford, and Sheriff of that shire and Essex in 1201, two years before his death. The second Richard was a leader under Simon de Montfort in the Baronial war, and one of the twenty-five nobles chosen to govern the realm. "And in 18 John, with Robert Fitz Walter, went over into France for more aid. Nor returned he to his due obedience, upon the death of King John, as many other did; but continuing still in arms with the fiercest, was taken prisoner in the battle of Lincoln, 1 Hen. III. Moreover after this, being a person of a haughty spirit, he was in

---

* This is an error. The office of Chief Banneret of London was held in fee by the chastiliary of Castle Baynard—*Blount's Tenures.* (See *Baynard.*)

† This must be wholly imaginary. "Not only is there no proof that William the Conqueror ever was at Rome, but every presumption is against it."—*The Conqueror and his Companions,* by J. R. Planché.

the Tourneament at Blithe in 7 Hen. III., contrary to the King's prohibition;' for which, his Lands were seised. But, afterwards, he became of a better temper."—*Dugdale.* Accordingly, in 1236 we find him Justiciar of the King's Forests in nineteen different counties; and five years later Sheriff of Essex, and Governor of Hertford Castle, as his father had been. He died s. p. about 1257: and his "noble inheritance" was divided between his three sisters: Margery, married to Hugh de Bolebec in Northumberland, who had Stansted Hall: Aveline, married to William de Forz, Earl of Albemarle; and Philippa, married to Hugh de Playz.

The name, epitomized to Muschet, continued for more than two hundred years longer in Scotland. "The family of Montefixo or Muschet were Lords of Cargill, near Cupar, of which lands they had a grant from William the Lion.. They were considerable benefactors to the Abbey, and failed in the male line towards the middle of the fourteenth century, when one of the three coheiresses became the wife of Sir John Drummond, ancestor of the Earls of Perth. · By him she had, with other issue, Annabella, Queen of Robert III., and mother of James I. of Scotland."—*Andrew Jervise.* But the Muschets long survived the. extinction of the House of Cargill. William Muschet *de Montefixo* was slain at Otterburn in 1386. James Mushet of Tolgarth is mentioned in 1476: John Mushet held of the Earl of Monteith in 1494, and two others of the name George and Robert Muschete, occur in 1509.—*Registrum Magni Sigilli Regum Scotorum.*

. **Maleherbe:** in modern phraseology, *mauvaise herbe*—a weed. Unpromising as this name may sound, it yet takes the highest rank for seniority among, its ·Norman compeers. "The house of Malherbe," says the *Nobiliaire de Normandie,* "is one of the most ancient of the province. If we may put faith in·a Latin title deed cited by Duchesne, and taken from the History of Vincentius, it descends from a Danish noble, the companion-in-arms of Rollo. Raoul de Malherbe was one of the knights that accompanied William the Bastard when he conquered England in·1066. His descendants formed seven principal branches, namely, those of the Seigneurs de Bouillon-d'Arry; de Missy; du Bois d'Escure: de Fresnay: d'Armanville: de la Pigacière: and de Digny: and finally that of the Marquises de Malherbe. The present head of the family" (this was written ·in 1862) "is· Dominique Henri de Malherbe, General commanding the sub-division at Alençon." They bear *Ermine* six roses *Gules,* three, two, and one. · One of the branches displayed only three roses.

. Far different was the bearing of the English Malherbes. They adopted, in a chastened and mortified spirit, a coat interpreting the noxious significance of their name, viz., *Or* a chevron *Gules* between three nettle-leaves erect *proper.* No Sir Ralph Malherbe is entered in Domesday; but seven of the family occur in the· *Liber Niger.* ' The Malherbs of Finniton in Devonshire were, according to Prince, "a very antient tribe, that flourished there and at Winton-Malherb from near the time of the Conquest down to the last age; about thirteen generations following, some of which were knights." Ralph de Malherbe held of William de Tracy in 1165. In Somersetshire "the manor of Kingston was, in the time of Henry II., the possession of the family of Malherbe, who were lords also of Shipham, Rowborough, and many other adjacent manors. But in the ninth year of Richard I. Robert Malherbe made a grant of this lordship to Milo de Sancto Mauro, from whence the place was afterwards called Kingston-Seymour."—*Collinson's Somerset.* Another Robert Malherbe is found in the county, c. 1272.—*Rotuli Hundredorum.* Was it one or other of these Roberts who bestowed upon Croxton Abbey two bovrates in the Fee of Griseley?— v. *Nichols' Leicester.* Druettus and Drogo Malherbe were seated in Northampton-shire, temp. Hen. III. and Ed. I. (Hundred Rolls): and Michael and his son Nicholas in Kent, where they have left their name to Boughton-Malherbe. John and Richard Malherbe, at the same date, were resident in Bedfordshire. Four under-tenants of the name held of Simon de Beauchamp there in 1165. "Rain-thorpe in Norfolk was given in 1189 by Richard I., to Oliver Malherbe. Sir Ralf Malherbe was Lord in 1280."—*Blomfield.* Contemporary with him was a William de Malerbe, a land-owner both in Norfolk and Lincoln (*Rotuli Hundredorum*), probably descended from the Roger who held of the Bishop of Lincoln in 1165. Candel-Malherbe preserves the name in Dorsetshire: as does Cricket-Malherbe, held under the Barons Montacute, in Somersetshire. Hugo de Malherbe held of Roger de Mowbray in Yorkshire (Liber Niger). John Malerbe of Hoton was a benefactor of Newnham Priory (Mon. Angl.): and either he, or another John Malherbe, was part-founder of Thurnholme Priory, Lincolnshire, in the time of King John. Again, a John de Malherbe married the sister and heiress of Roger de Montbegon, who brought him the castle and honour of Hornby*·in Lancashire, and left an only daughter and heiress, Clementia, married to Eudo de Longvilers.—*Bain's Lancashire.* In Scotland, Sir Gilbert de Malherbe was executed as a traitor, having engaged in 1320 in a conspiracy against Robert Bruce. Eustace Malherbe of Stamford was Assessor of the King's tax there in 1305.

Mare: already given, as La Mare.

Musegros: from Mucegros, near Ecouen. This name, so largely repre-sented in England, is repeated further on in its modernized form of Musgrave; and the heralds, ignoring its origin, labour to affiliate it to the German *Graf.* They declare that, like Land-grave, Burg-grave, Mar-grave, &c., it is "a name of office:" and as *Mews* in old days meant the cage or place where hawks were kept while mewing (moulting), and in after times came to signify a stable, boldly announce that "Musgrave or Mewsgrave is clearly either the keeper of the

* Hornby was in later times the castle of E. Stanley, Lord Monteagle, ob' 1529; and his challenging motto, Glav (Glaive) et Gant, may still be read on the N. wall of the keep.

King's hawks or the King's equerry." In support of this etymological vagary, they tell us that once upon a time an Emperor of Germany or Archduke of Austria (we will accept either) had a beautiful daughter who was courted by two valiant nobles. Each of them had done him such " singular good service that he did not care to prefer one to the other." At last it was agreed that they should ride at the ring for the princess ; and whichever succeeded in carrying it off should marry her. Musgrave triumphantly drove his spear through the ring, became the Emperor's son-in-law, and in memory of his exploit, had the six golden annulets now borne by the Musgraves of Westmorland granted him for his coat of arms. But these annulets, like those of the neighbouring house of Lowther, simply indicate the suzerainty of the De Viponts, Barons and Hereditary Sheriffs of Westmorland, who bore *Gules*, three annulets *Or*. Both these families held of them.

Robert de Mucelgros is mentioned about 1080 (Ordericus Vitalis, 576) and Roger de Mucelgros, in 1086, was a tenant-in-chief in Herefordshire (Dom.) where he has left his name to Lude Muchgros. His descendants spread far and wide. Charlton Musgrove in Somersetshire was, with other manors, held by Richard de Mucegros in the time of King John ; and he was also farmer of the county of Gloucester. Robert de Mucegros married Helewise, one of the coheirs of the Barony of Malet ; and though Charlton passed away through an heiress in the beginning of Edward I.'s reign, the name, as Musgrave, long continued in the county. John Musgrave was Sheriff of Wiltshire, where he had large estates, 2 Ric. III. Another John had been during five years Sheriff of Devon under Henry III. At the same date, Richard Muchgros, of Muchgros in Longdon parish, Worcestershire, "was much esteemed." Robert de Musegros held Kemerton of the Honour of Gloucester. His grand-daughter and heiress married John de Ferrers, Baron of Chartley.—*Atkyn's Gloucester*. Richard Musgrove, joint Lord of Shelton and Knotting in Bedfordshire, obtained a pardon for his participation in the death of Gaveston in 1313 : and Thomas de Musegros, in 1316, was one of the lords of Claydon, Williamscote, Prescott, and Blechingdon, Oxon.—*Palgrave's Parliamentary Writs*.

Only one of these, the Northern house of Musgrave, is still resident in the county where it first took root, and is found as far back as our records ·extend. Its name is familiar to us from many an old Border legend and ballad. " Little Musgrave who was his foot-page," and his " bonny horse Grisell," figure in the exploits of Johnnie Armstrong, the Robin Hood of the moss-troopers, whose last pathetic words on his "departing night" are preserved in Scott's Minstrelsy. Then we have Sir Michael Musgrave, the disappointed lover of Lady Dacre's fair daughter Isabel, who fought and killed his successful rival, Sir John Armstrong, on his wedding day ; and was himself hewn to pieces "as small as flesh into a pot," by the wrathful kinsmen of the slain bridegroom. Above all, there is the fairy legend of the Luck of Eden Hall. In the grounds of their old manor house, there is a well of pure spring water, dedicated by tradition to St. Cuthbert, and embanked by the smooth fresh greensward that fairies love to use as their dancing floor. Accordingly, one night, a servant that had gone out to draw water surprised a company of elves that had joined hands in a dance measure, and were disporting themselves merrily in the moonlight. Close by the margin of the well stood a curiously enamelled glass in the form of a chalice, and the servant, watching his opportunity, darted upon it and secured it. The fairies, in great commotion, broke up their revels and crowded round him; making every imaginable attempt to get it back: but the man held his prize fast, till at last, wearied with their fruitless efforts, they relinquished it to him, and fled away, singing as they went

> " If that glass either break or fall,
> Farewell the luck of Eden Hall! "

This fairy goblet, still safe and unbroken, though, as I have been told, flawed by a slight crack, is kept as a valued heirloom at Eden Hall.

The pedigree—I am loth to return to the region of dry matter-of-fact—commences with Peter de Musgrave, living in the time of King Stephen, who gave their name to Great and Little Musgrave, which, " so far back as we have any account, belonged to this ancient family."—*Nicolson and Burn's Westmorland.* His grandson, Sir Adam, was high in favour with William de Vipont, to whom King John had given the barony of Appleby, and held Musgrave of him by cornage.* Sir Thomas Musgrave was a baron by writ in 1350, but the summons was never again repeated to his descendants. He was an active and gallant soldier in the Border wars; and one of the commanders at the victory of Nevill's Cross; twice Warden of the West Marches (in 1341 and 1372): Governor of Berwick and sole Justiciary of Scotland in 1342; Constable of York in 1359, and Eschætor of the three Northern counties in 1368. At length, during his second Scottish campaign in 1379, he was taken prisoner, and only released when Lord Nevill and some others became sureties for his ransom. He died five years afterwards. Second in descent from him was the Sir Richard who has the credit of having killed the last wild boar in Westmorland; and a huge tusk, that had been buried with him as a trophy, was actually found in his tomb at Kirkby Stephen. In the time of Henry VI., Thomas Musgrave acquired Eden Hall, ever after the residence of the head of the house, through his wife Joan Stapleton; and left four sons, Richard, John, Nicholas, and William, of whom came the four families of Eden Hall, Musgrave Hall, or Fairbank, Hayton, and Crookdake.

A cadet of the first named house, another Thomas, who was Captain of Bew-

---

* " A kind of grand serjeanty : the service of which tenure is to blow a horn when any invasion of the Northern enemy is perceived : and by this many hold their land north of the Pict's wall."—*Cowell's Interp.*

castle at the end of the following century, had been charged by one Lancelot Carleton with having offered to surrender it to the Scots, and making it "a den of thieves, and a harbour and receipt for murderers and felons." He elected to clear himself according to the old custom that had been handed down to the Borderers from their Norse forefathers, and to have his cause "openly tried by way of combat before God and the face of the world: and to try it on Canonby Holme, before England and Scotland, upon Thursday in Easter Week, A.D. 1602." The laws regulating these encounters are minutely given,* but we are not told which champion proved himself in the right.

It was the nephew of. this challenger who became the first Baronet of Eden Hall—Sir Richard, created 1611. The next heir, Sir Philip, fought stoutly for the King in the Civil War, and was one of the "persons of quality" taken prisoner in 1645 at the battle of Rowton Moor, near Chester; "a gentleman," says Lord Clarendon, "of noble extraction and ample fortune, who lived to engage himself again in the same service, and with the same affection ; and after very great sufferings to see the Restoration." He had commanded in chief in Cumberland and Westmorland, where he raised a regiment, and been governor of the city and castle of Carlisle ; and was no sooner released from captivity through the good offices of his uncle Lord Wharton, than he took service under the Countess of Derby, who appointed him her lieutenant in the Isle of Man. He conducted its defence bravely and skilfully, but was at last forced to surrender on honourable terms. In 1660 he had the grant of a Baron's patent, but it was never taken out. When the King came home and "enjoyed his own again," Sir Philip was prepared with a long list of grievances ; "but it was well," says Surtees, "with this Country, when the wrongs of a country gentleman, notorious for his fearless opposition to the successful faction, amounted to no more, *flagrante bello*, than an account of out-houses damaged, victuals wasted, and corn eat up green by the troopers' horses." Nor was he left, like so many others, without the slightest recognition of his services. He was named Constable of Carlisle, and received "some other reparation." The present baronet is his direct representative.

Two other baronetcies have been granted to the family ; one—a baronetcy of Nova Scotia to the Musgraves of Hayton in 1638 : the other in 1782, to an Irish branch seated at Tourin, in the county of Waterford.

Musard. Ascuit, Hascoit, or Hasculphus Musard, holds a great barony in Domesday. Enisand Musard and Hugh Musard also appear there, the latter

---

* They were "to fight on foot : to be armed with jack, steel cap, plaite sleeves, plaite breeches, plaite socks ; two swords, the blades to be one yard and half a quarter in length ; and two Scotch daggers or dirks at their girdles. Two gentlemen to be appointed in the field, to view both the parties, to see that they be both equal in arms and weapons, according to this indenture ; the gentlemen then to ride to the rest of the company, and leave them but two boys under 16 to hold their horses"

holding of the Countess Judith. There is a difference of opinion as to their origin. If, as M. de Ste Marie (Recherches sur le Domesday) conjectures, they belonged to the Musards who were lords of Sauxelles and Issondun-sur-Creuse, in La Marche, up to the seventeenth century, they probably came to England under the banner of Roger de Poitou, who had married the daughter of their feudal suzerain, Audebert, Count de la Marche.˙ The author of the 'Norman People' (quoting Lobineau, Hist. Bret. ii. 117) says they were the sons of Hasculph, Viscount of Nantes in Brittany, and this opinion is supported by the fact that Enisand Musard had vast grants in Yorkshire from Alan le Roux of Brittany, Earl of Richmond, with the feudal dignity of Constable of Richmond. It was his grandson Roald who founded Easby Abbey in 1152 (Mon. ii. 649); and from him, it is suggested, descended the Yorkshire families of Richmond and Burton: the latter name having been taken from the seat of their seigneurie. Hasculph, the elder brother, was seated in Derbyshire, where his son Richard was Baron of Staveley, and his grandson, Hasculph II., on the occasion of the marriage of Henry II.'s daughter, certified that he held fifteen and a half knight's fees. This latter Hasculph died 33 Henry II., and was succeeded by Ralph, who was High Sheriff of Gloucester 17 John, and continued Sheriff till 9 Henry III. His home was at Misarden or Musarden in that county, which had taken its name from the Musards, and continued in their possession for about two hundred and forty years; that is, from the Conquest till the end of Edward I.'s reign. "He married Isabel, the widow of John de Nevill, without the King's License, and paid one hundred Marks for his Transgression. He built a Castle at Misarden, and the old ruins of a place in Misarden Park is at this Day called Musard's Castle. He was a Baron of the Realm, and this Manor, in ancient Records, is called the Barony of Misarden. He dyed 14 Henry III., and was succeeded by Robert his Son, who dying without Issue, Ralph Musard was his Brother and Heir, and being under-age at his Brother's Death, he was given in Ward to Jeffrey Despencer, who in consideration thereof paid five hundred Marks to the Crown. Ralph dyed 49 Henry III., and left John his Son and Heir, who had Livery of the Manor of Misarden 15 Edward I., and dyed two years after.

"Nicholas Musard, Uncle to John, and younger Brother of Ralph, had Livery of this Manor 17 Ed. I., and dyed without Issue 29 Ed. I.; whereby Sir Nicholas Frescheville, Son of Amicia, his eldest Sister then dead, and Margaret his Sister then living, and Joan, Wife of William de Chelardiston, the Daughter and Heir of Isabel, his third Sister then dead, were his Heirs."—*Atkyn's Gloucestershire.*

"Musard" is said to be "an opprobrious cognomen, signifying one who muses; literally a muser, a gaper, and used in the sense of a dull, lazy fellow, until after Chaucer's time."—*A. S. Ellis.*

Moine: "The family of Moygnes, Moynes, or de Monacho, held Owre Moyne, or Moyne-Ogres, very early after the Conquest. In the reign of Edward I.

it was found that Ralph Moyne held this manor of Owers by service of serjeancy of the kitchen, and his ancestors had held it from the time of Henry I., by gift of that king, by the said service."—*Hutchins' Dorset.* The last male heir, Sir John Moygne, died temp. Ed. IV., leaving two daughters, of whom one was married to Sir William Stourton. The Moines gave as their arms Barry of six, *Or* and *Vert.* " Their crest, a demi-monk with a penitential whip in his hand, alludes to the name, and not to one of them being whipped out of a monastery when the other issue male failed, as some have imagined. Some have deduced them from the Mohuns of Somerset, which, though it be a gross error, has taken such deep root, that the Lord Stourton still quarters the Mohun arms for those of Moygnes, though they are very different.

" A branch of this family had Sibton-Moyne, co. Gloucester. Another was seated in Essex in the reign of Henry II. Another in Cambridge and Huntingdon, in the reign of Henry III."—*Ibid.* In Essex they held Eystan (Easton) of the King in chief, and in Wiltshire, Maddington, both " per les services d'estre achateur del kuysine de Roy, et Lardiner de Roy a temps de coronements de Royes et de Reynes d'Engleter." Sir John le Moygne of Maddington, the last male heir, was Lardener at the coronation of Henry V. See *Hoare's Wilts.*

" Monk's Hall, in Blackburn Hundred, is supposed to take its name from a family who resided here as early as Edward III. They were sometimes called Le Moine and sometimes De Monkys, according to the language used in the charter. Henry de Moniaic occurs in the charter by which Accrington was granted, to Kirkstall Abbey."—*Baines Lancashire.* He does not give their arms.

" In the neighbourhood of Oundle, in Northamptonshire, stands Barnwell, a little Castle, that formerly belong'd to Berengarius le Moigne, that is, Monk."— *Camden.* In Cambridgeshire their seat was at Weston; and in 1282 Sir John le Moine also held Moine's Manor in Norfolk; "in 1334 his heiress Margaret had it, and was wife of Sir John de Sutton of Wivenhoe." Wreningham, in the latter county, appears to have been owned by another branch, that, " about 1261, ended in three co-heiresses."—*Blomfield.* Sawtrey-Moigne, in Huntingdonshire, was long their residence; and some of their tombs remain in the church. John le Moygne was Sheriff of Cambridgeshire and Huntingdonshire 38 & 39 Henry III.; William de Moygne four years later; and others of the name occur in the list in the reigns of Edward I., Edward III., and Richard II. This was the last occasion on which they are found; and they were certainly extinct before 1433, as their name is missing among those of the " Gentry of the Shire," returned by Henry VI.'s Commissioners.

In Devonshire we find the Le Moines, or Monks, seated at Potheridge, near Torrington, temp. Ed. I. " They continued there for fifteen or sixteen generations, having married heiresses, or co-heiresses, of Tilley, Estcott, Rishford, Trenchard, Crukerne, Grant, Champernowne of Inswerke, Wood, and Plantagenet, Viscount Lisle. It seems not improbable that the first of the Le Moynes, who was of Potheridge, might have been a younger son of the family who gave name to Shipton Moyne, in Gloucestershire."—*Lysons.* But their coat was entirely different; for they gave *Gules* a chevron between three lions' heads erased *Argent,* and eschewed the crest of the monk and his penitential whip. The brother of the last Sir Thomas Monk of Potheridge was the famous General Monk who brought about the Restoration, and was rewarded with the Dukedom of Albemarle.* He inherited Potheridge from his childless elder brother, and rebuilt the old house with great splendour, but it has since fallen to ruin. He married his sempstress, Anne Clarges,† and had an only son named Christopher, with whom his honours expired in 1687. The wife of this second Duke, Lady Elizabeth Cavendish (afterwards Duchess of Montagu) was one of the co-heiresses of the wealthy Duke of Newcastle, but brought him only a child that died in infancy.

Montrauers, or Maltravers: seated in Dorsetshire. "Hugh Maltravers witnessed Henry I.'s charter to Montacute, and 5 Stephen William Maltravers gave 1000 marks of silver and £100 for the widow and lands of Hugh de la Val during the term of fifteen years, and then to have the benefit of her dowry and marriage. John (temp. Hen. III.) was Custos of the King's forests this side Trent, and claimed to have of every forester in the Forest of Savernake and elsewhere in the county of Wilts, at his death, his horse, saddle, and horn, bridle, sword, bow, and barbed arrows."—*Hutchins' Dorset.* Their home was at Wellcombe, and several manors in the county, Lytchet Maltravers, Loders Maltravers, Worth Maltravers, as well as Stapleford Maltravers in Wiltshire, Henford Maltravers in Somersetshire, and Childrey Maltravers in Berkshire— testify to their possessions. Sir John Maltravers was Seneschal of the Household to Edward I.,‡ and another Sir John his son, who served in the Scottish wars, and was taken prisoner at the battle of Bannockburn, had summons to parliament as John Maltravers, sen., in 1327. He was the Lord Maltravers whose name in history is blackened by a celebrated crime. Edward II., after his

---

* Oliver Cromwell added the following curious postscript to one of his letters to Monk; "There be that tell me there is a certain cunning fellow in Scotland call'd George Monk, who is said to lie in wait there to introduce Charles Stuart : I pray you use your diligence to apprehend him, and send him up to me."

† It appeared in evidence at a trial at the King's Bench in 1700, that Anne Clarges was the daughter of a farrier in the Savoy, married to one Thomas Ratford ; and that she and her husband sold wash-balls, powder, gloves, &c., at the sign of the Three Spanish Gipsies in the Royal Exchange. About 1647, "she being sempstress to Monk, used to carry him linen." Her husband either died or deserted her two years afterwards ; and she was married to the General in 1652.

‡ "If this John, whom Dugdale represents to have been a rebel baron 1 Henry III., and to have died 24 Edward I., be one and the same person, he must have been a very aged man indeed ; as those periods comprehend a space of eighty years."— *Banks.* Nichols, more probably, gives two Sir John Maltravers, father and son.

deposition, had remained for some time in the custody of the Earl of Leicester, from whom, being found too lenient a gaoler, he was transferred to the keeping of Lord Berkeley and Lord Maltravers, and by them conveyed to Berkeley Castle. But as Lord Berkeley, again, "used more courtesie," than was desired, he was replaced by a sterner spirit, Sir Thomas Gournay, who, with Maltravers, remained in charge of the King to the end.   Being haunted by the fear of a rescue, they hurried their poor prisoner away secretly to Corfe Castle, and from thence to one strong place after another, keeping him constantly on the move, and always travelling by night, till, judging that all trace of him must be lost, they brought him back to Berkeley.   Meanwhile the Earl of Kent was plotting to release his brother; and the Queen and the Bishop of Hereford wrote "sharp letters to his keepers, blaming them greatlie for that they dealt so gentlie with him, and kept him not streictlier;" and the Bishop added an enigmatical line, which by a change of punctuation might be made to bear two exactly opposite meanings;

"Edwardum occidere nolite timere bonus est."

They had little trouble in reading the riddle, and set themselves to their suggested task, trying various means of getting rid of the King, without leaving any marks of violence.   At last they hit upon a fiendish device, and put him to death with such revolting cruelty that his shrieks and wails "moved many within the castell and the towne of Berkeley to compassion."

The House of Lords, however, judged that Maltravers had not himself laid hands on the King, but employed Gournay and Ogle as his deputies; and although sentence of death was passed upon him in 1330 by the same parliament that condemned Edward's assassins, it was for a different crime—the murder of the Earl of Kent.   Maltravers had in the meantime made his escape to Germany, where he remained for many years.   At last, in 1345, he voluntarily came and surrendered himself to Edward III., on his landing in Flanders; and "for his special services there, where he lost all his goods, and suffered great oppression," obtained the King's free permission to return to England and abide the decision of the next Parliament.   Six years later, he received a full pardon, with a fresh writ of summons; and in 1352 was appointed Governor of the Channel Islands. He founded a hospital in Guernsey, and died in 1364, five years after his only son John, who, like himself, had been summoned to parliament in the first year of the King's reign.   John, too, had a son who died early in life, and his two daughters became their grandfather's heirs.   Joan, the eldest, was twice married, but childless; and thus the barony devolved on Eleanor, the wife of John Fitz Alan (a younger son of the Earl of Arundel) Marshal of England in 1377, and summoned to parliament in the same year as Lord Maltravers.   Their grandson succeeded as twelfth Earl of Arundel; and the two titles were jointly conveyed in 1580 to Thomas Howard, Duke of Norfolk, by Lady Mary Fitz Alan, sole heiress of the eighteenth Earl.

A younger branch, which survived the elder only by twenty years, descended from Robert, believed to have been an uncle of the elder Lord Maltravers. His grandson, Sir John, married a Dorsetshire heiress, Elizabeth Sifrewast, who brought him Hooke and Crowel, and was succeeded by another Sir John, whose two daughters inherited. One of them conveyed Hooke to Sir Humphrey Stafford.

Merke. " Adelolfus de Merc " held in Essex 1086 under Eustace Earl of Boulogne ; and his estate of Tollesbury was still held by one of his descendants, Henry de Merk, in 1251. This name, variously given as Merkes, Markes, and Mark, was derived from Marc in Normandy. Geoffrey de Marco and his sons are mentioned by Ordericus Vitalis (591). It is still retained by many places in Essex. There is Le Marck, or Marks Hall, in the parish of Leyton, Mark's Tay (held under the Mandevilles "from the earliest times"), the parish of Markes Hall, Merks in Dunmow (possessed since the days of the Conqueror), and others. The family was wealthy, numerous, and greatly sub-divided ; but the pedigrees furnished by Morant are disjointed and incomplete. Aitropus, or Eutropius, and Simon de Merc occur in the *Rotuli Curiæ Regis* of 1194–98 : and the latter is also entered in the Monasticon as a benefactor of Thornton Abbey. He and his son Ingelram held Marks, in the parish of Great Dunmow, of the King *in capite* of his Honour of Bologne, and had certainly three, if not more, successors in the male line. Henry de Merc, who held the fee of Shotgrove (including Tollesbury) in the time of Henry III., is also credited with three generations of heirs ; the last, another Henry, was living in 1291. Mark's Tey passed through Alicia (apparently the heiress of Thomas Markes) to William de Tey in the following century. In 1226 Sir Walter de Merc held lands in Blanche Roung of the King *in capite,* and was succeeded by William his son. John de Merc (probably the grandson) received from Ed. I. in 1296 the whole manor of White Roding, thence called Merks, with remainder to his sister, Cicely de Hastings. She held this manor " by the service of keeping two lanar falcons, or hawks, for heron-hawking ; and a greyhound trained to make a heron rise, from Michaelmas to the Purification, for the King's use."—*Morant.* Comberton-Marks, in Cambridgeshire, likewise belonged to them. Eustace de Merc, in the time of Cœur de Lion, founded a small monastery in honour of St. Thomas at Roese's Cross (now Royston) in that county.

We find this family in many other parts of England. Philip Mark was a man of great note, and Sheriff of the counties of Nottingham and Derby during the latter part of King John's reign, and the first seven or eight years of Henry III. " He held the township of Bulwell by demise of King John, and had the Manor of Melbourne committed to him, and the Farm of Bulwell, to sustain him as long as he had this manor, 12 Hen. III., for life."—*Thornton's Notts.* Peter Markes was joint Sheriff from 1210 to 1216. They bore Per pale *Ermine* and *Azure,* a lion rampant counterchanged, in a bordure *Sable* bezantée ;

—evidently derived from the coat of the Mercs of Essex: *Gules* a lion *Argent* within a bordure indented *Or.* In Northamptonshire, "Alons de Merke, in the hydarium of Hen. II., was certified to hold nearly two hides in Evenley, part of the Wodhull fee."—*Baker.* Henry de Merc was of Kent 1194–98 (*Rot. Curiæ Regis*). Robert de Merc held lands at Winchester in 1148 (Winton Dom.) Eudo and William Marc witness King Stephen's grant to Southampton Priory, of which William himself was a benefactor; and either this or another William occurs with Roger Markes in the chartulary of Tichfield Abbey (Mon. Angl.) Two seals of this family are preserved in Camden's Visitation of Huntingdon in 1613: that of "William de Merc of Chesterton, father of Egidius and Hugh de Merc," a fesse: and that of Giles de Merc, Party per pale, a cross moline. The last mention I have found of the name is in 1459, when Thomas Merke was Archdeacon of Norwich.

Murres: In a satirical poem of 1204: the "*Bible* de Guiot de Provins:" there is a mention of this, or a very similar, name:

> " Oncques certes deça la mer
> Ne vi un si cortois baron
> Qui fut Morises de Troon
> Et qui fu Renauz de Nevers? "

In the *Monasticon Anglicanum* Reginaldus des Mores witnesses a grant of Galfrid Camerarius de Clinton to Bretford in Warwickshire, and a William de Murrers occurs in the chartulary of Thickhead Priory. Geoffrey de Mores, about 1272, in the *Rotuli Hundredorum.* In the succeeding century, William Morers married one of the three sisters and co-heirs of Sir Robert Ashton, who held Sutton in Dorset and some manors in Somersetshire 12 Ed. III.—*Hutchins' Dorset.* Richard de Murers held of the Percy fee in Lincoln (*Testa de Nevill*) as well as in Yorkshire, where he was Lord of Elvington (*Kirkby's Inquest*). In 1253 he had a charter of free warren at Elvington; and the family possessed several other estates in the county. His son and heir William held at Thoxton of the Honour of Richmond; and at Thurstanby of Henry de Percy; Peter de Murers at Catton-cum-Soka of the Honour of Chester; and Ralph de Morers was Lord of Wilton, Lasingby, and Lackenby.—*Ibid.* In the list of the "Gentry of Cheshire," made in 1443, I find the name of "Johannes Mores de Trumpington."

Mortiuale; for Martival or Martivaus. This family bore *Argent*, a cinque-foil *Sable*, pierced of the field, and held Noseley in Leicestershire of the Earls of Leicester "by an annual acknowledgment of a rose flower." It was probably, as well as their own bearing, in honour of the rose or cinquefoil of their suzerains the Beaumonts. Ralph de Mortivall, in the time of King John, witnesses a charter of the last of these Earls; and, in a previous generation, William de Mortivall had granted some lands to St. Mary's Abbey at Leicester with their consent. Anketill Martivaus was Sheriff of Warwickshire in 1240 and 1241; and

Sheriff of Leicester in 1258. "His son, Sir Anketill, founded a chantry in the chapel of his mansion house at Noseley, which was afterwards enlarged by his son Roger to a collegiate church."—*Nichol's Leicestershire.* This little college was founded in honour of the Ascension of Our Lord and the Assumption of the Blessed Virgin; "which festivals had been ever the especial favourites of Roger de Martival from his attaining years of discretion." He became a churchman, having entered Merton College in 1280, and been the donor of several valuable MS. to its library; and was first Archdeacon of Leicester, then Dean of Lincoln, and lastly, Bishop of Salisbury from 1315 to 1329. Fuller includes him in his list of "Worthies;" and says, "Now seeing Bishop Godwin hath nothing more of him than his name and date, it is charity further to inform posterity that he was the last heir male of his house, and founded a college at Nowsley." His heiress was his sister Joyce, married to Sir Robert de Sadyngton of Sadyngton in Leicestershire some time Chancellor of Ireland; and their daughter Isabel brought Noseley to one of the Hastings family. Leland's account is somewhat different: "Noseley longid to the Blaketes: and an Heire general of them about Edward the 3. Tyme was married to Roger de Martevalle that founded the little College of Noseley. This Noseley and other Landes thereaboute cam onto 2 Doughtters of one of the Mortevilles, whereof one was married onto Hugh Hastinges, the other was a Nunne, and alienid much of her Parte." This may have been a younger sister of Isabel de Sadyngton, whose husband was not Hugh, but Sir Ralph de Hastings, Sheriff of York and Governor of York Castle in 1377.

Monchenesy. Hubert de Monte Canisi held a barony in Suffolk in 1086 (Domesd.) and bore *Or* three inescutcheons *Vair.* This Hubert was a benefactor of the monks of Eye, Thetford, and St. Albans; to the latter he granted the church of Edwardeston in Suffolk, "whereupon," says Dugdale, "it became a cell of that great Abbey." He must either have lived to be almost a centenarian, or have had a son of the same name who is confounded with him in the "Baronage," for Hubert de Montchensie is spoken of in 1140, seventy-four years after the Conquest. The next mentioned is Warine, who married Agnes, the daughter of Pain Fitz John, at that time one of the first barons of the realm, and left three sons: of whom the two elder, Ralph and William, were both knights, and Hubert, the youngest, a priest. Nothing further is said of Ralph; but William received from Henry II. a grant of the town of Winfarthing * in Norfolk; attended Cœur de Lion into Normandy in 1195, and in the following reign gave forty marks and a palfrey to be exempted from a similar expedition beyond sea. He died

* The famous "Good Sword of Winfathing," long preserved in the church, was "counted of so great virtue, that there was a solemn Pilgrimage used unto it, with large Giftes and Offeringes, with Vow Makinges, Crouchings, and Kissinges; it served to find things that were lost and Horses that were stolen or else run astraye; it helped also unto the Shortning of a Married Man's Life, if that the Wyfe that was

6 John, leaving his son William a minor, "who lived," says Dugdale, "not long after; for 15 John Warine de Munchensi (his Uncle I suppose) gave a Fine of two thousand marks (a prodigious Sum for that Time) for Livery of his whole Inheritance, and to be quit of those debts which he owed the Jews." He seized and kept possession of Keymes Castle in Cardigan Bay, "won great renown" at the battle of Xaintonge, and died in 1255, "being then reputed one of the most Noble, Prudent, and Wealthy Men of all the Realm." By his wife Joan, one of the great Pembroke heiresses, he left one son, William, who it would appear chiefly resided at Winfarthing, where he had a park well stocked with deer, but also held lands in Essex, Kent, Gloucestershire, Northamptonshire, Herts, and Bucks; in all fourteen and a half knight's fees. He was among the discontented barons that rose in arms against Henry III.; one of the chief commanders at Lewes in 1264; and in the following year summoned to the parliament they called in the King's name. "But not long after this, being taken at Kenilworth in that notable surprise made by the Forces of Prince Edward, a little before the Battell of Evesham, his Lands were seised and given to William de Valence; who had married his Sister. Whereupon his Mother undertook to bring him in before the Feast of St. Hillary, to stand to the judgment of the King's Court in pursuance of the Decree called *Dictum de Kenilworth ;* but being not able to perform it within the compass of that time, by reason of his sickness, she promised to bring him in upon that very day: where, and at which time he had such fair respect for his Sister's sake, that William Valence her Husband freely restored them to him again." This was only the prelude to the free pardon he received from Edward I., with the additional privilege "that he might keep Dogs to hunt the Hare, Fox, and Wilde Cat in the King's Forests." He twice served with the King's army in Wales; and on the second of these occasions, in 1289, lost his life in attacking Rees ap Griffith's fastness at Drossellan; for, "endeavouring to demolish that Castle by undermining it, he was with divers others overwhelmed in the fall thereof." He had no son; and his brother-in-law, De Valence, "then claimed to possess himself for the third time of his estates; and tried, though in vain, to bastardize his only child, Dionysia. She married her guardian, Hugh de Vere."—*Blaauw's Baron's War.* But she left no children; and the long coveted inheritance reverted to her aunt, and thus to her aunt's husband, De Valence.

The manor of Boughton Monchensie, that once formed part of this great barony, retains its name in Kent.

Mallory: or De Maloure. "Maloures or Malesoures was near St. Brieux

---

wearye of her Husband should sett a Candle before that Sword regularly every Sunday for the space of a whole Yeare. It was thro' the Suttilty of the Parson and the Clerk made a precious Relique full of Virtue, and able to do much, but specially to enrich the Box and make fat the Parson's Pouche."—*Blomfield's Norfolk.*

in Brittany. Durand de Malesoure lived c. 1040. He had two sons, who came to England in 1066: 1. Adam Fitz Durand, who held in Essex, 1086; and 2. Fulcher de Maloure, whose barony was in Rutland, and who held in Northants from the Countess Judith at the same date." (Bridge's Northamptonshire.)— *The Norman People.* The Mallores were seated for many generations in Leicestershire, where they affixed their name to Kirkby Mallory. "The first of the family," says Nichols, "that I have met with was Geoffrey, father of Sir Anchitel Mallory, who, being governor of the town and castle of Leicester under Robert Blanchemains in the time of his rebellion against Henry II., marched thence to Northampton, and after a sharp fight, having defeated the burghers there, returned to Leicester with the spoils and plunder of that town; for which his lands being forfeited, they were in 1174 seized by the King. Nor was he ever restored to them; but Henry his son, paying a fine of sixty marks to King John, obtained a restitution of this manor of Kirkby Mallory, and all his father's lands in this county and Warwickshire." Thomas Malesoures was several times knight of the shire during the reign of Edward II.; and in that of his successor, Sir Anketill Mallore sold Kirkby Mallory. His eldest son, Sir Thomas, was of Bramcote, Warwickshire, in right of his wife, the heiress of the Grendons, but had only one child, Elizabeth, married to Sir Robert Ever. The male line was, however, continued till 1512, when John Mallory was slain at Therouenne, or Tournay, leaving five daughters. This elder branch of the house was seated at Walton-on-the Woulds; but there were also Mallorys of Swinford, bearing different arms; of whom was John Mallory, High Sheriff of Leicestershire 15 Ric. II., 4 Henry V., and 3 Henry VI. Swinford had come to him by his marriage with the eldest co-heiress of the Revells, who also brought him Newbold Revell in Warwickshire. He appears to have been a younger son of the Northamptonshire branch (see above), and his line ended with his great grandson Nicholas, High Sheriff of Leicestershire in 1502, whose co-heiresses, Dorothy and Margaret, had both for their first husbands two gentlemen of the name of Cave.

The family also held Botley in Warwickshire of the Botelers of Overston from the twelfth to the fifteenth century. "The place where the Malores most resided," says Dugdale, " was Walton-on-the-Would in Leicestershire; though they were likewise owners of Botley in this county," where Tachebrook Mallory retains their name, and continued in their possession till Henry VI.'s time. Simon Malore is styled Lord of Drayton in 1277; and tenth in descent from him was Nicholas, High Sheriff in 1502, who left only two daughters. Winwick in Northamptonshire was another of their possessions, and they were also landowners in Rutland and Cambridgeshire, where Sir William Mallory is returned as one of the gentry of the county in 1433, and Sir Anthony was three times High Sheriff in the reigns of Henry VII. and Henry VIII. The last I find mentioned is another William, who served the same office 6 & 17 Elizabeth. Sir Peter Malorey, who married Matilda, the co-heir of Stephen de Bayeux, and the widow of Elias de Rabayn, was one of the "knights called as assistants" to.the Parliament held at Salisbury by Edward I. in 1296. He was one of the Justices of the Common Pleas in 1291, and in that quality had summons to parliament. Another "Peter de Malure is noticed, who, 35 Ed. III., was one of those who, holding lands in Ireland, had summons to attend a great council then convened to meet at Westminster, to deliberate upon the affairs of that kingdom. But with regard to the descent of these persons, or their connection with each other, there is no proof to establish the same."—*Banks.*

Sir Christopher Mallory (son of Sir William and a daughter of Lord Zouche) acquired great estates in North Yorkshire and the co. of Durham by his marriage with Joan, daughter and co-heir of Robert Conyers of Hutton Conyers, the last representative of the elder branch of that great Norman house. "There be two Lordshipps lyenge not very far from Ripon, that is Norton Conyers and Hutton Coniers. Norton hathe Northeton Coniers, and Malorie hath Hutton Coniers. Thes Lands cam to theyr Aunciters by two Dowghters, Heirs Generall of that Coniers."—*Leland.* This must have been in the very first years of the fourteenth century ; for his great grandson, William Mallory, was living in 1444, when he succeeded his father-in-law at the "Place caullyd Highe Studly, a little from Fontaines." He, too, had matched with a co-heiress, Dionysia Tempest, whose elder sister, by a curious coincidence, was the wife of Richard Norton of Norton-Conyers. It does not, however, appear that he abandoned his old manor house at Hutton, for it continued to be the chief seat of his descendants until the end of the sixteenth century. Both his son and his daughter-in-law founded chantries in Ripon Cathedral, where many of the family were buried. Leland mentions "a Tumbe of one of the Malories in the Southe Parte of the Crosse in a Chapel, and without, as I heard, lyeth diverse of them under flate Stones." They flourished for nine descents in Yorkshire, multiplying so rapidly that one of them, burdened with eighteen children and fifteen brothers and sisters, was compelled to sell—"at a time when changes of property were seldom thought of or voluntarily effected "—two of their most ancient estates, Trefforth and Washington in the co. of Durham. Unlike their neighbours the Nortons, the Mallorys took part with the Crown in the Rising of the North, and Sir William, then the head of the family, and High Sheriff of the county in 1592, was brother-in-law to Sir George Bowes of Streatlam, Queen Elizabeth's ruthless " marshal north of Trent." He was very keen in advancing the Reformation, which had made but scant progress in the Ripon district, and was employed by the Ecclesiastical Commissioners at York " to pull downe the gilden tabernacle " in the Cathedral. Yet one of his grandsons, Christopher Mallory, suffered persecution as a Roman Catholic, being arrested on the Tower Wharf in 1628, "whilst looking curiously at the ordnance": and also charged with inducing a Londoner named Lancaster to leave his property to two foreign monasteries. "Soon after, the strange story crops up that Mallory had acted in a play at the house of Sir John York of

Goulthwaite, a convert to Popery. It is gravely stated that Mallory performed the part of the devil, and in that character carried off King James on his back to a supposed hell, alleging that all Protestants were damned."—*J. R. Walbran.* Though he stoutly denied both accusations, he was actually detained for some little time in prison. His nephew, Sir John, commanded two regiments for the King during the Civil War, and, as governor of Skipton, held that castle for three years, and during that time brought over a troop of horse from Ripon, and drove out Sir Thomas Mauleverer and his men, who had taken possession of the town." During his absence from home, his own house at Hutton Conyers was, according to tradition, set upon and partly destroyed by the Parliamentarians. "Sir John, of course, was a marked man, and was obliged to lay down as a composition for his estates the large sum of £2,219." His son William proved the last of "this ancient and well allied family," and died in 1664. On his death the estates reverted to his brother-in-law George Aislabie, who "came to his end in a very unfortunate manner. Miss Mallory, his wife's sister, had been to a party at the Duke of Buckingham's house on Bishop hill, and was escorted home to Aislabie's house by a brother of Sir Edward Jenings of Ripon. By some mischance they could not get in, and so Mr. Jenings was obliged to take the lady to the residence of his brother-in-law, Dr. Watkinson. On the following day Jenings told Aislabie that it was hard Sir John Mallory's daughter must wait at George Aislabie's gates and not be admitted. This produced a quarrel and a challenge, and the two met at Penley Croft, close to the city, the signal of the meeting being the ringing of the minster-bell to prayers on a good Sunday morning. Mr. Aislabie was killed."—*Ibid.* For about one hundred years—till 1781—his posterity continued at Studley. The last heir had the rare good fortune of adding to his possessions Fountains Abbey, with its beautiful domain, and his daughter and grand-daughter successively inherited them. The latter, Miss Lawrence—one of the few great heiresses on record that never chose to marry—left them in 1845 to the father of the present Marquess of Ripon, the representative of Sir William Robinson, who had married Mary, daughter of George Aislabie, and the heiress of Studley.

A branch of the Yorkshire Mallorys, descended from a younger son who became Dean of Chester, and died in 1644, survived in Cheshire till 1795.

Marny; anciently written De Mareni, and sometimes De Marinis; a name probably derived from the fief of Marreiny in Normandy (mentioned in the Exchequer Rolls, about 1180). This family held Layer Marney, in Essex, from the time of Henry II. to that of Henry VIII. The first mentioned is " William de Marney, who about the year 1166 held a knight's fee under Henry de Essex of the Honour of Hagnet. Werry de Marinis was excused by a writ of King Richard I. from paying scutage for that King's ransom. In 1263, William de Marny obtained leave from Henry III. to impark his Wood of Lire within the precincts of the Forest of Essex."—*Morant.* The principal man of the family was Sir Henry Marney, "a person of great wisdom, gravity, and of singular fidelity to that prudent prince, King Henry VII., and one of his privy Council." He had both courage and abilities, and pushed his fortunes at Court with unvarying success in two different reigns. He commanded for Henry VII. at the battle of Stoke against the Earl of Lincoln, and afterwards fought the Cornish rebels under Lord Audley at Blackheath. Under Henry VIII. he was again a Privy Councillor, a Knight of the Garter, Captain of the King's Guard, Keeper of the Privy Seal, and finally—the year before he died—a peer of the Realm. He had received a large share of the forfeited estates of Edward Stafford, Duke of Buckingham, and commenced building "a great and capacious house" at Layer Marney, of which the quadrangle was intended to· be one hundred feet square. But the gate-house alone is now standing, and is probably the only part of his great work that was ever completed. It is eight stories high, commanding "a beautiful and extensive prospect out a great way to sea and all round, though this is a flat country."—*Morant.* His barony was of the very briefest duration. He was created Lord Marney of Layer Marney in 1522, and was succeeded in 1523 by his son, with whom it expired in 1525. This second Lord Marney, who has been one of the Esquires of the Body to the King, and Constable of Rochester, was the last of his race. Two daughters were his co-heirs, Catherine, first married to George Ratcliffe, and afterwards to Thomas Lord Poynings, and Elizabeth, wife of Lord Thomas Howard, a son of the third Duke of Norfolk, who was created Viscount Howard of Bindon in 1559.

Mountagu: or Montagud (de Monte Acuto): from Montaigu-les-Bois, in the arrondissement of Coutances, Normandy, which remained in the possession of the family till the death of Sébastien de Montaigu, s. p. in 1715.—(*Recherches sur le Domesday*). Two of this name appear in Domesday: Ansger and Drogo de Montaigu; both richly endowed; but the former left no heir.· Drogo's barony was in Somersetshire, where two of the manors he held in 1086, Shipton and Sutton, still retain his name. Shipton Montagu was the head of the honour. He had come to England in the train of the Earl of Mortaine, and received from him large grants of lands, with the custody of the castle, built either by the Earl or his son William, in the manor of Bishopston, and styled, from its position on a sharp-topped hill, Monte Acuto. In 13 John, his grandson Drogo II. certified that he held ten and a half knight's fees in the Western counties. The first baron by writ was Simon de Montacute, "a right valiant chieftain and a wise," who did good service in the wars of Scotland and of Gascony, was Governor of Corfe Castle and Beaumaris, and Admiral of Edward I.'s fleet. The King bestowed upon him the hand of a princess of royal Danish blood, Aufrick, daughter of Fergus King of Man, who, seeing her brother and all her kindred overcome by Alexander III. of Scotland, had fled into England with the charters of her island, for protection and assistance. Simon, with the King's aid, reconquered her sovereignty, and it continued with their descendants till his great-grandson sold his rights to Lord Scrope. It is evident, however, that it had at least once passed out of their possession, for we find mention of a second conquest in 1342 by William, Simon's grandson, who was crowned King of Man by Edward III. This William de Montacute, created Earl of Salisbury in 1337, was a famous soldier and statesman in Edward's reign, and first earned the King's gratitude by seizing Roger Mortimer in Nottingham Castle, and sending him prisoner to London. For this he was rewarded with numerous grants, including many of Mortimer's forfeited estates, a pension of £1000 a year, and the manor and castle of Werk, to be held by the service of defending it against the Scots. It was there that, in 1341, Froissart tells us the King fell in love with the beautiful Katherine de Grandison, Countess of Salisbury. David, King of Scotland, then returning home with a victorious army laden with spoil, stopped on his way to invest Werk, and ordered a general assault. The Earl's brother, Sir Edward, a most gallant soldier, was in charge as castellan; his Countess was also in the Castle, and showed such a brave spirit, that "instead of receiving courage from others, she added heart to all." She went about among the soldiers, distributing gold and silver, with many engaging and encouraging words, and further promises of reward, telling them that "King Edward their lord would presently come to their relief." The Scottish assault was bravely repulsed; but that night, Sir Edward, mindful of the Countess' jeopardy, sought a messenger who would make his way to the King at York, and acquaint him with their condition. He threw down a purse of gold, as the reward of whoever would adventure for this service, with his best gelding to carry him; but the undertaking seemed desperate, and no hand was put out to take it up. Then Sir Edward declared that for the sake of the Lady of the Castle, and for theirs, he would do the errand himself. "For I have such knowledge of you," added he, "that I doubt not you will make a shift to hold out till my return." When darkness fell, he sallied out, and it rained so hard, that the Scottish sentries kept under shelter, and he passed through their army unperceived and unhurt. At daybreak, he was half a league away, and meeting two Scots driving cattle to the camp, pricked them with his spear, and cried, "Now go your ways, and tell your King that I am Edward Montacute, who have this night broke through his camp, and am now going to direct the King of England hither with his army;" and so set forward "on the spur." On receiving this message the Scottish King renewed the assault with redoubled fury; but the brave Countess and her little garrison again beat him back; and finding that he had wasted ten days before the Castle, he took his baron's advice to return home; and next morning re-crossed the Tweed with his whole force. That same day, at noon, King Edward arrived, and pitched his camp where the Scots had lain; and when he had put off his armour, declared he would "see the Castle, and give a visit to the noble lady the Countess of Salisbury," whom he had not seen since her marriage.

And when the Countess, hearing of his coming, had the gates set open, and came forth to greet him, in the full flush of her triumph, and radiance of her beauty, the King lost his heart to her then and there; and it is the cognizance of her garter, picked up by him at a Court revel with the warning words, " Honi soit qui mal y pense," that has now been for upwards of five centuries worn by one of the proudest orders of chivalry in Christendom.*

The loyal castellan, Sir Edward, was summoned to Parliament in the following year. He was very eminent in the French and Scottish wars, and married the King's cousin, Lady Alice Plantagenet, one of the co-heiresses of Thomas de Brotherton, Duke of Norfolk; but left only one daughter, Joan Countess of Suffolk, who died childless.

The Earl of Salisbury, however, fairly outshone his brother in renown; for " of his valorous deeds worthily to write," says Walsingham, "would be a work of great commendation," and some magnitude. He had been early retained to serve the King in peace and war for the term of his natural life, and scarcely a month of it was left unemployed. He lost an eye in the wars of Scotland, was taken prisoner in France, and narrowly escaped execution by the good offices of the King of Bohemia, fought the Saracens at Algeziras, succeeded the King's uncle as Earl Marshal of England, was Governor of the Channel Islands, Constable of the Tower, and Admiral of the Fleet. He died of a fever, brought on by the hurts and bruises he had received at a great tourney held at Windsor in 1344; and his fair widow ended her days in the sisterhood of St. Albans. The next Earl was—if that were possible—more completely a soldier than even his father had been, for his whole life may be described as one prolonged campaign. He fought at Cressy, and led the rear-guard at Poitiers, where he had a savage contention with the Earl of Warwick as to which of them should shed the most French blood. When mustering his men between Dover and Sandwich for the French war in 1359, he told them plainly he never meant to return alive, except he came as a conqueror; ": Wherefore," said he, " if there be any among you unwilling to partake with me in whatever God shall please to send us, honour or dishonour, peace or war, life or death, that man hath my free will to depart:" but not a man went. He was first married to Joan

---

* This is the version given by Froissart, Polidore Virgil, &c., of the foundation of the Order, and seems to me the most probable; but there is at least one other (see *St. John*), and the story has been very generally doubted. M. Fournier plausibly objects the Countess's age, being " sixty at the time;" but I am at a loss to divine how he arrives at this conclusion. When she was besieged at Werke Castle, Froissart says she had been married fourteen years; and in those days of early marriages, we may safely assume that she was not more than thirty—perhaps hardly as much. The Order was founded three years afterwards, in 1344. Her husband died of injuries received at the jousts that preceded its institution; and her son, who succeeded as second Earl of Salisbury, was then only fifteen years of age.

Plantagenet, the Fair Maid of Kent, but divorced on account of her pre-contract with Sir Henry Holland; and his second wife, one of the Mohun co-heiresses, brought him only one son, who, by a cruel fatality, was slain by his own hand at a tilting match at Windsor 6 Richard II. His nephew John thus became his successor. This, the third Earl of Salisbury, was the son of Sir John de Montacute, a person of great note in his time," and one of the heroes of Cressy, and his wife Margaret, the heiress of Thomas Lord' Monthermer, son of Ralph, Earl of Gloucester and Hereford, by Joan of Acres, the daughter of Edward I. She brought him, with other great possessions, her father's barony of Monthermer, and he had been summoned to parliament in her right by Edward III. Earl John was, like all his race, a soldier, "always in the hottest medley," and one of the chief men among the Lollards. He was a great favourite of Richard II., stood faithfully by him to the very end, and even conspired with the Earls of Kent and Huntingdon to get rid of his supplanter. All three accordingly presented themselves at Windsor Castle, disguised as Christmas mummers, with the intention of murdering the new King; but the plot leaked out, and they fled in hot haste to Cirencester, where they were seized and summarily put to death by the townspeople. All Salisbury's possessions escheated to the Crown by attainder; but Henry IV., moved by compassion for his widow and children, granted them a maintenance, and restored a great part of the estates to his son Thomas, who was reinstated in his Earldom in 1409. He was the fourth and last Earl of the blood of Montacute, and the greatest of all who bore the name; for none of his warlike predecessors ever rose to the height of his superb renown. The "mirror of all martial men," it was from him the greatest captain of the age first learnt the art of war; and his life was so crowded with exploits and achievements, that to recount them all would be to narrate anew the whole glorious reign of Henry V. The King trusted and rewarded him above all men; named him Lieutenant General of Normandy; gave him, with many Norman castles and manors, the entire county of Perche; and sent for him when he was lying on his death bed at Vincennes. There, with his last words, he solemnly "recommended his affairs" to his two uncles, the Dukes of Bedford and Gloucester, and to the "renowned Salisbury," and the former, as soon as he became Regent, accordingly appointed the Earl Vicegerent and Lieutenant of the King in France, Brie, and Champagne. He did " not sleep in his great office of trust;" but was unwearied in his efforts to maintain the dearly-won supremacy of England; and as long as he lived to be the soul of the war, her power was never humbled before her enemies. His name alone struck them with dismay; for he had made it a name of fear to their ears; and years and years after his time they still vividly remembered

> "What a terror he had been to France."

At last, as he stood at a grated window in a tower overlooking the siege of

Orleans, he was struck by a cunningly-aimed shot that carried away half his face, and killed Sir Thomas Gargrave by his side.

> "Salisbury—
> How far'st thou, mirror of all martial men,
> One of thy eyes, and thy cheek's side struck off?
> *　　　　*　　　　*　　　　*
>
> In thirteen battles Salisbury o'ercame,
> Henry the Fifth he first trained to the wars,
> Whilst any trump did sound, or drum strike up,
> His sword did ne'er leave striking in the field."
> —*Henry VI., Part I., Act* i.

He died eight days afterwards, and his body was taken home to be buried, by his express desire, in his own church of Bisham in Berkshire, where all his forefathers had lain. He had married "a very fair Lady," Eleanor Holland, sister and co-heir of the same Earl of Kent who had perished with his father at Cirencester, and left an only child, Alice de Montacute, in her own right Countess of Salisbury, who married Sir Richard Nevill, the eldest son of Ralph, first Earl of Westmoreland by his second wife Joan de Beaufort, and transmitted her heroic blood to her son the King maker. (See *Nevill.*)

The existing house of Montagu descends from a Northamptonshire squire who died in 1517, and lies buried in Hemington church. "Collins and others have deduced this Thomas Montagu from Simon Montagu, who is stated to have been younger brother to John, third Earl of Salisbury, and uncle to Thomas, the fourth and last Earl. Unfortunately there is no proof of the existence of this Simon, nor of any of the intermediate generations. But the late Mr. Thorpe (and it seems Mr. Anstis concurred in this opinion) suspected this family to be descended from James Montagu, a natural son of Thomas, the last Earl of Salisbury. This James lies buried in the church of Ludsdowne in Kent, of which place he derived the manor from his father. The bordure round the arms of the present family favours this idea. The question is now of little consequence : a proud family may be content with such a mark once in seven centuries."—*Sir Egerton Brydges.* Sir Edmund Montagu, the actual founder of the family, was the younger son of Thomas (though he lived to inherit whatever patrimony there may have been), and chose the law as his profession. He rose rapidly and steadily into great repute ; obtained a seat in the House of Commons, and such "authority, account, credit, and countenance" there, that once, when Henry VIII. was angered at the delay of one of his subsidy bills, he sent for Montagu, and crying, "Ho ! Will they not let my bill pass?" laid his hand on his head as he knelt before him, and said, "Get my bill to pass by such a time to-morrow, or else by such a time this head of yours will be off." Under this extreme pressure, Montagu "wrought so effectually," that the bill was got through the House even before the time prescribed. In 1539 he was named Chief Justice of the King's Bench, and six years afterwards Chief Justice of the Common Pleas, "a descent in honour, but an ascent in profit;" declaring that he was now an old man, and loved the kitchen before the hall, the warmest place best suiting with his age. In politics he was less successful; for, though able and active, and ever solicitous to trim his course towards the winning side, he compromised himself irretrievably in the cause of Lady Jane Grey, and was thrown into the Tower by Queen Mary, in spite of his tardily-proffered allegiance. He was only pardoned on payment of a heavy fine, and having been at the same time deprived of his Chief Justiceship, spent the rest of his days in retirement at his house of Boughton, in Northamptonshire, where he died in 1563. He had received very large grants when "the golden showers of Abbey-lands rained amongst great men" at the Sequestration, and bequeathed to his son Edward property in thirty-two parishes lying in four different counties.

This second Edward Montagu was the common ancestor of all the different branches of the house. From his eldest son, Edward, sprung the Dukes of Montagu; from his fourth son Henry the Dukes of Manchester and Earls of Halifax; and from his seventh son, Sir Sidney, the Earls of Sandwich.

Edward, the eldest son, who was created in 1621 Lord Montagu, a man "easy of access, courteous to all, yet keeping the secrets of his own heart," was "exceedingly beloved" in the county, and so hospitable that twelve hundred people were "fed, cheered and comforted by his beneficence." But he was "no friend to changes, either in church or state," and when the Civil War broke out, was imprisoned in the Savoy by the Parliament, where he died at the age of eighty-one. The next Lord was the father of two sons; 1. Edward, who was—as the story goes—dismissed from his post at Court for making love to Queen Katherine of Braganza, and fell at the siege of Bergen in 1665, unmarried; and 2. Ralph, termed "the most successful and unscrupulous of the entire house. He was employed as Minister in France, and as appears from Barillon's papers, received fifty thousand crowns from Louis to ruin Danby, who was dreaded and detested by France. This ruin he accomplished by reading in the House letters from Danby to the French Court asking for money in consideration for a treaty. Out of such disgraceful gains as these rose the pile of Montagu House, till lately occupied by the British Museum, which Lord Montagu built for his town house, intending to make of Boughton a miniature Versailles."—*Great Governing Families of England.* In this he certainly was successful, for he not only built a spacious palace in the French style, but emulated the splendours he had admired at Versailles by landscape-gardening on the grandest scale. The avenues he designed and planted—one of them six miles long—are still the pride of the county. From the time he first entered the House of Commons he had played a great part in political life, and no one was more zealous and active in furthering the Revolution of 1688. On their accession, William and Mary created him Earl of Montagu and Viscount Monthermer, and Queen Anne, in

1705, further conferred upon him the titles of Duke of Montagu and Marquess of Monthermer. He died four years afterwards, leaving only one surviving son, by his first wife, Lady Elizabeth Wriothesley (the widow of the last Earl of Northumberland), John, with whom the line closed. This second Duke had married one of the co-heiresses of the great Duke of Marlborough, Lady Mary Churchill, who brought him three sons, all of whom died early, and three daughters. The youngest of these, a second Lady Mary, proved to be the heiress, and was the wife of George Brudenell fourth Earl of Cardigan, who took the name of Montagu when her father died in 1749, and was himself created Duke of Montagu and Marquess of Monthermer in 1766. But their only son died in his father's lifetime, and once more the inheritance passed to a daughter, Elizabeth Duchess of Buccleuch, and from her to her second son, Lord Henry Scott, who succeeded to one of his grandfather's baronies, and bore his name.* He, again, left no heir male, and on his death in 1845 "the miniature Versailles" reverted to the son of his elder brother, the present Duke of Buccleuch.

Henry Montagu, the ancestor of the Dukes of Manchester, trod the same path to eminence that his grandfather had followed; for he, too, was a subtle and successful lawyer, and Lord Chief Justice of England. He succeeded Sir E. Coke in 1616; and in 1620 obtained from the Duke of Buckingham the staff of Lord Treasurer for a "consideration" of £20,000;† but held it for little more than a year, after which he had to resign in favour of the Earl of Middlesex, and to accept the inferior office of Lord President of the Council in exchange. During that year, however, he had received the titles of Baron Montagu of Kimbolton and Viscount Mandeville; Kimbolton Castle in Huntingdonshire, which he had purchased from the Wingfield family, having once been the property of the Mandevilles. Charles I., not long after his accession, further created him Earl of Manchester; and in 1628 he again exchanged his office for that of Lord Privy Seal, which he held for the rest of his life. "He was," says Lord Clarendon, "a wise man, and of an excellent temper, of great industry and sagacity in business." He left six sons; 1. Edward, his successor; 2. Walter, who was a Catholic priest, and Abbot of St. Martin's, near Pontoise; 3. James, the Puritan member for Huntingdon; 4. Henry, died s. p. 5. George, also a Puritan, who sat for Huntingdon in the Long Parliament, and was the grandfather of the celebrated Lord Halifax; and 6. Sidney, who never married.

* This barony has been revived in favour of another Lord Henry Scott, the second son of Walter, fifth Duke, who was created Lord Montagu of Beaulieu in 1885.

† "When Montagu was asked what the treasurership might be worth a year, he replied, 'Some thousands of pounds to him who after death would go instantly to heaven, twice as much to him who would go to purgatory, and a *nemo scit* to him who would venture to a worse place.'"—*Ibid.*

Edward, second Earl of Manchester, was one of the leaders of the popular party in the Civil War; but, Lord Clarendon tells us, "most unfit for the company he kept. He was of a gentle and a generous nature, civilly bred : had reverence and affection for the person of the King; lov'd his country with too unskilful a tenderness; and was of so excellent a temper and disposition, that the barbarous times, and the rough part he was forced to act in them, did not wipe out, or much deface, those marks." He was "in the van of the Puritan minority in the House of Lords;" impeached with the five obnoxious members of the Commons in 1642; and entered with heart and soul into the service of the Parliament. He commanded a regiment at Edgehill ; and the next year, as leader of the army raised by the seven associated Eastern counties, gained success after success, defeating the Earl of Newcastle at Horncastle, and carrying the city of Lincoln by storm. Cromwell, whom, "being his countryman, he had raised from a low fortune," was second in command; and jealousies and differences sprang up and grew between them, till, after the second battle of Newbury, the future Lord Protector formally charged the Earl with treachery and cowardice. The enquiry that followed led to the so-called Self-Denying Ordinances, that deprived Manchester of his command. He was Speaker of the House of Lords, but never took his place in parliament after the King's execution ; aided in the Restoration, and sat in judgment on the regicides. He died in 1671, having survived his eldest son. Charles, third Earl, his grandson and successor, who was in arms for the Prince of Orange, and for a short time his principal Secretary of State, was created Duke of Manchester in 1719, and is now represented by the seventh Duke.

Charles Montagu, Earl of Halifax, the younger son of a younger son (his grandfather had been the fourth brother of the second Lord Manchester) was left to make his own way in the world. While still at Cambridge, he wrote a poem that attracted the attention of the witty Earl of Dorset, who invited him to London ; and two years later gained his first celebrity by publishing (with his college friend Prior) a parody on Dryden's Hind and Panther. It was not, however, till he was elected a member of the Convention Parliament that he was fairly launched in the political arena; for he had always intended to enter the Church. "At thirty," says Macaulay, "he would have gladly given all his chances in life for a comfortable vicarage and a chaplain's scarf; at thirty-seven he was First Lord of the Treasury, Chancellor of the Exchequer, and a Regent of the Kingdom, and this elevation he owed not at all to favour, but solely to the unquestionable superiority of his talents for administration and debate." He was the first financier of his time, and two of his financial operations are still remarkable—the modest loan of one million in 1672 that was "the germ of the largest National Debt ever known ;" and the great re-coinage of silver in 1698. He was created Lord Halifax on the recommendation of the House of Commons in 1700, and Earl of Halifax and Viscount Sunbury by George I. in 1714, but died, without posterity, nine months afterwards. His barony had been secured by reversion to his nephew George Montagu, who in the same year received the two higher titles from the Crown, and transmitted them to his only son, the last heir-male of the family.

The Earls of Sandwich, the only other existing branch of the Montagus, descend from Sir Sidney, the youngest brother of the first Earl, who bought from Sir Oliver Cromwell Hinchingbrook, their present seat, near Huntingdon. Edward, his son, fought by Cromwell's side in the Civil War from the age of eighteen, and earned such rapid promotion that he was a brigadier when "not two months more than twenty years old:" but it was as a sailor that his principal reputation was to be gained. In 1656 he was appointed joint Admiral of the Fleet with Blake, and after the death of the latter, had the sole command, "in which," says Lord Clarendon, "he was discreet and successful." He had remained the staunch supporter and personal friend of the Protector; but, on the downfall of Richard Cromwell, he listened to the overtures made to him by Charles II., and agreed to use the Commonwealth fleet in forwarding the Restoration. In these negotiations, he acted independently of Monck, and even made it a condition that they should be kept secret from him, a reticence which Monck never forgave. He brought the King over to England, and two days after the joyful landing at Dover, the George and Garter were presented to him on board his ship, then riding in the Downs. In July following, he was created Earl of Sandwich and Viscount Hinchingbrook, made Master of the King's great Wardrobe, Admiral of the Narrow Seas, and Lieut.-Admiral to the Duke of York, Lord High Admiral of England. Two years after this, he was the King's proxy at his marriage, and brought back the new Queen; but the latter part of his life is chiefly noteworthy for his successes at sea. In 1665, when the Dutch and English fleets had been engaged for thirteen hours off Leostaff, Sandwich, with his blue squadron, fell upon the enemy's centre, divided their fleet in half, and turned the scale of victory. Eighteen men of war surrendered on that occasion; and in the course of the same year he captured twelve others, with a host of merchant men, and one thousand prisoners. He fell in 1672, during the second Dutch war, serving as Vice-Admiral under the Duke of York. One Sunday night in May, the united French and English fleets were lying sociably together off Solebay, in Suffolk, and "great jollity and feasting" was going on, when the Earl broke in with the unwelcome suggestion that it would be well to weigh anchor and get out to sea, for "as the wind stood, the fleet rode in danger of being surprised." The advice was not taken, and so ill received by the Duke of York, that he retorted by a taunt implying that the Earl was afraid. The surprise he foreboded actually occurred on the following day, when De Ruyter attacked the allies unawares, and utterly defeated them. Sandwich, in his ship, the Royal James, was the first to sail out and interpose between the advancing enemy and the unprepared fleet, and singly and successfully engaged several of their ships. No one, however, came to his relief; the Duke chose to abandon him to his fate; and when he saw his own Vice-Admiral, Sir Joseph Jordan, sail past him to join his commander, he cried out, "We must fight it out alone to the last man!" and loyally kept his word. He defended himself till noon, and sunk three of the Dutch fire-ships; but a fourth, under cover of the smoke, succeeded in grappling the Royal James, and set her aflame. Of her crew of one thousand men, the greater part lay dead or dying on deck, and the slender remnant got away in the long boat. But the Earl, with the Duke's taunt of the night before still ringing in his ears, disdained to save his life, and remained behind to perish, the last man left in his burning ship. Twelve days after the battle, his body, recognized by the star on his coat, was found floating in the sea off Harwich, and buried with public honours in Westminster Abbey. From his eldest son, Edward, descends the present and eighth Earl; Sidney, the second, married the heiress of the Wortleys, adopted their name, and was the father-in-law of the eccentric authoress, Lady Mary Wortley Montagu.

Mountford: from Montfort-sur-Rille, near Brionne, in the arrondissement of Pont Audemer. The site of their castle can still be traced near the present town. This great baronial house derived from a common ancestor with the Bertrams, Oslac, Baron de Briquebec, who lived in the tenth century. His son Thurstan de Bastenberg was the father of Hugh Barbatus—Hugh with the beard —whom both Dugdale and Sir Henry Ellis believe to have been the companion of the Conqueror. But Wace expressly tells us that he had been slain in a private quarrel soon after William became Duke of Normandy—in those early and evil days " when the feuds against him were many, and his friends few; when the barons warred upon each other, and the strong oppressed the weak. A mighty feud broke out between Walkelin de Ferrières, and Hugh Lord of Montfort; I know not which was right and which wrong; but they waged fierce war with each other, and were not to be reconciled; neither by bishop nor lord could peace or love be established between them. Both were good knights, bold and brave. Once upon a time they met, and the rage of each against the other was so great that they fought to the death. I know not which carried himself most gallantly, or who fell the first, but the issue of the affray was that Hugh was slain, and Walkelin fell also; both lost their lives in the same affray, and on the same day." This combat is mentioned by William de Jumièges. It was therefore another Hugh—his son Hugh II., who furnished fifty ships and sixty knights for the expedition to England, and was the " Constable " spoken of by Ordericus at the battle of Hastings; for the De Montforts were hereditary Marshalls of Normandy. He had gained his reputation in arms twelve years before, when he had been one of the leaders at the famous battle of Mortemer. Wace describes how he helped to save William Malet's life (see p. 262) and " he is one of the four knights named by Guy, Bishop of Amiens, as the mutilators of the body of Harold at the close of the conflict; but I need only here repeat my utter disbelief in so improbable a statement, supported by no other contemporary writer."—*Planché.* He received a barony of one hundred and thirteen English manors, with a large proportion of Romney Marsh; and "was one of the barons intrusted by the Conqueror with the administration of justice throughout England, under Bishop Odo and William Fitz Osbern in 1067; and by the Bishop himself, Hugh de Montfort was made Governor of the Castle of Dover, the chief fortress in Odo's own Earldom, and the key of the kingdom. His absence on other duties with the Bishop south of the Thames was taken advantage of by the Kentish malcontents, and led to the assault of the Castle by the Count of Boulogne. The attempt failed, through the loyalty of the Royal garrison and the personal hostility to Eustace entertained by the townsmen from the recollection of the fatal affray in 1051."—*Ibid.*

This second Hugh de Montfort died a monk in the Abbey of Bec, but at what date is not exactly known. He had been twice married, and left two sons; but both were childless, and his daughter Alice was his heir. The elder, Hugh III., died on pilgrimage. The second, Robert, who in 1099 commanded the Norman army in Maine, took part with Robert Curthose against Henry I., and being "called in question for his infidelity," begged permission to go to the Holy Land, and joined the Crusaders under Bohemund, receiving a hearty welcome and a high command as *Strator Normanici exercitus hereditario jure.* He never returned home, and had perforce left the whole of his possessions in the King's hands. They must, however, have been given back to his sister Alice— perhaps because she was the wife of the King's cousin, Gilbert de Gant; for "by reason of her being so great an Inheritrix," their son bore her name of Montfort, and was styled Hugh IV. He joined in the rebellion of Waleran Earl of Mellent, whose daughter he had married, and spent fourteen years of his life in prison— "no man," says Dugdale, "interceding for his enlargement, in regard what he had done was without any provocation." Fourth in descent from him comes Peter de Montfort, who, "puffed up with ambition," took a leading part in the Baron's War, and was one of the council of nine authorized to exercise regal power after the victory of Lewes. More than this; in the Commission soon after appointed "to reform and settle the Kingdom, there was a more especial power given to this Peter than any of the rest, viz. : That whatsoever he should swear to do, the King must be obliged to it. During the time of his continuance in power, certain it is, that he did much mischief;" but his reign and his life ended together in the disastrous rout of Evesham, when the Prince of Wales "came down upon those rebellious Barons like terrible Thunder," and he fell by the side of his great namesake, Simon Earl of Leicester :—

> "le fleur de pris
> Qui taunt savoit le guerre!"*

* This famous Earl was in no wise connected with the baronial De Montforts. His father, Simon the Bald, who first came to England in King John's time, and

. "In him this family was in the Meridian of its glory, which thenceforward daily faded." Yet his son was "in no whit abridged of his ancient Patrimony," being admitted to grace by the Dictum of Kenilworth, though he, too, had been in arms with the barons, and taken prisoner at Evesham. The next heir, John, who went to the wars of Gascony with Edward I., had summons to parliament in 1295, and was succeeded in his barony by his two sons. The youngest, Peter, was in priest's orders when his elder brother died, but " was so dispensed with that he took to the World and became a Knight," married Margaret de Furnivall, and, as we shall presently see, still further emancipated himself from the austerity of his earlier years. His wife brought him an only son, named Guy, between whom and Margaret de Beauchamp, daughter of Thomas Earl of Warwick, a marriage was arranged "for the better founding of a firm league of friendship between them and their Posterities, in regard that many Suits had been betwixt their Ancestors, by reason that their Lands, in divers places, lay continuous." There was an additional compact, which settled these questions to the Earl's advantage, for it so happened that the young heir died before his father, and left no posterity. Failing issue by Guy and Margaret, Montfort's castle and estate of Beldesert in Warwickshire, with many other lands, were to go to the said Thomas, Earl of Warwick, on Sir Peter's death. " But all this while Sir Peter was living, and having had issue by an old Concubine, Lora de Ullenhalle, took care for their advancement, as may appear by those Lands they enjoyed." These illegitimate descendants flourished at Coleshill, co. Warwick, till the attainder of Sir Simon Montfort in the time of Henry VII.

The name is kept by Wellesbourne Montford in Warwickshire.

Maule : from the town and lordship of Maule, in the Vexin Français, eight leagues from Paris, which belonged to this family for four hundred years. The Sires de Maule are " frequently mentioned by Ordericus Vitalis, and their history has been preserved by. Duchesne, from the time of Guarin, who lived c. 960, father of Ansold, father of Peter Lord of Maule."—*The Norman People.* "Roger, the last Lord of Maule, was killed at the battle of Nicopolis in Hungary, fighting against the Turks, 1398 : and his coat of arms, which is the same with that borne by the Earls of Panmure, was set up in the church of Notre Dame in Paris. His only daughter and heiress was married to Simon de Morainvilliers, Lord of Flaccourt."—*Wood's Douglas.* Guarin de Maule, a younger son of Ansold, Sire de Maule, came over in the Conqueror's army, and received as his guerdon the manor of Hatton, and some other lands in Cleveland. One of his two sons, Robert, attached himself to David Earl of Huntingdon, and followed his fortunes when he became King of Scotland. He

---

achieved his fortune by marrying Amicia de Beaumont, the eldest co-heiress of the Earl of Leicester (see *Beaumont*) was the great-grandson of an illegitimate son of Robert, King of France, who had the town of Montfort by gift of his father, and thence assumed his surname.

had grants in the Lothians, and his son, who fought at the battle of the Standard in 1138, further received from the King, in free gift, the lands of Foulis in Perthshire. Sir Peter de Maule, third in descent from him, about the year 1224 married Christian de Valognes or de Valoines, an heiress thrice-told, for she brought him one splendid inheritance after the other. From her father, William de Valognes, she had, first, the two baronies of Panmure and Benvie, and other lands both in England and Scotland: then, on the death of Christian Countess of Essex (the grand-daughter of Gunnora de Valognes), ten years later, the whole of the great possessions of the De Valognes in the counties of Cambridge, Essex, Norfolk, and Suffolk, came to be divided between her, " Lora, her aunt, and Isabel, her cousin:" and lastly, she succeeded to the estates of Sibilla de Valognes, widow of Robert de Stuteville. In the fifteenth century, Sir William Maule claimed the great barony of Brechin in right of his grandmother Jean Barclay; but as the better part of it was annexed to the crown of Scotland in 1437, the share he secured was by no means a large one. His descendant, Patrick Maule of Panmure, who went to England with James VI. as one of the gentlemen of his bedchamber, and faithfully followed Charles I. in all his battles and his subsequent captivity, was created Earl of Panmure and Lord Maule of Brechin in 1646. The fourth Earl, true to his family traditions, joined the Jacobite rising in 1715, and was taken prisoner at the battle of Sheriffmuir, but rescued by his brother Harry, and soon after escaped abroad, forfeiting alike lands and honours. His was said to be " the largest of the confiscated properties;" and at two different times, the government offered to restore it to him, provided he would return home and take the oath of allegiance to the House of Hanover. But this he stedfastly refused to do; and he died, as he had lived, an exile, in 1723. He left no children. His brother Harry, who was next in succession, had by his two marriages no fewer than eight sons: but they all without an exception died unmarried. The third of these, William Maule, who by the death of his two elder brothers became the head of the house, was created Earl of Panmure and Viscount Maule (in the peerage of Ireland) in 1743; and was enabled, in 1764, to re-purchase his ancestral estate of Panmure, which he settled on the son of his sister Jean, George Earl of Dalhousie, "in life rent, and then to the Earls second and other sons in their order." At his death in 1782, this settlement was impugned by the heir-male, Thomas Maule (grandson of Henry Maule, Bishop of Meath) but the Court of Session decided in favour of Lord Dalhousie. When the Earl died five years afterwards, the Maule estates accordingly devolved on his second son, William Ramsay, who took the name and arms of Maule, and was created Lord Panmure in 1831. His son, Fox Maule, succeeded his brilliant cousin, the late Marquess of Dalhousie, as eleventh Earl in 1852, and died, a childless widower, in 1874. Thus the English barony of Panmure soon followed the fate of the previous Scottish and Irish honours.

Monhermon, for Monthermer. It is doubtful whether this name should stand on the list. We hear nothing of it till 1296, when Ralph de Monthermer, "a plain Esquire," made a stolen love-match with the daughter of Edward I., Lady Joan Plantagenet, commonly called Joan of Acres. She was then the newly-made widow of Gilbert de Clare, Earl of Gloucester and Hertford, and invested with all his honours and possessions; but, probably well aware that she should never obtain her father's consent, hazarded the dangerous step of marrying without license. The imprudent couple at once fell under the ban of the King's displeasure, who punished them for their offence by the sequestration of her castle and honour of Tunbridge and all other estates. Monthermer, however, was a gallant soldier, who fought his way into the good graces of his war-like father-in-law by his valour in the Scottish wars, and was reinstated and summoned to parliament as Earl of Gloucester and Hertford *jure uxoris* in 1299. In the following year we find him on the Roll of Carlaverock, and though not styled by these titles, bearing the chevronels of Clare in lieu of his own green eagle :—

> " Cely dont bien furent aidiés,
> E achievées les amours,
> Après granz doubtez e cremours,
> Tant ke Dieus le en volt delivre estre,
> Por la comtesse de Gloucestre,
> Por ki long tens souffri granz maus.
> De or fin o trois chiverons vermaus
> I ot baniere soulement;
> Si ne faisoit pas malement
> Kant ses propres armes vestoit,
> Jaunes ou le egle verde estoit,
> Se avoit nom Rauf de Monthermer."

It would appear—though Dugdale does not allude to it—that he and the Princess had been much indebted to the good offices of Anthony Beke, Bishop of Durham, for their reconciliation with the King. He served in all the Scottish campaigns, and became such a favourite with Edward, that when Robert Bruce was crowned King at Scone, he had a grant of all Annandale, with the title of Earl of Atholl (forfeited by an adherent of the Bruce) and the lands and fees of all those that held of the Earldom. The Princess Joan died in 1307, and her Earldoms of Gloucester and Hertford devolved—as, according to modern usage, they should have done twelve years before—on her son Gilbert de Clare, and there is no further mention of the Scottish title, as, in his summons to parliament in 1308, and in the various grants he received from the new King in 1309, he is styled only Ralph de Monthermer. He was taken prisoner at Bannockburn, but "found favor in regard of former accidental familiarity with the King of Scots, in the Court of England, and was pardoned his fine for Redemption, who thereupon returned into England, and brought the King's

Target, which had been taken in that fight, but prohibited the use thereof." He died about 1325. He had a second wife, Isabel de Valence, widow of John de Hastings, and the second of the four great Pembroke heiresses; but his only two sons were by his first marriage. Thomas, Lord Monthermer, the eldest, was killed in a seafight with the French in 1340, leaving an only child, Margaret de Monthermer, who, by her marriage with the Earl of Salisbury's second son, conveyed the barony to the Montacutes. Edward, the younger, was summoned to parliament in 1337; but on that single occasion only; and nothing is known as to his posterity.

· **Musett**; in Duchesne's list, Muffet: Leland gives it Muschet, which is the more correct version. This family bore *Argent* two bars between six leopards' faces *Gules*, three, two, and one. William Muschet held of the Bishop of Ely in 1165 (Lib. Niger), and was Sheriff of Cambridgeshire 2 Ric. I., as was William "filius John Muschet" 6, 9, 11, and 12 Ed. III. Muschetts, a small manor still held under the Bishop of Ely, retains their name. Adam de Muschet, about 1240, held under Robert de Waledom at Great Peatling in' Leicestershire (Testa de Nevill). John Musket was Lord of Heccecomb, Somersetshire, in 1316 (Palgrave's Parl. Writs). Robert Muschett of Gloucestershire and Hertfordshire, Ralph Muskett of Hertfordshire only, in the time of Edward I. (Rot. Hundred.). At the same date "Dominus William Muschett" was a considerable proprietor in Kent, and held land in Huntingdonshire (Ibid). Roger Mushett gave some land at Benney to the Preceptory of Temple Rothley. (Mon. Angli.) In Dorsetshire, John Muskett held in Winterborne-St. Martin 20 Ed. III., and during the same reign Gerard Muschet married Joan, daughter of Ralph Brett, Forester of Blackmore, and sister and heir to another Ralph, but left only a daughter.—*Hutchins' Dorset.* The name occurs in Scotland from a very early period, but was there used as a familiar form of Montfichet. "The corruption of names, arising from a tendency to abbreviate, and to adopt leading sounds, is conspicuous in the following instances, some of which occur in the Ragman Roll[*]—Montfichet is transformed into Muschet, Montalt into Mouhat or Mowat: Vache into Veitch, Baddeby into Baptic,' Vermel into Wermel, Grosseteste into Grozet."—*W. Chambers.*

Meneuile: long seated in the counties of Durham and Northumberland. Milburn, a member of the Morpeth barony, was held of it by knight's service, by Robert de Meneville: see *Mackenzie's Northumberland.* In the former county their manor-house at Sledwish, near Whorlton, and within a few fields of the Tees, was granted to them at an early date by the old Lords of Barnard's Castle; they also held Winston, &c., and one of them, Robert de Menevill, received from King John the hand of Agnes de Dyvelstoun (Dilston) a Northumbrian

---

[*] The instruments of homage to Edward I. the "Hammer of the Scots," now preserved in the State Paper Office, are usually known by the uncouth title of the "Ragman Rolls." ·

heiress. Another Robert, Sheriff of Durham in 1339, acquired the Lordship of Horden by purchase from Sir Thomas Holland in 1343; and left three sons, of whom the youngest alone was married, and had an only daughter, Isabel. This Isabel, generally called the Lady of Horden, became the heiress, and the estate passed to her son by her second husband, Sir William Claxton. Probably the William de Meyneyvyle who was twice High Sheriff, first in 1364 and again in 1370, was one of her uncles. The family appears seated at Sledwish in the following century, and finally came to grief in the first year of Queen Mary's reign.

. "Ninyan Menvill was a partisan of Dudley, Duke of Northumberland; and, it should seem, joined in proclaiming Lady Jane Grey Queen on the death of Edward VI.; for he was attainted 'of high treason committed at Durham House on the 10th of July, I. Mary, in company with John, Duke of Northumberland, Andrew Dudley, and John Gayts, Knights, and others.' Menvill escaped with life, fled, and was outlawed. The Dudleys found favour in the eyes of Elizabeth; and perhaps by a natural revulsion of feeling, all those who, for whatever cause, had suffered under the late reign, seemed entitled to grace and mercy from a successor who had herself tasted of the bitter cup of persecution. Menvill was restored in blood and estate in the first of Elizabeth, whilst the temporalities of the See were in the Crown. Yet it seemed doubtful whether Menvill ever recovered possession of Sledwish. The Crown, I apprehend, sometimes granted these patents of reversal without much minute inquiry into existing circumstances, and the parties interested were left to fight out their battle as they might."—*Surtees.* At all events, there is no further record of the Menvilles in the county histories. Their old manor-house is thus described: "Sledwish Hall, lonely and sequestered, is a place of ghastly gray renown. There are tales of secret passages and concealments; and some years ago the bones of an infant were found carefully deposited in a stone coffin in an adjoining field. The circumstance only infers that some of the Catholic residents here might bury their dead privately with their own ceremonies, and some persecuted priest may very possibly have found refuge here during the horrors of the Popish plot." Yet it was for conspiring to place a Protestant princess on the throne that poor Ninian Menville was attainted and outlawed.

Surtees believes the family to have been "a branch of the Lords Menill of Cleveland." But the two names are certainly distinct; for "Dominus de Meneuilla 1 feod. lig.:" is found in Duchesne's *Feoda Normanniæ.*

Manteuenant: for Maucovenaunt, according to Leland's more correct reading; though the true spelling is Mauconvenant. This family is entered in the *Nobiliaire de Normandie*, and gave as their arms *Gules* nine roses *Argent.* Their seigneurie of Sainte Suzanne was in the district of Argentan; and Charles Adolphe de Mauconvenant, Marquis de Sainte Suzanne, sat among the nobles of the Cotentin in the Assembly convoked in 1789, for the Election of the States General.

The first mention of them in England is in 1156, when Mauger Malevenant served as Sheriff of Sussex and Surrey. Nicolas de Maucovenant held of William Fitz Alan in Shropshire in 1165 (Liber Niger). William Malcuvenant was a tenant of Patric Earl of Sarum in Wiltshire (Ibid.), and witnessed the foundation charter of his Priory at Bradstock (Mon. Angl.). Geoffrey de Maucovenant held half a knight's fee at Easington in Cleveland of Margaret Lady Ros of Werke, one of the co-heiresses of Peter de Brus, Lord of Skelton (Kirkby's Inquest). In 1314 he was one of the Commissioners of Array in the Wapentake, and summoned for service against the Scots (Palgrave's Parliamentary Writs). Robert Maucovenant is found in Lincolnshire temp. Ed. I. (Rot. Hundred.), where both he and Laurence Maucuvenant held in Carleton of the Percy fee (Testa de Nevill).

Manfe; more rightly Maufe, according to Leland's reading, or Malfey. This name is twice found in the Norman Exchequer Rolls 1180–95. Alexander Malfe was a benefactor of Sawtrey Abbey in Huntingdonshire. (Mon. Angl.) William Malfed held three knight's fees of Richard de Aquilâ in Sussex (Liber Niger) and Simon Malfe, of Northamptonshire occurs 1194–98. (Rotuli Curiæ Regis): Roger Malfe, of the latter county, in the *Rotulus Cancellarii* of 1203. Another William Malfe, or Maufee, was certified as one of the Lords of the townships of Ripe, Chiddingley, Hoadley, Operton, and Landport, all in the County of Sussex, in 1316.—*Palgrave's Parliamentary Writs.* Geoffrey and Simon Malfey, Suffolk, c. 1272.—*Rotuli Hundredorum.* John Maufe was among the Barons and Knight Bannerets taken prisoners at the battle of Bannockburn. Oliver Malfe held one knight's fee of the Honour of Gloucester; and John de Maufe another of Roger de Quincy at Haselbury, Northamptonshire.— *Testa de Nevill.* In the Camden *Roll of Arms,* Maufe bears *Argent* a Lion rampant *Sable* between nine escallops *Gules.*

Menpinçoy, for Montpinçon, in Leland's list Mountpinson; a baronial family, from Montpinçon, near Evreux. The Baron de Montpinson, Bailliage de Vere, and another De Montpinson, Bailliage de Domfront, took their seats in the great Assembly of the Norman nobles in 1789. "Ralph de Montpinson was Dapifer to William the Conqueror. (Ord. Vit.) His son Hugh, who married a daughter of Hugh de Grentemesnil, and his grandson Ralph, are also mentioned by Ordericus. Philip de Montpinson witnessed 1132 the foundation charter of Fountains Abbey, York (Mon. v. 306). The family appears afterwards in Lincoln, Essex, Hertford, Norfolk, Wilts; and in 1165 the barony of Montpinson in Normandy consisted of fifteen knight's fees. (Feod. Norm. Duchesne)."—*The Norman People.* They bore *D'argent a une lion de sable, a une pinzon de or en le espaule.* Fulk de Montepincernoun, first of the name, "by marriage with Agnes, only daughter and heir of Ralph Facatus, shortly after the Conquest, obtained several lordships in Norfolk, where the family continued to flourish till 7 Ed. II., when William the son of Sir Gyles, sold his estates. From that time till the reign of Edward IV. the Montpinsons continued in a state of obscurity. The first who rose to any public notice in Wilts was Robert Mompesson, who by marrying the heiress of Godwyn and Bonham obtained considerable property; his son John 18 Edward IV. was Sheriff of Wilts, and in the first year of the usurper Richard, his name was put in the commission for raising forces in the county. He bore the arms as above given, which he must have derived from the Norfolk family, and most probably was well aware of his descent from them.

"The family was dispersed so widely over the West of England that I fear a very correct pedigree cannot be obtained."—*Hoare's Wilts.* I will at least give the one furnished by Sir Richard himself, and by Hutchins, in his *History of Dorset.*

Robert Mompesson of Bathampton, Wilts, the husband of Alice Godwine of Gillingham, was the grandfather of Drew, who died in the lifetime of his father John (the Sheriff of 1478 and 1482), leaving three sons, John, Richard, and Thomas. John's line ended in the ensuing generation, but Richard, seated at Maiden Bradley, and Thomas, seated at Corton, were both represented till the last century.

Richard's posterity was transplanted into Dorsetshire by his son's marriage with the heiress of Durnford, where the six following generations had their abode. The last heirs were two brothers, neither of whom were married. Thomas, the eldest, died in 1767, having outlived Henry, the younger, some forty-four years. Henry, whose lungs were affected, had been ordered to winter in a milder climate, and was on his way to the South of France when he was attacked and murdered by a band of robbers near Calais. He was at the time in company with Mr. Sebright and two other English gentlemen. "Being wounded, but not mortally, by a pistol shot, he fell, and might probably have survived had he not, by looking up too soon, been observed by the robbers just as they were going off, on which they returned and cut his throat. They belonged to the former band of the famous Cartouche."—*Hutchins' Dorset.*

The Corton branch had continued in Wilts, where John Mompesson served as High Sheriff in 1508, and Edward Mompesson in 1540. The two last mentioned by Hoare were members of parliament. Thomas was returned in 1661 for Wilton; in 1678 for New Sarum; in 1681 for Old Sarum; in 1688 for the county; and in 1695 again for New Sarum; while Charles represented Wilton and Old Sarum from 1698 to 1705. Thomas, who was knighted in 1661, held Pilesdon Court, Dorset, in right of his wife Dinah, daughter and coheir of Sir Hugh Windham, Bt.; and was one of the Commissioners of the Privy Seal in 1697.

Maine, "or Mayenne, from Mayenne in Maine, a powerful baronial house, of which Walter de Mayenne occurs in 976 (La Roque, i. 159, 160). Judael of Mayenne had a vast barony in Devon 1086, and his family long continued there. In 1165 Walter Fitz Juel de Mayenne (de Meduana) held a barony of twenty-one knight's fees in Kent."—*The Norman People.* Judael appears in Domesday as Judhel de Totenais, so named from his barony of Totness. "Nothing is known of this person but that he possessed the baronies of Totness and Barnstaple, which intimates that he was high in the Conqueror's favour."—*Lysons.* M. Delisle mistakes him for one of the house of Toeni. He was probably grandfather of the Juhel de Meduana who witnesses one of the Empress Maud's charters to Geoffrey de Mandeville. Dugdale mentions a Walter de Meduana "amongst these who were witnesses to the grant, made by William de Braose to the monks of S. Florence at Salmure (Saumur) in France, whereof King William the Conqueror and Maud his Queen were some of the number." He also speaks of the other Walter, who lived in the time of Henry II., and upon the assessment made upon the marriage of the King's daughter, certified to a barony of twenty knight's fees *de veteri feoffamento* and nine *de novo.* He cannot have been fond of campaigning, for the only further notice of him to be met with is, that he was fined in 1171 for not joining the expedition to Ireland, and again in 1186 "in regard he was not with the King's army at Galway." Nothing more is known of him than that he married the widow of Roger Earl of Hereford, who survived him and enjoyed his inheritance. But there must be some mistake in the name, for there is no Roger Earl of Hereford to be found in the Bohun pedigree.

Nicholas de Meduana, of Dorset and Somerset, occurs in the Great Roll of the Pipe of first Richard I. According to Lobineau, "Juhel de Mayenne, Seigneur de Dinan" in 1197, bore on six escutcheons six mullets pierced of six points; a coat entirely different from any of those borne by the English families of this name. One of them—the Maynes of Teffont-Ewyas, claim, by Burke's account, to descend from "Joel de Maine, of King's Nymet, temp. Hen. I.:" another, settled in the neighbourhood of Stirling since the commencement of the fifteenth century, received the title of Baron Newhaven in 1794, but it expired with its first holder. This Sir William was the sixth son of William Mayne of Powis, co. Clackmannan, the husband of three wives and the father of twenty-one children, "in whose house the cradle is said to have rocked for fifty years." I need scarcely add that the family is not extinct, though Powis passed through one of his granddaughters to the Alexanders.

Mainard. "Mainardus homo Rogeri Pictavensis," is mentioned in Domesday as an under-tenant in Essex and Lincolnshire; and either he or another of the name held in Wilts, Hants, and Norfolk, before the Conquest. "M. Mainart or Mainard, Ralph, John, and the estate of the Mainards in Normandy are spoken of in the Norman Exchequer Rolls, 1180–1198."—*The Norman People.* The early notices of this family are very scanty. "In the hydarium of Henry II. Maynard was certified to hold one hide and half in "Cherleton" (Charlton), but as the paramouncy of his estate is withheld, no clue is furnished for tracing it to the Domesday lord. Maynard does not occur among the feudatories of the Barony of Wahull in the *Liber Niger*, and it may therefore be presumed that family had not then acquired interest here."— *Baker's Northamptonshire.* Croxton Abbey held five bovates in the fee of Griseley, the gift of Robert Maynard, senior: and John Mainard had property in Fencot and Moorcot 7 Ed. I.—*Bullington and Ploughley's Oxfordshire.* Edward Maynard, in the previous reign, sold to the monastery of Sheppey some lands at Milsted, in Kent.

The pedigree of the Viscounts Maynard only commences in the following century with John Mainard of Axminster in Devonshire, who served in France under the Black Prince, and was appointed Constable of Brest in 1352. Sixth in descent from him we find another John Maynard, sitting in Queen Mary's first Parliament as Burgess for St. Albans, and numbered among the thirty-nine stout Protestants who were indicted in the King's Bench for absenting themselves from the House rather than join in accepting the Pope's authority in the realm. He had two sons, 1. Ralph; and 2. Sir Henry, father of the first Lord Maynard.

Ralph's descendands lived at Sherford, in the parish of Brixton, which passed from them to the Drakes. A younger son named Alexander settled at Tavistock, and was the father of Sir John Maynard, Serjeant-at-law, described by Fuller as "one of the biggest stars of the constellation of pleaders; the bench seeming sick with long longing for him to sit thereon." He was a man of high character and ability, and took an earnest part in the struggle against Popery that culminated in the Revolution of 1688. He lived to be upwards of ninety, and to be presented at Court after King William's landing. The King, on being told of his great age, observed that he must have outlived all the lawyers that had been his contemporaries. "Ay, and I might have outlived the laws themselves," replied the old man, "but for the happy coming of Your Majesty." His son left two coheiresses; one married to Sir Henry Hobart (ancestor of the Earl of Buckinghamshire), the other to the Earl of Stamford.

The other successful cadet, to whom we must now revert, Sir Henry Maynard, an able and ambitious man, had achieved his fortune more than one hundred years before as Secretary to the Lord Treasurer Burghley. He purchased the old estate of the Lovaines, Estaines-in-Turri, or Little Easton in Essex; thus seating himself in the county where the original mention of the name is found, though the manor held by the Mainard of Domesday—Wickford, is in an altogether different district. He sat as member for St. Albans in three of Queen Elizabeth's parliaments, in another as knight of the shire, and served as Sheriff during the last year of her reign. He was knighted either by her or King James—authorities differ on this point—and died in 1610. The eldest of his eight sons, William, "being one of the most considerable persons in the county, appears in the list of the first baronets" the following year; was created

Lord Maynard of Wicklow in Ireland in 1620; and Lord Maynard of Estaines in the English peerage in 1628. His successor, the second lord, " was one of those truly worthy patriots who did not run headlong with the incendiaries of the last century" (Morant wrote in 1766) "but were for taking proper measures to deliver this nation from the Tyranny of the Army, and restoring peace to these distracted Kingdoms; for which he and the rest of these patriots were impeach'd of high treason in 1647." Among them was his uncle Sir John Maynard, M.P. for Lostwithiel, who, for "exerting himself that the army might be disbanded," was expelled from the House of Commons, and committed to the Tower as a traitor.*

Lord Maynard was a zealous promoter of the Restoration, and Charles II., on ascending the throne, wrote to commend him with his own hand. "I do assure you there is no man upon whose affection and unbyassed resolutions to serve me I do look with more confidence then upon yours; and therefore you may reasonably presume that my kindness is proportionable. I hope it will not be long before I have a good occasion to manifest it." Nor had he, in common with other suffering loyalists, to rest content with fair words and empty promises; for the King named him Comptroller of his Household, with a seat in his Privy Council; and James II. retained him both at this office and at the Council Board. The direct line ended with his grandson Charles, the last of another family of eight sons, of whom five died young, and three successively bore the title. None of them ever married. Charles, who thus became the sixth Lord Maynard, and lived a bachelor to the ripe age of eighty-five, obtained a Viscountcy in 1766, with remainder to his nearest kinsman in blood, Sir William Maynard of Walthamstow (descended from Secretary Maynard's third son). On his death in 1775, Sir William's son, Sir Charles (Sir William himself had died three years before) accordingly succeeded to this new honour, and transmitted it to a nephew named Henry, with whom it expired in 1865. There had been an heir male, for this last Viscount had a son who died the year before him, leaving two little daughters. To the eldest, Frances Evelyn—then barely four years old—he bequeathed the whole of his estates; and she married in 1881 Francis Greville Lord Brooke, son of the fourth Earl of Warwick.

Morell. This name is by some writers conjectured to have been the *sobriquet* of a dark-complexioned man. John Morel was seated in Norfolk in 1086 (Domesday) and another—if not the same Morel, occurs in Northumberland nine years afterwards. "In the year 1095, Robert Mowbray, Earl of Northumberland, and his party, marched into Bamborough Castle for security, on the approach of the royal troops to chastise them for their treason. The

---

* This was one of the unfortunate men whose opinions were in advance of their time. Had he lived nearly two centuries and a half later, he would have been an honoured member of the Peace Society, and accounted an earnest—if over-zealous— reformer of abuses in expenditure.

King, William Rufus, besieged it in person. As traitors never think themselves safe anywhere, Mowbray secretly fled for sanctuary to St. Oswin's shrine at Tynemouth, where he was taken prisoner. His steward and kinsman, Morel, with a courage that would have done honour to a better cause, defended the Castle in the absence of his unfortunate lord. He defended it against all the forces of the King. The King had turned the siege into a blockade, and raised a fortress near it called Malvoisin, *i.e.* Bad Neighbour, some time before the Earl fled. Morel, not terrified by so many bad neighbours, still held out, with an astonishing perseverance and resolution, to the surprise of the King, who, beginning to be uneasy, tried to effect that by policy, which he could not do by force. He ordered the Earl to be led up to the very walls, and a declaration to be made, that if the Castle did not surrender, his eyes should be instantly put out. This succeeded to his wish. Morel no sooner beheld him in this imminent danger, than he consented to yield upon terms. For his fidelity and affection to his lord, and his gallant defence, the King took him into his Royal protection and favour. A god-like action, thus generously to reward a faithful enemy!" *Wallis' Antiquities of Northumberland.* Another John Morel (no doubt his descendant) held a fief in Northumberland in 1165. (Liber Niger). Robert Morel witnesses Jordan de Chevrecourt's grant to Pontefract. (Mon. Angl.) William Morel, in the time of Henry III., held one knight's fee at Newton-Morrel, near Gilling, of the Honour of Richmond.—*Gale's Richmondshire.* The coat of Sir William Morele, " les armes de France ove un lyon recoupée d'argent ung bende de goules," is entered in 1322 on the roll of the battle of Boroughbridge.—*Palgrave's Parliamentary Writs.* In the same year Lucas Morel, resident in the Hundred of Hinckford, testified as "being blind and exceeding fourscore years of age."—*Ibid.*

The name extended throughout England. Middleton Morel was their seat in Northumberland. Ralph Morell held one knight's fee in Roding-Morell, Essex, of the Honour and Castle of Aungre (Ongar). Geoffrey Morell was the owner in 1317 ; "and the year following a fine passed between him, Joan his wife, and Alan Morell."—*Morant.* Another manor in the parish of Gosfield, in the same county, was named from them ; and some of the family "were living in Hedingham Sible as low as the reign of Henry VIII." In the time of Henry I., " Morel de Heddendon" held of the barony of Robert de Ewyas.—*Duncumb's Herefordshire.* Nicholas Morrel, of Lincolnshire, occurs in the *Rotulus Cancellarii* of 1202.

Mainell, or De Grente-mesnil, from Grente-mesnil (now Grandmesnil) in the arrondissement of Lisieux. Hugh de Grente-mesnil, " a brave Souldier," fought stoutly at Hastings, and "was that day in great peril : his horse ran away with him, so that he was near falling, for in leaping over a bush the bridle rein broke, and the horse plunged forward. The English seeing him ran to meet him with their hatchets raised, but the horse took fright, and turning quickly round brought him safe back again."—*Wace.* Two years after the battle he was appointed, with

Odo, Bishop of Bayeux, William Fitz Osbern, and others, one of the Justiciars of England during the King's absence in Normandy. He was Viscount of Leicestershire and Hampshire, and according to Domesday, held one hundred and four Lordships, of which two-thirds, with the Honour of Hinckley—in right whereof he was Lord High Steward of England—were in Leicestershire. He lived to be a very old man, and in 1094, " being grown aged and infirm, he took upon him the habit of a Monk; and within six days afterwards departed this life, whereupon Bernard and David, two Monks of St. Ebrulfe's " (a Norman monastery he had restored and endowed), " having seasoned his Corps with Salt, and wrapped it in an Hide, conveyed it to Normandy, where it was honourably buried on the South side of their Chapter-house."—*Dugdale.* His elder sons left no posterity: but from the fourth, Ivo, descended Hugh de Grentemesnil, whose daughter Petronill became his sole heir, and brought to her husband, Robert Blanchmains, Earl of Leicester, the Honour of Hinckley and the Hereditary Stewardship of England, which afterwards passed, through her daughter Amicia, to the Montforts. This Countess Petronill left a singular bequest to the church of Leicester—a coil of her own hair, twisted into a rope, by which she desired that the lamp always kept alight in the choir might be suspended. It is further recorded of her, that when she was taken prisoner with her husband at Leicester, " desirous of lessening the prize which their enemies had obtained, she drew from her finger a ring set with a precious stone of great value, and threw it into the river."—*Bullington and Ploughley's Oxon.*

A branch of the Meynells is of very early date in Yorkshire: but how—or if at all—related to Hugh the Justiciar, we are not informed. "Stephen, Sire de Mesnil, temp. William I., obtained great estates in York and Notts. His son Robert and grandson Stephen joined in the foundation of Scarth Abbey, York (Burton, Mon. Ebor. 357). Hence the Lords Meynil of York. Gilbert,[*] second son of Stephen I., was of Notts 1130, and was ancestor of the Meynells of Meynil Langley."—*The Norman People.* The first Lord Meinill was Nicholas, great grandson of the second Stephen, who, for good service in the Welsh wars, had a debt of one hundred marks remitted to him by Edward I., besides a grant of free warren on all his lands in Yorkshire. He afterwards served in the Scottish campaigns, and had summons to parliament in 1295. Five years previously, he had brought a charge against his wife of an attempt to poison him, and though she is said to have successfully cleared her character, would never see her again. The barony became extinct with his son Nicholas in 1322: but was re-granted in 1336 to an illegitimate son of the same name, who married a daughter of Lord Ros of Hamlake, and left an only child, Elizabeth. She married John, second Lord D'Arcy, conveying this second Barony of Meinill to her descendants, with

---

[*] One pedigree of the Meynells calls this Gilbert a younger brother of the Hugo de Grentemesnil who was in the Conqueror's army, and yet makes him by a manifest absurdity, the father of Robert Meynell, mentioned in 1165 !

whom it remained till 1418, when it fell into abeyance among the sisters of the eleventh Lord D'Arcy.

Gilbert, the ancestor of the Meynells of King's Langley, was the father of Robert, who 12 Hen. II. held five knight's fees of Ralph Fitz Herbert. One of these was Langley in Derbyshire. His son William was seated there, and bore the arms of his feudal suzerains, the Fitz Herberts; to which Hugo, the next heir, Steward to the Earl of Derby, added the horse-shoes of the Ferrers. Hugo's grandson, who represented Derbyshire in Edward I.'s fifth parliament, married an heiress, the daughter of Robert de la Ward, Steward of the Household to Edward I., and again changed his coat of arms for the Vair, *Ar.* and *Sa.* of the De la Wards, which his descendants continued thenceforward.

In the next generation, Hugh Meynell, who fought at Cressy and Poictiers, was a baron by writ 1 Ed. III.; but the summons was not repeated, either to his son or his grandson. With the latter the elder line failed; but a younger brother, William, of Yeavely and Willington, was the direct ancestor of Hugo Meynell Ingram, of Hoar Cross in Staffordshire, at whose death in 1871 the family became extinct. The name of Ingram was taken on account of the great inheritance of the Viscounts Irvine, which eventually came to the descendants of the third of the five sisters of the last Viscount, Elizabeth Ingram, married in 1782 to Hugo Meynell, younger, of Bradley.

Maleluse; for Maules, or Meulles; (Leland gives it Meulos:) from Meulles, near Orbec, in the arrondissement of Lisieux. Baldwin de Meules or de Molis, whose estates in Devonshire fill eleven columns of Domesday, was of the blood royal of Normandy, being the younger son of Gilbert Crespin, Earl of Brionne and of Eu, whose grandfather was Duke Richard Sans Peur. Count Gilbert, "illustrious alike in his fore-fathers and his descendants," had been one of the early guardians of the Conqueror, and was waylaid and murdered in 1040 as he was peaceably riding near Eschafour, expecting no evil. His two young sons, for whom a similar fate was apprehended, were conveyed by their friends to the court of Baldwin of Flanders, then "the common protector of banished men;" and his lands seized and appropriated. Count Baldwin harboured the fugitives for thirteen years; till, on the occasion of his daughter Matilda's marriage with Duke William, his son-in-law, at his intercession, restored to them the Norman fiefs that their father had held. Richard received Orbec and Bienfaite, and Baldwin Sap and Meules. Both brothers were in the Conqueror's army, and both are mentioned by Wace, the elder as

"Dam Richard ki tient Orbec,"[*]

and the younger as the "Sire de Sap."

[*] The name of this Richard is one of the principal omissions on the Battle Roll. Of his blood was the splendid and far-famed lineage of De Clare, Earls of Hertford, Gloucester, and Pembroke.

⁛ This Sire de Sap, who received from his Royal kinsman the great barony of Oakhampton, comprising one hundred and sixty-four West country manors, and the Hereditary Shrievalty of Devon, is variously called in Chronicles Baldwin the Viscount, Baldwin the Sheriff, Baldwin of Exeter, Baldwin de Sap, Baldwin de Meules, Baldwin Fitz Gilbert, or Baldwin de Brionne, "to the bewilderment of readers unversed in Norman genealogy." The King further entrusted to him the custody of the dearly-won city of Exeter, and of the great castle that he was directed to build there, to make room for which as many as forty-eight houses had to be cleared away. He died at about the same time as his elder brother—before 1090; and a miraculous story is told in 1091 by one Walkeline (afterwards known as St. Aubin, Bishop of Angers), of his appearance after death. Walkelin, then a parish priest, had been sent for in the middle of the night to shrive a sick man; and on his way home, was alarmed at hearing the tramp of approaching soldiers, believing that he was about to encounter some of Robert de Belesme's men, marching to the siege of Courcy Castle. He prudently determined to keep out of sight; and attempted to hide himself under some medlar trees until they had gone by. But he was suddenly confronted by a giant bearing a mighty club, who cried in a voice of thunder: "Stand! Not a step further!" and the priest, frozen with terror, remained rooted to the spot; the grim club-bearer standing by his side. Then, in the bright moonlight, a long and lamentable procession passed before his wondering eyes; a procession of the dead, bemoaning the evil that they had done in their time. There were many he had known in life, both men and women; his own brother Robert; former neighbours and friends; great barons and Seigneurs; Bishops, Abbots, and priests—some who had been regarded as saints upon earth—yet all alike bowed down with anguish, groaning, and bewailing the excruciating torments of purgatory. Amidst the ghastly throng he recognised the dead faces of two great men that had not long before passed away, Richard and Baldwin, the sons of Count Gilbert of Brionne.

Baldwin had been twice married; but of his wives the Christian names only are known. Albreda, the first, was a kinswoman of the Conqueror's; "the King gave him his aunt's daughter to wife," as one of his sons states in a memorial addressed to the Duke of Normandy, and quoted by Ordericus; Emma, the second, was probably the "wife of Baldwin the Sheriff" that is entered in Domesday. He had three sons; Richard, his heir; Robert, who received in 1090 his grandfather's town and castle of Brionne; and William; besides three daughters, of whom Adeliza alone survived him.

Richard, generally known as Richard Fitz Baldwin, who succeeded as Baron of Oakhampton and Sheriff of Devon, died s. p. in 1137, and was first buried at Brightly, but by desire of his sister Adeliza subsequently transferred to Ford Abbey. She was his sole heiress, and in her own right Sheriffess of Exeter and Baroness of Oakhampton. She was the wife of Randolph Avenel, by whom she had an only child, Maud, who succeeded to her barony and was twice married; first to Robert d'Avranches; and secondly to another Robert, a bastard son of Henry I. By her first husband she had one daughter named Hawise; by the second another named Maud; "Which Daughters, by each Husband, being great Heirs, and in Minority at their respective Fathers' Deaths, were by King Henry II. committed to the Custody of Reginald de Courtenay. He therefore discerning the advantage he had by thus being their Guardian, took Hawyse (the elder) for his own Wife; and match'd Maude (the younger) to William de Courtenay his own Son by a former Wife."—*Dugdale.* No more complete or compendious arrangement could have been devised for securing the great Barony of Oakhampton to his posterity!

Another of the name, Roger de Meulles, who in 1086 held three manors in Devonshire under Baldwin the Viscount, founded a venerable West-country house that is still in existence. It is clear that he must have been a kinsman of his suzerain's, but there is no evidence to show that he was his son, as the family pedigree would lead us to believe. His posterity was seated in Cornwall as well as in Devon and Somerset, the name gradually lapsing into Moels, Mules, and Moyle. Dugdale mentions another Roger de Meules in the time of Stephen; but begins his account nearly one hundred years later with Nicolas, who married one of the co-heiresses of James de Newmarch, in whose right he possessed Cadbury and Sapeston in Somersetshire. He further received considerable grants in Devonshire from Henry III.; and "was in such high esteem with the King, that James his Son and Heire was by special Command admitted to have his Education with Prince Edward, Hugh de Giffard and Bernard de Savoy (his Tutors) being required to receive him, with one Servant, and to find him Necessaries." As "a stout and expert soldier," Nicolas was throughout his life employed in offices of trust and importance; having at different times served as Constable of eight royal castles, Lord Warden of the Cinque Ports, Governor of the Channel Islands, and Seneschal of Gascony, where he gained a signal victory in 1243 over the King of Navarre, and took him prisoner on the field. His eldest son died before him; and the second, Roger, was his successor, and the father of John, a baron by writ in 1299, with whose three sons the line terminated. The last of them, John, fourth Lord Moels, died in 1377, leaving two daughters, Muriel, married to Sir Thomas Courtenay, and Margaret, Lady Botreaux, between whom the estates were divided and the barony fell into abeyance.

The present family of Mules is derived by Burke from a second son of Nicholas, second Lord Moels, who, as Dugdale expressly informs us, died s. p. 9 Ed. II. But, setting aside this impossible ancestor, they are lineally descended from Sir John Mules, living before the reign of Richard II., and married to the heiress of the Flavells, "who brought the manor of Ernsborough and a goodly patrimony to him," which afterwards passed away through heiresses.

Memorous: a singular name. John de Mumuru' held one half a knight's fee in Purteshull, Gloucestershire, of the Honour of Gloucester, and half a fee of William Stuteville.—*Testa de Nevill.*

This is the only occasion on which I have met with it: unless, indeed, we stretch a point, and agree to recognize it under a disguise. Henry and William Muneno, about 1200, witness a deed of Andrew Fitz Milo at Stokesay.—*Eyton's Salop.* A charter from Roger de Momery to Bishop Roger de Meyland is preserved in the muniment room of the Chapter of Lichfield.—*Staffordshire Historical Collections;* vol. vi. p. 2.

Morreis; presumably from the fief of St. Maurice in Normandy. The families of this name were numerous. "Morris Court in Bapchild," Kent, took its name from one of them, and was long their residence. They were extinct there before the end of Henry IV.'s reign.—*Hasted's Kent.* John Morice, Moricz, Moriz or Moryce, Knight or Banneret, was a man of note and influence in the reign of Edward II. He was knight of the shire for Bedford in 1322 and 1327; twice also Conservator of the peace for the county; summoned to attend the great Council at Westminster in 1324; and the same year appointed one of the Commissioners of array for Bedfordshire and Buckinghamshire, "empowered to raise and march certain detachments of hobelers and archers for service in Gascony."—*Palgrave's Parliamentary Writs.* We there meet with two more John Morices who were his contemporaries; John Morice of Cambridge, a burgess for Cambridge in 1307, 1324, and 1327; and John Morice, who served as knight of the shire for Huntingdon in 1319 and 1322. He was probably the ancestor of the John Morys whose name appears on the list of the Gentry of Huntingdon in 1433.

Morleian Maine. I believe that here, as in the case of Mountmartin Yners (see Introduction, p. xiii.), a letter has accidentally disappeared, and that we should read "Morlei and Maine." There are thirteen instances of names thus joined together in Holinshed's copy, though for the sake of convenience, I have always separated them, and shall do so now.

The Morleys were a Norfolk family; and two of the name—Ingulf and Morell de Morley—witness the foundation charter of Windham Priory in the time of Henry I. They first come into notice during the reign of Edward I., when Sir William de Morley, who had served in the Scottish wars, was summoned to parliament as a baron. His son Sir Robert, named by Edward III. Admiral of the Fleet from the Thames mouth Northwards, was the gallant commander that won the greatest victory ever yet obtained over the French at sea; "the like Sea-fight having never before been seen." This was on Easter Day, 1341, when Lord Morley attacked and well nigh annihilated the enemy's fleet off Sluys in Flanders; and the following year "sayling with that Fleet unto Normandy, and other Ships from the Cinque-ports, he burnt Fourscore Ships of the Normans, with three Port-Towns, and other Villages." Twice again—in 1348 and 1355—he was in command of the victorious Northern fleet; nor were his services less freely rendered on shore. They extended over a period of thirty-two years, during which he participated in the glories of Cressy, for his first campaign in France was undertaken in 1327, and the eighth and last in 1359. He died while attending the King thither again in the following year, being then Constable of the Tower. He was twice married. His first wife, Hawise, sister and heir of John le Mareschal, had brought him the hereditary office of Marshal of Ireland and the barony of Rie, comprising the hundreds of Eynsford and Fourhow, with other estates in Norfolk, besides lands in Essex and Herts. Two of her manors, Swanton-Morley in Norfolk, and Hallingbury-Morley in Essex, still bear his name. His second wife was Joan de Tyes; and by each marriage he had a son: 1. Sir William, Marshal of Ireland in his mother's right; 2. Sir Robert, "styled cousin and heir of Sir Robert de Montalt, formerly Steward of Chester," and twice mentioned in the French wars, whose line expired with his great-granddaughter Margaret, the wife of Thomas Radcliffe.

His eldest son and his grandson, successively Barons Morley, were, like him, engaged in the King's service in France; and the grandson, Sir Thomas, fourth Lord, arriving at Calais in 1380 "with divers other English Lords, rode with his Banner display'd" in full feudal state. But to this banner it would appear there was another claimant. "In 1395," Blomfield tells us, "there was a Cause in the Court of Chivalry between Sir John Lovell, Plaintiff, and this Sir Thomas, concerning the arms of Morley, *Argent* a Lion *Sable*, claimed by Lovell as heir to the Lords Burnell, who bore the said Arms; Maud, sister and heir of Sir Edmund Burnell, having married John, Lord Lovell, his grandfather. Lord Morley pleaded that the Arms belonged to his Ancestors from the Conquest, time out of mind, without Impeachment, except by Nicholas Lord Burnell at the siege of Calais, who claimed against Sir Robert de Morley his Ancestor; to whom the Arms were adjudged by the Constable and Marshal, and that they had borne them ever since. It seems certain, however, that the ancient arms of the Morleys were *Argent* a Lion *Sable*, sometimes double-queued, and are those of Roger de Cressi, assumed by the Morleys, who inherited from him." Morant gives them *Argent*, a lion passant between two bars *Sable*, thereon, three bezants. The Burnell lion was crowned.

The next in succession, a second Sir Thomas, was retained to serve Henry V. with ten men-at-arms, and thirty archers; "and being with him in France, at the time of his death, bore one of the Banners of Saints which were carried at his solemn Funeral." He was the father of Robert, sixth and last Lord Morley, who died in 1442, leaving as his sole heiress a baby daughter, Alianor, little more than ten months old. She carried the barony to William Lovell, the second son of William, Lord Lovell and Holland, and it passed to their son Henry, who died s. p., "unhappily slain at Dixmuyde in Flanders in

1489;" and then to their daughter Alice, the wife of Sir William Parker, standard-bearer to Richard III. Her son was summoned to parliament as Lord Morley in 1555; and his line continued till 1686. The old barony then fell into abeyance. Dugdale, I should observe, always spells the name "Morle."

There was, it appears, a Welsh family that bore it; for Williams, in his *History of Monmouth*, tells us that "the daughter and heir of Sir John Morley of Raglan married Thomas Gwillym-ap-Jenkin, and brought Raglan and a great estate belonging to it."

The title of Earl of Morley was granted in 1815 to Lord Boringdon, descended from a very old Devonshire family that bore the name of Parker, but was wholly unconnected by blood with the earlier Lords Morley, and bore different arms.

Maine: a duplicate. (See p. 301.)

Maleuere: from Maulevrier,* near Rouen. In the Bayeux Inquest "feodum Malevrier in Asnières debet servitium dim. mil." "Helto de Mauleverer held in Kent in 1086, and 1120 Helto, his son, witnessed the charter of Bolton, York (Mon. ii. 101)."—*The Norman People.* · "Robert de Roumeli (who, after the forfeiture of Earl Edwin, was the first grantee of his lands in Craven), gave to this second Helto and his wife Billiholt the manors of Bethmesley, Hawkswick, and East Malham, which their descendants continued to hold as feudatories of the Honour of Skipton. Helto's son, 'Wil'mus Maleporar,' who was in possession at the time of the marriage of Matilda, daughter of Henry I., and his grandson, also William, 21 Hen. II. are both mentioned in the Black Book of the Exchequer. In the same year the son of this second William, Helto, gave Hawkswick to the monks of Fountains; and this grant was confirmed by Aaliza de Roumeli. Allerton and Bethmesley continued in the direct line of this family till William Mauliverer, who had three sons, Ralph, Henry, and William, gave the latter to his third son, from whom descended in succession William, Giles, and William, which last had Sir William Mauliverer, knt., father of Sir Peter Mauliverer, who lived in the reign of Edward III., and left two daughters and co-heiresses, Alice, married to Sir John Middleton of Stockeld, and Thomasine to William de la Moore, of Otterburne, by whom he had Elizabeth, his only daughter and heiress, who, marrying Thomas Clapham, brought the manor of Bethmesley into that family. The

---

* There appear to be several places of this name. "Lamartinière (1735), who gives Maulevrier as the name of a little town in Anjou, of a parish in the Pays de Caux in Normandy, and of a forest in the same province, says of the first-named place, 'Cette ville a été bâtie par Foulques Néra, qui la donna à un de ses chevaliers, qui prit le nom de cette terre et la transmit à sa postérité.' Both places are found in Aubert de la Chenaye Des Bois (*Dict. de la Noblesse*), who also gives Maulevrier, a property and seigniory in Burgundy, possessed in the fourteenth and fifteenth centuries by a branch of the house of Dumas-Marcilly."—*R. S. Charnock.*

eldest son of this match was John Clapham, a "famous esquire" in the wars of York and Lancaster, and a vehement partisan of the house of Lancaster, in whom the spirit of his chieftains, the Cliffords, seemed to survive."—*Whitaker's Craven.* The Mauleverers bore *Argent* three greyhounds cursant *Sable*, collared of the first: *armes parlantes*, in allusion to their name; and had their burial-place in the church of Bolton Priory, where they had founded a chantry. Beneath this is the vault where, according to tradition, they and their descendants were always interred upright :—

> "There, face by face, and hand by hand,
> The Claphams and Mauleverers stand :
> And in his place among son and sire
> Is John de Clapham, that fierce esquire,
> A valiant man and a name of dread
> In the ruthless wars of White and Red ;
> Who dragg'd Earl Pembroke from Banbury Church,
> And smote off his head on the stones of the porch."

Allerton-Mauleverer, between Boroughbridge and Wetherby, was their residence for more than five hundred years; and several of the family appear on the roll of High Sheriffs of the county. The first of these, who bore the remarkable name of Halvatheus, served 8 Henry V.; John Mauleverer 13 Henry VIII.; and Sir Thomas 6 Edward VI. The latter had been knighted at Flodden, and was succeeded by his cousin and son-in-law Sir Richard, again Sheriff 31 Elizabeth, who was the father of a second Thomas, created a baronet in 1641. Yet this newly-honoured Sir Thomas turned traitor, sat on the King's trial, and signed his death-warrant. The fifth baronet, who died unmarried in 1713, was the last of the line; and Allerton-Mauleverer passed to his stepfather Lord Arundell.

Other branches there had been, seated at Allerton-Gledhow, Potter-Newton, and Woodersome; and one of the last-named house, who married a Cleveland heiress in the time of Edward IV., was still represented at the end of the last century. Arncliffe (i.e..Erne or Eagle Cliff), "the dark hill, steep and high," that, clothed with its hanging woods, looks down upon the ruins of the old Carthusian Priory of Mount-Grace, is one of the peaks of the so-called Alps of England, and was the ancient domain of the Colevilles of the Dale. Joan, sister and co-heir, of Sir John de Colevile, brought it to Sir Richard Mauleverer, whose descendants held it for upwards of three hundred years. "This family," says Longstaffe, "wore the field sable, and collared the greyhounds of the *Malus Leporarius* with gold. They give the greyhound as a device in a variety of ways, and had another beautiful badge, the maple-leaf; but I suspect that it is a Colville one, and not paternal. William Mauleverer, in time of Elizabeth, was the genealogist of the family; but it would have been extraordinary indeed had he escaped the temptations of his age. His waverings have their interest.

In 1581, at the age of twenty-four, he prefixes some verses to the well-known fiction, which generally passes as the pedigree of Mauleverer. In 1584, he signs the true pedigree in the Visit. of Yorkshire. The said fictitious pedigree is in fact brought down to 1587, and in 1591 it is emblazoned on vellum, certified "*par me, Lancaster Herald at Arms*," and sealed with that unscrupulous herald's coat. In 1601, at the age of forty-five, Mauleverer reverts to the truth, and elaborates with proofs *in extenso* for every generation, "my pettigree collected and contrived out of myne ancient and newe evidences." It had been well had the Elizabethan heralds' contrivances been triumphantly refuted by every family in the same way. The last male heir, Timothy Mauleverer, died in 1794.

Maudut, from Mauduit, near Nantes. Some have sought out an ungracious meaning to this name, affirming that it signifies *maledoctus*, or evil-taught. Geoffrey Maudit held in Wilts *in capite* 1086, and his brother William held a barony in Hampshire at the same date. The latter was afterwards Chamberlain to Henry I., and received from that King the hand and estates of one of his wards, Maud de Hanslape, who brought with her the feudal Barony of Hanslape in Bucks, "the castle and honour of Porcestre" (Porchester) and "Bergedone" (Berwedon) "in Com. Rutl. with the whole Soke, which Queen Maud gave to the before-specified Maud." Their descendants held their Buckinghamshire barony "by the service of Chamberlain to the King in his Exchequer:" and one of them, William Mauduit, having married Alice de Newburgh, the daughter of Waleran, fourth Earl of Warwick, his son succeeded to that Earldom on the death of Margery, the last heiress, in 1263, "with the Castle and honour of Warwick, and all the manors and lands thereto belonging." It was one of the fairest inheritances in England, but he only possessed it during four years, and left no son to succeed to it when he died. His only sister Isabel married William de Beauchamp, the "Blind Baron" of Elmley, and thus brought the Earldom of Warwick into the family that made it so famous. Isabel afterwards took the veil in the convent she had founded at Cokehill. Walton-Mauduit in Warwickshire took the name, as did Easton-Mauduit and Gaston Mauduit in Northamptonshire.

Castlethorpe in Bucks is the site of "the ancient Castle of the barony of Hanslape, taken and demolished in 1217 by Foulkes de Brent, when it was garrisoned against the King by its owner William Mauduit, one of the rebellious barons. It exhibits traces of very extensive buildings."—*Lysons.*

The descendants of the Wiltshire baron long continued seated at Somerford Mauduit in that county, and one of them had summons to parliament as a baron of the realm. This was John Mauduit, who served as Sheriff 3 Ed. III., was Constable of Old Sarum, and died in 1347, leaving a son, "of whom," says Dugdale, "I have not heard what became. But there was another John Mauduit, who had his residence at Wermenstre in Com. Wiltes;" and bequeathed a great inheritance to his little granddaughter Maud (then only nine years' old) at his death in 1364.

Mountmarten, from a town so named in Normandy. "Mountmartin *près la mer* was held of the Honour of Mortain, and was situate within the jurisdiction of the Vicomté of Cerences."—*T. Stapleton.* The fair of Montmartin, established before 1082 by Robert Count of Mortain, had some celebrity, and was much frequented by the Bretons. Jordan de Montmartin occurs in the Norman Exchequer Rolls, during the last years of the twelfth century. The name remained in the Duchy till 1789, as it was then borne by one of the nobles of the Côtentin assembled for the election of the States General.

The earliest notice that I have found of it in England is in the thirteenth century, when Jordan de Montmartin received from Henry III. a grant of Trianstone in Kent. He was dead before 1251, and the land had passed to Ospringe Hospital.—*Archæologia Cantiana.* The next in date, Matthew, served Edward I. in his Scottish wars, and is the "Mons. Mathy de Montmartyn" who in 1303 appears on the "Roll of the Magnates and others who had served under the King at the siege of Stirling, &c. :" and was "Del houstel le Roi demorantz a Dunfermelyn." In 1307 he had license " to enclose and krenellate his manse of Burn" (Borne, as it appears in Domesday, now Westbourne) on the extreme western boundary of Sussex, adjoining Hampshire (Sussex Archæologia). In neither county, however, can I find any further trace of the family, with this one exception, that John de Monte Martino was Prior of Lewes in 1319. Two years after that, Ponsard de Montmartin occurs in Essex. He was summoned from the Hundreds of Dengie and Thurstable to attend the muster at Newcastle-on-Tyne for service against the Scots: and in 1324 received a summons to the great Council at Westminster.—*Palgrave's Parliamentary Writs.* But I have not succeeded in discovering anything more concerning him, or any descendants of his.

Mantelet, or Montellis: Duchesne gives it Mantel. William de Montellis is mentioned in Normandy about 1198. The name, as Mantel, dates from the Conquest in England. "Turstin Mantel was a baron in Buckinghamshire 1086 (Domesday): where he also held some land under the Earl of Mortaine; and in 1115 King John granted Tottenhoe, in the same county, to Ralph Mantel. In 1210, Osbert Mantel is mentioned as enfeoffing Robert de Beauchamp; and another (if not the same, Ralph Mantel, as the deed is undated) granted Tottenhoe to Snelsham Priory; his son William and his brother Geoffrey witnessing the deed."—*Lipscomb's Bucks.* No further account of them is to be found in that county. In Northamptonshire, "the Mantells had an interest in Rode as early as the reign of Henry II., where, and at Hartwell, &c., insulated individuals are continually emerging at detached periods ; but no regular descent can be verified prior to John Mantell, who in 1446 levied a fine of the manor of Heyford in fee simple. Both Bridges and Vincent confound him with his grandson of the same name who died in 1503. Walter Mantell, the next in succession, was knighted. His son, John Mantell, sallying forth in a nocturnal frolic with his brother-in-law, Lord Dacre to chase the deer in Sir N. Pelham's park at Laughton in 1541, encounter'd three men, one of whom was mortally wounded in the affray. He and his associates were tried for murder and executed; and their estates escheated to the Crown. To complete the irretrievable ruin of the house, his son Walter Mantell engaged in the Kentish insurrection headed by Sir Thomas Wyatt, and being taken prisoner with him, was sent to the Tower, and soon after executed in Kent, and attainted."— *Baker's Northants.* His uncle and namesake, who had purchased the site of Horton Priory in 1553, suffered in the same cause in the same year at Seven Oaks, and his estate also fell under attainder. It was, however, restored to his son Matthew by Queen Elizabeth, and was still held by his descendants when Hasted's *History of Kent* was published in 1790. The name is sometimes given as Mantle. They bore *Argent* a cross engrailed between four mullets *Sable.*

In Essex, Robert Mantell held Little Maldon of the Honour of Peverell and founded a Cistercian Monastery at Bilegh in 1180. He was Sheriff of the county for twelve consecutive years—from 1169 to 1181; and Mathew de Montell (probably his son) filled the same office during four years of King John's reign. John Mantell appears as Sheriff in 1208: Mathew again (joined with him) in 1214; and with Robert Mantell in 1215; Robert alone in 1219. Another Mathew left a widow named Cecily, who held Little Maldon in 1289; but this is the last time their name appears in the history of the county.— *Morant.*

Miners: in Duchesne's list, by the accidental omission of the first letter, this appears as yners. A Herefordshire family of this name (extinct in the male line since 1765) claims to have been seated at Treago, in that county, from the time of the Conquest: but their pedigree only begins in the fourteenth century with John de Miners, Constable of the Castle of St. Briavel under Edward II. The name, however, is found much earlier, as Gislebert and Henry de Mineriis occur in Palgrave's *Rotuli Curiæ Regis* of 1198. They held of the Honour of Breteuil in Normandy. (*Duchesne.*)

Here, as in so many other instances, I am disposed to adopt Leland's earlier reading, which gives this and the next name as " Manclerke et Maners."

The house of Manners takes its time-honoured name from Mesnières, near Rouen. "The family of Mesnières long continued in Normandy, Ralph and Roger de Mesnières being mentioned in the Exchequer Rolls of 1198, and William de Mesnières in 1232, whose descendants continued to be of consequence till about 1400, when the male line ceased. Richard de Manieres came to England 1066, and in 1086 held of Odo of Bayeux, Borne, Kent, and Benestede, Surrey (Domesd.). He was father of Tirel de Manieres, who, with

Helias de St. Saens, a neighbouring noble, devoted himself to the cause of William Clito, the dispossessed heir of Robert of Normandy, and the legitimate heir to the throne. These faithful adherents of Clito lost their estates, and had to endure extreme sufferings on his behalf. On his death-bed he recommended them to his uncle, Henry I., who accepted their submission. Tirel de Manieres, who was surnamed 'Peregrinus,' or the Wanderer, from his adventures with William Clito, granted the church of Benestede, Surrey, to St. Mary Overy temp. Hen. I. (Mon. ii. 85), and gave the manor of Benestede in free marriage with his daughter to William, Earl of Salisbury. Hugh de Maniere, his son, was also surnamed 'Peregrinus,' and with his son Richard 'Peregrinus' or de Manieres, made grants in Hants to Waverley Abbey (Manning and Bray, ii. 146). He had another son, Robert, who is mentioned in the charters, and whose gift, as well as that of his brothers, was confirmed by Eugenius III. in 1147 (Mon. Angl. ii.). In 1165 this Robert held part of a fee in Northumberland; and his sons, Walter and Thomas de Maners, witnessed a charter of William de Vesci 1178 (Mon. ii. 592). Their elder brother Henry had issue Reginald de Manieres, who witnessed a charter of Hugh, Count of Eu, temp. John (Mon. ii. 921), and as ' De Maisneris' is also mentioned in Normandy 1198 (Magn. Rotul. Scaccarii Normanniæ). From him descends the house of Manners of Ethel, Northumberland; and from another branch Baldwin de Maners, a baron by writ in 1309."—*The Norman People.*

Etal, the original seat of the family, was held of the barony of Wooler; and in 1277 Sir Robert de Maners had a writ of military summons to "go against Llewellyn Prince of Wales, according to the service he owed of two knight's fees in the county of Northumberland; but being infirm, Sir Robert Talebois·served for him." His grandson and namesake, "one of the principal persons of the county certified to bear arms by descent from their ancestors," was a soldier of some note in Border story. He fought at Nevill's Cross, was Warden of the Marches, and Constable of Norham, gallantly beating back the Scots when they had all but surprised the castle, and nearly a score of their men had scaled the walls, and gained a footing on the battlements. It was he who obtained "license to embattle" from Edward III. in 1342, and built the castle that—now a picturesque ruin—still bears his sculptured coat of arms, and stands above the village of Etal on the Till. Third in descent from him was another Sir Robert, a stout Yorkist throughout the Wars of the Roses, and rewarded with grants both of land and money by Edward IV. and the King-maker, the crowning achievement of whose life was his marriage. His wife, Eleanor de Ros, one of the greatest heiresses in the country, was of the true "old conquering blood," the sister and coheir of Edmund, last Lord Ros, and eventually his sole representative. She brought him the accumulated baronies of Ros, Hamlake, Vaux, Trusbut, and, above all, Belvoir, with its broad domain, and the noble castle enthroned above, holding sway and sovereignty over all (see vol. i., p. 117). Thenceforth the little

Border castle was deserted. The family, transplanted into Leicestershire, at once took rank among the greater barons, and the son of the heiress of Belvoir, George, Lord Ros, matched with the blood royal. The Lady Ros was Anne, sole child of Sir Thomas St. Leger, by Anne of York, Duchess of Exeter, the eldest sister of Edward IV. In honour of this great alliance, their son George was granted an augmentation of his arms, adding the Royal lions and fleur de luces of France and England in chief, was named a Knight of the Garter, and created Earl of Rutland by Henry VIII. in 1525. The new Earl received besides a splendid grant of Abbey lands, including part of the estates of Kirkham and Rievaulx, two monasteries founded by his ancestor Walter Espec, who had vainly vowed to "make Christ his heir." He commenced rebuilding Belvoir Castle, and died in 1543, leaving behind him a good name as "a noble house keeper, a tender father, and a kind master."· The third Earl, "a profound lawyer, and a man accomplished with all polite learning," was, as Camden tells us, intended by Queen Elizabeth to succeed Bromley as Lord Chancellor, but died before him. Roger, fifth Earl, married a daughter of the famous Sir Philip Sydney; but he and his brothers Francis and George—both successively Earls of Rutland—all died childless, and the title devolved in 1641 on John Manners of Haddon, grandson of the Sir John with whom the beautiful Vernon heiress ran away (see vol. iii., p. 215). This Earl John was father of another John, who during his lifetime had been called up to the House of Lords as Lord Manners of Haddon, succeeded him as ninth Earl in 1679; and "as the head of a family which had contributed greatly to the Revolution," was created Marquess of Granby and Duke of Rutland in 1703. He himself was far from having sought this mark of Royal favour by any endeavour of his own :—least of all by a diligent attendance upon the Queen. He hated Court life, and loved the country, living almost entirely at Belvoir, where he royally kept up the old English hospitality. So strong was his prejudice against London, that, when he married his eldest son to a daughter of the patriot Lord Russell, he stipulated, by an article in the settlements, that his daughter-in-law "should forfeit some part of her jointure, if ever she lived in town without his consent." To this marriage we owe some of Rachel Lady Russell's best letters; and from it sprung, in the second generation, the soldier Marquess of Granby, one of the most popular men of his day, whose name—constantly held out as an attraction to the public—"is familiar to us on the sign boards of old inns." Nor was his great popularity undeserved. He was not only a gallant and victorious commander, but a just, generous, and humane man. No general could be more careful of his men: The commissariat was very faulty; but whenever the soldiers found themselves in bad quarters, he provided them with food and necessaries out of his own pocket, and kept an open table for the officers. His first campaign was against the Jacobites in 1645, ending with Culloden; his next with the British contingent in Germany, where he led the cavalry charge at Minden with brilliant courage and signal success ;—a forcible

contrast to the vacillating conduct of his superior officer, Lord George Sackville.[*]
He was appointed to succeed the latter in the chief command, and greatly distinguished himself on all subsequent occasions, for throughout the war, he and his Englishmen were invariably chosen for the post of greatest honour and greatest danger. On his return home, he was appointed Master-General of the Ordnance, and in 1766 Commander-in-Chief, with a seat in the Duke of Grafton's cabinet. But he resigned all his offices when the Government took proceedings that he deemed unconstitutional against John Wilkes. He never lived to be Duke of Rutland, but died, when scarcely past the prime of life and at the very height of his reputation, in 1770. The present and seventh Duke is his great-grandson.

One of his younger brothers, Lord George, took his mother's name of Sutton (she had been the sole heiress of Robert Sutton, last Lord Lexinton) on succeeding to her inheritance, and became the founder of two new families. He was the father of five sons; of whom Charles, the fourth, became Lord Archbishop of Canterbury in 1804, and the youngest, Thomas, was created Lord Manners on being appointed Lord Chancellor of Ireland in 1807. The Archbishop's son of the same name was Speaker of the House of Commons for seventeen years, and on retiring from office in 1835 received the titles of Baron Bottesford and Viscount Canterbury. Both titles continue; but the Lords Manners have dropped the additional surname of Sutton.

Mauclerke: illiterate. It is hard to conceive what amount of ignorance could have warranted this designation, at a time when, as a rule, no layman was able either to read or write. But in those warlike times, when men used their sword instead of their pen, and churchmen only were scholars, it was deemed almost ignominious for a knight to condescend to book-learning. He had to give his time and thoughts to far other matters, if he meant to hold his own and fight his way in the rough and turbulent world he lived in. This characteristic contempt of letters is well pourtrayed by Shakespeare in *Henry VIII.*, where the Duke of Buckingham, speaking of the " butcher's cur," Wolsey, scornfully exclaims

> "A beggar's Book
> Outworths a noble's blood."

Buckingham was, as Johnson styles him, one of the " ancient unlettered martial nobility."

A Walter Mauclere occurs in Normandy 1180-95, and Hubert Malcler is entered in the *Rotuli Hundredorum* of 1198. But the name is not common:

---

[*] They had been on bad terms in the army; yet when summoned as a witness on Lord George's trial for cowardice, he, with great generosity, did all that was in his power—as far as truth permitted—to soften and extenuate the evidence he had to give.

though Bardsley (*English Surnames*, p. 506), tells us that, "corrupted into Manclerk, it still exists." "Mantelake's or Manclerks" manor had its name from some of its former Lords, tho' I meet with none of them of that name."— *Blomfield's Norfolk.* Walter Mauclerk, Bishop of Carlisle, was Treasurer of the Exchequer to Henry III., and bought Horncastle, Lincolnshire, of Ralph de Rhodes. He was Sheriff of Cumberland for the first seven years of that reign: afterwards resigned his see, and in 1246 entered the convent of Friars-Preachers at Oxford.—*Matthew Paris.* Godfrey Mauclerk was Mayor of Leicester in 1286, and another Walter occurs in the same county.—*Nichol's Leicester.* Perhaps the same who held at Shapwick-Champayne, Dorsetshire, 32 Ed. I.— *Hutchins' Dorset.* Thomas Mauclerk, of Northumberland, was summoned to attend the great Council held at Westminster in 1324.—*Palgrave's Parl. Writs.* The most distinguished bearer of this *sobriquet* was Peter de Dreux, of the blood royal of France, who in right of his wife Alice was Duke of Brittany and Earl of Richmond, but forfeited his English honours in 1235, by his adherence to French interests.

Maunchenel; for Montchevrel. " Joannes de Montchevrel one feod. lig: " occurs in Duchesne's *Feoda Normanniæ.* The family continued in the Duchy in the last century; for Ourcin de Montchevrel is named in the great assembly of the " Order de la Noblesse " held in the Church of St. Stephen at Caen, 1789, for the election of the States General. In 1685 Henry de Mornay was Marquis de Montchevreuil, and bore Barry *Argent* and *Gules*, a lion rampant *Sable* crowned *Or.* (v. Anselme). But in England I have searched for the name in vain.

Mouet; for Monet or Monei, from Monnay, Normandy. "William de Monay was a benefactor to Bliburgh, Suffolk, before the time of Henry II. (Mon. ii. 593). Robert de Monei held a fief from Bigot, Earl of Norfolk, in 1165. (Liber Niger.) "—*The Norman People.* The fee held by William was at Brigg. In Yorkshire, " Henri de Monnaie witnesses the original grant of the manor of Allerton, probably about 1190: " and a family of the name—Monet of Hadlesby, continued in the county in the seventeenth century."—*Thoresby's Leeds.* Robert Monay was of Oxfordshire in the time of Edward I.—*Rotuli Hundredorum.* William de Mony is entered in the *Testa de Nevill* as holding part of a knight's fee at Clinton, in that county, of Guy Fitz Robert and Bardolt Fitz Roger: and Walter de Munet as holding by serjeanty at Munet in Staffordshire.

Meintenore: for Meintemore. In 1194 (6 Ric. I.) Henri de Mentemore of Northants and Warwickshire, Walter de Mentemore, of the latter county, and John de Meintemore of Oxfordshire occur in the *Rotuli Curiæ Regis.* Richard and Robert de Myntemore, Kent; and Hugo and Roger de Mentemos, Bucks, are found in the *Rotuli Hundredorum* of the reign of Edward I. The latter has left their name to Mentemore, in that county.

Meletak: Male Kake according to Leland's version; a name that has suffered much transmutation in spelling. The true form is Malecache, but we find it given as Malechac, Malecake, Maletak, Maletoc, Melkay, Malekahe, &c., &c. It is a *sobriquet*, the reverse of Bonekake (John Bonekake held in Kent 38 Hen. III.) but I have no idea of its meaning.

It occurs as early as the reign of Stephen, when Roger de Maletoc (this is the sole occasion on which I find it given with a *de*), witnesses a deed of Randle Gernons, Earl of Chester.—*Ormerod's Cheshire.* Not long after, a charter of Henry Pudsey, the son of another Prince Palatine, Hugh, Bishop of Durham 1153–89, is witnessed by "Alano Malecache" (v. *Surtees' Durham*): probably the same Alan Malekake who is mentioned as a benefactor of Fountains Abbey and Rosedale Priory. He was a Yorkshireman, in some way connected with the Amundevilles, for the two oxgangs of land in Wheldrake that he bestowed on Fountains had been the gift of Helewise de Amundeville; and may likewise have been of kin to Richard Malebisse, two of whose charters to Whitby he witnesses as "Alano Malechac." His own grants to Rosedale in Rydale, as enumerated by Burton, accurately describe the locality of his property. He gave "lands and pasture in Loketon, liberty of hewing timber in his wood of Stayndale, all his land from Abunescard to Nordrane, that is nearer Liteldale, in Ketelthorpe, and all his meadow in Mideldayl, in Pykeringe meadow, extending in length from Pykeringe water to the water of Costa."—*Mon. Elcor.* His son William, who confirmed these gifts, must have been the William Malekake who held three bovates of land at Pickering in the time of Henry III.—*Testa de Nevill.* At the same date, Galfrid Malecake held eight bovates at Lokinton.—*Ibid.* William witnesses a great number of grants to Whitby; and another William—no doubt his son—who occurs in the Hundred Rolls of 1272, gave some land at Lokinton to the Abbey. Thomas Malecake, between 1293 and 1296, married Alice, widow of John de Armenters of Stowe.—*Baker's Northants.* Richard Malecak' was of Little Smeaton, Yorkshire, in 1378.—*Rotuli Collectorum Subsidii Regi a laicis.* Aschetin de Malecake witnesses Theobald Fitz Pagan's grant to Wickham Abbey, in the same county.—*Mon. Angl.* The arms of the Malecakes (as given by Robson) were *Vert* a saltire lozengée *Or.*

Manuile. Manneville always stands—in Domesday and elsewhere—for Magneville or Mandeville, a name that has been already given. But it is very possible that Monneville may be here intended.

Nigel de Monneville was a tenant *in capite* in Yorkshire 1086 (Domesd.) "He was the son of Ralph de Monteville (a vill in the Roumois) who was a party, with Helisendis his wife and Hugh Fitz Baldric, to the deed of his kinsman Gerald de Roumare, "soldier in Christ."'—*A. S. Ellis.* He married Emma, one of the daughters and co-heirs of William de Arques, who held Folkestone under Bishop Odo: and died soon after Henry I.'s accession, leaving an only child, Matilda, who inherited the whole of the great barony of Folkestone, and was given in marriage by the King to Riwallon d'Avranches. "The Mundevilles of Berkswell, in Warwickshire, were either descended from a son of Nigel by another wife, or from one of his brothers; Ralph and William."—*Ibid.*

Mangisere: Leland's version is Mangysir. Anselme mentions a Henry de Montgisart, whose daughter Eschive became the wife of Renaud III., the last of the house of "Soissons d'Outremer." (Histoire Généalogique ii. 523). Here, again, I have to record a case of utter failure. No name at all resembling it in England have I been able to meet with.

Maumaisin; or rather as Leland gives it Mauveysin: *Malus vicinus:* an ominous name. "This family is considered to have been a branch of the ancient Counts of the Vexin (Wiffen, Mémoires de la famille de Russell, i. 49). In 1070, Ralph Malvoisin, Sire de Rosny, (who occurs as "Malusvicinus" in Suffolk 1086) gave lands to the Abbey of St. Evroult, Normandy (Ord. Vitalis, 604). Hugo Malusvicinus, founder of Blithburgh Priory (Mon. i. 468) appears in Stafford 1130 (Rot. Pip.) Henry Malveisin in Salop and Stafford 1165 (Lib. Niger). Gilbert Malveisin was of Normandy at this time (Mém. Soc. Ant. Norm. viii. 266). Ridware Mauvesyn still bears the name of this family."—*The Norman People.* Berwick Maviston, in Shropshire, was held by a branch of the Mauveysins. "The return upon the death of Saer Mauveysin in 1283 states that he held a knight's fee under Richard Fitz Alan by service of Castle-guard at Oswestry, with one horseman, not heavily armed, for forty days in time of war." —*History and Antiquities of Shropshire.* Their principal seat was at Mavesine-Ridware, in Staffordshire, which was first owned in the time of King John by William Mauveysin (son of the founder of Blythburgh Priory), and continued in their possession till the beginning of the fifteenth century. The last heir, Sir Robert Mavesyn, was "slain in 1403 at the battle of Shrewsbury, *ex parte regis,* as his monument in Mavesine Ridware saith; and well might be called Malvoisine; for (as the report of the country is) going towards the battle of Shrewsbury, he met with his neighbour Sir William Handsacre going also into the said battle, either of them being well accompanied by their servants and tenants; and upon some former malice, it might seem, or else knowing the other to be backed by the contrary party, they encountered each other, and fought as it were a skirmish, or little battle, when Mavesyn had the victory, and, having slain his adversary, went on to the battle, and was there slain himself. The said Sir Robert left behind him two daughters, Elizabeth and Margaret, who were his heirs; Elizabeth was married to Sir J. Cawarden, knt., and Margaret was married to Sir William Handsacre, son of the aforenamed Sir William, to whom she brought her purparty in recompense of the death of his father slain by hers."— *Erdeswick's Staffordshire.* "The old manor house of Maveyson-Ridware," adds his editor Dr. Harwood, "is entirely demolished, except the gate-house, in which is an old chamber said to have been an oratory. The ancient part of the church contains several monuments. Some of the tombs of the Mavesyns were opened, at different periods during the last century. The stone coffin in which was deposited the body of Hugo, the founder of Blythburgh Priory, was raised in 1785, after it had remained undisturbed for upwards of six hundred years. The altar tomb of the last Sir Robert is very handsome; his figure is armed and helmed, with a great sword on one side and a dagger on the other." The Mavesyns bore *Gules* two bendlets *Argent.*

Mountlouel: Maulovel in Leland's copy. Humbert, Seigneur de Montluel, and Alix de la Tour his wife, founded the church of Montluel in 1289. Jean de Montluel (probably in default of heirs male) granted the Seigneurie to Henry de la Tour in 1325. (Anselme, vol. ii. 17, 20.)

In England we first meet with the family in Yorkshire. According to the *Testa de Nevill,* " Robert de Maulovel was among those who held of the King as of the Honour of Tickhill in the reign of Henry I."—*Hunter's South Yorkshire.* They bore *Vert,* three wolves passant *Or,* in allusion to their name.*

It was either this Robert, or his son of the same name, that married the heiress of Rampton in Nottinghamshire, Pavia, daughter of Nigel de Rampton, and left (according to Thoroton) four sons, Stephen, Robert, Roger, and Richard. Stephen died early, and the custody of his son Robert was given to Roger, "who took care of him in his infirmity, when all his other friends left him," and obtained from him a "chartel" or grant of some land at Rampton. When, however, Robert came of age, in King John's time, he declared that "he was not in his own power when he made that chart, nor knew his own sense," and claimed back the property. This was dealing hard measure to his uncle, for I find, from entries both in the *Rotuli Cancellarii* and *Rotuli Curiæ Regis* of that reign, that he held land in four different counties, Leicester, Lincoln, Notts, and Derby. Roger recouped himself with an heiress, for in 1209 he "gave account of a swift running palfrey and two leis of greyhounds, for having the King's letters deprecatory to Maud de Muschans, that she should take him for her husband."

Robert's grandson married Elizabeth, daughter of Sir Thomas de Longvilers, and eventually the heiress of her family, as the children of her brother Sir John both died s. p. Her son Stephen proved the last heir male of the Maulovels, and through his daughter—another Elizabeth—Rampton passed to John Stanhope, whose son Sir Richard further succeeded to the great Longvilers inheritance in 1398. It was this marriage that first brought the Stanhopes from Durham into Nottinghamshire, and Rampton continued to be their seat for six successive generations, till Saunchia Stanhope conveyed it to the Babingtons in the time of Henry VIII.

Maurewarde: for Maurouard, as it is given on the Dives Roll, or Malruard, as written in Domesday; an unmistakeable nickname, which I am

---

* Wolves must have been plentiful in Normandy, judging from the names given in connection with them. Besides the above, we find Trancheloup, Heurteloup, Gratteloup, Cul de Loup, Piedeloup, &c.

quite at a loss to explain. When, in many cases, it was˙ subsequently turned into Malregard—under which form, we are told, it lingered on for several centuries — it clearly signified Evil Eye. But the original Maurouard or Malruard could admit of no such sinister interpretation.

Geoffrey Malruard founded the family in Somersetshire, where Norton-Malreward * has kept his name. He held Twertona (Tiverton) in 1086 of the Bishop of Coutances; and his descendants "were people of eminence and distinction in the county, and in Dorset and Devon; but their principal seat was at this Norton, where they had free-warren in their estate. In a chartulary of Kington Abbey in the county of Wilts, Sir William Malreward is set down as one of the principal benefactors to that monastery. Geoffrey Malreward confirmed the grant."—*Collinson's Somerset.* He further informs us that the name was, "in after days, contracted to Marwood." It is still borne by Kingston-Maureward in Wiltshire, Winterborne Maurewarde in Dorsetshire, and Godeby Maureward in Leicestershire. The latter was acquired by Geoffrey Maureward, towards the end of Henry III.'s reign, through his marriage with Ada, only daughter of Sir Adam Quatremars of Overton-Quatremars, the last male of his house. It had been previously known as Godeby-Quatremars; and a marginal comment inserted in Burton's History by Mr. Peck gives a disagreeable account of its climate :

> "Every day a shower of rain,
> And upon Sundays, twain :
> Anglia ventosa ; si non ventosa, venenosa."

But, whether in rain or shine, the Maurewards remained there for six generations : the last was Sir Thomas, living 5 Richard II.—6 Henry VI. His only child Philippa married Sir Thomas Beaumont, a younger son of John, fourth Lord. This Sir Thomas twice served as knight of the shire for Leicester, 1 Hen. IV., and 8 Hen. V. ; and was High Sheriff of Warwick in the latter year.

---

* A very grotesque etymology of Norton Malreward has, according to Collinson (*History of Somerset*), "prevailed from time immemorial" in the popular mind. "Sir John Hautville" (who gave his name to the adjoining *vill* of Norton-Hautville) "was a man of prodigious strength. and withal a great favourite with King Edward I. who frequented his house in this neighbourhood. The King, having one day expressed his desire of knowing the extent of Sir John's manhood, and seeing a specimen of his abilities, the knight undertook to convey three of the stoutest men in His Majesty's army, up to the top of Norton Tower. This he effected by taking one under each arm, and the third in his teeth. Those under his arms made some resistance, for which Sir John squeezed them to death ere he reached the summit : but the other in his teeth was carried up unhurt. For this feat of strength the King gave Sir John all his estate lying in the parish of Norton, observing at the same time it was but a *small reward*, whence, say they, comes the surname of this parish of Norton !" The trifling circumstance that two of "the stoutest soldiers in his army" were killed in the process seems to have attracted no attention at all.

There are traces of the family in other counties. Walter Maureward and Ivetta Marreward are found in Lincolnshire, about 1272 (*Rotuli Hundredorum*) : and in 1292 William de Maureward held Somerby and some other lands of Philip Marmion "by the service of one knight's fee and suit of court at his honour and castle of Tamworth." Copsi Maureward, in the time of Henry II., witnesses William Breton's grant to St. Mary's Abbey, York.

Monhaut : already given, as Mohant.

. **Meller,** or **Mellers.** William de Mesleriis, Eguerrand, Fromund, Simon, and Walter de Meuleriis, are mentioned in the Norman Exchequer Rolls during the last years of the twelfth century. In England two under-tenants of the name occur in 1165 : Richard, holding two knight's fees, and Humphrey, holding one, both of William de Abrincis. A William de Millières witnesses Richard de Builli's foundation charter of Roche Abbey, York, in 1146, as well as that of Boxgrave, in Sussex.

"Humphrey de Millers held one knight's fee of William de Abrincis in Overston (Liber Niger) and received the manor of Overston in marriage with William's sister Felicia. He left two sons, William, and Ralph, rector of Overston; which William also had two sons, William, and Humphrey, rector of Overston, and a daughter, Felicia, who, on the death of her brothers without issue, became their heir. She was succeeded by her son Gilbert, who was a clerk, and is sometimes called Gilbert de Wyarville, and sometimes Gilbert de Millers. In 1257 he obtained a license of hunting in the counties of Northampton, Nottingham, and Derby; but in 1270 the King arraigned an assize against him, and in 1276 his manor of Overstone was in the hands of the Crown."—*Baker's Northamptonshire.* There was a family of this name in Norfolk, where Robert de Milliers "was enfeoffed of Gonville's Manor by Roger de Montealt; he held it at half a fee of Roger's castle of Rising; it afterwards belonged to Godfrey de Milliers. Hugh de Meliers held Fenthall temp. John, and when one of his sons became a monk in St. Benet's Abbey, Alice de Meliers, his widow, gave two parts of the tithes of her demesnes here to that house; in 1294 Sir Hugh, their son, was lord; and after him Richer de Meliers. William de Meliers, 2 Richard II., held one fee in Wymondham and Rising."—*Blomfield.* Roger de Millers was of Dorsetshire, temp. Ed. I. ; (*Rotul. Hundred.*) where, according to the *Testa de Nevill,* he held in King's Winterborne some land that had been Thomas Maufilart's. The name continued in the county for many generations. John Meller, 2 Elizabeth, acquired from the Earl of Pembroke Winterborne-Came, where (as appears from the pedigree) his father and grandfather had been seated before him : and, some years later, Upcerne and Little Bridy. His son Sir Robert in 1620 bequeathed £20 a year to the poor of Cerne and Upcerne. "During the Rebellion, Sir John Meller compounded, and paid £693 13s. 4d. for being a Commissioner of Array. John his son, 1651, compounded for delinquency £630, but was excused. 1 Jac. II.

c. 7, an Act passed to enable Edward Meller to sell lands for the payment of debts. He died without issue, 1699, at Cheneys in Bucks, where he retired after having alienated the 'greater part of his estate. Vulgar tradition, founded it may be merely on the name, says, the ancestor of this family was miller to the Abbot of Abbotsbury. We have no other account of their extraction, which does not seem to be great: however, in the reign of Elizabeth they made many purchases of Abbey lands, viz. Little Bridy, Winterborne Came, Winterbourne Faringdon, Upcerne, &c., and were remarkable for depopulating most of them. They were first seated at Winterborne Came, where was their place of burial."— *Hutchins' Dorset.* They bore *Azure* four mascles in lozenge *Or.*

Mountgomerie: from a hill fortress so named in the diocese of Lisieux.[*] Its lords ranked high among the nobles of Normandy. The first that came to England, Roger de Montgomeri, who styled himself proudly, "Northmannus Northmannorum," was related to his sovereign through his maternal grandmother, Weva, the wife of Turolf, Lord of Pont Audemer, who had been a sister of the Duchess Gunnor. During Duke William's minority, he was in banishment at Paris, having, by some means or other, made himself obnoxious to the regents of the Duchy, but early became the chosen favourite of his young prince, by whom, says Wace, "he was accounted a great friend." He went with him to the Angevine war; was named by him Viscount of Hiesmes; called to his counsels before the invasion of England; contributed sixty vessels to his fleet, and received the command of the right wing of the Norman army at the battle of Hastings.[†] "William sat on his war-horse and called out Rogier, whom they name De Montgomeri. 'I rely greatly on you. Lead your men thitherward and attack them from that side. William, the son of Osbern, the seneschal, a right good vassal, shall go with you and help you in the attack, and you shall have the men of Boulogne and Poix and all my soldiers:' (mercenaries)."— *Wace.* The ground thus pointed out for the charge was the steepest and most difficult part of the hill, skirted on one side by the gorge of the Malfosse: but Roger and his division did their work gallantly, and were the first to break through the English stockade. Roger himself had a hand to hand encounter with one of the champions of the Saxon army. "An English knight," says Wace, "came rushing up, having

---

[*] "The name of this castle enjoys a peculiar privilege above all others in Norman geography. Other spots in Normandy have given their name to Norman houses, and those Norman houses have transferred those names to English castles and English towns and villages. But there is only one shire in Great Britain which has had the name of a Norman lordship impressed upon it for ever."—*Freeman.*

[†] Mr. Planché, in *The Conqueror and his Companions,* points out that according to Ordericus Vitalis, Roger was not present at the battle at all, having been left behind in Normandy as governor of the Duchy. Mr. Freeman asserts this to have been "a plain though very strange confusion between Roger de Montgomeri and Roger de Beaumont" on the part of Orderic.

in his company 100 men, furnished with various arms. He wielded a Northern hatchet" (*hache noresche*) "with the blade a full foot long : and was well armed after his manner, being tall, bold, and of noble carriage. In the front of the battle where the Normans thronged most, he came bounding on swifter than the stag, many Normans falling before him and his company. He rushed straight upon a Norman who was armed and riding on a war-horse, and tried with his hatchet of steel to cleave his helmet : but the blow miscarried, and the sharp blade glanced down before the saddle-bow, driving through the horse's neck down to the ground, so that both horse and master fell together to the earth. I know not whether the Englishman struck another blow : but the Normans who saw the stroke were astonished, and about to abandon the assault, when Rogier de Montgomeri came galloping up, with his lance set, and heeding not the long-handled axe, which the Englishman wielded aloft, struck him down, and left him stretched upon the ground. Then Rogier cried out, 'Frenchmen strike ! the day is ours !'"

Roger de Montgomeri was magnificently rewarded. He received first the two Earldoms of Arundel and Chichester, with the city of Chichester, the castle of Arundel, and seventy-seven Sussex manors; and soon after he had a grant of the city of Shrewsbury, and nearly the whole of Shropshire, comprising "the entire Earldom of Mercia, and all the demesne of the Saxon monarchs. The shortest way of stating Roger's vast property in Shropshire, is to observe that of four hundred and six manors, if we have counted them rightly, into which the property of the county in lay hands was divided, all but forty-nine were holden under him."—*Owen and Blakeway's Shrewsbury.* He parcelled them out among his own dependants, and built his castle at Shrewsbury, on a hill above the Severn, commanding the only isthmus by which the town could be approached by land. Besides all this, eighty other manors of his are enumerated in different counties. (Domesday.) "But," mournfully says Dugdale, "after the Normans became so victorious, they thought the whole realm of England too little recompense for so great and hazardous an enterprize ;" and Roger, deeming it a pity that his good sword should lie idle in its sheath, asked and received from the King a grant to himself and his companions, of whatever territory they "could by power and force obtain from the Welsh." The position of his county involved constant dealings with those dangerous neighbours, and the new Earl of Shrewsbury probably considered it as much his policy as his business to complete the work of the Conqueror by the further conquest of Wales. He was, however, far from effecting this, though his campaign was brilliant, and to a certain extent, successful. He brought under his rule a large share of Powis Land which he christened Montgomeryshire ; and to protect this new Border possession, built a strong fortress that also bore his name. Like the castle of Peverel in the Peak, it was "a simple vulture's nest on a crag," standing in a wilderness that had been some Englishmen's hunting ground in the time of King

Edward; but a town grew up around it, and was called by the Welshmen, from one of Roger's lieutenants, Tre-Vauldwin, or the town of Baldwin.

Within his Earldom, he held rights only less extensive than those of his neighbour Hugh Lupus; and his government is praised by Ordericus. "This earl," he says, "was wise and moderate, and a lover of justice, and delighted in the company of wise and modest persons." He died in 1094, having survived the Conqueror six years, though considerably his senior, and been for a short time in arms against William Rufus; and was buried with great state in the abbey he had founded at Shrewsbury. He had been twice married. His first wife, Mabel de Belesme, was the heiress of a house that had long been notorious for its wickedness; and in which the lust of cruelty was said to be an hereditary taint in the blood, transmitted from generation to generation. She certainly did not discredit her ancestry. "She was," says Ordericus, "a sanguinary woman, vindictive, cunning, and cruel; oppressing her vassals, and fattening on their spoils." Among other misdeeds, she poisoned her husband's only brother, in mistake for some one else whom she had wished to be rid of. Once, when seized with some terrible "distemper" in her face, she snatched a little child from its mother's breast, and held its mouth to her loathsome cheek. The poor baby sucked it, and "quickly died;" but Mabel was cured. She lived for fifteen years after this, to die at last by the hands of four brothers whom she had wronged in their inheritance. She was slain in her own chamber at Bures in Normandy, as she was resting on a couch after her bath; her infuriated murderers hacking her body to pieces with their daggers. Her son Hugh, with sixteen of his knights, was in the town at the time; but the night was dark and stormy, and the country under water from the overflow of the rivers, and the murderers, by breaking down all the bridges after them, escaped unharmed into Apulia. She left four daughters and five sons: 1. Robert de Belesme; 2. Hugh, of whom presently; 3. Roger de Poitou, so called from the country of his wife (see Vol. 3, p. 40); 4. Philip the Clerk, originally intended for the Church, who went with Robert Curthose to the Holy Land, and "made a good end" before the walls of Jerusalem in 1099; and 5. Arnulph, who married the daughter of a King of Ireland, and vainly strove to filch his father-in-law's crown. He built the castle of Carew in Pembrokeshire, and was, according to Leland, the ancestor of the Carews.

The second Countess of Shrewsbury, Adelais de Puisay, was in all respects (except her noble birth) the exact opposite of her predecessor; a gentle, religious woman, whose only son Ebrard was chaplain to William Rufus and Henry I.

On Earl Roger's death, his eldest son Robert took the great Belesme inheritance in Normandy and Maine; and Hugh, surnamed for his valour Le Preux, succeeded as second Earl of Shrewsbury, but bore the title only a very few years. When "the black fleet of Norroway," commanded by Magnus Barefoot, appeared off Anglesey, the two great Norman Earls of Chester and Shrewsbury gathered their forces to defend the threatened coast; and Hugh Le Preux, riding down to the shore to reconnoitre, and conspicuous on his prancing charger, was singled out by a Norse archer and shot through the heart. In his death agony he sprung from his saddle, and fell headlong into the sea; the savage Northmen shouting in glee, "Leit loupe!" (let him leap.) His death was a grievous calamity to Shropshire, for he left no heir, and his ferocious brother Robert came over from Normandy to reign in his stead. Hugh—though said to be the gentlest of Mabel's sons—had been very cruel: men spoke of his having maimed and blinded the hostages that he received; but Robert is described as nothing less than an incarnate fiend. It is difficult to give credit to all the stories told of him: how he impaled men and women on sharp stakes: how, under pretence of playing with his own little godson, he thrust out his eyes with his thumbs: and how, though very greedy of gain, he would never suffer his captives to be redeemed, preferring to gloat over their torments rather than to pocket their ransom. "The greatest slaughter of men," says Dugdale, "was his chiefest delight." He built himself a stronghold at Brugge-North (Bridgnorth) where, during four ruthless years, he lorded it over the unhappy Welsh, making the country ring with such tales of horror, that the "marvels of Robert de Belesme" passed into a proverb. Happily, this "inexorable butcher" took part with Robert Curthose, and after a fierce struggle, had to surrender to Henry I. in the guise of a suppliant, bringing in his hand the keys of Shrewsbury Castle, and was for ever banished the kingdom. All his honours and lands were seized, with those of his brothers Roger and Arnulph, and he went back to Normandy in a frame of mind best described by Ordericus in the words of Scripture—"Woe to the inhabiters of the earth, for the devil is come down upon you in great wrath!" Never weary of conspiring, he fought against the King at the battle of Tinchebrai, and only came back to England, a dozen years afterwards, as his captive. Then, "at length he who had so long tormented others in prison, perished himself in the prison of King Henry." His eyes were put out, and he was shut up for the rest of his life in Cardiff Castle, to rot away forgotten in one of the ghastly *oubliettes* of those days. It is said that, to put an end to his misery, he tried to starve himself to death; but "Fame, which had so long waited as his attendant, knew not whether he was alive or dead: yea, the very day of his decease is lost in oblivion." By his wife Agnes, daughter of Guy Count of Ponthieu, he left one son, William Talvace, who, deprived of the great estates of his father, eventually succeeded to those of his mother, and was the ancestor of the Counts of Ponthieu and Alençon, extinct in the male line in 1225. None of his posterity ever returned to this country.

The Scottish house of Montgomery claims to descend from a son of Philip the Clerk * (see p. 328), who, exiled at the same time as his uncle Earl Robert, went

* It is well known that Philip had a daughter named Maud, who was Abbess of Almenesches: but there is no evidence whatever that he had a son. "The Earls of Eglintoun are presumed to be descended from this family of Montgomeri, but no

to Scotland, and took up his abode in Teviotdale. Robert de Mundegumberi is often mentioned in the reign of Malcolm IV., and obtained from Walter the Steward of Scotland the manor of Renfrew, still held by his posterity. Sixth in descent from him was John de Montgomerie, who took Hotspur prisoner at the battle of Otterburn in 1388, and married Elizabeth, sole heir of Sir Hugh de Eglinton, who brought him the baronies of Eglinton and Ardrossan. Their grandson was created Lord Montgomerie about 1448: and Hugh, third Lord, became Earl of Eglinton in 1507. The male line failed with the fifth Earl, another Hugh, who in 1611 obtained a fresh grant of his title, with reversion to the children of his aunt Lady Margaret Montgomerie, the wife of Robert Seton, first Earl of Winton. Her son Alexander, called for his intrepidity "Grey Steel," therefore succeeded as sixth Earl, taking the name of Montgomerie, and is the lineal ancestor of the present Lord Eglinton, who also bears his paternal title of Winton.

A younger brother of the second Baron became the founder of an Irish family. His descendant in the fifth generation was created Viscount Montgomery of Great Ardres, co. Down, in 1622: and the next in succession received the Earldom of Mount-Alexander; but both titles became extinct in 1758. From Robert, the second brother of the first Viscount Montgomery, are derived the Montgomerys of Grey Abbey, in the same county.

Manlay: an entirely English name. "The manor of Manley in Cheshire was possessed in the reign of Henry III. by a family who assumed the name of the township, and held it as mediate lords under the Dones of Crowton."— *Ormerod.* It probably here stands for Maulay (see p. 245).

Maulard, Maillard, or Mallard. I first met with this name in Cheshire, where Richard Mailard is mentioned in William de Meschines' grant to Chester Abbey. It is unmistakeably Norman. Henri Mallard was one of the one hundred and nineteen "gentilshommes de Normandie" who, in 1423, defended Mont St. Michel against the English. Walter Maillard held of the King by serjeanty at Bradwell; William Mailard one knight's fee at Sutton in Nottinghamshire.—*Testa de Nevill.*

Mainard: a duplicate.

Menere: or Menières; Louis de Menières, Seigneur de la Gaudinière, is mentioned by Père Anselm as living in 1670. In England, Gilbert de Minières held three parts of a knight's fee of the Archbishop of York, t. Henry II.—*Gale's Richmondshire.* William de Mineres gave some land near Culertune to the

---

proof has ever been made, and though in 1696 there existed a Comte de Montgomeri in France, an Earl of Montgomery in England, a Montgomery Earl of Eglintoun in Scotland, and a Montgomery Earl of Mount Alexander in Ireland, the link has yet to be found which would legitimately connect these noble families with that of the great Earl of Shrewsbury."—*Planché.*

Templars. — *Mon. Angl.* Ralph de Meyners held three knight's fees at Houghton, in Sussex, of the Honour of Warrenne. — *Testa de Nevill.* William de Meneres was Vicar of Bishop-Middleton, co. Durham, in 1310.

In Scotland " we find Alexander de Meyners, son of Robert, Chancellor of Scotland, holding the lands of Durrisdeer in Annandale, early in the twelfth century." — *McDowell's Dumfries.* Sir David de Meynneres, in 1248, was of the retinue of the Queen of Scotland. Sir Robert de Meygners is mentioned in 1255 among the heads of the English party, to whom Henry III. accredited his envoys to the Scottish Court, the Earl of Gloucester, and Mansell his chief secretary. " They were," says Tytler, " despatched for the purpose of dismissing those ministers who were found not sufficiently obsequious to England." He sat in council with the Scottish magnates assembled at Roxburgh, when Henry III. was received by the youthful King and Queen, and " the government of Scotland was re-modelled. * * * A regency was now appointed, which included the whole of the clergy and nobility who were favourable to England, to whom was entrusted the custody of the King's person, and the government of the realm for seven years." — *Ibid.* Of these regents Sir Robert was one. " Alisaundre de Meners" (in all likelihood his son) was present at the meeting of the Estates of Scotland, convened in 1289 at Brigham-on-Tweed, and signed the letter of congratulation addressed by them to Edward I. on the proposed marriage of " their dear Lady and Queen," the Maid of Norway, to Prince Edward. In 1296 he was taken prisoner at Dunbar Castle, and committed to the Tower, from whence he was only released in 1297 on condition that " he shall attend the King with horse and arms beyond seas." Sir John de Lisle received a grant of " the lands in Scoleswode at Hardenes that had been the property of William, son of Alexander de Meners." This Sir William de Meygners occurs in the time of David II. and Robert II. At the same date, Sir Alexander de Meygners held Redhall near Edinburgh, and the Perthshire barony of Glendochwere, both of which he surrendered to Robert II., who granted them in 1375 to Robert Earl of Fife and Menteith. The following year the King bestowed the barony of Enach in Nithsdale on Robert, son of John de Meygners. Johanneta de Meygners is likewise mentioned. — *Palgrave's History and Affairs of Scotland.*

Martinast, for Martinvast. Many place names in the Côtentin appear to be derived from St. Vast. Besides Sifrewast or Chiffrevast, which we shall meet with further on, there are Sottevast (which gave its name to a branch of the great house of Mandeville), Thollevast, Hardinvast, Barnevast, Brillevast, Vasteville, Le Vast, and St. Vaast La Hougue, a sea-port about seven miles from Barfleur, memorable for the great sea-fight of 1692. Martinvast, where the ruins of its seignorial castle may still be seen, is about four miles from Cherbourg. " It passed to Richard de Martinvast, a Nottinghamshire Esquire. He did service with the commune of Cherbourg." — *Sir Francis Palgrave.* A Richard de Martinvast, and his uncle Norman de Martinvast, occur in Northamptonshire in 1130' (Rot. Pip): and another Richard in Rutlandshire in 1194 (Rot. Curiæ Regis). Ralph de Martinvast witnesses a deed of Robert Blanchemains, who was Earl of Leicester 1169–1190 : and Henry II. confirmed to Leicester Abbey one yard of land in Humberstone, the gift of the said Ralph. Juliana, daughter of Robert de Twyford, Lord of Burton Lazars about 1170, brought his estate to her husband, Robert de Martinvast.—*Nichol's Leicestershire.* This is the last occasion on which the name occurs in the county. William de Martiwaste was Sheriff of Bedfordshire and Buckinghamshire 13 Hen. III.

In Normandy the Seigneurie of Martinvast was still held by the family in the fifteenth century. One of them was beheaded for high treason under Louis XI.—*M. de Gerville.*

Mare : repeated for the third time.

Mainwaring : the modern form of Mesnil-Garin, a well-known Norman family. Ranulph de Mesnilgarin was Lord of Mesnilgarin near Coutances, and in 1086 held twelve lordships in barony from Hugh Lupus. (Domesd.) This Ranulph affords one of the exceptional instances of a Domesday patriarch now represented by heirs-male ; but then his posterity almost assumed the proportions of a tribe. "Altogether the house of Mainwaring threw out the extraordinary number of at least fourteen different branches, besides the three bastard branches of Nantwich, Croxton, and Great Warford. In nine other counties they occur : viz. Berks, Gloucester, Kent, Devon, Lancaster, London, Salop, Stafford, and Worcester ; in some of which families of several generations subsisted."— *Ormerod's Cheshire.*

Their original seat was at Warmincham, where the two sons of Ranulph, Richard and Roger, succeeded each other, and were in turn benefactors to Chester Abbey ; the one in 1093, the other previous to 1119. Roger's son and heir, Sir Ralph, was Justice of Chester in the latter part of Henry II.'s reign, and married Amicia, the daughter of his Earl, Hugh Kevelioc. This great alliance is one of the chief illustrations of the family ; but the legitimacy of the bride is hotly contested by Sir Peter Leycester, and appears at the best to have been doubtful. The county historian "conjectures her to have been the Earl's daughter by a first but unproved marriage, and consequently of half blood only to Randle Blundeville, and to the four sisters who were co-heiresses of the lands of the Earldom."

Sir Roger, the issue of this marriage, was the father of Sir Thomas, and Sir William, ancestor of the Mainwarings of Over-Peover. Sir Thomas was the heir, but his line expired with his son, who left three co-heirs, Maud, Margery, and Joan. Maud, as the first born, conveyed Warmincham to her husband, Sir William Trussell, the younger, of Cubbleston, of the Northamptonshire house of Marston-Trussell.

The lords of Over-Peover thus succeeded to the representation of the family, and adopted the coat of the elder house. Their township, first held by the Ranulphus of Domesday, had been granted by Sir Roger Mainwaring to his second son in the time of Henry III. for the annual rent of one soar sparrow-hawk; and continued in the name till quite the end of the eighteenth century, or very nearly six hundred years. "Over Peeover," says Sir Peter Leycester, "hath near unto it that stately house and great demesne, which hath been the continued seat of that great name of the Mainwarings, from whence there is none of the great races of that name (though they be many) but do desire to derive their original. And well may they do so; for, saith Mr. Cambden, here that notable, antient family of Menilwarin, commonly called Mainwaring, is seated; out of which Raulf married the daughter of Hugh Kevelyock, Earl of Chester." Several of their ancient monuments remain in the church; but the fifth lord of the manor, who first bore the arms of the head of the house, lies in Acton Church, where, by his will (made in 1393 before departing for the wars of Guienne), he desired to be buried, "with his picture in alabaster to cover his tomb:" bequeathing to it at the same time "a piece of Christ's cross, which the wife of his half-brother Randle had then in her keeping." This half-brother, styled by the Earl of Chester *armigerum suum*, was his successor, and served as Sheriff in 1412 :—one only of the many members of this family to be found on the roll.

Several Mainwarings took part in the Civil War: one, a grandson of Sir Randle, thirteenth in succession at Peover, was killed at the siege of Chester fighting for the King: another, of the Whitmore stock, served for the Parliament under General Skipton: and a third, belonging to the Kermincham branch, was a distinguished leader on the same side, and defended Macclesfield against the Royalists under Col. Lee.

The sixteenth heir of this ancient house, Sir Thomas, was created a baronet at the Restoration; but the line only continued for three more descents; and Sir Henry, the last of his race, died unmarried in 1797. Peover passed away by his will to an utter stranger in blood, the son of his mother's second marriage with the rector of Walthamstow; and the old home that had been the cradle of the Mainwarings for so many centuries thenceforward knew them no more. The adopted heir, Thomas Wetenhal, took his half-brother's name, and a baronetcy followed in the next generation.

But the good old Cheshire house survived, and has flourished for yet another hundred years, though no longer in its native County Palatine. The Mainwarings of Whitmore, in whom the representation of the Randulphus of Domesday is now vested, descend from the tenth lord of Peover, Sir John, who, though he died at the age of forty-five, was already blessed with a family of thirteen sons and two daughters. Edward, the ninth son, married in 1518 the heiress of Whitmore, and settled in her Staffordshire home, where his posterity have taken root. The house was garrisoned for the Parliament during the Civil War; and in the '45, Edward Mainwaring put himself at the head of his tenantry, and marched to Derby to oppose the Jacobites. James, a cadet of this house, bought Bromborough, near Chester, about the end of the seventeenth century; thus bringing back the old name to the county where it had so long been held in honour: but in 1850 his descendants migrated to Otley Park, in Shropshire, that had come to them through a Kynaston heiress.

Matelay. This, as well as the following name, I first lighted upon in the Hundred Rolls of the time of Edward I., occurring under the various forms of Matelasch, Matelask, Matelaw, Matelay, Matelasc, Mateslask, &c., and chiefly in Norfolk. It is, however, likewise found in Kent; and in 1322 Richard · Matelask was a townsman of Cambridge. But there can be no reasonable doubt that it was taken from Matelase (now Matelask) in the parish of North Erpingham, Norfolk. " This was in the Conqueror's time a berewite or hamlet dependant on Saxthorp, three furlongs long and two broad, and Godric kept it for the King. William de Wendevall held it temp. Henry I."—*Blomfield's Norfolk.* I think we may therefore fairly dismiss Matelay into the disgraced category of interpolations

Malemis. Another obvious nickname, of which in modern French the meaning would be no less clear. There are constant allusions in the Norman names (some of them we have already seen) to peculiarities or deficiencies of costume.* But I apprehend that " mis "—in the sense of " dressed "—is altogether of later date. ·

In the *Rotuli Hundredorum* of the reign of Edward I. the name is spelt Malemeis. John, the son of Thomas Malemeis, of Kent, was then in ward to Robert de Aguylon. Henry Malemeis occurs there at the same date. But this is only a contraction for Malemains, as the coats assigned by Robson to Malemeis, Malmys, or Malennys clearly prove. The first, *Argent* a bend engrailed *Purpure*, is one of those borne by the Malemains; and the second *Argent* a bend engrailed *Vert*, merely a repetition with different tinctures. A " Ricardo Malamusca " witnesses a deed of Baldwin de Rosei's in Norfolk, which, from the design of the seal, may be assigned to the latter part of the twelfth, or the beginning of the thirteenth century.

Maleheire. The name of William Maheure is on the Roll of the Assizes taken at Stratford by Geoffrey Fitz Peter and his associates, 10 Ric. I. William de Malhovers held one piece of land, with the advowson of the Chapel of St. Mary Magdalen at York, by the service of finding benches for the county ۰court.—*Testa da Nevill.*

---

* In addition to Al Chapel, Tort Chapel, &c., we find Saumauntel, Curtmantel (Henry II. was so named for introducing a new fashion in cloaks), Curthose, Curtepy or gaberdine, Blancapel or Blanch-Cape, Couvre-chef, Tornemantel (was this the old form of "turn-coat?"), Courtemanche, Wastehose, Grisegonelle (grey coat), Brustechapun (ugly hood), &c.

Moren: a name of frequent occurrence in Normandy. Four Morins— Morin de Vaumeray, Morin de Litteau, Morin d'Auvers, and Morin de la Rivière, took their places among the nobles in the Assembly of 1789 ; and the two latter are now represented by the Count d'Auvers and the Marquis de la Rivière. The Morins de Tourville, ennobled in 1719, bear *Or* a cross engrailed *Sable.*

In England, " Morinus " held a barony in Devonshire, and " Moran " was a tenant of Hugh Lupus in Cheshire.—*Domesday.* Robert Morin or Marin, in 1165, held six fees of Earl Simon in Lincolnshire, and two others of the Archbishop of York in Richmondshire : and Thomas Morin held one fee of old feoffment of William de Ros in Kent.—*Liber Niger.* Was this the " Morin de Chitehurst " entered in the same record as the tenant of the Earl of Arundel in Sussex ? William de Morin is also to be found there, holding of the Abbey of Winchcomb in Gloucestershire. Thomas and Ralph Morin were joint Sheriffs of Northamptonshire in 1183. Ralph, with Gilbert Morin occur in 1189–90 in Buckinghamshire and Bedfordshire ; as does another Yorkshire tenant of the Archbishop's, William Morin, who must have been Robert's son (Rot. Pip.). Ralph Morin was of Bedfordshire about 1272 (Rot. Hundred.). Robert Morin served as High Sheriff of Leicestershire in 1323.

That this family was numerous and influential appears incontestable ; but it is somewhat strange how few traces of it survive. Newnham-Murren, adjoining Wallingford in Oxfordshire, was one of their seats ; and Richard Morin bequeathed some of his land there, with his body for burial, to Reading Abbey. In Nottinghamshire, three brothers of this name, Robert (perhaps the Leicester Sheriff), Ralph, and William de Moran, married, temp. Ed. I., the three heiresses of Oliver de Lovetot, Lord of Coleston. Joan de Lovetot, who was the wife of Robert, and probably the elder sister, inherited Coleston, and her great-granddaughter Agnes transferred it to the Thurvestons or Thorotons. They gave their name to Moryn's Hall, where John Moren, the father of Agnes, " lived most of his time."—*Thoroton's Notts.*

Melun: for " Malaon, the arms of which (*Argent*, a lion rampant *Gu.* crowned *Azure*) are preserved by Robson, and correspond with those of the Viscounts de Mauleon of Poitou, a branch of the Carlovingian Viscounts of Thouars."—*The Norman People.* Savaric de Malleon was Constable of Porchester Castle in 1216, and Seneschal of Poitou and Gascony in 1222. He held Petersfield and Mapledurham (part of the Honour of Gloucester) by grant of King John. It was this Savaric who in 1216 was left by the King in charge of . the city and castle of Winchester, just after Pentecost, the holy time chosen by the Bishop of Winchester, who was with the King, for excommunicating Lewis and all his favourers. Upon the departure of the King, Savaric set fire to the suburbs of Winchester. Then followed the siege of the castle, which at last by the counsel of Savaric was given up to Lewis ; upon which followed the

surrender of all the Hampshire castles."—*Woodward's Hants.* In 1229, after
the death of Waleran Teutonicus, he became Warden of the Isle of Wight. " He
was," says Worsley, " a Poictevin, and had been very serviceable to the King
during the war with France ; but afterwards, on some discontent, changing sides,
became extremely troublesome."

As far as it relates to Savaric, the name would be an obvious interpolation ;
but it occurs in England during the previous century. William de Mallion
witnesses a charter of Coeur de Lion's to Norwich in 1193.—*Blomfield's Norfolk.*

·   Marceaus ; for Monceaux (v. Leland): the "Sire de Monceals" of the
Roman de Rou. He "descended from the ancient lords of Maers and Monceaux,
Counts of Nevers. Landric IV. became Count of Nevers c. 990 by marriage,
and had a younger son Landric of Nevers, Baron of Monceaux, grandfather of
William de Monceaux, who is mentioned by Wace in 1066. He appears as
William de Moncellis in the Eastern Domesday, and as William de Nevers in
Norfolk 1086. His descendants occur in Sussex, but chiefly in Yorkshire and
Lincoln."—*The Norman People.* There are several *communes* of this name in
Normandy ; but Monceaux, near Bayeux, is probably the one meant. This
name is frequently to be found in the earlier muniments of Battle Abbey ; for
a branch of the family, soon after the Conquest, settled at Bodiham, in its
immediate neighbourhood. Part of his estate there was granted by William de
Monceaux to the Abbey, at some date previous to 1200. In 1278, the Lord of
Bodiham was Henry Wardedu, a cadet of the De Monceaux, who, having been
placed under the guardianship of the Earl of Eu (Anglicized Ou) was thence
called Ward de Ou, and transmitted this singular appellation to his children. He
held four knight's fees at Bodiham, Penhurst, &c., and was a knight of the shire
in 1302. He, too, was a benefactor of the Abbey ; and his eldest son, Sir
Nicholas, who succeeded in 1315, assumed the cowl and joined the community.
The inheritance thus passed to his brother Richard, and at Richard's death in
1343 to his daughter and sole heir Elizabeth Wardedu, married to Sir Edward
Dalingruge—the same Sir Edward who, by licence of Richard II., built Bodiham
Castle in 1386.

According to the Battle chartulary, the De Monceaux who gave their name
to Hurstmonceux in the same county, had themselves derived it from a Hampshire
heiress. Her ancestor, " William de Monceaux, held three knight's fees of
ancient enfeoffment at Compton-Monceaux. The tenure was by serjeanty under
Thomas Maudut, who held immediately of the King. Walter de Monceaux also
held land in Compton by service of marshalry."—*Woodward's Hampshire.*
This line had ended in a "distaff," or female heir, married to a Sussex landowner, Hurst or Herste, of Hurst. He adopted her name both for himself
and his homestead, which was destined to become the site of the magnificent
castle of the Fiennes.' It was, for some considerable time, the seat of his
descendants, one of whom, Waleran de Monceaux, entertained Henry III.

there in 1264. A great hunting party was held in the park in honour of this Royal visit, at which a noble of the King's train, Roger de Tournay, accidentally lost his life. About the time ot Edward III., Maud de Monceaux brought Hurstmonceaux to the Fiennes'. Quarum-Monceaux, in Somersetshire, must have formed part of the original estate. Dru de Monceaux, who, in the beginning of the twelfth century, married Edith, daughter of Earl Warren and the mysterious Gundreda, long believed to have been the Conqueror's daughter, probably belonged to this Hampshire house. Edith had been first married to Gerard de Gournay, whom she followed on the pilgrimage to Palestine from which he never lived to return; and Dru possessed the Honour of Gournay during the minority of her son Hugh.

In Lincolnshire, Sir Alan de Monceaux, at about the same date, founded Nun Coton Priory, "more especially for the souls of Stephen Earl of Albemarle and of Hawise his wife, and endowed it with the whole town of Coton. He followed the fortunes of the Earl, and shared his possessions in Yorkshire as well as Lincolnshire."—*Poulson's Holderness.* In the former county, his descendants were mesne-lords of Barmston for three hundred years; their tombs were to be found in the church, and a stained glass window bearing their red cross still remained in 1620: but all have now disappeared. Thomas de Monceaux received a writ of military summons 4 Ed. III. He was the grandson of a Sir Robert, whose wife, Hawyse de Monceaux, Lady of Lisset, had been an heiress and a kinswoman; and the second son of a Sir Ingram who, dying in 1291, left the eldest in ward to the King. But the boy lived only a few years, and Thomas then succeeded. He himself died in 1345, and was followed by three generations of John, and lastly, by William de Monceaux, with whom the direct line ended in 1446. He, again, had married an heiress, Margaret Fauconberg, then the widow of John Constable, but had no children: and his sister Maud carried Bramston to Sir Brian de la See. Two uncles, Robert and Alexander, were living 1420–29; another, William, was a priest.

After the loss of their Yorkshire fief, I find no other notices of them in that county; but it has been plausibly suggested that the name survives in Lincolnshire under the modernised form of Monson. "Thomas de Monceaux d. 1345, seized amongst others of the manors of Killingholm, Keleby, &c., Lincoln (Inq. p. Mort.). His son, Sir John de Monceaux (or Monson) d. 1363, seized of Burton and Keleby, Lincolnshire, which continued in this family t. Elizabeth. John Monceaux or Monson was of Lincoln 1378: sixth in descent from whom was Sir John Monson, who was possessed of Burton and Keleby at his death in 1593. From him descended the Lords Monson, Viscounts Castlemaine, and Lords Sondes."—*The Norman People.* No hint of this descent is, however, afforded us by the genealogy of the Monsons. Nor does the coat of De Monceaux, *Or*, a cross moline *Gules*, in the slightest degree resemble theirs, though the tinctures coincide. Lord Monson (now Viscount Oxenbridge) bears *Gules*

II.   z

two chevronels *Or*, and is derived from "John Munson, denominated of East Reson, co. Lincoln, and living in 1378." This would be the John de Monceaux of that date (see p. 337), who was the grandson of Thomas, and died in 1381; but the subsequent descent, as given by Collins, in no wise corresponds with Poulson's account. The heiress Maud is passed over in silence; and the regular succession of John Monsons is carried on for three more generations, all seated at Carlton, near Lincoln.[*] Yet, in spite of these discrepancies, I am inclined to endorse the opinion I have above quoted, as to the true origin of the family. It is at least more easy to accept than the suggestion of "some antiquaries"—I would rather term them humourists—who pretend to derive Monson from the German *Münzen* (coins). The regicide Viscount Castlemaine, who was the sole bearer of the title, belonged to the house of Carlton. Earl Sondes descends from Lewis, second son of the John Monson who was created Baron Monson of Burton in 1728, by his wife Lady Margaret Watson. She was the youngest of the four daughters of Lewis, first Earl of Rockingham, who had married Catherine, eventually sole heiress of Sir George Sondes of Lees Court, Kent, and received the title of Viscount Sondes in 1714. His eldest son, who bore it, died before him, and both his two grandsons were childless. The last of them, Thomas, third Earl, who survived his brother but a few months, devised his whole estate to his cousin Lewis Monson, on condition that he assumed the name and arms of Watson. This he accordingly did in 1745; and in 1760 he was created Lord Sondes. The fifth Lord was promoted to an Earldom in 1880.

One other brief notice of the De Monceaux occurs in Cumberland. Amand de Monceaux, during the reign of Richard II., was three times Sheriff and three times knight of the shire: but, after this, the name is never met with again.

Maiell. Roger Mahell witnesses the Earl of Sussex's foundation charter of Boxgrave Priory, Sussex (Mon. Anglicanum) in the time of Henry II. "Ricardus Mihial" occurs in the Norman Exchequer Rolls during the following reign.

The subsequent notices of the name are scanty enough. Richard Le Mahill, in 1242, was one of the jurors with Earl Patric, when he and Walter Cumin deposed on oath "that they were neither of counsel or aid when on their part any people were sent to attack or lay waste the King of England's land in Ireland or elsewhere, to the King's dishonour."—*Calendar of documents relating to Scotland.* "In 1321, lands alienated in Kirkby to Matthew Meyell were not held of the King, but of Lucy Meyell, by the service of one rose-flower a year." —*Nichol's Leicestershire.* "Walteri Mayll," in 1433, appears in the list of Huntingdonshire gentlemen; and John Meyell of Stratford among the Gentry of Warwickshire, at the same date.

* Many of them lie buried in South Carlton Church; and on one of their monuments (date 1593) the crest given is a pun on the name, "a Moon griping the Sun *Or*," with the motto, *Prest pour mon pais*, which they still use.

According to Robson " Maiell" bore *Argent* on a chevron *Sable* three cinque-foils of the field.

Morton. Macy de Moritania held a barony in 1066; and in after times the name of Morton or Morteyne became widely spread. But I think this entry rather refers to the Conqueror's half-brother, Robert, the " Comes Moritoniensis" of Domesday, born of Herleva's marriage with Herluin de Conteville. When her base-born son became Duke of Normandy, he lost no opportunity of raising her kinsfolk from their humble estate, to the discomfiture and mortification of his haughty relatives on the father's side. Most of all he took pleasure in promoting his brothers to the level of the scornful nobles who looked down upon them ; and on the exile of William the Warling, he bestowed upon Robert the county of Mortain.

Robert, we are told, "loved him much," and proved through life his faithful liegeman. William of Malmesbury describes him as of "a heavy, sluggish disposition," and wanting in decision of character ; but he was not cruel, and had all the courage of his race in the field. He contributed one hundred and twenty vessels to the fleet that invaded England, and joined the expedition with all his knights and retainers, bringing "great aid." He is three times represented in the Bayeux Tapestry ; first, sitting at meat on his brother's left hand, the evening after their landing ; next, in council with him and Odo ; and lastly, directing the building of the *castellum* erected at Hastings. According to tradition, the consecrated banner of St. Michael de Periculo Maris, brought from the monastery of the Mount in Normandy, was borne before him in the battle ; during which, as Wace tells us, he never went far from the Duke's side. We may judge that he did his part well, for he was rewarded with the lion's share of the spoils of England. No other grant equalled, or even approached his in magnitude ; for his possessions stretched across the whole breadth of the island, and reached the Land's End. With the title of Earl, he had the entire county of Cornwall (two manors and the church lands alone excepted) comprising two hundred and forty eight manors ; fifty-four in Sussex, besides the borough of Pevensey; seventy-five in Devonshire, forty-nine in Dorsetshire, ten in Suffolk, twenty-nine in Bucking-hamshire, thirteen in Hertfordshire, ten in Wiltshire, ninety-nine in Northampton-shire, and one hundred and ninety-six in Yorkshire, besides smaller grants in five other counties, making a grand total of seven hundred and ninety-seven lordships. One account—Dugdale's—carries the number up to eight hundred and two. He built a castle on the rock of Dunheved (now Launceston) as his chief seat in Cornwall : but he had another, with a market, at Trematon ; a third fortress at Montagud, near Yeovil, in Somersetshire ; and a fourth at Pevensey in Sussex, where he repaired the old Roman stronghold. There is little to record of him during the Conqueror's reign, beyond a successful repulse of the Danes in Lindsey, where he and the Count of Eu had been left in command ; but in 1087 we find him pleading at the King's deathbed for the pardon and release of their brother Odo. William granted his petition with undisguised reluctance. "My brother Odo," he declared, "is not a man to be trusted; he is ambitious, prone to fleshly lusts, and of enormous cruelty. If set free he will bring confusion to the realm, and ruin to thousands." These dying words were prophetic. Odo rose in rebellion against the new King within a year of his accession; and Robert, being strongly opposed to the separation of the Duchy, where he still retained his county of Mortain, joined him in attempting to place Robert Courtheuse on the throne. The two brothers were besieged by Rufus in Pevensey Castle, and, after holding out for six weeks, surrendered themselves to the mercy of their nephew, and were banished the realm. "Perhaps Robert sailed away for the last time, a broken man, from the very spot where he had landed."—*A. S. Ellis.* His vast domains were forfeited, and according to the obituary of his father's abbey of Grestain in Normandy, where he was buried, he died in the following year. By his wife Matilda, the daughter of Earl Roger de Montgomerie, he had an only son William, and three daughters; Agnes, first offered in marriage to William de Grentemesnil, but afterwards the wife of André de Vitré; Denise, married to Guy de La Val; and Emma, married to William Count of Toulouse.

William, the heir, was restored to the greater part of his father's possessions, and the Earldom of Cornwall. But he remained a malcontent; for he expected, and audaciously demanded, his uncle Odo's great Earldom of Kent. It must have been he, and not, as Dugdale infers, his father, who, on the very day and hour that William Rufus died "by the glance of an arrow" in the New Forest, saw the apparition described by Matthew Paris. He himself was hunting in another part of the forest, and had lost sight of his attendants, when, in a lonesome place, he was confronted by "a very great black Goat, bearing the King all black and naked and wounded through the midst of his Brest. And adjuring the Goat by the Holy Trinity to tell what that was he so carried, he answered, 'I am carrying your King to Judgment: yea, that Tyrant, William Rufus; for I am an evil spirit and the Revenger of the malice he bore to the Church of God: and it was I that did cause this his slaughter, the Protomartyr of England, St. Alban, commanding me so to do, who complained to God of him for his grievous oppressions in this Isle of Britain, which he first hallowed.'"

The black goat conveyed these tidings of deliverance to most unwilling ears: for the Earl had hated and envied Henry Beauclerk from childhood, and could ill endure to see him ascend the throne. Before long, he was openly in arms against him, and, espousing the cause of Duke Robeft as his father had done, was punished as he had been for his treason—deprived of his title and estates, and sent out of the kingdom. He then raised the standard of revolt in Normandy; was besieged by the King in his castle of Tinchebrai: and led the van with determined valour in the decisive battle fought beneath its walls. But he was worsted, taken prisoner, and carried to the Tower of London, where he spent the rest of his life in captivity. His eyes were put out by the King's order. No one can tell how or when he died: and Dugdale "can find no mention of either Wife or issue that he had."

Noers. Gilbert de Noyers witnessed a charter of Duke Richard to Fontanelles, 1024 (Neustria Pia, 166). William De Noiers or De Nuers was an under-tenant in Norfolk, 1086 (Domesday) ; and "the manor of Gothurst, or, as it is now called, Gayhurst in Buckinghamshire was, at the time of the Norman Survey, held under the Bishop of Bayeux by Robert de Nodariis, or Nowers, whose family not long afterwards became possessed of it in their own right."— *Lysons.* Almaric de Noers, in the time of Henry III., held one knight's fee of William de Say, "being (as it may be presumed) the same which Walter Giffard, Earl of Buckingham, 12 Hen. II., then certified that Hugh de Nuers held of him in that county."—*Banks.* His son William married the heiress of Stoke-Goldington, and was the father of another Almaric, who is included by the above writer in his *Barones Pretermissi.* "In 24 Ed. I., he was one of those eminent persons who had summons to attend the great council then ordained to assemble at Newcastle-upon-Tyne. In the year following, his name is mentioned as one of the knights of the shire for the county of Bucks, being then written Amary de Nowers. He died 2 Ed. II., seized of the manors of Gothurst, Weston, and Stoke Goldington in Buckinghamshire, and of Cestre Parva, in the county of Northampton. Joan his wife died shortly after, 4 Ed. II., being then seized of the manor of Lathebury, and of a part of the manor of Cainho, in the county of Bucks."—*Ibid.* His son John acquired a great Bedfordshire estate through his wife Grace, daughter and heir of Robert Fitz Neale, or Nigel, the last Lord of Salden, who brought him four sons. Yet the line ended with his grandson Almaric, who died in 1408, without issue. Three grand-daughters remained. "Agnes and Grace died nuns ; and Joan Nowers became heir to her father and brother ; she married Sir Robert Nevill, who had Gothurst in her right, and died possessed thereof in 1426, leaving issue ; in whose heirs-general (if legitimate) is vested the representation not only of Almaric de Nodariis, who flourished temp. Ed. I., but of the co-heirship of the ancient barony of Albini, of Cainho ; together with that of the old and famous barony of Percy."—*Ibid.*

The William de Noers of Domesday had the custody of thirty-three of the Conqueror's manors in Norfolk, and is said to have stood high in his favour. "Ralph de Nuers held Swanton-Nuers (Nowers) of the Bishop of Norwich, and witnesses a deed of Robert Fitz Ralph in the time of Hen. II. He was probably the same Ralph who held at that time of William de Abrincis in Kent one fee of the old feoffment. Milo de Nuers, 10 Ric. I., conveyed part of his interest there to Roger de Kerdeston. Simon de Nuers was living 35 Hen. III.: Sir Robert de Nuers held in 1327 ; and his son John in 1361. The manor of Nuers came to Sir William Oldhall, living 1437."—*Blomfield's Norfolk.* This must have been through John de Noer's grand-daughter Margery, who is mentioned in *Nichol's*

Leicestershire. The De Nuers held in Knossington, in that county, of Robert de Tateshall.

Neuile; one of the illustrious names

"Familiar in our mouths as household words,"

that sound with a trumpet-note through the pages of English history. Few—. probably none—of our great historic houses can rank with the Nevills in their pride of place. They represent, in direct male descent, the sovereign Earls that ruled the North in early Saxon times; "were barons from the time for which records first exist" [*] under the Norman kings; and swayed the destinies of the country at their will in the wars of York and Lancaster. In the fullest and truest sense of the word, they were "princes in the land;" foremost in the council and the field, unsurpassed in arms, splendid in hospitality, and ruling in feudal power and supremacy a territory more important than some of the kingdoms of the Heptarchy. Their domain, in the county of Durham alone, extended for forty miles along the valley of the Tees, and seven hundred knights held their fees of the great Honour of Raby. "This Saxon line," says their historian, Henry Drummond, "surpasses all others in England by the greatness of its alliances, honours, and possessions. It has furnished a Duke of Bedford, Marquess of Montacute, Earls of Northumberland, Westmorland, Salisbury, Kent, Warwick, and Montacute; Barons Nevill, Furnivall, Latimer, Fauconberg, Montacute, and Abergavenny; two Queens; a Princess of Wales; a mother of two Kings; Duchesses of' Exeter, Buckingham, Norfolk, Warwick, York, Clarence, and Bedford; Marchioness of Dorset; Countesses of Northumberland, three Westmorland, Arundel, Worcester, Derby, Oxford, two Suffolk, Rutland, Exeter, Bridgewater, and Norwich; Baronesses Ros, three Dacre, three Scrope, Daincourt, Mountjoy, Spencer, Fitzhugh, Harrington, Hastings, Conyers, Willoughby de Broke, Hunsdon, Cobham, Strange, Montacute, and Lucas; nine Knights of the Garter, two Lord High Chancellors, two Archbishops of York, Bishops of Durham, Salisbury, and Exeter, Ambassadors, Speaker of the House of Commons, &c." The list reads like a peerage-roll.

The Nevills derived their name from the Norman fief of Neuville-sur-Touque, and "descended from Baldric Teutonicus, who with his brother Wiger came to Normandy c. 990 to offer his services to the Duke (Ord. Vitalis, 479)."—*The Norman People.* It is said that the first who came to England, Gilbert de Nevill, commanded the Conqueror's fleet; and they bore on a canton of their arms a galley, or ancient ship, in memory of this ancestor. Strangely enough, his name is not written in Domesday. The family became widely spread, and was numerous in Lincoln (where they held baronial rank) and elsewhere; but its greatness emphatically belongs to the North. The admiral's grandson, Geoffrey,

---

[*] I am here quoting Sir Harris Nicholas.

married Emme, the heiress of a great Northern baron, Bertram de Bulmer, who brought him the splendid dowry of Brancepeth Castle in the county of Durham, and Sheriff Hutton in Yorkshire, with a whole train of estates and manors, dependent on these two great fees. Their son Henry died s. p., and his sister Isabel, reversing the custom that gave rich Saxon wives to the Norman conquerors, transferred all these possessions to her Saxon husband, the Lord of Raby.

Robert Fitz Maldred, Lord of Raby, was the heir male of the ancient sovereigns of Northumberland, whose authority extended from the Humber to the Tweed. He descended from Earl Uchtred, the son-in-law of Ethelred II., by his earlier marriage with Sigen, daughter of Styr, the great Danish chief who "gave to St. Cuthbert Darlington and its appendages." She brought him two sons, Eadulf (Adolf) and Gospatric. Eadulf eventually succeeded to his father, but was slain by Siward the Dane, who had married his niece, and usurped the sovereignty on his death. Thus Gospatric, the younger son, was never Earl of Northumberland, as by right of blood he should have been. He was the father of Uchtred, Lord of Raby in the reigns of the Confessor and Conqueror, who (probably because, like the other Northern nobles, he had refused to join Harold's standard at Hastings) was apparently left undisturbed in the new Norman settlement.

Raby, the head of the Honour of Staindropshire, was held of the Church of Durham. As its name implies, it was a Danish settlement, and had been the residence of Canute the Great,* who, in his penitential old age, undertook a

---

* It has been ascertained beyond all doubt, from contemporary evidence, that Canute's mansion was close to Staindrop, and tradition has always pointed out Raby Castle as its site. The county histories are unanimous in adopting this opinion ; and one of the towers has been pointed out by Hutchinson and others as probably dating from the Danish times. Its form is unique in England ; but I have heard that there are two similars towers in the Castle of Egeskov, in the island of Funen, Denmark. There was a curious custom connected with its tenure. The Lord of Raby annually offered a stag to the Prior of Durham on St. Cuthbert's Day (September 18th) with great ceremony and "winding of horns ;" accompanied by a stately train befitting the occasion. Ralph Lord Nevill, about 1290, claimed the right to be each time entertained by the Prior with as many servants as he chose to bring ; but the monks refused to receive the offering on such terms, and, snatching the huge candlesticks from the altar, belaboured Lord Nevill's retainers with them so heartily that they beat a retreat, leaving the stag behind them. Ralph's son not only revived the dispute, but put in an additional claim for a night's lodging and a breakfast ; and the Prior, "knowing him to be powerful, and that the country durst not displease him, and to gain his favour, in regard he had no small interest at Court, was content that for one time he sh⁴ perform it as he pleased, yet so that it might not be drawn into example. And so Lord Nevill having carried his point brought but few with him, and those more for the honour of the Prior than a burthen ; and shortly after dinner took his leave, but left one of his servants to lodge all night and to breakfast there,

barefoot pilgrimage to the shrine of St. Cuthbert, and offered on·the altar Staindrop and Staindropshire, comprising Raby and eleven other manors. Under William Rufus, it was forcibly appropriated by Ralph Flambard, the "Firebrand Bishop" of Durham, but Dolfin, the son of Uchtred, being the husband of the Bishop's niece Adelicia, peaceably succeeded his father at Raby; and Flambard repented and made restitution before his death, restoring Canute's gift by charter to the convent. Three years afterwards, in 1131, Algar, then Prior of Durham, by another charter confirmed Dolfin in the possession of Staindropshire; and the Honour of Raby was held by sixteen generations of his descendants for the space of something over five hundred years, till it finally passed out of the family in 1569. Since that time, the castle has been owned and inhabited by the Vanes, and thus, throughout the long lapse of ages reaching down from the days of the Confessor to our own, there has always been a hearth-fire alight within its venerable walls. This Dolfin was the father of Maldred, and the grandfather of Robert, who married the Norman heiress.

Geoffrey, the son of Robert and Isabel, in accordance with the Normanizing fashion of the time, took his mother's name of Nevill, but retained his own coat of arms, the famous silver saltire that was to bear the proudest quarterings in England. His great-grandson Robert acquired a great territory in Yorkshire through the "fair and gentle" Mary of Middleham, who was the heiress of Robert Fitz Ranulph (see *Richmond*), and lived a widow for forty-nine years after his death. Ralph, the next in descent, is chiefly known for his quarrel with Bishop Beke, who twice summoned him to go with horse and arms to Scotland, while he alleged that his tenure was only to defend the patrimony of St. Cuthbert, and that he had no right, for King or Bishop, to go beyond Tyne or Tees. He was the father of two sons; Robert, "the Peacock of the North," slain early in life in a Border fray; and Ralph, the hero of Nevill's Cross, and the first layman ever buried in Durham Cathedral. He was one of the two chief commanders in the great victory that turned back the threatening tide of Scottish invasion; and carried his young son John (then barely five years old) with him to see the battle. John Lord Nevill lived to do honour to this early training, and to eclipse his father's renown; for he is computed to have won, in the course of his soldier-life, eighty-three walled towns, castles and forts; and far from restricting his services to the Palatinate, as his ancestor had.done, carried arms even against the Turks. He was retained by the Duke of Lancaster to serve him in peace and war; attended Richard II. to Scotland with a train of three hundred archers and two hundred men at arms; was at different periods Warden of the East Marches, Governor of Bamborough, High Admiral of

---

protesting that as a son and tenant of the Church, he would not be burthensome to it by bringing a great train: for, 'What does a breakfast signify to me? Nothing.'"— *Dugdale.*

England. Lieutenant of Aquitaine and Seneschal of Bordeaux, and one of the Founder Knights of the Garter. In 1378, having obtained from Bishop Hatfield license to castellate " touz les tours, mesons, et mures de son manoir de Raby," he encircled the old irregular pile with the greater part of its stately coronal of towers, and made it what Leland found it nearly two centuries afterwards, " the largest Castel of Logginges in al the North Cuntery." As it had been the cradle of the race, so it continued to give his designation to the head of the family, who, though at the same time Lord of the castles of Middleham, Brancepeth, Snape and Sheriff Hutton, was invariably styled *Dominus de Raby*, —in common parlance, Dan Raby, or Daraby, as Leland gives it.

This Lord Nevill was twice married. His first wife, Maud de Percy, brought him (besides three daughters) two sons; Ralph, the first Earl of Westmorland; and Thomas, who married the heiress of the last Lord Furnival, and in her right was summoned to Parliament in 1383 as Lord Furnival, but left no male issue. By his second wife Elizabeth, daughter and heir of Lord Latimer (whose arms appear on one of the stone shields of the inner gate-house at Raby) he had another son named John, who bore his mother's title of Latimer and died s. p. in 1430; and two daughters, on whom the barony did not devolve. (See *Latimer.*)

Ralph, the son and heir, was a man of unusual talent and ambition, who played his part ably and skilfully through life, and built up the fortunes of his house to the highest point of prosperity. "The strong light in which Shakespeare brings out Westmorland in his Henry IV. and Henry V. is a proof that he was even then remembered as a subtile and powerful agent in the intrigues of his age."—*Surtees.* He was appointed Constable of the Tower and created Earl of Westmorland in 1397, but soon deserted the failing fortunes of Richard II., and, turning towards the kindling star of Lancaster, became one of the principal instruments in placing Henry IV. on the throne. The new King showered dignities upon him. He was made a Knight of the Garter, invested for life with the Honour and county of Richmond, and created Earl Marshal of England, with a provision in the patent that "whereas in times past all other Marshals had borne a staff of wood, he should bear a staff of gold." By his second marriage he became the brother-in-law of the King, and never wavered in his allegiance to the Red Rose. He defeated the Percies at the battle of Shrewsbury, where Hotspur's headlong career was brought to a close; and put down a second Northern insurrection at Shipton Moor without striking a blow. In the next reign, he went as Earl Marshal with Henry V. to Agincourt, followed by five knights, thirty lances, and eighty archers. Surtees remarks that " Shakespeare preserves the consistency of his character by making him wish, as any reasonable man would do before the commencement of so doubtful a battle :—

"'Oh that we now had here
But one ten thousand of those men in England
That do no work to-day.'"

This elicits one of the finest passages in the play, Henry's rejoinder, commencing—

> " Who's this that wishes for more men from England?
> My cousin Westmorland ? No, my fair cousin ;
> If we are mark'd to die, we are enow
> To do our country loss; and if to live,
> The fewer men, the greater share of honour ! "

The Earl died in 1426, full of years and honours ; and lies buried under " a right statelie Tumbe of alabaster " in the choir of his own collegiate church of Staindrop. His effigy rests between those of his two wives. He is in full armour ; a strikingly handsome man, such as we might conceive the father of the Rose of Raby to have been ; and wears round his neck the collar of SS as the badge of Lancaster. He had no less than twenty-one children ; nine by his first Countess, Lady Margaret Stafford, and twelve by the second, Joan de Beaufort, the daughter of John of Gaunt, and the widow of Lord Ferrers. To this latter family the Earl showed a decided preference, for he first dismembered the splendid heritage of the Nevills by settling upon them his great Yorkshire estates. The royal Joan had brought him eight sons. Of these, the three youngest died s. p., and Robert, the fifth, was Bishop of Durham ; but the four elder brothers, Richard, Earl of Salisbury, William, Earl of Kent, George, Lord Latimer, and Edward, Lord Bergavenny, each became the founder of an illustrious house. They soared to the highest offices of the state ; and " were, perhaps, at that time, both from their opulent possessions, and their individual characters, the most potent family that has ever appeared in England."—*Hume.* As they were allied to the House of Lancaster through their mother, so were they allied to the House of York through the youngest and fairest of their sisters. Cecily Nevill, the last born of these twenty-one children, was remarkably beautiful, and called in the neighbourhood the Rose of Raby. She married in her early youth Richard Plantagenet, Duke of York, and was the mother of Edward IV. and Richard III.* This marriage

---

* Cecily of Raby is quoted by Fuller as " the clearest instance of frail human felicity." She lived to see three of her descendants Kings of England, and her granddaughter Elizabeth Plantagenet, the " White Rose of York," unite the rival houses as the Queen of Henry VII. But, "from the violence of the times in which she lived, and the greatness of her connections, few women suffered greater misfortunes and endured more sorrows than she did. Her character was basely calumniated, but none seem ever to have believed her guilty of the crimes laid to her charge ; so, that, when stripped of everything which she possessed, her husband attainted, and herself a widow, she was still safe and respected, though defenceless, in the midst of her enemies."—*H. Drummond.* In her latter years she professed herself a Benedictine nun, but resided in her own house, where the order of her day has been accurately recorded. She rose at seven, heard mattins and mass before breakfast, and dined at eleven, passing all the intermediate hours in her chapel ; she then gave audiences for an hour, slept for a quarter of an hour, and returned to her devotions till " the first

shaped the politics of the Nevills, for thenceforward they espoused the cause of their brother-in-law, who placed his reliance on their power to set him on the throne of England; "and became," says Surtees, "the chief agents in the destruction of their kindred blood of Lancaster." To write their history would be simply to recapitulate the chequered and bloody story of the Wars of the Roses; and I can here afford but a scanty account of their fortunes and career.

1. Richard, the eldest son of the Earl's second marriage, was the husband of the heiress of the Montacutes, Alice, only child of Thomas Earl of Salisbury, who brought him the baronies of Montacute and Monthermer, and the Earldom was revived in his favour in 1442. This was but one of several grants and distinctions conferred upon him by Henry VI.; yet he was among the foremost to desert his cause. He fought and won with his brother-in law the first pitched battle between the contending Roses at St. Albans; and was constituted Lord Great Chamberlain after the victory of Northampton in 1460; but his campaigns ended with the disaster of Wakefield. Here—again with the Duke of York—he was taken prisoner, beheaded, and his head set up by the side of the Duke's over the gates of York. He left many children. One of his sons was slain at Wakefield; another was Archbishop of York and Chancellor of England; John, the third, was Marquess of Montacute; and Richard, the eldest, was the

"Proud setter up and puller down of Kings,"

who married the heiress of the Beauchamps, and is renowned in history as the "stout Earl of Warwick." The portrait of Richard Nevill the King Maker, "the greatest and last of the old Norman chivalry—kinglier in pride, in state, in possessions, than the King himself," has been so often and so eloquently drawn, that his splendid presence has grown to be familiar to us. We see him with his body guard of six hundred retainers in russet coats, embroidered with the Ragged Staff of Beauchamp before and behind; with his "exceeding great household," daily feeding thirty thousand mouths at his various castles and manors;* and his special pursuivant, called the Warwick Herald, assigned to him for his service in his martial exploits. We see him "ever in favour" with the commons, and so popular that every one was proud to wear his badge: "no man," reports Sir

---

peale of evensong." At five she supped; and after supper indulged in a little "honest mirthe" with her gentlewomen; at seven she drank a cup of wine, took "her leave of God for al nighte" in prayer, and by eight o'clock was in bed, where she thus spent eleven consecutive hours. She must otherwise have passed many a cold spring and autumn evening in the dark, as fires and candles were only allowed in her household from All Hallow's Day to Good Friday.

* "Of his extraordinary hospitality also doe I find this observ'd, that at his house in London six Oxen were usually eaten at a breakfast, and every Tavern full of his meat; for who that had any acquaintance in his Family should have as much sodden and rost as he could prick upon a long Dagger."—*Dugdale.*

Philip de Comines (who visited him when he was Captain of Calais) "esteeming himself gallant, whose head was not adorn'd with his Ragged Staff, nor no door frequented, that had not his white Crosse painted thereon." We see him the great commander of his age, leading the van at Northampton, and seizing the King himself at the first battle of St. Albans. We see him turning the tide of victory at Ferrybridge, where, "receiving some loss, whereat divers were staggered," he stabbed his horse before the King's eyes, in token that where he fought there could be no retreat, and crying, "Let him flee that flee will, I will tarry with him that will tarry with me," kissed the cross of his sword to confirm the vow. We see him crowning and discrowning King after King at his will and pleasure; raising and dispersing armies by the sole magic of his name; and last of all, we see him in the closing scene, on that fatal Easter Sunday in 1471, when he fell by the hand of Sir Roger Kynaston at the battle of Barnet. "Though fought between blood-relations," says Mr. Drummond, "no combat was ever more sanguinary or cruel." He was attainted after his death, and both his Earldoms forfeited. He had received from Henry VI. a grant of pre-eminence above all the Earls of England, and held Crown lands of the annual value of fourscore thousand crowns, in addition to his own inheritance of Middleham, and the great Beauchamp estates.

Two daughters only had been born of his marriage: Isabel, Duchess of Clarence; and Anne, married first to the Lancastrian Prince of Wales, Edward, the son of Henry VI., and then to the Yorkist King, Richard III. Isabel was the mother of the last male Plantagenet, Edward, Earl of Warwick and Salisbury, who suffered on the block in 1499, "a victim to the jealousy of the House of Tudor," and two daughters, Margaret, restored as Countess of Salisbury by Henry VIII., but also beheaded, who was the wife of Sir Richard Pole, and is now represented by the house of Hastings; and Winifred, who left children only by her second husband, Sir Thomas Barrington. Of her, too, descendants remain. Anne Nevill, the younger sister, whose life, bound up with each of the conflicting dynasties, was "full of state and woe," left none. She pined away and died within a year of the death of her only child, Edward, Prince of Wales, King Richard's son.

John, Marquess of Montacute, the brother of the King-Maker, had inherited their mother's great estates, and was summoned to parliament by Henry VI. in 1460, and again on his accession by Edward IV., as Lord Montacute. He had rendered good service to the House of York, and when Henry Percy, third Earl, fled into Scotland with the Lancastrian king in 1467, he was himself created Earl of Northumberland. Two years later, however, he had to relinquish the title in favour of the dispossessed heir, Henry Percy's son, who, then a prisoner in the Tower, tendered his allegiance to Edward, and was re-instated in his Earldom. John Nevill received in compensation the Marquessate of Montacute. He changed sides with his brother, fell with him at the battle of Barnet, and, like him, was sentenced to attainder and confiscation after death. His eldest son George had been created Duke of Bedford two years before, as the intended husband of the King's daughter, Lady Elizabeth Plantagenet; but this sudden collapse of his fortunes reduced him to beggary, and for this reason, having no means to maintain the ducal dignity, he was degraded from all his honours by Act of Parliament in 1477. Neither he nor his brother John were ever married; and five sisters alone remained, to whom Henry VIII. restored the inheritance. They were : 1. Anne, married to Sir William Stonor; 2. Elizabeth, married first to Lord Scrope, and then to Sir Henry Wentworth; 3. Margaret, married first to Sir John Mortimer, and secondly to Charles Brandon, Duke of Suffolk; 4. Lucy, married first to Sir Thomas Fitz William, and secondly to Sir Anthony Browne; and 5. Isabel, married to Sir William Hudlestone.

2. William, the second son of the Earl of Westmorland by Joan de Beaufort, married the heiress of Thomas, sixth Baron Fauconberg, and was summoned to parliament in her right in 1429. Like all the rest of the Nevills, he was an excellent soldier, and was rewarded for his valour at Towton by being named High Admiral of England, and created Earl of Kent in 1463. He died the same year, leaving three co-heiresses, among whose descendants the Barony of Fauconberg remains in abeyance ; Joan, married to Sir John Bethune ; Elizabeth, married to Sir John Strangeways ; and Alice, the wife of Sir John Conyers.

3. George, the third son of the same marriage, inherited several of the Latimer estates from his father, and had summons to parliament in 1469 as Baron Latimer, but in the latter years of his life became an idiot. The title was borne by his son, grandson, and great-grandson, with whom the line closed in 1577. This last Lord Latimer left four daughters : 1. Katherine, Countess of Northumberland ; 2. Dorothy, Countess of Exeter; 3. Lucy, married to Sir William Cornwallis; and 4. Elizabeth, married to Sir John Danvers, who became his co-heirs. Nevertheless, there remained a male heir, Edward Nevill, descended from the second Lord, who should have been Lord Latimer, and sought to recover the Earldom of Westmorland from James I., but was obliged to content himself with having both titles inscribed on his tombstone in Eastham church. It is believed that his two sons had died before him.

4. Edward, the fourth son of the same marriage ; Lord Bergavenny by right of his wife, Lady Elizabeth Beauchamp, sole heiress of Richard, Earl of Worcester and Baron Bergavenny : of whom presently.

I now return to the children of the Earl of Westmorland's first marriage with Lady Margaret Stafford, the elder line that remained seated at Raby, and continued there for six generations more. By the division of the estates (see p. 346) they had lost a great part of their patrimony, and with it much of their ancient power and importance, but still ranked foremost among the potentates of the North. When the great Catholic rising was being concerted in 1569, it was at their castle of Raby, in the same hall where the seven hundred knights that held of the Nevills had been wont to assemble, that the gentlemen of the North met in council. Besides the Earl of Northumberland, there were present old Norton and his sons, Markinfield, Swinburne, and about one hundred more. "They were," says Froude, "all uncertain, * * * there was no resolution any where. They had all but broken up, and 'departed every man to provide for himself,' when Lady Westmorland, Lord Surrey's daughter, threw herself among them, weeping bitterly, and crying 'that they and their country were shamed for ever, and that they would seek holes to creep to.' The lady's courage put spirit into the men." The die was cast; "and at four o'clock the following afternoon, Sunday, November 14th, as the twilight was darkening, Northumberland, Westmorland, Sir Christofer and Sir Cuthbert Nevill, and old Richard Norton, entered the city of Durham. With sixty followers armed to the teeth behind them, they strode into the cathedral; Norton with a massive gold crucifix hanging from his neck, and carrying the old banner of the Pilgrimage, the Cross and streamers and the Five Wounds. They overthrew the communion board; they tore the English bible and prayer-book to pieces; the ancient altar was taken from a rubbish heap where it had been thrown and solemnly replaced, and the holy water vessel was restored to the west door; and then, amidst tears, embraces, prayers, and thanksgivings, the organ pealed out, the candles and torches were lighted, and mass was said once more in the long desecrated aisles." But the rebellion, begun with such enthusiasm, was short-lived and unsuccessful. Though the insurgent leaders gathered together a force variously estimated at from eight thousand to fifteen thousand men, and marched as far south as Tadcaster, they met with no support, and their solitary feat of arms was the capture of Barnard Castle. By the middle of December the discouraged army was broken up, and the two Earls were riding for their lives "in a blasting North wind that swept across the moors, with snow and sleet lashing in their faces," to seek refuge in Scotland. Here Lord Westmorland, "to be the more unknown, changed his cote of plate and sword with Jock o' the Syde," than whom, says Maitland,

"A greater thiefe did never ryde;"

and was harboured by the Kerrs at Ferniherst till he could make his escape to Flanders. He never returned home, but lingered on for thirty years in exile and dire poverty; sharing a slender Spanish pension with forty or fifty of his banished followers that "daily came to meat with him;" most anxious to obtain his pardon, and pining for his native land. But Elizabeth, who had taken possession of his estates, proved inexorable from first to last; and he died, neglected and forgotten, a very old man, in 1601. His wife, who had remained in England, subsisted on a grudging pittance doled out to her by the Queen; but at her death in 1593, his four daughters—the daughters of so princely a house—were literally left in want of bread. There had been no son; and, on the accession of James I., Edward Nevill (as we have seen) put in his claim as heir male, pleading that the last Earl's fall was caused "by his service and affection for the King's mother." This was undeniable, and in Queen Elizabeth's lifetime James had not only been profuse of promises, but had even written a letter to Nevill, styling him Earl of Westmorland. But now promises and precedent alike went for nothing; his petition was handed over to the Judges, who declared the Earldom forfeited by attainder; and in 1624 it was conferred on Francis Fane, the eldest son of Sir Thomas Fane and Mary, Baroness Le Despencer, the then heir general of the house of Abergavenny.

This was an act of injustice. Edward Lord Bergavenny (see p. 349) had transmitted his title to his son, grandson, and great-grandson, and the latter was the father of Mary Fane. He had no other child; and, on his death in 1586, she claimed the barony, as having been held by tenure of the Castle of Bergavenny from the time of Henry III. But she had a cousin, another Edward Nevill, to whom, as the unquestioned male heir, it was adjudged by the House of Lords; and the King, as "some satisfaction" to the disappointed heiress, granted her the Barony of Le Despencer, that had been held by one of her ancestors.

To this Edward, fourteenth Baron of Bergavenny by tenure, and to his posterity, it is evident that, on the failure of the elder branch of Latimer, the Earldom of Westmorland should have belonged. Had the attainder been reversed, it must have been his by birthright. From him the present head of the family is directly derived; and thus descends, in an unbroken male line extending over nearly thirty generations—a lineage such as scarcely any other house in England can boast of—from Uchtred, Earl of Northumberland in the reign of Ethelred II. George, the twenty-fourth baron, was created Earl of Abergavenny in 1784, and the present and fifth Earl received a Marquessate in 1876.

Newmarch; from the castle of Neumarché in Normandy, which, about 1060, was seized by Duke William, to the prejudice of its inheritor, Geoffrey de Newmarch. (Ord. Vitalis.) Geoffrey's son Bernard was one of the Conqueror's companions-at-arms, and witnesses one of his charters to Battle Abbey. He obtained his share of the spoil—a Welsh principality—by his own good sword; for, as Freeman expresses it, "he used a soldier's licence to appropriate the territory of Brecknock." The history of its conquest is thus narrated:

"Bernard Newmarch came to this district, according to the *Annales Cambriæ*, . in 1091, in pursuit of Rhys-ap-Tewdwr, ruler of 'the right hand part'—a phrase which is the exact equivalent of the old Welsh *Deheu-barth*—and at Brechenauc Rhys-ap-Tewdwr was slain. It is said that Maenarch had ruled Brycheiniog in peace, and that his son Bleddyn-ap-Maenarch was ruler when the Normans arrived. Fitz Hamon had just taken possession of Glamorganshire, and now Newmarch conquers Brycheiniog. He approaches Brychan's stronghold, the *Gaer*, from the North, but, finding the place too strong, makes as if for the Eppynt Hills along a ridge parallel with the river Eskyr. The British troops were on the opposite side, where the lane called *Heol-y-Cymry* runs in the same direction.

"It is stated by Jones (History of Brecon) that Newmarch, unaware of the presence of the Welsh troops, crossed over through a wood, called after the event *Cwm-gwern-gâd*, now corrupted into *Cwmgwingad*, that the Welsh rushed upon them with fury, but that the Normans, with better discipline, stood firm against the onset, and in the end won the field. The Welsh were dispersed, the brave Rhys-ap-Tewdwr slain near a well called to this day *Ffynon-pen-Rhys;* and Bleddyn-ap-Maenarch also fell. With this defeat ended for ever the British lordship of Brycheiniog. Newmarch immediately settled down as lord of the district, adding one more to the redoubtable Lords Marchers. He moved the seat of government from the spot where Brychan and his successors had dwelt— the Gaer on the Eskir, now a knoll crowned with stately trees—and built his castle near the confluence of the Honddu and Usk, a place which probably even then was called Aberhonddu. Of the existence of a town or even of a village on this spot before Newmarch's conquest we have no information, so that the town of Brecknock and its castle must be viewed as the creation of the Norman freebooter."—Nichol's *Counties and County Families of Wales.*

Bernard lost no time in parcelling out the lands of his new province among the followers that had helped him to win it ; and established himself so firmly at Brecknock "that no efforts of the natives could dislodge him." His position was further strengthened through an alliance with a Welsh princess, Nesta, the daughter of Griffin-ap-Llewelyn. " By marrying a Welsh wife he took the most likely course to reconcile his vassals to the rule and exactions of a foreigner. Crushed to the dust by the iron heel of the conqueror, robbed of their inheritance in kind to feed his pampered men-at-arms, subject to constant insult and frequent injury from a contemptuous and cruel soldiery of foreign speech and foreign manners, it was still some small consolation to the warm though sinking heart of the Welshman that in the frowning castle of Aberhonddu there was one lady of the blood of the Cymry, though it might be one of the line of Trahaern the Usurper, and herself of more than doubtful morals, she was still the descendant of Anarawd, son of that Rhodri the Great who, two hundred years before, was King of all Wales, and deemed ' the pride and protector of the Cymry.' " —*Ibid.*

Yet it was through this same Welsh wife, whose Royal blood was to reconcile his unwilling subjects to their thraldom, that his son's connection with Wales was severed. Her life was shamelessly profligate ; and the son, Mael, as he grew to manhood, was stung by the sense of his mother's dishonour. " For," says Dugdale, " taking notice that his mother did play the Adultress ; watching one night for her Paramour, he maimed him grievously, and then let him go with shame. And that this Act of his so enraged his Mother, that, in revenge thereof, she made her address to the King, and publickly took her Oath, that this Mael her Son was not begotten by her Husband, but by another with whom she had at that time private familiarity. Moreover, that the King thereupon took occasion to bereave him of his whole Inheritance; and caused Livery to be made of it to Sybil her Daughter, whom she affirmed to be the child of her Husband, and that he married her to a noble Knight of his Court, called Miles, the son of Walter Constable of Gloucester. Which Miles was afterwards by Maud the Empress advanced to the Earldom of Hereford." Countess Sybil had five sons, but they all died s. p. and the county of Brecknock and Gower-land were conveyed by the second of her three co-heiresses to Philip de Braose.

It is satisfactory to know that Nesta had qualms of conscience. Her husband, whose confessor was a monk of Battle, had given some land and a ruined church near Brecknock to the Abbey; and she, "being sick," added a part of her own inheritance in Herefordshire. With these and other contributions in lands and tithes, the church was restored, and a Priory founded as a cell to Battle Abbey, which in process of time became a flourishing community.

Adam de Newmarch, presumably a kinsman of Bernard's, "though how allied to him," says Dugdale, "I find not," appears as a benefactor of Nostell Priory at its foundation in the time of Henry I., and held Whatton in Nottinghamshire and other lands in Yorkshire of the Honour of De Gand. Next comes another Adam (no doubt his son) for whose custody William de Newmarch paid £93 16s. in 1160. This William held a barony in Hampshire, which when "he afterwards fell into the infirmity of Leprosy," was transferred in 1204 to Godfrey de St. Martin. His former ward was at that time a knight, and Lord of Whatton, where he was followed by four generations of successors, till, through the daughter of the last heir, they were amalgamated with another line seated at Bentley in Yorkshire. Of this latter house was a second Sir Adam, who was twice summoned to Parliament, first by Henry III. in 1260, and four years later by the insurgent barons. He had been taken prisoner when "advancing his Banner against the King at Northampton," and deprived of his estates, those in Lincolnshire being granted to William de Gery, and those in Yorkshire to Robert Foliot. But the victory of Lewes retrieved his fortunes, and though again captured at Kenilworth, "yet had he the benefit of that favorable Decree called *Dictum de Kenilworth*." His son, in 1314, received a writ of military summons, and had free warren in all his Yorkshire demesne, where the next heir, Roger, obtained a weekly market and yearly fair at the capital manor, Wymersley. Roger's son Ralph married Elizabeth de Newmarch, the heiress of Whatton, and was the father of the last male heir, Robert, whose daughter Elizabeth carried the whole inheritance to John Nevill of Althorpe in Lincolnshire. "The said Elizabeth, her grandmother, overliving her Son Robert, had," says Thoroton, "a mind to disinherit her," but did not succeed. These Newmarches bore *Argent* five fusils in fesse *Gules:* five fusils in fesse being, we are told, the coat of the Bee-Crespins and Grimaldis.

This by no means completes the list of collaterals. There was a William de Newmarch of Northumberland, dead before 1130 (Rot. Pip.) and a Henry de Newmarch, who held a barony of nearly seventeen knight's fees in 1165 (Lib. Niger); and in one of his charters to the Monks of Bermondsey, speaks of his grandfather Winebald, and Winebald's sons, Roger and Milo, as former benefactors of the Abbey. His brother James had succeeded him in 1204, but did not very long survive; as in 1215 the estates lying in Berkshire, Somersetshire, Dorsetshire, Wiltshire, and Gloucestershire, were divided between this last lord's two daughters and co-heirs, Isabel, the wife of Sir Ralph Russell, and Hawise, first married to John de Botreaux, and then to Nicholas de Moels. Cadbury was the head of this barony.

Norbet; Newbet in Leland's list; most probably Nerbert. William de Nerbert, in 1165, held four knight's fees of the Earl of Gloucester in Gloucestershire.—*Liber Niger.* Philip de Nerbert one in Devonshire, at Berry-Norbert.—*Testa de Nevill.* This he had, it would appear, inherited from William. " Bury-Nerbert, sometime the seat of Willihelmus Nerbert de Bury (such evidence of the name I have seen divers) but in this age of Berry or Bury de Nerbert."—*Westcote's Devon.* From them it passed to the Berrys. " Monuments of both families are in the old church ; and hard by, fallen sadly from its high estate, is the old manor-house."—*Worth's Devon.* It is said to date from the reign of Edward IV. : and was once rich in external decorations, friezes, and mouldings, elaborately carved in stone, and bearing the arms of the Plantagenets and Bonvilles. All were removed a few years ago by the proprietor (the late Mr. Basset) " to ornament a building in his garden at Waterhampton ! "

According to a Survey by Inquisition of the county of Glamorgan, preserved in the Record Office, and probably taken in 1262, Philip de Nereberd then held four fees, including East Orchard, and Nerberd Castleton Castle, of which building some part yet remains.

Norice, or Norreys. " Petrus Norreis " is found in the Norman Exchequer Rolls, about 1198, and several of the name in England at the same date. " Henry le Norreys was seized of estates in Notts, which on his death King John granted to Alan le Norreys, his brother."—*The Norman People.* From him (according to the same authority) came the Norreys' of Speke in Lancashire, whom Dugdale affirms to be the ancestors of the Lords Norris of Rycote and the Earl of Berkshire, now represented by the Berties. " They were," he says, " of Speke, *in com. Lanc.* long before King Edward the Third's time, and most of them Knights." John, the second son of Sir Henry Norris of Speke, is said to have lived in 1361 at Bray, in Berkshire, where he was succeeded by a son and a grandson.

But I fear that " those gentle historians who dip their pens in nothing but the milk of human kindness " (as Edmund Burke aptly describes the heralds), have dissimulated the true origin of the Lords Norris. Their undoubted ancestor was Richard de Norreys, the favourite cook of Henry III.'s Queen, Eleanor of

Provence, who was rewarded in 1267 by a grant of the manor of Ocholt in Berkshire, "subject to a fee farm rent of 40^s and stated to have been an encroachment from the forest."—*Lysons.* One of his descendants, John, who impartially served the Red and White Rose, having been Master of the Wardrobe to Henry VI., and Esquire of the Body to Edward IV., built the present mansion of Ockwell during the former reign. "A large bay window full of coats of arms in stained glass, shows those of the abbey of Abingdon, with the mitre, and of the family of Norreys, several times repeated, with their motto 𝔉𝔢𝔶𝔱𝔥𝔣𝔲𝔩𝔩𝔶 𝔰𝔢𝔯𝔟𝔢." —*Ibid.* The line, which could boast of some very gallant soldiers, ended with Francis, second Lord Norreys, who was created Earl of Berkshire by James I., and the barony passed through his grand-daughter, Bridget Wray, to the Berties. Her son was the first Earl of Abingdon.

Newborough. Henry de Newburgh (so named from the castle of Neufbourg, in Normandy, where he was born) was the younger son of Roger de Bellomont Earl of Mellent, and the brother of Robert, afterwards Earl of Leicester (see *Beaumont*). He himself obtained the Earldom of Warwick towards the latter end of the Conqueror's reign, "when," says Dugdale, " King William, having begirt Warwick with a mighty ditch, for the precinct of its walls, and erected the gates at his own charge, did promote this Henry to the earldom, and annexed thereto the royalty of the borough, which at that time belonged to the crown." Here, "upon the site of the tower illustrated by the traditions of Guy, the great opponent of the Danes," he built his castle, which, enlarged and strengthened during the long succession of its powerful lords, became one of the most renowned of English fortresses, and remains " the glory of the Midland shires." William Rufus further bestowed upon him all the lands that had belonged to his Saxon predecessor Thurkill, whose daughter and heir Margaret, Leland tells us, he had married. Ordericus, on the other hand, asserts that his wife was a sister of Rotrode, Count de la Perche, and one of his sons (the Bishop of Evreux) certainly bore the name of Rotrode. But he was probably twice married, for it was only through the former alliance that his descendants could lay claim to the right they invariably asserted of representing the famous Guy. The Bear and Ragged Staff, that had been handed down as Guy's device, was first assumed by Henry de Newburgh, and has ever since been continued as the badge of all the successive Earls of Warwick.

No tradition has struck deeper root in the hearts of Englishmen than the heroic legend of Guy of Warwick; and though he is sometimes treated as a mythical champion, there seems to be no rational ground for doubting his existence, nor his good service against the Danes. His story, as told by Dugdale, is copied from an account written about 1395, and has thus acquired all the adjuncts and *couleur locale* belonging to that period, which, however strangely interpolated upon its Anglo-Saxon groundwork, do not necessarily discredit it.

Guy, whose " memory for his great valour hath ever since been, and is still as famous," and whose name was honoured even in the far East, was the son of Siward of Wallingford, and acquired the Earldom of Warwick by marrying the only child of Rohand, "a famous warrior inrich't vith great possessions" in the time of Alfred. Soon after, he set forth on a pilgrimage to Jerusalem. During his absence, in the third year of the reign of Athelstan, the Danes made one of their accustomed inroads, landed on the South coast, wasted and burnt the country nearly up to the gates of Winchester, where the King had taken refuge, and sent two of their chieftains " to desire him to resign his crown, or else that the dispute for the kingdom should be determined in a single Combat by two Champions for both sides." The King, being hard pressed, accepted these terms, and "calling together his nobles, offered that province" (Hants) "for a reward to him that should conquer the Danish champion Colbrand." He further "enjoyn'd a Fast of three dayes," and "with earnest prayers and abundant teares," waited for the coming deliverer. But none presented himself. Earl Rohand, "that most valiant of a thousand," was dead; Earl Guy beyond seas; and Colbrand, the Dane, was a ferocious giant, whom all dreaded to encounter. At last, on the Eve of St. John the Baptist, a good angel appeared to the King in a dream, and bade him go up, with two churchmen, to the top of the Northgate (where the Hospital of the Holy Cross was afterwards founded), staying there till the hour of prime, and " then he should see divers poor people and pilgrims enter thereat, amongst which there would be a personable man in a Pilgrim's habit, barefooted, with his head uncovered, and upon it a Chaplet of white Roses; and that he should entreat him for the love of Jesus Christ, and the devotion of his pilgrimage, and the preservation of all England, to undertake the Combat." The King went as directed, and " espying one neatly clad in a white short sliev'd gown reaching to the midleg, with a Garland of Roses upon his head " (to our ideas there is something very festive in the Palmer's attire), "and a large staff in his hand, but looking wan and much macerated by reason of his travelling barefoot, and his beard grown to a very great length," laid hold of his coat, and offered him entertainment. This the Palmer refused; then the King, opening his heart to him, " told how Olaus King of Denmark and Golavus King of Denmark had besieged him there for nearly a twelvemonth," and how sorely he stood in need of a champion to maintain his right. " ' Oh my Lord the King,' saith the Palmer, ' you may easily see that I am not in any condition to take upon me this fight, being feeble and weakned with dayly travail: alas! where are your stout and hardy Souldiers, that were wont to be in great esteem with you?' 'Ah!' quoth the King, ' some of them are dead, and some are gone to the Holy Land; I had one valiant Knight which was Earl of Warwick, called Guy: would to God that I had him here, for then should this Duel be soon undertaken, and the War finisht:' and as he spoke, tears fell from his eyes." The Palmer, moved by his distress, accepted the office of champion; then, in great joy, "they brought him into Church with ringing of bells, and *Te Deum* was begun with cheerful voices;

and they entertained him with meat and drink, as also with bathing, putting apparel upon him; and for the space of three weeks cheered him up with the best refreshments." When the appointed day arrived, the Palmer rose betimes and heard three masses; then "armed himself with the King's best harness," was girt with the sword of Constantine the Great, and holding in his hand the lance of St. Maurice, rode forth, "the most proper and well appointed knight that ever they saw," to meet Colbrand the Dane. The giant came "so weightily armed that his horse could scarce carry him, and before him a Cart loaded with Danish axes, great Clubs with knobs of iron, Steel Lances, and Iron Hooks to pull his adversary to him" (a curious description of the weapons in use during the fourteenth century): and as soon as he saw the Englishman, called out to him to "get off his horse, and cast himself down with submission. But the Palmer, arming himself with the sign of the Cross, and commending his soul to God, put spurs to his Horse to meet the Gyant." The latter unhorsed him; and the blows aimed by the Palmer could, by reason of his height, reach no further than his shoulder; then Colbrand "smote at him with a square bar of steel," but he interposed his shield, struck the club out of the giant's hand, and while he stretched out his arm to take it up, cut off his hand. The combat went on notwithstanding, till "in the evening of the day," the Dane fainted from loss of blood, and the Palmer cut off his head with an axe: "and going to the Cathedral to give thanks to God, offer'd up his weapon at the high altar (long kept in the vestry there, and called by the name of Colbrand's Axe), and resumed his pilgrim's habit, refusing all reward. The King being importunate to discover his name," and the Palmer consenting to reveal it to him only, under oath of secrecy, "they walked out alone in a bypath to a certain Crosse at some distance from the Citie, and there, humbly bowing himself to the King," he confessed he was Guy of Warwick. "From whence the Earl bent his course to Warwick: and coming thither not known of any, for three days together took Almes at the hand of his own Lady as one of the XIII poor people unto which she dayly gave relief herself, for the safety of him and her, and the health of both their souls. And having rendered thanks to her, he repaired to an heremite that resided amongst the shady woods hard by, and abode with that holy man till his death; and then succeeded him in his cell, and continued the same course of life for the space of two years after; but then discerning death to approach, he sent to his Lady their wedding Ring by a trusty servant, wishing her to take care of his burial; adding also, that when she came she should find him lying dead in the Chapel before the Altar; and moreover that within XV dayes after she herself should depart this life." The place of his retreat is still called Guy's Cliff. By his neglected wife he left a son named Reynburn, who was followed by Wolgeat, then by Wigod, and lastly, by Alwyne (cotemporary with Edward the Confessor), who is called Alwinus Vicecomes in Domesday, "either because he did exercise the power and authority of Earl Leofric (his uncle) here in Warwickshire, or else that he had the custody of the county to the King's immediate use. He left issue Turchill, who was a great man in that age, but no more really Earl than his father or Ancestors had been." It is clear that neither father nor son took part with Harold, for at the date of Domesday, Turchill "continued possess'd of vast lands in this Shire, yet thereof was neither the Borough nor Castle of Warwick." His son, however, never enjoyed his inheritance, which passed to his daughter Margaret, the wife (according to Leland) of the first Norman Earl of Warwick, to whom, after this long digression, we now return.

He was, says Dugdale, " of great familiarity with Henry, the King's youngest son, and one that stuck closest to him, upon the death of William Rufus, for obtaining of that Crown; and so ever afterwards." He founded St. Sepulchre's Priory; and "began the making of Wedgenock Park, following therein the example of the King Henry, who made the first park at Woodstock that ever was made in England." His son Roger, who espoused the cause of the Empress Maud, was the father of William and Waleran, who in turn succeeded to his Earldom and possessions—certified 12 Hen. II. to amount to one hundred and five knight's fees, in those days an enormous fortune. But Waleran "had much ado a great part of his time touching his inheritance; there starting up one who feigned himself to be his brother, Earl William, deceased in the Holy Land, which occasioned him no little trouble and vexation." The line ended with his grandson Thomas, sixth Earl, who died s. p. in 1242, leaving the Earldom to his only sister Margery. She was at that time married to John Mareschal (brother, as some say, of William Mareschal, Earl of Pembroke), but she lost her husband the year following, and at once became an object of speculation as a marriageable heiress. Henry III. forthwith issued his mandate to the Archbishop of York and William de Cantilupe, desiring them to seize her castle of Warwick, " forasmuch as the said Margerie being one of the most noble Ladies in England, and possesst of a Castle extraordinarily strong situate also towards the Marches, it would be most perilous she should take to husband any person whatsoever of whose fidelity the King had not as great confidence as of his own;" threatening that, "in case she should be so rash as to do otherwise, the same Castle and lands should be for ever forfeited to the King and his heirs." She was not even allowed the customary privilege of buying the liberty to marry as she pleased by payment of a heavy fine: but forcibly urged "as from the King" to give her hand to "one of his domestic servants in his special favour," John de Plessetis. The match, as may be supposed, was utterly distasteful to her, and she delayed giving her consent as long as she dared; yet, before the year was out, she had become the wife of the upstart favourite. Even then, the King was not wholly satisfied. "As there was," says Dugdale, "extraordinary means used about wooing and winning this great Lady to marry with John de Plessets, so there was not wanting suspition that, being such an heir, she had been strongly solicited by some; and that possibly by reason of the weakness of her Sex, she might have been wrought upon to contract herself privately with another. Wherefore to make sure work, the King got a Bond of her with a Deed to boot whereby she obliged herself that if it could be justly proved that she had so contracted marriage with any other before, all her lands and possessions should be forfeited." Poor Margery had no children; and when she died (about 1263) the vast inheritance of the Newburghs passed to her cousin William Mauduit, and four years later to his sister, Isabel de Beauchamp. They were the children of her aunt Lady Alice, the only daughter of Waleran, fourth Earl of Warwick.

This illustrious branch of the Beaumonts has left its name to Winfrith Newburgh, a manor and hundred in Dorset, where some descendants of the first Earl of Warwick continued till 1541. "His fifth son, according to Dugdale, but his third, according to Camden (probably two of the elder brothers died young), inherited his father's lands in Normandy, was seneschal and justiciary of that duchy, and a great benefactor to the abbey of Bec, where he became a monk, and dying 1158, was buried in the chapter house there. Of his marriage we find no account. This was, probably, the same person who is styled dapifer and justiciar of Normandy by Du Chesne, in his Norman Chronicle, and the same to whom King Henry I. gave Winfrith."—*Hutchins' Dorset.* His son and heir Roger founded Bindon Abbey in 1172, where most of his descendants had their sepulture, and married Maud Arundel "sometimes styled Countess of Sarum," who must have been a very considerable heiress, for in 1245 her son Robert paid £15 for "fifteen knights fees of R. Arundel." Robert, "among other illustrious nobles, was party to a treaty of peace between King Richard I. and Tancred King of Sicily, on the occasion of the passage of the former to the Crusades in the Holy Land."—*Ibid.* Six more generations succeeded him at Winfrith. "Sire Robert de Newborgh," in 1322, "is enrolled amongst the Knights Bachelors taken in arms against the King at the battle of Boroughbridge, and in the following summer submitted to a fine of £100, in consideration of which his life was saved." His descendant William, less fortunate, was made prisoner at Gast near Tewkesbury, and there beheaded in 1430. The last heir, Sir Roger, was Sheriff of Dorset and Somerset 8 Hen. VIII., and died the same year, leaving his great estate to his daughter Christian, the wife of John, second Lord Marney.

In Leland's time, "the Genealogie of the Newborows and the name of Heires General that they maried with be yn Glasse Windows in a Parlour in the Maner Place at Est Lilleworth." This manor house has long since disappeared, for the castle now standing at Lullworth was built in 1600 by Viscount Bindon, partly out of the ruins of Bindon Abbey.

Neiremet; in Leland's copy, Nairmere. "Hugo de Nemore Herbert," or Bosc-Herbert, was a tenant in chief in Dorsetshire, and William de Nemore an under-tenant in Suffolk 1086. (Domesday). The former, called *Hugo de Bosco* in the Exon Domesday, was the ancestor of the barons of Halberton in Devonshire, and of a family of long continuance in Dorset: but none of his posterity bore the name of Nemore.

I have never succeeded in finding any mention of it elsewhere.

Neile. This may possibly stand for "Néel-le-Viconte," as he is styled in the Chronicle of Normandy, the famous Néel de St. Sauveur "called, on account of his valour and skill, his bravery and noble bearing, Chef de Faucon—Noble Chef de Faucon was his title."—*Wace.* He ruled a great Norman fief as Viscount of the Côtentin, and led the men of his territory at the Battle of Hastings, where he "exerted himself much to earn the love and good will of his lord, and assaulted the English with great vigour. He overthrew many that day with the poitrail of his horse, and came with his sword to the rescue of many a baron."—*Ibid.* The *cri de guerre* of the men of the Côtentin, he tells us, was "St. Sauveur! St. Sauveur! Sire de St. Sauveur!" Yet his French commentator, M. Le Prévost, doubts whether Néel was actually present on the occasion. "His presence at Hastings is vouched by no one else. Domesday is silent: but this does not appear conclusive, as he might have died in the interval; and M. de Gerville quotes on the subject M. Odolent Desnos, *Histoire d'Alençon*, where it is stated that Néel was killed in 1074 in a battle near Cardiff. The last Néel de St. Sauveur died in 1092, as appears by an account of his relation, Bishop Jeffrey de Mowbray's desire to attend his funeral: *Mem. Ant. Norm.* i. 286, ii. 46. One of his two daughters and heiresses married Jourdain Tesson; the other was mother to Fulk de Pratis."—*Taylor.*

Though Néel le Vicomte is not entered in Domesday, the name is there amply represented. Two Nigels held by barony; Nigèl de Stafford (see *Toesni*) and *Nigellus Medicus*, the Conqueror's physician, who had estates in Hants, Wilts, Hereford, Shropshire, &c. Eight others were sub-tenants; *Nigel homo Episcopi Dunelmensis* in Lincolnshire: *Nigel homo Episcopi Linc.* in Notts; *Nigel homo Ivonis Taillgebosc* and *Nigel homo Juditæ Comitissæ* both again in Lincoln; *Nigellus quidam serviens Rotberti Comitis de Moritania, Nigellus Miles*, a vassal of Roger de Poitou, and two other Nigels, both very richly endowed, whom I suspect to be one and the same person, as the entries exactly correspond in many cases.

Nigel, the vassal of the Earl of Mortaine, held, jointly with Richard de Surdeval, the whole of his Yorkshire lands, by what rent or service is not known. "This Nigel is called Nigel Fossard. He was the ancestor of a race of Lords of Doncaster who continued to possess the interest he enjoyed there till the reign of King Henry V. His rights are now vested, by a grant of King Henry VII. in the corporation of Doncaster. The name of the Earls of Mortaine does not afterwards appear, but the descendants of Nigel are represented as holding in chief of the king, and were amongst the barons of the realm.

"Nigel held much of the Mortaine lands in other parts of the county. Besides the manor and soke of Doncaster, he had Rotherham, held of him by the family of Vesci."—*Hunter's South Yorkshire.*

" How he acquired the name of Fossard, which means more frequently grave-digger than ditcher, does not appear. It might have become a family surname, though, of course, with this meaning when first given. 'Fossarius' holds lands of the Count of Mortaine at Berkhempsted (Domesd.)."—*A. S. Ellis.* Nigel held in all ninety-one Yorkshire manors : and "as became one so favoured by fortune, was a most liberal benefactor to St. Mary's Abbey, York. His charter is witnessed by Robert Fossard, Aschitell de Bulmer, and Walter Fossard ; the first and last, no doubt, being his own sons, the younger one giving precedence to an important tenant. This grant is so prodigal, that we may suspect it was made on his death-bed when stricken with remorse (Old Mon. i. 394).

" Robert Fossard succeeded his father, and, by heavy fines, regained all his lands, except Doncaster, after the forfeiture of William Count of Mortaine, and became a tenant *in capite* of them. Doncaster, the King retained for twenty years."—*Ibid.*

Hunter, likewise, calls Nigel Fossard's son Robert, and says his grandson and great-grandson were both named William. Dugdale arranges the succession differently, inserting Adam Fossard as the next heir to Nigel, and thus making Robert his grandson. But all authorities are agreed that the line ended with a William Fossard in the fourth generation. Their barony, in 1165, consisted of thirty-four knight's fees. One of them had done good service with "the stout Northern Barons" at the Battle of the Standard, and been taken prisoner with King Stephen at Lincoln. The last William served in the French war of 1173, and followed the King to Normandy in 1194. His only daughter and heiress Joan was the wife of one of the heroes of Cœur de Lion's crusade, Sir Robert de Turnham, whose feats of arms in the East are chronicled by Peter de Langtoft, a rhyming Yorkshire monk—

> " Robert de Turnham se mene noblement,
> La terre souz maryne ad conquis nettement."

He was one of the commanders of the fleet at the siege of Cyprus in 1191, and afterwards Governor of the island. The King, on his arrival at Jaffa, despatched him and five other of his best knights with a challenge to the Soudan, inviting the infidel to come out to meet him in the open field, and cross swords in single combat. " When the King was in prison in Germany, Sir Robert was sent with the King's harness to England, and for his good service in this journey was discharged of his share of the levy for the King's ransom. On the death of King Richard he delivered up to John the castle of Chinon, where the treasure lay : and having founded an abbey at Begham in Sussex, died about 1210."—*Hunter.* This brave knight had no son, and his daughter Isabel—the second heiress of Doncaster—was reserved to an ignoble fate.

According to Dugdale, she was the guerdon given by King John to Peter de Manley for the murder of his nephew Arthur.

The old castle of the Fossards at Doncaster had disappeared even in Leland's time. "The Chirche of S. George," he tells us, "stands in the very area wher ons the Castelle of the towne stoode, long sins clene decayid. The dikes partely yet to be seene, and foundation of parte of the waulles."

The author of "The Norman People" believes this to have been "a Frank, rather than a Norman family, perhaps from Fossard, near Fontainebleau:" thus happily dispensing with the unsavoury derivation from *Fossarius*, or grave-digger.

Normauile, for Normanville; "a branch of Basset of Normandy, descended from Hugh Fitz Osmond, who held in capite in Hants in 1086. From him came the barons of Normanville, a younger branch of whom held the barony till about 1500. (La Roque, Maison d'Harcourt.)"—*The Norman People.* Gerold de Normanville was a benefactor of Battle Abbey: his grant of "Bocestepe" was confirmed by Henry I.; and in one of the charters of Henry, third Earl of Ewe, he is styled *Dapifer meus.* Norman de Normanville, according to the *Liber Niger,* was a baron of Sussex in 1165. "Not long after the Conquest, the Normanvilles held the towns of Empingham and Normanton in the county of Rutland. A Family of eminent note in those days for military affairs; for I find that about the latter end of King John's reign Ralf de Normanville was sent by the King with forces to the defence of Kenilworth Castle against the rebellious barons; and paid sixty marks, one Dextrarium (horse for the great saddle) and Palfrey for having the Farm of the Co. and Free Warren at Empingham. In 5 Hen. III. the King ordered Henry de Nevill to deliver from Clive Forest six Oaks and six Furchias for the building of a certain Hall by him design'd to be built at Empingham. His son Thomas left an heiress Margaret, whose husband, William de Basing, died Lord of this manor 9 Ed. II."—*Wright's Rutland.* Normanton sounds like an Anglicized Normanville. It is added that they were also seated at Kenarton, in Blackburn Hundred, Kent; and several branches existed in Yorkshire, where Ralph de Normanville was joint Sheriff in 1203. One of them was "dependant on the Percies" in Craven, and held Coniston from the time of Ed. II. till 1 Henry VIII., when it was sold by Sir John de Normanville.—*Whitaker's Craven.* In South Yorkshire we find Avice de Normanville holding land at Brinsworth 4 John; and her descendant Ralph 44 Henry III. had a grant of free warren at Brinsworth-Thribergh, and held Dalton in the same county, as well as Stainton in Lincolnshire. The heiress of the Normanvilles married Ralph Reresby early in the reign of Edward II. The last male heir, Sir Adam, "must have been an aged man at the time of his decease in 1316; for as early as 1279 he presented a rector to the church of Thribergh. And this fact must, I fear, entirely destroy the credit of a romantic story connected in village tradition with the first settlement of the Reresbys at this place. This tradition speaks of the plighted vows of the beautiful heiress of Thribergh at a cross, the fragment of which is still to be seen in a lane near the village; of the journey of her knight to the Holy Land; of a rumour reaching Thribergh of his death; of the lady's unwillingly allowing herself to be betrothed to another lord; of her visiting the cross on the morning of her intended nuptials, and of her meeting Reresby there in palmer's weeds; and finally, of her union with him in fulfilment of her earliest vows. Whatever little truth there may be in this tradition, which has been handed down, as supposed from the time, it is clear that the heiress of Normanville, through whom the inheritance passed to the Reresbys, was no heiress at the time of her marriage."—*Hunter's South Yorkshire.* I cannot see why this fact should "entirely destroy the credit" of Margaret de Normanville's love story. Even though she was not then Lady of Thribergh, she may have met her lover—a lover evidently unacceptable to her family—in secret at St. Leonard's Cross, and plighted her troth to him there on the eve of his departure for Jerusalem. Nothing was heard of him for years after, during which she waited with patient constancy, till at last, convinced that he was dead, she agreed to give her hand to another. On the very night before her wedding, she received a mysterious message bidding her repair to the old trysting place, where she found a travel-stained pilgrim in whom she recognized her true knight. The tale seems familiar to us, for it is found in many forms and in many places.

These Normanvilles bore *Argent* on a fesse between two bars gemelles *Gules*, three fleurs-de-lis *Or.* The motto of their representatives the Reresbys was "Mercy, Jesu!" The latter held Thribergh till the end of the seventeenth century, when they ended ignobly with a Sir William Reresby, who gambled away the whole of his property, and became a tapster in the King's Bench prison. He is said to have staked and lost the estate of Dennaby on a single main.

Thoresby, in his *History of Leeds*, gives the pedigree of a Reginald de Normanville, to whom the Conqueror gave the Barony of Laxton, and the custody of the Forest of Sherwood. His son Ralph[*] left an only daughter, Basilia, married to Robert de Caus, Caux, or Calx, by whom she had a son and two daughters. The son's line ended in the next generation; and the two daughters, Matilda and Constance, thus became co-heirs, and married two brothers; Adam Fitz Peter, named De Birkin from the place of his residence; and Thomas Fitz Peter, styled De Leedes. The name, however, long continued in the county; for Edmund Normanvyle is on the list of the gentry of Notts furnished to Henry VI. in 1433.

The latest notice I have met with of the Normanvilles is in Hunter's *South Yorkshire.* He gives the pedigree of Sir John Normanville of Kilnewick, and

---

[*] This must be the Sir Ralph who witnesses John Fitz-Matthew's grant to Worksop, and was a benefactor of Sawtrey Abbey, Huntingdonshire.

nine generations of his descendants, of whom the last, Thomas, was nineteen years old in 1585. Sir John's son, Sir Ralph, had married Agnes, daughter and heir of Sir Stephen Walleis of Little Haughton. The family was afterwards seated at Billingley.

The name extended itself in Scotland. In the *Monastic Records of Teviotdale*, I find that Hugh de Normanville, the husband of Alicia de Berkeley, gave to Melrose Abbey some land " on the confines of Rutherford." His successors, John and Thomas, were also benefactors of Melrose. Thomas bestowed on them " his land called the Ploughgate *inter les denes*, for which they were bound to pay him, at Roxburgh fair, a pair of gilt spurs."

Neofmarch, for Neufmarché, already given as Newmarch.

Nermitz; variously spelt Nermits, Nernuyt, Nernewtes, Nernieut, Neyrnut, Neinmuth, &c. The first mention I find of this family is in the time of Hen. I., when Robert Nernoit was of Berkshire (Rot. Magn. Pipæ). In the following century Maud, second daughter and co-heir of Geoffrey Bellew, married a Neyrnut. Their son, Milo, is mentioned in 1210, and was one of the Collectors of the Aid demanded by Henry III. " In 1299, John de Neyrnut held his lands under the Honour of Wallingford, belonging to Edmund Earl of Cornwall; and in 1320 they were settled on Sir John Neyrnut for life, with remainder to his sons, John, William, Thomas, and Edmund, and their respective heirs in tail; but in default of issue passed by the marriage of Margaret, daughter and heir of Sir John Neyrnut, to John Hervey of Thurnley, co. Beds." (ancestor of the Marquesses of Bristol).—*Lipscomb's Buckinghamshire*. This Sir John was seated at Burnham in Bucks, and died 1373. He bore *Sable* a lion rampant between six billets *Argent:* but Edmondston gives a rather different coat for Nernieut or Nernewtes; *Gules*, a lion rampant *Argent* within a border gobonated *Argent* and *Sable*. Westbury-Nernewtes, in the parish of Ashwell, Hertfordshire, and Upton-Nervets, or Nermits, in Berkshire, still recall the name.

Nembrutz. No name that bears even the faintest resemblance to this has come within my knowledge. It may possibly be a distortion of Newburgh.

Oteuel. Ralph de Ottevile held of Richard Morin of Newnham Morin in Oxfordshire. This is the one solitary occasion on which I have met with the name. There are, indeed, two De Otteles entered in the *Testa de Nevill:* Adam, who held *in capite*, and Walter, a tenant of Earl Ferrers: but in both these instances Ottele stands for Otley. Robson gives the arms of the Ottewells (of Ireland) as *Argent*, three Cornish choughs *Sable.*

Olibef: in Leland's list Gilebof; from Quilleboeuf in Normandy. This name is variously spelt in the *Monasticon*. Walter Oildeboef witnesses Margerie de la Ferté's confirmation charter to Motesfont Priory, Hants; Hugo, Ralph, William, Gerard, and Walter de Wildebuf occur in the chartulary of Bismede Priory in Bedfordshire; and Reginald de Weldebef, Oldebef, Wellebuf, or Waldefef witnesses several of the charters to Brecknock. " The Waldeboefs," says Camden, "were among the principal fellow-soldiers of Bernard de New-march." Llanhamlach, three miles from Brecon, "in the rich valley of the Usk, was the happy portion which fell to the first Walbeoffe.· Of the castle or house he built we know nothing, except that it stood on a spot in the close vicinity of the present house. The Walbeoffes, though for several generations they inter-married with the best families, both Norman and British, were not a prosperous race, nor were they a race that deserved prosperity. What wealth they possessed was at last squandered by a certain John, whose son Charles, when he came to the nominal inheritance, found himself a needy man, and sold his patrimony to a gentleman named Powel. He had a considerable family, but what ·became of them and their descendants we cannot tell. The name seems to have long disappeared from Breconshire. They bore *Argent* three bulls passant in pale *Gules*, armed and ungled *Or.*"—*Nichols, Annals of Counties and County Families in Wales.*

In the *Rotulus Cancellarii* 3 *John* Oliver de Welleboeuf occurs in Notts and Derby. I also find mention of a family of Oldbeif or Ouldbeif in Kent. "About A. D. 1435 John de Skeffington added greatly to the family property by his marriage with Margaret, daughter and heiress of William Oldbeif and Maud his wife. This lady brought into the family the Oldbeif coat, which appears upon the shields at Tunbridge: *Azure* a bend *Or*, cotised *Argent*, between six mullets pierced of the second."—*Archæologia Cantiana.* David Wildeboef and Amicia de Wildeboef occur in Huntingdonshire temp. Ed. I.—*Rotuli Hundredorum.*

Olifant: see *Olifard.*

Olifant (derived from ·*elephas*) signifies an elephant's tusk mounted as a horn, which was one of the ancient symbols of command. In the Chanson de Roland, when the paladins are beset in the narrow gorge of Roncesvalles, Olivier urges Roland to summon Charlemagne by winding his horn:

"Cumpainz Rollanz, sunez vostre olifan!"

At the third blast, sixty thousand horns respond to the call; but they are styled *corns* or *graisles;* Roland's alone is the *olifant.*

Osenell; for Oseville or Doseville, as it stands in Leland's list; named from Osseville in Normandy. Roger de Oseville is found in the Norman Exchequer Rolls of 1189–93;—probably the same Roger mentioned in the grant of the Earldom of Sadberge to Hugh Pudsey, Bishop of Durham, by Cœur de Lion, as holding half a knight's fee at the former date. Margaret de Osenvill of Lincolnshire, and Sewall de Oseuill and his uncle Alexander in Essex, are both found at about the same time in the *Rotuli. Curiæ Regis.* Joan de Osevilla, the widow of William de Rugdon, occurs as a benefactress in the chartulary of Lacock Abbey. Ralph de Osulvilla held in Bedfordshire 1130 (Rot. Pip.) and another Ralph is mentioned in 1200 in Northamptonshire.—*Rotuli Curiæ Regis.* At the close of the same century, Walter Doseville held Hothorp, in the latter county, of the fee of St. Edmund, and married Margaret, the eldest of the four sisters and co-heirs of William de Kirkby, who brought him Stoke Mandeville, in Leicestershire, Oakley Parva, &c., in Northamptonshire, and Munden in Hertfordshire. His son John had succeeded him in 1316, but presumably left no heir, as his son-in-law Edward Trussell was in possession in 1330. Yet the name remained. Henry de Oseville, in 1322, "was, in consideration of his continuance with the King, exonerated from contributing to the fine imposed upon the knights and esquires of the counties of Essex and Hertford."—*Palgrave's Parl. Writs.* He served as knight of the shire for Herts in the second parliament held by Edward III. Robert de Oseville, of Buckinghamshire and Oxfordshire, received a summons for military service in 1322, and another to attend the great Council at Westminster in 1324.—*Ibid.* In Oxfordshire the family had been seated during the previous century; for Sewall de Osseville, in the time of Henry III., held two knight's fees in Wendlebury (*Testa de Nevill*), and was a benefactor to the Knights Hospitallers of St. John of Jerusalem.—(*Mon. Anglicanum.*)

Oisell; from Oissel-sur-Seine,* about eight miles from Rouen. Robert de Ossel held the fourth part of a knight's fee in the bailiwick of Loudes; (Duchesne) and the family continued in the last century. "Le président d'Oissel" was one of the Norman nobles assembled in 1789 in the Cordeliers at Rouen for the election of the States General. In England Simon Doisell witnesses a charter of John de Limesey to Hertford (a cell of St. Albans). (Mon. Angl.) Robert Oisell held of the Bishop of Winchester in 1165 (Liber Niger): Matthew Oisel is mentioned in Wiltshire and Somersetshire in 1194, and John Oisel and Gerard Oisel in Northamptonshire in 1198.—*Rotuli Curiæ Regis.* Another Matthew Oisel attests Edward II.'s confirmation charter to Tichfield Abbey, Hampshire. (Mon. Angl.) John Oysel, of the same county, was Burgess for Farnham in the Carlisle Parliament of 1307: and Henry Oisel, in 1313, was returned for Dorchester. Nicholas Oisel, in 1316, was certified Lord of Cames-Oysell, Hants.—*Palgrave's Parl. Writs.* At the same date, Geoffrey Oisel was Lord of Newton-subtus-Onesborgh, and Roger Oisel of Burton-upon-Yore, both in Yorkshire. Richard Oisel was one of the Justices appointed to perambulate the forests in the counties of Nottingham, Cumberland, and York.—*Ibid.* This Richard Oysel, in 1305, was Bailiff of Holderness, Steward of the royal manor of

---

* An adjoining island is said to have been one of the famous strongholds of the Northmen in the ninth century; and the Dukes of Normandy had a palace there where they sometimes resided. "The land of Oissel is named in a grant from King Henry I. to Roland, to which were annexed the duties of Chamberlain, namely, to find rushes for the bed-chamber, and a bed of down."—*Gage's Suffolk.* At the time of the Conquest it was held by Corbuzzo, father of Robert and William, tenants *in capite* in Norfolk, Suffolk, and other counties (Domesday).

Burstwick, then the "Head of the Seignory," and Eschætor of Edward I. North of the Tweed. When Robert the Bruce's Queen fell into the hands of the English King after her husband's defeat in that year, Richard Oysel was desired to provide for her entertainment at Burstwick, and she was consigned to his safe custody by letters of the Privy Seal. The King ordained " qe ele gisse en la plus bele maison du manoir a sa volonté." She was to have a lady of honour and a waiting woman, " bien d'age et avisez :" two equally steady pages, an exemplary foot boy : and a " valet of good bearing and discreet, to keep her keys." Besides this modest household, " three greyhounds were to be kept for her diversion in warren and park." She was removed to Windsor on the accession of Edward II., two years afterwards.—*Poulson's Holderness.* Richard Oisell had been deprived of his office before 1321, when he is spoken of as the " former Bailiff of Holderness." In a Roll of Arms, temp. Ed. III., I find entered " Richard Oysell port d'argent ove une sautour engrelee et quatre choughes de Cornwaille de sable."

Gilbert, son of Robert Oysel of Plumpton, in the parish of Spofforth, was a benefactor of Fountains Abbey. According to *Kirkby's Inquest* Roger de Oisell held at Aysgarth in Wensleydale of Nicholas de Gerdeston and Mary de Nevill— the "fair and gentle Mary of Middleham," who was the widow of Robert de Nevill of Raby, and the eldest daughter and co-heir of Ralph Fitz Ranulph, Lord of Middleham—and at Thoraldby of her sister's husband, Robert de Tateshale.

Ivo Oisel, of Shropshire, occurs in the Pipe Rolls 1155–58 : and Henry de Hosoll held part of a fee of Hugh Wac, Lincoln, in 1165.—*Liber Niger.*

Olifard. Hugo and William Olifard occur in Hampshire and Northamptonshire in 1130 (Rotúl. Pip.) and 1165 (Liber Niger). William Olifard, of Huntingdonshire, in the time of Edward I. (Rot. Hundredorum.) No other mention of the name has come under my notice in England; but it was very early transplanted beyond the Tweed, and still flourishes in Perthshire under its Scottish pseudonym of Oliphant. The first of this family on record, David Olifard, "served in the army of King Stephen against the Empress Maud in 1141. A conspiracy was formed against her; she escaped from Winchester, attended by King David I. Surrounded by the enemy, David was rescued by Olifard, although in the adverse party, on account of the King having been his godfather. Olifard concealed him so dexterously as to elude a strict search, and conveyed him in safety to Scotland. David gave to the companion of his journey the lands of Crailing and Smallham in Roxburghshire; and he had the honour of being the first Justiciary of Scotland of whom any record appears. In this important character he acted during the year 1165, and continued to act for several years under William III."—*Douglas' Peerage of Scotland.* The first three generations of his descendants succeeded him as ·Justiciaries of Lothian, and one of them, a Sir Walter Olifard who lies buried in the choir of

Melrose Abbey, was among the guarantors of the treaty concluded in 1237 between Alexander II. and Henry III. His grandson Sir William was first called Olifant, and was in charge of the last Scottish castle that opened its gates to Edward I. The Constable of Stirling, Sir John de Soulis, then absent in France, had committed it to his keeping as a gallant and experienced soldier. But he had only a feeble garrison; and when he found himself beset by the great English· host, he sent a message to the King, telling him that he could not surrender the fortress without forfeiting his honour as a knight, pledged by oath to Sir John de Soulis; but that, if a truce was accorded him, he would go over to France, obtain the required permission from his master, and ·return to deliver it up. This was in true accordance with the laws of chivalry; and Edward, at any other time, might have entertained the proposal; but now, exasperated and "full grim" at the obstinate resistance he had encountered, he would not listen to it for a moment. "Let him surrender the castle," he replied, "or hold it at his peril." Olifant could hope neither for support or relief; the only man in Scotland who had refused to acknowledge Edward's sovereignty—William Wallace—being a hunted outcast that

> "In mores and mareis with robberie him fedis;"

and he stood single-handed against desperate odds. Yet he never hesitated or faltered in his duty. He strengthened his walls as best he might, brought to bear his engines of defence, and prepared to hold out to the last extremity. Edward battered the fortress with thirteen "great engynes of all the reame the best," and stripped the refectory of St. Andrews of its leaden roof to make his missiles. But for some time the lofty walls bore the brunt unscathed; the gallant little garrison sallied forth to fire the faggots heaped up to choke the castle fosse, and hurled stones and javelins from the ramparts with deadly effect upon the besiegers. The old King, riding round the lines, was struck with a javelin which lodged in the plates of his armour; and plucking it out with his own hand, shook it defiantly in the air, crying aloud that "he would hang the villain that had hit him." No youthful soldier exposed himself with greater "fire and temerity;" and once again he narrowly escaped with his life, when his horse, scared at the fall of a large stone, reared and fell back with him. Week after week, however, the siege went on with little or no result, till Edward, determined to bring it to a close, called together his best men, and wrote to desire the sheriffs of York, Lincoln, and London to furnish him with as many balistæ, quarrells and bows and arrows as they could hastily collect; further ordering the Constable of the Tower to give up those he had in keeping. He had two monster machines, the "Ram" and the "Wolf," constructed to overtop the battlements and discharge vast stones and balls of lead upon the inner works; he cut off all communication from without, and set the roofs alight by flights of arrows tipped with Greek fire. At last, after three months, the work was accomplished; a yawning breach had opened in the crumbling walls; the outer ditch was filled up with stones and faggots, and the scaling ladders placed for a general assault. The heroic garrison could offer no further resistance. All that was left of it consisted of a few score of famine-stricken men, mounting guard over heaps of ruin and rubbish, and reduced to the direst depths of distress. They offered to capitulate, and asked for terms; but Edward would accept nothing short of an unconditional surrender. Nor did he spare the men who had fought so well a single humiliation in the painful pageant of feudal submission that was to follow. Sir William Olifant, with twenty-five knights and gentlemen that had been his companions-at-arms, appeared before the King, as he sat in state surrounded by his nobles, in the piteous guise of penitents, bare-headed, bare-footed, stripped to their shirts, with halters round their necks, and falling on their knees at his foot-stool, with clasped hands implored his clemency. Then, and then only, did Edward vouchsafe to pronounce them exempted from further ignominy, and give out the order, "·Let them not be chained." But Olifant, as the leader, was sent to the Tower, and retained in captivity for four years.

This brave man's son married a daughter of Robert Bruce—Elizabeth, the youngest of them; and her brother David II., in 1364, erected the lands of Gask —to this day the property of the Oliphants—into a free barony. A few more descents brings us to Sir Laurence, of Aberdalgy, the first Lord Oliphant, created probably by James II. in 1458, but certainly prior to 1467, when he sat as a peer in the Scottish parliament. There were in all eleven barons of the name, though the direct line closed with the fifth Lord, who dissipated the greatest part of his patrimony, early in the 17th century. He had an only daughter, Anne, to whom he conceived the peerage must descend; but, wishing it to be held by the heir-male, Patrick Oliphant, he resigned his honours and estates in favour of the latter. This settlement was not, however, ratified by the Crown, and Anne Oliphant asserted her claim before the Court of Session. Charles I. was present in court when the cause was decided in 1633, and it was ruled that Lord Oliphant's deed barred his daughter's succession, but could not dispose of the peerage, to which, again, Anne Oliphant had no right. "Both the heir-male and heir-female were excluded by this decision; and the dignity declared to be at the King's disposal, who determined that the heir-male should have the title of Lord Oliphant, and that Sir James Douglas, husband of Anne Oliphant, should be called Lord Mordingtoun, with the precedency of Lord Oliphant."—*Ibid.* The title thus conferred on Patrick continued to be borne by his descendants till 1751, when William, eleventh Lord, died s. p., acknowledging as his heir Laurence Oliphant of Gask. But he, having been engaged in the Jacobite rising of 1745, was attainted, and did not assume the title. "No person has voted as Lord Oliphant at elections of representative peers since 1750. John Oliphant of Bachilton was styled Lord Oliphant: he died in 1781, leaving a posthumous daughter."—*Ibid.* Two Perthshire families, the Oliphants of Gask and Oliphants of Condie, still carry on the ancient name.

Orinal, for Orival or *De Aurea Valle;* from Orval, a fief in the Vicomté of Coutances. Regnault d'Orval, about the time of the Conquest, witnessed the foundation charter of L'Essay, and gave to the Abbey his church of Orval. "The Honour of Lithaire was held for two generations by a family who derived their local surname from this fief: thus Rainaldus de Orivallo, contemporary with Robert Courteheuse and King Henry I., established in 1115 a cell at Orval, for the residence of a certain number of monks from the abbey of L'Essay, *maxime pro ipsius anima atque uxoris sue Matildis.* He left issue three sons, William, Hugh, and Robert, and a daughter married to Roger *filius Episcopi;* of these the eldest son was tenant of the Honour in 1172. On the roll of 1180 Robert L'Angevin, the fermor of the Vicomté of the Côtentin, rendered accompt of the issue of the land of William de Aureavalle. from the feast of St. Michael to the Circumcision of our Lord, 29 Hen. II., in which same regnal year Adam de Port gave 1000 marks to the King for livery of his wife's inheritance in Normandy, as also that he might be restored to the King's favour and do his homage. This baron, who derived his local name from Port-en-Bessin of the fee of the Bishop of Bayeux, appears to have been thrice married; his first wife was the Countess Sibilla, widow of Milo, Earl of the county of Hereford, and daughter and heiress of Bernard de Novo-Mercato, a powerful baron of that county, whose fief Adam de Port reported to the Exchequer, 14 Hen. II., with the nomenclature of the knight's fees held of the old and new feoffment; at which date his father, John de Port, Lord of Basing in Hampshire, was still living. Not long after, A.D. 1172, an accusation of treason was brought against him, and not appearing to the summons to abide his trial, he was banished the realm, when his barony in the county of Hereford escheated to the crown, and ever after continued to be described in the records of this and the following reigns, as *feodum Adæ de Port fugati* or *fugitivi.* By the Countess Sibilla he had no issue. His second wife was Mabilia de Aureavalle, whose inheritance in Normandy he has been shown to have obtained in 1180, and by whom he had a son named William de Portu, who had possession of the Honour of Lithaire in the second year of the reign of King John, and who eventually inheriting the land of the family of *S'to Johanne* through descent from Muriel, sister of William and Robert St. John, who had intermarried with his maternal ancestor *de Aureavalle,* thereupon assumed that local surname. The third wife of Adam de Port was sister of William de Braose." —*T. Stapleton.* How it was that Mabel became the heiress of Orval is left unexplained. The fief was confiscated by Philip Augustus.

Robert de Aurea Valle—perhaps the above-mentioned Robert—was of Devon in 1130 (Rot. Pip.) and Peter de Orival, who occurs there about 1272 in the *Rotuli Hundredorum,* was no doubt his descendant. Walter Dorival, at the same date, is found in Kent.

Orioll. Matthew de L'Oriel, or L'Oriol, and Robert L'Orle, occur in the Norman Exchequer Rolls 1180–95. In England I find an old Lancashire family named Orrell, though Baines seems to assign to them a Saxon origin. "Richard de Horul held half a carucate in thanage and a render of 10ˢ· together with the service of finding one judger of old. As these possessions were drengages, it would seem that the Horuls were descended from the thanes of the Domesday Survey, and they were ancestors of the Orrells of Turton, who had also property in the adjoining township of Dalton in the time of Henry VIII. Orrell Hall is now a large farmhouse." One of the family built Turton Tower. "The expense, it is said, was so exorbitant as to cripple the Orrells, and they were never able to recover from its effects. After many struggles, they first mortgaged the township, and subsequently sold it to the celebrated Humphrey Chetham. Several of the Orrells still reside in Turton and the neighbourhood."—*Illustrated Itinerary of Lancashire.* The township of Orrell retains their name. I cannot find that it belongs to any place in Normandy; but there is a town called Loriol on the Rhone. Oriel, the ancient name of the Irish county of Lowth, which gives the title of Baron to Viscount Massareene, is merely the Anglicized form of the Celtic Orgial or Argial.

Camden speaks of "the famous family of the Orells" of Turton-Tower. A Robert Oriol witnesses the foundation charter of Northampton Priory (Mon. Angl.).

Pigot: or Picot. This name is seven times registered in Domesday; though probably in more cases than one as a duplicate. Among the tenants-in-chief, we find:

Picot, *Hants,* 50 b. *Yorksh.* 309 b.
Picot de Grentebrige, *Cambr.* 200.

As under-tenants:

Picot, *Surr.* 35, 35 b. ter. 44 b. 50 b. 151 b. *Heref.* 187. *Cambr.* 190, 190 b. bis. 191, 194 bis. 195, 197 ter. 200, 201 b. 202 passim. 202 b. *Northampt.* 227. *Stafford.* 247, 255 b. *Shropsh.* 258 passim 258 b. ter. *Yorksh.* 309 b. passim. 310 b. 321 b. 322 b. 328 b. *Essex,* 67, 68.

Picot, homo Alani comitis, *Yorksh.* 310 b. *Linc.* 347 ter. (see Vol. 2, p. 208).
Picot, Rogerus, *Chesh.* 264 b.
Picot Vicecom. de Exesse, *Cambr.* 201 b.
Picotus, *Sussex,* 25. *Cambr.* 190 passim 193 b. *Essex,* 3 b.

Of these, the greatest landowner was Picot de Say, who held twenty-nine lordships in Shropshire alone, and whose real name was Robert de Say, Ficot or Picot having originally been a *sobriquet.* (See *Say.*) "Picot (called *Miles* to distinguish him from his suzerain) who held of him in his barony of Clun" (Eyton), was probably his relative. Another Picot held of Roger Fitz Corbet in Worthin; and his descendant Ralph Fitz Picot (living 1180) acquired Aston, now Aston-Pigot, in that vicinity, through his wife. Others of the name were contemporary with Ralph (*Ibid.*).

The Sussex Picots were benefactors of Battle Abbey. About the end of the twelfth century, Gilebert, the son of Fulk, the son of Warine, whose father had come over with the Conqueror, gave "a piece of land in a field E. of the windmill" (a windmill is still to be found on the same site); and "Adam his brother, William and Petronilla, children of Laurence; Adam the son of Adam; and Stephen (whose deed is dated 1304) son of the second Adam," all occur in its chartulary. They appear to have been seated in its immediate neighbourhood.

"Picot de Grentebrige," the other Domesday Baron, was Sheriff of Cambridgeshire, and had very large possessions in different counties. "Picot bore rule in Cambridge, and Eustace in Huntingdon; and the amount of wrong wrought at their hands seems to have far surpassed the ordinary measure of havoc. Among the other sins of Picot, the Survey charges him with depriving the burgesses of Cambridge of their common land. Yet he too appears as an ecclesiastical benefactor. A church and monastery of regular canons arose at his bidding in honour of St. Giles within the bounds of the old Camboritum, and strangely as the building has been disfigured in later times, some small relics of the work of the rapacious Sheriff still survive. The foundation for a Prior and six regular Canons was made in 1092 at the prayer of his wife Hugolina de Gernon."— *Freeman.* The head of his Honour was at Brunne, where the moat of his castle, with a few other traces of the building, yet remain.

His son, Robert Fitz Picot, forfeited the barony by conspiring against Henry I., by whom it was granted to Pain Peverel, said to be the husband of Robert's sister. Robert, we are told, had a younger brother, "Saher de Say, who is stated to have taken refuge in Scotland, and obtained grants from Alexander I., named after him Sayton. Alexander, his son, was a baron of Sayton and Winton (Chalmers, Cal. i. 517; Douglas, Peerage). From him descended the Lords Seyton or Seton, Earls of Winton and Dunfermline, Viscounts Kingston, and (under the name of Gordon) Marquesses of Huntley and Dukes of Gordon." — *The Norman People.* In the genealogy given by Burke, this Saer, the ancestor of one of the most illustrious houses in Scotland, is called the son of Dougall, whose father first assumed the name of Seyton in the time of Malcolm Canmore. But when I find that Dougall, living in the reigns of Edgar and Alexander I. (1098-1124) is married to a daughter of De Quinci, Earl of Winchester, Constable of Scotland, I may surely be permitted to doubt! Saier de Quinci received his Earldom from King John about 1210, and it was his second son, who, by marrying the Princess Helen, became in her right Constable of Scotland.

Saer's descendant Christopher, the brother-in-law of Robert Bruce, is distinctly stated to have been of English lineage. v. *Ridpath's Border History.* Yet no family was ever more thoroughly Scottish in heart and deed, or suffered more cruelly from the English invasion. Christopher himself was hanged, drawn, and quartered as a traitor in 1306 at Dumfries; his brother John underwent the same fate at Newcastle; and Sir Alexander Seton, Governor of Berwick in 1333, saw his son Thomas—"a comely and noble-looking youth "—hanged before his own eyes at the gates of the town !

But it is with Picot, or Pigot, that we have here to do. Though many families' have borne and still bear the name (twenty-three coats of arms are assigned to it in Burke's Armoury), one only of them can trace a descent from a Domesday tenant. This was Roger Picot, tenant in fee of Broxton, co. Chester, in 1086 : whose line has been carried on uninterruptedly to the present time. Gilbert, his grandson, acquired several other Cheshire manors through his wife Margaret, daughter and heir of Robert de Rullos ; and for many generations their descendants were Lords of Butley, and great benefactors of Chester Abbey. John Pigott, Justice in Eyre, who was Justiciar of Chester in 1401, and Serjeant-at-Law for the counties of Chester and Flint 1400-9, married another heiress, Agnes de Wetenhall, and left two surviving sons : John, Lord of Butley ; and Richard, seated at Chetwynd in Shropshire, the immediate ancestor of the existing family. John's posterity continued at Butley till the time of Edward VI., when the last heir died, and the place was sold by his three daughters. "A junior branch, seated at Bonisall in Cheshire, and afterwards at Fairsnape, Lancashire, was still extant in 1746 "—*Ormerod's Cheshire.*

Richard had been transplanted into Shropshire by his marriage with Joan, daughter and co-heir of Sir Richard de Peshale of Chetwynd. From him descended a long line of wealthy squires, who constantly occur as Sheriffs of the county, and held Chetwynd for twelve generations. Richard Pigott, who sold his inheritance in 1774, it is said "for an old song," and afterwards lost a great part of the purchase money abroad, was the graceless youth that made the wager recorded in Burrow's Reports under the title of "The Earl of March *versus* Pigott." He and the son of Sir William Codrington, sitting one evening over their wine at Newmarket, "agreed to *run their father's lives* one against the other, Sir William being a little turned of fifty, and Mr. Pigott upwards of seventy." But it turned out that poor Mr. Pigott had died in his distant home in Shropshire at two o'clock in the morning of that very day ; his hopeful son being altogether unacquainted with the state of his health. On this, young Pigott refused to pay the five hundred guineas he had staked ; but found that he had to reckon with the notorious Duke of Queensberry (then Lord March), who, having taken Mr. Codrington's bet, brought an action against him for the amount, and recovered it. "Lord Mansfield decided that the impossibility of a contingency is no bar to its becoming the subject of a wager, provided the impossibility is unknown to both the parties at the time of laying it."—*Burke.* Mr. Pigott died at Toulouse in 1794, having survived both his foreign wife and his son, and was succeeded by his uncle William, Rector of Chetwynd and Edgmond. A branch of these Pigotts is seated at Doddingshall in Buckinghamshire.

Two other families, now either extinct or lost, dated from the time of Henry I.; and though both seated in the same county, appear, as far as I am able to judge, to have been entirely distinct. Sir Ralph Picott, living under Richard I. and King John, who has left his name to two manors in Essex still called Picotts, "descended from a Picott who was Sewer to Alberic de Vere in Henry I.'s time. Sir Ralph's son Sir William in the reign of Henry III. held of the King in *capite* by the service of keeping one spar-hawk in the King's court at the King's cost. Sir Ralph, his son, obtained in addition 'that the King was to find him maintenance for three horses, three boys or grooms, and three greyhounds; and the said Ralph was to change the Spar-hawk at his own charge.' He had two sons, William and Robert, which last was of Pateswic, and dying in 1334 was buried in Dunmow Priory of which he was a benefactor. John, son of William, was his heir, and sold the estate in 1349."—*Morant's Essex.*

The other Picots—sometimes called De Heydon—held Kingston and Ratcliffe-on-Soar, in Nottinghamshire, of Henry I. *in capite* by the Serjeantry of keeping his hawks. (I may observe, that this coincidence of tenure is the one point of contact between the families.) Peter Picot, in the reign of Henry II., held Heydon in Essex by Grand Serjeantry; "that is, by the Lords of it serving or waiting at the Coronation of the Kings of England with a bason and towel, to wash the King's hands before dinner, and to have for fee the Bason, Ewer, and Towel." He was followed by John; by Peter; by Thomas, who had freewarren in Kingston and Ratcliffe 37 Hen. III.; and lastly by Sir Peter Picot, who survived both his sons, and died in 1313, leaving as his heirs his sister Isabella Touke and his nephew Simon de Seneville.

Pery: in Duchesne's copy, Pecy. One letter has in either case been left out, for Leland's list enables us clearly to identify the name. We there find this and the preceding one given as "Pygot et Percy," and come upon one of our great historical houses, "that, like Cæsar's, has been artificially preserved to the present time."—*Freeman.* The name, "grotesquely construed in England," says Sir Francis Palgrave, "as signifying Pierce-eye," was taken from Percy, a fief near Villedieu in the Côtentin. An Elizabethan herald, named Glover, "derives this family from Mainfred de Percy, a Danish chief, who is said to have lived before the time of Rollo, and whose descendants, named alternately Geoffrey and William de Percy, continued in succession Lords of Percy, until the last William de Percy of Normandy went to England, temp. William I., and founded the English house of Percy. But Percy did not belong to any private family; it was part of the ducal demesne; and consequently it is difficult to believe that the name of De Percy could have existed. In point of fact, it is not mentioned in any record till shortly before the English Conquest, and it had probably been assumed not long previously, for in 1026 the estate of Percy was still part of the demesne of the Duke, who granted it, with other domains and castles, by a charter of that date, to his spouse in dowry."—*The Norman People.* William and Serlo de Percy came over in the time of the Conqueror, but neither of them are mentioned at the battle of Hastings: and from a passage in the cartulary of Whitby Abbey, quoted by Dugdale, it appears that William de Percy accompanied his sworn brother-in-arms, Hugh Lupus, to this country, the year afterwards. He was surnamed, from his whiskers (rarely worn by the close-shaven Normans) Alsgernons; and "being much beloved by the King," appears in Domesday as a great landowner, holding a barony of thirty knight's fees, including some lands that had belonged to a Saxon lady, whom, "as very heire to them, in discharging of his conscience," he afterwards married. Hugh Lupus, on becoming Earl of Chester, transferred to him his great domain of Whitby in the East Riding, where he re-founded the Abbey of St. Hilda's, and appointed his brother Serlo the first prior. He accompanied Robert Curthose on the first Crusade, and died in 1096 at Montjoye, as they came in sight of Jerusalem. The line ended in 1168 with his grandson William, who left only two daughters. Maud, the eldest, was the wife of William de Newburgh, Earl of Warwick, by whom she had no children; her sister Agnes thus became sole heiress, and was married by Queen Adeliza (the second wife of Henry I.) to her brother Josceline de Louvain, a younger son of Godfrey with the Beard, Duke of Nether Lorraine and Count of Brabant. Though the bridegroom came of the sacred blood of Charlemagne,* the bride stipulated that he should take either her name or arms; and he chose the first alternative, calling himself Percy, but retaining the ancient azure lion of Hainault; in order, it is said, to transmit his claim to his father's principality in default of succession to his elder brothers.† Queen Adeliza granted them, as her marriage gift, the Honour of Petworth, comprising twenty-one knight's fees, in Sussex; and their son Henry founded the illustrious house of Percy, Earls of Northumberland, that endured close upon five hundred years, and extended through eighteen renowned generations. Its name is written on every page of the history of England, for, during all these centuries, there was scarcely a war or insurrection in which a Percy was not to be found fighting in the foremost rank. They died on the battlefield, the scaffold, or in prison; and their titles perished again and again under attainder. The first baron by writ was Henry de Percy, summoned to parliament by Edward I. in 1299: and he, too, was the first of the family who struck root in Northumberland. Ten years later, he purchased from Anthony Beke, Bishop of Durham, the great Northern barony of the De Vescis, with the strong frontier fortress of Alnwick; and his son further obtained from Ed. III.

---

* "Not only throughout the Middle Ages, but long after that era, there was a species of mystical pre-eminence attached to the Carlovingian lineage, which those who could claim the honour nourished, though often in silence. God alone can bestow the prerogative attached to renowned ancestry, no human power can impart or destroy the prerogative: it is specially and directly created by the Almighty's hand." —*Sir Francis Palgrave.*

† From his elder brother are descended the Electors of Hesse Cassel, and the mother of the Princess of Wales.

the castle and barony of Warkworth. From that time forth, the Percies were repeatedly March-Wardens, and ever busied in "regulating" the feuds and raids of the wild Border country.

This second Lord Percy was a soldier of the first rank, who fought and won at Halidon Hill, and led one of the divisions of the victorious army at Nevill's Cross, when David II. was taken prisoner, and the famous Black Rood of Scotland offered at St. Cuthbert's shrine. The next Lord married Lady Mary Plantagenet, the great-granddaughter of Henry III., and had two sons, who both received Earldoms from Richard II. The younger, Sir Thomas, a companion in arms of the Black Prince, was created Earl of Worcester in 1397, and impartially served both Richard and his successor by sea and land; till joining in his brother's rebellion, he was taken prisoner at the battle of Shrewsbury, and beheaded the following day. He died s. p. The elder brother, Henry, created Earl of Northumberland on the occasion of the King's coronation in 1377, was the King-maker of his time:

> "Northumberland, the ladder wherewithall
> The vaunting Bolingbroke ascends my throne."

He succeeded in dethroning Richard II., and received as his requital a grant of the Isle of Man, to be held by the tenure of carrying, at each coronation, the sword with which the new King had landed at Holderness. But when he next attempted to change the dynasty in favour of the young Earl of March, he was utterly routed at Shrewsbury; and though then pardoned and restored by the King, rose again in rebellion the following year and was slain at a second overthrow at Bramham Moor in 1403. His head was set up on London Bridge, and his quarters over the gates of London, Lincóln, Berwick, and Newcastle.[*] His son Hotspur—the first knight of his age, still lives before our eyes in Shakespeare's brilliant portrait;

> "I saw young Harry, with his beaver on,
> His cuisses on his thighs, gallantly armed,
> Rise from the ground like feathered Mercury,
> And vaulted with such ease into his seat,
> As if an Angel dropt down from the clouds
> To turn and wind a fiery Pegasus,
> And witch the world with noble horsemanship."

Nor is he less familiar to us as "the Persé owt of Northumberlande" of Chevy Chase, the noble old ballad founded on the battle of Otterburn, where he was taken prisoner by the Scots in 1388. His captor, Sir John de Montgomerie, built a castle with the money paid for his ransom. His last field was at Shrewsbury, where he fell fighting by his father's side in 1403. Both his son

---

[*] By his second wife, Maud de Lucy, the widowed Countess of Angus, he acquired the whole of her great Cumberland property (though she brought him no children) as well as the estates of her first husband. See p. 203, and Vol. 3, p.

and grandson died, as he had done, in battle: and both of them in the service of the House of Lancaster; the second Earl at St. Albans, the third Earl leading the van of Queen Margaret's army, sword in hand, at Towton. Three more brothers of the latter—he was one of a goodly band of nine—laid down their lives in the same cause; one, Sir Richard, being slain with him at Towton; another (created Lord Egremont in 1449) in the King's tent at Northampton; and the last, Sir Ralph, at Hedgeley Moor, near Chillingham Castle, crying, as he fell, "I have saved the bird in my bosom!" (his fealty to King Henry.) This third Earl of Northumberland had acquired, by his marriage with Eleanor, grand daughter and heiress of the last Lord Poynings, the three ancient baronies of Poynings, Fitz Payne, and Brian; but all his honours were forfeited, his son thrown into the Tower, and his Earldom transferred in 1467 to Lord Montague by the triumphant Yorkist King. After two years, however, the young heir made his submission, took the oath of allegiance to Ed. IV., and was released and re-instated; Lord Montague receiving the Marquessate of Montague in exchange for the Percy Earldom. Again, in the next generation, Sir Thomas Percy was executed at Tyburn for taking part in the Pilgrimage of Grace in 1537: and thus, on the death of his childless elder brother, the sixth Earl, (Anne Boleyn's lover), a few months afterwards, his son, being attainted in blood, was unable to inherit. The estates were transferred to John Dudley, Earl of Warwick, who was created Duke of Northumberland by Ed. VI.: and once more it appeared that the house of Percy-Louvain had come to an end. But once more it was only for a time; for no family ever had a better right to their old war cry of "Esperance!" The crescent moon of their crest was the true type of their fortunes, that never waned but to shine again. Within less than twenty years the new Duke was beheaded for conspiring to place his daughter-in-law on the throne, and the son of the unhappy Sir Thomas was restored by Queen Mary, and created Earl of Northumberland anew in 1557.

He, like his father, died the traitor's death on the scaffold. In 1569, he and the Earl of Westmorland, who were both by position and family the hereditary leaders of the North, placed themselves at the head of the great Catholic conspiracy so long and bitterly remembered as the Rising of the North. It seems certain that he, at least, entered into it unwillingly, urged on by his wife, Lady Anne Somerset, for "she," writes Lord Hunsdon to Cecil, "is the stouter of the two, and doth harden him to persevere, and rideth up and down with the army, so that the grey mare is the better horse." When the enterprize ended in disaster and their followers dispersed, the two Earls, with Lady Northumberland, made their way across the Border into Liddesdale, where the poor Countess had to be left behind at the house of a Scottish moss-trooper, described as "not to be compared to an English dog-kennel." Another Border thief, Hector of Hardlawe—a name ever after infamous in Border story—betrayed the Earl to the Regent Murray, who delivered him up to the tender mercies of Elizabeth.

He was beheaded at York in 1572. On this occasion, a reversionary clause in the new patent preserved the honours of the house to his brother. But he, led by the inborn habit of rebellion that seemed inveterate in his race, in his turn conspired for Mary Queen of Scots, with whom he had fallen deeply in love, and in 1584 was thrown into the Tower, where, the next year, he was found one morning dead in his bed, with three pistol bullets in his body. In the next generation, the ninth Earl shared the same fate, except in the manner of his death, for he was accused of complicity in the Gunpowder Plot (in which one of his nephews had taken part) and fined and imprisoned by the Star Chamber. The fine imposed was £30,000: an enormous sum at that time, for which he vainly strove to compound by the offer of Syon, that had been granted to him by Queen Elizabeth in 1602. No less than fifteen years of his life were spent in the Tower, but not altogether unhappily, for with his fellow-prisoner Sir Walter Raleigh, he devoted himself to abstruse scientific studies, which earned for him, in those unlettered days, the name of the Wizard Earl. His son sided with the Parliament against Charles I., and with his grandson the curtain dropped upon the varied vicissitudes of their story, by the final extinction of the Percies in the male line.

Jocelyn, this last and eleventh Earl, died in 1670 at Turin, in the very flower of his age—a young man barely twenty-six; and with him descended to the grave the world-famous name he bore. He left one only child; a little daughter of four years old, Lady Elizabeth, known as "the great Percy heiress," who was three times a wife, and twice a widow, before she was seventeen. On this baby girl, in her own right Baroness Percy, Lucy, Poynings, Fitz Payne, Bryan and Latimer, were centred all the possessions, and—with the sole exception of the Earldom—all the honours of her house. It was a heavy burden to be laid on so youthful a head; and from the day that she was left an orphan, she was singled out for contention by the cupidity of the world. Match-makers were lying in wait for her from her earliest years. She was scarcely thirteen when Charles II. wrote a coaxing letter to the Countess of Northumberland, asking the hand of the Percy heiress, then "of full age," for his son George Fitz Roy (by Barbara Villiers, Duchess of Cleveland) whom, as a preparatory measure, he had created Earl of Northumberland five years before. This usurpation of her lost husband's title was scarcely likely to propitiate the Countess; and the proffered alliance was rejected. A few months afterwards, in 1679, Lady Elizabeth was married to the heir of one of the greatest fortunes in the kingdom, Lord Ogle, son of the Duke of Newcastle; a lad but a few years older than herself; who died within a twelvemonth. Her second husband, Thomas Thynne, to whom she seems to have been only "contracted," was murdered by another jealous aspirant, Count Königsmark: and she became Duchess of Somerset in 1682.

The winner of this great prize, Charles Seymour, the "Proud Duke" of Somerset, was a man who, from his extravagant eccentricities, might in the present day run the risk of being considered insane. His pride of birth and rank was nothing short of a mania. He had an almost overwhelming sense of his own dignity; and, aping the seclusion observed by Oriental monarchs, shunned to expose himself to the profanation of vulgar eyes. When he took the air in his State coach, running footmen preceded him to warn every one else off the road. His daughters never sat down in his presence; and when, suddenly aroused from an after-dinner nap, he found that one of them had been guilty of this gross breach of etiquette, the offence never passed out of his mind, and he remembered it against her even in his will. Again, when his second wife, Lady Charlotte Finch, once tapped him familiarly on the shoulder, he was amazed beyond measure, and severely rebuked her for her forwardness. "Madam," said he, "my first Duchess was a Percy, yet she never dared to allow herself such a liberty." Not content with the old manor house of the Percies at Petworth, he transformed it into a palatial mansion, built on a scale of grandeur proportioned to his aspirations; and when the Percy heiress came of age, induced her to release him from the engagement to take her name and arms, which he had entered into on their marriage. She brought him no less than thirteen children; (of whom several died in infancy); and appears in a great fresco, painted by La Guerre at Petworth House, as Juno, seated on a triumphal car, and surrounded by her numerous family. Yet one son only lived to be married—Algernon, Earl of Hertford; and one daughter only left children—Lady Catherine, the wife of the well-known statesman, Sir William Wyndham. The son married a Thynne, by whom he had one daughter—another Lady Elizabeth; and one son, George Viscount Beauchamp, a lad of great promise, who was carried off by the small-pox in 1744 at Bologna at the early age of nineteen. The daughter, who thus remained the only surviving child, was older than her brother, and at the time of his death had been already four years married to Sir Hugh Smithson of Stanwick, in North Yorkshire.* But though this second Lady Elizabeth now became heiress to her grandmother's Percy baronies, a settlement made by that same grandmother (who had died in 1722) excluded her from the succession of the

---

* Sir Hugh Smithson has been called an apothecary's son; but it was in reality the first Baronet's brother, Bernard, who was an apothecary in the City, as appears from the grant of arms which they jointly received in 1663. It seems unaccountable that they should have owned no paternal coat, for they belonged to a very respectable family in Yorkshire. The elder, a rich London merchant, who acquired Stanwick in the North Riding, had obtained his baronetcy for his loyalty during the Civil War. Yet Sir Hugh was very far from being considered a fitting match for the Duke of Somerset's grand-daughter; and a letter from the old Duke, strongly opposing Lady Elizabeth's marriage, is still preserved at Alnwick. The solitary *bon-mot* with which George III. was ever credited was made when the newly-created Duke applied in vain for the Garter, and exclaimed: "I am the first Northumberland that was ever refused the Garter!" "Rather say," rejoined the King, "the first Smithson that ever asked for it."

greater part of the Percy estate. Whether deterred by her own example from burdening another woman with so great an inheritance, or because she (not unnaturally) preferred her own daughter to her yet unborn grand-daughter, the Percy heiress decreed that two-thirds of her domain should pass to that daughter's son, Sir Charles Wyndham, in case her own sons died without heirs male. Accordingly, immediately after young Lord Beauchamp's death, we find the old Duke writing eagerly, with his own cramped and trembling hand, to the then Prime Minister, Lord Granville, to ask for the Earldom of Northumberland and Barony of Cockermouth for his grandson; assuring him that the Wyndhams would never be a burthen to the Crown, as they would "have more than £20,000 *per annum*, to support these titles, of the Northumberland estate."* The King agreed to grant the Earldom, but only as a reversion, whenever Sir Charles should come into the property.† "Lord Hertford represented against it; at last the King said he would give it to whoever they would make it appear was to have the Percy estate; but old Somerset refused to let anybody see his writings, and so the affair dropped; everybody believing there was no such settlement."—*Horace Walpole.* However, when the old Duke died in 1748, this famous settlement was brought to light; and his son and successor, Algernon, seventh Duke, naturally wishing the title of Northumberland to go to his own daughter, Lady Elizabeth Smithson, actually succeeded,

---

* Twenty thousand a year was at that time an enormous' fortune. About sixty years before, Lord Macaulay tells us there were only three subjects in England possessed of such an income : the Duke of Ormond, who had £22,000 a year; the Duke of Buckingham, who had £19,600; and the Duke of Albemarle, who left £15,000 a year, and £60,000 in money.

† Earl Granville writes, Nov. 23, 1744, that he is "commanded by the King to assure you in his name that he is ready and willing to comply with your request, in granting the Earldom of Northumberland and Barony of Cockermouth to Sir C. Wyndham, with the remainder which you propose, in case your Grace and the Earl of Hertford should have no issue. But, as it is His Majesty's opinion that the Earldom of Northumberland would be rather a burden to Sir C. Wyndham than an advantage, until such time as, by God's will, the estate should come to him, His Majesty has commanded me to acquaint you, that the only method in which he thinks this affair can at present be carried into execution is in the following manner, viz. : That your Grace should take out a patent for the Earldom of Northumberland and Barony of Cockermouth to yourself and heirs male of your body; and in failure of such issue (which at present Lord Hertford and his possible issue must be), then remainder to Sir C. Wyndham, &c.; remainder to his brother Percy Wyndham Obrien, &c. : remainder to their sister, &c. ; according to what your Grace desires in your letter, and conformably to what, as far as I can recollect, was your intention, when an affair of this nature was in agitation some years ago " (evidently when Lady Elizabeth married) "viz. : that the Wyndham family should have the title of Northumberland, when a considerable part of that great and ancient estate should devolve on them."—*Petworth MS.*

through his great influence at Court, in obtaining two separate Earldoms in 1749, with remainder, the one to his son-in-law, the other to his nephew. On his death, a few months afterwards, Sir Hugh Smithson accordingly succeeded to the Earldom of Northumberland, with Syon, Northumberland House, Alnwick, Warkworth, and the estates in Northumberland, while Sir Charles Wyndham succeeded as Earl of Egremont, with Petworth, the Honour of Egremont, Top-clyffe, Wressel, Leconfield,* and the great Yorkshire fief, part of which had come to the Percies by grant of William the Conqueror. The second had very considerably the lion's share, for the Northumberland property, though of great extent, was at that time scarcely cultivated, and of comparatively little value. But on the first devolved the honour of representing the family; for he took the name and arms of Percy, and being created Duke of Northumberland in 1766, was the direct ancestor of the present Duke. The old Percy baronies, however, passing in the female line, were, on the death of Hugh, third Duke, transferred to his nephew, John Murray, seventh Duke of Atholl, whose mother was Lady Emily Percy.

Two years before he died, the first Duke had obtained the title of Lord Lovaine, with remainder to his second son Lord Algernon, who inherited it in 1786, and was created Earl of Beverley in 1830. His son George, second Earl, succeeded to the Dukedom in 1865, on the death of his cousin Algernon, fourth Duke, who had been called up to the House of Lords as Lord Prudhoe in 1816. It is to this Duke Algernon, who was a man of singular taste and knowledge, that the admirable restoration and fine new buildings of Alnwick Castle are due.

Perepount: from Pierrepont, near St. Sauveur, in the Côtentin, which, up to the seventeenth century, continued in the possession of the family. Louis de Pierrepont, in 1690, received from Louis XIV. the barony and marquesate of Biars; and some of the name are still to be found in Lower Normandy. They were originally divided into three branches, of which the first bore Paly of six, *Or* and *Azure*, a chief *Gules;* the others, *Azure* a chief indented *Or;*—in the latter case nearly the same arms as those originally borne by the English house.

Three brothers of this name occur as under-tenants in Domesday: " Reinaldus de Perapund " in Norfolk: and Godfrey and Robert "de Petroponte" in Suffolk. The two latter held in addition about nine thousand acres in Sussex under Earl Warren, to whom, as there is some reason to believe, they were very near of kin (*W. S. Ellis, Sussex Archæologia,* vol. xi.). Rainald's son William held four thousand more acres in the county, and founded the powerful family of Poynings (see p. 55). Godfrey's estates eventually passed to Robert's successors. Henstead

---

* The manor of Leconfield, near Beverley, was granted to Henry de Percy by his brother-in-law, Peter de Bruce, to be held by the curious tenure, " That, every Christmas Day, he and his heirs were to repair to Bruce's castle at Skelton, and lead the lady of that castle by the arm from her chamber to the chapel to mass ; and thence to her chamber again ; and after dining with her, to depart."

in Suffolk, part of his great manor of Wrentham, was called from him Henstead-Perpound's.

Robert, the progenitor of the great house of Pierrepont, held one of the largest, if not the largest manor in Sussex, Hurst-Pierpoint, extending over several different parishes, which was transmitted to his descendants in unbroken male succession for nearly three centuries.   Hugh, Robert, and William, who witness a deed of their suzerain's in the Lewes chartulary previous to 1148, were probably his sons.   Hugh left only a daughter named Beatrix, married to William de Warren, Lord of Wirmegay.   Robert appears in the *Liber Niger*, as well as Simon de Pierrepont, with whom he (or another Robert) went to the siege of Acre under Cœur de Lion.   One of Simon's grandsons, Guy, was Lord of Glazeley in Shropshire, and adopted the name of his manor, where his posterity continued for five generations.   At the same date, John de Perpund held land by serjeantry in Nottinghamshire; and another Simon, ten knight's fees of the Earl Warren (Testa de Nevill).   This Simon died s. p.: and was succeeded by his brother Sir Robert, who sided with Henry III. against the barons, and was taken prisoner at the battle of Lewes.   It was his marriage that transplanted the family to Notts; for his wife Annora, the sister and sole heir of Lionel de Malavers or Mauvers, brought him Holme—since Holme Pierrepont, and a great estate in that county.   On his seal first appears the present coat of Pierrepont: *Argent* semée of cinquefoils *Gules*, a lion rampant *Sable*, " probably adopted by his father, who may have married a Clifton, a Nottinghamshire family, whose arms resemble these in all but tinctures."—*W. S. Ellis.*   Yet it is certain that Sir Robert's eldest son Simon, and Simon's heiress Sibilla, who carried away Hurst-Pierpont and the Sussex estates to the Uffords, used the original coat of their house, as borne by Robert de Pierrepont at the siege of Acre (see Dansey's *Crusaders*): *Azure* a chief chequy *Or* and *Gules;* which (with the chequers of Warren added in honour of their suzerain) was that retained by two of the French families of this name (see p. 381).

Sir Robert's second son and namesake, who, on Simon's death, became the head of the family, bore his father's coat, and, succeeding to his mother's inheritance, settled at Holme-Pierrepoint.   He fought in Scotland with Edward I.: and several of his descendants, in their turn, rendered good service in the field.   One was among the foremost at Halidon Hill: another, a stout Yorkist, was knighted by Edward IV. after the battle of Barton: and a third was made a Knight Banneret in 1513 for his valour at the sieges of Tournay and Therouenne.

The last Simon de Pierrepont of Hurst had received a summons to parliament in 1293, but, as I have already said, left no son.   A second peerage was granted by Charles I. to Robert Pierrepont, who was created Baron Pierrepont of Holme-Pierrepont and Viscount Newark in 1627, and Earl of Kingston in the ensuing year.   The family property had by this time been largely increased, notably by purchases of Church lands; and the new Earl is described as "a person of excellent parts and ample Fortune." He was in addition an ardent loyalist; yet Clarendon has "a pleasant story, which administered some mirth" at Court, to tell of his parsimony. The King was in great need of subsidies: and "there were two great men who lived near Nottingham" (where he then was) "both men of great fortunes and of great parsimony, known to have much money lying by them, Pierrepont Earl of Kingston, and Leake Lord Dencourt. To the former the Lord Capel was sent: to the latter, John Ashburnham of the Bedchamber, each of them with a letter, all written with the King's hand, to borrow of each five or ten thousand pounds. Capel was very civilly received by the Earl, and entertained as well as the ill accommodations in his house, and his manner of living, would admit. He expressed, with wonderful civil expressions of duty, ' the great trouble he sustained, in not being able to comply with His Majesty's commands;' he said, ' all men knew that he neither had, nor could have money, because he had every year, of ten or a dozen which were past, purchased a thousand pounds land every year; and therefore he could not be imagined to have any money lying by him, which he never loved to have. But he said he had a neighbour' (Lord D'Eyn-court) ' who lived within a few miles of him, who was good for nothing, and lived like a hog, not allowing himself necessaries, and who could not have so little as twenty thousand pounds in that scurvy house in which he lived :' and concluded with great duty to the King, and detestation of the Parliament, and as if he meant to consider further of the thing, and to endeavour to get some money for him, which though he did not remember to send, his affections were good, and he was afterwards killed in the King's service."

This happened the very next year—in 1643. Mrs. Hutchinson (in her *Memoirs of Colonel Hutchinson*) gives the following account of his death, which however singular, is "assuredly true," being attested by other authorities : " My lord, professing himself to him " (Captain Lomax, one of the Parliamentary committee) " as rather desirous of peace, and fully resolved not to act on either side, made a serious imprecation on himself in these words: ' When,' said he, ' I take arms with the king against the parliament, or with the parliament against the king, let a cannon bullet divide me between them :' which God was pleased to bring to pass a few months after : for he, going to Gainsborough, and there taking up arms for the king, was surprised by my Lord Willoughby, and after a handsome defence of himself, yielded, and was put prisoner into a pinnace, and sent down the river to Hull; when my Lord Newcastle's army marching along the shore, shot at the pinnace, and being in danger, the Earl of Kingston went up on deck to show himself and to prevail with them to forbear shooting ; but as soon as he appeared, a cannon-bullet flew from the King's army, and divided him in the middle, being then in the parliament's pinnace, who perished according to his own unhappy imprecation." The Royalist version of this melancholy affair is that the attack upon the pinnace was a bold attempt at a rescue by Sir Charles Cavendish. He "demanded the Earl," and, "receiving a refusal, discharged a drake at the boat, which unfortunately killed the Earl and his servant, who were 'placed as a mark to his friend's shot.'"

His son and heir, a zealous Royalist, was created Marquess of Dorchester in 1644, but as he had no male heir, this new title expired with him in 1680. Three grand-nephews successively inherited the Earldom; one of them holding it for only two years; and the last, Evelyn, fifth Earl, received a renewal of the extinct Marquessate in 1706; and further, in 1715, the Dukedom of Kingston. He had one son who died before him, and three daughters, of whom Lady Mary, the eldest, was perhaps the cleverest, and without question the most eccentric, woman of her day. She married Edward Wortley Montagu; and in 1716 accompanied him on his embassy to Constantinople, whence she has the credit of having imported into England the native practice of inoculation, as a protection against the small-pox. She had first experimented on her own little boy, then three years old. On her return home, she had "the pre-eminence of wit and beauty at the Court of George I.:" and was at one time the fast friend of Pope; but their intimacy resulted in a bitter and life-long quarrel. At length, on the plea of ill-health, she left her husband to live abroad, and spent twenty-two years in Italy, only coming back to England when she became a widow in 1761—the year before her own death. She was then seventy-two, yet "she has," writes Mrs. Montagu, "more than the vivacity of fifteen, and a memory that is perhaps unique. When Nature is at the trouble of making a very singular person, Time does right in respecting it. Medals are preserved, when common coin is worn out." Horace Walpole's account of her is very uncomplimentary. "Lady Mary Wortley is arrived: I have seen her: I think her avarice, her dirt, and her vivacity, are all increased. Her dress, like her languages, is a galimatias of several countries: the groundwork rags, and the embroidery nastiness. She needs no cap, no handkerchief, no gown, no petticoat, no shoes. An old black-laced hood represents the first: the fur of a horseman's coat, which replaces the third, serves for the second: a dimity petticoat is deputy, and officiates for the fourth: and slippers act the part of the last. When I was at Florence and she was expected there, we were drawing *Sortes Virgilianas* for her: we literally drew

'Insanam vatem aspicies.'

It would be a stronger prophecy now, even than it was then." Her celebrated Letters were not published till after her death.

Her brother, William Lord Newark, though he only lived to be twenty-one, left a son of his own name who succeeded his grandfather as Duke of Kingston; and a daughter, Lady Frances, married to Philip Meadows.

This second and last Duke married, late in life, when he was enfeebled both in body and mind, one of the former Maids of Honour of the Princess of Wales,

Elizabeth Chudleigh. She was the daughter of a captain in the army, who belonged to a good Devonshire family, and had served under Marlborough, but left his family in straitened circumstances, and Mr. Pulteney (afterwards Earl of Bath), being a friend of her mother's, procured for her a place at Court. She proved a brilliant success ; for she was " of enchanting beauty and quick wit, with great readiness of repartee :" aiming (as she herself said) on all subjects to be "short, clear, and surprising." She hoped to have married the Duke of Hamilton, but he broke off the engagement ; and, piqued and disappointed, she made a clandestine match with Captain Hervey, "a young seaman just out of his teens." The marriage was performed at night, by the light of a solitary tallow candle stuck into an empty bottle ; and remained a profound secret, unacknowledged either by bride or bridegroom. They were too poor to afford to lose her salary ; and though she had two children (who died young) she continued to be Miss Chudleigh, the Maid of Honour. She presently took a hearty dislike to her young husband, and was never at ease till he had gone to sea, with "a fair wind down Channel" to speed him on his way ; and, to make matters worse, her former admirer, the Duke, renewed his suit, which she was obliged to reject. She then went with a party of friends to the church where her marriage had taken place, and while the others engaged the clergyman's attention, furtively tore out the leaf of the register on which it was entered. Not long after, however, she managed to have the entry replaced, for Captain Hervey had meanwhile succeeded to the Earldom of Bristol, and as he was in wretched health she looked forward to becoming a Countess Dowager, with an ample jointure. In this she was disappointed ; the Earl recovered ; and with his collusion (as was then believed) she was publicly married in 1769—twenty-five years after her first stolen wedding—to the Duke of Kingston. The Consistory Court of London had shortly before declared her free from any previous matrimonial contract ; and the King and Queen, with all the great officers of State, "honoured her by wearing her favours."

The weak old man whom she had inveigled into matrimony died four years afterwards, leaving her everything he possessed :—the estates for her life only, but the personalty absolutely—on condition she did not marry again. It was a lamentable close to the history of a proud and honoured race, for he was the last of his lineage, and with him expired a seven-hundred-year-old name.

The Duchess' life had always been disreputable ; but it now became so openly and outrageously licentious, that she had to escape from the clamour of the scandal it excited. She sailed for Italy in a splendid yacht, and met with a triumphal reception at Rome, where the Pope, knowing nothing of her story, treated her as a princess. But she was quickly summoned home by the startling news that a sentence in the Ecclesiastical Court had established the validity of her first marriage, and that the Duke's heirs were about to prosecute her for bigamy. The banker at Rome (who was in their interest), at first refused to advance her money for her journey; but she stationed herself at his door, pistol in hand, and compelled him, *vi et armis*, to give her what she required. On her arrival at Kingston House, she found friends ready to espouse her cause;—among others, Lord Mansfield and the Duke of Newcastle; and the next night went to a masked ball in the· character of Iphigenia. Her trial took place before the House of Lords, in Westminster Hall; and was attended by vast crowds, including Queen Charlotte and the Princess of Wales. She appeared in widow's weeds, "a bale of bombazine," attended with two waiting-women, "mourning maids of honour to support her when she swoons at her dear Duke's name," Horace Walpole calls them; a physician, an apothecary, a secretary, and a formidable array of counsel. She was then a large, shapeless woman of about fifty-six, with no traces of her former beauty; but she went through her part well, and never lost her presence of mind, even when the terrible record of her past life was unfolded by the Attorney General. She was found guilty, but claimed her privilege as a peeress, and was discharged without any punishment. "The wisdom of the land," writes Horace Walpole, "has been exerted for five days in turning a Duchess into a Countess, and yet does not think it a punishable crime for a Countess to convert herself into a Duchess. After a paltry defence, and a speech of fifty pages (which she had herself written, and pronounced very well) the sages, in spite of the Attorney General (who brandished a hot iron) dismissed her with the single injunction of paying the fees, all voting her guilty, but the Duke of Newcastle—her neighbour in the country—softening his vote by adding ' erroneously, not intentionally.' So ends the solemn farce. The Earl of Bristol, they say, does not intend to leave her that name, nor the house of Meadows a shilling." Yet she retained her fortune, and escaping the writ *ne exeat regno*, travelled all over the Continent, everywhere splendidly entertained as Duchess of Kingston, till she finally took up her abode in Paris, where she died in 1788.

It was not till then that the Duke's nephew, Charles Meadows (the second son of his sister Lady Frances), entered into possession of the Kingston estates, "by devise from the Duchess," and took the name and arms of Pierrepont. All the honours had become extinct at the Duke's death; but two of them were revived in his favour in 1796, when he became Viscount Newark and Baron Pierrepont; and, ten years later, he was created Earl Manvers. He is now represented by his grandson.

A branch of this family once existed in Wales. "Gileston or Gilston, to which there was a manor or lordship attached, was so called from Sir Giles Pierpont, one of Bernard Newmarch's knights. Joyce, daughter and heir of John Pierpont *alias* Parkville, married Walter or Watkin Gunter, eighth in descent from Sir Peter, a contemporary of Sir Giles."—*Jones' Brecon.*

Pershale. This name is interpolated, for it was taken from the manor of Pershall, in the parish of Eccleshall, Staffordshire. The family has been generally derived from Robert Fitz Gilbert de Corbeuil, who held Pershall from

Robert de Stafford by the service of a knight's fee; but another account (which I have copied from Erdeswick's county history) is entirely different. "Sir John Swinnerton gave the manor of Pershall to Sir Richard his son (a younger son no doubt) who thence took the name of Pershall about 55 Henry III. The Pershalls bore the *Argent* a cross formé fleury *Sable* of the Swinnertons, adding a canton *Gules* charged with the wolf's head of Hugh Lupus."

Power; "Poher, or Poncaer, descended from the Lords of Poncaer in Brittany. A branch settled in 1066 in Devon, with Alured de Mayenne; and in 1165 Ranulph Poer held three fees of his barony (Liber Niger). Bartholomew Poher, at the same time, was Lord of Blackborough, Devon, and father to Robert Poher, who settled in Ireland."—*The Norman People.* According to the Peerages it was, however, Roger, not Robert de la Poer, who went with Earl Strongbow to the conquest of Ireland, and received vast grants of territory. "It may be said without offence," writes Giraldus Cambrensis, "that there was not a man who did more valiant acts than Roger le Poer, who, although he were young and beardless, yet showed himself a lusty, valiant, and courageous gentleman, who grew into such good credit, that he had the government of the country about Leighlin, as also in Ossory, where he was traiterously killed; on whose slaughter a conspiracy was formed among the Irish to destroy the English, and many castles were destroyed." The Poer estates were of magnificent dimensions, extending from near Youghal to Cork Harbour, where the celebrated headland guarding its entrance still bears the name of Poor Head. The S. transept of Cloyne Cathedral is also called after them Poor Aisle. Among the most ancient writs to be found in the Irish Rolls Office are those summoning Nicholas le Poer, Baron of Waterford, to parliament in 1378, 1381, and 1383. His great grandson Richard was re-created in 1535 Lord Le Poer, Baron of Curraghmore; and was the father of John, Lord Le Poer, described by Sir Henry Sidney in his account of Munster to the Lords of the Council in 1575, as living "in shew far more honourably and plentifully than any other of his calling that lives in this province. The day I departed from Waterford, I lodged that night at Corragmore, the house that the Lord Power is baron of, where I was so used, and with such plenty and good order entertained (as adding to it the quiet of all the country adjoining, by the people called Power Country, for that surname has been since the beginning of Englishmen's planting inhabitants there) it may be well compared with the best ordered country in the English Pale." It was the boast of the family that "though dwelling in a country continually disturbed by convulsions and civil wars, they never once suffered forfeiture, or engaged in rebellion against the Crown:" and for this reason they received rough treatment at the hands of Cromwell. Two of their castles, Kilmeadon-on-Suir, and Don Isle (an almost impregnable fortress built on a steep crag on the sea coast) were captured and demolished. The lord of Kilmeadon was strung up, without either trial or shrift, on one of his own trees; and the heiress of Don Isle, after a splendid defence, was betrayed by one of her own gunners, and perished miserably in the flames that consumed her castle. Curraghmore, their most ancient possession, was saved by the quick-witted daughter of the Baron, who, seeing her father resolved to defend the place to the last extremity, contrived to lock him up in his own dungeon; and, throwing open the castle gates, went out to meet Cromwell with its keys in her hand. When questioned about her father, she explained that he was "unwillingly absent;" and that she had taken upon herself to surrender unreservedly to the Parliament, and therefore claimed, as her due, confirmation of the property and his protection at all times. "Cromwell, thus baffled, was constrained to sign the proper letters." It must have been John Lord Le Poer who was thus left chafing in confinement while his daughter made terms with the invader. His son Richard was created in 1673 Viscount Decies and Earl of Tyrone; but both titles expired with the third Earl in 1704. His only daughter Catherine, in her own right Baroness Le Poer, married Sir Marcus Beresford, who received the Earldom of Tyrone in 1746, and was the father of the first Marquess of Waterford.

The mother of Sir Marcus, Nichola Hamilton (the youngest of the three co-heiresses of Lord Glenawley) was the heroine of a celebrated ghost story, of which the first perfectly authentic account was published in 1880 by the Reverend B. W. Savile, one of her descendants. On the morning of the 15th of October, 1693 (a date faithfully treasured up in the family), she came down to breakfast deadly pale and in evident distress of mind, with a black ribbon bound round her wrist, which from that day forwards she never removed. Her husband anxiously inquired what was the matter; but she entreated him, with the greatest earnestness, to ask no questions. During the day a messenger brought them word that their neighbour, John, second Earl of Tyrone, had died suddenly in the night. He was Lady Beresford's kinsman; and in early life, having both been left orphans under the care of the same guardian, they had seen a great deal of each other. She was deeply affected; and as her husband was endeavouring to console her, she suddenly turned to him, in the midst of her grief, and told him she was expecting another child, and that it would be a son—her first son, for as yet she had only daughters. The prophecy came true; and in due time Sir Tristram was made happy by the birth of an heir. He died seven years afterwards, in 1701; and Lady Beresford re-married General Gorges, by whom she had four other children. In 1713, a large party assembled at her house to celebrate her birthday, for which she had made great preparation, and evinced a degree of solicitude that seemed altogether unaccountable. She appeared among her guests in the highest spirits; declaring that she felt uncommonly happy in keeping her forty-eighth birthday. An old clergyman, who was one of the company, here unfortunately interposed. "No, my Lady," he said, "you are mistaken; your mother, Lady Glenawley, and I, used to have many disputes concerning your age; and to-day I am able to prove myself in the right, for last week I happened to go to the parish where you were born, and took the opportunity of searching the register. You are only forty-seven to-day." Lady Beresford turned ghastly pale, and cried, "Then you have signed my death warrant!" She at once withdrew to her own room, and, sending for her young son Sir Marcus, and one other intimate friend, for the first time in her life told the story of Lord Tyrone's apparition to her on the night of his death, twenty years before, with all its now well-known details. She awoke to find him sitting by her bedside; and was so thoroughly convinced she was dreaming, that nothing short of the touch of his hand would serve to assure her of his actual presence. As his fingers closed round her wrist, every nerve and sinew shrank, and, though ice-cold, they left an indelible mark, as if from the gripe of red-hot pincers. He bade her hide it from every living soul, as long as she herself should live. Then, rising from his seat, he walked across to a bureau that stood on the other side of the room, and laid his hand upon it. " Look at this," he said, ".when the morning comes. You will find another proof;" and there, again, she saw the impress of a man's hand, deeply burnt into the wood. He told her that she would bear a son, and die on her forty-seventh birthday. " I thought," added she, " that I had outlived the fatal date. But I bless God that I am no longer afraid of death. I have learnt the truth of revealed religion, and can depart in peace." Then she desired her friend, as soon as she was dead, to take the ribbon from her arm, and to show it to her son. She died within the hour; and her wrist was found exactly as she had described it, with every nerve and sinew shrunk and withered away, and branded by the clasp of four fiery fingers. The bureau, retaining the scorched print-marks of a man's hand, is still in existence in Lord Clanwilliam's house of Gill Hall in the county Down; and Lady Beresford's portrait, painted with the mysterious black ribbon round her wrist, is to be seen at Curraghmore.

The name of Poer or Power is widely spread in Ireland. "The Poers of Belleville Park, near Cappoquin; the Powers of Affane and Mount Rivers, in the same vicinity; the Powers of Gurteen, midway between Clonmel and Carrick, are the chief representatives of this honourable name in the county of Waterford."—*Sir Bernard Burke.* Several branches remained seated in England. In Worcestershire the Poers held of the honour of Gloucester, and affixed their name to Pyriton Power. Robert de Poher was seven times Sheriff of Leicestershire under King John, and held five and a half knight's fees in the county. Richard le Poer occurs in the Hundred Rolls of 7 Edward I. as a landowner in Oxfordshire, where his descendants "continued for many ages;" Thomas Poure, a minor (the son of Sir Thomas Poure), died in 1407; his heiress was his sister Agnes Wyneslowe.—*Bullington and Ploughley's Oxon.*

Gentischieve le Poer held considerable property in Oxfordshire during the reign of John; and his descendant Sir Walter founded a house of charity dedicated to St. John at Oxford; after which, taking a journey to the Holy Land, he was absent for many years. The college, believing him to be dead, ventured upon altering some of his statutes, which provided for the reception and entertainment of pilgrims; and when he at length returned, so changed with age and travel that none might know him, and knocked at the gate of his hospital, he found it closed against him. He asked for alms, and was refused and turned away; but a poor scholar, compassionating his wan and weary looks, followed him out and put a piece of money into his hand. Then, drawing a ring off his finger, he asked the young man—a rather reluctant emissary—to take it to the Warden, who instantly recognised it. "God's mercy!" he cried; "it is the ring of our founder!" Having thus announced his presence, Sir Walter lost no time in discharging the vials of his wrath upon the disobedient fraternity, whom he sentenced to instant expulsion, and only pardoned when they had made the most abject submission, and most solemn promises of good conduct for the future. "The restoration of the Fellows of St. John's is said to have given rise to the choir music in the open air."—*Bullington and Ploughley's Oxfordshire.*

Painell, or Paganel, a great baronial family in Normandy. "The various accounts of it, either by Dugdale, or the county historians of places where they held lands, are so contradictory to each other, that to endeavour to reconcile them to any degree of correctness would require more consumption of time and expense in the investigation of public records, than would compensate any author for the undertaking."—*Banks.* I, for one, should be far from coveting such a task, even if I possessed the ability that it would require: and must therefore content myself with groping through the maze by the help of others:—quoting what appears to me the best authorities on this perplexing subject.

"The surname of this family, Painel or Paynell, in the Latin of the time "Paganellus," is a diminution of Pain or Paganus, and, as was the custom of the time, was no doubt first applied for distinction to a Pain Fitz Pain during his father's life-time, and happened, as in this case, to be perpetuated as a surname by his descendants."—*A. S. Ellis.*

"Paienal des Moustiers-Hubert" is mentioned in the Roman de Rou as fighting side by side with Avenal des Biarz and Robert Bertram at the battle of Hastings: "Many men," it is added, "fell before them." His fief was in Calvados, near Lisieux, where the site of the castle of Moustiers-Hubert may still be traced. Ordericus tells us that William Paganel was one of the great men who died about the same time as the Conqueror. It is, however, Ralph Paganel, presumed to be his younger brother, who appears in Domesday as one of the tenants in chief of the King: "and from this it seems likely that William, desiring to remain in Normandy, got as his reward those lands in the Côtentin which his descendants enjoyed: the Conqueror, moreover, it is known, gave his wife as dowry the fief of Briqueville-sur-Mer (Cart. Mont. S. Michel).

"What Ralph obtained was the entire estate of Merlesweyn, who had been Sheriff of Lincolnshire the year King Edward died, of which the bulk was in

Lincolnshire, but some portions in the South, and ten manors were in Yorkshire. Drax he seems to have fixed upon as his residence in Yorkshire, as there was a castle here in King Stephen's time which he may have built."—*Ibid.* In 1088, "that critical year for Rufus, when the whole kingdom was in confusion," we find Ralph Paganel Sheriff of Yorkshire, a staunch adherent of the King's, and on very bad terms with his neighbour the Bishop of Durham. The Bishop complained that his lands were invaded, his messengers arrested, and their horses killed under them, free passage through the county denied him, and all loyal subjects incited to injure him; till at length "Earl Alan, Earl Odo, and Roger Le Poictevin made oath to conduct the Bishop to the King and back if justice were not done him. They arrived at the court, then at Old Sarum, and the Bishop was heard before the King in council, and entreated to be restored to his see. Archbishop Lanfranc told him he had never seen writ of the King's to dispossess him of it: but he replied, ' I have seen Roger (Ralph) Paganel, who is here present, and he, by the King's writ, dispossessed me of the whole of my Bishopric within the county of York.' During the angry dispute that ensued, Paganel said it were fitting the King held his Earls to their pledge made to the Bishop, but Rufus bade him ' Be silent,' and the prelate was banished."—*Ibid.*

Paganel was a benefactor of the Church, and one of his last acts, "inflamed (as he says in his charter) by the fire of divine love, desiring to treasure up in heaven what I can after this life receive hundredfold:" was to bestow the desecrated Priory of the Holy Trinity, York, on the monks of Marmoutier, with a princely gift in lands, tithes, and advowsons. Some part of it had been the property of his wife Matilda (believed to have been the daughter and coheiress of Richard de Surdeval) and she and his four sons, William, Jordan, Elias, and Alexander, gave their assent to the grant. The eldest, William, must have been the son of a former marriage, as it was Jordan who succeeded to Matilda's inheritance; and when he had died s. p., it passed to the youngest brother, Alexander (Elias having become a Benedictine monk.) "These brothers had married two sisters; the former Gertrude (widow of Robert Mainill), the latter Agnes, daughters of Robert Fossard: and from Jordan, younger son of Alexander, descended the Paynells of Boothby Pagnell, Notts, who continued there until the reign of Elizabeth, when Francis Paynell sold the estate to Lord Burghley."—*Ibid.*

William Paynell of Drax, the eldest of these four brothers, married Avicia, one of the co-heiresses of William de Meschines, and left an only daughter Alice, who successively brought the great Paynell fief to Richard de Courci and Robert de Gaunt. Her first marriage was childless; but by her second husband she, again, had an only daughter, either Avice or Adeline, who married a son of the Gloucestershire magnate, Robert Fitz Harding, and was the mother of Maurice de Gaunt. He took his grandfather's name ; and died s. p. in 1239.

The elder line of Alexander Paynell's descendants ended in a similar way with a grand-daughter named Trethesenta, the wife, first of Geoffrey de Luttrel, and then of Henry de Newmarch.

Contemporary with these four brothers was Fulk Paynell, whom Dugdale adds to their number as a fifth son of Ralph Paynell, but "was apparently a younger son of William Paynell of Moutiers-Hubert, Ralph's elder brother."— *Ibid.* He married one of the greatest heiresses in the kingdom, Beatrix, sole daughter of William Fitz Ansculph de Pinkeny, who held a vast barony of ninety-one manors in 1086, and had his seignorial castle at Dudley in Staffordshire. All—or nearly all—this broad domain passed to their son Ralph Paynell, a zealous adherent of the Empress Maud, by whom he was appointed Constable of Nottingham. Dugdale accuses him of instigating the Earl of Gloucester to enter the defenceless town of Nottingham, which was "miserably plundered and then burnt by the Soldiers." He was succeeded by his eldest son Gervase, who in 1138 held Dudley Castle for the Empress, and certified in 1165 to upwards of fifty-six knights' fees. He was "one of the principal barons of the court of Hen. II.;" but having joined the King's rebellious sons in 1173, his castle was demolished by Royal command. He had no son. By his wife Isabel de Beaumont, daughter of Robert Earl of Leicester, and widow of Simon de St. Liz, Earl of Northampton, he left only one surviving child, Hawise, who carried Dudley Castle and his great possessions to her first husband, John de Someri, and re-married Roger de Berkeley. Gervase was the founder of Dudley Priory. A very early heraldic seat of his (date 1187) shows the two lions passant adopted from him by his descendants the De Someris.

William Paynell, whom Dugdale styles his brother, was the husband of another considerable heiress. "By marrying Juliana de Bahantune," Eyton tells us that he "acquired Bampton and other estates in Devon and Somerset, parcel of the Domesday Barony of Walter de Douai, sometimes called 'Walter de Bahantune.' Thus, in the reign of Stephen, there were two Baronies of Paynell, one seated at Drax, the other at Bampton." He adds that "when the elder male line of Paynell of Drax expired in the reign of Henry II.," the whole of the estates did not pass to the heiress, Alice, but "Drax itself, and many associated estates, went to other collaterals whose claim was in a male line, viz.: as descended from William Paynell of Bridgewater and Bampton, the husband of Juliana de Bahantune.

"The heirs of Paynell (of Drax, Bridgewater, &c.) adhered to Philip of France in the reign of John, and so lost their English estates, though one of the family was reclaiming a part of them as late as A.D. 1261."—*Domesday Studies, Somerset.* Dugdale tells us nothing of this. He says that William's son Fulk was forced to fly the country for "some great offence" in the reign of Henry II., and only recovered his barony on payment of one thousand marks at the accession of King John; but soon after was suspected of disloyalty, and had to give his son as a hostage. Further, that he was followed by three successive Williams, of whom the last left his sister Auda de Balun his heir in 1258. But three generations can scarcely be compressed into a span of about forty years; and I think it is obvious there can only have been the one William with whom the line ended.

Another William, his contemporary, the son of Fulk Paynell of Carleton in Yorkshire (it can scarcely by any possibility have been the same?) successfully claimed the escheated lands of his ancestors in 1261, and the next heir, John, paid the great sum of 1,312 marks for their redemption in 1272.

The deeper we plunge into the maze of this "very tangled story," the more hopelessly we find ourselves bewildered and involved. Drax had passed to Hugh Paynell (perhaps, as Dugdale suggests, another son of William and the Bahantune heiress), who in 1207 held six knights' fees there of the gift of King John, and was afterwards in arms against him. From him, no doubt, descended "Sir John Paynell, who had his principal seat at Drax in Yorkshire, and had summons to parliament from 28 Ed. I. to· 12 Ed. II." But Banks has·some doubt of his identity; for in these writs of summons he is never described as "of Drax"; hence "it may be questioned whether they refer to this John, or another John who seems to have been Lord of Otteley." The latter, mentioned in the parliament of 28 Ed. I., and again in that held at Lincoln, subscribed the famous letter thence addressed to the Pope as *Johannes Paynel dominus de Otteley.* May not the same John have been Lord both of Drax and Otteley?

Another baron of the name, *Will' Paynel de Tracington,* affixed his seal and signature to the same document, and from various statements (quoted by Banks) "may be reasonably inferred to have been John Paynell of Otteley's brother. John was, at all events, his heir, and on his death in 1316 succeeded to his Wiltshire manors of Littleton-Paynell and Knighton-Paynell, with other lands in Surrey and Sussex. When John himself died two years afterwards, they passed to his daughter Maud, who is said to have been the wife of Sir Nicholas de Upton.

. Many other scions of this preponderant house are incidentally mentioned, of whom I am quite incompetent to furnish an account. There was Adam Paynell (assigned by Dugdale as an additional son to the prolific Bahantune heiress), living in the time of King John, and married to the widow of William Fitz William, a sister and coheir of Robert Bardolf, Lord of Hoo in Kent, and Castle Carleton in Lincolnshire, who left a son and successor named Ralph. There was Richard Paynell, "one of the richest and most potent Barons in Yorkshire (v. *Thoresby*) who had his *aula* at Hooton," named from him Hooton Paynell. There was Sir William Paynell, who carried off Margaret de Gatesden, the wife of Lord Camoys, and compounded with her husband for a sum of money, receiving in return "a formal grant in writing under his seal, quitting unto him all his right and title to her." Banks thinks this may have been the Sir William Paynell of Tracington, who was a baron by writ in 1299; but the widow of the latter was certainly Ela de St. John.

In one instance only does the name appear to have been of long continuance. The family of Boothby Paynell, near Grantham, descended from Alexander Paynell and Agnes Fossard, survived till the close of the sixteenth century. They had adopted the bend of the Fossards, and bore it till 1308, when they exchanged it for the coat of another heiress, who brought them their Nottinghamshire seat. "There was one Bouthby," says Leland, "of very auncient tyme, the Heire generale of whom was maryed to Paynelle, and thereby rose much the Paynelles." They then assumed the two chevrons of the Boothbys, and made of this manor house their favourite residence. When Leland wrote, a dark cloud of sin and shame rested on the brave old name that reached so far back in the centuries, and had held so proud a place in the days gone by. I give the story in his own words. "The chief House of the Paynells had over a 900. Markes of Land by the Yere; and it was welle conservid on tille about the tyme of Henry the 5. Then John Paynelle the Father and John his Sunne, both Knighttes and great Lechers, began to decline; for John the Father began to selle, and John the Sunne begat abhominably a Doughter of his owne Doughter, and John the Father apon this sold all the Landes, parte owte of hand and parte in reversion : and John the Sunne dyid afore the Father, and yong John's Doughter fled to other partes of Englande for shame, and at the last married one Dines, a Wever, by whom she had Children : and after a 3. Descentes the Lands of the Dines cam by an Heire generale to one Bosson a Knight; and his Landes he also now cum to V. Sisters heires generales, whereof one is Wife to Richard Paynelle, now Owaner of Boutheby. Bosson was a Man born in Nottinghamshire, and had part of his Landes lying not far from Newark-on-Trent, and part lying in Yorkshire. Old Sir John Paynelle had a secunde Sunne callid Geffrey; he was Servant to the Quene of England, and yn good Estimation. Wherapon thinkking his Brother's Doughter dede, he made so importune sute, that at the laste he found meanes by the King, that the Duk of Bedford was content that Geffrey should buy of hym al such Landes as Sir John Paynelle the Father had sold unto him, the which was the beste peace of the Lande.

"But about the Tyme that Geffrey had payid for the Landes, came Dyne's Wife, Doughter to Yong Sir John Paynelle, and by a color got possession of Baroby a Manor of a 80. Poundes by the Yere, a Mile from Grantham; and so made clayme to the residew : so that at the last composition was made, that she should have of the Landes that the Duke of Bedeford had the Lordship of Baroby and Dunnington; and the residew to remain to Geffrey Paynelle, the whiche was great Granntfather to Paynell now dwelling at Boutheby.

"Though the Paynelles were Lordes of the Castelle of Newport-Painel in

Buckinghamshire, yet they had a great mynde to ly at Boutheby; wher they had a praty Stone House withyn a Mote."

With this scandal the family history virtually closes; for little remains to be told. Boothby Paynell was sold in the reign of Elizabeth; and according to one account, passed to the Harringtons: while another branch, seated at Fishtoft, near Boston, had become extinct in 1592. No wills or other records of the Paynells are forthcoming in the ensuing century.

Perche, or rather, as Duchesne gives it, Péché,* or Sin—surely the most unaccountable in all the *répertoire* of Norman nicknames. *Willielmus Peccatum* was a Domesday under-tenant in Norfolk, Suffolk, and Essex: in the latter county he held Netherhall of Richard Fitz Gilbert, Earl of Clare, whose kinsman he is believed to have been. "A very wicked fellow surely," opines Morant; "the name signifying Sin in the abstract." Yet he very possibly inherited it from an ancestor; and it was uncomplainingly borne by a long succession of descendants, churchmen as well as laymen. Richard Peché was Bishop of Coventry 1162–82, and another of the same name was Archdeacon of Malpas in Cheshire. Its evil significance, too, was lost, as, in the course of time, it lapsed into the homely and harmless form of Peachey or Peach.

Ralph Peche (perhaps William's son) about 1113 received from Roger, the second son of the Earl of Clare, the manor of Birdbrook in Essex; one of those granted by Gilbert Lord Peche to Edward I.: and in 1134 Hamo Peche, in right of his wife Alice, one of the four sisters and coheirs of William Peverell, was Lord of Brunne in Cambridgeshire, and held a barony of his own in Suffolk of twelve knights' fees. He was Sheriff of Cambridge from 1164 to Easter 1166: and paid scutage on nineteen fees in 1168. He was followed by two sons, Geoffrey and Gilbert. Gilbert's wife was "a sister of that famous Fitz Walter, who led the Barons' party in the time of King John. On Fitz Walter's banishment, she had to find hostages for her loyalty. One of these hostages was her own daughter Alice."—*Eyton's Shropshire.* Her son, Hamo II., went on pilgrimage to Jerusalem, and died on his journey, either going or returning. The next in succession, Gilbert II., for some reason or other, disinherited his two elder sons. "By his first wife, Matilda de Hastings, he had two sons, John and Edmund. The said Matilda died apparently about 1264–5, or during the period of Montfort's usurpation. Gilbert Peche re-married Joan, daughter of Sir Simon de Grey, on whose children he contrived to settle the bulk of his estates. The residue of his Barony he gave to King Edward I., probably about

---

* "One of the most singular rebuses I have seen occurs in a window in the chapel at Lullingstone, co. Kent, the seat of Sir Percival Dyke, Bt. It is that of Sir John Peché. In this instance the arms of the personage are surrounded by a wreath composed of two branches of a peach tree, bearing fruit, every peach being marked with an old English "e": Peach-é. It is curious that this device proves the true pronunciation of the name, which was formerly supposed to be Peche."—*M. A. Lower.*

the year 1284.* He died in 19 Edward I."—*Ibid.* Banks tells us that he had been summoned to parliament in 1260; yet this barony devolved neither on the despoiled sons of his first marriage, nor on those born of the second, whom he had "advanced" to the better part of the inheritance. The strangeness of the story is enhanced by some evidence adduced by Eyton to prove that John, the ill-used eldest son, was a voluntary sufferer. "In 1274 Gilbert Peche enfeoffed John, his son and heir, in the Essex manor of Plecheden. John was seized thereof five months, but then settled it on his father Gilbert, and on Gilbert's wife Joan, conjointly: with remainder to the heirs of Gilbert by the said Joan. . . . I take it, then, that the Gilbert Peche who had military summons as a baron in 1299, and who was Lord of Great Thurlow, Suffolk, in 1316, was eldest son of Gilbert Peche II. by Joan de Grey, and the founder of a new barony.

This third Gilbert (whom Dugdale confuses with his father) diligently attended Edward I. in his Scottish campaigns, and received a commission "to raise as many men-at-arms and foot-soldiers as he can" in 1322. He also served in Gascony. No successor is mentioned to his barony (of 1299): yet, according to Banks, he left two sons, Gilbert and Simon. Gilbert, called by Morant Sir Geoffrey (there is a Geoffrey Peche mentioned in Palgrave's *Parliamentary Writs*, as holding some lands in Norfolk in 1316,) died in 1353, having survived his only son, and of his two daughters only one left descendants. This was Catherine, married first to John Aspel, and then to Sir Thomas Nutbeme, Nutbrane, or Nutborne.

"What became of the right heirs of Gilbert Peche II. is," says Eyton, "a matter of conjecture." Edmund, the youngest, occurs in the *Parl. Writs* as Lord of Felsham, Suffolk, in 1316: and John must have been the Sir John Peche, "descended from Gilbert Lord Peche," who acquired Lullingstone in the previous century. His two sons, Sir William and Sir John, accompanied Edward I. to Scotland, and were knighted at Carlaverock. Another Sir William was Sheriff of Kent in 1462 and 1463, with the custody of Canterbury Castle. The last of the family, Sir John, was a man of some note, and lies buried under a magnificent monument in Lullingstone Church. He was Sheriff in the reign of Henry VIII., a Knight Banneret, and Lord Deputy of Calais. His estates passed through his sister Elizabeth to the Harts (an old Hertfordshire family): and from them in 1738 to the Dykes. It is noteworthy, that the coat of the Peches of Lullingstone, *Azure* a lion rampant *Ermine*, la queue furchée, crowned *Or*, was entirely different from that of the baronial Peches.

Two other knights of this family were summoned to parliament in the same year by Edward II; but in neither case can they be affiliated with any certainty

---

* "In those days," says Camden, "the English nobility brought up the ancient Roman custom in the time of their Emperors, of making their Princes their heirs, whenever they were out of favour. This Castle (Brunne) was burnt down in the Barons' War of Henry III.'s time, being set on fire by one Ribald de Lisle."

to the Lords Peche of Brunne. Of one of them, Robert Peche, nothing is absolutely known except this summons as a baron in 1321. Nor had he, it seems, any heir—at all events, no successor. The other, Sir John Peche, Knight Banneret, of Wormleighton in Warwickshire, was, on the contrary, constantly employed in public affairs. He was one of the justiciaries of his county in 1317: Conservator of the Peace in 1320: a Commissioner of array in Staffordshire, Warwickshire, Leicestershire, Northamptonshire and Rutland in 1322 : Captain of Dover Castle and Lord Warden of the Cinque Ports in 1323: and received several writs of military summons. But the summons to parliament was never again repeated, either to the grandson who was his successor, or to the next heir. This last Sir John was of Shenington in Gloucestershire; and in 1385 attended John Duke of Lancaster to Spain, where he is supposed to have died in the following year. He left two daughters and co-heiresses; Joan, died s. p. ; and Margaret, married to Sir William Montfort of Coleshill in Warwickshire. His arms, *Gules* a fesse between six cross-crosslets *Argent*, in chief a label of three points, seem to denote some suzerainty of the Earls of Warwick; and are again unlike those borne by the Peches of Brunne : *Argent* a fesse between two chevrons *Gules*.

Others of the name there were in different counties, as to whom information is wanting. Who was the *Dominus* Thomas Peche summoned from Suffolk to attend the great Council at Westminster in 1324? Who were the two Hampshire knights, Sir John and Sir Gilbert Peche, that took part in the famous tournament at Stepney? v. *Woodward's Hampshire.* Who was Sabina Peche, Forester of the Fee of Selwood in 1225? v. *Phelps' Somerset.* Who, Bartholomew Peche, Sheriff of Dorset and Somerset in 1252, that has left his name to Cowley-Pecche (now Peachey) in Middlesex? He had a grant of free-warren there in the following year.

Pauey. Froissart gives this as an Italian name. He tells us that Sir Aymery de Pavey, a Lombard, was appointed by Edward III. Governor of Calais; and that a French Lord, Geoffrey de Charney, "bethought him how Lombards naturally be covetous; wherefore he thought to get the town of Calais * * * : and by reason of the truce they of St. Omer's might go to Calais, and they of Calais to St. Omer's, so that daily they resorted together to do their merchandises. Then Sir Geoffrey secretly fell in treaty with Sir Aymery of Pavy, so that he promised to deliver into the Frenchmen's hands the town and castle of Calais for 20,000 crowns. This was not done so secretly but that the King of England had knowledge thereof; then the king sent for Aymery de Pavy to come into England to Westminster to speak with him, and so he came over, for he thought that the king had not had knowledge of that matter, he thought he had done it so secretly. When the king saw him, he took him apart, and said, Thou knowest well I have given thee in keeping the thing in this world that I love best, next my wife and children, that is to say, the town and castle of Calais; and thou hast sold it to the Frenchmen, wherefore thou well deservest to die. Then the Lombard knelt down, and said, Ah noble King, I cry you mercy; it is true that you say; but, Sir, the bargain may well be broken, for as yet I have received never a penny. The king had loved well the Lombard, and said, Aymery, I will that thou go forward on thy bargain, and the day that thou appointest to deliver the town, let me have knowledge thereof before : and on this condition I forgive thee thy trespass." Sir Aymery thankfully agreed; and accordingly when, at the time appointed—the first night of the New Year—Sir Geoffrey presented himself with his "five hundred spears," he found the King and Sir Walter Manny, with three hundred men-at-arms and six hundred archers, ready to receive him.

No doubt this double-dyed traitor came from Pavia. Yet the name is found in Normandy. Roger Pavé or de Pavia occurs there in the Exchequer Rolls of 1180–95 : and two families of the name, Pavée de Provenchère, and Pavée de Vendeuvre, still continued at the end of the last century.—*Nobiliaire de Normandie.*

The name does not appear to have been very common in England. Walter Pavey is mentioned in 1222 in the *Domesday of St. Paul's.* Thomas Pavi and Alice his wife occur in Staffordshire in 1272, (*Pedes Finium*) and N. Pawei in the *Hundred Rolls* of the same date. Henry Pavey of Chippenham, and John Pavey, each again married to an Alice, are found in Kent in 1319.—*Kent Fines.* Richard Pavey was among the Esquires who were in the retinue of Thomas Earl of Arundel at Agincourt in 1415. The earliest mentioned is "Ricardo de Pavee," who in 1183 witnesses Robert de Stafford's charter to Bordesley Abbey. *The Staffordshire Chartulary.* They occur at a later date in several other counties. Two of the name, William Pavey, obt. 1725, and Mary, wife of Robert Pavey, obt. 1770, lie buried in Bruton churchyard.—*Phelps' Somerset.* A small tablet of very ancient date, suspended in the centre arch of Stapleford Church, and inscribed with the old version of the first Psalm, bears the name of William Pavie. The two first lines of the translation run thus :—

> "The man is blest that hath not bent
> To wicked rede his care."

There was a family of the name seated at Plaitford in Wiltshire. Elizabeth, daughter of Thomas Pavey of Plaitford, who, early in the last century, married William Fox of Farley, in the same county, was the grandmother of the first Lord Ilchester and the first Lord Holland. Pavey of Norfolk bore *Sable* a fesse crenellée *Argent* between three eagles displayed *Or.* Another coat assigned to the name is *Ermine* on a fesse *Gules*, three martlets *Or.*

END OF VOL. II.

LONDON :
PRINTED BY WILLIAM CLOWES AND SONS, LIMITED,
STAMFORD STREET AND CHARING CROSS.